ST. MARY'S COLLEGE OF MARYLAND
ST. MARY'S CITY, MARYLAND 20686

SO-AHZ-714

The Mississippian
Emergence

The Mississippian Emergence

Edited by Bruce D. Smith

Smithsonian Institution Press Washington and London

To James B. Griffin

© 1990 The Smithsonian Institution
All rights reserved.
Printed in the United States of America
93 92 91 90   5 4 3 2 1

Library of Congress
Cataloging-in-Publication Data

The Mississippian emergence / Bruce D. Smith, ed.
     p. cm.
   Includes bibliographical references.
   ISBN 0-87474-844-5
   1. Mississippian culture. 2. Indians of North America—Southern
States—Antiquities. 3. Indians of North America—Mississippi River
Valley—Antiquities. 4. Mississippi River Valley—Antiquities.
5. Southern States—Antiquities. I. Smith, Bruce D.
E99.M6815M56   1990
975'.01—dc20   89-22000

♾The paper used in this publication meets
the minimum requirements of the American National Standard
for Permanence of Paper for Printed Library
Materials Z39.48 1984.

Robin Gould, Editor
Janice Wheeler, Designer
Craig A. Reynolds, Production Editor

For permission to reproduce individual illustrations appearing in this book, please
correspond directly with the owners of the works. The Smithsonian Institution
Press does not retain reproduction rights for these illustrations or maintain a file
of addresses for illustration sources.

Contents

List of Illustrations   xi

List of Tables   xiv

Foreword by Stephen Williams   xv

Contributors   xviii

1 Introduction   1

Bruce D. Smith

    Archaeological Chiefdoms and the Eastern Woodlands   1

    The Analogy-Homology Dilemma   2

    Nested Black Boxes   3

    Selective Multiple-Level Comparison   3

**2 Powell Canal: Baytown Period Adaptation on Bayou Macon,
Southeast Arkansas**   9

John House

    Introduction   9

    Physical Setting   9

    Cultural and Temporal Context   11

    Excavations at Powell Canal   12

    The Formal-Spatial Structure and Past Community Patterns of Powell Canal   13

    Technology   15

    Subsistence and Seasonality   16

    Bioarchaeology   18

    Baytown Period Adaptation on Bayou Macon   19

    Comparative Discussion   19

    Conclusion   22

**3 The Toltec Mounds Site: A Ceremonial Center in the Arkansas
River Lowland**   27

Martha Ann Rolingson

    Location and Environmental Setting   27

    History of Research in Central Arkansas   28

    Research at the Toltec Mounds Site   29

    Site Description   31

Mound Construction and History   31
Material Culture   34
Stratigraphy   36
Mound Function   37
Internal Settlement Plan   37
Settlement Pattern   39
Comparisons with Lower Mississippi Valley Sites   39
The Place of Toltec Mounds Site in Lower Valley Prehistory   44

**4 The Zebree Site: An Emerged Early Mississippian Expression in
Northeast Arkansas**   51
Phyllis Morse and Dan F. Morse
The Baytown Period Dunklin Phase Component   53
Big Lake Phase Artifacts   55
Environment and Subsistence   59
The Big Lake Phase Village   61

**5 Range Site Community Patterns and the Mississippian
Emergence**   67
John E. Kelly
Introduction   67
 The Range Site   69
Location and Environmental Setting   69
The I-270 Investigations   71
Archaeological Overview   72
The Late Woodland-Emergent Mississippian-Mississippian Sequence at
the Range Site   74
Changing Community Patterns at the Range Site   79
The Patrick Phase (A.D. 600–750)   79
The Dohack Phase (A.D. 750–850)   87
The Range Phase (A.D. 850–900)   93
The George Reeves Phase (A.D. 900–950)   97
The George Reeves-Lindeman Phase Transition   101
The Lindeman Phase (A.D. 950–1000)   104
The Lindhorst (A.D. 1000–1050) and Stirling (A.D. 1050–1150)
Phases   105
Changing Community Plans and Cultural Process   106

**6 The Emergence of Mississippian Culture in the American
Bottom Region**   113
John E. Kelly
Introduction   113
Location and Environmental Setting   113
Chronological Framework   115
A Cultural-Historical Framework for the Late Woodland-Mississippian
Transition in the American Bottom   117
The Patrick and Sponemann Phases (A.D. 600–750)   117
The Collinsville, Loyd, Dohack, and Range Phases (A.D. 750–900)   126
The Merrell, Edelhardt, George Reeves, and Lindeman Phases (A.D.
800–1000)   130
The Lohmann and Lindhorst Phases (A.D. 1000–1050)   136

Previous Models of Mississippian Emergence in the American
Bottom   139
   Local Evolution Explanations   139
   Migration-Contact Models   142
An Alternative Model   143
Future Research Directions   146

7 Emergent Mississippian in the Central Mississippi Valley   153
Dan F. Morse and Phyllis Morse
Introduction   153
Ceramic Complexes and Temporal Control A.D. 700–1200   155
   The Baytown Period   155
   The Varney Horizon   156
   The Beaker Horizon   157
   The Matthews Horizon   158
The Emergence of Mississippian Culture A.D. 700–800   158
   The Dunklin Phase   158
   The Baytown Phase, Plum Bayou Culture, and Flat-Based, Shell-
      Tempered Ceramics   159
   The Hoecake Phase   162
Early Mississippian Culture: A.D. 800–1000   163
The Evolution of Mississippian Culture: A.D. 1000–1200   166
Theories of Origin and Development   169

8 Explaining Mississippian Origins in East Tennessee   175
Gerald F. Schroedl, C. Clifford Boyd, Jr., and R. P. Stephen Davis, Jr.
Introduction   175
Environment   177
Culture Chronology   178
Woodland Period   180
Emergent and Early Mississippian Periods   185
The Woodland-Mississippian Transition   189
Conclusions   192

9 Mississippian Emergence in West-Central Alabama   197
Paul D. Welch
Introduction   197
Environment   198
Mississippian Emergence along the Central Tombigbee River   199
   History of Research   199
   Chronology   200
   Miller III Culture   203
   Summerville Culture   206
Mississippian Emergence along the Black Warrior Floodplain   209
   History of Research   209
   Chronology   210
   West Jefferson Culture in the Moundville Area   211
   Moundville I Culture   212
Mississippian Emergence in the Bessemer Area   214
   History of Research   214
   Chronology   215
   West Jefferson Culture in the Bessemer Area   215
   Bessemer Phase Culture   217
Conclusion   218

10 Mississippian Emergence in the Fort Walton Area: The Evolution of the Cayson and Lake Jackson Phases   227

John F. Scarry

    Introduction   227

    Fort Walton Mississippian   228

    Prior Archaeological Research   229

        Moore and Brannon: The Early Investigators   229

        Willey: Synthesis and Foundation   230

        The Post-Willey Era   230

    Culture History in the Southern Portion of the Fort Walton Area   231

        The General Fort Walton Chronology   231

        Woodland   231

        Early Fort Walton   232

        Middle Fort Walton   232

        Late Fort Walton   232

    Woodland-Mississippian Culture History in the Upper Apalachicola
Valley and the Tallahassee Hills   233

        The Parrish Lake Phase: Early Weeden Island in the Upper
Apalachicola Valley   233

        The Wakulla Phase and Late Woodland in the Tallahassee Hills   234

        The Cayson Phase   235

        The Lake Jackson Phase   237

    Models of Fort Walton Emergence   238

        General Considerations   238

        The Emergence of the Cayson Phase: Subsistence Costs and
Information   239

        The Emergence of the Lake Jackson Phase: Demographic Expansion
and Elite Alliances   242

    Conclusions   245

11 Trade and the Evolution of Exchange Relations at the Beginning of the Mississippian Period   251

James A. Brown, Richard A. Kerber, and Howard D. Winters

    Introduction   251

    The Place of Trade in Mississippian Period Studies   252

    Trade and Society   252

    Trade and Redistribution   253

    Prestige Goods Economy   255

    Models of Trade and Social Change   256

    The Context of Trade Between A.D. 800 and 1200   257

    Raw Material Sources and their Identification   258

    Artifact-Oriented Research   262

    Trade in the Southeast   263

    Prestige Goods   264

        Long-Nose God Maskettes   264

        Spatulate Celts   264

        Repoussé Copper Plates   265

    Utilitarian Goods—The Mill Creek Hoe Case   265

    Fall-off Curve Study   268

    Shell Bead Valuables   270

Contexts of Production   270
    The Organization of Production   270
    Spheres of Utility and Value   272
    Factors of Distribution   273
Summary and Conclusions   274

List of Illustrations

1. The location of settlements and regions considered in this volume   4
2. The environmental setting of the Powell Canal site   10
3. The location of the 1980–1981 excavation units at the Powell Canal site   12
4. The distribution of features at the Powell Canal site   14
5. Principal ceramic vessel forms at the Powell Canal site   15
6. Central Arkansas physiographic regions and archaeological sites   28
7. The location of mounds within the earthen embankment at the Toltec site   31
8. Stratigraphic profile of Mound B at the Toltec site   32
9. Chronological chart of excavated mounds in the lower Mississippi Valley   40
10. The location of lower Mississippi Valley sites discussed in the text   41
11. The location of the Zebree site within the eastern lowlands of the central Mississippi Valley   52
12. Dunklin phase ceramics from the Zebree site   54
13. Basic shell-tempered wares found at the Zebree site   55
14. Ceramic, lithic, bone, and shell artifacts found at the Zebree site   57
15. The settlement plan of the Big Lake phase village at the Zebree site   62
16. The upper American Bottom   68
17. The Range site and its catchment area   70
18. The extent of excavation areas at the Range site   72
19. Internal floor area information for small rectilinear structures at the Range site: mean and standard deviation values   75
20. The distribution of Patrick phase structures and occupation areas at the Range site   78
21. The distribution of features for Patrick phase settlements at the Range site   80
22. The distribution of features for Patrick phase occupation area P-3 at the Range site   81
23. The distribution of features for Patrick phase occupation area P-4 at the Range site   82
24. The distribution of features for Patrick phase occupation area P-5 at the Range site   83
25. The community organization of the P-5 occupation area at the Range site   84
26. The distribution of features for Patrick phase occupation area P-6 at the Range site   85

27. The distribution of features for Patrick phase occupation area P-7 at the Range site   86

28. The distribution of Dohack and Range phase structures and occupation areas at the Range site   87

29. The distribution of features for Dohack phase occupation area D-4 at the Range site   89

30. The distribution of features for Dohack phase occupation area D-2 at the Range site   90

31. The distribution of features for Dohack phase occupation area D-5 at the Range site   91

32. The distribution of features for Dohack phase occupation area D-3 at the Range site   92

33. The distribution of features for Dohack phase occupation area D-1 at the Range site   93

34. The distribution of features for Range phase occupation area R-4 at the Range site   94

35. The distribution of features for Range phase occupation area R-3 at the Range site   95

36. The distribution of features for Range phase occupation area R-5 at the Range site   95

37. The distribution of features for Range phase occupation area R-2 at the Range site   96

38. The distribution of features for Range phase occupation area R-1 at the Range site   97

39. The location of George Reeves and Lindeman phase occupations at the Range site   98

40. The distribution of George Reeves phase occupation and features at the Range site   100

41. The George Reeves-Lindeman phase transition at the Range site   99

42. The distribution of Lindeman phase features at the Range site   102

43. The late Lindeman phase occupation of the Range site   105

44. Early Mississippian occupation areas at the Range site   106

45. The distribution of M-1 phase features at the Range site   107

46. The American Bottom   114

47. The biotic communities of the upper American Bottom   115

48. Lithic resources of the American Bottom   116

49. American Bottom chronology   117

50. Late Woodland period radiocarbon assays for the American Bottom   118

51. Emergent Mississippian period radiocarbon assays for the American Bottom   119

52. Early Mississippian period radiocarbon assays for the American Bottom   120

53. Selected sites within the American Bottom   121

54. The Cahokia site   122

55. The distribution of Patrick and Sponemann phase sites within the American Bottom   123

56. The distribution of selected early Emergent Mississippian period sites (A.D. 750–900) within the American Bottom   125

57. Selected ceramic attributes for the Pulcher and Late Bluff traditions of the American Bottom   127

58. The Dohack phase community plan at the Westpark site   129

59. The distribution of selected late Emergent Mississippian period sites (A.D. 900–1000) within the American Bottom   132

60. George Reeves phase community plans at the George Reeves and Westpark sites   133

61. The Merrell phase community plan at the Robinson's Lake site   134
62. Lindeman phase community plans at the Schlemmer and Marcus sites   134
63. The Edelhardt phase community plan at the BBB Motor site   135
64. The distribution of Early Mississippian period sites in the American Bottom   138
65. Map of the central Mississippi Valley showing the distribution of sites yielding Varney Red ceramics, Plum Bayou-related materials, shell-tempered flat-based vessels, and beakers   154
66. Radiocarbon dates plotted by horizon   155
67. Archaeological sites in east Tennessee discussed in the text   176
68. Physiography of east Tennessee   177
69. Composition of Mississippian I and II ceramic assemblage groups at Martin Farm (40MR20)   186
70. Location of Mississippian I and II site components in the lower Little Tennessee River valley   187
71. Map of west-central Alabama, showing the three study areas   197
72. Locations of central Tombigbee sites mentioned in text   199
73. Chronologies of the central Tombigbee, Moundville, and Bessemer areas   200
74. Radiocarbon dates for Late Woodland phases in the central Tombigbee area   201
75. Locations of Moundville I mound sites   210
76. Locations of Bessemer area sites mentioned in text   214
77. The Fort Walton area, showing major sites and subareas   228
78. General chronology for the Fort Walton area   231
79. Relative change in site density in the Apalachicola Valley and Tallahassee Hills   234
80. Change in diversity of decorated ceramic assemblages in the Apalachicola Valley   234
81. Relationship of inheritance rules and status differentiation to decision-making   242
82. Geography of common minerals and important resource zones   259
83. Distribution of valuables of the A.D. 1000–1200 period   261
84. Distribution of copper artifacts among Mississippian period sites   262
85. Mill Creek chipped stone hoe blade forms   266
86. Distribution of Mill Creek hoe blades   267
87. Fall-off curve of the total number of Mill Creek hoe blades in counties within 20 km intervals from the quarry source   268
88. Fall-off curve of the average number of Mill Creek hoe blades in county centers within 20 km intervals from the quarry source   268

List of Tables

1. Estimated In Situ and Total Capacities of Pit Features at the Powell Canal Site   16
2. Carbonized Plant Remains from Powell Canal Site Features   16
3. Faunal Remains from Powell Canal Site Features   17
4. Demography of Powell Canal Site Burials   18
5. Radiocarbon Dates from the Toltec Mounds   34
6. Characteristics of Excavated Mounds in the Lower Mississippi Valley A.D. 1–1150   42
7. Excavation Research Strategies at the Zebree Site   53
8. Range Site Radiocarbon Assays   73
9. Summary of Range Site Community Dimensions and Features   88
10. Excavated Sites with Patrick and Sponemann Phase Occupations   124
11. Excavated Sites with Early Emergent Mississippian Occupations   126
12. Excavated Sites with Late Emergent Mississippian Occupations   131
13. Excavated Sites with Early Mississippian Occupations   137
14. Radiocarbon Dates circa A.D. 700–1200 in the Central Mississippi Valley   156
15. Selected Sites Reported with Major Varney Red Ceramics in the Central Mississippi Valley   160
16. Beakers Reported from the Central Mississippi Valley   168
17. East Tennessee Culture Chronology for the Woodland and Mississippian Periods   178
18. Alternative East Tennessee Culture Chronology for the Woodland and Mississippian Periods   179
19. Middle and Late Woodland Period Radiocarbon Dates   180
20. Hamilton Burial Mound Complex Radiocarbon Dates   184
21. Early Mississippian Period Radiocarbon Dates   185
22. Ceramic Frequencies of the Cofferdam and Gainesville Phases   201
23. Differences Between Cofferdam and Gainesville Base Camps   202
24. Radiocarbon Dates for Summerville I Phase Components   203
25. Health Status of Catfish Bend, Cofferdam-Gainesville, and Summerville I Mortuary Populations   205
26. Radiocarbon Dates for Fort Walton Components   236

Foreword

So here we have another volume drawn together by Bruce Smith on Mississippian societies. His *Mississippian Settlement Patterns* volume gave us in 1978 a general overview of Mississippian site demography across the Southeast, broadly considered. The volume in hand examines current knowledge about what has been a rather intractable subject for more than a century—Mississippian origins.

A brief review of research on this question of Mississippian origins provides a historical context for the present volume. We owe to William Henry Holmes the name "Mississippian" and to Frederic Ward Putnam and Cyrus Thomas the first academic publications on these societies. We should not forget the major contributions to our broader view of Mississippian by a host of late nineteenth-century amateur reporters, such as Charles C. Jones and his brother, Joseph, in Georgia and Tennessee; Gates P. Thruston, also in Tennessee; W.B. Potter and Edward Evers in Missouri; and Clarence Bloomfield Moore who swept the whole field from Georgia and Tennessee to the broad Mississippi drainage. Nor should we forget all the BAE field minions working for Thomas or even the astute *early* nineteenth-century reporters at Cahokia, for example.

But it is enough to say that by the 1920s the breadth and fabric of Mississippian was quite well known in some regards. The overall plans of dozens of sites had been documented and numerous cemetery burials with their attendant pottery vessels excavated. Ceremonial accouterments for rituals in stone, copper, shell, and even wood were well known. We had become aware of the glitzy *beigabe* and the towering earthen monuments upon which the temples had stood. In contrast, we had only snippets of knowledge about their domestic residences and their basic way of life.

This situation would change with the onset of the Thirties and the Depression. Out-of-work farmers were recruited in government-sponsored archaeological projects at a time when a depressed economy could not support new products of manufacture. As a result, the only growing inventories to be found were in archaeological laboratories, where workers fought to keep ahead of processing demands. Although these efforts concentrated upon good-sized sites of any period from Oklahoma to Georgia and from Florida to southern Illinois, the large sites with mounds tended to get special attention, and these large sites were mostly Mississippian.

The mound excavations were of considerable significance; for the first time whole structures could be carefully excavated. Mississippian pyramidal mounds were stripped of their construction levels and the structural features on the successive exposed "floors" were mapped to show the outline of perishable buildings that had once stood there. In the village areas not one but dozens of domestic structures were uncovered, as were the often surrounding palisaded walls. Site plans that showed more than just the mound structures were produced.

The Thirties data bonanza cried for integration: concepts like Hopewell and Middle Mississippi were not enough. To accomplish this end, a Southeast regional conference was inaugurated in 1937 both to share data and to order that same data. There was considerable agreement on the overall picture, less as to the means best suited to order it. The McKern system was favored in the Midwest, but the two major syntheses that appeared, that by James A. Ford and Gordon R. Willey in 1941 and that by James B. Griffin in 1946 (but presented in December 1941), differed in their adherence to McKernian philosophy. Ford and Willey espoused a chronological system, the core of which was a four-fold periodization: Burial Mound I and II, Temple Mound I and II. Griffin, not a pure McKernian despite his Michigan post, used a mixed system. It went from Paleo-Indian, including what would now be called Archaic, to Neo-Indian. The latter included Early and Middle Woodland and Middle Mississippi. The terms Early and Late Mississippi were also used in the text with chronological meanings.

Thus it would be Griffin who by his terminology would clearly signal the beginning of the search for Mississippian origins, but Ford and Willey were definitely very concerned about both the beginning and the end of Mississippian. So by World War II the study of major cultures was starting to come to grips with long-term developmental "history" too. At the very time these syntheses were being forged, two of the participants, Ford and Griffin, would in the fall of 1939 join with Philip Phillips in a survey of the Lower Mississippi Valley. Some years later (1951), in the first major report of that field work, they would state that one of the major goals of the survey had indeed been to try to get a handle on the problem of Mississippian origins.

The first Lower Mississippi survey summary volume was less than happy about the results of their search. While the resulting volume and its discussion of the problem (Phillips et al., 1951: 445–54) has become an indispensible document for Mississippian research, the authors admitted almost complete failure. The only really "early Mississippian" materials were found at the bottom of the last test pit they dug in 1947 at the Rose Mound in Arkansas. They found no single center of origin; indeed they felt that they had probably falsified that hypothesis, although they did not use those modern terms. They said instead that "We are becoming increasingly doubtful that a single center exists any-

where. We envisage rather a number of centers in which this culture [Mississippian] was developing more or less simultaneously along parallel lines with continuing interaction between them" (Phillips et al., 1951: 451).

Bruce Smith says abut the same thing in a somewhat more elegant way in the Introduction that follows. When multiple centers for Mississippian development are mentioned, I think of my short-lived Petri dish hypothesis; after all where else to generate a good Mississippian *culture* hypothesis. I suggested to friends, not too loudly, that an analogy for Mississippian development could be that of a basic culture, spread across the Petri dish of the Southeast, then rising from it would be individual peaks and developments to represent regional cultures, such as Cahokia, the Ohio Confluence, and the Cumberland Basin. But then you need a very unbiological communication system between those regional developments, and other things break down in the model too.

Maybe we need a whole new way of looking at this problem, and I offer you, not really in jest, the world of chaos and those charmings bits named "fractals." My leader into that strange new world is James Gleick and his challenging book *Chaos: Making a New Science* (NYC: Viking, 1987). He takes readers through a polychrome world of spell-binding "new" beauty and then tells them that this has to do with the way some feel the world may really be constructed. Yet the simplest thing he is saying is that we tend to force regularity into our understanding of the world since it is the only method we know, in the other direction lies chaos. How can we predict and find laws if we are not in control of all the systems within our models?

In characterizing the problems of dealing with nature that produced results that were sometimes erratic, Gleick (1987:65) says, "no good ecologist ever forgot that his equations were vastly oversimplified versions of real phenomena. The whole point of oversimplifying was to model regularity. Why go to all that trouble just to see chaos?" Does this tell us something about the failures of systems analysis to very successfully model archaeological problems? I should think so, since most computer studies have had to put so much regularity in their programs that the results hardly resemble the hard data that we know exists from archaeological sites. And what about the data that has been destroyed, not by our ineffective recovery techniques, although that is a problem too, but destroyed by the forces of nature that leave us grasping only a very small percentage of the cultural residue? Remember there is no way to predict what percent will ultimately be preserved.

I realize that this may not be a very upbeat way to introduce some very interesting views of where we are in 1990 in understanding the tangled pathway which leads through what I have called the Good Gray Cultures that span the gap from post-Hopewellian times to the Heydays of Mississippian. This six-hundred-year period, from about A.D. 300 to A.D. 900, is one of the least known times in the last three-thousand years of Eastern prehistory. We have few data points and not surprisingly rather few C14 dates as well.

From Time's crucible we have, so far, only a few worthwhile scraps of data. We must treasure them and wait for some more lucky strikes such as the mother lode from the Illinois-based I-270 project that has, in one blinding flash, revealed some four-thousand years of prehistory in the American Bottom in very considerable detail. Our new hits will need to be major projects and long-term ones too, such as the Toltec program described herein by Martha Rolingson. A few judicious test pits, even randomly stratified, just will not accomplish what is needed.

So with this all ahead for the wary reader, I salute this very necessary attempt to fill the gap; this fine effort will, I trust, spur others to do likewise.

Stephen Williams
Peabody Professor of American Archaeology
Harvard University

Contributors

C. Clifford Boyd, Jr., Department of Sociology and Anthropology, Radford University, Radford, Virginia

James A. Brown, Department of Anthropology, Northwestern University, Evanston, Illinois

R. P. Stephen Davis, Jr., Research Associate, Research Laboratories of Anthropology, University of North Carolina, Chapel Hill, North Carolina

John House, Arkansas Archeological Survey, University of Arkansas at Pine Bluff, Pine Bluff, Arkansas

John E. Kelly, Archaeology Program, Southern Illinois University, Edwardsville, Illinois

Richard A. Kerber, Department of Anthropology, Northwestern University, Evanston, Illinois

Dan F. Morse, Arkansas Archeological Survey, State University, Arkansas

Phyllis Morse, Arkansas Archeological Survey, State University, Arkansas

Martha Ann Rolingson, Arkansas Archeological Survey, Toltec Mounds Research Station, Scott, Arkansas

John F. Scarry, Bureau of Archaeological Research, Division of Historical Resources, Tallahassee, Florida

Gerald F. Schroedl, Department of Anthropology, The University of Tennessee, Knoxville, Tennessee

Bruce D. Smith, Department of Anthropology, National Museum of Natural History, Smithsonian Institution, Washington, D.C.

Paul D. Welch, Department of Anthropology, Oberlin College, Oberlin, Ohio

Howard D. Winters, Department of Anthropology, New York University, New York, New York

Introduction

Research on the Origins of Mississippian Chiefdoms in Eastern North America

ARCHAEOLOGICAL CHIEFDOMS AND THE EASTERN WOODLANDS

The broad and conceptually difficult terrain that stretches between tribal societies and state-level organizations (Feinman and Neitzel 1984) is often assigned the general label of "chiefdom" or "ranked society." The chiefdom concept still serves as a valuable abstract polity profile in studying societies that are neither egalitarian tribes nor states, and chiefdoms remain a quite active area of research inquiry in archaeology and ethnohistory (e.g., Earle 1987; Hudson et al. 1985; Drennen and Uribe 1987).

While in some ways not as conducive to archaeological inquiry as Oceania, with its island isolation and rich ethnohistorical record, the eastern woodlands region of North America in many respects still provides excellent opportunities for research on archaeological chiefdoms. This is particularly true in addressing the question of origins; in attempting to gain an understanding of the historical developmental transformation from tribes to chiefdoms, from principally egalitarian societies to ones exhibiting institutional inequality. The East is unlike many other areas of the New World, where chiefdoms developed only to be subsequently covered and masked by the indigenous evolution of state-level societies. The pre-European contact "Mississippian" chiefdoms of eastern North America initially emerged in river valley settings across a broad expanse of the East during a three-century span from A.D. 750 to 1050. A subsequent four centuries of complex and shifting chiefdom-level culture history has only partially masked and erased evidence of this emergence. And contrary to still popular diffusionist "south-of-the-border story" scenarios, the Mississippian emergence of A.D. 750–1050 was an independent pristine process of social transformation, uninfluenced by Mesoamerican state-level societies. Uninfluenced and unobscured by state-level societies, the Mississippian emergence also has a considerable interpretive challenge inherent in its pluralistic character. In many respects, the Mississippian emergence represents a broad scale, extremely complex, and parallel set of paradoxically discrete yet interconnected historical developmental sequences. Taking place within river valley settings that were widely scattered across the eastern woodlands, the Mississippian emergence encompassed semi-isolated societies that exhibit a broad diversity of cultural and historical backgrounds. Yet they were connected by a network of communication and exchange networks that followed both river and overland routes. On the surface, the societies involved in the Mississippian emergence arrived at generally comparable chiefdom levels of organization, seemingly by roughly similar developmental pathways.

But below this surface similarity, the degree to which the historical developmental sequences of different river valleys parallel each other is still far from clear. It is also far from clear to what degree this broadly similar process of cultural transformation was due to developmental interaction between river valley societies in transition, as opposed to their independent response to similar developmental constraints and opportunities. When viewed as a broadly distributed yet interconnected set of river valley societies mutually involved in a "rapid" three century historical episode of social transformation, the Mississippian emergence can be seen to represent a quite challenging cultural example of the analogy vs. homology, or process vs. history, dilemma.

THE ANALOGY-HOMOLOGY DILEMMA

In its purest form, the overarching homology or historical relatedness position considers the Mississippian emergence to have initially occurred in one core or heartland area and then to have rapidly spread across the east through adaptive radiation. Joseph Caldwell (1958) provided an early, very articulate presentation of this position. Armed with maize agriculture and associated technological innovations, and driven by demographic growth, newly emergent Mississippian groups expanded outward along prime real estate river valley corridors. Displacing and assimilating the societies they encountered (and so somewhat diverging from the heartland cultural mainstream), and often valley hopping considerable distances to establish site-unit intrusion colonies, predatory Mississippian groups remained culturally tethered to the heartland by the strong bonds of history, of common ancestry. From this adaptive radiation perspective, similarity between Mississippian groups over broad geographical areas could be attributed to homology (historical relatedness) while patterns of regional variation could be explained in terms of (social) reproductive isolation, assimilation, and divergent evolution in transit, in response to differing local cultural and environmental landscapes.

Rather than viewing the Mississippian adaptive radiation purely in demographic terms, involving the actual rapid outward expansion and colonization by biological descendant populations of heartland polities, it is also often explained in terms of the rapid outward spread of elements of the new cultural complex—things and ideas rather than colonists (e.g., technological innovations, new crops, new belief systems) along routes of communication and exchange, from society to society. When viewed from this cultural homology perspective, the Mississippian emergence could be interpreted as resulting both from opportunities provided by introduced innovations, and the pressure on recipient societies or societal subgroups to maintain parity with similarly empowered competitive groups or subgroups, either within the societies in question or adjoining them.

The analogy or process position, in its purest form, stands in polar opposition to the homology solution to the large spatial scale aspect of the "rapid" Mississippian transformation. When considered from an analogy perspective, the widespread cultural-developmental similarities of Mississippian societies are perceived and explained in terms of independent and isolated cultural response to similar challenges. While certainly not presenting this position in polar or dogmatic form, Jon Muller (1986) outlines it quite eloquently. Existing in generally similar river valley settings across the East, and having generally comparable economies, Late Woodland populations on the brink of the Mississippian emergence were similarly organized and similarly armed in terms of quivers of alternative adaptational responses to both internal and external events. When faced, over broad areas, with comparable problems, such as landscape partitioning and density dependent population-resource imbalance, they found similar solutions and followed parallel developmental pathways. The apparent broad-scale similarity of both the Mississippian emergence and Mississippian chiefdoms thus could be alternatively explained as not so much reflecting historical relatedness or cultural homology, but rather as the comparable adaptation of societies having the same starting point and facing the same challenges.

There is a wide theoretical middle ground between these polar opposites, occupied by a rich variety of explanatory variations on homology and analogy, and as the regional data sets of the East for the period A.D. 750–1050 expand and improve, it becomes ever more evident that the developmental sequences of different regions may well not cluster around a single scenario solution at either pole or in between. Rather, they could well form a multidimensional array of distinct historical sequences arranged in, as yet, poorly understood patterns of similarity and exhibiting different mixtures of demographic expansion, social reproductive isolation, and interpolity developmental interaction. There is no single, simple, all encompassing and comforting theoretical explanation for the Mississippian emergence. Rather, Mississippianists are faced with the cold reality of a large interconnected set of nested developmental back boxes resting in the interpretive shadow of the homology-analogy dilemma.

NESTED BLACK BOXES

Carrying the general label "Mississippian emergence A.D. 750–1050" the largest, all inclusive developmental box contains a geographically arranged set of regional or regional system boxes of different sizes, each carrying a label such as "American Bottom," "Coles Creek," "Central Mississippi Valley." Each of these is connected to others by interaction-exchange lines of communication and movement of people, objects, and ideas. These regional system boxes in turn each contain a set of smaller scale geographically arranged individual polity-level boxes, which are similarly interconnected through lines of human interaction. Individual polity boxes in turn are filled with interconnected individual community or settlement boxes of varying size and nature, which in turn contain interconnected societal subunit boxes containing basic economic unit (household) boxes.

While this nested black box metaphor for the Mississippian emergence is overly static and mechanistic, it does serve to both suggest and illustrate many of the difficulties involved in developing explanatory models of the Mississippian emergence, as well as providing a frame of reference for the content and organizational structure of this edited volume. Until fifteen years ago, almost all of these nested developmental boxes at all levels were tightly closed, and in the absence of information, explanatory models were universal, broad brush-stroke speculative scenarios. This total closure situation has changed somewhat, as reflected in the ten chapters that follow this introduction, with excavation and regional synthesis opening, to varying degrees, scattered boxes at different nested levels. The expansion of our view into the developmental black boxes of the Mississippian emergence will, I am sure, continue in the future as it has to this point—in a rather random and scattered manner, dictated to a considerable degree by the placement of impact zones and associated mitigation funding. Mississippian emergence boxes, comprising separate pieces of a set of related developmental puzzles, will not be consistently opened at a particular nested level, nor will they be either equally distributed across the East or advantageously clustered within a single regional system or individual polity box. Given

this current and continued pattern of almost random box opening within the shadow of the homology-analogy dilemma, consideration of the Mississippian emergence, of necessity, should be conducted within a multilevel comparative framework that seeks out and accommodates information from the full range of nested levels, ranging from basic economic unit households up through regional systems. In addition, while the A.D. 750–1050 Mississippian emergence is at least fleetingly observed in many areas, general explanatory inquiries should concentrate on those developmental boxes that have been most successfully and most completely opened.

SELECTIVE MULTIPLE-LEVEL COMPARISON

Given the above general frame of reference for approaching a better understanding of the Mississippian emergence, the content and structure of this edited volume comes into focus. The chapters that follow are not meant to provide a topically or geographically comprehensive overview of the Mississippian emergence. Rather, they comprise a set of successfully and relatively widely opened developmental black boxes from a range of different nested levels, that when taken together serve to cross-illuminate the Mississippian emergence from a number of different angles. While Chapters 2 through 5 represent well-opened nested boxes below the level of polity, and Chapters 6 through 11 are scaled above the level of polity, this dichotomy reflects more than the traditional division of site level vs. regional level consideration. The four sites considered in Chapters 2 through 5 (Powell Canal, Toltec, Zebree, and Range) were all investigated with an explicit overriding focus on understanding settlement structure and internal organization. With this organizational research focus dictating excavation strategy within settlements having clearly patterned artifact and feature sets under good temporal control, the results, in my opinion, provide the clearest, most detailed pictures yet available of the Emergent Mississippian period below the polity level. The sequence of four sites considered in Chapters 2 through 5, however, are nested at different levels within geographically separated and culturally distinct polities distributed along the Mississippi Valley (Fig. 1).

Dating about A.D. 600, the small, apparently seasonally occupied, Powell Canal site, discussed by John House in Chapter 2, in fact predates the Mississippian

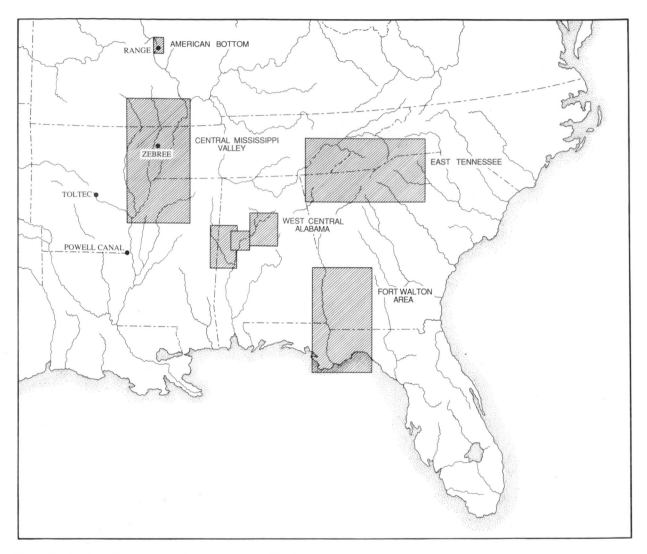

Fig. 1. The location of settlements and regions considered in this volume.

emergence, and provides the best view of a Late Wood-land habitation settlement in the lower Mississippi Valley to date. As such, Powell Canal, along with the limited number of comparably excavated settlements in the central Mississippi Valley (e.g., Late Woodland components at Zebree and Range), provide the essential comparative baseline for consideration of the subsequent transformation to chiefdom-level organization. In also addressing the obvious normative issue of representativeness and comparability, House employs his analysis of Powell Canal as a point of departure for a consideration of broader issues of regional patterns of settlement, community organization, technology, subsistence, and biocultural adaptation at the A.D. 700

baseline of the Mississippian emergence. Clearly, any adequate understanding of the Mississippian emergence will rest in part both on a more accurate characterization of its loosely integrated segmentary tribal Late Woodland forebearers, and in a more accurate measure of the degree of similarity between the tribal foundations extant in different regions. The unique nature of Powell Canal underscores how little is known regarding the Late Woodland baseline from which chiefdoms developed.

At the other end of the spectrum, in terms of within-polity developmental boxes, the Toltec site, described by Martha Rolingson in Chapter 3, represents one of the most carefully documented central settlements of the A.D. 750–1050 Emergent Mississippian period. Surrounded by a large earthen bank, the Toltec center exhibits a clear internal plan, with a total of 18 mounds bordering two central open areas or plazas. Mound construction began by A.D. 800, early in the Emergent Mississippian period, and mounds appear to have served primarily as foundations for residential structures. Given this early temporal placement, the level of planned and directed corporate labor mound construction, and the apparent residential substructural function of many of its mounds, Toltec stands out as the earliest well-preserved and well-documented center in the Mississippian pattern yet described. Similar, as yet undiscovered, central mound centers on a time scale comparable to that of Toltec are expected to have existed, likely largely obscured now by subsequent stages of mound construction. Large-scale corporate labor and social inequality, as evidenced by organized centers not exclusively devoted to corporate mortuary activities, are often considered hallmarks of Mississippian chiefdoms. Few burials were encountered during excavation of the Toltec site, and no evidence of status-related differential treatment of the dead has been recovered. Interestingly, the outlying Plum Bayou culture settlements for which Toltec served as a political and religious center appear to have been small hamlets and homesteads, and the Plum Bayou economy was based not on maize, but on indigenous eastern North American seed crops and wild species of plants and animals.

The Toltec mound center and its imbedded implications regarding corporate labor and status elevation highlight a range of issues centering on the various societal roles of mounds and mound centers and their sociopolitical meaning. Accordingly, Rolingson uses the Toltec mound center and its imbedded sociopolitical implications as a frame of reference for a broadly comparative chronological, structural, and functional consideration of mounds and mound centers in the Mississippi Valley. In detailing the long and complex history of mounds and mound centers in the lower Mississippi Valley, and the wide variety of distinctly different if not clearly understood societal roles they played across space and time, Rolingson underscores the interpretive dangers in overly facile uniform translations of corporate labor and earth moving into general sociopolitical pigeon holes. It is within the context of these mounds and mound centers that a central, if often ideologically masked, issue of the Mississippian emergence is most

directly addressed—the dual transition from a corporate role for such centers and their resident practitioners, to one focused on a particular central societal subgroup, and from a religious mortuary function to a more clearly secular and political one. Inherent in this issue is whether or not, as is popularly supposed, the restricted authority positions of corporate religious or ceremonial practitioners served as a spring board to permanent power positions and chiefdoms. Paul Welch provides a provocative discussion of this topic in Chapter 9.

Moving up the Mississippi Valley from Toltec, the Zebree site (Chapter 4) and the Range site (Chapter 5) provide the most completely and carefully described examples of Emergent Mississippian period habitation settlements yet excavated.

Described by Phyllis Morse and Dan Morse in Chapter 4, the Zebree site was the focus of testing and large-scale excavation over four field seasons that uncovered evidence of a Late Woodland (Dunklin phase) winter village of perhaps 40 people. This Dunklin phase village was overlain by an Emergent or Early Mississippian (Big Lake phase) planned community of perhaps 100–140 people, distributed in household clusters bordering a central plaza, which in turn contained a large central post. As summarized in Chapter 4, detailed comparative analysis of the material culture and feature technology of these pre-emergent and emergent Mississippian communities at Zebree provides an illuminating characterization of the nature and implications of the technological aspects of the Mississippian emergence, and their possible relationship with the documented increasing importance of maize. In the unfortunately still largely inaccessible multivolume site report on which Chapter 4 is based, the Morses comprehensively detail the dramatic changes in technology, production, and community organization that shaped the Mississippian emergence.

In Chapter 5, John Kelly describes and illustrates a series of 28 temporally discrete communities that span 500 years, from A.D. 600–1100, at the Range site. Continuing the pattern documented at Powell Canal and Zebree (Dunklin phase) the initial Late Woodland settlements at Range exhibited no overarching internal organization in terms of structure or feature distribution, making it difficult to establish contemporaneity of structure occupation, or the composition of the settlements at any one point in time. Subsequent emergent

Mississippian settlements at Range, however, show clear evidence of increased planning and internal complexity. In a remarkable expansion on the Dunklin-Big Lake transition at Zebree, John Kelly is able not only to document the initial appearance of an overall planned and center-focused community by A.D. 800 (and associated changes in feature and material culture technology) but to also follow the continuing development and increasing complexity of community plans at the Range site. Like the Zebree project, Kelly's work at the Range site demonstrates the value of large-scale excavation of community plans as providing invaluable access to evidence of sequential change in the spatial organization of society in periods of "rapid" social transformation. The Zebree and Range site excavations convincingly illustrate that evidence of emerging social inequality and changing social roles is not solely to be found in the analysis of differential treatment of the dead, or the development of mound centers, but can also be observed in the shifting organization and control of space and societal subgroups at the community level.

While Chapters 2 through 4 represent well-opened developmental black boxes below the polity level, and indicate the advantages in opening and comparing similarly varied settlement and center "boxes" across the East, Chapters 6 through 10 underscore the importance of careful comparison of well-opened emergent Mississippian puzzle boxes above the level of individual polity.

Sharing similarly impressive success in resolution of problems of fine-grain temporal control, the regional system chapters summarize the available information for the A.D. 750–1050 period of interest from five widely separated and quite distinct environmental and baseline culture history settings. Forming a rough north-south transect, Chapter 6 by John Kelly covers the American Bottom, and Chapter 7 by Dan Morse and Phyllis Morse the central Mississippi Valley, while Chapter 8 by Gerald Schroedl, Clifford Boyd, and Stephen Davis addresses Mississippian origins in east Tennessee. In Chapter 9 Paul Welch looks at parallel developmental trends in three adjacent areas of west-central Alabama, while John Scarry considers the evolution of simple and complex chiefdoms within the Ft. Walton regional system of north Florida and adjacent portions of Georgia and Alabama in Chapter 10.

Variously informed by the partially opened developmental black boxes at different nested levels within their regional areas of consideration, Chapters 6 through 10 provide in many respects an interesting array of diverse perspectives and differing approaches to the homology-analogy dilemma and the Mississippian emergence at and above the polity level. At the same time, however, these regional system level considerations of the Mississippian emergence share a similar emphasis on the dual importance of the pre-Mississippian baseline cultural contexts as framing developmental pathways, while local, if often similar, challenges and opportunities, both internal and external, influence the course of social transformation.

The analogy-homology dilemma is confronted directly by John Kelly in his Chapter 6 consideration of the emergence of Mississippian culture in the American Bottom. After describing previous local evolution and migration-contact models of Mississippian origins in the region, Kelly updates and supplements an alternative "integration" model he first proposed a decade ago. Explicitly in situ, Kelly's explanatory model also recognizes interaction with other regions as an integral aspect of the transition process. Similarly, while focusing on the interrelationships between demographic growth, sedentism, and the shift to maize agriculture, Kelly also considers internal changes on the cultural landscape. He argues that certain community features and symbols played a central role in facilitating and legitimizing the growing authority of some lineages, as reflected in the controlled and structured organization of space and people.

In Chapter 7, Dan Morse first addresses the difficult question of temporal control of Late Woodland and Emergent Mississippian archaeological complexes in the central Mississippi Valley, a region of rich environmental and culture-historical diversity. Beginning with a consideration of pre-emergent Late Woodland phases (Dunklin, Baytown, Hoecake), he then traces the development of Mississippian culture in the central valley, moving from area to area within the region as dictated by the data available for different time periods. Morse recognizes the Cairo Lowland area, and particularly the large "Range-like" Hoecake site, as being of paramount importance in understanding the origins of Mississippian culture in the central valley. But because information from the Cairo Lowlands area and the Hoecake site itself is relatively limited, he is restricted to largely viewing it within the context of better known areas to the south. Zebree serves as the primary focus of his pre-A.D. 1000 (early period Mississippian) Varney horizon discussion, while the Cherry Valley phase dominates his consideration of the early middle period Mississippian Beaker horizon. Avoiding any simplistic explanations, Morse points out that the Central Valley witnessed a number of concurrent but distinctive developmental sequences, and suggests that the Cairo Lowland, representing the only independent emergence recognized to date in the region, played a central role in the Mississippian emergence.

Like Kelly and Morse, Schroedl, Boyd, and Davis (Chapter 8) provide a detailed reassessment of the chronology and culture history of the Late Woodland-Early Mississippian transition. They also face the analogy-homology dilemma and discuss a number of explanations for the Woodland-Mississippian transition in the east Tennessee region that range from pure homology (migration-invasion) through cultural homology and migration—in situ combinations, to near pure analogy (in situ cultural development with minimum external influence). This final near pure analogy option for interpreting the Mississippian emergence in east Tennessee has become the general consensus model over the past fifteen years. Schroedl, Boyd, and Davis outline a number of possible interpretive variations on this in situ approach before focusing on the interrelationships between demographic growth, the shift to corn agriculture, and sociopolitical partitioning of the landscape as the primary transformational processes generated from within the culture systems of the region.

In Chapter 9, Paul Welch considers the Mississippian emergence in three adjacent study areas located in west-central Alabama. After dealing with difficult issues of chronology and culture history, and describing in detail the Woodland-Mississippian transition in each of the three adjacent areas under consideration, Welch compares their different developmental trajectories. Viewing the emergence of Mississippian culture in west-central Alabama in terms of changes in social integration and subsistence, Welch proposes that the shift to maize agriculture preceded and precipitated hierarchical social organization in both the Moundville and Bessemer areas, while in the central Tombigbee area, the adoption of agriculture came after a form of social ranking had occurred. Correspondingly, Welch speculates that in the Bessemer area, this process involved

the promotion of a sanctified role to a politically and economically dominant position, while in the Tombigbee area a political and economic role acquired a modest degree of sanctification.

Paralleling Paul Welch's comparison of Mississippian development in three adjacent areas of west-central Alabama, John Scarry (Chapter 10) considers both the initial emergence of simple (Cayson phase) chiefdoms in the Apalachicola River valley subarea of the Ft. Walton region, and the subsequent development of a complex (Lake Jackson phase) chiefdom in the adjacent Tallahassee Hills subarea. Scarry considers Cayson phase chiefdoms to have developed in adaptive response to demographically driven population-resource imbalance within the Apalachicola and Chattahoochee river valleys.

The subsequent fissioning of an emergent Ft. Walton chiefdom in the Apalachicola Valley led to the establishment of an early Lake Jackson phase simple chiefdom in the adjacent Tallahassee Hills subarea. Population growth continued within the Tallahassee Hills, but because of its quite different agricultural landscape, eventual population-resource imbalance led to the formation of the Lake Jackson complex chiefdom.

In a concluding chapter, Jim Brown, Richard Kerber, and Howard Winters specifically address a long-neglected aspect of the Mississippian emergence—the evolution of the exchange relations that formed the lines of influence, interaction, and communication between nested black boxes of Mississippian development. Recognizing that exchange is the major means by which small-scale agricultural societies carry on external relations, and arguing that trade was pervasive, Brown, Kerber, and Winters focus on the relationship between the origins of Mississippian society and the development of trade networks. Taking issue with the restrictive centralized polity model that has dominated perspectives on Mississippian societies and origins, Brown, Kerber, and Winters detail the role that a prestige goods economy played as a vehicle for emerging complexity on an interregional developmental scale. They argue very strongly in this concluding chapter that the Mississippian emergence cannot be adequately understood by focusing exclusively on the individual development of black boxes at different nested levels, but must also take into consideration the processes by which prestige goods economies facilitated and fueled the parallel interactive transformational processes within different regions. Conceptually, the approach taken by Brown, Kerber, and Winters clearly provides substantial resolution of many aspects of the analogy-homology dilemma.

Taken together, the ten chapters that follow provide, in my opinion, a compelling demonstration of the need to simultaneously consider and pursue explanations of Mississippian origins on a number of nested levels. They also highlight the need and the opportunity for a wider comparative dialogue, a more pluralistic approach to understanding the origins of Mississippian chiefdoms. In order to fully utilize and adequately interpret the wide range of information available from different regions of the East, multiple, if partial, explanations from a variety of theoretical perspectives should be encouraged. Models that focus on different aspects of the developmental process and which are framed at different temporal scales and analytical levels are a necessary aspect of gaining a better understanding of the initial development of ranked agricultural societies in the East.

REFERENCES CITED

Caldwell, Joseph
1958   *Trend and Tradition in the Prehistory of the Eastern United States.* American Anthropological Memoir 88.

Drennen, Robert D., and Carlos A. Uribe (editors)
1987   *Chiefdoms in the Americas.* University Press of America, Lanham, Maryland.

Earle, Timothy K.
1987   Chiefdoms in Archaeological and Ethnohistorical Perspective. *Annual Review of Anthropology* 16:279–308.

Feinman, Gary, and Jill Neitzel
1984   Too Many Types: An Overview of Sedentary Prestate Societies in the Americas. In *Advances in Archaeological Method and Theory,* vol. 7, edited by M. B. Schiffer, pp. 39–102. Academic Press, New York.

Hudson, Charles, Marvin Smith, David Hally, Richard Polhemus, and Chester DePratter
1985   Coosa: A Chiefdom in the Sixteenth-Century Southeastern United States. *American Antiquity* 50:723–737.

Muller, Jon
1986   *Archaeology of the Lower Ohio River Valley.* Academic Press, Orlando, Florida.

Powell Canal

Baytown Period Adaptation on Bayou Macon, Southeast Arkansas

INTRODUCTION

Phillips, Ford, and Griffin's (1951) archaeological survey in the lower alluvial valley of the Mississippi River in 1940–1947 had as one of its major goals the identification of pre-Mississippian cultures in a region that had come to be considered a "heartland" of Mississippian culture. By the conclusion of their research, a succession of pre-Mississippian "Baytown" cultural entities had been identified and Mississippian culture in the lower Mississippi Valley had been given a cultural-historical context. In the concluding chapter of their landmark study (Dunnell 1985), the authors directed attention to the great number of "middle Baytown" sites located throughout the lower Mississippi Valley. Seeing possible precursors of Mississippian community and settlement patterns among these sites, Phillips et al. (1951:440–443, 448) cautiously inferred Baytown period population growth and the increasing importance of maize agriculture. "Middle Baytown" corresponds to what we now know as the Baytown period in the lower Mississippi Valley sequence, the interval A.D. 300–700 (Phillips 1970:20).

The early recognition of the pivotal position of the Baytown period in the development of lower Mississippi Valley cultures would seem to have placed reconstruction of adaptation during this interval high on the agenda of archaeological investigation in this part of the Southeast. Nonetheless, data relevant to social organization, subsistence, and biological adjustments of Baytown period societies have been slow in accumulat-

ing. The 1981 investigations at the Powell Canal site on Bayou Macon in southeast Arkansas, however, yielded an unusually well-rounded data base pertaining to human adaptation in the Mississippi River floodplain at ca. A.D. 600 (House 1982a). The Baytown component at Powell Canal, dated immediately prior to the A.D. 700 baseline for the pan-regional emergence of Mississippian culture, which is the focus of this volume, may serve as a point of departure for reviewing available evidence pertinent to reconstruction of human lifeways throughout the central and lower Mississippi Valley on this time level and for considering patterns of pre-Mississippian adaptation to the resources, habitat zonation, and settlement pattern constraints of the largest river valley in North America.

PHYSICAL SETTING

The Powell Canal site is located on the east bank of Bayou Macon in a backswamp area 4 km west of the present day course of the Mississippi River (Fig. 2). The portion of Arkansas in which the Powell Canal site is located has been included in the Tensas Basin subdivision of the lower Mississippi Valley (Fisk 1944, fig. 1; Phillips et al. 1951, fig. 1). About 3 km west of the site is Macon Ridge, an extensive insular remnant of braided Arkansas River terrace surface correlated with the waning of Early Wisconsin glaciation in the Rocky Mountains (Saucier 1974:18). The mean annual temperature in southeast Arkansas is about 18 degrees C

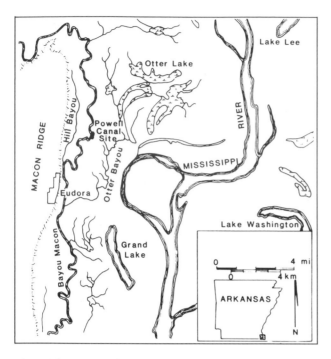

Fig. 2. The environmental setting of the Powell Canal site.

(64 degrees F) and the frost-free growing season averages about 230 days. Mean annual rainfall is about 1,320 mm (52 inches). Rainfall is generally abundant throughout the year but summer droughts are known to occur (Rheinhold 1969). The Powell Canal site is located on soils of the Sharkey-Bowdre association, developed in clayey alluvium deposited in slackwater areas by the Mississippi River (Cloutier and Finger 1967:2–4).

The Powell Canal site locality is characterized by a complex hydrology that is of crucial importance to interpreting past aboriginal adaptation. Bayou Macon was described in 1937 as

> a sluggish stream located between Bayou Barthlomew and the Mississippi River. It heads in Desha County, Arkansas, about six miles east of Winchester and flows south through South-eastern Arkansas and North-eastern Louisiana, emptying into the Tensas River (Lemley and Dickinson 1937:17).

Although the present day main channel of the Mississippi River is only 4 km east of the Powell Canal site, the drainage of the locality is toward the Tensas River and ultimately toward the Ouachita-Black River and Red River. This hydrological peculiarity is accounted for by the fact that the floodplain of an aggrading stream slopes away from the stream because of natural levees adjoining it (Fenneman 1938:91). Prior to historic artificial levee construction, the entire area was within the overflow of the Mississippi River at times of high water. Historic flood records (Patterson 1964) indicate a definite seasonal peak in flooding along this portion of the Mississippi River in March-April. Early nineteenth-century surveyor's notes examined by Frances B. King (1982a) indicate evidence of floodwaters as much as 2.2 m deep in the Powell Canal locality. The site itself, however, may have been flooded only infrequently because it is significantly higher than most of the surrounding area. Macon Ridge, some 3 km west of the Powell Canal site, rises approximately 6 m above the floodplain and did not go under even during the near-record flood of 1927 (Daniel 1977:85). It would probably have been a conveniently near and secure flood refuge for prehistoric inhabitants of the Powell Canal site.

The theoretical energy subsidy represented by nutrient-bearing floodwaters has been singled out by Smith (1978) as one of the most culturally important ecological characteristics of Southeastern floodplain environments. Another hydrological aspect of the environment that may have been significant to aboriginal inhabitants of the Powell Canal site is the fact that when the annual Mississippi flood stage began to fall, it would have been streams like Bayou Macon that carried the floodwaters out of thousands of square kilometers of inundated terrain. Again, historic flood records indicate that the draining of Mississippi River floodwaters down Bayou Macon would typically have taken place in April through June. Finally, Bayou Macon, because of its hydrological characteristics, may have functioned as a communication link between separate major drainage basins. In *The Forked River,* historian Stanley Faye (1942) reviewed early colonial sources portraying flood-season Bayou Macon as "a western Mississippi" and an aboriginally recognized transportation route. During high water, the upper end of Bayou Macon would have been connected to the Mississippi River, and would have led more-or-less directly to the heart of the Tensas Basin, to the Tensas-Ouachita confluence, and to the Troyville site.

A reconstruction of early nineteenth-century vegetational patterns in the Powell Canal site locality employing U.S. General Land Office survey records was prepared by King (1982a). This reconstruction reflects, to a varying extent, all of the variety of river bottom vegetational communities recognized by Braun (1950: 290–297) and others. The surveyor's notes mention "cypress swamp" in several locations. Low areas were covered by a wet forest dominated by hackberry (sugarberry) while better-drained ridges must have been forested by sweetgum and oak. The distinctive loessal soils of nearby Macon Ridge, in contrast, supported a mixed oak-hickory forest type. In such an environment, a variety of potentially important wild plant food resources would have been present in floodplain lakes and other habitats (King 1982a:14, table 4).

Animal species in Southeastern floodplain environments have been summarized by Shelford (1963) and species distributions and other general information about Arkansas mammals have been summarized by Sealander (1979). The Powell Canal site is on the Mississippi Flyway with a seasonal potential for economically significant harvests of waterfowl (Smith 1975: 128–129). The lower and central Mississippi Valley was characterized in former times by an especially abundant and high quality fish resource (Rostlund 1952; Lambou 1959). It is likely that in late spring when Mississippi River floodwaters began to drain out of thousands of square kilometers of forested backswamps, there were predictable concentrations of fish in distributary channels such as Bayou Macon.

CULTURAL AND TEMPORAL CONTEXT

The Baytown period (A.D. 300–700) has been defined in somewhat negative terms as "a slightly murky interval between the decline of Hopewellian and the consolidation of Coles Creek culture in the south" (Phillips 1970:20), and Baytown has been referred to as one of a group of "good gray cultures" prevalent on a post-Hopewellian time level in this portion of the Southeast (Williams 1963:297). In the central Mississippi Valley Baytown period components are characterized by a comparative lack of items attributable to long-distance exchange and indeed give an overall impression of simplicity and uniformity, although burial mounds appear to be associated with some components (Morse and Morse 1983:181–199; House 1982b:42). Morse and Morse (1983:192) have suggested that Baytown period settlement pattern data are consistent with a model of segmentary tribal organization (Sahlins 1968, cf. Brain 1971:64). Extended family households have been pro-

posed (Morse and Morse 1983:184) and alternative settlement system models include residential mobility with dispersal and nucleation by season (Morse and Morse 1983:186) and logistical strategies (see Binford 1980:18) involving relatively stable settlements (Jeter 1982:98). Below about latitude 33 degrees north, the apparent greater complexity of aboriginal cultures on this time level is exemplified by the spectacular scale of mound building at the Troyville site (Walker 1936) and the recent find of two polychrome ceramic human effigies at the Gold Mine site in northeastern Louisiana (Jones et al. 1979). The north-south dichotomy of aboriginal cultures between the central and lower Mississippi Valley has recently been emphasized in the redefinition of Troyville culture (Belmont 1984).

Perhaps because of a sampling bias against "good gray cultures" (Stoltman 1978:722; Jeter 1982:98; Morse and Morse 1983:181) data pertaining to Baytown period subsistence, community patterns, and human skeletal biology were, until very recently, sparse to nonexistent for most portions of the central and lower Mississippi Valley.

In general, subsistence appears to have emphasized hunting, fishing, and foraging with perhaps very limited horticulture involving squashes and native North American cultigens. There is a paucity of evidence of maize (Byrd and Neuman 1978), and Morse and Morse (1983:186) have proposed a subsistence base of "almost anything edible" for the Baytown period Dunklin phase in the central Mississippi Valley. The introduction of the bow and arrow toward the end of the Baytown period may have augmented hunting efficiency (Brain 1971:61–62; Byrd and Neuman 1978:15).

Turning to a temporal perspective, utilitarian ceramics provide evidence for strong cultural continuities from Marksville (100 B.C.–A.D. 300), through Baytown, into the Coles Creek period (A.D. 700–1100) in most portions of the area under consideration (Morse and Morse 1983:181). Indeed, it is as yet difficult to distinguish between Baytown and Coles Creek period assemblages in many regions (Rolingson 1982:19). Platform mound construction and the development of hierarchical settlement systems appear to have accelerated throughout much of the lower Mississippi Valley during the Coles Creek period (Brain 1978; House 1982b), coeval with the emergence of Mississippian culture in the central Mississippi Valley and elsewhere in the East. Recent data from the Toltec site near Little Rock, Arkansas provide evidence of the in situ development of Plum Bayou culture from Baytown culture and indicate that large-scale mound and earthwork construction on that site began by A.D. 700–800 (Chapter 3, this volume).

Within southeast Arkansas there is a definite concentration of Baytown period occupation along Bayou Macon. Many of the sites, including Powell Canal, are extensive middens and a few are associated with small mounds (Rolingson 1973; Lemley and Dickinson 1937). Several of the most intensively occupied of these sites are associated with areas of Sharkey clay and other backswamp soils that would be considered among the least suitable soils in the region for technologically simple horticulture (Baker 1973).

Aboriginal ceramics and other temporally diagnostic artifacts recovered at the Powell Canal site in 1980–1981 appear overwhelmingly to represent a single cultural assemblage. The core of the ceramic complex consists of Baytown Plain (79 percent of all sherds), Mulberry Creek Cord Marked (11 percent), Alligator Incised *var. Alligator* (5 percent), and Salomon Brushed *var. Salomon* (2 percent). The occurrence of sherds of the distinctive Mulberry Creek Cord Marked *var. Eudora* in the majority of cultural features of the site helps to tie the otherwise somewhat disparate feature content assemblages into a single cultural complex. *Eudora,* defined during the course of the Powell Canal investigation, is characterized by widely spaced, thickcord impressions in diagonally oriented plats on jar exteriors, often associated with carefully executed crisscross overstamping (House 1982a, fig. 31). Additional types and varieties occur in frequencies of less than 1 percent. The occurrence of Woodville Zoned Red *var. Woodville* in the Powell Canal ceramic collection supports the assignment of the Baytown component to the late Baytown period "Woodville Horizon" (Belmont and Williams 1981) and a date of A.D. 600 (Belmont 1982:107; unless otherwise stated, ceramic types and varieties referred to in this chapter are as defined by Phillips [1970:37–238]). Three organic samples submitted for radiocarbon analysis during the investigation, yielded disparate age assays ranging from 300 to 1100 radiocarbon years B.P. and are of little value in dating the late Baytown occupation at Powell Canal. Artifacts recovered at the Powell Canal site, in addition to ceramics, include square and contracting stemmed dart points, corner-notched arrow points, grooved

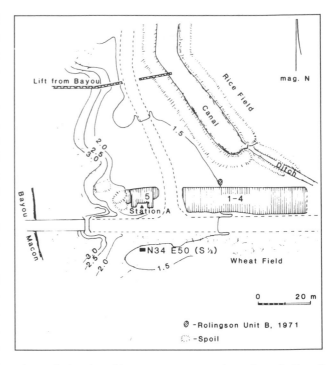

Fig. 3. The location of the 1980–1981 excavation units at the Powell Canal site.

plummets, cobble tools, modified bone and antler items, and a single tentatively identified marine shell bead associated with a burial.

Although the Powell Canal artifact assemblage corresponds well to the formal definition of "Baytown culture" offered by Rolingson (1982), southern affinities are also conspicuous. Belmont (1982:106) includes the Powell Canal site along with the Marsden and Western Deasonville phases as northern and late expressions of the newly redefined Troyville culture.

EXCAVATIONS AT POWELL CANAL

The Powell Canal site consists of an area of surface artifact concentration and midden extending some 270 m along the east (left) bank of Bayou Macon. Except for the steep bayou bank on the west, the site is nearly level but the land on the east edge of the site slopes gently toward the east, away from the bayou. On the south end of the site is an aboriginal mound roughly 1.5 m in height by 15 m in diameter; it has never been investigated archaeologically. At the time it was first mapped in 1971, the Powell Canal site was approximately bisected by an east-west gravel road that crossed

Bayou Macon by a wooden bridge. It was the projected replacement of this bridge by the Arkansas Highway and Transportation Department that occasioned the 1980–1981 excavations that are the subject of this chapter. These excavations were concentrated north of the gravel road, between the road and the modern irrigation canal, which gives the site its name (Fig. 3). This portion of the site had been earlier tested by Martha Ann Rolingson (1971) during a National Park Service-sponsored survey of site destruction by agricultural practices. The two phases of excavation at the Powell Canal site in 1980–1981 consisted of initial testing in October of 1980, followed by intensive excavation in May 1981, to mitigate the impact of the projected bridge alignment.

The 1981 project research design emphasized recovery of data pertinent to past community patterns and subsistence. A total of 469 sq m were opened on the site, employing a combination of machine and hand excavation techniques. For convenience, the areas initially opened by machine stripping were designated Cuts 1-4 on the east and Cut 5 on the west. A single 1 by 2 m unit was excavated by hand south of the road. The excavations resulted in a 60 m long east-west transect of a north-south trending linear streamside site. A total of 700 liters of soil matrix from pit features was processed by water flotation employing a modified SMAP apparatus (Limp 1974; Watson 1976) operated on-site.

THE FORMAL-SPATIAL STRUCTURE AND PAST COMMUNITY PATTERNS OF POWELL CANAL

Prior to modern disturbance, the stratigraphy of the Powell Canal site seems to have basically consisted of a dark clayey artifact-rich midden some 50 cm in depth grading into sterile brown plastic clay, into which aboriginal features intruded from the overlying midden. There is, however, evidence of considerable disturbance and truncation of the original profile of the site as a result of historic road and irrigation canal construction. The alluvial clay soils forming the site matrix are prone to vertical cracking during dry times of the year, which would no doubt promote some vertical movement of cultural material and the observed lack of physical stratification in recorded midden profiles (Duffield 1970; Wood and Johnson 1978:352–358). A particu-

larly fortunate aspect of the pedology of the Powell Canal site, on the other hand, is the fact that the sediments composing the site matrix are derived from relatively unweathered material deposited in the quite recent geological past. It is to the consequently nearly neutral pH of this soil matrix that we owe the unusual preservation of 1,400 year-old subsistence and human skeletal remains at the site.

The distributions of major classes of cultural features at Powell Canal are presented in Figure 4. Aboriginal midden-filled pits, of which 12 were excavated, fell into three categories: flat-based cylindrical pits (7), bell-shaped pits (2), and round-based pits (3). There was a distinct clustering of flat-based cylindrical pits and bell-shaped pits (considered a transformation of the former, Morse 1980a:8–11) in the western portion of the excavation, at the crest of the bayou bank (Fig. 4). The three round-based pits were widely scattered in Cuts 1-4 where the overall pit feature density appears to have been much lower than to the west. Given the reconstruction of site stratigraphic processes presented above, it cannot be assumed that the pit features observed during the 1980–1981 excavations were the only ones ever present in the excavated area. They may be only those extending below the midden. Though pit feature contents varied, most of the pits yielded abundant and well-preserved ceramic sherds and faunal and floral subsistence remains.

Considerable effort during the excavations was expended in an attempt to delineate possible aboriginal house patterns on the site. A total of ten probable aboriginal post holes were recognized but these were scattered throughout the excavation and revealed no discernable alignments.

The third class of aboriginal feature recorded at Powell Canal was human burials. The four burials recovered during the 1980–1981 excavations were all located on the eastern periphery of the site between 55 and 65 m from the bayou bank. Three burials, 2, 3 and 4, constituted a tightly clustered cemetery group on the north edge of the Cuts 1–4 excavation unit. Burial 1 was located about 10 m to the southeast. Local residents who visited the site during the 1981 excavations reported that, during irrigation canal construction in the 1960s, two additional burials were exposed within a few meters of Burial 1. The adult inhumations reflected a basically similar burial program; all were wholly or partially extended, head to the east. Details

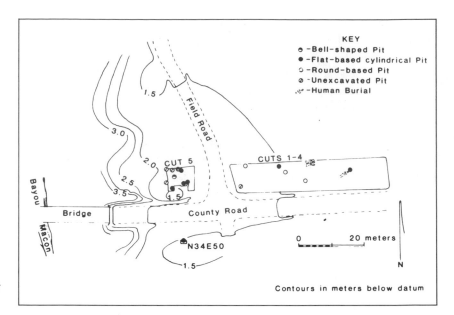

Fig. 4. The distribution of features at the Powell Canal site.

of the burial program, however, differed. Burials 3 and 4, an older adult male and female, respectively, were buried in an unusual prone (face-down) position, which may be a Deasonville cultural attribute (Phillips 1970:691; but see Morse 1973:2). The only grave good recovered from any of the Powell Canal burials was a shell bead from the throat area of the Burial 1 adult.

The most striking aspect of the Powell Canal site's formal-spatial structure, as revealed by the 1980–1981 excavations, is the functional variability encountered as one moves from west to east, perpendicular to the bayou bank. In contrast, analysis of feature and midden ceramic samples revealed little, if any, cultural-historical variability along this transect. The site's formal-spatial structure within the excavation area thus supports the interpretation that the array of cultural features exposed constitutes a single Baytown period "household cluster" (Winter 1976:25).

Following this line of thought, the cluster of flat-based pits in Cut 5—with their inferred food storage function—may represent an area where food was processed for storage. In light of the abundance of broken ceramics, ash, and food remains in the pit fills, this was probably also the area where food was cooked and consumed. It is probable that some of these pits were used in succession, rather than concurrently, representing successive seasons of occupation. It would be logical that a dwelling would have stood in close proximity to food preparation and consumption areas represented

by the Cut 5 pit feature cluster. The missing archaeological house pattern may have been located beyond the excavation—or it may not have involved alignments of postholes of sufficient depth to have extended below midden.

The round-based pits in the west end of Cuts 1–4 may represent a type of facility that was functionally distinct from that represented by the flat-based pits. The low artifact density in the fills of the round-based pits may also have functional significance because abundant artifacts were present in the overlying midden on this part of the site.

The cemetery area located some 60 m back from the bayou bank may have been used by the household or households whose principal living areas were immediately to the west on the crest of the bank. Though some biological differences were noted between the Burial 1 adult and those in Burials 2, 3, and 4 (see below), the common burial program and orientation support their being the product of a single cultural tradition.

Given the above interpretation of the formal-spatial structure of that part of the Powell Canal site within the excavation area, it appears likely that the household settlement itself may have had an overall elongated shape, its long axis perpendicular to the Bayou Macon bank line. This would be especially likely if the household settlement in the excavation area were just one of several such settlements along a few hundred meters of bankline at this point. This spatial configuration is

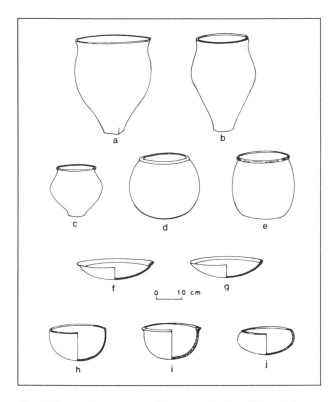

Fig. 5. Principal ceramic vessel forms at the Powell Canal site.

widespread among streamside settlement patterns; in geographical terms it represents a distortion of the locational lattice by linear resource localization (Haggett et al. 1977:104–105). The localized resource in this case would be Bayou Macon itself, representing a source of both transportation and food.

TECHNOLOGY

Ceramic vessel forms recognized during the analysis of the 4,455 sherds recovered at Powell Canal include tall vertical-sided jars, barrel-shaped beakers, cylindrical beakers with tightly constricted orifices, hemispherical bowls, shallow bowls, and incurvate-sided bowls (Fig. 5). The somewhat surprising diversity of ceramic vessel forms observed at Powell Canal is more characteristic of assemblages in the lower, as opposed to central Mississippi Valley on this time level (Hopgood 1969; Morse and Million 1980) and may indicate a commensurate complexity in the overall systemic cultural behavior with which these material cultural elements articulated (Griffin 1965). Vertical-sided, flat-based jars (Fig. 5a–b) were represented by the largest number of recovered

rims, constituting about one third of the series on which the attribute of vessel form was observed. These jars are considered to have been cooking vessels, although direct evidence of this function in the form of charred residue on a sherd interior was observed in only one instance. The overall shape corresponds to what Linton (1944:370–371) denominated the "Woodland" form and saw as an adaptation to residential mobility. Projection of the orifice diameters of vertical-sided jar rims in the types and varieties Baytown Plain *var. unsp.*, Mulberry Creek Cord Marked *var. Eudora*, and Alligator Incised *var. Alligator* indicates vessel capacities typically in the 10 to 20 liter range. This modality of cooking jar capacity supports the inference of extended vs. nuclear family households (Turner and Lofgren 1966; Million 1980; Morse 1980b:3). This inference, however, remains without corroborating evidence.

The diversity of recovered lithic tool forms mentioned above supports the inference of hunting, light-duty cutting, heavy-duty woodworking, and plant processing functions. Lithic raw materials identified include chert gravels, which might be derived from relatively local sources, and igneous rocks and hard sandstones derived from the Ouachita Province. The comparatively few bone artifacts recovered included three awls or other piercing implements, a large antler tine, which may have been used as a flint knapping baton, and fragments of a possible turtle shell rattle.

Overall morphology and other physical attributes of the 12 pit features excavated at Powell Canal support a model of storage pit function. The appropriateness of pits for storage of grain or similar foodstuffs has been reviewed by Morse (1980a:8–11). Experimentation has shown that partial germination of grain in sealed pits consumes available atmospheric oxygen, resulting in an anaerobic environment that inhibits further germination, and the growth of insect pests and aerobic bacteria. Frances B. King (personal communication, 1982) has suggested dried or smoked meat or fish or tubers of lotus or arrowhead as possible candidates for specific foods stored in pit features at Powell Canal. Remains of the two plants mentioned were recovered from pit fills at the site (see below).

Given the assumption of a storage function for Powell Canal pit features, estimation of the modality, and range of the food storage capacity represented might give some idea of the relative economic impor-

Table 1. Estimated In Situ and Total Capacities of Pit Features at the Powell Canal Site

Feature Number	Category	In Situ Capacity [1] (liters)	Total Capacity [2] (liters)
3	Large, bell-shaped	758.3	1376.0
8	Small, round based	57.5	346.9
10	Small, flat based	69.4	263.3
11	Small, flat based	25.5	268.5
13	Small, flat based [3]	205.7	577.5
14	Small, flat based	23.3	324.3
19	Small, flat based	175.8	429.8
22	Small, flat based	114.6	250.8
24	Small, flat based	25.5	188.1
25	Small, round based	88.1	291.3
26	Small, flat based	61.1	493.7
28	Small, round based	35.7	170.9

[1] In situ capacity: estimated capacity of the remaining portion of feature below level at which it was defined archaeologically.

[2] Total capacity: estimated original capacity derived by adding in situ capacity to the cylindrical volume obtained by projecting the diameter of feature (at level it was archaeologically defined) upward to the estimated elevation of prehistoric ground surface (1.40 mbd).

[3] Feature 13 is somewhat bell-shaped.

Table 2. Carbonized Plant Remains from Powell Canal Site Features

Wood Charcoal		62.4 g
Hickory nut shell (cf. *Carya ovata*)		40.1 g
Other		
Chenopodium sp.	Chenopod	2 seeds
Diospyros virginiana	Persimmon	2 fragments
Euphorbiaceae	Euphorb	1 seed
Galium sp.	Bedstraw	1 seed
Gramineae (Poaceae)	Grass	3 seeds
Nelumbo lutea	Lotus	1 seed
Polygonum sp.	Knotweed	1 seed
Rubus sp.	Blackberry/raspberry	1 seed
cf. *Sagittaria latifolia*	Arrowhead	1 tuber

cf. = compares favorably

(data from King 1982b, table 15)

tance of food storage to the Baytown period population at Powell Canal. Table 1 presents estimates of in situ and "total" capacity for each of the 12 pit features excavated. These pairs of estimates, in situ capacity and total capacity, should be considered minimal and maximal, respectively. Their approximate nature is obvious but they provide a basis for intersite comparison of storage pit capacities. At Powell Canal the estimated storage pit capacities range from 171 liters to 1,376 liters with a mean of 325 liters. These Powell Canal site figures will be compared with storage capacity estimates for other sites in a following section of this chapter.

Because pit feature contents constitute one of the major types of units employed in the analysis of the Powell Canal data base, explicit consideration of the cultural formation processes involved (Schiffer 1976: 28) is in order. The physical attributes of the pit fills support a model of storage pit "discard" by prompt backfilling after final use. If a primary storage function assumes a considerable time lapse between initial excavation of a storage facility and its final use and "discard," it is logical to assume that the soil removed during the excavation of the pit would not be readily available for backfilling. Rather, surface soil with a rich admixture of recently deposited cultural debris would be the most readily available fill material. The marked variability observed between pit fills within even very small areas on the site supports the inference that the

pit content assemblages tend to represent short-term outputs of the cultural system involved. The motive for prompt backfilling cannot be directly inferred. Perhaps open pits in a settlement area were seen as hazardous.

Storage of food has profound implications for the ecological adjustment of human populations. It extends the time-utility of seasonal peaks in resource availability. It also implies close ties to specific loci on the landscape. In the case of Powell Canal, acceptance of the proposition of food storage on-site implies a predictable schedule of reoccupation or at least revisits.

SUBSISTENCE AND SEASONALITY

Analysis of recovered floral and faunal specimens by Frances B. King (1982b) and Holly Ann Carr (1982) of the Illinois State Museum provided extremely valuable information on both aboriginal subsistence and seasonality of occupation at the Powell Canal site. These specimens are in every case from pit features attributed to the Baytown period on the basis of artifactual content.

The recovered floral remains identified by King (Table 2) reflected utilization of floodplain resources. They included many species available in open or disturbed floodplain habitats and some species such as arrowhead and lotus, which were procured from aquatic habitats. Seasonality indicators from most features suggest spring-summer occupations. Feature 13, a small bell-shaped pit in the Cut 5 cluster, however, contrasted with the other pit features in producing the over-

Table 3. Faunal Remains from Powell Canal Site Features

TAXA: Mammalia		Fragments	MNI[1]
Sylvilagus sp.	Rabbit	1	1
Sylvilagus aquaticus	Swamp rabbit	6	4
Sylvilagus floridianus	Eastern cottontail	7	5
Rodentia	Rodent	2	2
Sciurus sp.	Squirrel	6	3
Sciurus carolinensis	Eastern gray squirrel	10	2
Tamias striatus	Eastern chipmunk	3	1
Marmota monax	Woodchuck	1	1
Castor canadensis	Beaver	1	1
Sigmodon hispidus	Common cotton rat	5	3
Neotoma floridana	Eastern woodrat	1	1
Oryzomys palustris	Rice rat	2	2
Procyon lotor	Raccoon	6	3
Mustela frenata	Long-tailed weasel	1	1
Ursus americana	Black bear	3	2
Odocoileus virginianus	Whitetail deer	65	6

Total Number Mammal Taxa: 16

TAXA: Aves		Fragments	MNI[1]
Anas platyrynchos	Mallard	1	1
Aix sponsa	Wood duck	1	1
Meleagris gallopavo	Turkey	2	2
Passeriformes	Passerines	4	1

Total Number Bird Taxa: 4

TAXA: Pelecypoda		Fragments	MNI[1]
Amblema plicata	Three-ridge mussel	1	1

Total Number Mussel Taxa: 1

TAXA: Osteichthyes		Fragments	MNI[1]
Amia calva	Bowfin	477	42
Lepisosteus sp.	Gars	211	11
Lepisosteus osseus	Longnose gar	1	1
Lepisosteus platostomus	Shortnose gar	4	1
Lepisosteus spatula	Alligator gar	4	2
Borosoma cepedianum	Gizzard shad	2	2
Esox sp.	Pickerel	12	4
Cyprinidae	Minnows	1	1
Catostomidae	Suckers	9	4
Ictiobus sp.	Buffalos	7	5
Ictiobus cyprinellus	Bigmouth buffalo	4	4
Ictiobus bubalus/niger	Smallmouth/black buffalo	3	3
Ictiobus/Carpoides	Buffalo/carpsucker	1	1
Carpoides sp.	Carpsuckers	1	1
Carpoides carpio	River carpsucker	3	3
Catostomus commersoni	White sucker	5	4
Ictaluridae	Catfishes	16	6
Ictalurus sp.	Catfish	28	1
Ictalurus natalis	Yellow bullhead	5	4

		Fragments	MNI[1]
Ictalurus sp.	Catfish	28	11
Ictalurus nebulosus	Brown bullhead	13	4
Ictalurus melas	Black bullhead	9	5
Ictalurus nat./neb./mel.	Bullhead	17	7
Ictalurus furcatus	Blue catfish	2	2
Ictalurus punctatus	Channel catfish	6	5
Pylodictus olivaris	Flathead	2	2
Perciformes	Spiny-ray fishes	1	1
Percidae	Perches	1	1
Centarchidae	Basses	144	18
Micropterus sp.	Bass	27	12
Micropterus dolomieui	Smallmouth bass	1	1
Micropterus salmoides	Largemouth bass	3	1
Lepomis sp.	Sunfishes	15	8
Lepomis cyanellus	Green sunfish	1	1
Lepomis macrochirus	Bluegill	1	1
Amploplites rupestris	Rock bass	2	2
Pomoxis sp.	Crappie	10	4
Pomoxis nigromaculatus	Black crappie	5	3
Aplodinotus grunniens	Drum	5	3

Total Number Fish Taxa: 38

TAXA: Amphibia		Fragments	MNI[1]
Anura	Frogs	2	1
Rana sp.	True frog	2	1
Rana catesbeiana	Bullfrog	1	1
Caudata	Salamanders	2	1

Total Number Amphibian Taxa: 4

TAXA: Reptilia		Fragments	MNI[1]
Chelydridae	Snapping turtles	5	2
Chelydra serpentina	Common snapper	2	1
Kinosternidae	Mud and musk turtles	1	1
Kinosternon sp.	Mud turtle	4	1
Sternothaerus sp.	Musk turtle	1	1
Testudinidae	Pond and box turtles	25	2
Terrapene carolina	Carolina box turtle	20	1
Chrysemys/Graptemys	Slider/map turtle	11	3
Chrysemys sp.	Sliders	12	4
Gyraptemys geographica	Map turtle	2	2
Lacertilia	Lizards	2	1
Serpentes	Snakes	23	4
Colubridae	Nonpoisonous snakes	1	1

Total Number Reptile Taxa: 13

[1] Sum of individual feature MNIs

(data from Carr 1982, table 20)

whelming bulk of the hickory nut shell fragments identified, suggesting fall-winter occupation. Traces of hickory nut shell and persimmon seeds in other features may represent remains that had previously been incorporated in the soil at the site and were introduced into the pits with the soil used for fill. *No remains of maize or any other cultigens were identified.*

Faunal remains identified by Carr (Table 3) include a great variety of species including mammals, birds, reptiles, amphibians, and fish. Despite this overall diversity of taxa, faunal resource exploitation is decidedly oriented toward aquatics, especially fish and turtles. Both the species present and the larger size of most of the fish elements identified suggest an emphasis on resource procurement in spring or early summer, at least in part to take advantage of the spring spawn. Bowfin is the predominant fish species represented, followed in importance by species of catfish and bass and other centrarchids. Feature 13 is again anomalous in producing the highest relative proportion of mammalian elements, especially deer, corroborating the floral data in suggesting fall-winter occupation. Even in Feature 13,

Table 4. Demography of Powell Canal Site Burials

Burial Number	Age	Sex	Comments
1	15–17 yr	Female	
1a	neonate		Possibly intrusive in Burial 1 grave
1b	18 months		Very fragmentary
1c	adult		Designates two adult elements from grave fill not assignable to Burial 1
2	40+ yr	Male	
3	40+ yr	Female	
4	18–25 yr	Female	Very fragmentary

however, fish remains comprise 61 percent of identified faunal elements. Both King and Carr concluded that the data under consideration strongly suggest spring-summer occupation. The proposition of year-round habitation of the Powell Canal site is not supported. There is reason to believe that because of its low-lying location, the site may have been rendered uninhabitable because of flooding by the Mississippi River during the high-water season in many years. Historic flood records suggest that this would typically have been in late winter or early spring.

BIOARCHAEOLOGY

Skeletal remains from Powell Canal, comprising a total of six individuals from four burials, were studied by Mark W. Blaeuer and Jerome C. Rose of the Department of Anthropology, University of Arkansas, Fayetteville (Blaeuer and Rose 1982). The four burials are considered to constitute part of a Baytown period cemetery despite an unexpectedly recent radiocarbon age assay of the left femur of Burial 4 (300 ± 100 B.P., UCR-1417). All of the skeletal individuals were recovered in somewhat fragmentary condition as a result of historic disturbance and the use of heavy earth-moving machinery during the 1980–1981 excavation. The Powell Canal bioarchaeological study was integrated into an ongoing study of the time table and bioarchaeological consequences of the adoption of maize agriculture in the central and lower Mississippi Valley and trans-Mississippi south (Rose et al. 1984). Employing a broad array of specific methodologies, Blaeuer and Rose's study was focused around three objectives: (1)

paleodemography, (2) paleoepidemiology, and (3) dietary reconstruction.

Blaeuer and Rose's study indicated that the Powell Canal skeletal sample, while small, exhibited a demographic distribution consistent with a normal human population (Table 4). Similar to the Troyville culture Goldmine site series studied by Berg (1982), both male and female adults at Powell Canal exhibited well-developed muscle marking but were well differentiated on the basis of maximum femur head diameters. The infection, osteophytosis, and osteoarthritis rates were all low to moderate. Evidence of trauma was confined to a healed fracture of a distal phalange of the left hand of Burial 1 and a suggestion of healed fractures of the left tibia and fibula of Burial 4. No evidence of trauma resulting from interpersonal violence was observed in the Powell Canal skeletal sample. Tooth enamel hypoplasias indicated periods of childhood dietary stress, probably annual in the case of the Burial 1 adult. Examination of dentition in the skeletal sample revealed comparatively high attrition rates but a low frequency of caries. These data plus microstriation patterns on molar occlusal surfaces observed with a scanning electron microscope indicated a diet high in collected foods with moderate to low fiber content, probable use of stone plant-processing tools, and no evidence of a reliance on maize. Microscopic compression fractures on the enamel surfaces of the Burial 1 molar examined indicate probable consumption of nuts in the season prior to death, suggesting that this burial represents the dead of a fall-winter occupation. Absence of such attrition on molar enamel surfaces of Burials 2 and 3 suggests that these individuals represent the dead of a spring-summer occupation (none of the recovered teeth of Burial 4 were suitable for analysis).

The bioarchaeological dietary indicators from Powell Canal corroborate the faunal and floral indicators, discussed above. Blaeuer and Rose (1982:84) emphasized the indicators of a high level of adaptive efficiency—defined as the presence of a minimum disease load and an acceptable demographic profile for reproduction—in the Powell Canal population and offered for testing in future excavations the hypothesis that the broad spectrum economic pattern of the Baytown culture operating in the high biomass environment of southeast Arkansas produced a high level of adaptive efficiency and a steady increase in population size.

BAYTOWN PERIOD ADAPTATION ON BAYOU MACON

Powell Canal is one of several Marksville and Baytown period components on Bayou Macon in the Mississippi River floodplain in southeast Arkansas that are characterized by extensive midden areas and high surface artifact densities. The 1980–1981 excavations at Powell Canal corroborated the impression of intensive occupation on the site and demonstrated the importance of this locus within the overall Baytown period settlement system of the region. The abundant recovered ceramics appear to represent a single cultural assemblage and encompass a great variety of decorative modes and a great diversity of vessel forms. This ceramic assemblage complexity suggests a commensurate complexity in roles and statuses and structural poses of the resident community. The recovered lithic assemblage indicates a broad range of technological behavior. The presence of numerous pit features suggests that food storage was considerably important in the prehistoric economy and a predictable schedule of reoccupation or at least revisits occurred. The presence of cemetery areas indicates another, less tangible, sort of investment in this locus by the prehistoric Baytown people—as does perhaps the unexcavated mound on the south end of the site. The demographic composition of the recovered burial population provides direct evidence that the prehistoric occupants of the site were not a task-specialized social segment but rather included the full sex-age range of a normal human society.

Despite the implied low degree of residential mobility, seasonality indicators do not support the proposition of sedentary year-round occupation. Rather, a spring-summer emphasis is indicated with limited fall-winter occupation. Even the design of the predominant cooking jar form may represent an adaptation to residential mobility (Linton 1944). King (1982b:64) suggested that the Baytown period settlement pattern at Powell Canal may have been characterized by aggregation of a group at a spring-summer base camp to harvest a concentrated, seasonally available resource, with a winter dispersal for procurement of scarcer and more widely spaced resources.

What resource might have allowed an aggregation of numerous households on the banks of Bayou Macon in late spring and summer? The faunal data recovered from pit features at Powell Canal indicate an orientation toward aquatic resources, especially fish. It has already been emphasized that the aquatic ecosystem available to the prehistoric inhabitants of the Powell Canal site was a Mississippi River ecosystem, not an isolated Bayou Macon ecosystem. The fish population in the Bayou Macon watershed would have been characterized by high biomass levels and would have been annually restocked from the Mississippi River, providing the possibility of perennial abundant catches with little risk of over harvesting. Furthermore, this biomass would be spatially concentrated on a predictable annual basis when Mississippi River floodwaters began to recede and drain down streams such as Bayou Macon. Historical flood occurrence data indicate that this draining of Mississippi River floodwaters would have typically occurred in late spring, precisely the major season of occupation indicated by the recovered faunal and floral data. Focused exploitation of such predictable seasonal fish concentrations is a feature of present-day adaptation by human groups in Amazonia (Bergman 1974).

The evident emphasis on fish notwithstanding, faunal and floral data from Powell Canal indicate a highly diversified floodplain subsistence base, consistent with Morse and Morse's (1983:186) characterization of "almost anything edible." One of the most intriguing results of the Powell Canal site investigations is the lack of support for the proposition of growing reliance on maize at this time level in this portion of the Mississippi Valley. While the absence of maize in the archaeobotanical samples from the site may be attributable to contingencies of preservation or to maize having been produced and consumed elsewhere in the settlement system, the low dental caries rate in the recovered skeletal population argues strongly that maize or other processed high carbohydrate foods were not consumed at Powell Canal, nor at any other locus in the settlement pattern. In this light, the association of the Powell Canal site and other major Marksville and Baytown components with poorly drained clay soils along Bayou Macon no longer appears anomalous.

COMPARATIVE DISCUSSION

It is appropriate at this point to consider the supralocal applicability of the forgoing reconstruction of Baytown culture and adaptation developed from the Powell

Canal site data. In other words, do the Powell Canal site data reflect patterns of settlement, community organization, technology, subsistence, and biocultural adjustment that are widespread in the central and lower Mississippi Valley at the A.D. 700 Mississippian emergence baseline? Although investigation—especially in nonmound sites and habitation midden areas—has as yet been comparatively limited, a multifaceted valley-wide data base for this time period has begun to emerge in recent years. It is possible to begin to identify some areas of similarity and dimensions of variability among Baytown period sites in this portion of the Southeast.

As noted earlier in this chapter, most researchers discussing the Baytown period have emphasized evidence of simply structured settlement systems and dispersed, seemingly independent extended family households. Though much of the mound and earthwork construction at the Troyville site is probably assignable to the Baytown period (Walker 1936; Belmont 1984:89–90; Neuman 1984:170–177), excavation in the lower valley since the 1940s has provided little additional support for the association of "temple mounds" and "small ceremonial centers" with Baytown period components (Phillips 1970:964–965). Site plans characterized by low platform mounds around an oval plaza, however, are present at certain sites with major Troyville components in the upper Tensas Basin (Belmont 1984:89). The degree of aggregation represented by the extent of midden area at Powell Canal and some neighboring sites on Bayou Macon appears to be somewhat unusual. An extensive Baytown period midden area, however, appears to be present on the Griffin site in Washington County, Mississippi (Weinstein et al. 1979, appendix A, 151–171). The circular array of small shell middens designated by Phillips (1970:549, figs. 77, 80, 133, 149) as the "Tchula Lake pattern" appears to be a pattern unique to the Yazoo Basin.

Relatively few excavated data pertaining to Baytown period community organization are yet available. A pattern of artifact and feature concentrations within a compact Barnes culture midden area ranging between 1,200 and 2,400 sq m in area at the Zebree site in Mississippi County, Arkansas is interpreted as a multifamily fall-winter village (Morse 1980b:23; Morse and Morse 1983:186). More typical well-preserved Barnes culture sites in that region tend to be surface artifact concentrations less than 1,000 sq m in area, consistent with the interpretation of a single structure, extended

family settlement (Morse and Morse 1983:184). A combination of hand excavation and machine stripping in an approximately 1 ha area at the De Rossitt site in St. Francis County, Arkansas revealed over 100 aboriginal pit features in four discrete clusters, each cluster about 20 m in diameter with a mean spacing of about 40 m between clusters, center to center (Spears 1978, fig. 4–2). These clusters particularly invite comparison to the Cut 5 pit feature cluster at Powell Canal. Though post holes abounded at De Rossitt, no house patterns or their relation to pit feature clusters could be discerned. General cultural-historical and functional similarities between pit feature contents at De Rossitt support the inference that the cluster represent contemporaneous family dwelling areas (Spears 1978:60–63, 88). At the Barner site in Coahoma County, Mississippi, an array of Peabody phase pit features appeared to be associated with a rectangular wall-trench house; one of the pit features yielded a radiocarbon date of A.D. 875 (Brookes 1980, fig. 1, 23). Bathtub-shaped fire pits at Greenhouse and Goldmine are attributed to intercommunity feasting by Belmont (1984:86–88).

No aboriginal house patterns were recognized at Powell Canal and evidence pertaining to Baytown period house forms in the lower valley is generally scarce. Evidence of a Barnes culture circular house made of poles, apparently with some sort of perishable covering (i.e., as opposed to daub) was recognized at Zebree (Morse and Morse 1983:189). The evidence of a "Mississippian" rectangular wall-trench house dating to the ninth century A.D. at the Barner site is unexpected but supported by the identification of a similar structure with Peabody phase associations at the nearby Bobo site (Brookes 1980:25). Though the Peabody phase dates later than the A.D. 300–700 span, which is the focus of this chapter, Brookes (1980) emphasized continuities with Baytown culture.

The articulation of cemetery areas with habitation areas in Baytown period community organization is as yet little known. Apparent communitywide burial mounds appear widespread (e.g., Moore 1910:341–349, 1913:39–44; Jones et al. 1979; Jeter et al. 1979:39). One suspects, however, that local cemeteries such as the one encountered in the excavation at Powell Canal are more typical but have not been recognized because of the prevailing lack of grave goods.

The frequency of pit features, especially cylindrical and bell-shaped, within the excavated area at Powell

Canal argues for the importance of food storage in local Baytown adaptation and for the ability of the Baytown economy to produce at least seasonal surpluses. The Powell Canal data are paralleled in this respect by evidence from many other central and lower Mississippi Valley sites on this time level; for example, Zebree (Morse 1980b:10), De Rossitt (Spears 1978, appendix J), Barner (Brookes 1980:15–22) and the Boyd site in Tunica County, Mississippi (Connaway and McGahey 1971, table 1). Interestingly, the data on size and suggested storage capacity, as well as general pit feature morphology, also seem to be within the same range among these sites. Though the available data do not permit detailed quantitative comparisons of past storage pit capacities, modalities in pit feature diameters between about 60 cm and 100 cm suggest storage capacities well under 1,000 liters. It is difficult to determine what significance should be assigned to specific modalities and ranges of storage pit capacity; they presumably reflect not only the nature of the foodstuff stored but also the relative economic importance of storage and the size of the food-sharing social unit (Morse 1980b:10). The inferred typical storage capacity on this time level contrasts with the 2,000 liter mean storage capacity estimated for Early Mississippi Big Lake phase pit features at Zebree (Morse 1980a:8).

Subsistence remains from Powell Canal support a model of spring-summer usage of the site with heavy reliance on aquatic fauna, especially fish. This faunal evidence, in conjunction with indications of prolonged and intensive occupation of the Powell Canal site, suggests an overall cultural orientation toward aquatic resources on the part of Baytown populations in the region. The Powell Canal data are consistent with the pattern noted by Springer (1980:199–202) of the relatively greater importance of fish in archaeological faunal assemblages from the lower, as opposed to central, Mississippi Valley throughout the last 2,000 years of the aboriginal sequence. The relatively few and, for the most part, limited available analyses of Baytown period faunal assemblages, however, provide little basis for systematic comparison among regions (in addition to Springer's 1980 study cited, available analyses include Butsch 1971, Brookes 1980, Medlock and House 1980, Morse 1980b, Olsen 1971, Parmalee 1966, and Walker 1936). The diversity of taxa represented has been alluded to. Fish remains are a conspicuous part of all of

these assemblages, although generally ranking well behind deer in any projection of meat yield. Brookes (1980:32, 44) and Rose et al. (1984:403) have argued for the major importance of fish in Baytown and Coles Creek period economies in some regions in the central and lower Mississippi Valley.

Evidence of floral subsistence at Baytown period sites in the Valley tends to emphasize use of nondomesticated plant species, though an early date for the introduction of squash is supported and there is scattered evidence for the utilization of native annuals (e.g., sunflower, maygrass, goosefoot, and knotweed), which may have been cultivated (Byrd and Neuman 1978). Some investigators have seen compelling indirect evidence for Baytown period agriculture in settlement pattern data (e.g., Brain 1971:59–65; cf. Neuman 1984: 213–214). Notwithstanding, associations of maize with pre-Mississippi period components in the central and lower Mississippi Valley have been few and equivocal (e.g., Fowke 1928, cited in Byrd and Neuman 1978; Klinger et al. 1983). There is accumulating evidence that starchy-seeded annuals such as maygrass may have constituted a carbohydrate staple by Coles Creek times (King 1985; Rose et al. 1984:404). These plant species were not identified at Powell Canal. It seems likely that horticulture and a spring-summer fishing focus would have been alternatives rather than complements within a single subsistence system because of similar seasonal scheduling. The backswamp, floodplain distributary location of the Powell Canal site, by no means represents the exclusive setting of Baytown period sites. In the central Mississippi Valley, Baytown culture components occur across a diversity of environments including extensive Pleistocene terrace surfaces as well as major river floodplains (House 1975:158, 1982b:42; Morse and Morse 1983, fig. 9.1). The environmental diversity of Baytown culture site locations would argue for a diversity of subsistence emphases that may or may not have been integrated into a distinct Baytown culture economic pattern.

Summarizing the comparatively limited bioarchaeological data from the lower Mississippi Valley, Rose et al. (1984:417) pointed to evidence of a comparatively high level of adaptive efficiency among Baytown period populations. At both Gold Mine and Powell Canal, high osteoarthritis rates suggest high levels of physical stress associated with a strenuous hunter-gatherer lifeway. An apparent yawslike treponemal infection identified in Coles Creek period skeletal populations from Morton Shell Mound and Mount Nebo (Robbins 1978; Giardino 1984:112–114; Neuman 1984:203–206) may be present at Gold Mine (Berg 1982). Rose et al. (1984:414) suggest that this condition may have been ubiquitous in the lush environment of the lower Mississippi Valley. Among the lower Mississippi Valley Baytown and Coles Creek period populations studied to date, the notably low frequency of trauma from interpersonal violence contrasts markedly with evidence from contemporary Fourche Maline populations to the west (Rose et al. 1984:409) and Late Woodland populations from the Illinois Valley (Buikstra 1977:80). To date, the single example from the central and lower Mississippi Valley on this time level appears to be an Alba point found embedded in skeletal elements of a Mount Nebo site individual attributed to the early Coles Creek component at that site (Giardino 1984:114–115). Although the significance of differing rates of interpersonal violence among various societies is unknown, the low frequencies observed for the lower Mississippi Valley on this time level contributes to an overall picture of adaptive success with little impetus for subsistence change.

CONCLUSION

Circa A.D. 600, on the eve of the Mississippian emergence baseline, which is the focus of this volume, Baytown populations were living in well-established, if seasonally occupied, settlements along the bank of Bayou Macon in the Mississippi River floodplain in southeast Arkansas. The archaeological data from the site suggest a seasonal focus on the exploitation of aquatic resources, at least a moderate level of organizational complexity, and a high level of adaptive efficiency. Archaeobotanical and bioarchaeological evidence concur in suggesting that the Baytown society represented at the site consumed little if any maize.

Although the Powell Canal site data base is unusually well rounded in terms of the recovery of diverse classes of archaeological evidence, results from this site are generally paralleled by those from diverse other Baytown period sites in the central and lower Mississippi Valley. A range of subsistence emphases and settlement system variability, however, appears to have existed. In particular, it seems likely that a seasonal fishing focus and an early nonmaize horticultural pattern may have been seasonal economic alternatives. The weight of accumulating archaeobotanical and bioarchaeological evidence appears to be answering in the negative the long-standing question of pre-Mississippian maize agriculture in the central and lower Mississippi Valley. Bioarchaeological studies done to date suggest that the Baytown and Troyville peoples may have enjoyed a level of adaptive efficiency comparatively high among eastern North American peoples in Late Woodland times. In geographic context, these cultures do indeed appear to represent a set of specific adaptations to the resources and zonation of habitats in the Mississippi alluvial valley.

While some broad outlines of Baytown period cultures in the central and lower Mississippi Valley have begun to emerge, we still have far to go in attaining a satisfactory reconstruction of major events and processes during this period. It will be noted that the picture of the Baytown period presented in the foregoing pages is unrealistically synchronic. Substantial progress has been made in recent years in understanding general patterns of adaptation to the natural environment but we still have little concrete evidence pertaining to social organizational and political features of Baytown period systems. The extent of hierarchical organization in settlement systems in the central and lower Mississippi Valley on this time level remains unknown. In contrast to the central Mississippi Valley, the archaeological record from the lower Mississippi Valley gives the impression of continuity and relative stability across the A.D. 700 baseline. It remains to be seen to what extent the organizational changes seen in the transition from Baytown to Coles Creek to Plaquemine (cf. Brain 1978) derive not from dynamics internal to the systems involved, but constitute response to demographic and political changes in the central Mississippi Valley and beyond.

ACKNOWLEDGMENTS

The 1981 excavations at the Powell Canal site were carried out by the Arkansas Archeological Survey under the sponsorship of the Arkansas Highway and Transportation Department. Burney B. McClurkan, Archeologist with the Arkansas Highway and Transportation Department, co-directed the 1980 testing of the site with Marvin D. Jeter, then Station Archeologist at the University of Arkansas at Monticello. The 1981 research program was coordinated by Dr. Charles R. Mc-Gimsey, Director of the Survey and W. Fredrick Limp, Survey Research Coordinator. I hope that this chapter adequately reflects the central role played in the total Powell Canal research effort by my specialist collaborators: Frances B. King, Holly Ann Carr, Mark W. Blaeuer, and Jerome C. Rose. Conversations with Dr. Rose during the writing of this chapter were very helpful. I am grateful to Sam Brookes and Robert W. Neuman for providing me with information and sources on Baytown period research in Mississippi and Louisiana. Responsibility for any shortcomings in this chapter, however, is mine. I wish to dedicate this chapter to the memory of James A. Scholtz who taught me to excavate Baytown sites in east Arkansas in 1966–67.

REFERENCES CITED

Baker, Charles M.
1973   An Environmental Study of Site Locations in Southeast Arkansas. Manuscript on file, Department of Anthropology, University of Arkansas, Fayetteville, and Arkansas Archeological Survey, University of Arkansas at Monticello.

Belmont, John S.
1982   Peer Review. In *Powell Canal: Baytown Period Occupation on Bayou Macon in Southeast Arkansas*, by John H. House, pp. 104–107 (Appendix D). Arkansas Archeological Survey Research Series 19.
1984   The Troyville Concept and the Goldmine Site. In *The Troyville-Baytown Period in Lower Mississippi Valley Prehistory: A Memorial to Robert Stuart Neitzel*, edited by Jon L. Gibson, pp. 63–96. Louisiana Archaeology 9.

Belmont, John S., and Stephen Williams
1981   Painted Pottery Horizons in the Southern Mississippi Valley. *Geoscience and Man* 22:19–42.

Berg, Richard
1982   Paleopathology of the Gold Mine Site. Manuscript on file, Department of Anthropology, University of Arkansas, Fayetteville.

Bergman, Roland Wallace
1974   *Shipibo Subsistence in the Upper Amazon Rainforest*. Ph.D. dissertation, Department of Geography, University of Wisconsin, Madison. University Microfilms International, Ann Arbor.

Binford, Lewis R.
1980   Willow Smoke and Dog's Tails: Hunter Gatherer Settlement Systems and Archaeological Site Formation. *American Antiquity* 45:4–20.

Blaeuer, Mark W., and Jerome C. Rose
1982   Bioarcheology of the Powell Canal Site. In *Powell Canal: Baytown Occupation on Bayou Macon in Southeast Arkansas*, by John H. House, pp. 72–84. Arkansas Archeological Survey Research Series 19.

Brain, Jeffrey P.
1971   The Lower Mississippi Valley in North American Prehistory. Manuscript on file, Arkansas Archeological Survey, Fayetteville.
1978   Late Prehistoric Settlement Patterning in the Yazoo Basin and Natchez Bluffs Regions of the Lower Mississippi Valley. In *Mississippian Settlement Patterns*, edited by Bruce D. Smith, pp. 331–368. Academic Press, New York.

Braun, E. Lucy
1950   *Deciduous Forests of Eastern North America*. Hafner Publishing Company, New York.

Brookes, Samuel Owen
1980   *The Peabody Phase in the Upper Sunflower Region*. M.A. thesis, University of Mississippi, Oxford.

Buikstra, Jane E.
1977   Biocultural Dimensions of Archeological Study, A Regional Perspective. In *Biocultural Adaptation in Prehistoric America*, edited by Robert L. Blakely, pp. 67–84. Southern Anthropological Society Proceedings 11.

Butsch, Elizabeth A.
1971   Vertebrate Faunal Remains from the Roland Mound Site, 3AR30, Arkansas County, Arkansas. Appendix to *Investigations at the Roland Mound Site, 3AR30, Arkansas County, Arkansas, 1966*, by James A. Scholtz. Report submitted to National Park Service, Southeast region by University of Arkansas Museum, Fayetteville.

Byrd, Kathleen M., and Robert W. Neuman
1978   Archaeological Data Relative to Prehistoric Subsistence in the Lower Mississippi Alluvial Valley. *Geoscience and Man* 19:9–21.

Carr, Holly Ann
1982   Preliminary Analysis of the Faunal Remains. In *Powell Canal: Baytown Period Occupation on Bayou Macon in Southeast Arkansas*, by John H. House, pp. 66–71. Arkansas Archeological Survey Research Series 19.

Cloutier, Hardy, and Charles J. Finger
1967   *Soil Survey of Chicot County, Arkansas*. United States Department of Agriculture, Soil Conservation Service in cooperation with the Arkansas Agricultural Experiment Station.

Connaway, John M., and Samuel O. McGahey
1971   *Archaeological Excavations at the Boyd Site, Tunica County, Mississippi*. Mississippi Department of Archives and History Technical Report 1.

Daniel, Pete
1977   *Deep'n as it Come: The 1927 Mississippi River Flood*. Oxford University Press, New York.

Duffield, Lathel F.
1970   Vertisols and their Implications for Archaeological Research. *American Anthropologist* 72:1055–1062.

Dunnell, Robert C.
1985   Archaeological Survey in the Lower Mississippi Valley, 1940–1947: A Landmark Study in American Archaeology. *American Antiquity* 50:297–300.

Faye, Stanley
1942   The Forked River. *Louisiana Historical Quarterly* 25(4):2–23.

Fenneman, N. M.
1938   *Physiography of the Eastern United States.* McGraw-Hill, New York.

Fisk, H. N.
1944   *Geological Investigation of the Alluvial Valley of the Lower Mississippi River.* U.S. Army Corps of Engineers, Mississippi River Commission, Vicksburg.

Fowke, Gerard
1928   Archeological Investigations II: Explorations in the Red River Valley in Louisiana. *Annual Report of the Bureau of American Ethnology* 44:399–346.

Giardino, Marco Joseph
1984   Temporal Frameworks: Archaeological Components and Burial Styles: The Human Osteology of the Mt. Nebo Site in North Louisiana. In *The Troyville-Baytown Period in Lower Mississippi Valley Prehistory: A Memorial to Robert Stuart Neitzel,* edited by John L. Gibson, pp. 47–124. Louisiana Archaeology 9.

Griffin, James B.
1965   Ceramic Complexity and Cultural Development: The Eastern United States as a Case Study. In *Ceramics and Man,* edited by Frederick R. Matson, pp. 104–113. Aldine, Chicago.

Haggett, Peter, Andrew D. Cliff, and Allan Frey
1977   *Locational Analysis in Human Geography* (second edition). John Wiley and Sons, New York.

Hopgood, James Finley
1969   *Continuity and Change in the Baytown Pottery Tradition of the Cairo Lowland, Southeast Missouri.* M.A. thesis, University of Missouri, Columbia. University Microfilms, Ann Arbor, Michigan.

House, John H.
1975   Summary of Archeological Knowledge Updated with Newly-Gathered Data. In *The Cache River Archeological Project: An Experiment in Contract Archeology,* assembled by Michael B. Schiffer and John H. House, pp. 153–162. Arkansas Archeological Survey Research Series 8.
1982a   *Powell Canal: Baytown Period Occupation on Bayou Macon in Southeast Arkansas.* Arkansas Archeological Survey Research Series 19.
1982b   Evolution of Complex Societies in East-Central Arkansas: An Overview of Environments and Regional Data Bases. In *Arkansas Archeology in Review,* edited by Neal L. Trubowitz and Marvin D. Jeter, pp. 37–47. Arkansas Archeological Survey Research Series 15.

Jeter, Marvin D.
1982   The Archeology of Southeast Arkansas: An Overview for the 1980s. In *Arkansas Archeology in Review,* edited by Neal L. Trubowitz and Marvin D. Jeter, pp. 76–131. Arkansas Archeological Survey Research Series 15.

Jeter, Marvin D., David B. Kelley, and George P. Kelley
1979   The Kelley-Grimes Site: A Mississippi Period Burial Mound, Southeast Arkansas, Excavated in 1936. *Arkansas Archeologist* 20:1–51.

Jones, Reca, Nina Helfert, Dwain Kirkham, and Woodrow Duke
1979   Human Effigy Vessels from Gold Mine Plantation. *Louisiana Archaeology* 4:117–121.

King, Frances B.
1982a   Vegetational Reconstruction Around the Powell Canal Site. In *Powell Canal: Baytown Period Occupation on Bayou Macon in Southeast Arkansas,* by John H. House, pp. 10–15. Arkansas Archeological Survey Research Series 19.
1982b   Archeobotanical Remains. In *Powell Canal: Baytown Period Occupation on Bayou Macon in Southeast Arkansas,* by John H. House, pp. 63–65. Arkansas Archeological Survey Research Series 19.
1985   Presettlement Vegetation and Plant Remains. In *The Alexander Site, Conway County, Arkansas,* edited by E. Thomas Hemmings and John H. House, pp. 49–57. Arkansas Archaeological Survey Research Series 24.

Klinger, Timothy C., Steven M. Imhoff, and Roy J. Cochran, Jr.
1983   *Brougham Lake: Archeological Mitigation of 3CT98 Along the Big Creek Enlargement and Diversion, Item 1, Crittenden County, Arkansas.* Historic Preservation Associates Reports 83-7. Fayetteville.

Lambou, Victor W.
1959   Fish Populations of Backwater Lakes in Louisiana. *Transactions of the American Fisheries Society* 88:7–15.

Lemley, Harry J., and S. D. Dickinson
1937   Archeological Investigations on Bayou Macon in Arkansas. *Texas Archeological and Paleontological Society Bulletin* 9:11–47. Reprinted 1964 in *Arkansas Archeologist* 5(2):21–39.

Limp, W. Fredrick
1974   Water Separation and Flotation Processes. *Journal of Field Archeology* 1(3–4):337–342.

Linton, Ralph
1944   North American Cooking Pots. *American Antiquity* 9:369–380.

Medlock, Raymond C., and John H. House
1978   Vertebrate Faunal Remains from Boydell (3A558) Mound A Salvage, 1978. Manuscript on file, Arkansas Archeological Survey, University of Arkansas at Monticello.

Million, Michael G.
1980   The Big Lake Phase Pottery Industry. In *Zebree Archeological Project: Excavation, Data Interpretation, and Report on the Zebree Homestead Site,* edited by Dan F. Morse and Phyllis A. Morse (Chap. 18). Report submitted to U.S. Army Corps of Engineers, Memphis District by Arkansas Archeological Survey, Fayetteville.

Moore, Clarence B.
1910   Antiquities of the St. Francis, White and Black Rivers, Arkansas. *Journal of the Academy of Natural Sciences of Philadelphia* 14:255–364.
1913   Some Aboriginal Sites in Louisiana and in Arkansas. *Journal of the Academy of Natural Sciences of Philadelphia* 16(1):7–93.

Morse, Dan F.
1973   *Nodena: An Account of 75 Years of Archeological Investigation in Southeast Mississippi County, Arkansas.* Arkansas Archeological Survey Research Series 4.
1980a   The Big Lake Household and Community. In *Zebree Archeological Project Excavation, Data Interpretation and Report on the Zebree Homestead Site, Mississippi County, Ar-*

kansas, edited by Dan F. Morse and Phyllis A. Morse (Chap. 21). Report submitted to U.S. Army Corps of Engineers, Memphis District by Arkansas Archeological Survey, Fayetteville.

1980b Other Aspects of the Barnes Occupation. In *Zebree Archeological Project: Excavation Data Interpretation and Report on the Zebree Homestead Site, Mississippi County, Arkansas,* edited by Dan F. Morse and Phyllis A. Morse (Chap. 17). Report submitted to U.S. Army Corps of Engineers, Memphis District, by Arkansas Archeological Survey, Fayetteville.

Morse, Dan F., and Michael G. Million
1980 The Barnes Ceramic Complex. In *Zebree Archeological Project: Excavation, Data Interpretation and Report on the Zebree Homestead Site, Mississippi County, Arkansas,* edited by Dan F. Morse and Phyllis A. Morse (Chap. 16). Report submitted to U.S. Army Corps of Engineers, Memphis District by Arkansas Archeological Survey, Fayetteville.

Morse, Dan F., and Phyllis A. Morse
1983 *Archaeology of the Central Mississippi Valley.* Academic Press, New York.

Neuman, Robert W.
1984 *An Introduction to Louisiana Archaeology.* Louisiana State University Press, Baton Rouge.

Olsen, S. J.
1971 Boyd Site: Report of Faunal Analysis. In *Archaeological Excavation at the Boyd Site, Tunica County, Mississippi,* by John M. Connaway and Samuel O. McGahey, pp. 65–77. Mississippi Department of Archives and History Technical Report 1.

Parmalee, Paul W.
1966 Appendix A: Animal Remains from the Banks Site. In *The Banks Village Site, Crittenden County, Arkansas,* by Gregory Perino, pp. 142–145. Missouri Archaeological Society Memoir 4.

Patterson, James L.
1964 *Magnitude and Frequency of Floods in the United States, Part 7. Lower Mississippi River Basin.* United States Geological Survey Water Supply Paper 1681.

Phillips, Philip
1970 *Archaeological Survey in the Lower Yazoo Basin, Mississippi 1949–1955.* Papers of the Peabody Museum of American Archaeology and Ethnology 60, Harvard University.

Phillips, Philip, James A. Ford, and James B. Griffin
1951 *Archaeological Survey in the Lower Mississippi Alluvial Valley, 1940–1947.* Papers of the Peabody Museum of American Archaeology and Ethnology 25, Harvard University.

Rheinhold, R. O.
1969 The Climate of Arkansas. In *Climates of the States,* pp. 522–537. National Oceanic and Atmospheric Administration, United States Department of Commerce.

Robbins, Louise M.
1978 Yawslike Disease Processes in a Louisiana Shell Mound Population. *Medical College of Virginia Quarterly* 14: 24–31.

Rolingson, Martha Ann
1971 Preliminary Report on Spring 1971 Testing in South-

eastern Arkansas. *Field Notes, Monthly Newsletter of the Arkansas Archeological Society* 79:11–13.

1973 Initial Draft of the Bartholomew Sequence for the Bartholomew Project. Manuscript on file, Arkansas Archeological Survey, Fayetteville.

1982 Baytown Period. In *A State Plan for the Conservation of Archeological Resources in Arkansas,* edited by Hester A. Davis, pp. SE17–SE18. Arkansas Archeological Survey Research Series 21.

Rose, Jerome C., Barbara Burnett, Michael S. Nassaney, and Mark W. Blaeuer
1984 Paleopathology and the Origins of Maize Agriculture in the Lower Mississippi Valley and Caddoan Culture Areas. In *Paleopathology and the Origins of Agriculture,* edited by Mark Nathan Cohen and George Armelagos, pp. 393–424. Academic Press, Orlando.

Rostlund, Erhard
1952 *Freshwater Fish and Fishing in Native North America.* University of California Publications in Geography 9.

Sahlins, Marshall D.
1968 *Tribesmen.* Prentice-Hall, Englewood Cliffs, New Jersey.

Saucier, Roger T.
1974 *Quaternary Geology of the Lower Mississippi Valley.* Arkansas Archeological Survey Research Series 6.

Schiffer, Michael B.
1976 *Behavioral Archaeology.* Academic Press, New York.

Sealander, John A.
1979 *A Guide to Arkansas Mammals.* River Road Press, Conway.

Shelford, Victor E.
1963 *The Ecology of North America.* University of Illinois Press, Urbana.

Smith, Bruce D.
1975 *Middle Mississippi Exploitation of Animal Populations.* Museum of Anthropology, University of Michigan, Anthropological Papers 57.

1978 Variation in Mississippian Settlement Patterns. In *Mississippian Settlement Patterns,* edited by Bruce D. Smith, pp. 480–504. Academic Press, New York.

Spears, Carol S.
1978 *The De Rossitt Site (3SF49): Applications of Behavioral Archeology to a Museum Collection.* M.A. thesis, University of Arkansas, Fayetteville.

Springer, James W.
1980 An Analysis of Prehistoric Food Remains from the Bruly St. Martin Site, Louisiana, with a Comparative Discussion of Mississippi Valley Faunal Studies. *Midcontinental Journal of Archaeology* 5:193–224.

Stoltman, James B.
1978 Temporal Models in Prehistory: An Example from Eastern North America. *Current Anthropology* 19:703–746.

Turner, Christy, and Laurel Lofgren
1966 Household Size of Prehistoric Western Pueblo Indians. *Southwestern Journal of Anthropology* 22(2):117–132.

Walker, Winslow
1936 *The Troyville Mounds, Catahoula Parish, Louisiana.* Bureau of American Ethnology, Bulletin 133.

Watson, Patty Jo
1976 In Pursuit of Prehistoric Subsistence: A Comparative

Account of Some Contemporary Flotation Techniques. *Midcontinental Journal of Archaeology* 1(1):77–100.

Weinstein, Richard A., Wayne P. Glander, Sherwood M. Gagliano, Eileen K. Burden, and Kathleen G. McCloskey
1979   Cultural Resources Survey of Upper Steele Bayou Basin, West-Central Mississippi. Manuscript on file, United States Army Corps of Engineers, Vicksburg and Coastal Environments Inc., Baton Rouge.

Williams, Stephen
1963   The Eastern United States. In Early Indian Farmers and Village Communities, edited by William G. Haag, pp. 267–235. Manuscript on file, National Park Service.

Winter, Marcus C.
1976   The Archaeological Household Cluster in the Valley of Oaxaca. In *The Early Mesoamerican Village,* edited by Kent V. Flannery, pp. 25–31. Academic Press, New York.

Wood, W. Raymond, and Donald Lee Johnson
1978   A Survey of Disturbance Processes in Archaeological Site Formation. In *Advances in Archaeological Method and Theory,* vol. 3, edited by Michael B. Schiffer, pp. 315–383. Academic Press, New York.

The Toltec Mounds Site

A Ceremonial Center in the Arkansas River Lowland

The Toltec Mounds site was recognized as an important mound center as early as 1894, when it was included in the *Report on Mound Explorations* by the Bureau of Ethnology (Thomas 1894). Despite this early interest, scientific investigation did not begin until 1966. The size and arrangement of mounds at the site has been the basis for assigning it to the Mississippian period, although the Toltec artifact assemblage clearly is not Mississippian. Recent investigations provide data for the formulation of a distinctive cultural pattern, termed Plum Bayou.

LOCATION AND ENVIRONMENTAL SETTING

The Toltec Mounds site (3LN42) is located in central Arkansas on the bank of an abandoned channel of the Arkansas River. This location is 20 km southeast of the point at which the Arkansas River emerges from the interior highlands into the alluvial plain of the Mississippi River. This is a strategic position in relation to the diverse resources of several physiographic regions (Fig. 6).

The site is near the apex of the Arkansas Alluvial Fan, a subdivision within the Mississippi Alluvial Plain physiographic province. The Arkansas Alluvial Fan has two sections, the Arkansas River Lowland and the Grand Prairie Ridge (Phillips, Ford, and Griffin 1951: 18–19). The Arkansas River Lowland is an alluvial bottomland of ridges and backswamps created by the shifting meander belt systems of the Arkansas River. The site is located on the natural levee of Plum Bayou, an older meander belt system of the river. In this older system, the river flowed south along the western edge of the alluvial fan. Near present-day Monroe, Louisiana, the Ouachita River joined the Arkansas and both rivers flowed into the present Ouachita River channel to join the Red River. Saucier (1974:23) hypothesized that the shift from this older meander belt system to the modern one may have taken place about 1,000 years ago. If this age estimate is roughly correct, then this ancestral system rather than the modern channel would have been an important route for canoe transportation to other regions. To the west, in the valley and upland, the course of the river has not changed. The recent environmental conditions characterized by hardwood lowlands of alternating ridges and backswamps are generally applicable to the period of occupation for the site.

The four adjacent physiographic regions are the Grand Prairie Ridge, 20 km to the northeast; the West Gulf Coastal Plain, 15 km to the west; the Ouachita Mountains, 22 km to the northwest; and the Arkansas Valley, while 30 km away, would have been easily accessible by boat up the Arkansas River. The Grand Prairie Ridge is an alluvial terrace with flat terrain. The topsoils are underlain by clay, so that drainage is poor, but it supported a tall grass prairie vegetation that was attractive to migratory wildfowl (Phillips, Ford, and

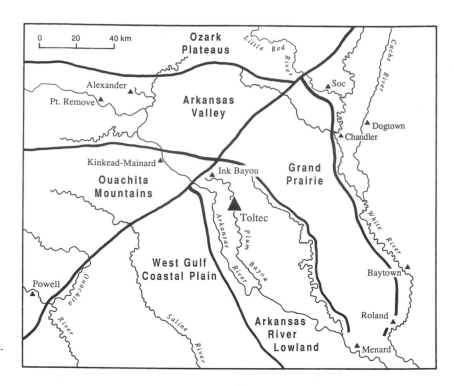

Fig. 6. Central Arkansas physiographic regions and archaeological sites.

Griffin 1951:19). The West Gulf Coastal Plain is characterized by flat to rolling terrain of poorly consolidated sand, clay, and gravels and was forested with pine and hardwood (Foti 1974). These gravels may have been a major source of chert used by the occupants of the Toltec Mounds site.

There are two sections in the Ouachita province, the Arkansas Valley and the Ouachita Mountains, both of which are forested with pine and hardwood (Foti 1974). The Ouachita Mountains are composed of sandstones, shales, and Arkansas novaculite deposits displaying maximum intensity of folding and faulting. Ridges are east-west trending, with the novaculite a common ridge marker. There are small areas of intrusive igneous outcrops (Thornbury 1965:281–282; Foti 1974). The Arkansas Valley section has a folded and faulted structure similar to the Ouachita Mountains but the terrain is more rolling than ridged. The predominant surface rocks are sandstones and shales. The Arkansas Valley province is topographically a trough separating the Ouachita Mountains from the Ozark Plateaus to the north (Thornbury 1965:281; Foti 1974). A small percentage of the lithics at the Toltec Mounds site are from sources in the Ouachita Mountains and Arkansas Valley.

HISTORY OF RESEARCH IN CENTRAL ARKANSAS

Central Arkansas is not a cohesive area physiographically and has not been viewed as a discrete archaeological region of study. There has been no long-term archaeological investigation in the central Arkansas area except for the Toltec Mounds site project. A central Arkansas region is here arbitrarily defined as a 100 km radius around the Toltec Mounds site (Fig. 6). This encompasses the majority of the Grand Prairie and the Arkansas River Lowland as well as portions of the West Gulf Coastal Plain, Ouachita Mountains, and Arkansas Valley. It also extends eastward into the White River Lowland, generally considered the western edge of northeastern Arkansas and the central Mississippi Valley, and westward into the Ouachita River valley and Caddoan region, neither of which would be considered central Arkansas.

Sites in central Arkansas were included in two early studies, Cyrus Thomas's (1894) report on the Bureau of Ethnology's mound exploration project and Clarence B. Moore's (1908, 1909, 1910) investigations along major rivers. The only site in central Arkansas actually excavated and reported prior to 1965 is the Menard site (Ford 1961), located at the southern tip of the

Grand Prairie. The Kinkead-Mainard site was excavated in 1932 but not reported until 1977 (M. P. Hoffman 1977). Both of these sites are late prehistoric to early historic period Quapaw phase sites (Fig. 6).

Archaeological surveys and testing prior to federal and private construction projects began with the Arkansas River Navigation Project in 1966 and 1967 (Scholtz and Hoffman 1968). In the ensuing 18 years, many construction projects have been preceded by survey and testing, but only two major excavations have been conducted. These are the Alexander site in the Conway water supply project and the Ink Bayou site in the Little Rock northbelt expressway corridor.

The Alexander site (Hemmings and House 1985) lies on the floodplain of Cypress Creek, a tributary of Cadron Creek that empties into the Arkansas River. Four major prehistoric components were identified at the Alexander site, dating to the Archaic, Marksville, Coles Creek, and Mississippi periods. The bulk of the site midden, along with pit features, post holes, and a small cemetery are attributed to the Coles Creek period and related to the Plum Bayou culture of the Toltec Mounds site.

The Ink Bayou site (McClurkan 1983; Waddell et al. 1987) is located on an abandoned oxbow lake of the Plum Bayou system, 20 km north of the Toltec Mounds site. It is a multiple component Plum Bayou culture site with a thin undisturbed midden, pit features, and post holes.

It is useful to extend the area of research interest beyond the vicinity of the Toltec Mounds site into areas where sites with Coles Creek Incised ceramics have been recognized. This information can be used to investigate the distribution of sites and define the Plum Bayou culture in a broader pattern. These include the Soc (Figley 1968), Chandler Landing (Moore 1910), and Dogtown sites (Schiffer and House 1975) on the Cache and White rivers to the northeast and the Roland (Baker 1974; Scholtz 1971), Menard, and adjacent Massey (Phillips, Ford, and Griffin 1951:267–272) and Baytown (McClurkan 1971) sites to the southeast on the White River. The Powell Mounds site (Scholtz 1964) is near the juncture of the Caddo and the Ouachita rivers. Upstream on the Arkansas River are the Point Remove site (Ashenden-Duncan 1980; Davis 1967) and the nearby Alexander site.

Diverse survey and minor testing projects in central Arkansas have produced a broad range of data, but no synthesis. One of the research domains of the Toltec Mounds project is the investigation of Plum Bayou culture settlement patterns. While considerable site data is accumulating, the quality of the site reports is varied and there have been no systematic settlement studies. It is evident that the Toltec Mounds site is unique to the central Arkansas region in terms of its size and earthworks. The other known mound sites in the area are generally small with no more than a few small mounds. Other major mound groups are found at a distance of 85 to 100 km and in other river systems.

RESEARCH AT THE TOLTEC MOUNDS SITE

The site was reported to the Smithsonian Institution in 1876 by Mrs. Gilbert Knapp, the landowner, and was known as the Knapp Mound group. Mrs. Knapp (1876a, 1876b, 1878:251) provided a brief description of the site, placing an emphasis on the embankment, which she termed a levee, the two largest mounds, and on the variety of stones that had been imported from as far away as Hot Springs. The first research at the Toltec Mounds site was in 1882 and 1883 by Edward Palmer for the Division of Mound Explorations of the Bureau of Ethnology under the general direction of Cyrus Thomas (Thomas 1894; Rolingson 1982a). All of Palmer's excavations were small and few artifacts of interest were recovered. Despite the artifacts, Cyrus Thomas considered that "these [earth] works form without doubt, the most interesting group in the state, and, in fact, one of the most important in the United States" (Thomas 1894:243). The name "Toltec" was first given to a local railroad station in the late 1880s and later used for the site.

Two published descriptions resulted from the work of the Bureau (Thomas 1894:243–245; Palmer 1917: 423–426). Additional letters, notes, and drawings are on file at the Smithsonian Institution (Rolingson 1982a). These records have proved to be invaluable to recent research because of the damage and destruction to the site features over the past 100 years. Most of the evidence for a late Mississippi period or early Quapaw phase occupation of the site comes from this data.

Professional interest in the site waned after the turn of the century. Clarence B. Moore (1908:557) visited Toltec, but did no investigation because of the lack of interesting artifacts. During the 1930s, archaeological excavations in Arkansas were focused on sites that could be worked with WPA funds or were pertinent to the interests of S. C. Dellinger of the University of Arkansas Museum, such as the bluff shelters of northwestern Arkansas and the Mississippian sites of northeastern Arkansas. Toltec was also outside of the area of the lower alluvial valley survey initiated in the 1940s by James B. Griffin, Philip Phillips, and James A. Ford (1951), and so it was not included in that classic study. It is briefly mentioned in a number of general studies of Mississippian culture, but all of the interpretation has been based on the nineteenth-century investigations (Larson 1971; Reed 1969; Shetrone 1930; Williams 1956).

A brief excavation was undertaken by the University of Arkansas Museum and the Arkansas Archeological Society in 1966 (Davis 1966). It was hypothesized that the ceramics should belong to a time period predating the construction of the mounds at Toltec. The ceramics were thought to be characteristic of a late Baytown to early Coles Creek complex despite the fact that the general characteristics of the site and mound arrangement suggested a Mississippian period temporal placement (Phillips 1970:916).

The Toltec Mounds site was acquired by the State of Arkansas in 1975 for development as an archeological state park. The following year the Toltec Mounds Research Project was initiated by the Arkansas Archeological Survey as a long range research program (Rolingson 1978a) that continues to the present. The overall Toltec research plan (Rolingson 1978a, 1982b: 54–62) contains eight research domains concerning the prehistory of the site and one domain relating to the historic period occupation, as well as a technical evaluation of archaeological research strategies.

The research domain of culture history focuses on the site's occupation and construction sequences, dates of occupation, and relationships to other regional cultures. The internal plan of the settlement, different activity areas and their social contexts, the technology of material culture, and mortuary patterns are all part of the intrasite variability research domain. The bioarchaeological domain addresses genetic relationships as well as environmental stress and adaptation as expressed in the nutritional and disease status of the Toltec burial population. Most of the data for these three research domains will be recovered through excavation.

Three research domains are concerned with the environment and man's interaction with it. One of these is the natural environment of the locality, including the history of the Arkansas River, the natural history of the site, middle nineteenth-century flora and fauna, and reconstruction of the prehistoric environment. The regional resources research domain will involve the identification of resources available in the adjacent physiographic regions and the recovery and analysis of evidence for the use of these. The research domain of subsistence strategies focuses specifically on the archaeological evidence of subsistence in the floral and faunal remains and the agricultural productivity of the locality.

Within the settlement system research domain, systematic site survey will allow the collection of data in the vicinity of Toltec and the identification of outlying sites. Research questions in this domain are concerned with the investigation of residential and specialized activity sites and a postulated hierarchical ranking of dispersed settlements. Data from all the above research domains are needed to investigate the sociopolitical-religious organization of Plum Bayou culture.

Major excavation and research were conducted at Toltec from 1978 through 1981 with funding provided by the Arkansas Archeological Survey and grants-in-aid from the Heritage Conservation and Recreation Service through the Arkansas Historic Preservation Program (Rolingson 1978b, 1980, 1982b, 1982c; Kaczor and Weymouth 1981). The site was found to have suffered extensive damage and destruction since 1850, and all but four mounds have been either reduced in height or destroyed. Because little information was available from the 1883 and 1966 excavations, one of the first goals of the long-term research project was to determine the nature, extent, and condition of the deposits and features in order to assess the applicability of various research approaches. As a result, initial testing at the Toltec site was distributed broadly across the site rather than concentrating in one area (Rolingson 1980, 1982b). The site was divided into six arbitrary sampling strata: (1) the large and visible mounds (A/Q, B, C, F), (2) remnant or leveled mounds, (3) the embankment, (4, 5) offmound areas of the east and west halves of the site, and (6) wooded or developed areas. Each of these six strata has had some excavation, generally in the nature of limited tests, with more effort expended on the remnant mounds than on any other single stratum. Areas for park development have also

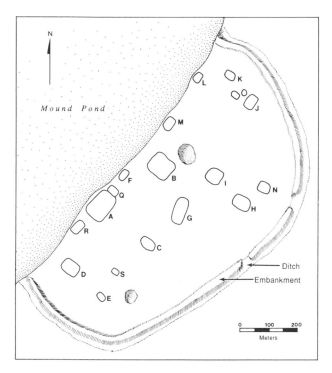

Fig. 7. The location of mounds within the earthen embankment at the Toltec site.

been tested. With these data, as well as several nineteenth-century descriptions, it is possible to identify and describe site features in some detail (Fig. 7).

SITE DESCRIPTION

During the nineteenth century the most impressive features of the site were an earthen wall and the two largest mounds. These were mentioned specifically in all early descriptions, while a number of low mounds were also noted. The embankment was prominent and the site was called a "fortification" (Bringier 1821:37) or a "triangular fort" (Nuttall 1821:98). It is difficult today to visualize how impressive this embankment must have been. Once 1,620 m long, 20 m wide, and 2.5 m high, it defined three sides of the site (with the lake on the fourth side) and enclosed 40 ha. The long east portion of the embankment had four gaps in it. The embankment probably had an exterior ditch along its full length.

Within the embankment were two immense artificial mounds and numerous smaller ones. The top of one of the large mounds was cultivated; artifacts and both

human and animal bone have eroded from it (Knapp 1878). The 1882 map of the site shows 16 mounds (Thomas 1894, pl. X). Mrs. Knapp (1876b) described the smaller mounds as having "tier upon tier of human and animal bones" as well as an abundance of adobe brick or daub.

Determining the nature and degree that modern land use has had in the destruction and alteration of site features is critical for the current research program briefly outlined above. All of the mounds except the highest one have been altered by houses, stock pens, outbuildings, cultivation, land leveling, and as sources of soil to be used in other places. Soil from the mounds and higher elevations has been used to fill surface depressions and borrow pits. The east third of the site, under intensive cultivation for several decades, has been altered by land leveling and sheet erosion. Because of the modern destruction to the upper levels of mounds and the site surface, research has focused on the early history and origins of the mounds rather than on later construction episodes.

MOUND CONSTRUCTION AND HISTORY

While most of the mounds at Toltec appear to have been destroyed in the last century, remnants do remain. Six of the mounds have been tested, providing information on their construction and use as well as on the nature of submound deposits. Although no prehistoric structures have been excavated, there is indirect evidence that they were present.

Mound B (Fig. 7) is 11.5 m high and has retained its quadrilateral shape, although the distinct flat top has been accentuated by cultivation. Mrs. Knapp noted that "It was certainly a place of sepulture, for human bones are found tier upon tier, mingled with those of deer and other animals" (Knapp 1878:251). A cut was made in the southeast corner of Mound B in the 1920s, and erosion has continued in that location over the decades. An excavation profile in this cut exposed the construction sequence for the upper two-thirds of the mound. Another test excavation adjacent to the northeast corner provides data on submound deposition.

A light scatter of midden and artifacts is present at the base of Mound B. A small basin-shaped hearth originates at an elevation hypothesized to be the pre-Mound B surface. The hearth and associated midden are thought to be either earlier than the mound or

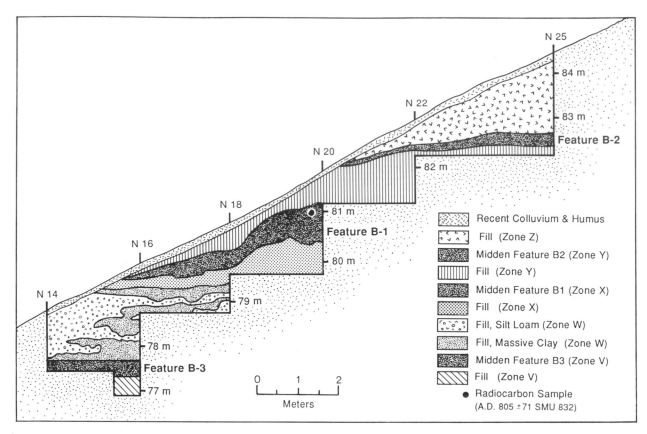

Fig. 8. Stratigraphic profile of Mound B at the Toltec site.

contemporary with the early stages of construction.

The lower 3 m of Mound B have not been tested. The upper 8 m have five soil zones of fill construction and three midden deposits (Fig. 8). The fill zones of mixed soil show distinct basket-shaped loads or small lenses. Few artifacts are present in these fill zones, which are caps rather than mantles. The emphasis in construction is on height.

There are three horizontal bands of concentrated midden in Mound B, each on the surface of a construction stage, at 3.8 m, 6.9 m, and 9.0 m above the mound base. They are distinct from the fill of the construction stages. Two are 20 cm thick while one is 70 cm thick. One of the middens contains sufficient amounts of daub to indicate a plastered building. The materials recovered from these three midden deposits suggest domestic activities, but artifact samples are small. These middens, which show no evidence of basket loading and do not appear to be redeposited midden hauled to the mound to be used as fill, are probably either

primary deposits of trash from buildings used as residences or may be redeposited midden from buildings that were pushed over to level the mound before additional construction.

Mound C (Fig. 7) is 4 m high and dome shaped, although this rounded appearance may partially be a result of modern use. None of the Mound C excavation units have cut into submound deposits, but a sample of submound materials was obtained adjacent to the mound. There is no evidence for stages of construction. Although the Mound C fill contained few artifacts, two shallow bowls were recovered from the upper levels of the mound. Neither specimen was apparently associated with either burials or buildings.

Two burials were found within the Mound C fill—an extended adult female in a poorly defined pit and a flexed male in a pit, which had then been filled with soil mixed with midden. There were no clearly associated grave goods. In addition, several burials, both in and adjacent to the mound, have been recovered by sporadic pothunting over the years. Because evidence of, or information on, burials anywhere else on the site is meager, the Mound C area is considered to be a mortuary precinct.

Mound D (Fig. 7) was reported in 1883 to be 1.5 m high, and over a meter still survives despite considerable use and damage during the historic period. The tops of later stages have been destroyed. It is interpreted as a quadrilateral platform with later additions increasing the length and width rather than the height.

A thin zone of midden predates mound construction. At the base of Mound D, on the plaza side, a partially exposed burned silt deposit with post molds in it probably represents a building floor. Four stages of mound construction have been identified, labeled 0 to III. Stage 0 is a thin fill zone over the burned silt building floor. The construction of Stage I over Stage 0 and adjacent middens provided the bulk of the mound height and initial size. Stages II and III of Mound D were both added to the west (off plaza) and south sides of Stage I.

Two dense concentrations of midden are associated with Mound D construction stages. One is associated with the premound burned silt deposit and Stage 0, while the other is on the slope of Stage II. Both are concentrated middens and are considered primary deposits associated with activities on this mound rather than as trash collected elsewhere and used for fill. These midden deposits provide indirect evidence that buildings on this mound were used as residences.

Mounds E, S, and G (Fig. 7) are all low mounds truncated by farming activities. One or two stages of construction have survived in each, and sealed middens can be linked to some of these mound stages. Based on a number of different lines of evidence, these three mounds are interpreted as low quadrilateral platforms, similar in form to Mound D. Each of these mounds has an occupation deposit beneath it, with a greater concentration of materials at the premound surface than in the buried deposits. The premound surface was not disturbed when mound construction began. Localized midden deposits have been defined beneath the mounds, and post molds, pits, and portions of structures were all found to be present.

Mound A (Fig. 7) is the great enigma of the site. Towering 15.0 m above the south plaza, it is the only mound not to have been denuded and cultivated. An excavation unit located 12 m southeast of the edge of the mound cut through a sequence of plow zone, slope wash zone, old ground surface, and midden. The artifact assemblages from these zones are useful in stratigraphic analysis.

The embankment, too, has suffered over the years. The northern third is nearly obliterated. The southern fourth is protected in woods, where it is still 2.5 m high with a shallow ditch on the exterior side. The middle section can still be identified on the surface by a change in soil color and texture, and some remnants stand above ground. A one-meter wide trench was excavated through one of these remnants. Two soil zones were found to be present, but apparently were associated with a single phase of construction. An inner core is composed of mixed soils while the exterior zone of the embankment is a homogeneous yellowish red silt loam. The original humus zone is present beneath the fill.

Few artifacts were found scattered through the fill during excavation of the embankment. No post molds were found, but the excavation was hardly adequate to verify the absence of such features. The excavation continued outside the embankment to recover evidence of a ditch. Instead of a ditch, an abandoned channel of the river was found. Running adjacent to the embankment for perhaps 600 m, this channel forms a natural ditch.

Six radiocarbon dates from five contexts (Table 5) and one archaeomagnetic date from an additional context have been obtained. Unfortunately, only one of these is a mound stage context. The other dates, however, do provide information on the premound occupation at Toltec, and the beginning of mound construction. One date of A.D. 211 ± 55 (SMU 1182) on a sample of humates from soil collected at the base of the embankment should predate its construction. Although it is a little earlier than expected, it is still within an acceptable range of interpretation.

The two dates from the base of Mound B and beneath Mound G are close in time and confirm the interpretation given to the context of the samples before the dates were received. The date from a hearth at the base of Mound B is A.D. 738 ±70 (SMU 1031) and from a post beneath Mound G is A.D. 746 ±75 (SMU 1027). The pre-Mound G post originates 28 cm below the premound surface at the base of the premound midden zone and thus is earlier than the start of mound construction. The relationship of the Mound B hearth

Table 5. Radiocarbon Dates from the Toltec Mounds

Context and Sample No.	Uncorrected		5730 year half-life		Tree-Ring Calibration (Damon et al. 1974)
	C-14 age	Calendar	C-14 age	Calendar	
Sub-Mound E SMU 1026	1148 ± 57	A.D. 802	1183 ± 57	A.D. 767	A.D. 820 ± 95
Sub-Mound E SMU 1025	1158 ± 48	A.D. 792	1193 ± 48	A.D. 757	A.D. 810 ± 70
Mound B SMU 832	1164 ± 50	A.D. 786	1199 ± 50	A.D. 751	A.D. 805 ± 71
Sub-Mound G SMU 1027	1224 ± 57	A.D. 726	1261 ± 57	A.D. 689	A.D. 746 ± 75
Base of Mound B SMU 1031	1232 ± 48	A.D. 718	1269 ± 48	A.D. 681	A.D. 738 ± 70
Sub-Embankment SMU 1182	1745 ± 48	A.D. 205	1798 ± 48	A.D. 152	A.D. 211 ± 55

to initial construction of the mound is less clear, however, because it is not underneath the mound but associated with a zone whose elevation appears to be below the base of the mound.

The single date recovered from a mound stage context is A.D. 805 ±71 (SMU 832), obtained on charcoal in the concentrated midden on the surface of a construction zone 6.9 m above the base of Mound B. This date is perhaps less useful for interpretation than the other dates because it is from a midden rather than a pit or a building post intruded into the mound stage surface. It is, nevertheless, reasonably consistent with the other dates.

The dates from beneath Mounds E and D are also quite similar. Two dates from one pre-Mound E pit, one on charcoal and one on humates, are in close agreement at A.D. 810 ±70 and 820 ±95 (Table 5) (SMU 1025, 1026). These samples are from a small pit containing charred twigs and branches that originated 26 cm beneath the premound surface. A single archaeomagnetic date from the base of Mound D is given as a range, from A.D. 815 to 915. It cannot be limited to a more specific date because the curve for the time period A.D. 700 to 1000 is not well established due to inadequate data in the south-central United States (Daniel Wolfman, personal communication). The context of the burned silt deposit from which the sample was taken appears to be at the base

of the earliest stage of mound construction.

Excluding the preembankment date, the radiocarbon dates cluster within 100 years, although the range of the standard deviations is 250 years. While there is certainly not enough chronometric data to establish a sequence of mound construction, the suggestion that there may be a difference in time between the middens beneath Mounds B and G and those beneath Mounds D and E is supported by differences in artifact content.

MATERIAL CULTURE

Plant and animal remains recovered during excavation of the Toltec site have only been partially analyzed. Flotation and waterscreen recovery techniques have been used on a systematic sample of excavation units and features, but these samples have not yet been analyzed. Preservation conditions vary drastically, with the best preservation of plant and animal remains occurring in the rich concentrated midden deposits associated with the mounds. It is hypothesized that a wide variety of wild plants and several domesticated plants were an important part of the diet.

The Alexander site (House 1985) provides some useful supplementary data. The major occupation is by the Plum Bayou culture in the A.D. 700 to 900 time period. It is a small, hinterland site in comparison with the Toltec Mounds center. The plant remains are predominantly those of native North American starchy seed-bearing annuals such as maygrass, chenopod, knotweed, and sumpweed, along with squash and gourd. Maize was not identified in the feature samples. The floral, faunal, and skeletal data indicate that a heavy reliance on wild animal and plant foods as well as some native cultigens existed.

The faunal remains from the Mound D excavations have been analyzed (R. W. Hoffman 1982). Deer, turkey, and raccoon make up 87 percent (by weight) of the faunal elements represented in this sample. Despite the dominance of these few species, a wide range of the fauna available in the vicinity is present in the archaeofaunal assemblage. The presence of species of both mixed deciduous forest and backswamp habitats reflect the mosaic aspects of the Toltec environment. Most of the fish and migratory wildfowl species represented are from backswamp or sluggish water habitats and would have been most readily available in the spring and summer. The turkey and deer of the deciduous forest would have been hunted in the fall and winter.

Artifacts made of bone are scarce in the collections. They include decorative items such as long bone pins with incising and small, thin perforated bone disks, as well as utilitarian awls and flakers. Among the bird species in the sample are pileated and redheaded woodpeckers, probably reflecting nonsubsistence use. Mantles and beaks of these birds were used in ceremonial paraphernalia in the Southeast and the practice could have considerable time depth in the area. The only animal effigy recovered is a bird head fragment, carved from trachyte porphyry, representing an owl.

Chert, in the form of waterworn cobbles, is the predominant raw material used for lithic artifacts. These can be obtained from river-deposited gravel beds in the Arkansas River Lowland and adjacent West Gulf Coastal Plain. Present in lesser but significant quantities are novaculite, quartz crystal, sandstone, igneous porphyry, and siltstone. All of these are readily available in the Ouachita Mountains region and along the fall line, only 20 km to the northwest. The most detailed analyses of lithics are of the Mound D sample (T. L. Hoffman 1982) along with a catalog of the large, private Chowning Collection.

The projectile point sample includes both arrow and larger dart points with arrows more common than darts. Most of the arrow points are barbed, expanded-stemmed forms that have long been termed "Scallorn" in the Mississippi Valley, although they deviate from the Scallorn type definition in the Caddoan area (Suhm and Jelks 1962:285). Rockwall points (Perino 1971: 84) are the most distinctive of the notched forms while the Honey Creek point (Derley 1979) is stemless. Honey Creeks are thin, well-chipped bifaces with a deltoid shape or slightly convex edges and base. The darts are predominantly small, gracile contracting-stemmed forms, classed as Gary Stemmed var. *Camden* or *Malvern*. Similar straight-stemmed forms are termed Means Stemmed var. *Means* or *Coy* (Schambach 1970:192–194, 202–206, 361–363). Both arrows and darts are found in most of the stratigraphic proveniences and arrow points are found in sealed, submound deposits.

Other chipped stone tools in the assemblage are knives and gravers or perforators, suggesting considerable working of wood and bone. Among these tools are bifacially flaked quartz crystal flakes and the tips of quartz crystals used as graving or cutting tools. Chipped adzes and celts made on cobbles are present. Ground and polished stone tools include a range of celt and adze forms made from the local sandstones, syenite, lamprophyre, and quartzites. Most of these specimens have been recovered in surface collections; specimens from the excavated submound deposits are rare. The restricted distribution may reflect chronological changes in use or differences in activity areas on the site. The most abundant pecked and ground stone tools are quartzite hammerstones. Small sandstone anvils and pitted stones are present but not abundant.

Distinctive, rare artifacts include grooved plummets and boatstones made of hematite or porphyry and rubbed and shaped galena cubes. Occasional fragments of mica and a thin piece of copper have also been found. Pipes are carved from a local red siltstone. Complete specimens are present in surface collections from the site and fragments have been found in the Mound D and E contexts. These appear to be similar to the modified platform stone pipes found by C. B. Moore (1910:344) at the Chandler Landing site on the White River.

The ceramic sample from excavated proveniences has a rather narrow range of decorated types, but additional types are present in surface collections. The ceramics are overwhelmingly plain and, when present, decoration is usually restricted to the upper rim of the vessel. Ceramics from the Mound D excavations are described in detail (Stewart-Abernathy 1980, 1982) and the distribution of types from the other mound excavations have been analyzed.

The type Baytown Plain accounts for over 90 percent of each of the samples from mound location excavations. The paste is tempered with grog or crushed sherds. One unusual aspect of the ceramics is the presence of crushed bone fragments in about 3 percent of the plain sherds. This is sorted out as a new type, Morris Plain. The amount of bone is usually quite low, with only one or two small fragments in the paste, which is predominantly grog tempered. This is not comparable to the bone tempering in the Caddoan area because it is found infrequently in both the paste and in the sample of sherds.

Vessel forms in both the plain and decorated ceramics are three general forms, hemispherical to shallow bowls, cylindrical to barrel-shaped jars, and recurved rim jars. Flat bases, either round or square, are present but infrequent.

The most common decorated type is Larto Red (Phillips 1970:98–101), although it may simply be more common because the red filming is over the body as well as the rim of the vessel. The percentage of this type varies considerably, with greater amounts present in submound deposits than in those associated with mound stages. Red filming is an infrequent mode on a number of decorated types, including Coles Creek Incised, Officer Punctated, and French Fork Incised.

Rim sherds with horizontal incised lines are typed as Coles Creek Incised in accordance with the expansion of the concept of Coles Creek as a decorative motif by Philip Phillips (1970:69). Most deviant from the original concept is a new variety, Keo, characterized by decoration limited to one or more lines incised in the lip of the rim. Several varieties have a combination of rim and lip lines. The differences in these are based on the number and spacing of lines and the presence of unmodified rims or those with a rim strap added. There are stratigraphic differences with the multiple-line motif and rim strap varieties occurring in the later deposits rather than the earlier deposits.

A new type, Officer Punctated, is established to recognize punctations restricted to the rim or lip of the vessel. Punctations on the rim have long been subsumed in other types, including Baytown Plain (Phillips, Ford, and Griffin 1951:79) but when there is so little decoration in the site sample, it assumes greater significance. Several varieties are based on the positioning and form of the rows of punctates, generally paralleling the differences in varieties of incising.

Several well-established types are present in the sample, including Alligator Incised, Evansville Punctated, French Fork Incised, Indian Bay Stamped, Mulberry Creek Cord Marked, Salomon Brushed, and Withers Fabric Impressed (Phillips, Ford, and Griffin 1951). These are each present in such small amounts that it is difficult to assess their significance.

Shell-tempered potsherds are also present in the mound excavation samples. All of these are plain with an abundance of crushed shell. These sherds are in sealed deposits beneath the mounds (D, E, G, S) and in stage-associated deposits (B, D) where there is no evidence for either animal or human mixing. They are considered to be part of the Plum Bayou assemblage because they are present in such diverse, sealed locations.

STRATIGRAPHY

There are several aspects to consider in sorting out the stratigraphy and occupational history of the site. First, the excavation samples of the mounds are small in terms of the total mound area and there is no direct data on buildings. This limits the interpretation of the deposits and associations of artifacts. Second, there may be occupations of the site prior to mound construction and after construction had ceased. Mounds may have been constructed at different times and changed as they were enlarged. Third, there may be functional differences in the mounds. Several uses are possible, such as a mantle over graves or as a platform for residence, religious building, charnel structure, or for graves. The use and form of a mound may have changed through time. Fourth, in addition to stylistic changes through time, there may be functional differences in the ceramics—a decoration may be associated with special use of the vessels.

Based on 16 proveniences that are considered sealed, primary, or short-term deposits, a stratigraphic analysis can be carried out. Mound fill zones or stages are of less use because they contain a mixture of weathered, older midden. Diagnostic artifacts that may help to delineate chronological differences are found in many of these sealed proveniences, although the artifact changes among these strata are slight. There are only slight differences in distribution among the arrow and dart points. The thin submound deposits beneath Mounds D and S contain a few dart, but no arrow, points. Both dart and arrow points are present in the submound deposits of Mounds G and E. Arrow points are dominant, but not exclusive, in the stage-associated middens.

There are some significant differences in the distribution of the ceramics despite the small amounts of diagnostic varieties. The French Fork Incised and multiple-line varieties of Coles Creek Incised occur together and have a restricted distribution in the middens associated with stages of Mound D, but not beneath it, beneath and associated with Mound E, and with the middle stages of Mound B. The one- and two-line varieties of Coles Creek Incised, Officer Punctated, and Larto Red have a greater distribution among the proveniences, but occur in greatest numbers in the middens beneath Mounds G, S, B, and A.

The presence of shell-tempered pottery in the sealed deposits beneath all five mounds as well as in the stage-associated middens is unexpected. It is certainly not common in the submound middens, but is consistently present and the distribution cannot be attributed to postdepositional mixing. There are no decorated shell-tempered ceramics in the sealed deposits.

A premound occupation of the site can be hypothesized although it cannot be delineated in these analysis proveniences. The presence of dart points, both small Gary Stemmed varieties and Means Stemmed, are indicators of this. Both arrow points and shell-tempered ceramics were part of the assemblage when mound construction began. The major differences are reflected not only in the artifacts associated with mound stages but also in the middens beneath mounds. Therefore, the beginning construction of Mounds D and E are considered later than the beginning of Mounds B, G, S, and perhaps A. This difference is tentatively supported by the radiocarbon dates, but the dates are so close together that the time difference is negligible. Mound construction probably began by the end of the eighth century A.D. There is also some evidence for an occupation of the site after mound construction had ceased. Decorated shell-tempered ceramics diagnostic of the late Mississippi period are present in surface collections and in graves intrusive into mound tops.

MOUND FUNCTION

Another important question is what the mounds were used for. One of the noteworthy aspects of the excavations has been the rare occurrence of human bone and evidence for mortuary practices. No localized cluster of burials in a cemetery has been found and the oral tradition of the site does not include reports of burials or of whole ceramic vessels that might have been placed with burials. Only three skeletons in or adjacent to Mound C have been excavated scientifically. There are reports of discoveries of other burials in both the Mound C and A areas. Based on this limited evidence, Mound C is considered a burial mound.

Mound D is interpreted as a platform used to support a domestic structure. The two sealed middens associated with stages are rich, greasy middens with no evidence of loading or weathering. They are interpreted as fresh trash thrown out from a domestic or residential structure on the mound. Mounds E and S also have rich middens adjacent to or under mound stages and these mounds are also considered platform foundations for residences. Based on the similarity of middens, the premound activities are thought to be residential, also. Mound G is more difficult to interpret because less has been excavated in relation to its size, but there are construction similarities to Mounds D, E, and S. This mound was notable to collectors for the abundance of artifacts present, thus, it is also considered a residential platform.

Mound B is distinct from the others because of its height. The excavations are inadequate for full interpretation, although stages of construction with associated layers of trash are recognized. These midden deposits would seem to indicate that this mound also supported a domestic structure.

INTERNAL SETTLEMENT PLAN

The general arrangement of features within the site is so orderly as to suggest internal planning of the settlement (Fig. 7). The mounds are placed to form two rectangles and the embankment parallels the arrangement, although the embankment corners are rounded. Two open areas or plazas are present, with Mound B in the middle. Ten mounds bound a rectangular south plaza, with Mound B at the northeast end. The only systematic sampling of an offmound area of the site is the portion of this plaza bounded by Mounds R, A,

C, S, E, and D. Most of the concentrated midden deposits are localized adjacent to and under the mounds with thinly scattered midden in the open plaza. A north plaza with Mound B at the southwest end is irregular in form if all nine mounds are used to define the border. If Mounds H and N are considered to be off the plaza, then the plan is more symmetrical.

Occupational debris is widely distributed across the site but the density varies from localized concentrations to light scatters. It is nowhere present in sufficient quantities to indicate the presence of a large or concentrated population. Most of the localized concentrations are associated with mound locations or with the edge of the south plaza. Midden is generally absent from the land adjacent to the embankment where the surface is low in elevation and drainage is poor. Certainly, modern activities have altered the pattern of occupation deposits. Prehistoric activities are also likely to have changed the pattern. There undoubtedly was more extensive sheet midden present over the site that was scraped up for use in mound construction.

There is evidence for large-scale community planning in the formal arrangement of mounds around quadrangular open spaces. Two principles appear to be in use for the placement of mounds, one in regard to celestial phenomena and the other in standardized distances (Sherrod and Rolingson 1987).

The alignment of mound positions with significant solar positions is the most obvious. Mounds A, G, and H are on an east-west alignment with the equinox sunrise and sunset observed from the centers of Mounds A and H. If the location of Mound A is used as a point from which observations are made, then the position of Mound B is aligned with the summer solstice sunrise. From Mound H as a point of observation, the position of Mound B is aligned with the summer solstice sunset and Mound S with the winter solstice sunset. Mound C appears to be slightly off the winter sunset position. Celestial north can be viewed from Mound E toward the position of Mound A.

While basic north-south and east-west alignments are present in the mound arrangement, they do not appear to establish the orientation of the plaza itself. Important solar positions in the sky appear to be marked by the positions of the mounds within the settlement plan. Environmental factors may also affect the orientation of the settlement, as the long axis parallels the lake bank.

With the second planning principle, standardized distances, the increment of distance used appears to be a module of 47.5 m, although the most common spacing of mounds is 95 m, or twice the module. Both Mounds A and H are important reference points for the standardized spacing of the mounds. Measured from the solstice observation point at Mound A, eight of the mounds on the south plaza are at an increment of the 47.5 m module. The length of the south plaza, from Mounds B to D is 380 m, or eight times the module. The length of the north plaza, from Mounds B to K, is 285 m, six times the module. Ten mounds on both plazas are positioned on increments of the module from Mound H. Thus, using the two observation points at Mounds A and H, nearly every mound on the site has standardized spacing.

The larger dimensions of the settlement also conform to the pattern. The length of the lake bank from the north point to the south point of the embankment is 950 m (20 times the module). The length of the embankment itself is 1,620 m (34 times). From the north end of the embankment to the first gap is 522.5 m (11 times) and from this point to the second gap is 237.5 m (5 times).

Both the solar alignment and the standardized spacing of mound positions are evidence that there were cultural guidelines for arrangement of a ceremonial center. Although the positions of the mounds mark the solar alignments, these had to be marked before construction was started. Observation of the movement of the sun would initially have been at ground level. The technique used to establish positions is likely to have been done with posts, as is evident at Cahokia where posts and mound edges mark the north-south alignment of major mounds and the site plan (Fowler 1969, 1975).

The distribution of midden and mounds at Toltec indicates that there was a relatively clean, open plaza edged with residences or residential platforms and one or more burial mounds. There is no evidence in support of a large, centralized population on the site. Organization and planning are evident in the arrangement of mounds around plazas, the selection of mound locations reflecting observation of celestial phenomena, the standardized distance in spacing of mounds, and the relatively short period of time for the beginning of mound construction.

SETTLEMENT PATTERN

The settlement pattern of Plum Bayou culture sites around Toltec Mounds is as yet known only superficially. While the research plan for the project established a 20 km radius study circle, a systematic site survey has not been undertaken. Numerous sites with the artifact assemblage of the Plum Bayou culture have been reported by amateur collectors and observed during cultural resource management surveys. These are located on the natural levees of the several streams draining the Arkansas River Lowland. Only one of these, the Ink Bayou site (McClurkan 1983; Waddell et al. 1987), has been excavated. It is considered to be a multiple component Plum Bayou hamlet adjacent to an oxbow lake. A portion of one structure was excavated and floral and faunal samples provide information on subsistence patterns.

A number of mound sites have been reported in the Toltec study circle. None are comparable to the Toltec Mound site itself, which is unique in the Arkansas River Lowland. Nearly all of these sites have been leveled as a result of intensive modern cultivation practices, and information regarding them is quite variable in terms of both quality and detail. They are reported as conical or dome-shaped mounds less than 3 m high with no clues as to the original form or function, and there are only general assessments of temporal placement.

Settlement pattern studies are planned in the near future and detailed comments must await such investigation. It is hypothesized that most of the population was scattered in the Toltec area locality with hamlets and households located on the higher elevations of the natural sandy loam levees of the small streams draining the area. The Toltec Mounds site, also with a rather small population, served as the religious and political center for this dispersed community.

Several contemporary sites are known in central Arkansas outside of the Arkansas River Lowland (Fig. 6). The largest of these is the Baytown site on the lower White River. While this is the type site for the Baytown culture, data on the site itself is superficial (McClurkan 1971). Nine mounds are known and the major occupation appears to have been contemporary with, or slightly earlier than, the Toltec Mounds site. The Roland (Baker 1974) and Menard (Ford 1961) sites on the White River are closer geographically, and perhaps also culturally, to Baytown than to Toltec.

Upstream on the White River and its tributaries are sites that are closely linked to the Plum Bayou culture by their artifacts. There are several small mound sites in the Dogtown site vicinity (Schiffer and House 1975), the Chandler Landing site (Moore 1910), and the Soc site (Figley 1968). The Soc site is especially interesting because it has Coles Creek Incised pottery, some of which is shell tempered. There are no mounds at this site.

The Alexander site, on a tributary of the Arkansas River, is well documented through extensive excavations (Hemmings and House 1985). Occupied at the same time as Toltec, it is a small settlement in the hinterlands. The nearby Point Remove site (Davis 1967) is notable because it is the last mound site going upstream on the Arkansas River until the Spiro site vicinity is reached. It, too, has Coles Creek Incised decoration on shell-tempered paste ceramics. In the Ouachita River drainage, the Powell Mounds site (Scholtz 1964) is of particular interest. Two mounds are present that are early Caddoan. The submound deposits contained Coles Creek Incised and French Fork Incised sherds.

The information used here is based on published reports of excavated sites. It suggests that there is a contemporary occupation throughout the central Arkansas area, as indicated by Coles Creek Incised pottery. How closely these sites may be related to the Plum Bayou culture of the Toltec vicinity cannot be determined without further research.

COMPARISONS WITH LOWER MISSISSIPPI VALLEY SITES

In order to understand the organization of a large site it is necessary to establish an internal site chronology and the sequence of construction and use of individual mounds. Not only may a settlement plan change through time, but the function of individual mounds may change. Much of the excavation on sites in the lower Mississippi Valley has been in nonmound areas and with an emphasis on establishing chronology on the basis of ceramic style changes. As a result, there are few sites with detailed descriptions of mound construction.

The focus of the present discussion is the chronological, structural, and functional details of mounds. The geographic area under consideration is limited to the Mississippi Alluvial Valley from the mouth of the Red

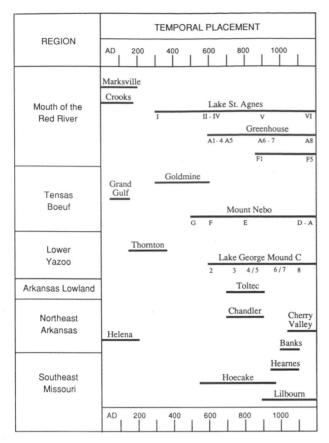

Fig. 9. Chronological chart of excavated mounds in the lower Mississippi Valley.

River on the south to the mouth of the Ohio River on the north. The time range is bracketed between A.D. 1 and A.D. 1150, from Middle Woodland to the end of the Early Mississippi period. A chronological chart of mound construction at 16 sites within this study area is given in Figure 9 and a simplistic synopsis of construction and use is given in Table 6. The locations of the sites are shown on Figure 10. The nature and quality of the data available for each site is dependent upon the preexcavation condition of the mounds, the extent to which excavations were carried out, and the amount of information contained in the published report. While each of the mounds is unique in construction and sequence of use, there are some trends evident, especially when the southern half of the valley is separated from the northern half, at about the mouth of the modern Arkansas and White rivers (Fig. 10).

In the southern half of the valley, four mounds date

in the early Marksville period, Marksville Mound 4 and Crooks Mound A and B in Louisiana and Grand Gulf in Mississippi. All are alike in that the initial mound is a flat-topped platform with subsequent additions of irregular or conical-shaped mantles. The use of these platforms as foundations for charnel houses as well as burials is likely, although specific evidence of post mold patterns is lacking. The sequence of mortuary processing activities and mound construction is different in each mound. The Grand Gulf mound differs in another respect in that burials were not preserved, although it has some characteristics of the other mounds.

The Thornton mound in Mississippi dates to the late Marksville period. It is a superimposed series of flat-topped platforms with middens on them. Patterns of post molds were not defined in the excavation trenches although post molds were common and the presence of buildings is likely. The few burials present are intrusive from subsequent occupations that did not add stages to the mounds. The mound at the Gold Mine site in Louisiana during the Baytown period is also a superimposed series of flat-topped platforms, but in this situation the primary mound function is mortuary, with burial pits from two of the platform surfaces intruded into the fill.

The Lake St. Agnes and Mount Nebo mounds in Louisiana and the Lake George Mound C in Mississippi are each multiple stage flat-topped platforms with the stages added over a long period of time. Burials in pits intrusive from a stage surface into the fill are present but only on occasional stages. Other stages may have no surviving evidence of the activity on that stage. One characteristic of these, as well as of Thornton and Gold Mine, is that they are asymmetrical constructions with enlargements made as lateral additions or aprons and caps, but not as symmetrical mantles. The forms of the early stages may be low and amorphous with a distinct raised rectangular platform shape appearing only in the middle and later stages.

The Greenhouse site in Louisiana is different from the others in that it is a multiple mound site while the others have only one to three mounds in use contemporaneously. The excavated mounds here have evidence of use as platforms for buildings with little use as mortuaries. Mound A building levels 1 and 2 were not excavated sufficiently to identify building patterns. At building level 3, the mound was 2.4 m high and had a building on it, as did levels 4, 6, and 7. Level

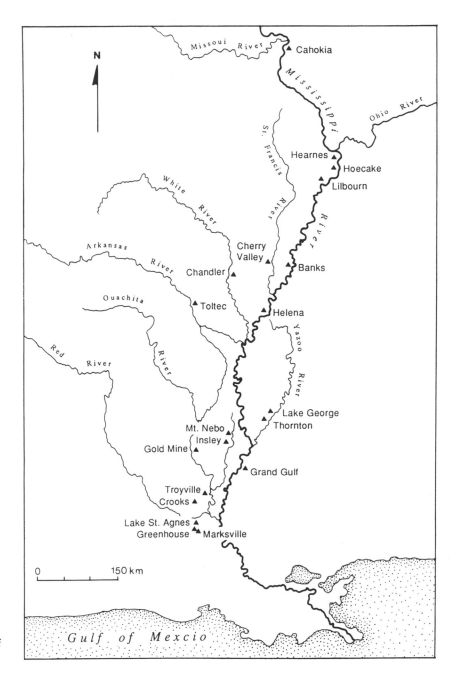

Fig. 10. The location of lower Mississippi Valley sites discussed in the text.

5 lacked evidence of a structure, but had eight burials. Mound F had at least five stages, most with evidence for buildings. Mound C, on the other hand, consisted of an 0.7 m thick deposit of midden with a localized area of 93 burials. These had been disposed of with little care or order. The deposit was capped with an artificially loaded soil. The locus designated Mound D had no constructed mound but was a midden accumu-

lation associated with a circular house. Mounds B, E, and G were not excavated. The chronological analysis by John Belmont (1967) places the initial site occupation about A.D. 300, but construction of Mounds A and E did not begin until about A.D. 600 and Mounds G and F were added about A.D. 900, with Mound C beginning about this time. Construction of mounds on the site had stopped by A.D. 1200. Internal planning of the

Table 6. Characteristics of Excavated Mounds in the Lower Mississippi Valley A.D. 1–1150

Site name	Characteristics	References
Marksville, LA	Mound 4: flat platform with burials; subsequent conical mantles with burials	Toth 1974
Crooks, LA	Mound A: flat platform with burials; subsequent conical mantles with burials	Ford and Willey 1940
	Mound B: flat platform with burials; subsequent conical mantle	
Lake St. Agnes, LA	Superimposed flat platforms; six stages; burial only in the first	Toth 1979
Greenhouse, LA	Mound A: superimposed flat platforms; seven stages with buildings; burials only in Stage 5	Ford 1951;
	Mound F: superimposed flat platforms; five stages with buildings	Belmont 1967
	Mound C: loaded soil containing burials	
Grand Gulf, MS	Flat platform with fired area on surface; subsequent irregular mantles; no burials	Brookes 1976
Gold Mine, LA	Superimposed flat platforms; four stages; burials in II and III	Belmont 1982a
Mount Nebo, LA	Superimposed flat platforms; seven stages; burials in second and seventh	Giardino 1982
Thornton, MS	Superimposed flat platforms; four stages; with middens	Phillips 1970:583–593
Lake George MS	Mound C only: superimposed flat platforms; five stages; two with burials	Williams and Brain 1983:38–56
Helena AR	Mound B: central subsurface tomb; subsequent single mantle	Ford 1963
	Mound C: subsurface tombs; subsequent mantles with additional tomb burials and group burials	
Chandler AR	Mound A: accretionary with burials throughout	Moore 1910
	Mound B: accretionary with burials throughout	
Hoecake MO	Story Mound I: subsurface log tombs; subsequent mantle	J. R. Williams 1974
	Brock Mound: accretionary with burials throughout	
Banks AR	Mound 3: subsurface pits and surface burials covered with platforms containing burials; subsequent mantle with burials and basin; final mantle with burials	Perino 1967; Morse and Morse 1983
Cherry Valley AR	Three mounds: charnel house on ground covered with mantle and burials	Perino 1967
Hearnes MO	Accretionary loading with burials	Klippel 1969
Lilbourn MO	Mound 2: superimposed flat platforms; three stages; rectangular building on top	Chapman et al. 1977
	Mound 3: superimposed flat platforms; three stages; no evidence of buildings found in tests	
	Mound 4: large rectangular structure on upper surface; remainder of mound not excavated	
	Mound 5: north half removed by machine; no features found except large post mold beneath mound at northwest corner	

Greenhouse site is evident in the position of Mound E aligned on the winter solstice sunset as observed from Mound A, and of Mounds G and A on the equinox position. These mounds are also placed at standardized distances from Mound A (Sherrod and Rolingson 1987).

The pattern in the northern half of the lower Mississippi Valley is different from that of the south. The mounds of the Helena Landing site in Arkansas are the only ones dating to the early Marksville period. These contained one or more subsurface tombs intruded into the ground from the premound surface. No platforms were constructed. Subsequent mantles of Mound C contained additional tombs and group burials. The final mound of both was a conical mantle.

The two Chandler Landing mounds in Arkansas, excavated by C. B. Moore in the early twentieth century, are now thought to date in the late Baytown period. Moore's description indicates that the mounds were accretionary, with burials scattered throughout. Bone was badly preserved and only occasional burials had grave goods. The Hoecake site in Missouri also dates primarily to the late Baytown period but is markedly different with some 30 or more mounds present. Two of these have been excavated. The Story Mound had subsurface tombs and a covering mantle. The Brock Mound had burials scattered throughout an accretionary fill. There is no indication of the concept of platforms as mortuary processing areas in either of the two mounds.

The Banks Mound 3 and the three Cherry Valley mounds in Arkansas and the two Hearnes mounds in Missouri date to the Early Mississippi period. In each of these the primary function is mortuary, although the specific processes are different. Banks Mound 3 has premound burial pits, a platform containing burials, and a covering mantle with burials. The three mounds at Cherry Valley began with a charnel house on the ground surface and subsequent mantles contained burials. The Hearnes Mound 1 is an accretionary mound with burials scattered through the fill. Both the Banks and Cherry Valley mounds have been radiocarbon dated and are apparently contemporary, about A.D. 1050 to A.D. 1150. The Hearnes mounds are assigned to the Early Mississippi period based on ceramic styles.

The Lilbourn site is a major Mississippi period civic-ceremonial site at which mounds have been excavated in recent years. The site had ten mounds with seven of these arranged around an open plaza in the classic Mississippian settlement plan. Four of these have been partially excavated and their construction is similar. The mounds are flat-topped platforms constructed in stages with evidence for buildings on some of the stages. The only burial that has been recovered is a single human skull on the south edge of Mound 4. The construction of the mounds is assigned to the Early Mississippi period of occupation. The analysis of the data is not presented in such a manner to determine the specific time of origin of individual mounds or the dating of the sequence of construction within the 500 years of occupation. The arrangement of mounds around a plaza with a north-south orientation of the long axis indicates internal planning for the community.

This sample of excavated sites is hardly adequate as a basis for drawing very many conclusions, given the geographic and chronological ranges involved. One safe conclusion is that the original form and use of a mound cannot be determined from its modern shape.

In the northern half of the valley, several mortuary patterns are present in the mounds of the late Baytown period and continue into the Early Mississippi period. The only platform apparently associated with mortuary processing is at Banks Mound 3 in the Early Mississippi period. There appear to be clear differences in construction and function of these burial mounds from the flat-topped substructure mounds of the Lilbourn site, although both are contemporary in the Mississippi period. It is doubtful, however, that conclusions should be based on the Lilbourn site alone. The initial dates for platform mound construction are not well documented in the northern half of the valley. The possibility that platform mounds used as residences were constructed prior to A.D. 900 should be investigated further.

In the southern half of the valley the flat-topped platform is present in the Marksville period and continues to be built through subsequent periods, but the conical mantle is abandoned and the function changes. Platforms without mantles are being constructed by the late Marksville period (Thornton). These platforms are the foundation either for mortuary activities that may include charnel houses or for residences, and the function of an individual mound may have changed through time.

The Toltec site mounds, interpreted as platforms for residences, are similar to the mounds at the Greenhouse and Lilbourn sites. At the Greenhouse and Toltec sites the platforms generally do not have intrusive graves on the platforms. They do have evidence of buildings, but it is difficult to identify the function of the structures without data from extensive excavations. Nevertheless, the use of platforms as foundations for buildings used as residences is earlier at the Greenhouse and Toltec sites than at the Lilbourn site. The data from the northern lower valley, however, simply may not be adequate for any firm conclusions in this regard. There is a significant difference between Lilbourn on the one hand and Toltec and Greenhouse on the other. Lilbourn is a nucleated settlement with a concentrated population within the settlement boundaries. The evidence from Toltec and Greenhouse indicates a small population within the settlement, with the people of the community mostly dispersed in smaller, outlying settlements.

In regard to internal settlement plan, the Greenhouse and Lilbourn sites also show the greatest similarity of these 16 sites to the Toltec Mounds site. The Greenhouse site has seven mounds arranged around a plaza that is oval to rectangular, with placement of mounds aligned to solar positions and standardized distances. The Lilbourn site has ten mounds, most of which are arranged around a rectangular open plaza on a north-south orientation. Conversely, at the Marksville site the five mounds inside the embankment are irregularly placed. The Lake George site has a rectangular arrangement, but most of the mounds were not constructed until after A.D. 1150 and Mound C is the only excavated early mound. At the Hoecake site there is no apparent formal arrangement of mounds.

This sample of sites with excavated mounds is too

limited for a discussion of the patterns of settlement design of ceremonial centers. Expanding the sample to include analysis of the plans of sites mapped during surveys does show some trends. The construction and use of platform mounds in the northern part of the valley is later and more restricted in time, therefore the pattern may be less variable. Ceremonial centers with multiple mounds generally have the mounds around an oval plaza area. The dominant mound tends to be on the west end of the plaza and face east or southeast (Phillips, Ford, and Griffin 1951:315–335). Other factors influencing the arrangement of mounds and buildings on the site appear to be topography and the requirements for fortification of the settlement (Chapman 1976; Reed 1969). Sites without mounds also show evidence of internal planning. At the Zebree site, the Big Lake phase village had a large post pit at the center of north-south and east-west transects. These define the four corners of the rectangular plan of the village. The orientation is likely to have been based on solar observations (Morse and Morse 1983:228).

In the southern half of the valley a general pattern is not as evident. Platform mounds used for either residences or mortuary activities are constructed over a longer period of time than in the north. The concept of an oval or rectangular plaza is present and topographic factors apparently influence their orientation, but centers are not fortified and boundaries are less clearly defined. A sequence of changes in site plans and positions of dominant mounds through time is postulated by Stephen Williams and Jeffrey Brain (1983: 402–408), based primarily on site survey data. The position of the dominant mound on the plaza shifts from east to south and finally to west through time and most sites remain small with only two to four mounds. The larger sites with multiple mounds are not constructed until after A.D. 1100, subsequent to contact with cultures to the north.

With the increased amount of data from investigations throughout the lower valley, it is evident that the internal spatial organization of settlements was not haphazard, but rather was complex and affected by a variety of factors. Topography or environment was one of the contributing factors. Recognition of the cardinal directions and seasonal position of the sun at the solstices and equinoxes appears to be another. These approaches to the investigation of settlement design have only begun and future research should produce some interesting ideas and interpretations.

THE PLACE OF TOLTEC MOUNDS SITE IN LOWER VALLEY PREHISTORY

The Plum Bayou culture has some aspects that are distinctive within the context of lower Mississippi Valley prehistory, while other aspects are typical. The subsistence pattern is typical for the time period with utilization of a diverse range of alluvial bottomland resources. Deer and turkey were hunted, while fishing and gathering nuts and other wild plant foods contributed to the diet. Although a number of cultigens were likely grown, there is no evidence indicating a primary dependence on maize.

The ceramics are predominantly clay tempered and plain and a limited number of vessel forms typical of the Late Baytown period in the lower Mississippi Valley occur. Decoration is simple incising or punctating with the motifs limited to the upper portion of the vessel. Larto Red is the dominant decorated type only at the Toltec Mounds site. Ceramics with shell-tempered paste are present, but not the diverse vessel forms usually associated with this tempering agent.

The abundance of lithics and the diverse range of raw materials utilized is unusual for sites in the lower Mississippi Valley. Most of the raw materials are available from the Arkansas River gravel deposits or from the Ouachita Mountains and can be found within 50 km of the Toltec Mounds site. The most unusual of these is the utilization of quartz crystal for tools. Artifacts such as modified platform pipes of red siltstone, and bird effigies, boatstones, celts, and plummets of igneous stones indicate a concern with stone carving and polishing. Galena, hematite, and limonite may have been used as sources of pigments. The abundance and diversity of materials are an indication that the occupants of the Toltec Mounds site probably controlled a local exchange network, but more information is needed to establish the extent of this network. A copper fragment and an incised section of conch shell are evidence for more distant trade relationships.

The Plum Bayou settlement pattern is dispersed and is generally typical of the late Baytown period in the lower valley. Most of the population apparently lived in hamlets, farmsteads, or seasonal camps. The few sites with one or two low mounds may be interpreted as small ceremonial centers, but the size of these sites is no larger than some sites without mounds. The large size of the Toltec Mounds site is outstanding among these settlements, although there is no evidence for a nucleation of population at this site. Rather, it is postulated that the residents were a moderate-sized group of the higher ranked members of the society.

There is no evidence for status differentiation in either burials or houses, but the excavation data is as yet quite limited. Although the material culture present on outlying sites is not as well documented as it is at Toltec, there appears to be a greater concentration at Toltec of the unusual raw materials and artifacts. This differential distribution of craft goods, natural resources, and higher quantities of exchange items can be interpreted as evidence for differential residential patterns with the higher ranked individuals of the society living at Toltec rather than in outlying settlements.

Excavation of six of the Toltec site mounds has provided information on their construction and use. Five of the six are substructural residence platforms. Most of these are low platforms, but one was built for height and therefore was conceptualized differently from the others. The period during which construction of many of these mounds was initiated appears to have been rather short, occurring about A.D. 800 to 900. Flat-topped platforms have a long and continuous history in the lower Mississippi Valley, but it is significant that the function changes. The earliest ones were used for mortuary processing and for burial, focusing on the corporate group. When platforms were used as residences, the focus shifted to a small group of individuals who had some degree of control over the corporate group. Data is limited, but as yet there is no evidence for status differentiation among the residential loci within the Toltec site. If the elite of the society were residing in this centralized location, then these differences would appear not within the site but between Toltec and the outlying sites, as is indicated by the distribution of material culture.

This shift in function may have started in the lower Mississippi Valley by A.D. 300 or 400, based on the evidence at the Thornton site mound and by A.D. 600 at the Greenhouse site. Some platforms continued to be used for mortuary purposes, such as Lake George Mound C and the Mount Nebo mound. There are parallels to this use of platforms for various activities in the Weeden Island culture of Florida and the Gulf Coast during the time period A.D. 200 to 900. At the McKeithen site in northern Florida (Milanich et al. 1984) three flat-topped platforms were constructed, each used for different purposes. Mortuary processing took place on one mound, while the burials were placed in another, and the third supported a residential structure.

The internal planning and earthwork construction at the Toltec Mounds site are among the more distinctive aspects of the culture and also can be interpreted as evidence for ranking individuals within the society. Planning is evident in the location of mounds within the site rather than in the orientation of the site as a whole. The positions of the mounds are based on both solar orientation and a standardized unit of measure. The Toltec site is not unique in these aspects—they are also present at the contemporary Greenhouse site and at other sites. Evidence for solar observations has been recognized in the organization of site plans, and considerable chronological and geographical ranges are indicated among sites, such as Poverty Point, Louisiana, Crystal River and McKeithen, Florida, and Cahokia, Illinois.

The magnitude of earthwork construction at the Toltec Mounds site is impressive. The construction of 18 mounds, of which four are quite large, may have continued over a period of 200 to 300 years. The mounds were not single units of construction, that is, they were enlarged in stages, so that no single stage represented a massive amount of labor. The 1,620 m embankment, however, may have been conceptualized and constructed as a unit. Whether intended as a defensive barrier or as a ceremonial boundary, it would not have been functional if it were constructed in segments over a long period of time. Neither a large number of people nor conscripted labor would have been required for its construction. Several large, multiple mound and earthwork sites were constructed sporadically during the 2,500 years preceding the Toltec site in the lower Mississippi Valley, including Poverty Point, Marksville, and Troyville, all located in Louisiana. Such major construction efforts became more commonplace after A.D. 1000.

The size of the Toltec Mounds site and amount of earthwork planning and construction can be interpreted as evidence for a long-term investment of labor by the community. The complexity of plan and details of construction and maintenance are evidence for a leadership that directed the activities. The range of knowledge reflected in the observation of celestial phenomena and earthwork construction is likely to have been restricted to a few religious leaders who also directed and organized the labor force during periods of construction. The structure of society would probably not have been egalitarian, but would have some hierarchical ranking of persons. The data is as yet too limited to reach even tentative conclusions about the complexity and form of ranked social structure, but it probably was not stratified into classes.

The Toltec Mounds site is the largest and most complex of the multiple mound sites in the lower Mississippi Valley during the period from A.D. 700 to 900, but there are four contemporary sites with monumental earthworks on a slightly smaller scale. The Greenhouse site, described above, is near the mouth of the Red River. The Troyville site (Neuman 1984:169–188) is poorly documented but may be a little earlier than, and contemporary with, Toltec. It is located at the juncture of the Arkansas-Ouachita River with the Red River and had ten or more mounds and an embankment. The Insley site on Bayou Macon in northeastern Louisiana, which had 14 mounds in an arrangement much as at Toltec, has not been excavated (Belmont 1982b). The Baytown site with nine mounds is near the juncture of the White River with the Mississippi River in east-central Arkansas. Poorly documented, it may be earlier than, as well as contemporary with, Toltec. There is a pattern to the locations of these sites. They are all west of the Mississippi River and near points of diverse environmental resources on major rivers. The cultures that produced them span the period from A.D. 300 to 1100, and maintained their own patterns of development. While they appear to have been relatively uninfluenced by other cultures, it is possible that the extensive exchange networks that are so clearly evident in subsequent centuries had their beginnings at this time.

Cultures in two other important loci outside of the lower Mississippi Valley were developing at the same time. One of these is the Cahokia location in the American Bottom, opposite the mouth of the Missouri River. Major mound construction at the Cahokia site is generally considered to have been initiated about A.D. 900. Construction of substructure platform mounds had ap-

parently begun at the nearby Pulcher site prior to A.D. 900 (Griffin 1977:487). It is possible that earlier efforts at mound construction at Cahokia have been obscured by the later earthworks and have not yet been sufficiently exposed in excavations.

The second locus is the Spiro site area on the Arkansas River in eastern Oklahoma. Small ceremonial centers at Spiro and other sites were established during the Evans phase, dated A.D. 700 to 950, with relationships to the Toltec site indicated by the ceramics (Brown 1984:12). The mounds and associated structures at these ceremonial centers, however, were used for mortuary activities. The extensive exchange network materials found with the later Spiro phase occupation (Brown 1983) may have a precursor in these earlier contacts and established routes along the Arkansas River.

Each of these aspects of Plum Bayou culture had earlier origins than their appearance at the Toltec Mounds site. The site is distinctive, however, for the combination of these elements of community planning and the magnitude of the site at this time period. It appears to be a forerunner of these aspects that are elaborated and expanded in the Mississippi Valley and throughout the Southeast in subsequent centuries. The Toltec Mounds site has been preserved with deposits moderately undisturbed, unlike other sites that have been badly damaged over the years. The research on the Toltec site and on the Plum Bayou culture has just begun and the research program is both ambitious and wide ranging. It will produce data important for understanding the development of complex societies in the Mississippi Valley.

REFERENCES CITED

Ashenden-Duncan, Alice
1980   Preliminary Speculations Concerning the Sherds From the Society Dig in 1967 at Point Remove. Manuscript on file, University of Arkansas Museum, Fayetteville.

Baker, Charles M.
1974   Roland Site Week-end Test Excavation. In *Emergency Surveying and Testing in the Lower White River and Arkansas Post Canal Area, Arkansas, 1965,* by Hester A. Davis and Charles M. Baker, pp. 58–63. Research Report No. 3. Arkansas Archeological Survey, Fayetteville.

Belmont, John S.
1967   The Culture Sequence at the Greenhouse Site, Louisiana. *Southeastern Archaeological Conference Bulletin* 6:27–34. Morgantown, West Virginia.

1982a The Troyville Concept and the Gold Mine Site. *Louisiana Archaeology* 9:63–96. Lafayette.

1982b Toltec and Coles Creek: A View from the Southern Lower Mississippi Valley. In *Emerging Patterns of Plum Bayou Culture: Preliminary Investigations of the Toltec Mounds Research Project*, edited by Martha Ann Rolingson, pp. 64–70. Research Series No. 18. Arkansas Archeological Survey, Fayetteville.

Bringier, Louis
1821 Notices of the Geology, Mineralogy, Topography, Productions, and Aboriginal Inhabitants of the Regions Around the Mississippi and its Confluent Waters. *The American Journal of Science* 3:15–46.

Brookes, Samuel O.
1976 *The Grand Gulf Mound (22-Cb-522): Salvage Excavation of an Early Marksville Burial Mound.* Archaeological Report No. 1. Mississippi Department of Archives and History, Jackson.

Brown, James A.
1983 Spiro Exchange Connections Revealed by Sources of Imported Raw Materials. In *Southeastern Natives and Their Pasts: A Collection of Papers Honoring Dr. Robert E. Bell*, edited by Don G. Wyckoff and J. L. Hoffman, pp. 129–162. Studies in Oklahoma's Past, Number 11, Oklahoma Archaeological Survey, Norman.

1984 *Prehistoric Southern Ozark Marginality: A Myth Exposed.* Special Publication, No. 6. Missouri Archaeological Society, Columbia.

Chapman, Carl H.
1976 Internal Settlement Designs of Two Mississippian Tradition Ceremonial Centers in Southeastern Missouri. In *Cultural Change and Continuity*, edited by Charles E. Cleland, pp. 121–146. Academic Press, New York.

Chapman, Carl H., John W. Cottier, David Denman, David R. Evans, Dennis E. Harvey, Michael D. Reagan, Bradford L. Rope, Michael D. Southard, and Gregory A. Waselkov
1977 Investigation and Comparison of Two Fortified Mississippi Tradition Archaeological Sites in Southeast Missouri: A Preliminary Compilation. *The Missouri Archaeologist* 38. Columbia.

Damon, P. E., C. W. Ferguson, A. Long, and E. I. Wallick
1974 Dendrochronologic Calibration of the Radiocarbon Time Scale. *American Antiquity* 39:350–366.

Davis, Hester A.
1966 Nine Days at the Toltec Site, the Society's Third Successful Dig. *Field Notes, Newsletter of the Arkansas Archeological Society* 20:2–5. Fayetteville.

1967 The Puzzle of Point Remove. *Field Notes, Newsletter of the Arkansas Archeological Society* 33:2–7. Fayetteville.

Derley, Jim
1979 The Honey Creek Point, a Prairie County Original? *Field Notes, Newsletter of the Arkansas Archeological Society* 170:5. Fayetteville.

Figley, Charles A.
1968 The Soc Site, 3WH34. *The Arkansas Archeologist* 9(3–4):41–58. Fayetteville.

Ford, James A.
1951 *Greenhouse: A Troyville-Coles Creek Period Site in Avoyelles Parish, Louisiana.* Anthropological Papers 44(1). American Museum of Natural History, New York.

1961 *Menard Site: The Quapaw Village of Osotouy on the Arkansas River.* Anthropological Papers 48(2). American Museum of Natural History, New York.

1963 *Hopewell Culture Burial Mounds Near Helena, Arkansas.* Anthropological Papers 50(1). American Museum of Natural History, New York.

Ford, James A., and Gordon R. Willey
1940 *Crooks Site, A Marksville Period Burial Mound in La Salle Parish, Louisiana.* Anthropological Study No. 3. Louisiana Geological Survey, Baton Rouge.

Foti, Thomas L.
1974 Natural Divisions of Arkansas. In *Arkansas Natural Area Plan.* Arkansas Department of Planning, Little Rock.

Fowler, Melvin L.
1969 The Cahokia Site. In *Explorations Into Cahokia Archaeology*, edited by Melvin L. Fowler, pp. 1–30. Bulletin No. 7. Illinois Archaeological Survey, Urbana.

1975 A Pre-Columbian Urban Center on the Mississippi. *Scientific American* 233:92–101.

Giardino, Marco J.
1982 Temporal Frameworks, Archaeological Components and Burial Types: The Human Osteology of the Mt. Nebo Site in North Louisiana. *Louisiana Archaeology* 9:97–124. Lafayette.

Griffin, James B.
1977 The University of Michigan Excavations at the Pulcher Site in 1950. *American Antiquity* 42:462–488.

Hemmings, E. Thomas, and John H. House (editors)
1985 *The Alexander Site, Conway County, Arkansas.* Research Series No. 24. Arkansas Archeological Survey, Fayetteville.

Hoffman, Michael P.
1977 The Kinkead-Mainard Site, 3PU2, a Late Prehistoric Quapaw Phase Near Little Rock, Arkansas. *The Arkansas Archeologist* 16–18:1–41. Fayetteville.

Hoffman, Robert W.
1982 *Animal Resource Exploitation Patterns at the Toltec Site: A Zooarcheological Study of the Mound D Sample.* Unpublished Master's thesis, Department of Anthropology, University of Arkansas, Fayetteville.

Hoffman, Teresa Lynn
1982 *Chipped Stone Tool Manufacturing Processes in Mound D at the Toltec Mounds Site (3LN42).* Unpublished Master's thesis, Department of Anthropology, University of Arkansas, Fayetteville.

House, John H.
1985 Summary and Conclusions. In *The Alexander Site, Conway County, Arkansas*, edited by E. Thomas Hemmings and John H. House, pp. 99–110. Research Series No. 24. Arkansas Archeological Survey, Fayetteville.

Kaczor, Michael J., and John Weymouth
1981 Magnetic Prospecting: Preliminary Results of the 1980 Field Season at the Toltec Site, 3LN42. *Southeastern Archaeological Conference Bulletin* 24:118–123. Gainesville.

Klippel, Walter E.
1969 The Hearnes Site: A Multicomponent Occupation Site and Cemetery in the Cairo Lowland Region of Southeast Missouri. *Missouri Archaeologist* 31. Columbia.

Knapp, Mrs. Gilbert

1876a   Letter of April 8 from Little Rock to Dr. Wm. H. Barry, Hot Springs. On file, Museum of Natural History Accession Number 5153, Smithsonian Institution, Washington.

1876b   Letter of April 11 from Little Rock to Professor Joseph Henry, Smithsonian Institution. On file, Museum of Natural History Accession Number 5153, Smithsonian Institution, Washington.

1878   Earth-works on the Arkansas River, Sixteen Miles Below Little Rock. *Annual Report of the Board of Regents of the Smithsonian Institution for 1877*, p. 251. Washington, D.C.

Larson, Lewis H.

1971   Settlement Distribution During the Mississippi Period. *Southeastern Archaeological Conference Bulletin* 13:18–25. Morgantown.

McClurkan, Burney B.

1971   A Brief Test at the Baytown Site (3MO1). *Field Notes, Newsletter of the Arkansas Archeological Society* 75:3–4. Fayetteville.

1983   *Archeological Survey and Testing Northbelt Expressway, AHTD Job # 60110, Pulaski County and Archeological Testing at the Ink Bayou Site, 3 PU 252*. Report submitted to the Office of State Archeologist by the Arkansas Highway and Transportation Department. Copies available from the Arkansas Highway and Transportation Department, Little Rock.

Milanich, Jerald T., Ann S. Cordell, Vernon J. Knight, Timothy A. Kohler, and Brenda J. Sigler-Lavelle

1984   *McKeithen Weeden Island: The Culture of Northern Florida, A.D. 200–900*. Academic Press, Inc. New York.

Moore, Clarence B.

1908   Certain Mounds of Arkansas and of Mississippi. Part I. Mounds and Cemeteries of the Lower Arkansas River. *Journal of the Academy of Natural Sciences of Philadelphia* 13.

1909   Antiquities of the Ouachita Valley. *Journal of the Academy of Natural Sciences of Philadelphia* 14:7–170.

1910   Antiquities of the St. Francis, White and Black Rivers, Arkansas. *Journal of the Academy of Natural Sciences of Philadelphia* 14:254–364.

Morse, Dan F., and Phyllis A. Morse

1983   *Archaeology of the Central Mississippi Valley*. Academic Press, New York.

Neuman, Robert W.

1984   *An Introduction to Louisiana Archaeology*. Louisiana State University Press, Baton Rouge.

Nuttall, Thomas

1821   *Journal of Travels into the Arkansa Territory During the Year 1819*. Thomas A. Palmer, Philadelphia. Reprinted in March of America Facsimile Series 63, University Microfilms, Ann Arbor.

Palmer, Edward

1917   Arkansas Mounds. *Arkansas Historical Association Publications* 4:390–448. Little Rock.

Perino, Gregory

1967   *The Cherry Valley Mounds and Banks Mound 3*. Memoir No. 1. Central States Archaeological Societies.

1971   *Guide to the Identification of Certain American Indian Projectile Points*. Special Bulletin No. 4. Oklahoma Anthropological Society, Norman.

Phillips, Philip

1970   *Archaeological Survey in the Lower Yazoo Basin, Mississippi, 1949–1955*. Papers of the Peabody Museum of Archaeology and Ethnology 60. Harvard University.

Phillips, Philip, James A. Ford, and James B. Griffin

1951   *Archaeological Survey in the Lower Mississippi Alluvial Valley, 1940–1947*. Papers of the Peabody Museum of Archaeology and Ethnology 25. Harvard University.

Reed, Nelson A.

1969   Monks and Other Mississippian Mounds. In *Explorations Into Cahokia Archaeology*, edited by Melvin L. Fowler, pp. 31–42. Bulletin No. 7. Illinois Archaeological Survey, Urbana.

Rolingson, Martha Ann

1978a   Research Plan for the Toltec Mounds Site, 3LN42. Manuscript on file, Arkansas Archeological Survey, Fayetteville.

1978b   Toltec Mounds Project: Preliminary Report on the 1978 Season. *Field Notes, Newsletter of the Arkansas Archeological Society* 162:1–12. Fayetteville.

1980   Toltec Mounds Research Project. *The Arkansas Archeologist* 21:35–56. Fayetteville.

1982a   Contributions to the Toltec Mounds (Knapp) Site Research by the Smithsonian Institution. In *Emerging Patterns of Plum Bayou Culture: Preliminary Investigations of the Toltec Mounds Research Project*, edited by Martha Ann Rolingson, pp. 71–86. Research Series No. 18. Arkansas Archeological Survey, Fayetteville.

1982b   Public Archeology: Research and Development of the Toltec Site. In *Arkansas Archeology in Review*, edited by Neal L. Trubowitz and Marvin D. Jeter, pp. 48–75. Research Series No. 15. Arkansas Archeological Survey, Fayetteville.

Rolingson, Martha Ann (editor)

1982c   *Emerging Patterns of Plum Bayou Culture: Preliminary Investigations of the Toltec Mounds Research Project*. Research Series No. 18. Arkansas Archeological Survey, Fayetteville.

Saucier, Roger T.

1974   *Quaternary Geology of the Lower Mississippi Valley*. Research Series No. 4. Arkansas Archeological Survey, Fayetteville.

Schambach, Frank F.

1970   *Pre-Caddoan Cultures in the Trans-Mississippi South: A Beginning Sequence*. Ph.D. dissertation, Department of Anthropology, Harvard University.

Schiffer, Michael B., and John H. House (compilers)

1975   *The Cache River Archeological Project: An Experiment in Contract Archeology*. Research Series No. 8. Arkansas Archeological Survey, Fayetteville.

Scholtz, James A.

1964   The Powell Site (3CL9): A Temple Mound Site in Clark County, Arkansas. Manuscript on file, University of Arkansas Museum, Fayetteville.

1971   *Investigations at the Roland Mound Site, 3AR30, Arkansas County, Arkansas, 1966*. Report to the National Park Service, Southeast Region by the University of Arkansas Museum, Fayetteville.

Scholtz, James A., and Michael P. Hoffman
1968 *An Archeological Survey of the Arkansas River Navigation Projects in Arkansas.* Report to the National Park Service, Southeast Region by the University of Arkansas Museum, Fayetteville.

Sherrod, P. Clay, and Martha A. Rolingson
1987 *Surveyors of the Ancient Mississippi Valley: Modules and Alignments in Prehistoric Mound Sites.* Research Series No. 28. Arkansas Archeological Survey, Fayetteville.

Shetrone, Henry C.
1930 *The Mound-Builders.* Appleton-Century, New York.

Stewart-Abernathy, Judith C.
1980 Descriptions of Types, Varieties, and Descriptive Classes for Mound D and Submound Midden Ceramics. Manuscript on file, Arkansas Archeological Survey, Toltec Mounds Research Station, Scott.
1982 Ceramic Studies at the Toltec Mounds Site: Basis for a Tentative Cultural Sequence. In *Emerging Patterns of Plum Bayou Culture: Preliminary Investigations of the Toltec Mounds Research Project,* edited by Martha Ann Rolingson, pp. 44–53. Research Series No. 18. Arkansas Archeological Survey, Fayetteville.

Suhm, Dee Ann, and Edward B. Jelks
1962 *Handbook of Texas Archeology: Type Descriptions.* Special Publication No. 1. Texas Archeological Society and The Texas Memorial Museum, Austin.

Thomas, Cyrus
1894 *Report on the Mound Explorations of the Bureau of Ethnology.* Annual Report of the Bureau of Ethnology, 1890–1891 12:17–742. Washington, D.C.

Thornbury, William D.
1965 *Regional Geomorphology of the United States.* John Wiley and Sons, New York.

Toth, Alan
1974 *Archaeology and Ceramics at the Marksville Site.* Anthropological Papers No. 56. Museum of Anthropology, University of Michigan, Ann Arbor.
1979 *The Lake St. Agnes Site: A Multi-component Occupation of Avoyelles Parish, Louisiana.* Melanges No. 13. Museum of Geoscience, Louisiana State University, Baton Rouge.

Waddell, David B., John H. House, Francis B. King, Mona L. Colburn, and Murray K. Marks
1987 *Results of Final Testing for Significance at the Ink Bayou Site (3PU252), Pulaski County, Arkansas.* Report submitted to the Arkansas Highway and Transportation Department by the Arkansas Archeological Survey, Fayetteville.

Williams, J. Raymond
1974 The Baytown Phases in the Cairo Lowland of Southeast Missouri. *The Missouri Archaeologist* 36. Columbia.

Williams, Stephen
1956 Settlement Patterns in the Lower Mississippi Valley. In *Prehistoric Settlement Patterns in the New World,* edited by Gordon R. Willey, pp. 52–61. Viking Fund Publications in Anthropology No. 23. Wenner-Gren Foundation for Anthropological Research. New York.

Williams, Stephen, and Jeffrey P. Brain
1983 *Excavations at the Lake George Site, Yazoo County, Mississippi, 1958–1960.* Papers of the Peabody Museum of Archaeology and Ethnology 74. Harvard University.

The Zebree Site

An Emerged Early Mississippian Expression in Northeast Arkansas

The Zebree site is located in Mississippi County, Arkansas within the boundaries of the Big Lake National Wildlife Refuge. It is on an area of relatively high ground near the western edge of Big Lake itself, close to the Missouri state line (Fig. 11). The site is located on an old surface of an earlier braided Mississippi River stage. Typical lowland topography, including some prairie soils, the recent levee soils of Little River, and a large shallow lake, form the immediate environment. The site, numbered 3MS20, was one of the first sites mapped by the Arkansas State University research station after the founding of the Arkansas Archeological Survey in 1967. Four seasons of excavation were subsequently conducted at the Zebree site, each with different research goals (Table 7; Anderson 1979).

Three archaeological sites in the wildlife refuge were tested by the Arkansas Archeological Survey in 1968 (Morse 1968) because a drainage ditch was being planned through the refuge. Dan Morse and a crew of two placed two test pits in an area of old potholes at Zebree. Three separate components were recognized at the site, showing occupation during Late Woodland, early period Mississippian and middle period Mississippian times. Early period Mississippian was previously unidentified in Arkansas and was recognized as highly significant. This component was stratigraphically distinct from the Late Woodland and middle period Mississippian components.

The discovery of significant stratified deposits at Zebree led to the funding by the National Park Service (Contract No. 14-10-7:911-21) of a major excavation at the site in 1969 (Morse 1975). Large contiguous areas of the site were dug in order to collect data on house patterns and community plans. Adequate and representative samples of artifacts from all three components were sought. Zooarchaeological samples were collected and identified. Hypotheses as diverse as the manufacture and function of the Zebree microlith industry, the date of the formation of Big Lake, and the nature and cause of cultural change to a Mississippian way of life were developed using data from this excavation. In particular, it was evident that the early period Mississippian Big Lake phase could not have developed from the preceding Late Woodland Dunklin phase (Morse 1977). Cultural processes including migration were examined to account for this development.

Final construction plans for a ditch to prevent the silting of Big Lake made funding available for one more field season at the Zebree site (Morse and Morse 1980). The U.S. Army Corps of Engineers and the Arkansas Archeological Survey cooperated to mitigate the destruction of the Zebree site (Contract No. DACW 66-76-C-0006). The previous excavations provided sufficient information for detailed data recovery strategies such as a 1 percent stratified systematic unaligned sample of 1-meter random squares, backhoe transects at judiciously chosen areas, and large area block excavations (Anderson 1976). Specialists hired to assist in recovering their own data in the field included an ethnobotanist, zooarchaeologist, and ceramic technologist.

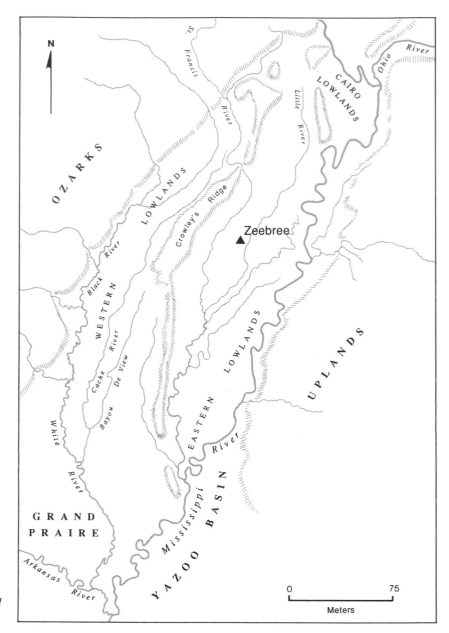

Fig. 11. The location of the Zebree site within the eastern lowlands of the central Mississippi Valley.

All samples were waterscreened, using mesh sizes from 1/16 to 1/4 inch. Flotation samples were automatically taken from each level and feature. Interaction between the nearby processing laboratory and field personnel was encouraged to maximize the range of samples recovered. A computer-generated map of the site was made of the different occupations using the random-square data. The botanical and zoological samples were studied to find both similarities and differences in diet of the three major prehistoric components. Tree-ring coring and cores taken from the lake beds were both used to increase environmental data (Bowers 1976, King 1980). The historic nineteenth- and twentieth-century components were also studied (P. Morse 1980a, 1980b). Two peer reviewers were flown in to review the excavations and make suggestions about data recovery (Smith 1976; Peebles 1976). A final report to the Corps was accepted in 1980 (Morse and Morse 1980).

An unexpected opportunity to add to the already re-

Table 7. Excavation Research Strategies at the Zebree Site

Year	Type of Excavation	Research Goal	Area Excavated in Square Meters
1968	Test pits	To assess significance of site	11
1969	Intuitive block unit and test pits	To collect as much diverse data as possible in a single season	180
1975	1% random sample test pits	To collect a representative sample of site and to investigate midden formation	55
1975	Backhoe transects	To locate site boundaries, to investigate stratigraphy, and to collect soil and pollen samples	490
1975	Block units	To expose high probability areas for house patterns, ditches, feature clusters, and flotation samples	494
1976	Bulldozer trenches	To collect as many artifacts as possible in a tight cultural context and in a short period, and to increase information on component locations	2,500

covered data was presented to the excavators in 1976. The ditch did not go through the site until July. An enlightened contractor, S. J. Cohen of Blytheville, Arkansas, loaned the use of heavy machinery to a group of volunteers headed by Morse and Anderson. The overburden was cleared and defined features were uncovered and excavated. This emergency salvage added to the artifact inventory and knowledge of community planning. The new ditch and levee system was mapped in relationship to the remnant of the Zebree site that still remains.

THE BAYTOWN PERIOD DUNKLIN PHASE COMPONENT

The Dunklin phase component underlay the later Mississippian and historic components and had been considerably disturbed by these later occupations. However, 62 features out of the 447 excavated were determined to date solely to the Dunklin phase by their contents (Morse and Anderson 1980:5–34). Radiocarbon dates derived from charcoal from three of these Dunklin features are A.D. 691±74, A.D. 829±70, and A.D. 863±84.

The most diagnostic artifact of the Late Woodland Dunklin phase is sand-tempered Barnes pottery (Fig. 12). Two Barnes pottery types are defined, Barnes Cord Marked and Barnes Plain (Williams 1954:204). A total of 35,072 sand-tempered sherds were recovered at the Zebree site in four or five major concentrations (Anderson 1980a).

Barnes ceramics were made from locally available backswamp clay tempered with windworn sand (Million and Morse 1980:16–20). The heavy sand temper created a paste that was apparently stiff and hard to work. The resulting shapes of the completed vessels were restricted to small, medium, and large conical jars and small circular bowls. A majority of the jars were completely cordmarked with a cord-wrapped paddle on the exterior surface. A very small number of Barnes vessels were fabric impressed. The larger jars usually have rim folds that would have strengthened the rim of the vessel. A majority of these jars measure about 13 to 24 liters in capacity and on the average are 30 cm in diameter and 40 cm high. This average Barnes Cord Marked jar becomes about 1,000 sherds when broken (Million and Morse 1980:16–19). Evidently such breakage was fairly frequent. It is obvious that the large number of sherds recovered does not necessarily indicate a large population.

An exceedingly small number of Dunklin phase sherds were otherwise decorated. One specimen of a small jar has a notched lip. One bowl rim sherd has an incised line and a series of minute notches resembling Officer Punctated (Rolingson 1982, fig. 22). Of two other punctated sherds, one has fingernail punctates and one has two rows of deep circular punctates. Five sherds have faint parallel incised lines

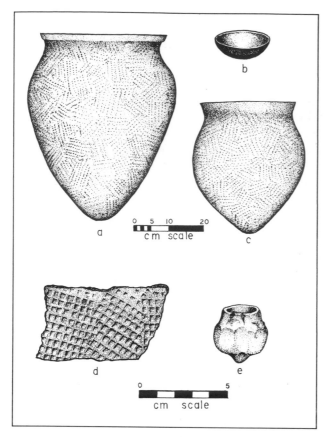

Fig. 12. Dunklin phase ceramics from the Zebree site; (a) large jar (33 l) with reinforced rim, (b) food bowl, (c) typical jar (13 l), (d) check-stamped decoration, (e) toy jar with nipple base, copying typical jars (from Morse and Morse 1983, fig. 9.3).

and engraving tools. Dunklin phase lithic material is scarce at Zebree. All lithic tools appear to have been curated and recycled. There was absolutely no evidence of the use of the bow and arrow in the Dunklin phase at Zebree, even though this technologically superior hunting device was already present elsewhere in the eastern United States.

Two antler projectile points were also found associated with the Dunklin phase (D. Morse 1980a:17-7). Four raccoon and bird bone awls could be assigned to this occupation. Again, the minimal number of other artifacts in comparison to the number of sherds appears to be significant. A small and mobile population is indicated by the relative paucity of artifact variety.

An incomplete circular house pattern was found in one of the four to five Dunklin phase concentrations at Zebree. A structure or windbreak about 4 m in diameter is indicated. Forty-six storage pits could be assigned to the Dunklin phase. The pit sizes range from 400 to 800 liters in capacity. These pits were circular in shape. Six pits were lined with double layers of mussel shell on the base and lower sides. Flotation samples from the contents of Dunklin phase pits were analyzed for evidence of subsistence. Wild plant foods such as wild bean (Strophostyles), sunflower, persimmon, wild grape, gromwell (Lithosperum), and false gromwell (Onesrediun) were present, as well as large amounts of charred acorn, black walnut, and hickory nuts (Harris 1980:239–250). Pollen samples were analyzed from two Dunklin phase pits. Ragweed, sunflower, fern, sweet gum, pigweed, sedge, hickory, smartweed, dogwood, and grass pollens were identified (Morse et al. 1980, table 6-3), although the pollen grains were not present in amounts deemed to be significant. One major research design developed before the 1975 Zebree excavation was to determine whether or not the Dunklin phase had corn agriculture. Not only was there no evidence of corn being either grown or consumed during the Dunklin occupation, but other plants grown elsewhere in the eastern United States, such as squash and marsh elder, were not present either. One sunflower seed and the presence of pigweed or goosefoot pollen are the only indications of possible Dunklin cultigens.

Fine screening of a total pit's contents resulted in the recovery of a faunal sample for the Dunklin phase that reflected the surrounding lowland riverine environment (Morse 1980a, table 17-2). Computation of the

over cord marking, which may simply be scraper marks. One small plain bowl has a scalloped rim lug, similar to those found on Coles Creek ceramics (Phillips 1970:186). A total of 93 check-stamped sherds resembling Wheeler Check Stamped (Phillips 1970:171) may all be from one vessel. The virtual lack of any decoration besides cord marking is typical of other Late Woodland occupations in northeast Arkansas (Spears 1978).

Only 22 projectile points were excavated at Zebree that could be assigned to the Dunklin phase (D. Morse 1980a, table 17-1). The points were crudely made of locally available Crowley's Ridge chert and quartzite. The variety of shapes included expanding stemmed, bulbous stemmed, side notched, corner notched, and rounded stemmed. Many can be considered a variant of Steuben (Perino 1985; Morse 1963). These Zebree points were all modified by use as cutting, scraping, minimum number of individuals, number of elements, pounds of meat per individual, and total pounds of meat available was made. Fish produced the most number of individuals and almost 25 percent of total meat weight. Birds and turtles each contributed 6 percent of meat by weight. Mammals still contributed most of the diet, particularly white-tailed deer, raccoon, and cottontail rabbit. Numerous species of mussels from Dunklin phase pits reveal a preference for a small stream habitat rather than a lake habitat (Morse 1980a, table 17-3). The faunal and floral remains both indicate a fall to spring occupation.

The Dunklin occupation at Zebree has been interpreted as a winter village composed of a maximum kin aggregate (Morse and Morse 1983:186). The four or five Dunklin midden concentrations may have been occupied either simultaneously or sequentially. The artifacts from the different middens appear to be contemporaneous. One central area, the highest portion of the site, has more debris than the other areas and may have been reoccupied more often. Computations from the sizes of Dunklin pots show that the typical small 7.5 liter jar could have fed about 10 individuals, the 13 to 24 liter jars could have fed 20 to 35, and one large jar measuring 33 liters could have fed up to 50 persons (Million and Morse 1980:16-9). The Dunklin winter village at Zebree may have had up to five extended family households at one time with 50 individuals as a maximum number. The actual number was probably smaller. These households probably lived as a more dispersed population in the Big Lake area during the rest of the year.

The lack of evidence of horticulture, the bow and arrow, or even of any exotic chert from outside the area of Crowley's Ridge indicates that the Dunklin phase occupation at Zebree was relatively isolated. A small number of grog-tempered Baytown vessels indicates some contact with other groups to the south and west. The Dunklin phase occupation at Zebree indicates the presence of a small tribal group with a minimal level of sociopolitical organization.

BIG LAKE PHASE ARTIFACTS

Radiocarbon dates for the Big Lake phase were run on nine carefully selected samples (Morse, Wolfman, and Haas 1980). The dates range from A.D. 810 to 1076; four of the dates were in the ninth century A.D., three

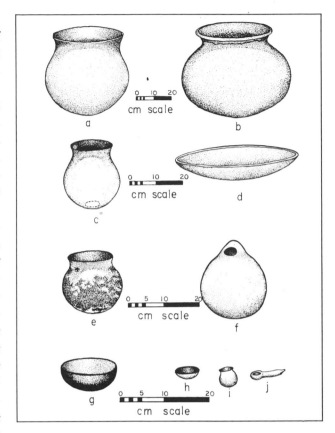

Fig. 13. Basic shell-tempered wares found at the Zebree site; (a) Mississippian Plain large jar with reinforced rim, (b) Varney Red Filmed large jar with reinforced rim, (c) Wickliffe funnel, (d) Varney Red Filmed salt pan, (e) typical Varney Red Filmed cooking jar, (f) Varney Red Filmed food bowl, (h) toy bowl, (i) toy jar, (j) toy ladle (from Morse and Morse 1983, fig. 10.7).

in the tenth century, and two in the eleventh. These are some of the earliest dates for the Mississippian period obtained in the eastern United States. The dates actually overlap with the Dunklin phase occupation. However, there is absolutely no evidence of cultural mixture. The Big Lake phase occupation was totally distinct from the Dunklin phase. Even when features contained combinations of the respective assemblages, the Dunklin phase sherds were demonstrated to be characteristic of a secondary rather than a primary deposit (Anderson 1980b:8–23). Potsherd size reduction increases with disturbance, and this was the case with Barnes ware in Big Lake features.

The pottery associated with the Big Lake phase at Zebree was all shell tempered (Fig. 13). There were 65,408 Big Lake phase sherds recovered and analyzed.

Shell-tempered pottery has long been one of the main cultural traits used in identifying an assemblage as Mississippian. The use of burned mussel shell in combination with backswamp clay produced a technologically superior paste (Million 1975:218–219). Weight of the paste was significantly reduced with the substitution of shell for sand. The older tradition of a conical shape to help distribute weight as the vessel was constructed gave way to a spherical shape that was much easier to construct and was also easier to use. Experimentation demonstrated that Mississippian paste was flexible and cohesive. It was therefore possible to manufacture a much larger variety of vessel forms that were also stronger and less apt to break.

The Big Lake phase ceramic assemblage consisted of a few simple forms that were sorted into three distinct wares or types (Million 1980). These categories were Varney Red, Mississippian Plain, and Wickliffe Thick. Sherds from the 1975 field season were both counted and weighed. Microscopic examination of the paste was used when thought necessary. Various by-products of pottery manufacture, such as coils and squeezes, were also identified. Varney Red pottery was first identified by Stephen Williams in southeast Missouri (1954:209). A heavy clay and hematite slip was applied to the interior surfaces of large shallow pans, small to large globular jars, and bowls. Hooded bottles were slipped on the exterior. The red slip was usually burnished with a polishing stone. Analysis of the random square data showed that sherds coated with Varney Red slip were consistently 1.5 to 2 times larger than unslipped sherds, showing that red filming actually made the vessels stronger and less likely to crumble (Anderson 1980b, table 8-4).

The Varney Red jar was the most common shape found (Fig. 13). The jars are globular in shape, with round bottoms and recurved rims. Three distinct size clusters were present, averaging 3.35 liters, 13.0 liters, and 52.2 liters in capacity. Large jars were far more difficult to manufacture (Holmes 1903:60) and may have functioned as cooking vessels to feed a large group on ceremonial occasions. They also may have been used for water or food storage. The medium-size Varney Red jar was the most common in number and obviously used for cooking. The small Varney Red jars often have nicks and chips on the rim from ladle damage. Three pottery ladles were found at the Zebree site. Most ladles were probably gourds. Small Varney Red jars were probably used both for cooking and serving. Loop handles for jars were very rare and probably dated late at the Zebree site.

The second most numerous Varney Red vessel shape was the salt pan (Fig. 13). These large, shallow, flat oval pans ranged from 10 to 26 liters in capacity. They were probably made in a mold such as a shallow basin or basket. Two pans found at Zebree of identical size indicate that such molds did exist (Million and Morse 1980:4–12). Molds were probably lined with fabric or grass to keep the coils from sticking to the exterior during manufacture. Grass impressions are found on the exterior of Zebree pans. Varney Red slip was heavily applied to the interior. The slip would help waterproof the vessel. The salt pan shape is often found near saline springs (Keslin 1964; Muller 1984).

The hooded bottle is a more unusual form. It closely resembles a gourd in shape, including a dimple in the center where the stem would have been (Fig. 13). The orifice is on the side. A capacity of over 4 liters is common. It has been proposed that these hooded bottles were used to store seed grain (Million 1980:18–22).

Untempered clay plugs or seals called Kersey Clay Objects, which may have functioned to seal these bottles, were found at Zebree. Grain stored in such an environment is safe from predators and the atmosphere is conducive to good seed preservation.

About 10 percent of the Varney Red vessels were simple, rounded base, molded bowls. They probably were used for food service. Toy bowls and jars were also found. They are crude copies of the larger forms.

Mississippi Plain is the basic utilitarian shell-tempered ware found in the eastern United States (Phillips 1970:130–135). The majority of the Mississippi Plain vessels at Zebree were large jars with capacities of over 50 liters. The jar rims are only slightly flared. No appendages or decorative treatments were found on these jars. Most Mississippi Plain bowl sherds were from simple, shallow, plain bowls. Many of these would have been individual food bowls. A toy ladle, seven miniature bowls, and seven miniature jars were also found. Bowls and toys were modeled instead of coiled.

Wickliffe Thick pottery (Phillips 1970:171–172) is a most unusual type. It is a highly specialized funnel made of coarse shell-tempered paste and has thick walls. It has two orifices on opposite ends of the vessel, one large and one small. Surface treatment can be cordmarked, incised, or thinly washed with red. The average capacity is about 5 liters. These vessels were crudely made and tended to break readily along coil lines. They

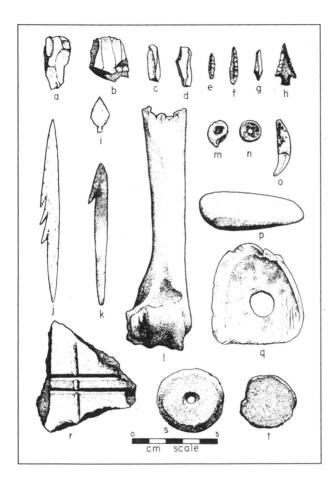

Fig. 14. Ceramic, lithic, bone, and shell artifacts found at the Zebree site; (a–g) microlith cores, blades, and drills, (h) Scallorn point, (i) gar scale point, (j–k) bone antler harpoons, (l) deer humerus flesher, (m) Anculosa shell bead, (n) conch shell bead, (o) raccoon canine pendant, (p) pottery polishing stone, (q) mussel shell hoe, (r) potsherd abrader, (s–t) pottery discs (from Morse and Morse 1983, fig. 10.8).

pottery clay. The shell temper in the clay had already been fired. Two 500 gm spheres of powdered hematite were found together in a pit, and were probably processed paint for red filming. They were coated with a clay cover. Many burned clay fragments were found at Zebree, some of which probably functioned as spacers used in a kiln. Spacer marks were found on some of the rim sherds. Pottery manufacturing tools found included shell-tempered pottery anvils, polishing stones, a flat cobble paint palette, and a bone and a shell scraper. Five curious small spud-shaped pottery objects may also be scrapers. These artifacts were not concentrated in one area. The pottery industry in the Big Lake phase was apparently part of the household economy. There is no evidence of craft specialization at the Zebree site.

Other artifacts were made of clay besides pottery (Fig. 14). Over 400 sherd abraders were found. A majority of these were made on recycled Barnes sherds, as the sandy Barnes paste was ideal for sharpening bone or wood tools. One-fourth of the abraders were made of shell-tempered sherds. Ornamental objects of clay include 12 disc or spherical-shaped beads, a perforated pottery pendant, and a clay labret. Portions of three shell-tempered pottery elbow-shaped pipes were discovered. Fifteen small crudely biconical pottery discoidals range in shape from thin to thick with some being perforated. Only one is deliberately tempered with shell. Sixty-four other pottery discs were recycled from sherds. A preference was shown for sherds with Varney Red slip. Similar discs were ethnographically observed in Indian gambling or guessing games (Culin 1907:45). Some discs were perforated and possibly were spindle whorls. Only one ground stone discoidal was found at Zebree. It was thick with a convex side and a small shallow depression in each center. It was made of sandstone. This style is associated with the Early Mississippian period at other sites (Perino 1971: 112–115). The stone and pottery discoidals were probably used in the chunkey game, where a spear was thrown at the rolling stone (Culin 1907:512).

The true arrowpoint was found at Zebree in Big Lake phase deposits. The economic advantages of the bow and arrow in hunting cannot be overemphasized. The increase in range possible with the bow, added to the hunting skills already present, must have provided considerably more game with less effort. The same bows and arrows also have similar advantages during raids or actual warfare. Eleven Sequoyah-like points (Perino

probably were used in salt production. Two pottery discs with multiple perforations may have functioned as strainers in the Wickliffe funnels.

Only 13 sherds were found in Big Lake phase deposits, which indicate possible cultural contact with contemporaneous Baytown or Hoecake phase cultures. Twelve of these sherds are Baytown Plain or Mulberry Creek Cord-Marked. One sherd with three lines on the exterior and one on the lip can be classified as Coles Creek Incised var. Greenhouse (Phillips 1970:72). This variety is dated as late by Phillips.

Evidence of the ceramic manufacturing process at Zebree included accidentally fired by-products, such as squeezes, coils, and a 64 kg sphere of shell-tempered

1985:351) were made on thin flakes with corner notches and serrations. Nine were made on locally available Crowley's Ridge chert, one on Crescent Quarry chert and one on a grey chert. Three Scallorn-like points (Perino 1985:344) may belong to a later component. Four Madison-like points, a simple triangular shape (Perino 1985:236) may also date later. One Haskell-like side-notched point (Perino 1985:174) was recycled into a drill. It may also date to the later Lawhorn phase. One gar scale was deliberately modified into a stemmed projectile point. Three bipointed bone awls may have functioned as points on a fish spear.

The large chipped Mill Creek chert hoe was found in Big Lake phase context. Thirty-five Mill Creek hoe chips with typical polish were present. The Mill Creek quarry in southern Illinois was a source for heavy agricultural tools throughout the Mississippian period in the central Mississippi Valley (Morse and Morse 1983: 205–207). Eight hoe chips of Tennessee Dover chert were also found. Their location at the site indicates that they may date to the later Lawhorn phase occupation at Zebree. The heavy chert hoe is indicative of an emphasis on agriculture and its possession was economically advantageous. A total of 13 mussel shell hoes were also recovered at Zebree.

Other objects indicate a sophisticated woodworking industry. Chipped chert chisels and adzes are present. Several are made of Crescent Quarry and Mill Creek chert. Eight ground stone adzes and celts made of limestone and basalt were found. A large trough abrader made of quartzite was probably used to manufacture celts and adzes. Small discoid chert choppers may also be woodworking tools. Orthoquartzite backed knives may have functioned as saws. Orthoquartzite outcrops on the western side of Crowley's Ridge, due west of the Zebree site.

Chert drills and perforators could have performed many functions. Many of these were recycled from points and knives. Of the 108 unifacial chert tools found, forms include transverse edge scrapers, concave edge scrapers or spokeshaves, and oblique-transversed edge scrapers. Ten graver tips were present on unifacial tools. Very few cores were found besides those for the microlith industry.

One of the most unexpected group of artifacts found at the Zebree site was the Cahokia microlith industry (Morse 1974; Fig. 14). Small specialized cores, blades, and cylindrical microlith drills were discovered in the Big Lake phase deposits during the first test dig at Zebree and their significance was recognized (Morse 1968). There is a specialized area at the Cahokia site where these artifacts are found in quantity (Mason and Perino 1961). Over 90 percent of the Zebree microlith artifacts are made on Crescent Quarry chert, which outcrops south of St. Louis, Missouri (Morse and Morse 1983:205). The rest are made on Mill Creek, Burlington, and Crowley's Ridge cherts and on Illinois novaculite. Specialized small columnar cores were knapped to produce blades. These blades were then made into microdrills. Almost 300 cylindrical and tabular microdrills were found at Zebree. The cylindrical microlith was probably hafted and used to drill shell and bone, especially shell beads.

Experiments using a cylindrical microlith hafted in a cane shaft showed that use of a bow drill made bead production much more efficient (Sierzchula 1980). Validation of the bead manufacture hypothesis was published by Yerkes (1983) when he examined cylindrical microliths under a high-powered microscope. Five cut and grooved sections of conch shell were found at Zebree, which were probably raw material for making beads. Only one conch shell bead was found at the site that could be definitely associated with the Big Lake phase. The conch shell was probably received in trade from the Cahokia site rather than directly from the Gulf Coast.

Microliths were not concentrated in one locality, but were found near or in all Big Lake phase habitation areas. This distribution implies that the shell bead industry was not the work of a few specialists, but part of the regular household economy.

Artifacts made of bone and shell were numerous and well preserved. Even fish scales were preserved in the Zebree midden. A mussel shell valve exhibited edge abrasion suggestive of use as a scraper, possibly on pottery. A deer rib also exhibited edge polish and is thought to have been used to scrape the outer surface of pottery vessels.

A large number of *Anculosa* shell beads were found that are ground flat and perforated. Three simple mussel shell gorgets were found, with no evidence of decoration. Bone beads, canine tooth pendants, and a raccoon mandible pendant were used as ornaments. Another type of adornment is indicated by four possible bone teeth from a scarifier.

The excellent state of bone preservation made interpretations about steps used in bone tool manufacture possible. Bone was usually grooved and then snapped. Antler batons for flint knapping were manufactured as well as antler tines modified for pressure-flaking tools. Bone awls numbered 15 and were presumably primarily used in working leather and a one-eyed awl may have been used to make nets. Bone chisels and bone fleshers show the versatility of this raw material.

The barbed bone or antler harpoon (Fig. 14) was an unexpected artifact type. Four such harpoons were found at Zebree (D. Morse 1980b, table 20.1). One is a triple-barbed specimen and the other three are single barbed. Similar artifacts had not been described elsewhere in the central Mississippi Valley. However, harpoons do occur at Cahokia, associated with the Fairmount phase (Perino 1950:60). These harpoons were probably used to catch large species of fish present nearby, including catfish, buffalo, and gar.

Bone fishhooks are another artifact representative of the fishing industry. An unfinished specimen shows that only one fishhook was made out of a section of long bone. A series of perforations were drilled along the edge to help carve out the blank. Another type of fishing technique is indicated by 13 different net impressions that were accidentally preserved in fired clay. Net openings are 5 by 20 mm, large enough to seine out smaller fish. Nets also could have been used to trap ducks similar to a technique used today by the State Game and Fish Commission.

ENVIRONMENT AND SUBSISTENCE

One major research focus of the 1975 Zebree site excavation was to see whether there was any significant difference between the subsistence patterns of the Dunklin and Big Lake phases. Various methods were used to gather subsistence data including the recovery of ethnobotanical and zooarchaeological remains, collecting pollen samples, coring the bed of Big Lake, a dendrochronological study of cypress in Big Lake and environmental reconstruction using early nineteenth-century General Land Office maps. The skeletal remains of both the Dunklin and Big Lake phase people themselves were also examined to see whether any inferences could be made from various pathologies and trace element analysis.

The date of the actual formation of Big Lake was important in interpreting subsistence patterns. Saucier

(1970) proposed that Big Lake and the St. Francis sunk lands were caused by alluvial drowning, when an abortive attempt by the Mississippi River to cut a new channel created new natural levees, which dammed up old braided stream channels. This event, the creation of a shallow lake, may have attracted Mississippian people to the area. To test this hypothesis, four sediment cores were collected in various areas of Big Lake (King 1980). We could not core beyond a sand layer. A radiocarbon date at the base of one core yielded a date of 180 B.P. Big Lake may either have been created or, more probably, modified by the New Madrid earthquake of 1811–1812. The pollen diagrams reflect the recent history of the area, showing a decline in oaks due to lumbering about 1905 and a subsequent decline in other tree species after drainage improvements in the area facilitated settlement in the 1920s.

Another approach to reconstructing the prehistoric environment was to use the observations recorded in the 1824–1840 General Land Office Survey field notes (Harris 1980). The entire region was recently cleared for agricultural use, destroying all natural vegetation except for the wildlife refuge. The early surveyors were instructed to record four witness trees at each section corner and two witness trees at each quarter section. The 120 sq mi area of the Big Lake Highlands, between the Right Hand Chute of Little River and the St. Francis River, were analyzed using this data. A map was then created using the witness tree data, combined with soil survey information and present topographic data.

The biotic communities available in 1840 and presumably available to those living at the Zebree site in the ninth and tenth centuries included open lake, cypress-tupelo, cypress-hardwood, cottonwood-willow-sycamore, sweetgum-elm-hackberry, and white oak-sweetgum plant associations (McGimsey 1984). In addition, a prairie was present near the Zebree site in prehistoric times (Guilday and Parmalee 1971). Once the nature of plant communities in the Zebree site area was established, inferences could be made concerning various plants and animals that are typically associated with these habitats. For instance, the open lake association of Big Lake has several zones including willow and buttonbush, knotweed, cattail, water parsnip, and water millet, floating leaf vegetation such as American lotus, water lily, and cow lily and finally free-floating vegetation such as water fern and duck weed (McGimsey 1984:10). The associated fauna would include catfish, buffalo fish, gar, frogs, turtles, fish-eating birds, migratory birds, and mammals such as muskrat, beaver, river otter, and mink. The white oak-sweetgum plant association is the most favorable for the production of acorns and thus the favored habitat of desirable game species such as white-tailed deer, wild turkey, and red and fox squirrels. This white oak-sweetgum habitat was located near the St. Francis River, about 15 mi west of the Zebree site.

The bone excavated at the Zebree site provided information on the species preferred by the inhabitants both for food and for raw material. The 1975 sample analyzed by Roth (1980, table 22-1), which dated solely to the Big Lake phase, numbered 108 individuals. Computations were made of the number of elements, minimum number of individuals, and the estimated meat yield. The sample contained only one extinct species, the passenger pigeon. The species list showed an emphasis on an aquatic habitat, particularly migratory birds and fish. A computation of species diversity showed emphasis on a diffuse economy rather than one focusing on a few food sources. Although the riverine, lake, and swamp microenvironments produced more individuals for food, the forest edge and deciduous forest microenvironments were the most important when computing total pounds of available meat. White-tailed deer was by far the most economically important species, followed by black bear, raccoon, and marsh and swamp rabbit. Habitat preference for both forest edge and deciduous forest species was somewhat greater during the Big Lake phase than for the Dunklin phase. This preference may reflect an increase in botanical community edges caused by the Big Lake phase peoples as they cleared land for agriculture. It may also reflect the effect of the bow and arrow causing more successful hunting.

There were 29 species present in both the Dunklin and Big Lake phase components. There was considerable overlap since a total of 44 species in all were identified in Roth's sample. His conclusion was that a wide variety of faunal resources continued to be exploited through time even after the advent of corn agriculture and the bow and arrow.

Analysis of ethnobotanical remains from Big Lake phase features revealed the presence of wood charcoal from cypress, willow, maple, oak, hickory, and leguminous wood (Harris 1976:63). Large numbers of charred acorn and hickory nuts were present. Grape, persim-

mon, hackberry, gromwell, chenopodium, and polygonum remains were recovered as well. Twenty-nine distinct Big Lake phase features produced corn, clearly indicating that corn was being grown and stored. The corn included both 12- and 14-rowed cobs of the North American Pop (Tropical Flint) race and 8- and 10-rowed Eastern Eight Row (Northern Flint) race (Blake 1984:46). A few Midwest Twelve Row cobs were present. The most similar assemblage of corn from the same time period comes from the Cahokia East Stockade area and dates to Late Bluff, Loyd, Merrell, and early Fairmount phases (Blake 1984, table 5-8).

Although corn was obviously a regular part of the diet in the Big Lake phase, it was apparently not as important as it was during middle period Mississippian. A stable carbon isotope analysis of human skeletons from Archaic and Woodland occupations, the Big Lake phase, and middle and late period Mississippian and historic components has been conducted in Arkansas and Missouri (Boutton et al. 1984). The three Big Lake phase skeletons analyzed had test results similar to earlier phases, indicating that corn was not sufficiently ingested to be picked up by the tests.

The importance of corn to the diet of Big Lake phase people in contrast to Dunklin diet cannot be overemphasized despite these test results. No trace of corn was found in undisturbed Dunklin phase deposits. A shift to maize horticulture would have led to many activities, including choosing special localities for the most desirable soils, clearing, cultivation, and guarding of fields, decisions about when to plant and harvest, conducting first fruit and harvest ceremonies, selecting and saving seed, and devising specialized food storage mechanisms. An increasing dependence on corn and the evolution of chiefdom societies in the southeastern United States are two phenomena that may be closely linked (See Chapter 7, this volume).

The large number of Varney Red salt pans present at Zebree and the absence of any salt springs in the area produced further investigations of the site environment. Ethnographic descriptions of primitive people making salt from leaching ashes (Schultz 1962:124–125) led to an investigation of the possibility of making salt from the American lotus, *Nelumbo lutea* (North 1975). Leaves and stems collected from Big Lake were dried, ground, burned, and then analyzed by atomic absorption. Both sodium and potassium were concentrated in the plant. Sodium chloride and potassium chloride could have been manufactured at Zebree by burning the lotus, leaching the ashes slowly through the Wickliffe funnel, and then evaporating the filtrate in the Varney Red salt pans. The Zebree site is a considerable distance from known salt springs. Salt is of considerable importance to people who are more dependent upon agriculture, and the use of such a substitute source is indicated.

One more line of evidence when studying subsistence is to examine the human skeletal remains themselves. It was hypothesized that a shift to using food that was low in protein and high in carbohydrates, such as corn, would have biological consequences such as decreased body size (Lallo 1973). A study of the Big Lake phase skeletal remains indicated that both males and females were taller than remains from later Mississippian sites (Powell 1980). Evidently dependence upon corn was not as complete at Zebree as in later phases.

An examination of Big Lake phase teeth showed an average of two to four dental caries per individual. These were concentrated in the molar and premolar areas. This pattern of dental pathology resembles those of other late prehistoric agricultural populations. Starchy foods such as cornmeal mush and hominy encourage bacterial activity, which causes such caries. Corn apparently was being eaten.

The teeth were also examined for evidence of enamel hypoplasia due to stress caused by nutrition or disease (Powell 1980). Grooves or zones of pitted enamel form on the teeth during childhood when such stress is encountered. The age when this occurs can be determined. The Big Lake phase sample showed such stress occurred from 3.0 to 4.5 years of age (Powell 1980, table 23-3), which is also true of later Mississippian populations. This observation may indicate the time of weaning, when children are often subject to disease, and possibly was connected to the use of corn.

Pathological infection of the tibia was observed in three out of eight Big Lake phase individuals. The percentage of those involved and the relatively moderate degree of infection indicated that the Big Lake phase population was healthier than those from later Mississippian sites, a possible indication of less dependency upon corn than was present later in time.

One more test done on Big Lake phase bone at Zebree was a trace element analysis to observe the levels of zinc, copper, strontium, and iron present using atomic absorption (Powell 1980). The results suggested that the Zebree inhabitants ate less red meat than a comparative sample from Mound 72 at Cahokia. This result was surprising given the evidence supplied by the zooarchaeological studies. Observations made on the Big Lake phase skeletal sample show the population was transitional between a way of life primarily dependent upon harvesting of wild foods and one dependent upon intensive agriculture. The diet reflected in the teeth shows a use of soft foods and less protein. However, the larger body size shows better nutrition than later populations. The results of the stable carbon isotope analysis reinforce this perception of a population that is transitional to more complete dependence upon corn agriculture.

THE BIG LAKE PHASE VILLAGE

The extent of the Big Lake phase village at the Zebree site was mapped using data from the random squares, backhoe transects, and analysis of contents of features. The village was rectangular, measuring approximately 100 by 124 m or 12,400 sq m in size. There were ditches around the perimeters, and the village was presumably fenced as well.

Nine partial or complete Big Lake phase houses were excavated at Zebree. These houses were rectangular and constructed with corner posts and wall posts 6 to 8 cm in diameter (D. Morse 1980c:21-1). Wall posts were spaced 20 to 30 cm apart. One house was constructed in a 60 cm deep basin. Only one house had obvious shallow wall foundation trenches. The total interior wall space was relatively small and varied between 6.6 to 11.4 sq m. The average house size was 8.5 sq m. The long axes of the houses were oriented 15 degrees to 35 degrees east of magnetic north and 55 degrees to 60 degrees west of north. There were no recognized interior features found in these structures.

The Big Lake phase houses are relatively small. Structures excavated at the Hoecake site in southeast Missouri are similar, with post construction within a rectangular pit 8 to 50 cm deep. The Hoecake houses are from 6.8 to 12.8 sq m, with an average of 9.2 sq m in size. These are exterior measurements as opposed to the interior measurements taken at Zebree, so the average house dimensions are probably quite similar. Similar house patterns were also found at and near the

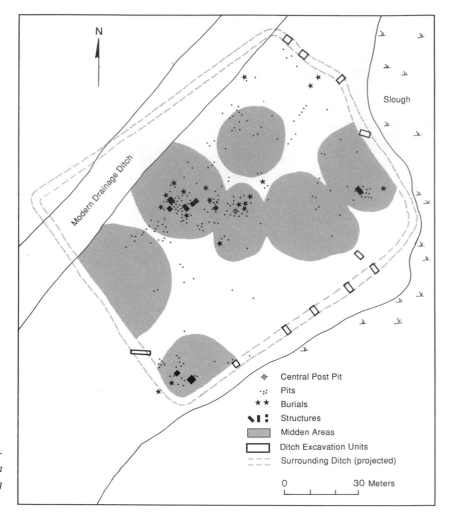

N

Slough

Modern Drainage Ditch

⊕ Central Post Pit
∴ Pits
★ ★ Burials
◥ ▌ ▐ Structures
Midden Areas
▭ Ditch Excavation Units
- - - Surrounding Ditch (projected)

0   30 Meters

Fig. 15. The settlement plan of the Big Lake phase village at the Zebree site, showing the location of those structures, midden areas, burials, and pits uncovered during excavation.

Cahokia site (Porter 1969, fig. 63). Houses from later Mississippian periods measure considerably larger in size, averaging 21.3 sq m at the Snodgrass site (Price and Griffin 1979) and 22.4 sq m at the Banks site (Perino 1966).

The small size of the Big Lake phase houses can be interpreted as reflecting a different kind of kinship and residence pattern than before, with a single nuclear family residing in each structure. This interpretation of occupation by a simple nuclear family of about five is evidently corroborated by the 3.5 liter capacity of the average cooking jar, which is interpreted to have fed five people on the average.

The houses at Zebree were not distributed randomly across the site. They were found in distinct midden clusters. Three major midden clusters were identified both by concentrations of artifacts and features and by

artifact density maps generated by data from the random square excavations. Excavations concentrated on two of these middens, labeled A and B. Two midden clusters, labeled D and E, were also discerned in the computer maps generated by the random square excavations. Two other areas, F and G, may be other household locations. Areas of low artifact density separated these midden clusters.

Sixty-eight cylindrical pits were associated with the houses in the midden areas (Fig. 15). These pits range in capacity from 1.36 to 3.9 cu m, and average about 2 cu m. They were slightly to moderately bell-shaped with flat bases. Two other pits were rectangular with flat bases and straight sides. These features all probably functioned as food storage pits. The average Zebree storage pit could have held 52 bushels of shelled corn. Ethnological data indicate that a nuclear family in

Mexico uses a minimum of 1 metric ton (39.4 bushels) of shelled corn during a year (Kirkby 1973:89). The average Big Lake phase storage pit could hold at least the minimum amount necessary for subsistence even allowing for some destruction due to underground storage. Experimental archaeology has shown that underground storage of grain is an effective technique (Coles 1973:39–40). When a pit is sealed, vegetational respiration produces carbon dioxide, which retards spoilage and germination. Even flooding does not affect all the stored food. The pits at Zebree were probably sealed with woven mats, caulked with clay. Fragments of fired clay with mat impressions were recovered. A large number of the other 270 Big Lake phase pits were basin shaped and circular. They may also have functioned to store food.

Two features, F-286 and F-429, may have been pottery-firing pits. Feature 286 was located on the southern edge of the site, away from any house cluster. It was 2.0 m in diameter with a flat base. Charred limbs were lying horizontally just above the base. A large pottery anvil and a toy bowl were in the fill, as well as large Varney Red and Wickliffe sherds. Feature 429 was on the northern edge of the site. It contained flat layers of sherds, burned clay, and charcoal. Pottery-firing sites would have been located away from house clusters, to prevent accidental burning of the village.

Burial pits were also found in the site. Thirty-one skeletons in 21 graves could be assigned to the Big Lake phase based on midden association. No grave goods were found with these skeletons. The Zebree skeletal sample was not representative of the total population, with no individuals aged between 1 and 15, and almost twice as many females as males (Powell 1980). Burial position was usually extended, with arms along the sides. However, a few individuals were flexed or semi-flexed, a burial position usually associated with Woodland and Archaic occupations in the central Mississippi Valley. One grave contained eight adult skeletons, four males and four females. Four of these skeletons lay on beds of mussel shells. Seven skeletons in the grave were oriented with skulls to the north, the other was pointed toward the west. This multiple burial feature was probably a charnel house and/or tomb. Unlike the tombs at the Hoecake site, it was not covered by a mound.

Backhoe trenches were placed perpendicular to the perimeter of the Zebree site to locate possible evidence of stockade ditches around the site. Definite evidence of ditching was found in these backhoe transects. Big Lake phase midden and features terminate where these ditch locations exist, showing that the area was ditched and probably fenced. However, these were not the wide and deep fortification trenches present around later Mississippian ceremonial centers (Price and Griffin 1979:37–40). The ditches at Zebree probably functioned to divert water from the site and to produce fill dirt to build up the village area. The existence of the ditches shows deliberate village planning, laying out a rectangular village with its corners oriented to the cardinal directions.

Two large borrow pits were found in the southern lower corner of the site. The fill from these capped a Dunklin phase midden. This may have taken place during the initial occupation of the site.

A deep pit, Feature 127, is interpreted as a central-post pit (Fig. 15). This feature was trench-shaped and shallow at one end and deep at the other. Such post pits are common at Cahokia (Fowler 1969:19). Large posts could be placed securely in the ground by laying them horizontally in a trench and then pulling them upright (Porter 1969:143). Such central posts are common at Early or Emergent Mississippian sites (Kelly et al. 1984, fig. 51). A central post may have been constructed by Big Lake phase people immediately upon their occupation of the site. The curious distribution of a rare Dunklin phase pottery type, Barnes Check Stamped, supports this conclusion. Only 93 Barnes Check Stamped sherds are known from the entire site (Anderson 1980:96). They are probably all from the same vessel. Seventy-one of these sherds are concentrated in the area where Feature 127, the post pit, is located (Fig. 15). The other 22 sherds are in the southern corner of the site, in the Midden B area. Dirt from the center of the site was probably carried over to this southern corner to build up the edge of the village.

A plaza or courtyard area probably was present in the center of the southern half of the site, south of Feature 127. The virtual absence of Big Lake phase artifacts in this 2,500 sq m area leads to this conclusion. No mounds were found at the site. However, the western edge of the site was destroyed in 1939 when a drainage ditch was dug, and it is possible that such a feature once existed at the site.

Mississippian communities were built according to definite plans. The Zebree site Big Lake phase village was constructed to fit the topographic contours of the environment, but these contours were also deliberately modified by village construction. The village area could have been laid out from a central point, where Feature 127 is located. The site is not aligned perfectly with the cardinal directions, as the north-south axis is shifted about 15 degrees clockwise. This orientation fits the site along the edge of a slough. The site boundaries were marked by ditches and were presumably fenced as well. Fill dirt from the ditches and some pits was probably used to elevate lower areas of the site such as Midden Area B. Separate house clusters were built within the site. These may represent kin cluster units such as separate lineages.

Approximately 100 to 140 individuals may have resided at the Zebree site at any one time, based on various estimates such as individuals per acre, number of cooking jars present, number of human bones found in the random squares and number of food storage pits found in the random squares (D. Morse 1980c, table 21-1). This was a significant population increase compared with the previous Woodland occupation. The site may have been occupied by the Big Lake phase as long as 200 years. There were probably individual farmsteads located near the site on areas of soil favorable to corn agriculture. These people would have attended religious ceremonies at Zebree and also found protection there if necessary.

There were no areas of craft specialization found at Zebree, although a concentrated effort was made to locate such areas. Tools and by-products of pottery making were found near each household. Varney Red salt pan sherds and Wickliffe Thick sherds are also found in all the major midden clusters. Microliths, cores, and Crescent Quarry chert debitage were also distributed in all the midden areas. Shell bead manufacture was obviously also a household task.

However, one interesting concentration was found in Midden A. Mammal bone was concentrated in this one midden, while fish and fowl were present in all the residential areas. Certain foods, particularly deer meat, may have been monopolized by a small segment of the population. Midden A may have been the residential area of a ruling lineage who retained certain desirable goods for themselves. Ranking individuals often retain scarce goods in a chiefdom (Peebles and Kus 1977:439).

The only true specialist at Zebree may have been the head of the ranking lineage. Such an individual could

have selected the site, laid out the plan of the village, and coordinated the labor of a large number during its construction. The Big Lake phase people apparently moved into the territory of the Dunklin phase, building their village immediately over the Dunklin midden. Their superior organization, more predictable economic base, and the military advantage of the bow and arrow may have helped them to successfully move into a new territory and survive. Mississippian culture had the potential to spread rapidly, with other less well organized groups either acculturating or being totally assimilated (Morse 1977:186). However, the inhabitants of the Zebree site themselves may not have had to "migrate" very far since there is a major cluster of emergent Mississippian sites along Pemiscot Bayou, including the major center known as Double Bridges (see Chapter 7, this volume). Based on the evidence at the Zebree site, the Dunklin phase did not independently evolve into the Big Lake phase. The Big Lake phase at the Zebree site is a fully emerged Mississippian expression although it dates somewhere within the ninth and tenth centuries A.D.

REFERENCES CITED

Anderson, David G.
1976   Excavation Strategies at the Zebree Site: 1975 Field Season. In *A Preliminary Report of the Zebree Project: New Approaches in Contract Archeology in Arkansas*, edited by Dan F. Morse and Phyllis A. Morse, pp. 30–43. Arkansas Archeological Survey Research Report 8. Fayetteville.
1979   *An Evaluation of Excavation Strategies Employed at the Zebree Site (3MS20) 1968–1976 Field Seasons.* Unpublished M.A. thesis, Department of Anthropology, University of Arkansas, Fayetteville.
1980a   *Zebree Archeological Project*, vol. 2, Appendixes. Submitted to Memphis District, U.S. Army Corps of Engineers by Arkansas Archeological Survey, Contract No. DACW66-76-C-0006.
1980b   Postdepositional Modification of the Zebree Behavioral Record. In *Zebree Archeological Project*, edited by Dan F. Morse and Phyllis A. Morse, chap. 8. Submitted to Memphis District, U.S. Army Corps of Engineers by Arkansas Archeological Survey, Contract No. DACW66-76-C-0006.
1980c   Field Strategies. In *Zebree Archeological Project*, edited by Dan F. Morse and Phyllis A. Morse, chap. 5. Submitted to Memphis District, U.S. Army Corps of Engineers by Arkansas Archeological Survey, Contract No. DACW66-76-C-0006.

Blake, Leonard W.
1984   Corn [at Zebree]. Manuscript on file, Arkansas Archeological Survey, Jonesboro.

Boutton, T. W., M. J. Lynott, J. E. Price, P. D. Klein, and L. L. Tieszen
1984 Stable Carbon Isotope Ratios as Indicators of Prehistoric Human Diet. In *Stable Isotopes and Nutrition*, edited by J. Turnlund and P. Johnson. American Chemical Society Symposium Series 1984.

Bowers, Lynn J.
1976 Tree-ring Dating at the Zebree Site in the Big Lake National Wildlife Refuge. In *A Preliminary Report of the Zebree Project, New Approaches in Contract Archeology in Arkansas*, edited by Dan F. Morse and Phyllis A. Morse, pp. 65–69. Arkansas Archeological Survey Research Report 8, Fayetteville.

Coles, John
1973 *Archaeology by Experiment*. Hutchinson and Company, London.

Culin, Stewart
1907 *Games of the North American Indians*. Bureau of American Ethnology Annual Report 24.

Fowler, Melvin
1969 The Cahokia Site. In *Explorations into Cahokia Archaeology*, edited by Melvin Fowler, pp. 1–30. Illinois Archaeological Survey Bulletin 7.

Guilday, John E., and Paul W. Parmalee
1975 Faunal Remains from the Zebree Site. In *Report of Excavations at the Zebree Site 1969*, by Dan F. Morse, pp. 228–234. Arkansas Archeological Survey Research Report 4, Fayetteville.

Harris, Suzanne E.
1976 Botanical Remains, Recovery Techniques and Preliminary Subsistence Results. In *A Preliminary Report of the Zebree Project, New Approaches in Contract Archeology in Arkansas*, edited by Dan F. Morse and Phyllis A. Morse, pp. 60–64. Arkansas Archeological Survey Research Report 8.
1980 1975 Features: Flotation Analysis Results. In *Zebree Archeological Project*, vol. 2: Appendixes, compiled by David G. Anderson. Submitted to Memphis District, U.S. Army Corps of Engineers by Arkansas Archeological Survey, Contract No. DACW66-76-C-0006.

Holmes, William H.
1903 *Aboriginal Pottery of the Eastern United States*. Bureau of American Ethnology Annual Report 20:1–237.

Kelly, John E., Steven J. Ozuk, Douglas K. Jackson, Dale L. McErath, Fred A. Finney, and Duane Esarey
1984 Emergent Mississippian Period. In *American Bottom Archaeology*, edited by Charles J. Bareis and James W. Porter, pp. 128–157. University of Illinois Press, Urbana and Chicago, for the Illinois Department of Transportation.

Keslin, Richard O.
1964 Archaeological Implications on the Role of Salt as an Element of Cultural Diffusion. *Missouri Archaeologist* 26.

King, James E.
1980 Palynological Studies of Big Lake, Arkansas. In *Zebree Archeological Project*, edited by Dan F. Morse and Phyllis A. Morse, chap. 14. Submitted to Memphis District, U.S. Army Corps of Engineers by Arkansas Archeological Survey, Contract No. DACW66-76-C-0006.

Kirkby, Anne V. T.
1973 *The Use of Land and Water Resources in the Past and Present Valley of Oaxaca, Mexico*. University of Michigan Museum of Anthropology Memoir 5.

Lallo, John W.
1973 *The Skeletal Biology of Three Prehistoric American Indian Societies from Dickson Mounds*. Ph.D. dissertation, Department of Anthropology, University of Massachusetts.

Mason, Ronald J., and Gregory Perino
1961 Microblades at Cahokia, Illinois. *American Antiquity* 26:553–557.

McGimsey, Charles R., IV
1984 Biotic Communities of the Big Lake Area. Manuscript on file, Arkansas Archeological Survey, Jonesboro.

Million, Michael G.
1975 Research Design for the Aboriginal Ceramic Industries of the Cache River Basin. In *The Cache River Archeological Project*, assembled by Michael B. Schiffer and John H. House, pp. 217–222. Arkansas Archeological Survey Research Series 8, Fayetteville.
1980 The Big Lake Pottery Industry. In *Zebree Archeological Project*, edited by Dan F. Morse and Phyllis A. Morse, chap. 18. Submitted to U.S. Army Corps of Engineers by Arkansas Archeological Survey, Contract No. DACW66-76-C-0006.

Morse, Dan F.
1963 *The Steuben Village and Mounds: A Multicomponent Late Hopewell Site in Illinois*. Anthropological Papers No. 21, Museum of Anthropology, University of Michigan, Ann Arbor.
1968 Preliminary Report on 1968 Archeological Excavations at the Big Lake National Wildlife Refuge. Manuscript on file, Arkansas Archeological Survey, Fayetteville.
1974 The Cahokia Microlith Industry. *Newsletter of Lithic Technology* 3:15–19.
1975 *Report of Excavations at the Zebree Site, 1969*. Arkansas Archeological Survey Research Report 4, Fayetteville.
1977 The Penetration of Northeast Arkansas by Mississippian Culture. In *For the Director: Research Essays in Honor of James B. Griffin*, edited by Charles Cleland, pp. 186–211. Anthropological Papers No. 61, Museum of Anthropology, University of Michigan, Ann Arbor.
1980a Other Aspects of the Barnes Occupation. In *Zebree Archeological Project*, edited by Dan F. Morse and Phyllis A. Morse, chap. 17. Submitted to Memphis District, U.S. Army Corps of Engineers by Arkansas Archeological Survey, Contract No. DACW66-76-C-0006.
1980b Other Big Lake Phase Artifacts. In *Zebree Archeological Project*, edited by Dan F. Morse and Phyllis A. Morse, chap. 20. Submitted to Memphis District, U.S. Army Corps of Engineers by Arkansas Archeological Survey, Contract No. DACW66-76-C-0006.
1980c The Big Lake Household and the Community. In *Zebree Archeological Project*, edited by Dan F. Morse and Phyllis A. Morse, chap. 21. Submitted to Memphis District, U.S. Army Corps of Engineers by Arkansas Archeological Survey, Contract No. DACW66-76-C0006.

Morse, Dan F., and David G. Anderson
1980 Descriptions of Features, 3MS20: 1968–1976 Field Seasons. In *Zebree Archeological Project*, vol. 2: Appendixes,

compiled by David G. Anderson. Submitted to Memphis District, U.S. Army Corps of Engineers by Arkansas Archeological Survey, Contract No. DACW-76-C-0006.

Morse, Dan F., Suzanne E. Harris, Alan Solomon, Lynne J. Bowers, and, Eric A. Roth
1980   Collection of Environmental and Subsistence Data. In *Zebree Archeological Project*, edited by Dan F. Morse and Phyllis A. Morse, chap. 6. Submitted to Memphis District, U.S. Army Corps of Engineers by Arkansas Archeological Survey, Contract No. DACW66-76-C-0006.

Morse, Dan F., and Phyllis A. Morse (editors)
1980   *Zebree Archeological Project*. Submitted to Memphis District, U.S. Army Corps of Engineers by Arkansas Archeological Survey, Contract No. DACW-76-C-0006.

Morse Dan F., and Phyllis A. Morse
1983   *Archaeology of the Central Mississippi Valley*. Academic Press, New York.

Morse, Dan F., Daniel Wolfman, and Herbert Haas
1980   Radiocarbon Dating. In *Zebree Archeological Project*, edited by Dan F. Morse and Phyllis A. Morse, chap. 11. Submitted to Memphis District, U.S. Army Corps of Engineers by Arkansas Archeological Survey, Contract No. DACW66-76-C-0006.

Morse, Phyllis A.
1980a The Forgotten Pioneers. In *Zebree Archeological Project*, edited by Dan F. Morse and Phyllis A. Morse, chap. 26. Submitted to Memphis District, U.S. Army Corps of Engineers by Arkansas Archeological Survey, Contract No. DACW66-76-C-0006.
1980b Later Historic Settlement Along Big Lake. In *Zebree Archeological Project*, edited by Dan F. Morse and Phyllis A. Morse, chap. 27. Submitted to Memphis District, U.S. Army Corps of Engineers by Arkansas Archeological Survey, Contract No. DACW66-76-C-0006.

Muller, Jon
1984   Mississippian Specialization and Salt. *American Antiquity* 49(3):489–507.

North, F. Chester
1975   Appendix 2: Determination of Sodium and Potassium in Nelumbo lutea. In *Report of Excavation at the Zebree Site, 1969*, by Dan F. Morse, pp. 235–237. Arkansas Archeological Survey Research Report 4, Fayetteville.

Peebles, Christopher S.
1976   Excavations at the Zebree Site: A Review of the Research Design. In *A Preliminary Report of the Zebree Project: New Approaches to Contract Archeology in Arkansas*, edited by Dan F. Morse and Phyllis A. Morse, pp. 69–76. Arkansas Archeological Survey Research Report 8, Fayetteville.

Peebles, Christopher S., and Susan Kus
1977   Some Archaeological Correlates of Ranked Societies. *American Antiquity* 42:421–448.

Perino, Gregory
1950   Cultural Clues from Cahokia. In *Cahokia Brought to Life*, edited by R. E. Grimm, pp. 59–61. Greater St. Louis Archaeological Society.
1966   *The Banks Village Site, Crittenden County, Arkansas*. Missouri Archaeological Societies, Inc. Memoir 1.
1971   *The Mississippi Component at the Schild Site (No. 4), Greene County, Illinois*. Illinois Archaeological Survey Bulletin 8

1985   *Selected Preforms, Points and Knives of the North American Indians*, vol 1. Points & Barbs Press, Idabel, Oklahoma.

Phillips, Philip
1970   *Archaeological Survey in the Lower Yazoo Basin, Mississippi, 1949–1955*. Papers of the Peabody Museum No. 60, Harvard University.

Porter, James Warren
1969   The Mitchell Site and Prehistoric Exchange Systems at Cahokia: A.D. 1000 ±300. In *Explorations into Cahokia Archaeology*, edited by Melvin L. Fowler, pp. 137–164. Illinois Archaeological Survey Bulletin 7.

Powell, Mary Lucas
1980   The Big Lake People: Skeletal Population. In *Zebree Archeological Project*, edited by Dan F. Morse and Phyllis A. Morse, chap. 23. Submitted to Memphis District, U.S. Army Corps of Engineers by Arkansas Archeological Survey, Contract No. DACW66-76-C-0006.

Price, James, and James B. Griffin
1979   *The Snodgrass Site of the Powers Phase of Southeast Missouri*. University of Michigan Museum of Anthropology Anthropological Papers 66, Ann Arbor.

Rolingson, Martha Ann
1982   *Emerging Patterns of Plum Bayou Culture*. Arkansas Archeological Survey Research Series 18, Fayetteville.

Roth, Eric A.
1980   Faunal Subsistence Patterns. In *Zebree Archeological Project*, edited by Dan F. Morse and Phyllis A. Morse, chap. 22. Submitted to Memphis District, U.S. Army Corps of Engineers by Arkansas Archeological Survey, Contract No. DACW-76-C-0006.

Saucier, Roger T.
1970   Origin of the St. Francis Sunk Lands, Arkansas and Missouri. *Geological Society of America, Bulletin* 81: 2847–2854.

Schultz, Harold
1962   Brazil's Big-Lipped Indians. *National Geographic* 121: 118–133.

Sierzchula, Michael C.
1980   *Replication and Use Studies of the Zebree Microlith Industry*. Unpublished M.A. thesis, Department of Anthropology, University of Arkansas, Fayetteville.

Smith, Bruce D.
1976   The Research Design of the 1975 Zebree Project: A Review. In *A Preliminary Report of the Zebree Project: New Approaches in Contract Archeology in Arkansas*, edited Dan F. Morse and Phyllis A. Morse, pp. 77–87. Arkansas Archeological Survey Research Report 8, Fayetteville.

Spears, Carol S.
1978   *The Derositt Site (3SF49): Applications of Behavioral Archeology to a Museum Collection*. Unpublished M.A. thesis, Department of Anthropology, University of Arkansas, Fayetteville.

Williams, Stephen
1954   *An Archeological Study of the Mississippian Culture in Southeast Missouri*. Unpublished Ph.D. dissertation, Department of Anthropology, Yale University, New Haven.

Yerkes, Richard
1983   Microwear, Microdrills and Mississippian Craft Specialization. *American Antiquity* 48:499–518.

Range Site Community Patterns and the Mississippian Emergence

INTRODUCTION

Based on over sixty years of archaeological investigations, including twenty-five years of intensive field work, Cahokia and its satellite communities in the American Bottom have been shown to represent the most complex prehistoric sociopolitical system to have developed north of Mexico. A number of models have been proposed to explain how the Cahokia system initially developed. Those models developed prior to 1980 basically incorporated in situ development and migration, and, to a large extent, were based on the available data from salvage excavations of the 1960s, as well as on the more focused research of the late 1960s and early 1970s at Cahokia. These models are examined in greater detail in the next chapter of this volume.

As a result of the FAI-270 archaeological mitigation project (I-270 project), the available archaeological data base for the critical five-century span (A.D. 600 –1100) that witnessed the initial development of Mississippian culture in the American Bottom has substantially expanded since the mid-1970s. This expanded and improved data base, particularly in regard to the timing of Mississippian development and associated changes in community organization and overall settlement patterning, has in turn encouraged a second generation of new and quite different models of Mississippian development.

Begun in 1975, the I-270 project was designed to identify and appropriately mitigate those archaeological sites situated within a 34 km section of the construction corridor of proposed Interstate 270 (now I-255) that extended from the Mississippi River near Columbia, Illinois north to an area just east of Cahokia Mounds (Fig. 16). Lasting two years and directed by the author, the initial pedestrian survey and site testing phase of the I-270 project was conducted through the Illinois Department of Transportation (IDOT) under the auspices of the Illinois Archaeological Survey (IAS) (Kelly et al. 1979). A variety of techniques, including magnetometer survey and phosphate analysis (McElrath and Williams 1981) were used in the initial evaluation of the 59 sites encountered within the I 270 alignment. Following initial site survey and evaluation, test excavations were conducted in order to more accurately establish the significance of the various sites and their eligibility for nomination to the National Register of Historic Places. Test excavations were conducted in 1976 and 1977 by IDOT archaeologists in coordination with the field school programs of a number of universities in Illinois. Full-scale excavation of sites within the project alignment, again involving a number of different universities in Illinois, began in the spring of 1978 and continued until 1982.

In addition to the 59 sites identified during the initial survey of the I-270 alignment, another 32 sites located in areas to be used for construction fill were investigated during the five-year program of large-scale excavation. A subsequent 5.8 mi extension of the project alignment required excavation of an additional 17 sites between 1984 and 1985 (Fortier and McElrath 1986).

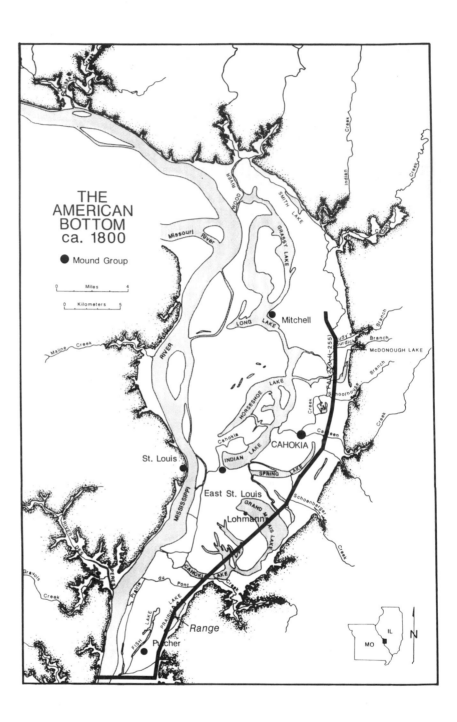

Fig. 16. The upper American Bottom.

An I-270 publication series consisting of separate site reports, along with a summary volume (Bareis and Porter 1984) provide a detailed record of the archaeological information recovered during the project.

A primary goal of the I-270 project was to obtain community organization information, and to do this, large earthmoving equipment was employed to expose extensive areas of most sites. As a result of these large-scale stripping operations undertaken during the I-270 project, changes in the size and internal spatial organization of settlements over a long span of prehistory were documented, and the patterns of temporal change in community plans provided an entirely new perspective on the nature and timing of cultural evolution in the American Bottom. The interpretive value of this community plan perspective in the American Bottom was particularly striking for the period from A.D. 600 to A.D. 1100: five centuries that spanned the initial Mississippian emergence.

This chapter focuses on a single settlement, the Range site, and its changing sequence of community plans over this 500-year period of rapid cultural change. Because of its size and organizational complexity, the Range site was recognized early in the I-270 project as having considerable potential for contributing to our understanding of the development of Mississippian culture in the American Bottom (Kelly et al. 1979; Bareis et al. 1977, 1981). While it is dangerous to make projections regarding a region's development from a single location, a site such as Range, with its inherent settlement complexity, does provide an important window from which to view larger scale developmental trends, while also providing some basis for their interpretation. The pattern of community plan change at the Range site from A.D. 600–1100 reflects demographic trends, as well as a number of social, economic, political, and religious transformations. As part of the economic change, a number of subsistence shifts documented at Range were also an integral part of the ongoing evolutionary process that ultimately culminated in the Cahokia variant of Mississippian culture.

THE RANGE SITE

Location and Environmental Setting

The Range site was initially recorded by Alan Harn in 1961 during one of a number of surveys carried out in the vicinity of Cahokia (Harn 1971). An outgrowth of the highway salvage work in the region at that time, these surveys were undertaken to provide some indication of the number and types of sites that existed outside of the main mound centers in the American Bottom. The following passages from Harn's field notes describe the Range site:

> Friday, August 25, 1961. Stopped and talked with a Mr. Floyd Range this morning. He farms a large area east of Dupo on a high ridge. He says numerous artifacts are found on the ridge, by several people in Dupo. The ridge is planted in beans and I won't be able to do much with it.
> Tuesday, September 26, 1961. Surface collected part of

the Range site. There is an enormous amount of material here. It has a very heavy late Woodland occupation and a slightly lighter Mississippian. Got a good sample of sherds and chert. Only two artifacts were procured, both being broken. A celt and a discoidal.

There are no records of any additional investigations at the Range site until the fall of 1975, when Ken Williams and I visited the site as part of the I-270 survey. Our initial investigations indicated a site encompassing approximately 10 ha with 70 percent of the site area located within the I-270 alignment corridor.

The Range site is situated on "point bar top stratum deposits of the upstream arm of the Prairie Lake meander scar" (White and Bonnell 1981), an abandoned channel of the Mississippi River (Fig. 17). The upper deposits of the point bar include the sandier soils of the Landes fine sandy loams soils series, which were restricted to the front slope and higher portion of the ridge. Soils on the back slope of the ridges were somewhat more clayey and belong to Riley silty clay loam series (Wallace 1978).

There are a number of different floodplain and upland environmental zones within a 5 km radius of the site. The floodplain, which comprises 69 percent of the area within the 5 km site catchment, can be further subdivided into terrestrial and aquatic habitats. Prairie Lake, which borders the site on the north and east (Fig. 17), is the most prominent aquatic feature in the Range site area, and would have been a major source of animal protein in the form of numerous species of fish and waterfowl. Nearby Fish Lake would also have provided abundant aquatic resources, as would the numerous marshes and sloughs along the lower terrace between Fish Lake and the Mississippi River (Fig. 17).

The terrestrial habitats would have been restricted to the higher and drier portions of the point bar that would also have contained well-drained soils often suitable for cultivation. The early land surveys indicated the presence of numerous fast-growing arboreal species such as cottonwood and willow along oxbow lakes such as Prairie Lake (Gregg 1975). The higher and more stable portions of the point bar may have developed into a bottomland prairie. There is some evidence (Pearsall 1982) to suggest that the site was under grassy, perhaps prairie, vegetation at about A.D. 600. Immediately east of Prairie Lake were the limestone-

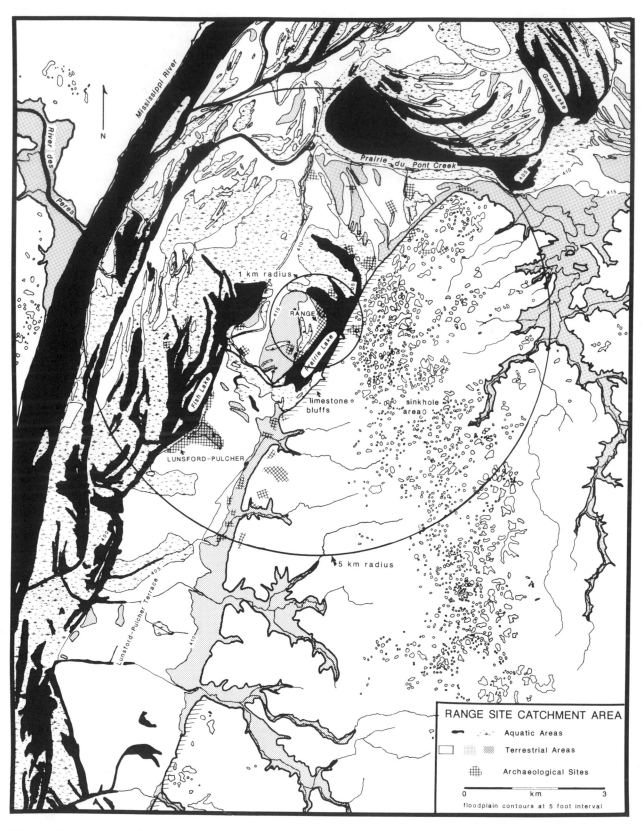

Fig. 17. The Range site and its catchment area.

faced bluffs. The adjacent uplands were quite varied and included sinkhole topography associated with the underlying limestone formations and more dissected stream valleys 3 to 5 km to the east. The underlying lithic facies in this area included raw materials such as limestone, sandstone, chert, and hematite. Oak interspersed with hickories and other plant species dominated the nearby uplands (Hus 1908). The oak-hickory taxa would have been important to the Range site inhabitants as a source of both house construction materials and hickory nuts and oak mast. Of the various animal species generally associated with the uplands, deer was perhaps the most important.

Thirty-three other sites have been identified within a 5 km radius of the Range site. Because only 3.5 percent of the area has been systematically surveyed, there are undoubtedly many more sites within this 5 km catchment. Twenty-one of the recorded sites have been excavated to varying degrees, and many contain cultural components coeval with those at the Range site. Prominent among those sites situated close to the Range site is the Lunsford-Pulcher site, a large Early Mississippian mound center (Snyder 1909; Fowler 1969; Freimuth 1974; Griffin 1977), which may have first been occupied during the Emergent Mississippian period (Fig. 17).

The I-270 Investigations

Initial work at the Range site during 1975 and 1976 included a controlled surface collection, contour mapping of the site, a magnetometer survey, the collection of phosphate samples, and test excavations (Kelly et al. 1987). Additional test excavations were conducted during the summer of 1977 by the University of Illinois, Urbana-Champaign, and a series of research problems pursued during the subsequent full-scale excavation of the Range site were outlined (Bareis et al. 1977, 1981). These research problems focused on the Late Woodland-Mississippian communities at the site and the extent to which they could contribute to our understanding of the Mississippian emergence in the American Bottom. An underlying premise of the initial Range site problem orientation was that a shift from a relatively egalitarian Late Woodland society to a more hierarchal Mississippian sociopolitical structure took place within the context

of a number of socioeconomic transformations, including the intensification of agricultural systems and the appearance of sedentary communities that were participating in a larger scale hierarchical settlement system.

In order to address these and other related aspects of the Woodland to Mississippian transition at the Range site, it was evident that large-scale stripping and the definition of house patterns and community plans would be necessary. Harn's initial surface collection at the Range site indicated both Late Woodland and Early Mississippian components, and our initial field work at the site suggested the presence of a series of village communities (Kelly et al. 1979:66). Part of the reason we suspected a series of villages was the unusually large area (4 ha) of Late Woodland and Emergent Mississippian occupation at the site in comparison with other known sites of that time period, such as the Knoebel site (Bareis 1976). The Knoebel site community plan, which consisted of structures arranged on opposite sides of an open area containing a large central post, also provided a set of general expectations for community plans at the Range site, and the large-scale stripping at Knoebel set the stage for a similar excavation approach to sites within the I-270 corridor.

Large-scale excavation of the Range site began in the spring of 1978 and continued on a year-round basis into the summer of 1981, when mitigation of the site was completed. As extensive areas of the Range site were exposed with large earthmoving machines, a complex and initially confusing array of pits, house basins, and other features were uncovered. These were defined, mapped, and excavated as they were exposed, with a total of over 5,500 such features recorded for the 4.5 ha excavated area (Fig. 18). The features indicated the presence of Archaic, Late Woodland, Emergent Mississippian, Mississippian, and Oneota occupations.

Some preliminary analysis and report writing was begun while the field work was still in progress. Mark Mehrer's master's thesis described the northernmost Mississippian occupation at the site (Mehrer 1982). The analysis and interpretation of the other cultural components at the Range site has continued to the present. Separate reports covering the Archaic, Early Woodland, and Middle Woodland components

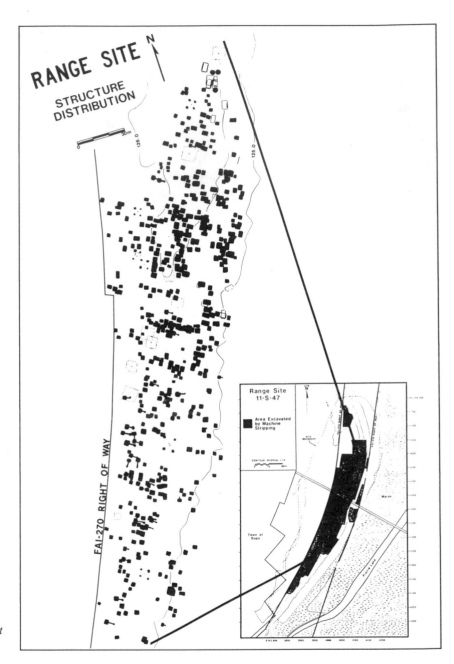

Fig. 18. The extent of excavation areas at the Range site.

at Range (Kelly and Fortier 1983), along with the Late Woodland occupation (Kelly et al. 1984) have been combined into a single published volume (Kelly et al. 1987). Another report (Kelly et al. 1989a) on the initial Emergent Mississippian phases (Dohack and Range) is forthcoming. Two other planned volumes will cover, respectively, the final two Emergent Mississippian phases (George Reeves and Lindeman)

and the Mississippian and Oneota occupations at the Range site. A summary volume on the site is also planned.

Archaeological Overview

While projectile points representative of the entire Archaic continuum were recovered during excavation

Table 8. Range Site Radiocarbon Assays

Phase	Community	Feature Class	Wood Charcoal Material Dated	Date (B.P.)	Date (A.C.)	ISGS No.
Patrick	P-1	Hearth	*Fraxinus* sp.	1430 ± 70	520	1020
		Hearth	cf. *Fraxinus*	220 ± 70	1730	1019
		Hearth	*Carya* sp.	modern		1021
	P-3	KHS	*Quercus* sp.	1160 ± 75	790	619
		KHS	*Quercus* sp.	1110 ± 90	840	626
		KHS	*Quercus* sp.	1070 ± 100	880	642
	P-6	EO	*Carya* sp.	1510 ± 75	440	853
		KHS	*Quercus* sp.	1080 ± 80	870	893
	P-8	KHS	*Betula* sp.	1100 ± 70	850	901
Dohack	D-2	SRS	*Quercus* sp.	960 ± 70	990	913
		SRS	*Quercus* sp.	990 ± 70	960	914
	D-5	SRS	*Quercus* sp.	1090 ± 70	860	905
Range	R-1	Pit	*Quercus sp.*	795 ± 75	1155	595
		Pit	*Quercus sp.*	810 ± 75	1140	646A
		Pit	*Quercus sp.*	810 ± 75	1140	646B
		SRS	*Quercus sp.*	1250 ± 130	700	651
		Pit	*Carya* sp.	1170 ± 75	780	776
	R-2	SRS	Salicaceae	880 ± 90	1070	623
		Pit	Salicaceae	880 ± 90	1070	627
	R-3	Pit	*Quercus* sp.	990 ± 75	960	620
		SRS	*Quercus* sp.	1040 ± 75	910	811
Lindeman	L-1	Pit	*Quercus* sp.	1010 ± 75	940	810
		SRS	*Carya* sp.	970 ± 75	980	824
Lindhorst	M-1	Pit	Salicaeae	910 ± 75	1040	577
Stirling	M-1	WTS	*Carya* sp.	950 ± 75	1000	569
		Pit	*Carya* sp.	870 ± 75	1080	570
		Hearth	*Carya* sp.	860 ± 130	1090	596
		WTS	*Carya* sp. (nut shell)	890 ± 75	1060	825

ISGS - Illinois State Geological Survey
KHS - Keyhole structure
SRS - Small rectilinear structure
WTS - Wall-trench structure
EO   - Earth Oven

of the Range site, it was not until the Late Archaic period that groups actually occupied the Range site locality for any length of time, as reflected by numerous pit features scattered across the entire length of the site. Based on the distribution of these pit features, eight discrete occupation areas were defined. In many respects the Late Archaic occupation of the Range site represents a less intensive extension of the Prairie Lake component at the Missouri Pacific No. 2 site to the south (McElrath and Fortier 1983) (Fig. 17).

No features were excavated at the Range site that could be assigned to either the Early or Middle Woodland periods. Evidence for Early and Middle Woodland utilization of the Range site was limited to diagnostic ceramics and lithics recovered from the plow zone and features of later occupational episodes.

By far the most intense utilization of the site oc-

curred during the Late Woodland through Early Mississippian occupations, which is the subject of interest here. It should be noted that portions of the site were used at some later date by Mississippian peoples as a mortuary area. The final prehistoric occupation was associated with the Oneota "incursion" into the American Bottom.

Although the Late Woodland, Emergent Mississippian, and Mississippian occupational episodes at the Range site frequently overlapped, forming an initially confusing pattern of over 5,000 features, it was possible to distinguish temporal components and communities by utilizing a number of standard archaeological techniques. Feature superposition consistently allowed the relative temporal position of ceramic assemblages to be established. The resultant ceramic sequence in turn was employed, along with the spatial patterning of approximately 600 houses and other features, to define a sequence of at least 28 temporally discrete communities for the 500-year span from A.D. 600–1100.

A total of 28 radiocarbon dates obtained on materials from a selected number of the 28 identified Late Woodland and Early Mississippian communities were of value in calendrically anchoring the sequence of occupational episodes at the Range site. But because of consistently large standard deviation values (Table 8), these radiocarbon age determinations were of little value in establishing either the calendrical date of any particular community, or how long such communities were in existence. The Late Woodland and Early Mississippian period communities at the Range site may have been in existence anywhere from only a few years to several decades in the case of the large villages.

The Late Woodland-Emergent Mississippian-Mississippian Sequence at the Range Site

The sequence of cultural phases at the Range site briefly outlined below is based on data derived from the site itself and from other sites in the region. Ceramic assemblages play the primary role in delineating each phase. Although not as temporally sensitive as ceramics, other classes of artifacts, as well as feature types, were also important in the delineation of different phases.

The Patrick Phase (A.D. 600–700)

Late Woodland occupation of the Range site was limited to the Patrick phase (A.D. 600–700). Patrick phase ceramic assemblages were dominated by grog-tempered, cordmarked jars and bowls. Decoration was generally restricted to interior lip impressions and occasional small lip lugs, effigy heads, or spouts. The lithic assemblage included a wide range of tools. Of particular importance was the presence of small stemmed and subtriangular arrow points, indicative of the initial introduction of the bow and arrow. Larger, expanding-stemmed points are also evident and may have been used as knives. Discoidals of clay and stone appear for the first time and are presumably the antecedents of the game known historically as chunkey. Pipes were also manufactured from clay

and stone. The most prevalent type of pipe was one characterized by an extended prow. Although most were plain, decoration was generally restricted to the bowl and included incising, nodes, and effigies. A number of the pipes were tempered with shell. This use of shell is somewhat anomalous because the first shell-tempered ceramic vessels were introduced from outside the area, some 100 to 200 years later. Shell was sometimes mixed with clay, however, and used to patch Patrick phase grog-tempered vessels.

The Patrick phase inhabitants of the Range site constructed three different types of structures: small rectilinear, large rectilinear, and keyhole. They also constructed screens. The small rectilinear and keyhole structures constructed at the Range site during the Patrick phase, with a mean floor area of 5 sq m (Fig. 19), were considerably smaller than those of the preceding Late Woodland phases in the region. Each house was constructed in a rectilinear basin with individual posts placed along the basin walls. Burned, and thus preserved, wall elements indicate the use of a variety of woods for posts and thatch covering. Post molds from several Patrick phase structures were outslanting, suggesting a wigwam type of construction. Almost half of the 81 Patrick phase small basin structures have an extended entry, and are referred to as keyhole structures. The small floor area and the general lack of any internal features or debris suggests that the primary function of most of these structures was as sleeping huts. If one allows 1.3 sq m per person based on the average minimum amount of space of two prone bodies, these dwellings could have housed from two to six individuals. This sleeping space value of 1.3 sq m per individual would seem to be an appropriate basis for estimating community population size based on total floor space of structures. A similar estimate of 1.5 sq m per individual has been obtained for small huts in Australia (Williams 1985). Other formulas for projecting population size from floor area are certainly available (e.g., Naroll 1962; Flannery 1972; Smith 1978), but are likely to be inappropriate because they are based on multiple-activity habitation structures.

Three large rectilinear structures of single-post construction and two screens were assigned to the Patrick phase. These undoubtedly were specialized facilities.

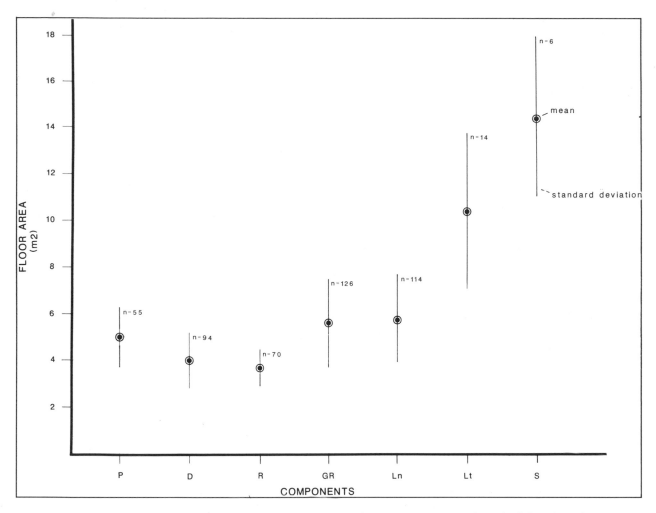

Fig. 19. Internal floor area information for small rectilinear structures at the Range site: mean and standard deviation values.

In addition to the structures, numerous features were excavated and undoubtedly used in the processing, cooking, and storage of subsistence items. There was, in fact, a very high ratio of pits to structures (22:1). Almost a tenth of these facilities were earth ovens, presumably used in the steaming of various food stuffs.

The Dohack Phase (A.D. 750–850)
This initial Emergent Mississippian phase is characterized by a number of major technological changes. Perhaps the most significant is a shift to limestone as a tempering agent. Many of the Late Woodland Patrick phase vessel forms, with emphasis on certain ceramic shapes such as jars with constricted orifices, dominate Dohack phase ceramic assemblages. Ac-

companying these changes in ceramic vessel forms and tempering materials were a number of subsistence changes. Maize appears for the first time as a major element in archaeobotanical assemblages. The same types of structures were present, with the small rectilinear type the most frequent (n = 102). The three keyhole structures were smaller in size, with the floor areas for both types reduced to 4 sq m (Fig. 19). The frequency of earth ovens and pits decreases relative to the Patrick phase at the same time that pits with rectilinear orifices become more abundant. Many of these changes in ceramic technology and feature frequency are thought to be related to the introduction, or increasing importance, of maize. While material cultural assemblages of Dohack phase communities at the Range site contain many of the artifacts commonly recovered from antecedent Patrick phase contexts (e.g., small arrow points, discoidals, pipes) these items decrease in ubiquity.

The Range Phase (A.D. 850–900)

The Range phase can be differentiated from the antecedent Dohack phase primarily on the basis of ceramic assemblages. There is a dramatic increase in the frequency of jars with plain necks, large bowls or pans, and jars with restricted orifices. Lip notching decreases in frequency while lip lugs become more frequent. Handles and stumpware vessel forms appear for the first time. In addition, vessels traded in from the northern half of the American Bottom become much more common. Again, some of these innovations may well be associated with the processing of maize. The high frequency of shallow bowls may be related to the preparation of "corn breads," and there is indirect evidence of possible log mortars in the form of small (30–50 cm) pits used to hold these items. The frequency of pits with rectilinear orifices continues to rise, while the ratio of pits to structures is comparable to the Dohack phase. Range phase communities have the smallest (3.7 sq m floor area) houses of any occupational episode represented at the Range site (Fig. 19).

In the artifactual assemblage there is a continued decrease in projectile points, discoidals, and pipes. The decrease in projectile points coincides with a decrease in deer. When considered in conjunction with the decrease in upland nuts, this suggests a deemphasis on upland species and perhaps a reduction of the subsistence territory. The decrease in pipes and discoidals may reflect a shift in their role from a more "secular" corporate use to one restricted to certain rituals in the community, under the control or direction of a specific individual.

The George Reeves Phase (A.D. 900–950)

Many of the trends of change in pit and house structures and material culture assemblages documented for the preceding Range phase continue into the George Reeves phase. Within the George Reeves phase ceramic assemblage, however, there is a notable increase in the representation of jars that have undecorated necks. These jars in fact occasionally have entirely plain surfaces. Some of these have constricted orifices and may represent bottles or prototypes for seed jars. Red filming appears on jars with plain necks and cordmarked bodies, but such red-filmed jars comprise only a small percentage (less than 1 percent) of the George Reeves phase ceramic assemblage. Interior lip impressions on ceramic vessels virtually disappear, while exterior decorations increase in frequency, often on thickened or appliqued lips. Thick, elephantine loop handles are also present on a small percentage of jars. Some shell-tempered jars are evident, but like a number of grog-tempered plain or red-filmed vessels, they are thought to be derived from sources outside the American Bottom region. The most notable of these nonlocal vessels is a grog-tempered, red-filmed, hooded frog effigy bottle.

Although polished hoe flakes recovered from Patrick, Dohack, and Range phase contexts suggest the possible earlier presence of agricultural tools, the first complete hoes, manufactured from Mill Creek and Burlington cherts, come from George Reeves phase contexts. Ceramic discs used as spindle whorls also appear for the first time in George Reeves phase contexts.

Houses increase in size (5.6 sq m floor area) during the George Reeves phase (Fig. 19), and there is also an increase in the range of variation in structure floor area. Continuing a trend first noted in the Dohack phase, there is a marked decrease in the ratio of pits to structures, and very few earth ovens are present. George Reeves phase communities at the Range site also have the highest frequency of deep straight-walled or expanded-walled pits with rectangular orifices.

The Lindeman Phase (A.D. 950–1000)

The Lindeman phase, marking the end of the Emergent Mississippian period, witnesses the culmination of a number of trends toward increasing diversity in ceramic assemblages and structures that began two centuries earlier. Cordmarking continues as the primary surface treatment for ceramics, particularly on large bowls, stumpware, and the lower body of most jars. The trend toward decreasing cordmarking of jars also continues, however, with some bowls and stumpware similarly lacking cordmarked surfaces. When present, other forms of plastic decoration are limited: punctation, exterior lip notching, effigy lugs or adornos, and loop handles. Ceramic spindle whorls are occasionally decorated with incised lines. One such disc represents a spider web. Red filming, initially occurring on jars and often over cordmarked surfaces during the George Reeves phase, also appears on other vessel forms during the Lindeman phase, including bowls, seed jars, and at least one hooded bottle. A new vessel form, the seed jar, also appears for the first time in Lindeman phase ceramic assemblages at the Range site, with decoration, when present, consisting of punctates encircling the orifice. This seed jar vessel form, like the hooded bottle and bowls with inverted lips, is a gourd or squash effigy.

The representation of extraregional vessels also increases dramatically during the Lindeman phase. The nonlocal shell-tempered jars in Lindeman phase assemblages have plain, cordmarked, brushed, and red-filmed (Varney Red Filmed) surface treatments. Other nonlocally manufactured red-filmed bowls, seed jars, and hooded bottles are also present in Lindeman phase ceramic assemblages, along with grog-tempered vessels, generally jars with cordmarked or plain surfaces. Several examples of red-filmed, grog-tempered hooded bottles have also been recovered.

White Burlington chert, acquired from quarry areas across the Mississippi River, becomes far more abundant in Lindeman phase lithic assemblages, and hoes of Mill Creek chert, derived from southern Illinois quarries, also increase in frequency.

The average size (5.8 sq m floor area) of structures and the variation in structure floor area continues to increase during the Lindeman phase. This overall increase in the average size of structures during the Lindeman phase may not be related to any increase in community population levels, but rather may reflect nondomestic activities and storage functions. A few Lindeman phase structures have large interior pits placed at one end, a pattern that becomes quite common in later Mississippian period houses.

The Lindhorst Phase (A.D. 1000–1050)
The ceramic assemblage of the Lindhorst phase reflects considerable continuity from the Emergent Mississippian period into the Mississippian period. While there is a slight decrease in limestone tempering, the increase in shell tempering is not significant and is generally restricted to nonlocal vessels, primarily those from the Cahokia area, but with some coming into the American Bottom from the south. There is also a marked decrease in vessels, particularly jars, having cordmarked surfaces, with a corresponding increase in plain undecorated surface treatment. Notched lips on jars disappear, and rims are often outflared or thickened at the lip. Red filming continues to be present on bowls, jars, and seed jars. Stumpware is still being manufactured, and along with ceramic "funnels," which appear for the first time in Lindhorst ceramic assemblages, may have continued to function as vessel supports.

Although the rectangular single-post basin construction of structures characteristic of Emergent Mississippian period communities at the Range site continues into the Mississippian period, wall-trench house construction becomes much more common during the Lindhorst phase, and constitutes an important marker of post-A.D. 1000 Mississippian period occupational episodes. The marked increase in structure size (Fig. 19) during this initial Mississippian phase reflects the continuation of a trend begun during the preceding Lindeman phase, with an increased allocation of interior house floor area to a storage function, as reflected by large, deep storage pits.

The Stirling Phase (A.D. 1050–1150)
The distinctive and diagnostic temporal markers for Stirling phase occupation of the Range site are Ramey Incised jars and Powell plain jars with rolled rims, which first appear in A.D. 1050–1150 contexts. Limestone continues as the most common tempering agent, even though the frequency of shell-tempered vessels increases from 8 percent to 34 percent in Stirling phase ceramic assemblages, and is employed across a number of different vessel forms, including bottles. Most of these shell-tempered vessels are probably derived from the Cahokia area. Cordmarked surface treatment continues on some limestone-tempered jars.

Stirling phase houses at the Range site are generally comparable to those of the preceding Lindhorst phase, exhibiting a slight increase in average size (Fig. 19), and a trend toward square as opposed to rectangular shape. It is possible that future fine-grain analysis of Stirling phase features and material culture assemblages might allow the further temporal subdivision of this one-century phase; and given the persistence of

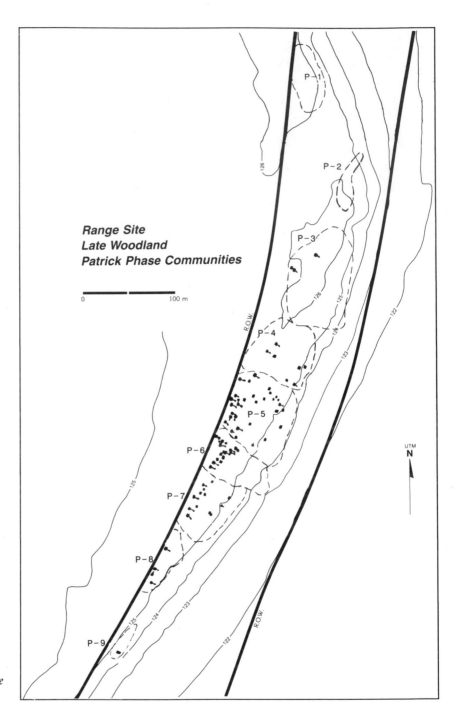

Fig. 20. The distribution of Patrick phase structures and occupation areas at the Range site.

the Pulcher ceramic assemblage, the establishment of a separate phase for this complex in this area of the American Bottom.

Summary
The above brief descriptions of the material culture

attributes and changing nature of pit and house features at the Range site over a 500-year span from A.D. 600–1100 outline the temporal markers employed in sorting out and seriating the overlapping confusion of community plans. These changes in material culture and site features, in addition to providing temporal markers, also represent the more salient technological and stylistic transformations that occurred both at Range and throughout the American Bottom. Against this general background of rapid and dramatic change, the evolution of community organization at the Range site can now be considered.

CHANGING COMMUNITY PATTERNS AT THE RANGE SITE

By employing the various temporally sensitive markers briefly outlined above, it was possible to identify and temporally seriate 28 different occupational episodes at the Range site, with each of these considered to represent a discrete community. Each of these 28 communities is identified by an alphanumeric designation. For example, the temporally ordered Patrick phase set of communities is designated P-1 through P-9.

The Patrick Phase (A.D. 600–700)

The sequence of nine Patrick phase occupational episodes at the Range site represents the most spatially extensive, and to a certain extent most intensive, utilization of this locale by human populations. A total of 1,872 Patrick phase features, including 86 structures, were identified within an area of 2.6 ha. The nine occupation areas (P-1 through P-9, Figs. 20–27) were defined on the basis of the spatial distribution of features, particularly the horizontal patterning of structures (Kelly et al. 1987).

Patrick phase occupational episodes at the Range site varied considerably in size and complexity, ranging from specialized, limited term encampments (P-1, P-2, P-9) through single family homesteads (P-3), and hamlets (P-4), to the largest village of over 35 structures (P-5). Homesteads were comprised of one to three structures, while hamlets generally had ten or fewer houses with no overall organizational pattern to their distribution. Villages contained numerous structures distributed about an open area or community square. Such villages are reminiscent of Flannery's (1972) compounds in some respects, while also sharing certain aspects of his village settlement type.

The two northernmost occupations (P-1, P-2) lacked structures and were interpreted as limited term occupations based on the low density of debris and limited diversity of tool types represented (Fig. 21). It was not possible to establish whether these occupational episodes were seasonal in nature or longer in duration. The two southernmost occupations (P-8, P-9) each contained several structures abutting the right-of-way. The major part of these occupations, however, might be located to the west, outside the right-of-way (and area excavated). It is possible that only a portion of P-8 was excavated, and that it was a more substantial, village-sized community.

The remaining occupational episodes at the Range site (P-3 through P-7) were more substantial settlements, with much higher debris density and a wider range of artifact types represented. Although there is no accurate and reliable method of measuring the actual duration of these settlements (P-3 through P-7), they undoubtedly were occupied for a number of years before abandonment. It is likely that these more stable settlements were involved in a system of shifting cultivation. Within the context of such shifting cultivation systems, the relocation of settlements is often attributed to an eventual reduction in soil fertility; it is not a factor in some floodplain settings such as the Amazon (Hames 1983; Gross 1983). A number of other factors are also known ethnographically to necessitate settlement relocation. Other resources such as water, firewood, and animals may become less abundant. Fields may become weed choked. Settlements may be threatened by external raiding or increasing internal hostility, or supernatural threats may be perceived (cf. Smith 1972). The P-3 homestead was the smallest of these longer term Patrick phase occupational episodes at the Range site. Covering a very large area, the P-3 settlement at Range included three structures and a great number of pits, and had a very high pit to structure ratio of 93:1 (Fig. 22). Presumably this represents the activities of at least two households over a relatively long period of time (e.g., 10–20 years). The low frequency of feature superpositioning appears to indicate that activities were consistently relocated over the duration of occupation.

The hamlet, P-4, included nine structures arranged in three separate clusters (Fig. 23), along with two large, single-post, rectilinear facilities. The low frequency of a common domestic artifact category (projectile points) at this P-4 settlement, along with the distribution of certain artifact classes such as pipes

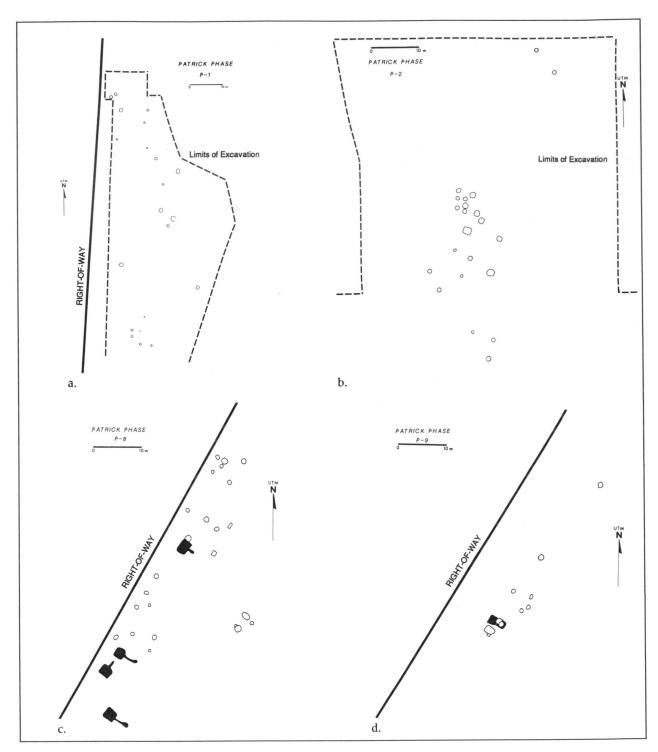

Fig. 21. The distribution of features for Patrick phase settlements at the Range site: (a) P-1, (b) P-2, (c) P-8, (d) P-9.

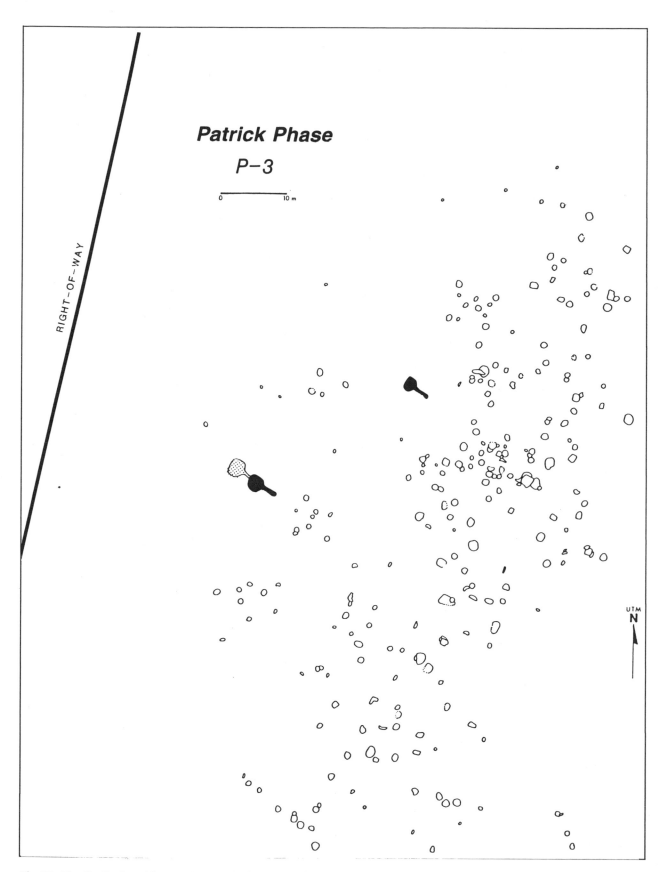

Fig. 22. The distribution of features for Patrick phase occupation area P-3 at the Range site.

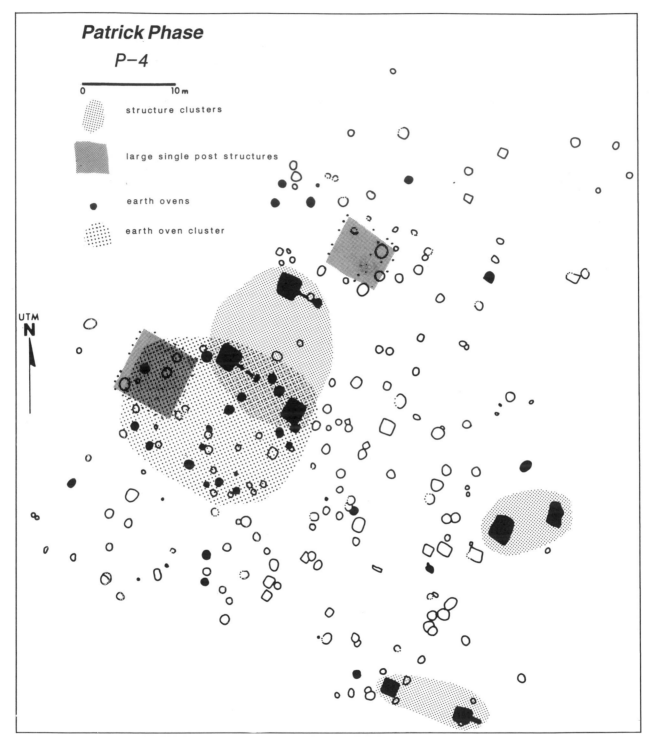

Fig. 23. *The distribution of features for Patrick phase occupation area P-4 at the Range site.*

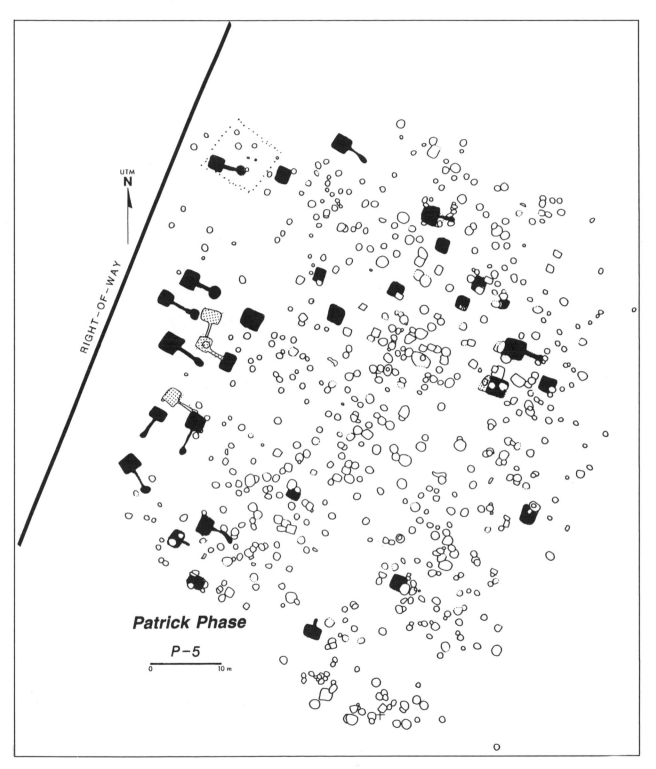

Fig. 24. The distribution of features for Patrick phase occupation area P-5 at the Range site.

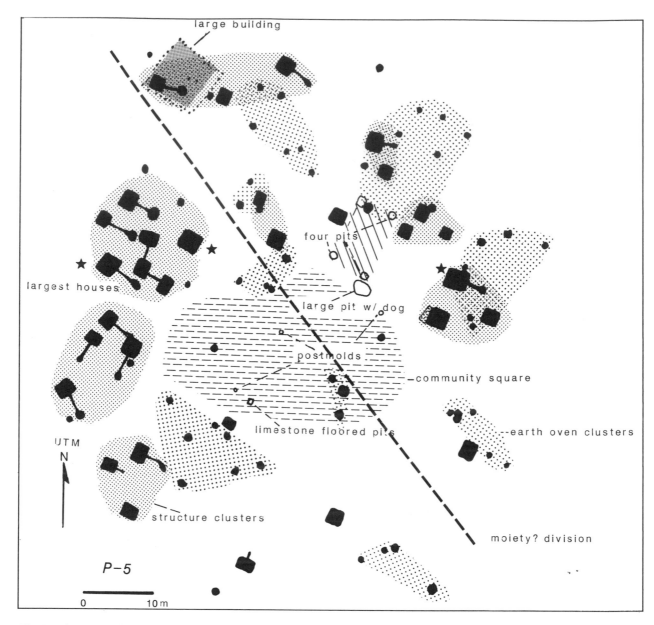

large building

largest houses

four pits

large pit w/ dog

postmolds

community square

limestone floored pits

earth oven clusters

structure clusters

moiety? division

UTM
N

P-5

0   10 m

Fig. 25. The community organization of the P-5 occupation area at the Range site.

and discoidals, suggests that P-4 may have filled a specialized role in a larger settlement system. A large number of earth ovens were concentrated just to the west of the southernmost single-post structure, and these earth ovens contained an unusually high frequency of bowl rims. Taken together, the large single-post structures with nearby earth ovens, and the abundance of pipes and discoidals, supports the possibility that this community's role was centered around activities involving games and the preparation

and serving of food. In certain respects it is strongly reminiscent of nodal communities (Emerson and Milner 1982) of the later Mississippian period.

Three Patrick phase settlements at the Range site were designated villages based on the number of structures and their organizational pattern (P-5 through P-7, Figs. 24–27). One of these village communities (P-6, Fig. 26), which extended to the west, outside of the right-of-way excavation corridor, was only partially excavated.

Composed of 33 basin structures distributed about a community square, the P-5 village (Fig. 24) was the largest of the Late Woodland communities identified at the Range site. A majority of the houses were distributed in a semicircle about the community square, the approximate center of which was marked by a large post mold. These structures were in turn grouped into a number of discrete clusters, interpreted as representing individual household units of nuclear families and perhaps in some instances extended kin units. Other features associated with the P-5 community provide additional insights regarding the spatial patterning and range of activities carried out by the Patrick phase inhabitants of this large village. Earth ovens, for example, were distributed in nine clusters located in close association with the household clusters (Fig. 25). This pattern of clustering was also present for some of the other features associated with the processing and storage of subsistence items.

The semicircle of structure clusters at the P-5 Patrick phase village could be further subdivided, roughly on a north-south axis, into two segments that may reflect a larger moiety division of the community (Fig. 25). Each of these "moiety" segments contained a large basin house that, on the basis of structure size and association, may mark the location of certain "moiety" leaders.

The largest building in the P-5 village community was peripherally located to the northwest along the axis of moiety division (Fig. 25), and may be associated with a particular segment of the community. Unlike the similar structures documented for the P-4 community at the Range site, this large single-post structure did not have any associated concentration of earth ovens, ceramic bowls, or discoidals. Thus, its actual community role is still not clearly understood.

Distributional patterns of limestone-floored pits, pipes, discs, and discoidals also provide clues regarding community patterns of integration. Of the six limestone-floored pits associated with the P-5 village, four formed a rectangle on the north side of the community square (Fig. 25). The fifth pit was situated on the opposite side of the square, while the sixth was located on the northeast margin of the community. The exact purpose of these facilities is unclear, although one functioned as an earth oven and there is some indication that the walls may have been lined

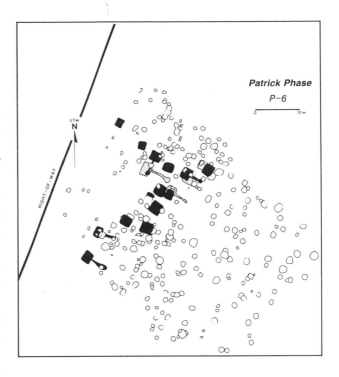

Fig. 26. The distribution of features for Patrick phase occupation area P-6 at the Range site.

with limestone slabs. The location of these pits is suggestive of some form of specialized, perhaps ritual use. The placement of slabs of "white" limestone may represent some form of purification similar to that of spreading white sand or clay over the temple floor or walls, the plaza, or the fireplace of the plaza evident among Southeastern groups (Hudson 1976). The symmetrical arrangement of the four pits is also reminiscent of the four-fold division of the world so well documented for historic Indian groups of the Southeast. The tight rectangular arrangement, however, precludes the formation of the associated cross. The location of this pit cluster on the edge of the community square points in the direction of its use or control by a segment of the community rather than by the community as a corporate unit, in that it is not centrally located. This group, however, is centrally located between the large basin structures. The largest pit in the P-5 village was located just to the south of the cluster of four limestone-floored pits (Fig. 25). It contained little debris, and to a large extent had filled naturally. Located within this pit were the remains of a female dog with several puppies in her birth canal. Nearby features contained discs and pipes that may have been used in ritual activities. In contrast with other Patrick phase communities, discs and pipes comprise a large portion of the artifacts of this settlement, while discoidals are relatively infrequent. The overall spatial distribution of these artifact types provides some additional insight concerning their role within the community (Kelly et al. 1987). Discs were distributed in eight clusters throughout the community; pipes were recovered from seven areas of concentration, which were primarily distributed around the margins of the community square and in one instance within the central area of the square. Discoidals were distributed in four groups around the margin of the square. Although these items were recovered from secondary refuse contexts, it is assumed that they were in general more apt to be deposited in areas where they were last utilized. These distributional patterns would seem to indicate the use of pipes and discoidals in the immediate vicinity of the square, perhaps in association with certain ceremonies. Based on their wider distribution through the community, discs appear to have had a less restricted use context.

The remaining Patrick phase community identified at the Range site, P-7 (Fig. 27), also identified as a village, was considerably smaller than P-5, and exhibited a slightly different configuration. Twelve structures were distributed about an open area, and there was some indication that two occupational episodes may have been involved. There was also a lower density of material, suggesting a more limited period of occupation. While discs were common, discoidals and pipes were not. Like the P-5 village, discs were distributed throughout the settlement.

The considerable range of variation in the Late Woodland Patrick phase utilization of the Range site locale, and the variety of different settlement types represented, allows for some insights concerning the nature of Patrick phase settlement systems within the American Bottom. The different types of settlements (specialized limited activity sites, homesteads, hamlets, villages of varying size and organizational complexity) should represent many if not all of the settlement types present in the region during the Patrick Phase. If the separation and seriation of these settlements is correct (Kelly et al. 1987), this also points to the dynamic and perhaps unstable nature of the settlement system. We see a shift from homestead to

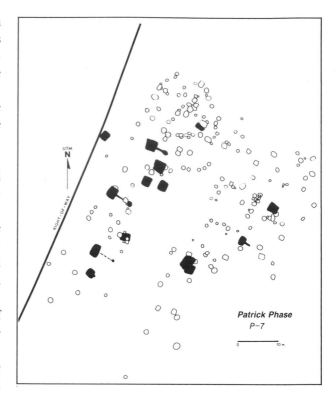

Fig. 27. The distribution of features for Patrick phase occupation area P-7 at the Range site.

hamlet to large multifamily community, presumably the result of fusion of smaller social units. On the other hand, the smaller settlement, P-7, at the end of the sequence, perhaps reflects the fissioning of a larger village-level community. Such a process or cycle of growth and collapse is characteristic of horticultural societies throughout the world (cf. Hames 1983). As such it is also reminiscent of the segmentary lineages of many tribal societies (Service 1971; Sahlins 1961).

There are several important aspects of the internal organization of the Patrick phase occupational episodes at the Range site that should be emphasized. First, the larger village-level communities are distinguished by the presence of multiple structure clusters, which probably represented household units. Further spatial and cultural divisions within the overall community plan perhaps indicate larger social units composed of a number of households. In addition, the community square is an important precursor to those evident in the subsequent Emergent Mississippian period villages at the Range site. Specialized buildings,

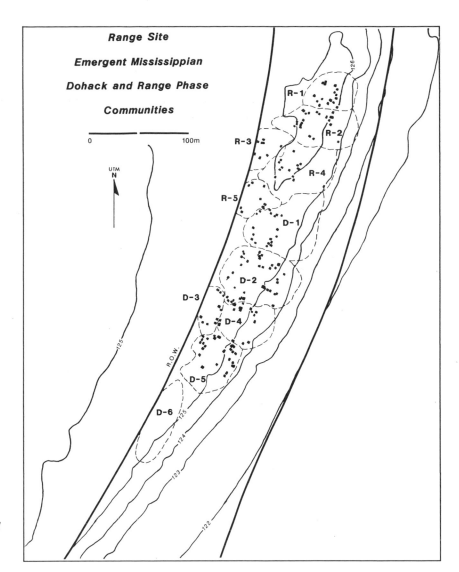

Fig. 28. The distribution of Dohack and Range phase structures and occupation areas at the Range site.

such as the large rectilinear structures and limestone-floored pits, are peripherally positioned in regard to the community and the community square respectively. The lack of strong centrality within the square suggests its sporadic control for and by certain segments of the community. This, perhaps more than any other aspect of these villages, characterizes the unstable nature of such settlements in comparison to later Emergent Mississippian communities at the Range site.

The Dohack Phase (A.D. 750–850)

In contrast to the preceding Patrick phase, which spanned a century (A.D. 600–700) and encompassed nine distinct occupational episodes at the Range site, the Dohack phase at Range is late and covers approximately the last five decades (A.D. 800–850) and a sequence of six Range site communities (Figs. 28–33). Extending over an area of only 1.2 ha, compared to the 2.6 ha occupational area of the Patrick phase at the Range site, the Dohack phase communities also exhibit a number of significant and abrupt changes in technology and subsistence (Kelly et al. 1989a). Because these changes occur so abruptly in the Dohack villages at the Range site, it is likely that there was an occupational hiatus separating the final Patrick community (P-7) and the first Dohack phase com-

Table 9. Summary of Range Site Community Dimensions and Features

Phase	Community	Dimensions (m) NE–SW	NW–SE	Area (ha)	Number of Houses[1]	Total Features
Patrick	P-1			.72	0	25
	P-2			.62	0	22
	P-3	111	68	.75	3	282
	P-4	67	58	.39	7	245
	P-5	88	71	.62	33	740
	P-6	37	25+	.24+	18	306
	P-7	48	38	.35	14	210
	P-8	41	10+		4	29
	P-9	40	16+		2	13
Dohack	D-1	72	51	.38	19	203
	D-2	52	60	.36	35	276
	D-3	49	19+	.09+	10	44
	D-4	45	53	.28	16	134
	D-5	62	47	.30	25	180
	D-6	82	27+		0	12
Range	R-1	37	46	.18	16	112
	R-2	36	78	.22	22	160
	R-3	46	29	.13	7	27
	R-4	66	78	.35	13	259
	R-4a				7	
	R-4b				5	
	R-5	36	38	.14	10	29
George Reeves	G-1	18	40	.07	8	14
	G-2	175	94	1.20	151	464
	G-3	6			2	4
Lindeman	L-1	144	72	.96	132	683
Lindhorst	M-1	46	18	.08	5	27
	M-2	24	10	.02	2	8
	M-3	31	14	.04	2	9
	M-4	17	23	.04	3	11
Stirling	M-1	39	15	.06	5	33
	M-3	5	4	<.01	2	7

[1] Excludes specialized structures

munity (D-2). Abundant evidence for this intervening time period, and a smoother and more gradual transition in material culture and subsistence between the Patrick and Dohack phases, is present at the recently excavated Sponemann site to the north.

Each of the six Dohack phase occupational episodes at the Range site was spatially discrete, and five of the six (D-1 through D-5) were defined on the basis of the distribution of structures and certain central features (Figs. 29–33). Located at the southern end of the site, the major portion of the sixth Dohack phase occupation area (D-6) lay outside of the right-of-way to the west, and was represented in the area excavated only by a number of pit features.

The five Dohack communities, for which relatively complete organizational plans were recovered during excavation (D-1 through D-5), can be characterized as villages of varying size and duration, and can be temporally ordered earliest to latest (D-2, D-5, D-4,

D-3, D-1) on the basis of a number of ceramic attributes. Each of these five Dohack phase villages at the Range site shared a common overall organizational plan, with structures distributed around a community square, the center of which was marked by some form of central feature(s). A pattern of distinct clusters of houses could also be discerned, and three of the communities had several specialized structures. Although pit features were dispersed throughout each community, there was some clustering suggestive of their association with particular structure-cluster household units. Information regarding the number of structures and features and the dimensions of each Dohack phase community at the Range site are presented in Table 9.

In the earliest three Dohack phase villages at the Range site (D-2, D-5, and D-4) (Figs. 29–31), the central features of community squares consisted of a set of four rectangular pits arranged to form a square.

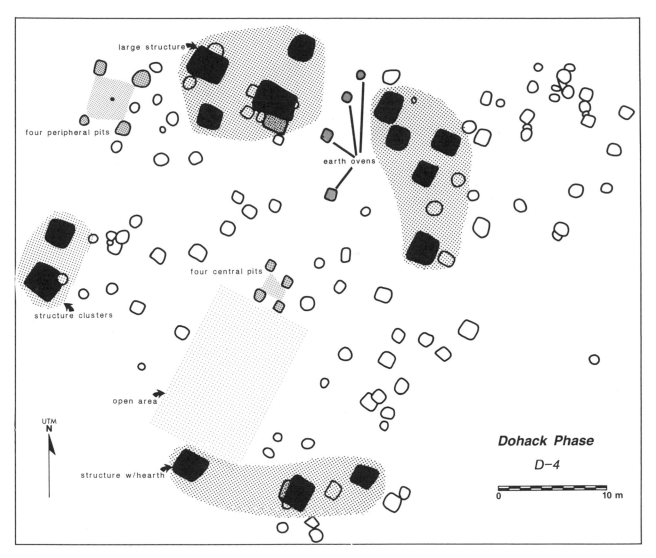

Fig. 29. The distribution of features for Dohack phase occupation area D-4 at the Range site.

The center of this pit configuration was marked by a large post mold in the D-2 and D-5 villages. In the later D-4 village the four central pits are located to the northeast of a structure with an internal hearth. Although other pits were distributed throughout the community square, the area between the four pits and this structure was totally devoid of any features. The area to the northeast of the central pit features was also devoid of features, with the exception of a linear arrangement of four earth ovens that extended into the gap between the two largest house clusters (Fig. 29). The other two house-cluster household units were located at the southern and western corners of the community square. Another set of four pits arranged in a square and centered on a large post mold was located near the largest house in the D-4 village, in the northwest corner of the community (Fig. 29).

The D-2 village was the largest of the Dohack phase communities at the Range site location (Table 9), and exhibits a very complex internal organizational plan. The four central rectangular pits marking the center of the community appear to have undergone a single episode of renewal and rebuilding, as

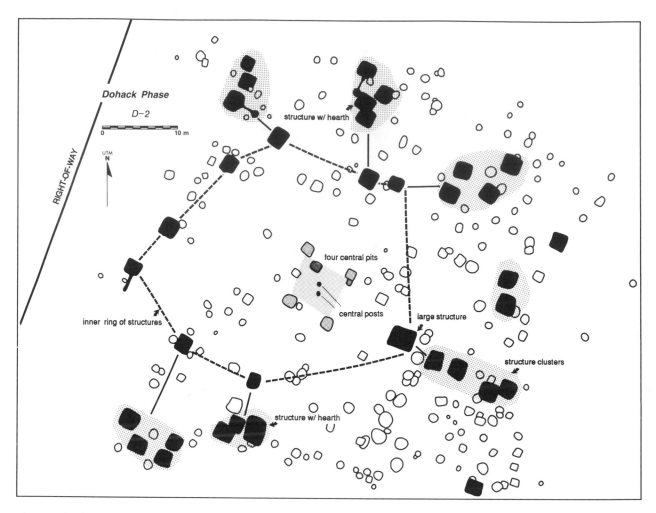

Fig. 30. The distribution of features for Dohack phase occupation area D-2 at the Range site.

reflected by the presence of two central post molds and two pairs of pits at the northern corners of the central complex of pits (Fig. 30). The pits defining the southern corners of this central complex were apparently rebuilt or renewed in the same location. The structures of the D-2 village were distributed in two concentric rings about the four central pits.

The innermost ring is composed of nine structures (Fig. 30). Except for the two paired structures that are located on the northern edge of the community square, these houses are spatially separated from each other. Eight of the structures in this inner ring form a semicircle about the four central pits along the south, west, and north sides of the community square. Located on the east edge of the community square, and aligned with the central pit features, the

final structure of this inner ring is the second largest structure in the village. Although this structure did not have an internal hearth, a large concentration of burned limestone was located on the house floor.

Beyond this inner ring of nine widely spaced structures, seven structure clusters could be discerned, with each containing two to four houses (Fig. 30). Two isolated structures are also present. Six of these structure clusters, each consisting of three or four houses, are in clear spatial association with a structure in the inner ring (Fig. 30). The three inner ring structures along the west side of the community square are located close to the western edge of the excavation area, and their associated outlying structure clusters are quite probably located outside the right-of-way to the west (Fig. 30). The only two

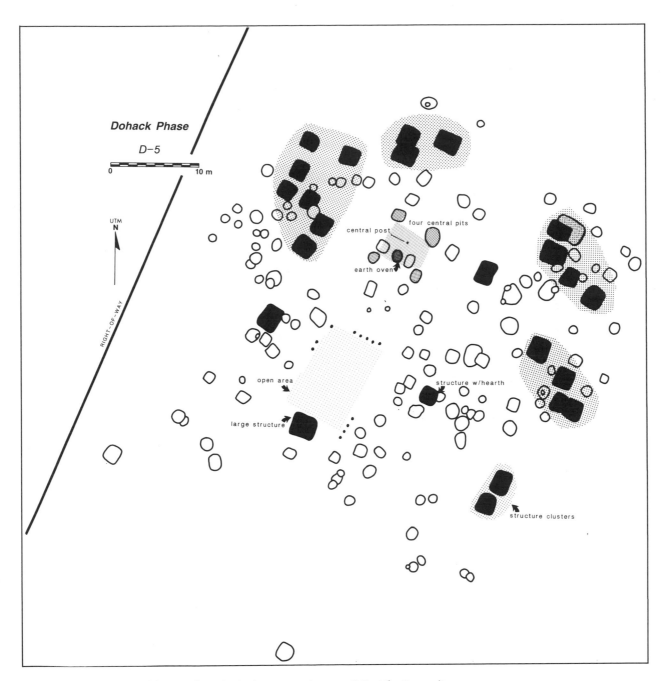

Fig. 31. The distribution of features for Dohack phase occupation area D-5 at the Range site.

structures with internal hearths in this D-2 village community are located across the community square from each other, on its southern and northern sides, with the southern hearth structure the largest house in the village.

In the subsequent, and smaller, D-5 village, the four central pits are actually located north of the square's center, and defined the northeast end of a corridor or community square that was essentially devoid of features. One of the largest structures of the community is located at the opposite (southwestern) end of this feature-free area, which is also defined along portions of its northwest, northeast, and southeast sides by a series of screens (Fig. 31). In addition,

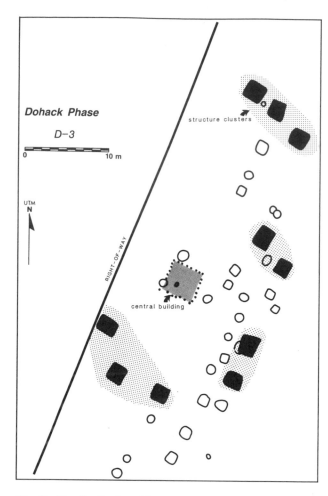

Dohack Phase

D-3

0   10 m

UTM
N

RIGHT-OF-WAY

structure clusters

central building

Fig. 32. The distribution of features for Dohack phase occupation area D-3 at the Range site.

two spatially isolated structures are situated on the northwest and southeast boundaries of this central feature-free area, on a 90 degree axis with, and balancing, the cluster of four pit features and large structure just described (Fig. 31). The remaining structures of this D-5 village were distributed in a semicircular pattern of five household clusters.

The final two villages of the Dohack phase, D-3 and D-1, are virtually identical in terms of community plans (Figs. 32, 33). Unfortunately a portion of the D-3 community extended to the west beyond the right-of-way excavation area, and as a result was not excavated. The approximate center of both of these settlements is marked by the presence of a large, square, single-wall post building approximately 4 m

on a side. The remaining structures are distributed around the central community square. While four clusters of structures are evident in both the D-3 and D-1 villages, the house clusters are relatively widely spaced, with considerable open area between them. In addition, neither of these final two village communities of the Dohack phase contain structures having internal hearths, and they have the smallest average structure size values for any of the Dohack phase occupations at the Range site.

In summary, the overall configuration of the Dohack phase villages described above is strongly reminiscent of the largest of the Patrick phase villages (P-5) (Fig. 25). The structure clusters undoubtedly represent households of varying size. The larger houses may be those of community leaders, while those having internal hearths may have been either residences of ceremonial practitioners or simply structures with specialized functions.

One of the most significant aspects of Dohack phase community organization is the consistent occurrence of central features associated with the village square. The central location of such facilities indicates that it is likely they were shared by all segments of the community, and suggests their village-level corporate status. The overall configuration of Dohack phase communities and their central corporate facilities also appears to embody certain symbolic elements that underlie Mississippian belief systems. The central fourfold pit complexes, often accompanied by a central post, could well reflect the initial emergence of the cross-in-circle concept, incorporated as part of the community plan, with these central community square feature complexes symbolic of the "cross" within a "circle" of houses. The large structures, especially those with hearths, may represent the precursor of temples or elite structures. The presence of fire is symbolic of the sun and its role as the source of life, while the cross-in-circle concept is part of the "fire-sun-deity" complex as defined by Waring (1965). Finally, the two different types of central facilities—below-ground storage pits and above-ground structures—may reflect the duality of the upperworld and underworld, another important theme in southeastern Indian mythology (Hudson 1976; Howard 1968; Waring 1965). Although only dimly reflected in the archaeological

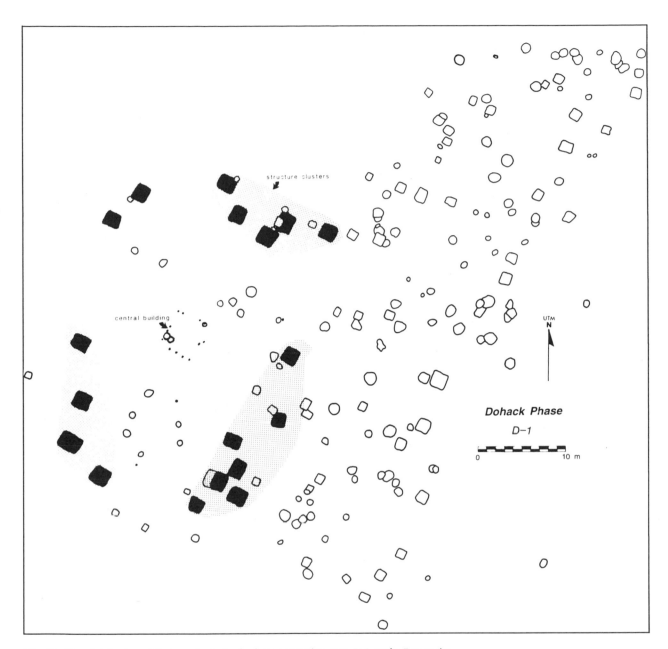

Fig. 33. The distribution of features for Dohack phase occupation area D-1 at the Range site.

record, these newly emerging symbolic elements were likely integrated with concerns and ceremonies centered on agricultural success and fertility, and functioned within a developing belief system that operated to bind and stabilize such agricultural communities.

The Range Phase (A.D. 850–900)

The six communities that can be assigned to the Range phase (Kelly et al. 1989a) extend over an area of approximately 0.8 ha, and are located immediately north of the preceding Dohack phase villages (Fig. 28). One of the five Range phase occupation areas (R-4) contained structures indicative of two commu-

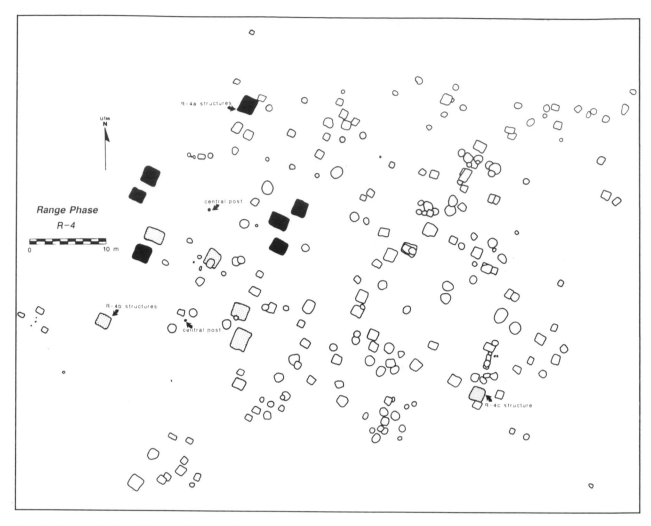

Fig. 34. The distribution of features for Range phase occupation area R-4 at the Range site.

nities, designated R-4a and R-4b. Two of the Range phase communities, R-1 and R-2, are small villages, and in general were similar in plan to the preceding Dohack phase villages. The remaining Range phase settlements (R-3, R-4, R-5) were designated as hamlets on the basis of fewer structures and a simple community plan. In all of the Range phase settlements, structures were distributed about a community square that had some form of central feature(s). Pit features were generally distributed throughout each settlement, with some clustering of pit features near structures.

Although most of the Range phase settlements were spatially separated, it was possible to order them temporally using certain ceramic attributes.

Based on available information, the R-4b hamlet was earliest in the sequence, followed by either R-4a or R-5 hamlets, the R-2 and R-1 villages, and the R-3 hamlet. The final Range phase settlement (R-3) overlaps with a portion of the large George Reeves-Lindeman village, and may represent the initial substratum for this later community.

The seven structures comprising the R-4a hamlet (Fig. 34) are distributed around a square having a central post. Six of the structures form two groups of three on opposite sides of the central square, while the seventh is isolated at the north end of the central square. The structures of the R-4b hamlet are distributed in a semicircle around three sides of a central square that has a small central post (Fig. 34). To the

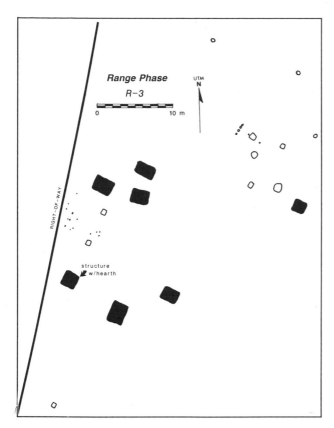

Fig. 35. The distribution of features for Range phase occupation area R-3 at the Range site.

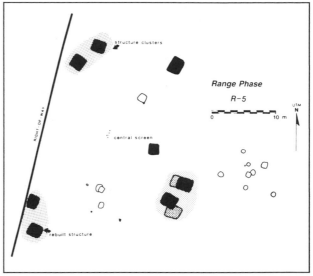

Fig. 36. The distribution of features for Range phase occupation area R-5 at the Range site.

east of these two hamlets an isolated structure with unknown community affiliation was designated R-4c. The other two Range phase hamlets (R-3, R-5) are located along the backslope of the ridge. The R-3 hamlet consists of two sets of three structures located at opposite ends of an open area containing two rectangular pits and numerous post molds. A seventh isolated structure is located to the east of the main group of six houses (Fig. 35). One of the structures in the southern house cluster contained a small internal hearth. The R-5 hamlet consists of four spatially distinct house clusters arranged about a central square. The approximate center of this square is marked by a short screen of four post molds (Fig. 36). An isolated structure impinged on the square's eastern edge. One of the two structures in the southwestern cluster of houses had been rebuilt twice, with one of these rebuilding episodes representing the largest structure in the community.

In the largest Range phase community, the R-2 vil-

lage, structures are arranged around three sides of a large community square. The approximate center of this square is marked by three large post molds. The 20 structures of the R-2 village form five distinct clusters (Fig. 37), with a single isolated structure, which had been burned, designated as R-2b. Within one of the structure clusters, houses are aligned in two parallel rows. Extending to the east from this cluster of aligned structures into the community square is an area completely devoid of features. The largest structure in the R-2 village community is located within one of the northern three structure clusters and at the apex of the arc of structures comprising the R-2 village. It had been rebuilt three times and contained several internal pit hearths. The initial construction phase of this structure was relatively small, and it had burned.

The small R-1 village (Fig. 38) is the next to final occupational episode of the Range phase. The overall plan of the settlement involves structures arranged in a semicircle about a community square. On the open or opposite side of the central square are three tightly grouped structures. Four large rectangular pits are located at the center of the community square, arranged in a square pattern about a large post mold. Each of the four central pits had been excavated twice, with the pit volume decreasing on each occa-

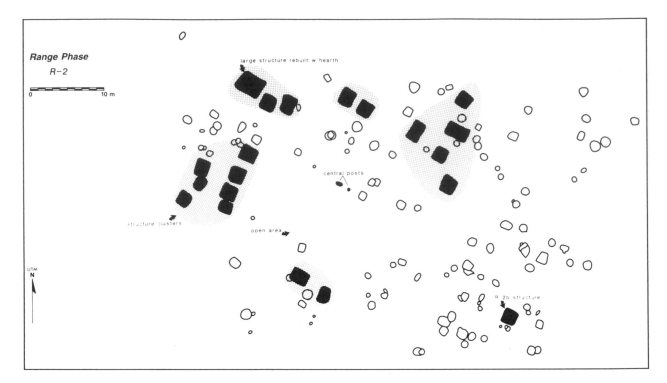

Fig. 37. The distribution of features for Range phase occupation area R-2 at the Range site.

sion. The central post had also been replaced once. Several smaller pits are also grouped within this central pit complex, along with a second large post (Fig. 38). These smaller pit features may have served as the location for log mortars. With the exception of the tightly clustered set of three structures to the northwest of the central square, the individual houses of this R-1 village form a continuous, although slightly irregular, distribution. The largest house within the R-1 village is situated at the apex of this semicircle. It had been rebuilt on one occasion, and contained two small interior pit hearths. A small earth oven was located adjacent to this building.

In addition to the four central pits located in the community square of the R-1 village, a second cluster of four rectangular pits is located just to the east of the R-1 semicircle of structures. Two small post molds may mark the center of this feature cluster. A large single-post building is located just to the south of this second cluster of four pits, and it may have been associated with them.

In comparing the Range phase communities at the Range site with the preceding communities of the

Dohack phase, a number of significant changes warrant discussion. Hamlets appear again during the Range phase and may reflect a continuation of the pattern of occasional community fissioning that was suggested during the Patrick phase.

Within the R-2 village, and to a certain extent in the R-1 village, clustering of structures suggestive of extended family households continues, although there is a more linear pattern in their distribution. Communities also continue to be organized around central open areas that contain central feature complexes. The dominant central feature complex of the Dohack phase, consisting of four rectangular pits surrounding a post, continues into the Range phase, and is joined by a new and less complex central feature—a single post. Although large basin houses occur occasionally in the earlier communities of the Dohack phase, they become a dominant element in the village community plans of the Range phase. These large structures, invariably centrally or apically situated within the community, also contain internal pit hearths and exhibit evidence of rebuilding. While all of these separate elements (large structures, internal hearths, evidence of rebuild-

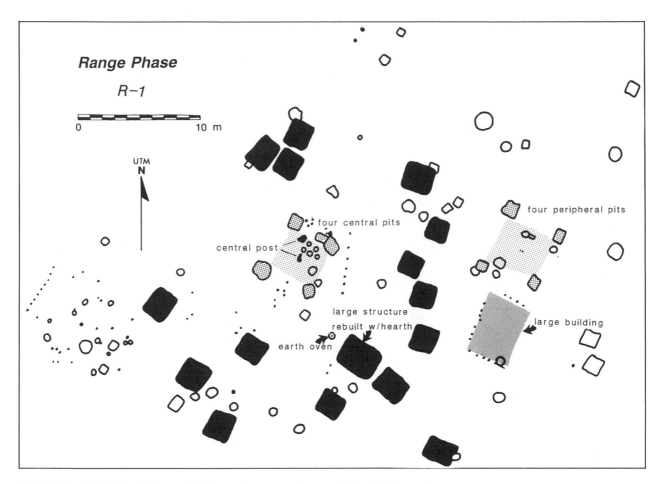

Fig. 38. The distribution of features for Range phase occupation area R-1 at the Range site.

ing, central or apical location) are represented in the Dohack phase communities, they do not occur all together in a single context. The coalescing of these elements within Range phase communities may reflect the consolidation of political authority and the sanctification of this authority through the presence of fire and the rebuilding or renewal of these structures. The evidence for the reexcavation of the four central pits of the R-1 village may also reflect ritual, busklike renewal. If this is the case, the large focal structures and central pit features might represent a significant forerunner of the plaza-platform mound configuration associated with Mississippian towns.

The George Reeves Phase (A.D. 900–950)

The communities of the George Reeves phase (Kelly et al. 1989b) extend over a much larger area (1.7 ha)

of the Range site than those of the preceding Range phase, forming a continuous distribution of structures and associated pit features (Fig. 39). The earliest George Reeves phase occupational episodes at the Range site consist of a smaller homestead and hamlet settlements. A pair of structures (G-3) 27 m south of the large G-2 village can be best characterized as a farmstead. To the north of the main occupation areas, seven structures form a hamlet (G-1) similar to the settlements at the George Reeves (McElrath and Finney 1987) and Westpark sites. The two sets of structures to the west of the main occupation areas (G-2a, G-2b) are difficult to interpret. It is possible that they are isolated homesteads similar to the G-3 homestead to the south. It is more likely, however, that they are outliers of the larger G-2 village.

Within the main settlement area of the George Reeves phase (G-2) (Fig. 40), structures are organized

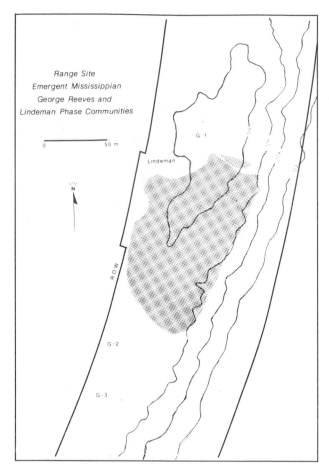

Fig. 39. The location of George Reeves and Lindeman phase occupations at the Range site.

around a series of courtyards, and are often arranged in linear patterns or rows. Each courtyard and its associated structures received a separate designation (e.g., G-2c). Although the main occupation area is considered as a single community here, there is undoubtedly some degree of time depth, and based on evidence of structure rebuilding and superposition along with certain distributional patterns, there were two episodes of settlement reorganization. This community persisted into the subsequent Lindeman phase.

The core of the George Reeves phase village was restricted to the southern two-thirds (G-2e to G-2k) of the main occupation area (Fig. 40). At the center of this core area a community plaza (G-2h) contained both a large (42 sq m) single-post building and a set of four large rectangular pits arranged in a square pattern around a central post at opposing ends of the plaza. This configuration of four pits would twice experience renewal/replacement; once during the George Reeves phase and once during the subsequent Lindeman phase of this main occupation area. The large building located at the northwest end of the community plaza also appears to have been rebuilt. Rows of structures border this central plaza on three sides, with the irregular line of structures behind the large single-post plaza structure, perhaps dating somewhat later within the George Reeves sequence. Another large 41 sq m square structure was located just southwest of the main plaza. It may have been used by those persons in this area of the village.

Moving outward from this central plaza, additional smaller courtyards bordered by structures are placed in a relatively symmetrical pattern. To the southwest of the central plaza, and paralleling it, are two small courtyards (G-2i, 2j). A third courtyard (G-2k) is contiguous to the southwest of these two. It is marked by a central post (Fig. 40). To the northeast of the central community plaza, two more courtyards (G-2f, 2g) parallel it, with each having the quadripartite pit arrangement. A third courtyard (G-2e) is contiguous to the northeast.

To the northeast of the main village area or core is the remainder of the village. It consists of a secondary plaza or courtyard (G-2d) that is contiguous on the northeast with the courtyard, G-2e (Fig. 39). A large, deep, limestone-floored pit is centrally located within this secondary plaza. The largest basin structures in the village demarcate the southwest corner of this plaza. Another large basin structure situated on the northeast edge of this plaza also fronts on the courtyard, G-2c, to the northeast. This courtyard is the northernmost part of the village and consists of four structure clusters distributed about this area, whose center was marked by the presence of a large post. Apparently the courtyard was shifted to the east and this post was removed and replaced by another post that marked the new center of this courtyard. Because there was little evidence to indicate temporal priority between this portion (G-2c and 2d) and the main area of the village, these are interpreted as contemporary units, perhaps representing two different social groups. The inhabitants of G-2c and G-2d were distantly related to the remainder of the community's inhabitants and were linked to them through those residing in the area about G-2e.

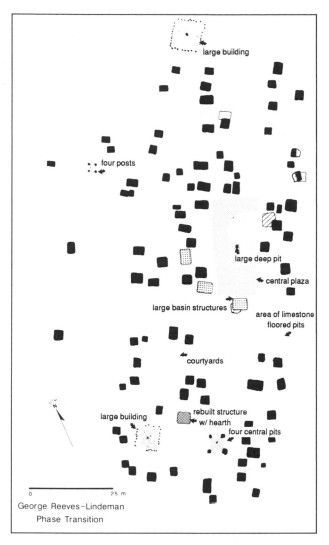

George Reeves–Lindeman
Phase Transition

Fig. 41. The George Reeves-Lindeman phase transition at the Range site.

Located to the north of the area G-2c was a large (31 sq m) square building that was enlarged to 42 sq m later during this phase and subsequently rebuilt during the Lindeman phase. It is undoubtedly similar to the large, square structure at the south end of the village in its overall size, peripheral location, and presumed specialized use by certain segments of the community.

This community pattern marks a dramatic break with earlier occupational episodes at the Range site in that it represents the amalgamation of a number of different kinship groups at a single location. More importantly, the overall configuration of the commu-

nity indicates a strong central focus. The central plaza, its attendant structures and internal features, forms a strong community core. This central plaza is in turn symmetrically flanked by a series of additional courtyards, each with its associated houses. I would propose that this community pattern reflects the spatial distribution of a series of ranked social groups, and represents the best evidence currently available for the initial emergence by A.D. 900–950 of a ranked form of sociopolitical organization in the American Bottom region. Although no mound construction is present, the large rectangular structure at the one end of the central courtyard is perhaps the chief's house. The four pits and central post located at the opposite end of the community plaza undoubtedly played the same ceremonial and symbolic roles as described for them earlier in this chapter. The northernmost and secondary plaza and courtyard are interpreted as a separate and subordinate social group. If the aforementioned ranking relates in any manner to kin relations, the former inhabitants are distantly related to those in the main village through the inhabitants of the northern courtyard G-2e.

The George Reeves-Lindeman Phase Transition

By A.D. 950, and the end of the George Reeves phase, the community organization of the G-2 village at the Range site changes, and these changes persist into the following Lindeman phase. There is a northward shift of the community as new structures are constructed to the north and the houses to the south of the central plaza are abandoned. The former plaza appears to have been split into two courtyards with a rectangular basin structure and internal hearth placed on the north edge equidistant from the large square building to the southwest and the quadripartite pit arrangement to the southeast. This configuration appears to have persisted into the initial part of the Lindeman phase with the basin house rebuilt on several occasions (Fig. 41). The large secondary plaza (G-2d) to the northeast of the central plaza (G-2h) of the G-2 village now occupies the center of the village (Fig. 41). The center of this plaza (G-2d) is marked by a large (2.7 cu m), deep rectangular pit. A lens of sand was placed just above the floor and may represent ritual purification. A pair of smaller pits with lime-

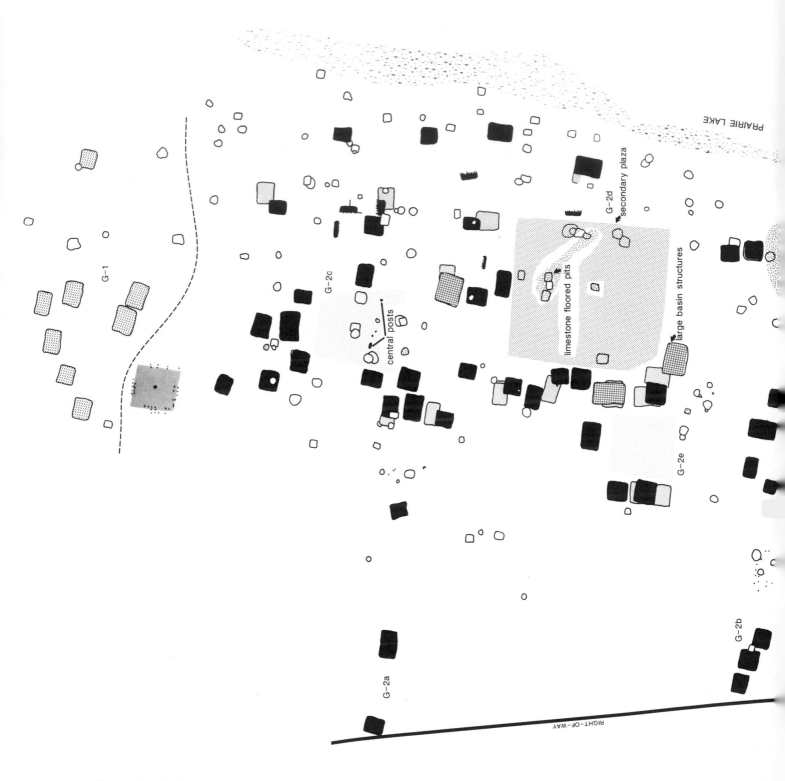

Fig. 40. The distribution of George Reeves phase occupation and features at the Range site.

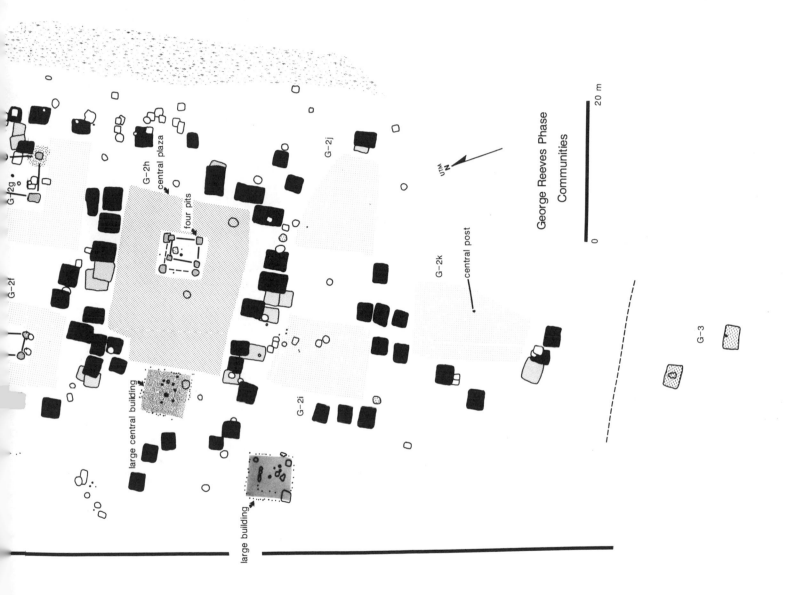

George Reeves Phase
Communities

G-2g
G-2h
central plaza
four pits
G-2f
G-2i
G-2j
G-2k
central post
large central building
large building
G-3

UTM N

0   20 m

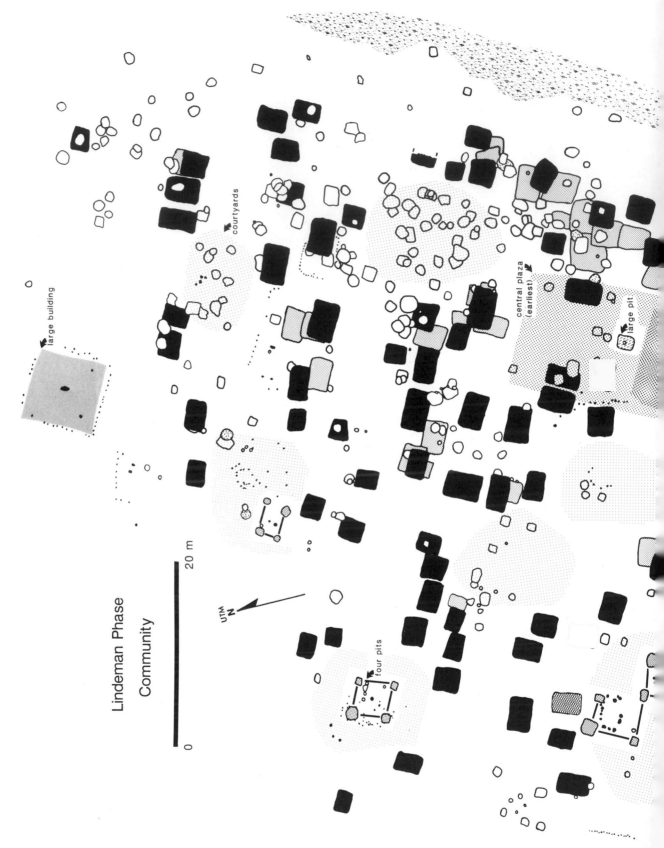

Fig. 42. The distribution of Lindeman phase features at the Range site.

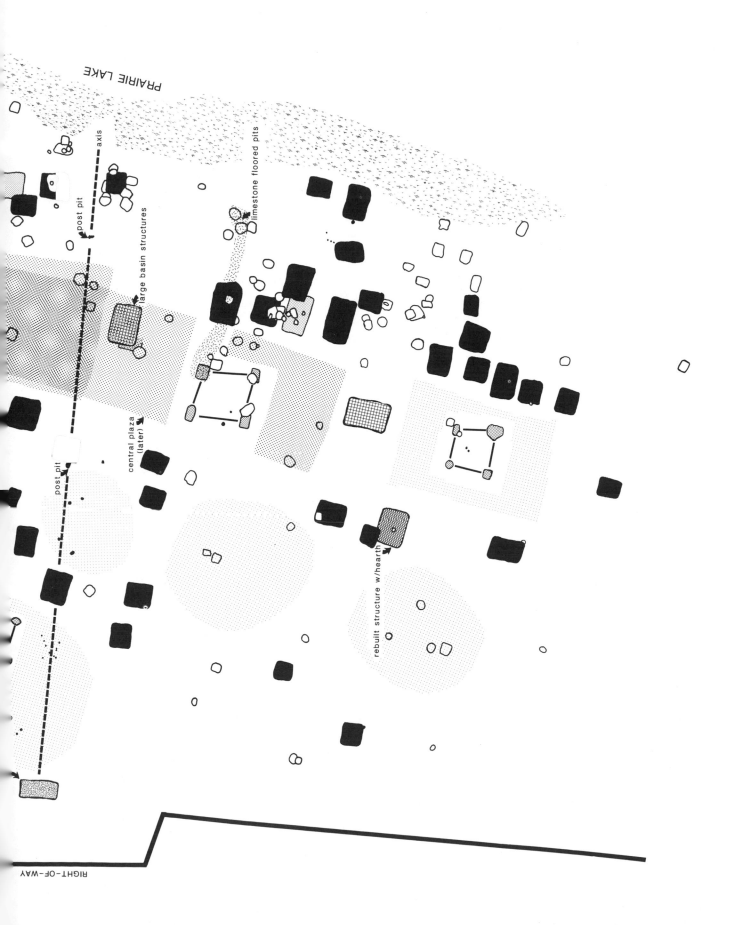

PRAIRIE LAKE

post pit

axis

large basin structures

limestone floored pits

central plaza (later)

post pit

rebuilt structure w/hearth

stone floors are located to the northeast of this central feature, and three more limestone-floored pits are located to the east of it. A large single-post basin structure is constructed at the south end of this courtyard, and another eight limestone pits are clustered to the south of this central structure. The use of limestone-floored pits in this area began earlier in the George Reeves phase and persisted into the Lindeman phase. A number of other houses are built along the northwest edge of the central area, and an additional series of courtyards with attendant structures are established to the northwest and northeast of the new central plaza. A large post appears to have marked the center of the northeast portion of the community (Fig. 41). The additional structures to the northwest of the main community (G-2a, G-2b) may have been part of the community reorganization that took place at this time.

Like the earlier G-2 village, the various courtyards of the new community configuration represent a number of different social groups. The central courtyard or plaza, with its larger bordering structures, undoubtedly represents the ranking lineage. In marked contrast to the earlier George Reeves and Range communities, however, the expected symbolic elements are not as obvious and are more difficult to interpret.

The Lindeman Phase (A.D. 950–1000)

The community plan described above for the end of the George Reeves phase persists into the early part of the Lindeman phase, followed by a number of dramatic changes in the existing community plan (Kelly et al. 1989b). The village continues to expand to the west, with new house construction concentrated in the northwest quadrant of the village, as structures in the southeast quadrant are abandoned. The overall configuration of the village was one of a semicircle of houses facing the lake (Fig. 42). The central courtyard or plaza had shifted slightly to the southwest, along with the largest basin structure in the community. Directly opposite this large central structure was the quadripartite arrangement of four pits. Courtyards with associated houses bordered this central structure to the northwest and southwest. Further north three other courtyards opened on the central plaza (Fig. 42), and additional courtyards were dispersed to the

northwest and northeast. In addition, two post pits placed along the northwest and southeast sides of the central plaza formed an axis that divides the community into nearly equal halves. When the axis formed by these two posts is extended to the west, it crosses the center point of the most unusual structure of the Lindeman phase community.

Rectangular in form and having the lowest width: length ratio (0.52) of any structure in the community, this building was symmetrically positioned at the western apex of the community (Fig. 42). The structure's floor was highest in the center and sloped markedly toward a series of irregular, broad, shallow wall trenches. Small posts were aligned closely in these "shallow trenches," but with substantial (.80–1.0 m) gaps separating them into a series of walls. This structure also yielded a high frequency of Monks Mound Red ceramics, most notably bowls. It also contained carbonized fragments of bald cypress wood (Parker 1989). In addition to its central location in respect to the entire community, this structure also faced an arc of structures to the east. The courtyard associated with this arc of structures contained four pits arranged about a post, with this pit and post feature complex offset to the northeast of the center of the courtyard. Another set of three pits, also organized around a post, were located just to the northwest of the first pit and post feature complex, with the two feature complexes perhaps sharing a pit (Fig. 42). The central post in the second pit and post feature complex was also part of an oval pattern of small pits or large post molds located within the surrounding cluster of pits. This oval post/pit pattern may represent a structure, or alternatively, may have been the rest for wooden mortars used in the "ceremonial" processing of corn. A basin structure, which had been rebuilt twice and contained a possible hearth, was located immediately to the northeast of this second pit and post feature complex.

It is difficult to establish whether or not this west-centrally located courtyard and the unusual structure associated with it was contemporaneous with the central plaza to the east. Based on ceramic assemblages, the central plaza appears initially to predate the west-central courtyard, with both undoubtedly contemporary at some point.

The four pit and central-post feature complex was also present in two other community courtyards,

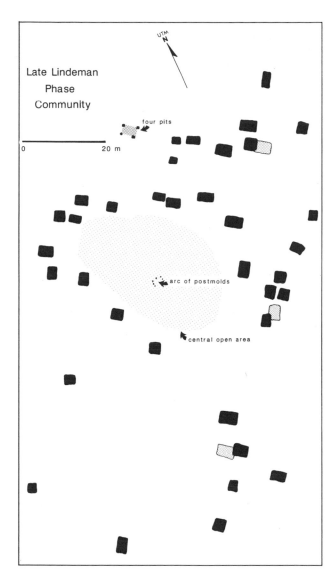

Late Lindeman
Phase
Community

four pits

0   20 m

arc of postmolds

central open area

Fig. 43. The late Lindeman phase occupation of the Range site.

lage. Because of their frequency and lack of evidence of any rebuilding within a fairly short period of time (the Lindeman phase spans only 50 years), they do not appear to have been "operational" for any extended period of time. Perhaps they fulfilled some dedicatory function, or reflected the assigned role of a particular social group in certain ceremonies. It is also possible that the individual pit and post elements of these feature complexes were not constructed simultaneously, but individually over a period of years. It would be difficult to substantiate such speculations without considerably more information from similar communities in the American Bottom.

Later in the Lindeman phase, this evolving community decreased considerably in size, with corresponding changes in overall organization. A majority of the structures were located in the northern half of the community, while structures to the south were primarily situated along the lake edge, and may represent a separate settlement. The northern group of structures form an arc open to the south, with the center of the central open area marked by a small arc of post molds, which may be part of a circular structure. To the east of this arc of structures bordering the open courtyard, a linear pattern of structures followed the lake edge, with another group of structures occurring to the northeast (Fig. 43). By this time the earlier large village, and its distinct organization, had dissolved. Presumably the former inhabitants and descendants of the large Lindeman phase village had been incorporated within the Pulcher mound center community, or established a new settlement at another location.

The Lindhorst (A.D. 1000–1050) and Stirling (A.D. 1050–1150) Phases

For the Early Mississippian period Lindhorst and Stirling phases, four distinct habitation areas (M-1, M-2, M-3, M-4) and at least one possible mortuary area can be identified at the Range site. While each of these Early Mississippian period habitation areas contains evidence of occupation during the Lindhorst phase, only two (M-1, M-3) continued to be inhabited into the early part of the Stirling phase. Each of these Lindhorst and Stirling phase occupational episodes includes several households that

both peripherally placed along the northwest margins of the village. While the symbolic meaning of the pits is assumed to have remained unchanged, their role within the community has changed. No longer are they community facilities, even though they still retain their central role in regard to particular community segments. They still play a corporate role, but not for the entire community. Based on ceramic indicators, it appears that these pit and post feature clusters were not in existence at the same time, but were constructed over the course of occupation of the vil-

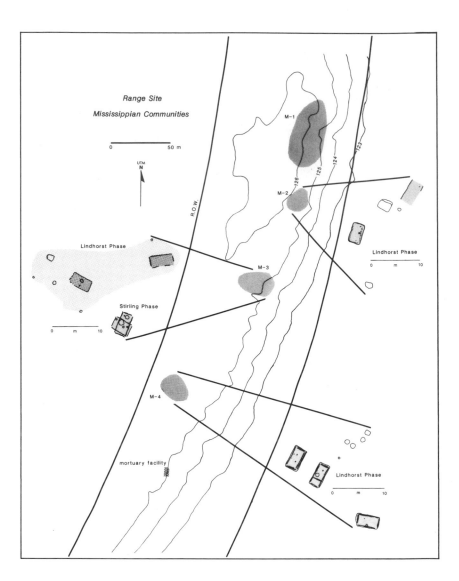

Fig. 44. Early Mississippian occupation areas at the Range site.

could be characterized as a farmstead (Fig. 44).

In addition, the northernmost habitation area of the Early Mississippian occupation of the Range site (M-1) included a somewhat unusual and specialized set of features (Fig. 45). Three circular single-post basin structures with hearths may well have been sweat lodges. A small rectangular wall-trench structure also had an internal hearth. A large rectangular wall-trench structure, which had been burned, was located nearby. It was found to contain a cylindrical hearth and an internal storage pit with a limestone slab-lined floor. A second, substantially larger square single-post structure with a central post pit was also present (Fig. 45). The exact purpose of the rectangular structures, and their relationship to the circular sweat lodges, remains somewhat problematical.

Mehrer (1982) identified two occupational components for the Early Mississippian period, with occupation A equivalent to the Lindhorst phase and occupation B the Stirling phase. He assigned some of the specialized M-1 area structures to the Lindhorst occupation component, and others to the following Stirling phase component. Alternatively, one could propose that based on the concentrated location of these M-1 area specialized structures between the Stirling phase features, they should all be assigned to the Stirling phase occupation of the site. I favor a third temporal placement of the specialized M-1 component, however, as a discrete occupational episode falling between the Lindhorst and Stirling phase farmstead

Fig. 45. The distribution of M-1 phase features at the Range site.

the later Stirling phase features. Regardless of their exact temporal placement, these structures represent a nodal community. Such settlements served as important integrative centers for scattered farmstead communities. It is certainly possible that the remaining early Mississippian farmsteads at the Range locality were contemporary with this specialized M-1 area cluster of nodal community structures.

CHANGING COMMUNITY PLANS AND CULTURAL PROCESS

The information base available to archaeologists interested in studying prehistoric cultural change is almost always limited to temporally and spatially isolated data sets of varying kinds that are relatively small and quite limited in terms of research potential. Often elaborate sampling schemes will be employed to argue for the representative nature of such scattered and disparate pieces of a cultural process puzzle. Rarely is an archaeologist presented with an information base such as that uncovered at the Range site—where a critically important 500-year span of cultural evolution can be viewed at the community level, through the analysis of a temporal sequence of over 28, essentially complete, community plans. Despite the complex overlapping of occupational episodes over a period of 500 years at the Range site, and the resulting difficulties of recognizing discrete communities within the confusion of five centuries of prehistoric construction of features, it was possible to identify and temporally order a series of distinct occupational episodes of varying size and complexity. Through the straightforward, if at times overwhelming, process of establishing the temporal placement of over 5,000 individual features based on their contents, it was possible to slowly reconstruct, piece by piece, the size, composition, and overall organization of a long sequence of communities at a particular archaeological locality.

Once these individual communities were defined in time and space, their organizational aspects and material culture assemblages provided a rich and remarkably complete information base for the analysis and interpretation of cultural change, and the Mississippian emergence, at the locality or community level.

While it is of course essential to address the question of Mississippian emergence at a larger, regional scale of analysis, which will be attempted in the following

settlements. The ceramic assemblages recovered from these specialized M-1 area structures place them late in the Lindhorst phase, temporally intermediate between the earlier Lindhorst occupational episodes and chapter, the careful and detailed analysis of change at the community level holds the promise of significantly illuminating critical aspects of this complex evolutionary process.

The Range site locality, which was occupied almost continually over the 500-year span of interest here, provided easy access to a variety of different environmental zones, with the adjacent oxbow lake providing an essential and inexhaustible source of meat protein. Other resources such as wood and lithic raw materials were located nearby in the uplands to the east, and were easily accessible through a small valley in the limestone bluffs on the opposite side of Prairie Lake. The soils of the site locality were fertile and well drained, and tillable soil areas of other nearby Prairie Lake point bar ridges were also easily accessible to the inhabitants of the Late Woodland and Emergent Mississippian communities of the Range site.

The most spatially extensive utilization of the Range site locality occurred during the Late Woodland Patrick phase (A.D. 600–800). This was also the period of most intensive utilization of the site, at least in terms of the high ratio of pits to structures. The nine Patrick phase occupation areas range in size and complexity from small specialized settlements through homesteads, hamlets, and villages of varying size and organizational complexity. This range of settlement types and their temporal ordering appears to reflect the cycle of settlement fusion and fission often found in locationally unstable food production societies. While a wide range of nondomesticated food items were available and procured locally, the cultivation of a variety of crops was an important element in their subsistence strategy, which presumably involved a system of shifting cultivation. Seed crops such as goosefoot (Chenopodium berlandieri), erect knotweed (Polygonum erectum), maygrass (Phalaris caroliniana), little barley (Hordeum pusillum), and sunflower (Helianthus annuus) were grown along with tobacco (Nicotiana). If present, maize was just another starchy seed crop of limited dietary importance. Based on the spatial clustering of structures and various types of pit features, household groups formed the basic subsistence unit in Patrick phase communities, with each household largely self sufficient and responsible for processing its own food. This pattern of economic self sufficiency at the household level continues through the Emergent Mississippian and Mississippian period communities at the Range site locality.

The large P-5 Patrick phase village (Fig. 25) contains several organizational elements that are important precursors for the subsequent Emergent Mississippian communities. The overall P-5 village plan consists of structure clusters distributed about a community square having a large post as a central feature. The P-5 village structure clusters reflect extended family household units. The overall distribution of these structure clusters suggests a higher level organizational duality within the village. The two largest basin structures are interpreted as representing the houses of the leaders of the two community segments. A number of other specialized facilities are also present in the community. These include a rectangular arrangement of four pits with limestone slab floors on the edge of the community square, and a large square building on the periphery of the community. The four pits are probably involved in ceremonies associated with the community square, while the peripherally located structure was probably restricted in use to certain segments of the community.

The transition from the Late Woodland into the Emergent Mississippian occupation of the Range site locality is marked by a number of significant subsistence and technological changes. Most notably, maize abruptly occurs in abundance in a large number of contexts. Approximately 72 percent of the initial Emergent Mississippian Dohack phase features contain maize. Many of the other technological changes occurring at this time are likely associated, to varying degrees, with the abruptly more important role of maize in the economy. Limestone becomes the tempering agent of choice. Bowls increase in frequency, and jar forms carry more constricted necks and orifices. There is a marked decrease in the ratio of pits to structures, and an increase in the number of pits with rectilinear orifices. Earth ovens become far less frequent. There is also a decrease in the floor area of structures, along with the virtual disappearance of keyhole structures. The density of structures per community increases, as more structures are constructed within a smaller area.

A number of important organizational elements of the preceding Patrick phase communities continue to be present in the five initial Dohack phase settlements that can be completely defined. Structure clusters continue to be distributed about a central area or community square. For the first time, however, the central area contains a central feature complex consisting of either a building or a set of four pits arranged in a square pattern. These community square central feature complexes are interpreted as corporate facilities that embody certain symbolic elements associated with the cross-and-circle, and therefore associated with agricultural fertility and ceremonies comparable to the historic busk. A distinct class of specialized structures also appears during the Dohack phase, identified both by size and the presence of internal hearths. The largest structure of the D-2 village is centrally located, while those D-2 structures having internal hearths are also centrally positioned (Fig. 30). This organizational pattern of specialized structures is interpreted as representing the ritual position of the inhabitants, as well as reflecting the overall organization of the village about a single individual. The Dohack communities having central structures (D-1 and D-3, Figs. 32, 33) lack the organizational elements discussed above. They fall late within the Dohack sequence and may represent another social division within the Prairie Lake locale.

While the Patrick to Dohack transition was marked by a number of abrupt and dramatic changes in community organization, Dohack villages differ from those of the subsequent Range phase in degree more than in kind. For example, there is an increase in jars with plain necks, a slight decrease in structure size, and an increase in pits with rectangular orifices. The appearance of stumpware, and the marked increase in bowls, particularly the large shallow variety, may indicate shifts in the methods of processing maize. While small villages similar to those of the Dohack phase occur at the Range locality during the Range phase, they are smaller, and hamlet level communities are also present. The two Range phase villages (R-1, R-2) present a consistent pattern of community organization. Again, structures are organized about a community square having central feature complexes. In contrast with the pattern of distinct structure clusters in Dohack and Patrick phase villages, Range phase structures reflect a relaxation of this clustering tendency, and a trend toward a linear configuration. The most important change involves the appearance of a centrally positioned structure in both Range phase villages (R-1, R-2). These apically positioned structures are the largest in the villages, and show evidence of having been reconstructed on several occasions. They also contain hearths, and at least one example of burning. These structures represent the coalescence of several disparate elements evi-

dent among the preceding Dohack communities. The position of community leader is now spatially united with certain ceremonies or rituals, which is not uncommon for ranked societies (Service 1971:162). The remaining structures of these Range phase villages are dispersed equally outward from this central facility, and undoubtedly their distance to this structure is indicative of social distance from the central individual in the community. In many respects the large structure associated with fire and rebuilding/renewal is a forerunner of the Mississippian platform mound.

In the subsequent George Reeves phase communities of the Range site locality, ceramics with plain surfaces predominate, and red-filming first appears on ceramics. Structures increase in size and the ratio of pits to structures is quite low. And while the George Reeves communities are far more extensive than those of earlier phases, there is also an increase in the level of density of structures, as villages become more tightly organized (Fig. 40). The large G-2 village was clearly evolving and being reformed as it crept northward over a considerable period of time. The G-2 community is of considerable importance in that it represents the initial appearance of a nucleated and tightly organized village community, which persisted into the following Lindeman phase. Organized around a central plaza containing a large square structure situated opposite a set of four pits, the community plan incorporated structures organized in linear patterns around a symmetrical plan of widely spaced secondary courtyards, some of which were marked by central post features or the quadripartite pit arrangements. To the north were a secondary plaza and courtyard, which probably represented another social segment that ultimately rises as the dominant portion of the village. This large village, with a tightly controlled overall settlement plan, reflects the nucleation of several social groups into a single community. The central plaza with its opposing central facilities represents the coalescence of two similar but different symbols. One is the above-ground (upperworld) building; the other the below-ground (underworld) pits. Thus, there is not only a coming together of different social groups but also those dual components of society necessary to bind them together. The large central structure may be the house of the community leader. The spatial distribution of the other structures and associated small courtyards may well reflect the relative social position of the inhabitants in regard to the centrally placed community leader. This overall community plan constitutes, in my opinion, clear-cut evidence of ranking within Emergent Mississippian society.

Toward the end of the George Reeves phase, and extending into the initial part of the Lindeman phase, this large nucleated village undergoes reorganization (Fig. 41). The overall community plan of a central plaza surrounded by a symmetrical pattern of smaller satellite courtyards persists, but with different constituent elements and a northward creep that represents the domination of this portion of the village. The central plaza is relocated to the northeast, and a new set of opposing central courtyard feature complexes is constructed, with the axis of alignment of the large basin structure and an associated large rectangular pit shifting 90 degrees. Several other large basin structures are constructed around this new central courtyard, as the surrounding village expands to the west and north. By the beginning of the Lindeman phase the village forms a wide semicircle bordering Prairie lake, and the central courtyard, with its opposing structure and a four pit complex, shifts to the south (Fig. 42).

At the same time, other ceremonial elements are added to the Lindeman phase community plan. At some point, two posts are placed on either side of this central courtyard, in alignment with an unusual rectangular structure positioned at the apex of the village. A large courtyard located to the northeast of this structure, and bordered by an arc of structures, contains a square set of four pits just to the east of its center point. Another group of adjacent pits incorporate the northwest pit of the first pattern of four to form a second rectangular set. This associated set of pit features and specialized structure may have formed the central community features for the village late in its history, when most of the occupation had shifted to the northeast. Two other courtyards located further to the north also contain square sets of four pits. These are peripheral courtyards and may very well fall later in time than those to the south, based on associated ceramic assemblages.

The late Lindeman phase occupation of the Range site locality consists of a smaller village organized around a central courtyard having a circular single post structure at its center (Fig. 43). Several smaller courtyards are located to the northeast.

The Early Mississippian utilization of the Range site was limited to a series of farmsteads and a specialized nodal settlement that played an integrating role for outlying farmsteads (Fig. 44). Undoubtedly many of the documented changes in the size and organizational complexity of the Range site communities after A.D. 900 are related to changes in the larger cultural landscape of the American Bottom, with the nearby Lunsford-Pulcher mound center perhaps exerting growing influence over the Range site and other similar communities. Cultural change and the Mississippian emergence at this larger regional level of analysis is the topic of the following chapter in this volume.

ACKNOWLEDGMENTS

The Range site investigations were successful because of the efforts of numerous individuals. This chapter is one of the products of their labor. The author would like to gratefully acknowledge the following individuals for their assistance in the investigations of this truly unique site. First and foremost I would like to acknowledge the support and cooperation of the United States Department of Transportation, Federal Highway Administration; the State of Illinois, Illinois Department of Transportation (IDOT); the Illinois Archaeological Survey; and the Department of Anthropology, University of Illinois. In particular, Earl Bowman, J. Paul Biggers, George Lammers, and Dr. John A. Walthall of IDOT were instrumental in overall support from their level. Dr. James W. Porter and Prof. Charles J. Bareis of the University of Illinois placed considerable confidence in my ability to carry out the investigations and were particularly supportive of my work in the field. Steve Ozuk and Dr. Mark Mehrer were a major asset in the successful completion of the field work and the subsequent reports. Almost 200 individuals played a role in the field and lab operations, in particular Mike Morelock, Roger Williamson, Dr. George Milner, Chris Szuter, and Joyce Williams helped immensely. The completion of the various reports have been due to the tireless efforts of Steve Ozuk, Mark Mehrer, Joyce Williams, Lucretia Kelly, Sissel Johannessen, Lucy Whalley, Kathryn Parker, Ned Hanenberger, and Dr. George Milner. Finally, I must thank Dr. Bruce D. Smith for his patience and his editorial abilities to make my thoughts intelligible. I alone, however, assume responsibility for the contents of this chapter.

REFERENCES CITED

Bareis, Charles J.
1976   *The Knoebel Site, St. Clair County, Illinois.* Illinois Archaeological Survey, Circular 1.

Bareis, Charles J., and James W. Porter
1984   *American Bottom Archaeology: A Summary of the FAI-270 Project Contribution to the Culture History of the Mississippi River Valley.* University of Illinois Press, Urbana.

Bareis, Charles J., James W. Porter, and John E. Kelly
1977   *Report of Investigations and Proposed Mitigation for the Range Site (11-S-47), St. Clair County, Illinois.* Department of Anthropology, University of Illinois at Urbana-Champaign, Archaeological Mitigation Project.
1981   Proposed Mitigation of a Portion of the Archaeological Data Within the Right-of-Way for FAI-270 in the American Bottom. In *Archaeology in the American Bottom: Progress Report of the Illinois FAI-270 Archaeological Mitigation Project*, edited by Charles J. Bareis and James W. Porter, Appendix A, pp. 177–216. Department of Anthropology, University of Illinois at Urbana-Champaign, Research Report 6.

Emerson, Thomas E., and George R. Milner
1982   Community Organization and Settlement Patterns of Peripheral Mississippi Sites in the American Bottom, Illinois. Paper presented at the 47th Annual Meeting of the Society for American Archaeology, Minneapolis.

Flannery, Kent V.
1972   The Origins of the Village as a Settlement Type in Mesoamerica and the Near East: A Comparative Study. In *Man, Settlement, and Urbanism*, edited by Peter J. Ucko, Ruth Tringham, and G.W. Dimbleby, pp. 23–53. Schenkman Publishing Company.

Fortier, Andrew C., and Dale L. McElrath
1986   Archaeological Investigations at the University of Illinois (1985–1986). *Illinois Archaeological Survey Newsletter* 1/2:7–9.

Fowler, Melvin L.
1969   Middle Mississippian Agricultural Fields. *American Antiquity* 34(4):365–375.

Freimuth, Glen A.
1974   The Lunsford-Pulcher Site: An Examination of Selected Traits and Their Social Implications in American Bottom Prehistory. Unpublished pre-dissertation paper, Department of Anthropology, University of Illinois-Urbana.

Gregg, Michael L.
1975   *Settlement Morphology and Production Specialization: The Horseshoe Lake Site, A Case Study.* Unpublished Ph.D. dissertation, Department of Anthropology, University of Wisconsin, Milwaukee.

Griffin, James B.
1977   The University of Michigan Excavations at the Pulcher Site in 1950. *American Antiquity* 42:462–488.

Gross, Daniel R.
1983   Village Movement in Relation to Resources in Amazonia. In *Adaptive Responses of Native Amazonians*, edited by Raymond B. Hames and William T. Vickers, pp. 429–449. Academic Press, New York.

Hames, Raymond B.
1983   The Settlement Pattern of a Yanomamo Population Bloc: A Behavioral Ecological Interpretation. In *Adaptive Responses of Native Amazonians*, edited by Raymond B. Hames and William T. Vickers, pp. 393–497. Academic Press, New York.

Harn, Alan D.
1971   *An Archaeological Survey of the American Bottom in Madison and St. Clair Counties, Illinois.* Illinois State Museum Reports of Investigations 21 (Part 2). Springfield.

Howard, James H.
1968   *The Southeastern Ceremonial Complex and its Interpretation.* Missouri Archaeological Society Memoir 6.

Hudson, Charles
1976   *The Southeastern Indians.* The University of Tennessee Press.

Hus, Henri
1908   The Ecological Cross-Section of the Mississippi River in the Region of St. Louis, Missouri. *Missouri Botanical Garden, Annual Report* 19:127–258.

Kelly, John E., and Andrew C. Fortier
1983   *The Range Site: The Archaic, Early Woodland, and Middle Woodland Components.* Department of Anthropology, University of Illinois at Urbana-Champaign, FAI-270 Archaeological Mitigation Project, Report 60.

Kelly, John E., Jean R. Linder, and Theresa J. Cartmell
1979   *The Archaeological Intensive Survey of the Proposed FAI-270 Alignment in the American Bottom Region of Southern Illinois.* Illinois Transportation Archaeology Scientific Reports 1. Illinois Department of Transportation, Springfield, and Illinois Archaeological Survey, Urbana.

Kelly, John E., Andrew C. Fortier, Steven J. Ozuk, and Joyce A. Williams
1987   *The Range Site (11-S-47): Archaic Through Late Woodland Occupations.* American Bottom Archaeology FAI-270 Site Reports 16. University of Illinois Press, Urbana.

Kelly, John E., Steven J. Ozuk, and Joyce A. Williams
1984   *The Range Site (11-S-47): The Late Woodland Component.* Department of Anthropology, University of Illinois at Urbana-Champaign, FAI-270 Archaeological Mitigation Project Report 63.
1989a   *The Range Site 2 (11-S-47): The Emergent Mississippian Dohack and Range Phase Occupations.* Department of Anthropology, University of Illinois at Urbana-Champaign, FAI-270 Archaeological Mitigation Project Report 81.
1989b   The Range Site 3 (11-S-47): The Emergent Mississippian George Reeves and Lindeman Phase Occupations. Manuscript on file, Department of Anthropology, University of Illinois at Urbana-Champaign.

McElrath, Dale L., and Fred A. Finney
1987   *The George Reeves Site (11-S-650).* American Bottom Archaeology FAI-270 Site Reports 15. University of Illinois Press, Urbana.

McElrath, Dale L., and Andrew C. Fortier
1983   *The Missouri Pacific #2 Site (11-S-46).* American Bottom Archaeology FAI-270 Site Reports 3. University of Illinois Press, Urbana.

McElrath, Dale L., and Joyce A. Williams
1981   An Assessment of the Archaeological Phosphate Survey on Sites in the FAI-270 Right-of-Way. In *Archaeology in*

the American Bottom: Progress Report of the Illinois FAI-270 Archaeological Mitigation Project, edited by Charles J. Bareis and James Porter, pp. 159–176. Department of Anthropology, University of Illinois at Urbana-Champaign, Research Report 6.

Mehrer, Mark W.
1982   *A Mississippian Community at the Range Site (11-S-47), St. Clair County, Illinois.* Department of Anthropology, University of Illinois at Urbana-Champaign, FAI-270 Archaeological Mitigation Project Report 52.

Milner, George R., Thomas E. Emerson, Mark W. Mehrer, Joyce A. Williams, and Duane Esarey
1984   Mississippian and Oneota Period. In *American Bottom Archaeology: A Summary of the FAI-270 Project Contribution to the Culture History of the Mississippi River Valley,* edited by Charles J. Bareis and James W. Porter. University of Illinois press, Urbana.

Naroll, Raoul
1962   Floor Area and Settlement Population. *American Antiquity* 27(4):587–589.

Parker, Kathryn
1989   Range Site Lindeman Phase Floral Remains. Manuscript on file, FAI-270 Archaeological Project, Department of Anthropology, University of Illinois at Urbana-Champaign.

Pearsall, Deborah M.
1982b   Phytolith Analysis of Soil Samples from the Range Site (11-S-47), St. Clair County, Illinois. Manuscript on file, FAI-270 Archaeological Report, Department of Anthropology University of Illinois at Urbana-Champaign.

Sahlins, Marshall D.
1961   The Segmentary Lineage: An Organization of Predatory Expansion. *American Anthropologist* 63:322–45.

Service, Elman R.
1971   *Primitive Social Organization: An Evolutionary Perspective.* 2nd edition, Random House.

Smith, Bruce D.
1978   *Prehistoric Patterns of Human Behavior: A Case Study in the Mississippi Valley.* Academic Press, New York.

Smith, Philip E. L.
1971   Land-use, Settlement Patterns and Subsistence Agriculture: A Demographic Perspective. In *Man, Settlement, and Urbanism,* edited by Peter J. Ucko, Ruth Tringham, and G. W. Dimbleby, pp. 1–17. Schenkman Publishing Company.

Snyder, John Francis
1909   Prehistoric Illinois. Certain Indian Mounds Technically Considered. *Journal of the Illinois State Historical Society* 1, 2:31–40, 47–65, 71–92.

Wallace, D. L.
1978   *Soil Survey of St. Clair County, Illinois.* United States Department of Agriculture Soil Conservation Service.

Waring, Antonio J., Jr.
1965   The Southern Cult and Muskhogean Ceremonial. In *The Waring Papers: The Collected Works of Antonio J. Waring, Jr.,* edited by Stephen Williams. University of Georgia Press, Athens.

White, William P., and Linda M. Bonnell
1981   *Geomorphic Investigations at the Range site (11-S-47).* Department of Anthropology, University of Illinois at Urbana-Champaign, FAI-270 Archaeological Mitigation Project Geomorphological Report 6.

Williams, Elizabeth
1985   Estimation of Prehistoric Populations of Archaeological Sites in Southwestern Victoria: Some Problems. *Archaeology in Oceania* 20(3):73–80.

The Emergence of Mississippian Culture in the American Bottom Region

INTRODUCTION

East of the present day city of St. Louis, Missouri, the valley of the Mississippi River abruptly broadens to form the American Bottom, an area of approximately 800 sq km, which witnessed, from A.D. 600–1100, the development of the most complex prehistoric sociopolitical system known north of Mexico. In this chapter, I want to review previous explanatory models for this developmental process, and to offer an alternative explanation. In order to discuss such developmental explanations, however, it is necessary to first provide an environmental, temporal, and spatial context for the Mississippian emergence in the American Bottom region, and to provide a brief outline of the cultural historical framework for the five-century span in question.

Location and Environmental Setting

When expanded to include the adjacent upland drainage catchment areas of Mississippi River tributaries (Fig. 46), the "greater American Bottom" region encompasses considerable environmental diversity and a wide range of inorganic and organic resources. Forming the western boundary of the American Bottom proper, the Mississippi River has shaped and reshaped its landforms since the end of the Pleistocene. As such the river has had a significant effect on the overall configuration of the biotic communities of the area.

Bordering the current channel and having a maximum width of 4 km, is a low terrace zone made up of a parallel series of ridges and swales produced by the river's relatively recent downcutting and incising. Clearly demarcated between the present day towns of Columbia and Cahokia, Illinois, as a result of geomorphological research associated with the construction of Interstate 270 (Figs. 17, 46; White 1983:9), the Lunsford-Pulcher terrace, which covers a considerable portion of the American Bottom, contains a complex series of superimposed abandoned channel meander loop oxbow lakes that mark the river's changing course from about 8000–1000 B.C. (cf. Munson 1974; Kelly et al. 1979; White et al. 1984).

The Wood River Terrace, which dates to the end of the Pleistocene, is primarily restricted to the northeast corner of the American Bottom (Hajic 1987). An extensive area across the northern floodplain may represent the filled channel for this terrace. It is incised by a series of meander loop oxbow lakes, including Long Lake, Edelhardt Lake, and McDonough Lake. Smaller terrace sequences, presumably related to this feature, can be found at a number of the valley openings along the eastern margins of the valley (e.g., Palmer Creek Terrace, Milner 1982).

Colluvial veneer and alluvial fan areas located at the base of the bluffs form the final major geomorphological element of the American Bottom (Fig. 46; White et al. 1984). These are a product of redeposition from erosional and stream processes associated with the uplands and hence are superimposed on the floodplain.

The biotic communities (Fig. 47) of the American

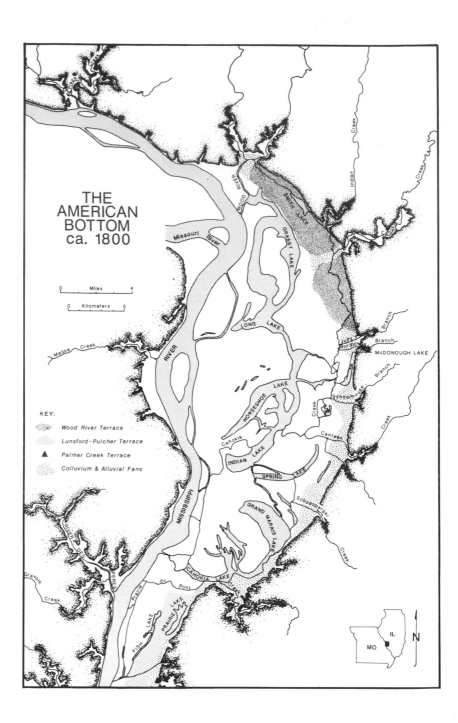

Fig. 46. The American Bottom.

Bottom were quite diverse during late prehistory, with reconstructions (largely restricted to the area of the American Bottom north of Dupo, Illinois) based on the early twentieth-century studies of Hus (1906) and Telford (1927), along with the early nineteenth-century land records of the U.S. Government (Gregg 1975; Welch 1975). As noted by Johannessen (White et al. 1984:39), the factors effecting the development of these communities include elevation, degree of annual submergence, and other aspects of drainage.

The major communities within the floodplain are the river edge zone, subject to annual submergence; the floodplain forest zone, with two linear elevation subzones (Welch 1975); the lake, slough, and pond zone, which includes the low wet areas adjacent to these aquatic areas; the bottomland prairie, which was quite

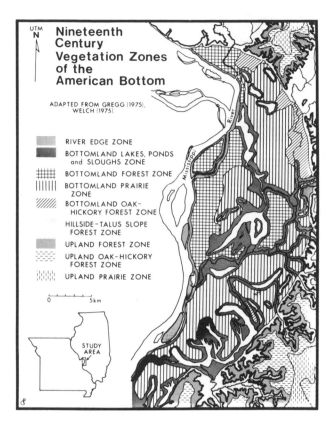

UTM
N

**Nineteenth
Century
Vegetation Zones
of the
American Bottom**

ADAPTED FROM GREGG (1975),
WELCH (1975).

▦ RIVER EDGE ZONE

▓ BOTTOMLAND LAKES, PONDS
and SLOUGHS ZONE

▤ BOTTOMLAND FOREST ZONE

▥ BOTTOMLAND PRAIRIE
ZONE

▨ BOTTOMLAND OAK-
HICKORY FOREST ZONE

HILLSIDE-TALUS SLOPE
FOREST ZONE

▨ UPLAND FOREST ZONE

UPLAND OAK-HICKORY
FOREST ZONE

UPLAND PRAIRIE ZONE

0   5km

STUDY
AREA

Fig. 47. The biotic communities of the upper American Bottom.

extensive at the time of land survey; and the floodplain oak-hickory zone, restricted to the higher and drier portions of the floodplain. The physiographic units that are transitional to the uplands include a distinct assemblage of the woody and herbaceous plants referred to as the bluff slope and stream drainage zone. Three zones dominate the uplands and include the upland forest zone with its mixture of oak-hickory and other woody species; the upland oak-hickory zone, not only quite extensive but also the most important resource zone of the uplands; and the upland prairie zone, dominating the higher and drier portions of the uplands.

Around the eastern edge of the American Bottom, the Illinois uplands are underlain by Pennsylvanian and Mississippian sandstones and limestones that often outcrop at the valley edge or in the upland stream cuts. These outcrop areas provided easy access to lithic raw materials such as limestone, sandstone, shales, and occasionally, cherts (Kelly 1984). With the exception of Cahokia Creek, the uplands are highly dissected by a series of small streams (White et al. 1984). Those por-

tions of the uplands underlain by the later Mississippian limestones have a sinkhole topography, with these formations also producing the numerous springs evident along the bluff face.

Along the western margin of the American Bottom, the Ozark uplands are also highly dissected. While containing many of the same sedimentary rocks as the Illinois uplands, the Ozarks are far richer in terms of mineral resources such as hematite (Holmes 1903; Kelly 1980), galena (Walthall 1981), and salt (Gates 1966), as well as having an extensive area of high quality chert—the Crescent Hills Quarry area (Fig. 48; Ives 1975). These cherts were extensively quarried throughout the prehistoric occupation of the American Bottom. The Meramec River drains an extensive area of the northeast portion of the Ozarks, providing the primary access to the lithic and mineral resources of the northern part of this region.

Chronological Framework

Although largely based on research conducted as part of the FAI-270 project, the Late Woodland-Mississippian chronological framework currently in use for the American Bottom (Fig. 49) is a revision of the 1972 Cahokia Conference chronology (Fowler and Hall 1975), and in fact reflects over 50 years of systematic investigations of the Late Woodland-Mississippian continuum in the region (Kelly 1987). More recent fieldwork at Cahokia by William I. Woods and his colleagues at Southern Illinois University-Edwardsville (SIU-E), and in the surrounding area by the University of Illinois-Urbana Champaign (UI-UC) under the direction of Charles J. Bareis will undoubtedly result in further refinement of this chronological framework.

The Late Woodland-Mississippian period sequence covers the period from A.D. 300 to A.D. 1300. This chapter will focus specifically on the five century portion of the sequence from A.D. 600 to A.D. 1100, which brackets the cultural transition from Late Woodland through Emergent Mississippian and into the Early Mississippian period. At the present time, this five-century span is represented by a series of cultural phases. These phases are defined primarily on the basis of their ceramic assemblages, which serve to differentiate them in time and space. In effect these represent a series of temporal slices ranging in thickness from 50 to 100 years. The ordering of these temporal slices

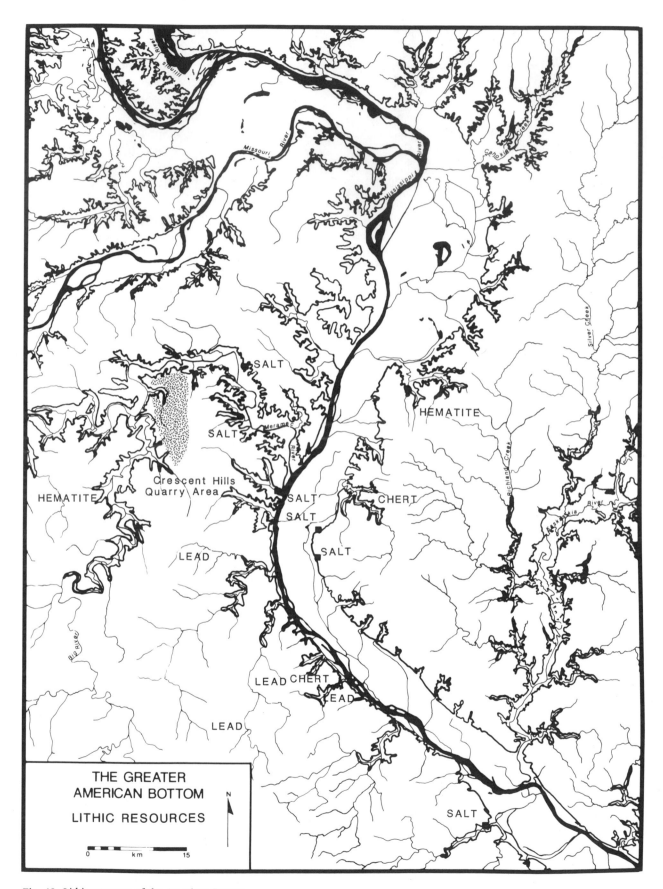

Fig. 48. Lithic resources of the American Bottom.

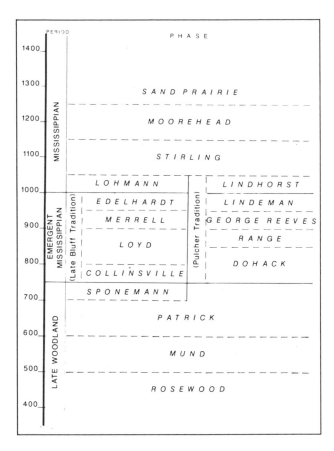

Fig. 49. American Bottom chronology.

is based primarily on ceramic seriation in conjunction with stratigraphic information. Radiocarbon dates in general support the chronological framework (Figs. 50, 51, and 52), but standard deviation values of 140–260 years substantially reduce their value. Clearly the 50-, 100-, and 200-year time spans assigned to phases in the current chronology are only approximations, as are their specific calendrical placement. Hall (1985b), for example, has proposed that the Emergent Mississippian and earlier Mississippian phases should all be moved up 50 years.

While the Late Woodland Patrick phase (A.D. 600–700) encompasses all of the American Bottom, two distinct ceramic "traditions" have been identified for the subsequent Emergent Mississippian period (A.D. 750–1000) (Figs. 49, 53). A "Late Bluff tradition" centered in the northern portion of the American Bottom near the Cahokia site (Fig. 54) subsumes a sequence of three phases: Loyd (A.D. 800–900), Merrell (A.D. 900–950), and Edelhardt (A.D. 950–1000). Recent investigations

in conjunction with the FAI-270 extension project to the north have identified two new complexes that fall between the Patrick and Loyd phases (Fortier 1988). A second, parallel, "Pulcher tradition" centered in the southern (Monroe County) portion of the American Bottom (Kelly 1987) consists of four phases: Dohack (A.D. 750–850), Range (A.D. 850–900), George Reeves (A.D. 900–950), and Lindeman (A.D. 950–1000). The Pulcher tradition in fact persists into the Early Mississippian period in this portion of the American Bottom, with the designation of the A.D. 1000–1050 Lohmann phase in the Late Bluff tradition area and the parallel Lindhorst phase in the Pulcher tradition area reflecting the continuing presence of two distinct ceramic tradition areas within the American Bottom.

A CULTURAL-HISTORICAL FRAMEWORK FOR THE LATE WOODLAND-MISSISSIPPIAN TRANSITION IN THE AMERICAN BOTTOM

In order to compare and evaluate the various explanations of Mississippian development that have been proposed for the American Bottom over the past 25 years, it is worthwhile to first selectively describe the culture history of the period of Woodland-Mississippian transition, focusing on five general areas of change that are central to any and all definitions of Mississippian:

1. Dramatic changes in technology and material culture,
2. A shift to maize-dominated field agriculture,
3. Interregional exchange,
4. An increase in the size and organization of sociopolitical units,
5. A marked increase in social differentiation.

Much of the archaeological information on which the following culture history is based was recovered during the FAI-270 project (Bareis and Porter 1984), resulting from the excavation of over 20 sites dating to the five-century span of A.D. 600–1100 (Figs. 53–64).

The Patrick and Sponemann Phases (A.D. 600–750)

The Patrick phase (A.D. 600–700) is the last of three sequent phases that comprise the Late Woodland cultural tradition in the region prior to the divergence of the Late Woodland into what becomes the Emergent Mississippian co-traditions in the American Bottom.

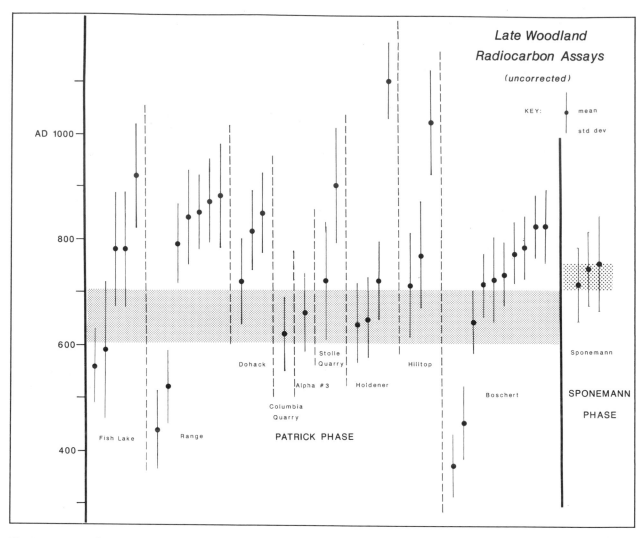

Fig. 50. Late Woodland period radiocarbon assays for the American Bottom.

This divergence begins at the end of the Late Woodland sequence in the upper part of the American Bottom with the Sponemann phase (A.D. 700–750). A coeval unit to the south has yet to be defined. In many respects the Patrick phase is the climax of Late Woodland cultural development. At least 28 sites in the American Bottom with Patrick phase components have undergone some form of excavation (Fig. 55). Patrick phase ceramic vessels are grog or grit tempered and cordmarked. In contrast with the preceding Mund phase (A.D. 500–600), Patrick phase ceramic assemblages are marked by an increase in the diversity of jar morphology, with incurve-necked vessels becoming much more frequent. Bowls appear in ceramic assemblages for the first time since the Middle Woodland. Decoration of vessels increases, with lugs, effigies, and spouts occasionally present, and interior lip impressions become the most common new decorative treatment. Ceramic and lithic pipes often exhibit a prow and in some instances are shaped into effigies such as turtles or frogs. Small, stemmed arrow points and discoidals appear for the first time.

In comparison with the preceding Mund (A.D. 500–600) and Rosewood (A.D. 300–500) phases, there is a marked increase in the number of Patrick phase sites that have been investigated, suggesting an increase in population after A.D. 600 (Kelly et al. 1984a). In addition, Patrick phase sites are located

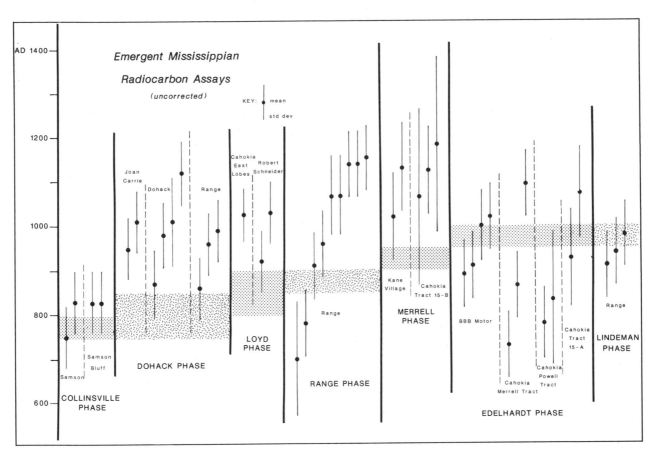

Fig. 51. Emergent Mississippian period radiocarbon assays for the American Bottom.

throughout the region, including both the adjacent uplands and the American Bottom proper (Fig. 55), in contrast with Rosewood and Mund phase settlements, which were mainly restricted to the uplands or adjacent to the bluff base.

Extensive excavations at a number of locations indicate a variety of different kinds of Patrick phase sites, ranging from small, limited term occupations to large multifamily settlements. This range of settlement types is based on the results of excavations at the Range site (see Chapter 5), where the community plans of nine Patrick phase settlements extending over an area of 2.6 ha were uncovered (Figs. 20–27). The 33 small (less than 8 sq m) single-post wall, rectangular basin structures comprising the largest of these Patrick phase settlements at the Range site (P-5) were distributed about a central open area (Fig. 25). A large post marked the approximate center of this community square. Those small rectangular basin

houses having extended ramps are referred to as keyhole structures. Clusters of two to seven structures and associated features can be discerned, indicative of family units and in some cases extended families. The spatial division of the village's family clusters into two units of comparable size may reflect a suprafamily social unit dualism such as moieties. Within each of these spatially discrete units, the largest houses (Fig. 25) may have been occupied by the leaders of their respective social divisions. A large (approximately 64 sq m) peripherally located structure may represent a facility used by a particular segment of the community, such as a men's group.

The nine Patrick phase settlement plans uncovered at the Range site represent a community's utilization of the location over an extended period of time (100 years) (Kelly et al. 1987). Of varying size and duration, these settlements likely reflect an economic base incorporating shifting cultivation in which settlements

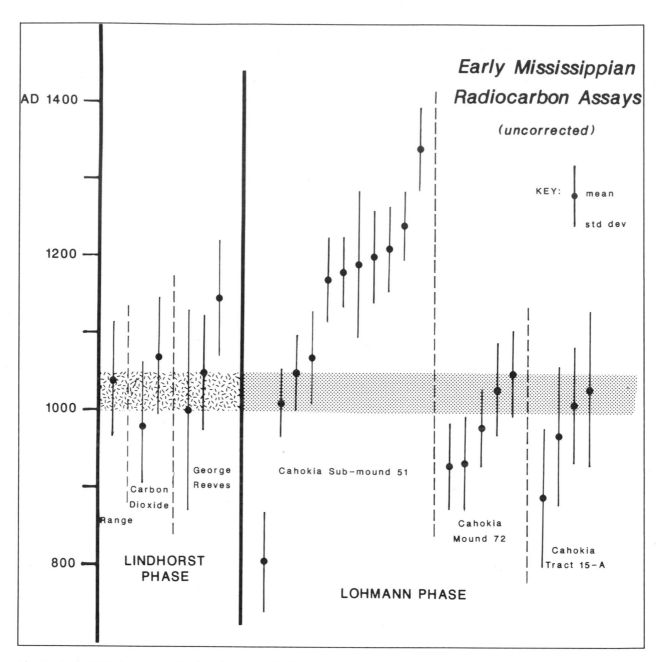

Fig. 52. Early Mississippian period radiocarbon assays for the American Bottom.

were abandoned after a number of years due to changes in available resources or even social conditions. Variability in settlement composition may also indicate relatively fluid patterns of community fusion and fission along shifting lines of internal alliance and dispute similar to that documented for present day tropical forest horticultural societies (cf. Hames 1983). Of the other excavated Patrick phase compo-

nents in the American Bottom, only those of the Schlemmer, Westpark, Fish Lake, A.G. Church (and possibly Dohack) sites produced evidence of structures (Table 10). In general these settlements correspond to the smaller settlement units evident at the Range site. They appear to represent either specialized, limited term occupations or individual household occupation episodes. Excavations at Fish Lake

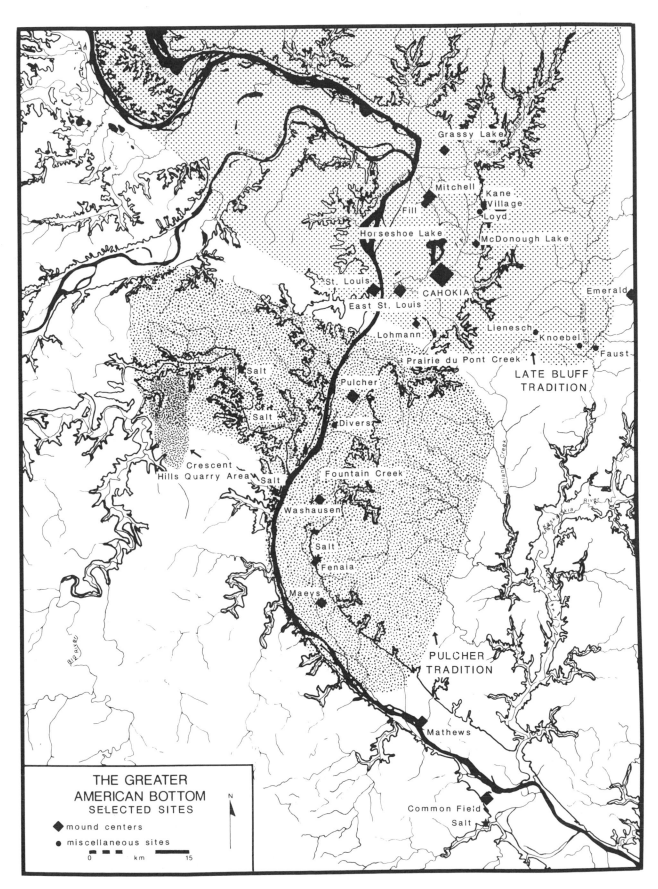

Fig. 53. Selected sites within the American Bottom.

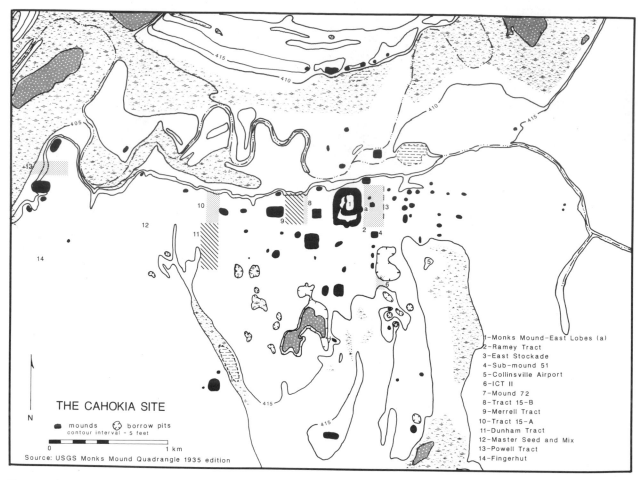

1-Monks Mound-East Lobes (a)
2-Ramey Tract
3-East Stockade
4-Sub-mound 51
5-Collinsville Airport
6-ICT II
7-Mound 72
8-Tract 15-B
9-Merrell Tract
10-Tract 15-A
11-Dunham Tract
12-Master Seed and Mix
13-Powell Tract
14-Fingerhut

THE CAHOKIA SITE

N

■ mounds   ⊘ borrow pits
contour interval - 5 feet

0   1 km

Source: USGS Monks Mound Quadrangle 1935 edition

Fig. 54. The Cahokia site.

and West Park revealed portions of what may be interpreted as villages. Features are often dispersed over areas of 0.1–0.2 ha, with pits frequently distributed in clusters.

Patrick phase populations in the American Bottom area depended on a wide range of wild plant and animal food resources (Johannessen 1987; L. Kelly 1987). In addition, a variety of indigenous crop plants were cultivated, including sunflower, lambsquarter, erect knotweed, maygrass, and little barley (Johannessen 1987). Tobacco was also common. There is little evidence of maize being grown by Patrick phase communities. Many of the large deep pits at Patrick phase settlements were undoubtedly used for the storage of both wild and cultivated plants. Earth ovens are a common feature at many Patrick

phase sites, and carbonized acorns and sunflower seeds have been recovered from some earth oven floors. Thin-walled ceramic jars, associated with earlier Late Woodland phases, were important in the boiling of starchy seeds of a number of indigenous cultigens (Braun 1983). By the Patrick phase, however, an increase in wall thickness of some cooking vessels may reflect a shift in plant processing and cooking methods. Large thick-walled bowls, for example, which first appear in Patrick phase assemblages, may have been used to parch seeds.

Very little information is currently available concerning Patrick phase mortuary programs. The lack of burial populations represents a serious gap in the archaeological record, both in terms of addressing the question of status differentiation within Patrick phase

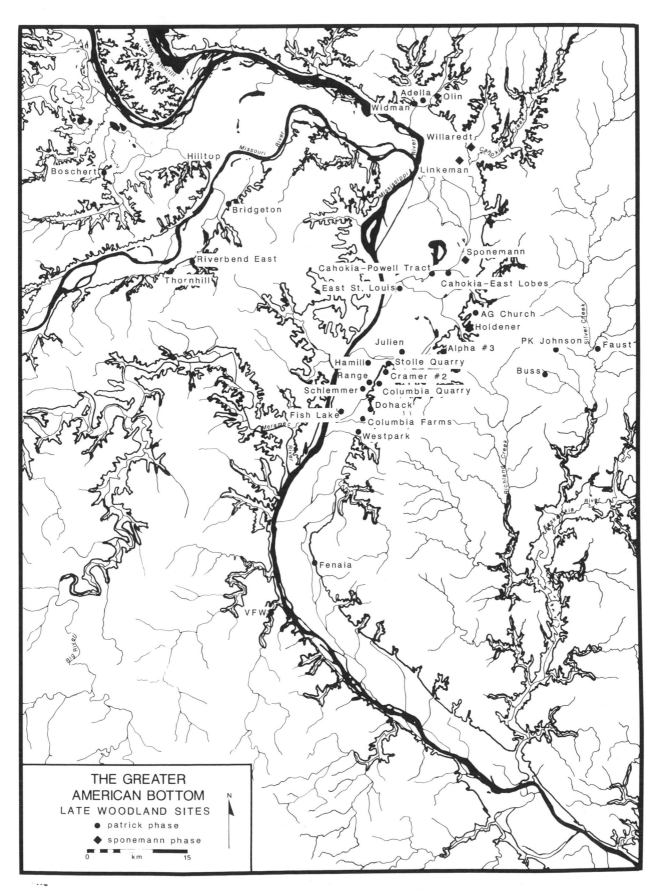

Fig. 55. The distribution of Patrick and Sponemann phase sites within the American Bottom.

Table 10. Excavated Sites with Patrick and Sponemann Phase Occupations

Site	Location	Results	Nature of Investigations	Reference
Patrick Phase				
Cahokia Powell Tract	American Bottom floodplain	Pit features	Highway salvage	O'Brien 1972
Cahokia Monks Mound, East Lobes	American Bottom floodplain	Buried deposits beneath mound	Testing	Williams 1975
Stolle Quarry	Bluffs above American Bottom	Pit features	Salvage	Hall and Vogel 1963
AG Church	Uplands above Canteen Creek	Pit features and structure	Salvage	Pauketat n.d.
Schlemmer	American Bottom floodplain	Pit features and structure	Salvage	Szuter 1979; Berres 1984
Westpark	Bluffs above American Bottom	Pit features and structure	Salvage	Kelly et al. 1989a
Hamill	American Bottom floodplain	Pit features	Salvage	Kelly et al. 1989a
Buss	Uplands, Ash-Loop Creek	Pit features	Salvage	Kelly et al. 1989a
PK Johnson	Uplands, Ash-Loop Creek	Pit features	Salvage	Kelly et al. 1989a
Range	American Bottom floodplain	Definition of 9 settlements	I-270 Project	Kelly et al. 1987
Fish Lake	American Bottom floodplain	Pit features and structures	I-270 Project	Fortier et al. 1984
Julien	American Bottom floodplain	Pit features	I-270 Project	Milner 1984a
Dohack	Uplands, Hill Lake Creek	Pit features and structures?	I-270 Project	Stahl 1985
Alpha #3	Uplands, Powdermill Creek	Pit features	I-270 Project	Bentz et al. 1988
Cramer #2	Uplands, Prairie du Pont Creek	Pit features	I-270 Project	Bentz et al. 1988
Columbia Farms	Uplands, Palmer Creek	Pit features	I-270 Project	Bentz et al. 1988
Columbia Quarry	Uplands, sinkholes	Pit features	I-270 Project	Westover et al. 1983
Holdener	Uplands, Schoenberger Creek	Pit features	I-270 Project	Wittry et al. 1982
Faust	Silver Creek terrace	Pit features	Highway salvage	Bareis 1968
Diekemper	Sugar Creek terrace	Pit features	Highway salvage	Bareis 1971
Widman	Terrace above Wood River	Pit features	Highway salvage	Wolforth 1988
Adella	Bluffs above Wood River	Pit features	SIU-E field school	Denny et al. 1978
Olin	Bluffs above Wood River	Pit features	SIU-E field school	Denny et al. 1978
Fenaia	American Bottom terrace	Pit features	Testing as part of Historic Sites Survey	Hendrickson 1979
Hilltop	Bluffs above Missouri-Mississippi floodplain	Pit features	Salvage	Shippee 1972
Riverbend East	Bluffs above Missouri River	Pit features	Salvage	Hunt 1974
Bridgeton	Missouri River terrace	Pit features	UMSTL field school	Wright 1986
VFW	Plattin Creek terrace	Pit features	Highway salvage	Nixon et al. 1983
Thornhill	Bluffs above Missouri River	Redeposited material in Mississippian features	Testing	Batsell-Fuller 1985
Sponemann Phase				
Sponemann	American Bottom floodplain	Pit features and structures	I-270 Project extension	Fortier and McElrath 1986
Willaredt	Bluffs above American Bottom	Pit features	Highway testing	Hawks 1985
Lindeman	Wood River terrace	Pit features	Testing	Bareis and Munson 1973

societies, and in providing a data base for broad-based bioarchaeological analysis. Most Patrick phase burials, isolated individuals or disarticulated body parts, have been fortuitously recovered from settlement storage/refuse pits. Contemporary mortuary sites in the lower Illinois River valley indicate little social differentiation within burial populations of this time period (Droessler 1981).

There is little evidence for extraregional trade within Patrick phase material culture assemblages. The evidence for interaction with nearby regions is best illustrated by the similarity in vessel forms and decorative modes. This area of shared ceramic form and design extends from the central Illinois River valley south along the Mississippi River to the mouth of the Ohio River and as far east as the Wabash River (Kelly 1985).

In the upper portion of the American Bottom, the newly defined Sponemann phase (A.D. 700–750) is the culmination of the Late Woodland cultural tradition. While it is considered by some (Fortier 1988) to be an Emergent Mississippian phenomenon based on the increased ubiquity index of maize (which occurs in 30 percent of the site features), it is clearly Late Woodland in terms of its ceramic assemblage and settlement plans. A large portion of the ceramic assemblage is Patrick phase with the remaining portion representing an assemblage exhibiting strong affinities with Late Woodland complexes in the Mississippi River Valley to the north (McGimsey and Conner 1985; Morgan 1985). The Sponemann phase represents the amalgamation of two ceramic traditions in the American Bottom with maize perhaps entering with groups from the north.

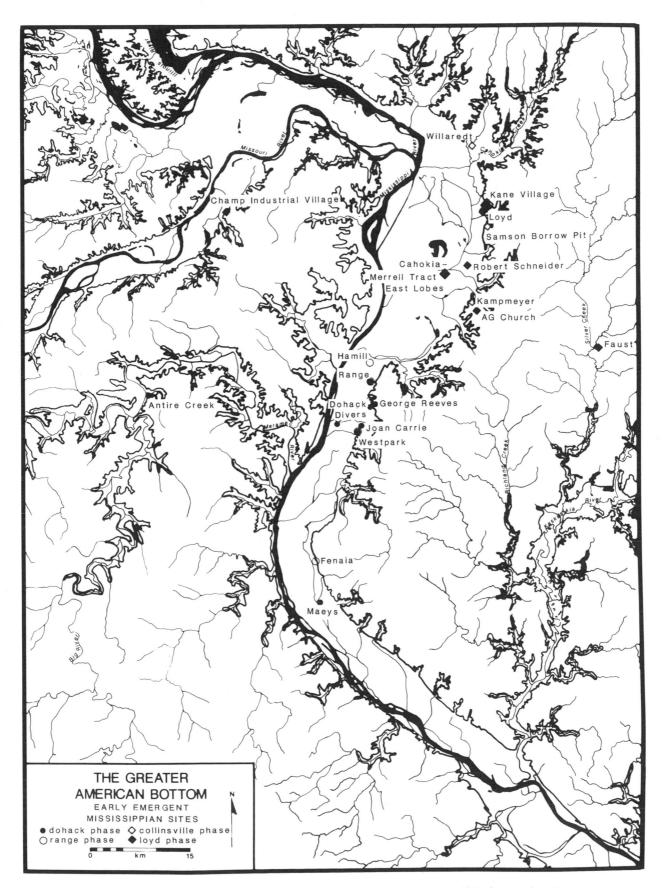

Fig. 56. The distribution of selected early Emergent Mississippian period sites (A.D. 750–900) within the American Bottom.

Table 11. Excavated Sites with Early Emergent Mississippian Occupations

Site	Location	Results	Nature of Investigations	Reference
Dohack Phase				
Dohack	Uplands, Hill Lake Creek	Pit features and structures	I-270 Project	Stahl 1985
Joan Carrie	Bluffs above American Bottom	Pit features	I-270 Project	Esarey 1980
George Reeves	Bluffs above American Bottom	Pit features	I-270 Project	McElrath & Finney 1987
Range	American Bottom floodplain	Definition of six settlements	I-270 Project	Kelly et al. 1989b
Westpark	Bluffs above American Bottom	Definition of one settlement	Salvage	Kelly et al. 1989a
Maeys	American Bottom floodplain	Pit features	Testing as part of Historic Sites Survey	Porter 1972
Divers	American Bottom floodplain	Features	Testing	Freimuth 1970
Antire Creek	Bluffs above Meramec River	Features?	Salvage	Lopinot et al. 1987
Range Phase				
Range	American Bottom floodplain	Definition of five settlements	I-270 Project	Kelly et al. 1989b
Fenaia	American Bottom terrace	Features	Testing as part of Historic Sites Survey	Hendrickson 1979
Westpark	Bluffs above American Bottom	Pit features	Salvage	Kelly et al. 1989a
Hamill	American Bottom floodplain	Pit features	Salvage	Kelly et al. 1989a
Collinsville Phase				
Kane Village	Bluff base American Bottom	Features	Salvage	Munson & Anderson 1973
Kampmeyer	Bluffs above American Bottom	Features	Salvage	Kelly et al. 1989a
Samson Borrow Pit	Bluffs above American Bottom	Pit features and structures	I-270 Project extension	Fortier 1988
Willaredt	Bluffs above American Bottom	Pit features	Highway testing	Jackson 1988b; Hawks 1985
Loyd Phase				
Cahokia Merrell Tract	American Bottom floodplain	Pit features and structures	Testing	Kelly 1980
Cahokia Monks Mound-East Lobes	American Bottom floodplain	Buried deposits beneath mound	Testing	Williams 1975
Loyd	Wood River terrace	Pit features	Salvage	Hall and Vogel 1963
Robert Schneider	American Bottom floodplain	Pit features and structures	I-270 Project	Fortier 1985
AG Church	Uplands, Canteen Creek	Pit features	Salvage	Pauketat n.d.
Faust	Silver Creek terrace	Pit features	Highway salvage	Bareis 1968
Champ Industrial Village	Terrace above Missouri River	Pit features	Salvage	Blake 1964

The Collinsville, Loyd, Dohack, and Range Phases (A.D. 750–900)

The term "Emergent Mississippian" is employed in the American Bottom to refer to those entities that bracket the A.D. 750–1000 transition from Late Woodland to Mississippian. To simplify discussion, the seven Emergent Mississippian period phases identified to date in the American Bottom will be summarized under 100-150 year temporal headings.

At least 20 sites having components dating to the time period A.D. 750–900 have been excavated in the American Bottom region (Fig. 56). When the Emergent Mississippian phases dating to A.D. 750–900 (Loyd and Collinsville in the Late Bluff tradition area, Dohack and Range in the Pulcher tradition area) (Figs. 49, 53, 56) are compared to the preceding Patrick and Sponemann phases, a number of dramatic changes are evident.

Perhaps the most notable change is the abrupt increase in the relative ubiquity and abundance of maize within initial Emergent Mississippian settlements. While rarely found in pre-A.D. 700 Patrick phase contexts, maize was present in over 50 percent of the sampled A.D. 800–900 features at sites such as Range, Dohack, and Joan Carrie (Table 11). As noted earlier, maize was present in about 30 percent of the features recently excavated at the Sponemann site (Parker 1986), which falls between the Patrick and Collinsville phases in the northern Late Bluff tradition area.

Although no "borderline" artifact complexes coeval to those documented at Sponemann and other sites in the north (Table 10) have yet been identified as falling between the Patrick and Dohack phases of the Pulcher tradition in the south, the dramatic differences between the Patrick and Dohack phases in terms of ceramics, features, and botanical remains

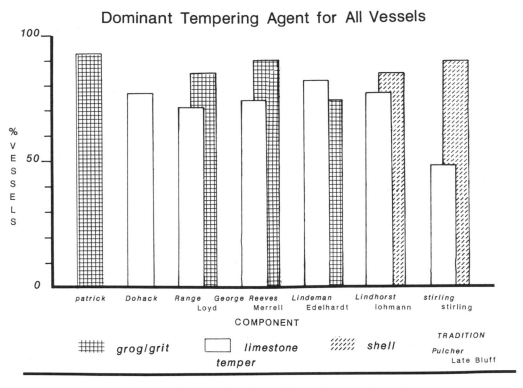

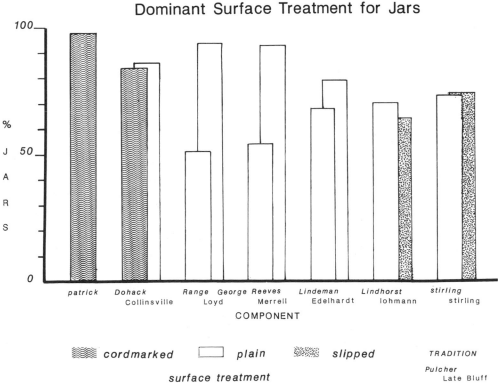

Fig. 57. Selected ceramic attributes for the Pulcher and Late Bluff traditions of the American Bottom.

certainly suggest the existence of such intervening complexes. The materials from the Antire Creek site in the lower Meramec Valley and the Westpark site across the Mississippi River in Illinois may provide such evidence (Table 11).

While grog and grit continue as the dominant tempering material within the Late Bluff tradition area of the American Bottom, Dohack phase ceramic assemblages of the Pulcher tradition exhibit a major shift to limestone temper (Fig. 57). This adoption of limestone as a tempering agent occurs at the same time or slightly earlier to the west of the American Bottom, in the northeastern Ozarks (Price and Price 1984). Farther south in the Ozark and Mississippi Valley areas of southeast Missouri and northeast Arkansas, a parallel shift to another carbonate, shell tempering, is taking place as early as A.D. 800 (Chapter 7).

To the north, in the Late Bluff tradition area of the American Bottom, many of the Loyd phase jars are manufactured from upland clays, identified through petrographic analysis as being associated with Madison County shales (Porter 1963, 1984). These fire to a distinctive color that can be readily identified. Many of the Collinsville phase jars appear to be manufactured from upland clays. Late Bluff jars of the Loyd phase are characterized by plain, incurved necks with small triangular lugs, while the Collinsville phase consists of plain necked jars with interior lip impressions, and some cordmarked jars and bowls. This is in contrast with the high frequency of cordmarked Pulcher tradition jars during the Dohack and Range phases. An increase in jars with plain necks, however, is evident by the Range phase (Fig. 57). A new vessel referred to as stumpware appears during the Loyd and Range phases. These funny footed funnels were probably used as vessel supports for jars (Porter 1974:612; Kelly 1980:414–415).

Like the Late Woodland Patrick phase, sites of the A.D. 750–900 Collinsville, Loyd, Dohack, and Range phases are distributed throughout the American Bottom proper and adjacent upland areas. Recent survey data suggests that the apparent trend of population growth observed for the Patrick and Sponemann phases (A.D 600–750), continues through the period A.D. 750–1000 (Kelly 1980).

While there are also strong continuities between settlement patterns and community plans of the Patrick phase and succeeding Emergent Mississippian phases of A.D. 750–900, there are also a number of changes that may reflect community response to increasing population levels and increased competition for various resources.

A range of settlement types, from homesteads to larger villages, which is quite comparable to the preceding Patrick phase, is evident for the A.D. 750–900 Emergent Mississippian phases, but the area occupied by larger settlements of this period decreases, with a concomitant increase in structure density levels from the Patrick phase through the Dohack and into the Range phase (Figs. 28–38). As yet, no large settlements dating to this time period have been excavated in the Late Bluff tradition area of the American Bottom, although the Loyd phase structures on the Merrell Tract at Cahokia may be part of a large village (Kelly 1980).

In terms of community plan, continuity is evident in the Dohack and Range phase villages at the Range site (Figs. 28–38) in that a central open area or community square is still present, and structures are arranged in small clusters around this central area. But the overall organization of the villages is more structured, and the symbolism extant in such settlements is more lucid.

In the five Dohack phase villages at the Range site, two types of central features are apparent. One consists of four large pits that are organized as a square, usually around a central post (Fig. 30). The second type of central feature is a large rectilinear structure (Fig. 33). In those communities with the four pits some type of larger specialized structure(s), often with a hearth, are centrally located within the central area (Fig. 30).

To date, the Range phase has only been identified from excavations at the Range site. Excavations at the Westpark, Fenaia, and Hamill sites (Fig. 56) may contain Range Phase components (Table 11).

Within the Range phase villages at the Range site (Figs. 34–38), two types of central features are evident in the central open area. The first is a group of four large pits situated around a central post (Fig. 38), which first appears in the Dohack phase. The second type of central feature is simply a large post (Fig. 37). As in the Dohack phase, there is a central basin structure, with the remaining structures distributed in a symmetrical fashion out beyond this facility

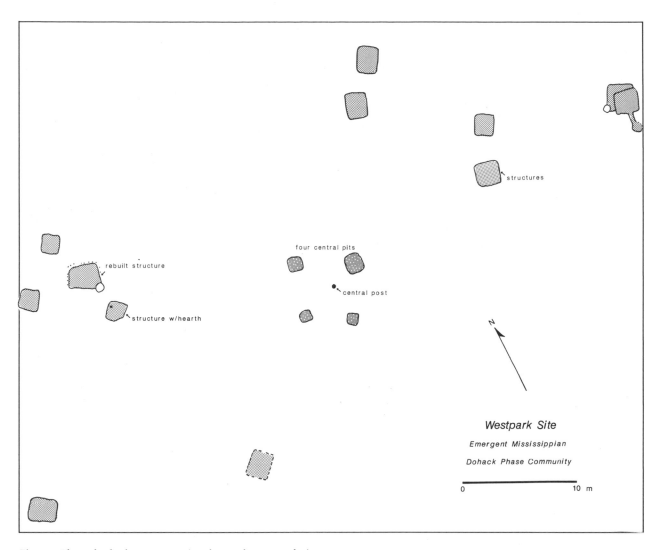

Fig. 58. The Dohack phase community plan at the Westpark site.

and around the community square. The Range phase villages are slightly smaller than those of the Dohack phase, with structures clustering, but often in a linear pattern.

Unlike comparable structures in the Dohack communities, the larger central structures were rebuilt on several occasions, and their small "pit" hearths also distinguish them from other structures in the village. This evidence of rebuilding and hearths is reminiscent of the rebuilding and ceremonial hearths associated with Mississippian platform mounds. In certain respects this complex can be viewed as the prototype for the later Mississippian platform mound complex.

The general community plans of the Range site for the period A.D. 800–900 presumably represent a single lineage village organization, and in many respects provide us with significant insights into the basis for such an authority structure. In part, the underlying basis for the development of such authority is likely tied to certain religious ceremonies and associated symbols. A central symbol is the cross-in-circle, as evinced by the four central pits or the large rectangular structure in the community square (Fig. 38). These, in turn, could represent the fire-sun deity that is indirectly associated with fertility in southeastern Indian belief systems (Waring 1985; Howard 1968; Hudson 1976). The various hearths, along with structure rebuilding, may also be symbolic of this deity, which is a fundamental element in fertility, and has ties to an annual cycle of rebirth. This of course is the essence of the historic busk ceremony (Hudson 1976).

The Westpark site provides the only other example of such a distinctive community pattern. A Dohack phase community (A.D. 750–850) at Westpark exhibited four central pits, a structure that had been rebuilt on a number of occasions, and a nearby structure with a small hearth (Fig. 58). All of the other known Dohack phase sites are smaller upland settlements that lack evidence of such central ceremonial features.

To the north in the Late Bluff tradition area, only smaller Collinsville and Loyd phase settlements have been investigated to date, except within Cahokia proper, where excavations were not extensive enough to delimit a complete settlement. Given the evidence on the Merrell Tract, a large Loyd phase village is expected.

By the beginning of the Emergent Mississippian period at A.D. 750, there is increasing evidence for exchange both within the American Bottom area proper, and involving the movement of materials between regions. Within the American Bottom region, Burlington chert from the Cresent Hills quarries was being procured. This included finished items such as small stemmed projectile points and woodworking tools such as adzes and chisels. Jars manufactured from Madison County shales were traded south (Kelly et al. 1989b), while vessels from the Pulcher tradition area have been found in Loyd phase contexts to the north (Kelly 1980). Ste. Genevieve cherts also have been recovered in Loyd phase contexts (cf. Kelly 1980; Fortier 1985). These were undoubtedly obtained from southern sources. The most important item involved in extraregional exchange during this period was the Mill Creek hoe. Evidence for the acquisition and use of such hoes, in the form of hoe flake by-products of tool resharpening, has been recovered from Loyd, Range, and some Dohack phase contexts. Except for a few shell- and grog-tempered vessels from Loyd phase contexts at Cahokia (Kelly 1980), there is little evidence for extraregional trade of ceramic vessels. Anculosa shell beads have also been recovered from Dohack and Range phase contexts (Kelly et al. 1989b). These shells are freshwater gastropods common to the lower Ohio drainage (Chmurny 1973). The only other exotic items that

have been recorded for this time period is a copper pendant recovered from a Dohack phase feature at the Range site (Kelly et al. 1989b), and small fragments of worked copper from Loyd phase contexts on the Merrell Tract at Cahokia (Kelly 1980).

The Merrell, Edelhardt, George Reeves, and Lindeman Phases (A.D. 800–1000)

Defined in terms of distinctive ceramic assemblages, these four tenth-century A.D. phases (Fig. 49) are characterized by a number of changes in both material culture and domestic architecture. An increasing diversity is evident in ceramic assemblages and in ceramic design elements. Structures continue to be built using single posts placed in rectangular basins, but there is both an increase in the mean size of structures, and a larger range of variation in structure dimensions.

In the Late Bluff tradition area, Merrell phase (A.D. 900–950) components have been identified at five sites: several areas at Cahokia, Kane Village, Radic, Robinson's Lake, and A. G. Church (Table 12; Fig. 59). Occupations of the subsequent Edelhardt phase (A.D. 950–1000) are evident in a number of areas of Cahokia, and excavation of Edelhardt phase components has also taken place at the BBB Motor, Knoebel, and Lohmann sites. An Edelhardt phase occupation has been identified at the Bridgeton site along the lower Missouri River (Wright 1986).

Within the Pulcher tradition area to the south, George Reeves phase (A.D. 900–950) components have been excavated at the George Reeves, Range, and Westpark sites, while Lindeman phase (A.D 950–1000) components have been investigated at the Range, Marcus, George Reeves, Schlemmer, Hamill, and Westpark sites (Table 12). The collection from the Caulk's Creek site along the lower Missouri River (Blake 1949) may represent the northwesternmost context of the Pulcher tradition during the George Reeves phase.

With the exception of Cahokia and the Range site, the only settlements known for the period A.D. 900–950 appear to be small hamlets of less than ten structures (Kane Village, Radic, Robinson's Lake, A. G. Church, George Reeves, Range, Westpark) (Figs. 60–61). The George Reeves phase settlement at the Range

Table 12. Excavated Sites with Late Emergent Mississippian Occupations

Site	Location	Results	Nature of Investigations	Reference
George Reeves Phase				
George Reeves	Bluffs above American Bottom	Definition of settlement	I-270 Project	McElrath and Finney 1987
Range	American Bottom floodplain	Definition of three settlements	I-270 Project	Kelly et al. 1989c
Westpark	Bluffs above American Bottom	Definition of settlement	Salvage	Kelly et al. 1989a
Caulk's Creek	Bluffs above Missouri River	Surface materials	Survey	Blake 1949
Lindeman Phase				
Range	American Bottom floodplain	Definition of settlement	I-270 Project	Kelly et al. 1989c
Marcus	American Bottom	Definition of settlement	I-270 Project	Emerson and Jackson 1987
George Reeves	Bluffs above American Bottom	Definition of settlement	I-270 Project	McElrath and Finney 1987
Westpark	Bluffs above American Bottom	Definition of settlement	Salvage	Kelly et al. 1989a
Hamill	American Bottom floodplain	Pit features	Salvage	Kelly et al. 1989a
Schlemmer	American Bottom floodplain	Definition of settlement	Salvage	Szuter 1979; Berres 1984
Merrell Phase				
Cahokia Merrell Tract	American Bottom floodplain	Pit features and structures	Testing	Kelly 1980
Cahokia Tract 15-B	American Bottom floodplain	Pit features and structures	Highway salvage	Vogel 1975
Kane Village	Bluff base American Bottom	Features	Salvage	Munson and Anderson 1973
Henderson	Uplands Wood River	Pit features	Testing	Hawks 1985
Robinson's Lake	American Bottom floodplain	Definition of settlement	I-270 Project	Milner 1984b
Radic	American Bottom floodplain	Definition of settlement	I-270 Project	McElrath et al. 1987
AG Church	Uplands Canteen Creek	Pit features	Salvage	Pauketat n.d.
Edelhart Phase				
Cahokia Merrell Tract	American Bottom floodplain	Pit features and structures	Testing	Kelly 1980
Cahokia Powell Tract	American Bottom floodplain	Pit features and structures	Highway salvage	O'Brien 1972
Cahokia Tracts 15-A and 15-B	American Bottom floodplain	Pit features and structures	Highway salvage	Hall 1975a; Vogel 1975
BBB Motor	American Bottom floodplain	Definition of settlement	I-270 Project	Emerson and Jackson 1984
Lohmann	American Bottom	Pit features and structure?	I-270 Project	Esarey with Good 1981
Knoebel	Silver Creek	Definition of settlement	Highway salvage	Bareis 1976
Lambert-St. Louis Airport	Uplands Coldwater Creek	Pit features	Salvage	Blake 1955
Bridgeton	Missouri River terrace	Pit features	UMSTL field school	Wright 1986

site appears to be the initial stage of a large village that persisted into the Lindeman phase. The Merrell phase structures identified at the Cahokia site (Merrell Tract and perhaps Tract 15-B) may in fact be part of a large community.

The large George Reeves phase village at the Range site is characterized by a large central plaza delineated by a linear distribution of structures along three sides (Fig. 40). A large rectangular single post building is located at the northwest end of this area, while a set of four pits arranged in a square about a central post are at the opposite end of the plaza. Both the building and pits were rebuilt or replaced on several occasions. This central area was flanked in a symmetrical fashion by a series of courtyards with associated structures. This community represents the nucleation of various settlements in the area into a single community, and the central plaza and its affiliated facilities represents the best evidence for social ranking at this time.

A greater variety of settlement types is known for the period A.D. 950–1000. Small, one to three structure farmsteads (Fig. 62) have been identified at a number of sites: Schlemmer, George Reeves, Westpark, Range, Marcus, and Cahokia (Powell Tract). A larger, 16 structure hamlet has been excavated at the BBB Motor site (Fig. 63), and a large village of 154 structures has been uncovered at the Range site. In addition, the 50 single post, basin structures of Tract 15-A at the Cahokia site presumably represent a portion of a large village. It was not possible to determine the size of other settlements of this time period

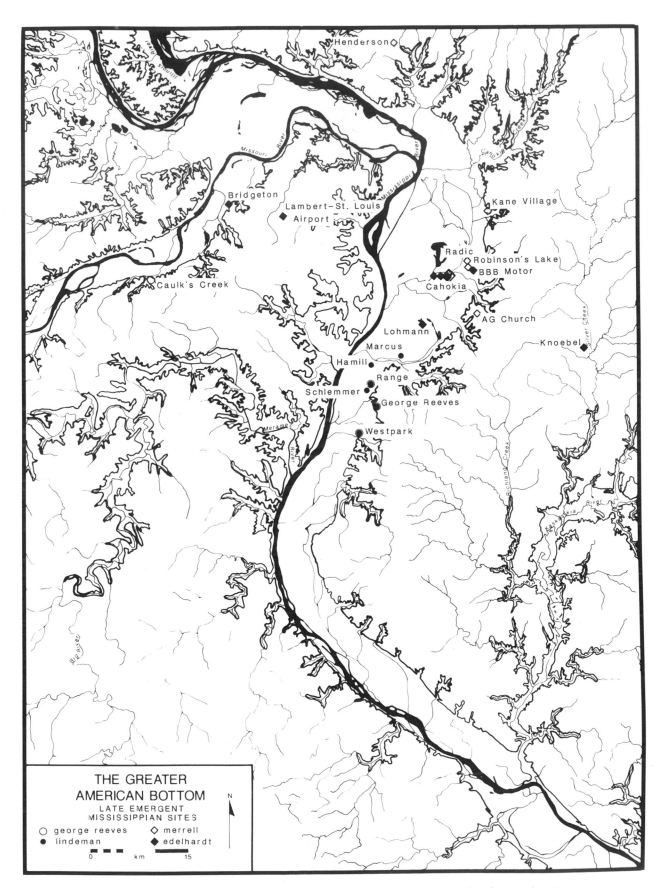

Fig. 59. The distribution of selected late Emergent Mississippian period sites (A.D. 900–1000) within the American Bottom.

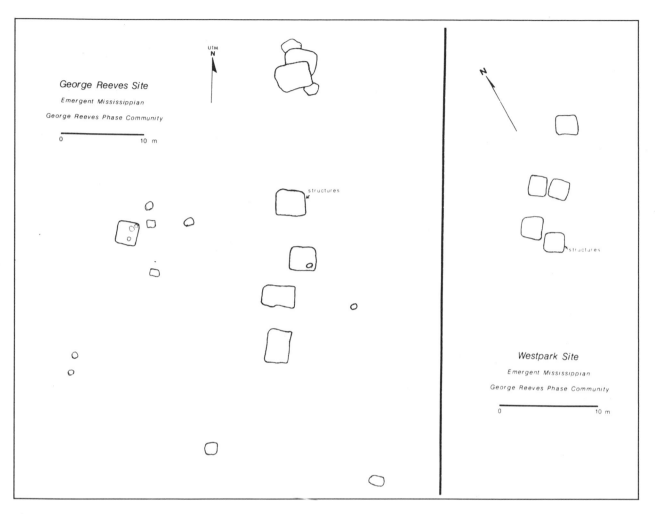

Fig. 60. George Reeves phase community plans at the George Reeves and Westpark sites.

identified in other areas of Cahokia or at the Lohmann site.

Of particular importance is the initial appearance of sizable villages with population that may have numbered in the hundreds during the period A.D. 950–1000. The large Lindeman phase village at the Range site (Fig. 42) differs in its configuration from the earlier George Reeves phase village. There is a shift in the location of the central plaza to a position on the lake side of the community at the end of the George Reeves phase, but also persisting into the initial part of the Lindeman phase. Except for a large rectangular pit, this area is devoid of any central ceremonial features. A large rectangular, single post basin structure is located to the southwest of this central pit. Other large basin structures flank the northwest edge of this plaza. In general

there is an expansion of the community to the northwest and northeast. The remaining structures are distributed around ten courtyards. Most of these smaller courtyards contain central features. Presumably, these courtyards are the focal point of certain social groups, such as lineages.

This expansion is more evident in the subsequent episode of the village, especially with additional structures in the northwest quadrant of the village. The central plaza shifted to the southwest, with four large rectangular pits arranged in a square and a large basin structure to the southwest. An unusual complex of structures and pits in a square configuration were associated with a large courtyard at the western edge of the village. While it is possible that these two central areas are contemporary, the west-

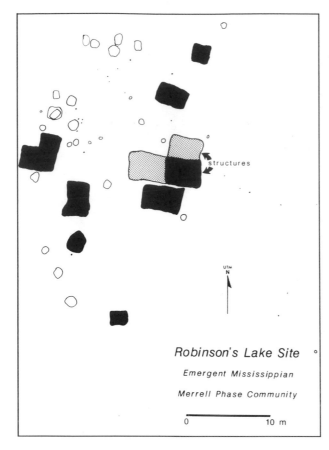

Fig. 61. The Merrell phase community plan at the Robinson's Lake site.

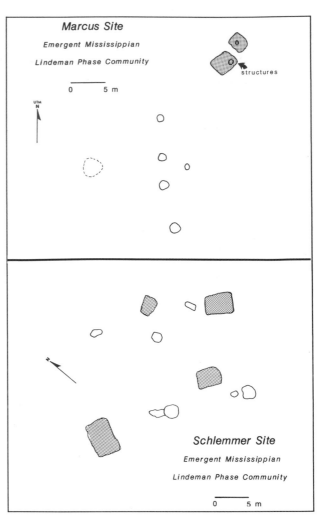

Fig. 62. Lindeman phase community plans at the Schlemmer and Marcus sites.

ern one may have subsequently replaced the one along the lake. Also of interest is the peripheral placement of four central pits in courtyards along the northwest margins of the village.

This change in community plan would appear to represent the coalescence of lineage level social groups in one location, beginning as early as the George Reeves phase (A.D. 900–950) in the Range site location. This lineage coalescence is certainly evident by the subsequent Lindeman phase, and in part may be a response to continued population growth in the American Bottom region.

Changes in the location of the central plaza presumably reflect certain political shifts, in that, for example, the death of a village chief necessitated a transfer of political authority. The seemingly clear pattern of ranking is not as prevalent during the subsequent transition and the Lindeman phase. There

may have been a movement of the village leader to a location such as Lunsford-Pulcher during the George Reeves phase, with the Range village assuming a new chief and a more subordinate role. Certainly the configuration of the Lunsford-Pulcher mound center with its large central mound and flanking smaller mounds points in this direction.

By the end of the Lindeman occupation, however, this village was reduced in size. This may indicate the dispersal of the village population into small social units, such as the numerous farmsteads recorded for this time period. At the same time, however, the presence of even larger settlements, such as Lunsford-Pulcher (Fig. 53), at about this period of time may

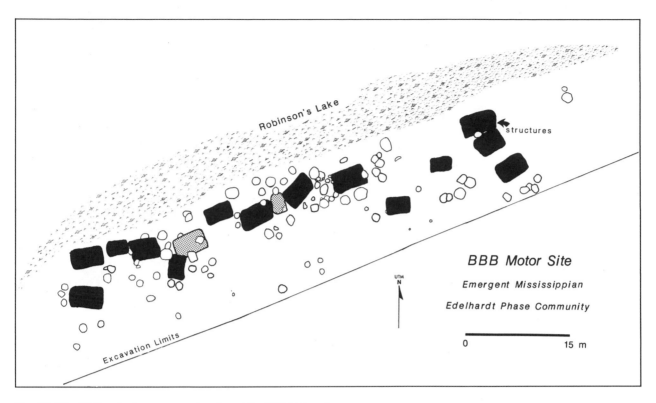

Fig. 63. The Edelhardt phase community plan at the BBB Motor site.

reflect the continued coalescence of lineage-level social units into even larger communities.

While there is at present little direct evidence for the construction of platform mounds in the American Bottom area prior to A.D. 1000, it would not be surprising if such evidence eventually was forthcoming, given the level of sociopolitical organization reflected in increasingly complex community patterns.

A series of single and multiple mound centers from Cahokia south to Prairie du Rocher may very well represent platform mounds constructed by Emergent Mississippian populations in these areas. Most of these mounds are relatively small when compared to the later Mississippian platform mounds. Farming has distorted their original shape so that it is difficult to conclude at this time that they were even platform mounds. Most of the sites involved are multicomponent sites with extensive Late Woodland, Patrick phase occupations. For those in the Pulcher tradition area, there is often an extensive Lindeman-Lindhorst occupation. These centers were first described by Porter (1974). It was subsequently noted (Kelly 1980) that these multimound centers were located in close

proximity to the Mississippi River and in a downstream position from the mouth of large streams exiting the Ozarks (Fig. 53). It was proposed at that time that these centers were constructed during the latter part of the Emergent Mississippian period. This is still a viable proposition, especially in light of the recent Range site data. This is more apt to be true in the case of the multimound centers such as Lunsford-Pulcher, Washausen, Maeys, and Mathews, in that they reflect occupations over an extended period of time. The configuration of mounds at the Lunsford-Pulcher site certainly reinforces the early placement of these centers.

The Late Bluff tradition area of the American Bottom likely witnessed changes in community patterning and sociopolitical organization similar to those just described for the Pulcher tradition area. While direct evidence is lacking, mound construction may also have begun in the Cahokia area by A.D. 950, based on other lines of evidence such as the unusually large basin structures documented at the Merrell Tract (cf. Kelly 1980).

By A.D. 1000, the end of the Emergent Mississippian period, there is clear evidence of increased interaction both within the American Bottom region and beyond. The exchange of ceramic vessels and lithic raw materials between the Late Bluff and Pulcher tradition areas persists. Mill Creek chert hoes appear to be traded into the region in even greater numbers, and Anculosa shell beads also continue to flow into the region. Shell-tempered jars, most likely originating in southeast Missouri, initially appear during the Loyd phase, but increase in frequency by A.D. 1000. In addition, there is some evidence for a local shift to the use of shell as a tempering agent by Edelhardt potters, as evidenced by the BBB Motor site ceramic assemblage (Emerson and Jackson 1984). Other exotic ceramic types such as Dillinger Cordmarked, Yankeetown Incised, Kersey Incised, and a variant of Larto Red-filmed in the form of hooded bottles, are coming into the American Bottom region from groups in southern Illinois, western Kentucky, and southeast Missouri (Kelly 1980; Emerson and Jackson 1984; Kelly et al. 1984b). Coles Creek ceramic types, originating in the lower Mississippi Valley, also appear for the first time at about A.D. 950 (Kelly 1980; Emerson and Jackson 1984).

While considerable residential and sociopolitical stability is evident among the various American Bottom communities of A.D. 950–1000, there is clear evidence of increasingly broader cultural and spatial patterns of interaction, at a number of different levels. While local exchange may focus on certain needed resources, extraregional exchange may have been designed to accommodate social and religious obligations.

The Lohmann and Lindhorst Phases (A.D. 1000–1050)

The A.D. 1000 time line marks the temporal boundary between the Emergent and Early Mississippian periods, with the Lohmann and Lindhorst phases representing the initial cultural manifestations of the latter period in the American Bottom. It is clear that the developmental antecedents of the Early Mississippian lie in the preceding complexes of the Emergent Mississippian period. In many respects the Stirling phase (A.D. 1050–1150) represents the climax of the Emergent Mississippian traditions in the region.

The ceramic trends (Fig. 57), established much earlier, that serve to distinguish and define the Late Bluff and Pulcher tradition areas also continued into the Early Mississippian period. By the end of the Stirling phase these traditions had merged. In the Late Bluff tradition area to the north, shell tempering had been assimilated into the ceramic manufacturing process by A.D. 1000. Ceramic design elements such as plain and filmed jar bodies also become prevalent by the Early Mississippian. To the south, limestone temper persists as the primary agent well into the Stirling phase, while jars with plain or filmed necks and cordmarked bodies persist into the Lohmann-equivalent Lindhorst phase.

In addition to the ceramic elements of construction and design that serve to distinguish the Emergent and Early Mississippian material culture assemblages in both the Late Bluff and Pulcher tradition areas, a shift to wall trench structures is also evident throughout the American Bottom region after A.D. 1000. Accompanying this alteration in construction mode were a number of other changes relating to structure size and the organization of space within structures. Structures increased in size during the Early Mississippian period, with this increase reflecting, in part, accommodation of internal storage facilities, which were almost entirely lacking in Emergent Mississippian structures.

A number of Lohmann phase occupations have been identified through excavation (Table 13). Farmstead settlements have been uncovered at the Turner site, and at least three sites in the I-270 extension (Fig. 64). Work at two single mound centers—Lohmann and Horseshoe Lake—have revealed evidence for Lohmann occupations. At Cahokia, excavations have exposed evidence for Lohmann materials in a number of areas, indicating that by this period Cahokia had emerged as a mound center supporting populations exhibiting considerable status differentiation, and had a number of different areas of residential habitation. Based on excavations carried out on the east lobes of Monks Mound, and within the associated reclaimed borrow pit under Mound 51 to the southeast of Monks Mound at Cahokia (Fig. 54), it appears that construction on the largest mound north of Mexico had begun by A.D. 1000, if not sooner (Kelly 1988).

In addition, the elaborate mortuary program centered on high status individuals interred in Mound 72 at Cahokia (Fig. 54) provides clear evidence of the

Table 13. Excavated Sites with Early Mississippian Occupations

Site	Location	Results	Nature of Investigations	Reference
Lindhorst Phase				
George Reeves	Bluffs above American Bottom	Definition of settlement	I-270 Project	McElrath and Finney 1987
Range	American Bottom floodplain	Definition of four settlements	I-270 Project	Mehrer 1982
Carbon Dioxide	American Bottom floodplain	Definition of settlement	I-270 Project	Finney 1985
Lunsford-Pulcher	American Bottom	Pit features and structure	Testing and salvage	Freimuth 1974; Griffin 1977
Westpark	Bluffs above American Bottom	Definition of settlement	Salvage	Kelly et al. 1989a
Lohmann Phase				
Cahokia Merrell Tract	American Bottom floodplain	Post pits	Research and testing	Kelly 1980
Cahokia Powell Tract	American Bottom floodplain	Pit features and structures	Highway salvage	O'Brien 1972; Ahler and DePuydt 1987
Cahokia Tract 15-A	American Bottom floodplain	Pit features and structues	Highway salvage	Hall 1975; Vogel 1975
Cahokia ICT-II	American Bottom floodplain	Definition of settlement	Museum salvage	Brown et al. 1986
Cahokia Sub-mound 51	American Bottom floodplain	Borrow pit fill	Testing	Chmurny 1973
Cahokia Mound 72	American Bottom floodplain	Mound excavation	Research	Fowler and Anderson 1975
Cahokia Monks Mound, East Lobes	American Bottom floodplain	Buried deposits beneath mound	Research and testing	Williams 1975
Fill	American Bottom floodplain	Pit features	Highway salvage	Porter 1974
Horseshoe Lake	American Bottom floodplain	Pit features and structure	Research and testing	Gregg 1975
BBB Motor	American Bottom floodplain	Definition of settlement	I-270 Project	Emerson and Jackson 1984
Lohmann	American Bottom floodplain	Pit features and structures	I-270 Project	Esarey with Good 1981
Turner	American Bottom floodplain	Definition of settlements	I-270 Project	Milner 1983
Olszewski	American Bottom floodplain	Definition of settlement	I-270 Project extension	Hanenberger 1986
Esterline	American Bottom floodplain	Definition of settlement	I-270 Project extension	Jackson 1988a
Willoughby	American Bottom floodplain	Definition of settlement	I-270 Project extension	Jackson 1987
Knoebel	Silver Creek terrace	Definition of settlement	Highway salvage	Bareis 1976
Lienesch	Uplands, Richland Creek drainage	Definition of settlement	Highway salvage	Bareis 1972
Christ	Bluffs above Silver Creek	Pit features and structures	Salvage	Kelly et al. 1989a
Lambert-St. Louis Airport	Uplands, Coldwater Creek	Pit features	Salvage	Blake 1955

development of substantial status differentiation within Cahokia populations by A.D. 1000 (Fowler 1974).

Lohmann phase residential areas have been identified in a number of different locations within Cahokia (Table 13), including portions of the Powell Tract, Tract 15-A, and the ICT-II Tract. Within Tract 15-A the residential area appears to be a continuation of the Edelhardt phase community. On the Merrell Tract, Lohmann phase ceramics were recovered from a large post pit, which may indicate the utilization of this area for special purposes. The Cahokia Woodhenge, however, originally assigned to the Fairmount phase (A.D. 900–1050) of an earlier cultural historical framework, is now thought to date to the late Stirling or early Moorehead phase (A.D. 1100–1200).

To the south, in the Pulcher tradition area, Lindhorst phase farmsteads have been excavated at the Range, Carbon Dioxide, and George Reeves sites (Table 13, Fig. 64). A nodal settlement (Emerson and Milner 1982) appears at the Range site and presumably persists into the Stirling phase. An intense occupation at the Lunsford-Pulcher site, documented as the result of salvage excavation by the author and under analysis by Charles Bentz, likely indicates a major mound center. Presumably by this period mound centers had developed at a number of larger sites within the American Bottom in addition to Cahokia, such as Lohmann, Horseshoe Lake, Lunsford-Pulcher, Maeys, and Washausen. This emergence of mound centers represents a continuation of the trend toward population nucleation and a coalescence of social units within the American Bottom. At the same time, however, there is some indication from upland surveys east of the Lunsford-Pulcher site (Koldehoff 1989) that there was a parallel increase in the presence of small social units (farmsteads) within the upland areas, especially along watershed divides,

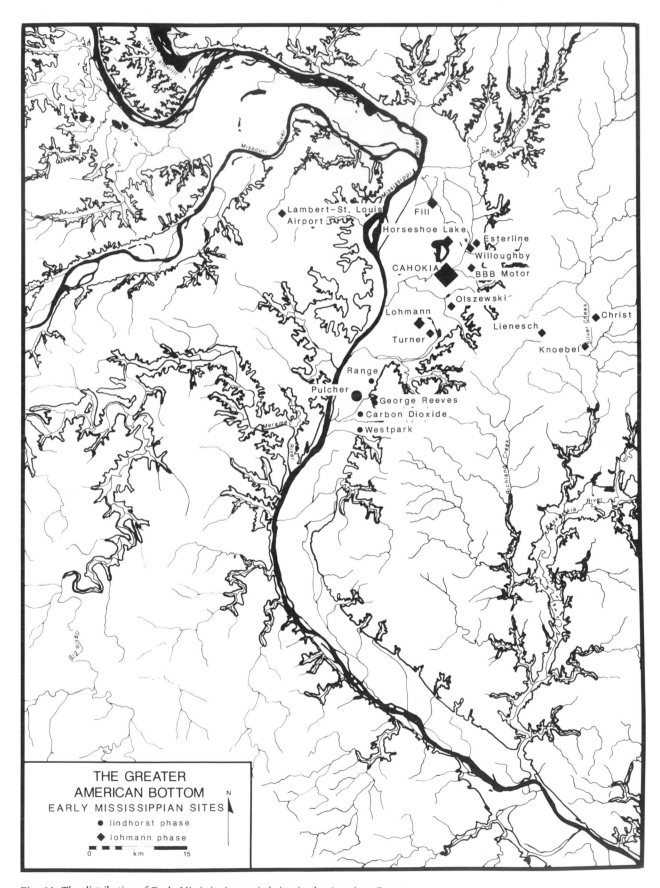

Fig. 64. The distribution of Early Mississippian period sites in the American Bottom.

suggesting a dispersal of population out of the American Bottom proper.

After A.D. 1000 the Emergent Mississippian period patterns of local and extraregional exchange outlined above appear to intensify. Burlington chert continues as the primary lithic raw material moving through exchange networks that operated within the American Bottom and beyond (Koldehoff 1987). Despite the availability of local cherts in the Pulcher tradition area, Burlington materials dominate the lithic assemblages, continuing a trend first evident during the George Reeves (A.D. 900–950) and Lindemann (A.D. 950–1000) phases. Burlington chert was used in the production of the flake tools which dominate Mississippian lithic assemblages, for the manufacture of microliths associated with the production of marine shell beads (Yerkes 1983), as well as for a large biface industry of hoes and woodworking tools, and a small arrowhead industry. Burlington chert was also exchanged as far south as northwest Mississippi during this period (Koldehoff 1987). Ceramic vessels from the lower Mississippi Valley also continue to be exchanged north into the American Bottom region (Kelly 1988). Mill Creek chert, in the form of hoes, continues to be an important item of exchange. Kaolin cherts from the Mill Creek quarry areas of southern Illinois also appear as projectile points (Fowler 1974) and perhaps hoes in American Bottom assemblages during this time period.

While much of the material exchanged both locally and interregionally had utilitarian purposes, the artifactual assemblages recovered from Mound 72 provide insights into another aspect of existing exchange networks. Caches of exotic projectile points, discoidals, mica sheets, marine shell beads, and rolled copper indicate the broad geographic reach of the interregional exchange network in high status goods during this time period. With the exception of copper and mica, outlying settlements in the American Bottom dating to this time period have also yielded the classes of material represented in the Mound 72 burial assemblage, but in much smaller quantities (Kelly 1989).

In addition to providing substantial evidence for the long distance exchange of elite grave goods, Mound 72 also provides the earliest clear and direct evidence for marked status differentiation and a mortuary program centered on an elite individual. Despite the presence of over 240 burials (Rose and Wells 1972), and abundant elaborate and exotic burial objects, Mound 72 is not solely an elite cemetery area, but rather appears to represent a monument to a particular authority figure and his larger social group. In fact, most of the individuals interred would appear to be the "retainers" of this high status individual (Fowler 1974). Despite the abundant burial goods present in Mound 72, it is a relatively small monument that appears early in Cahokia's history as a mound center.

Having provided a brief background summary of the culture history of the American Bottom area over the five-century span (A.D. 600–1050) that witnessed the in situ emergence of a ranked sociopolitical system fueled by maize centered field agriculture, I can now turn to a consideration of the various models of explanation that have been proposed for this complex trajectory of cultural development.

PREVIOUS MODELS OF MISSISSIPPIAN EMERGENCE IN THE AMERICAN BOTTOM

Over the past twenty-five years a number of models and interpretations have been proposed regarding the initial development of Mississippian culture in the American Bottom region. Until recently these explanatory models, and the question of Mississippian development in the region, focused on the large mound center of Cahokia. Porter (1974:6–8) provided a brief review of the then recent models of Mississippian development at Cahokia, identifying a basic dichotomy of local evolution vs. migration-contact explanations.

Local Evolution Explanations

The essential premise of local evolutionary models was that Cahokia was an in situ developmental phenomena emerging out of a local Late Woodland cultural context, with minimal external stimulus. Variations on such a local developmental theme have been presented by Fowler (1974), Benchley (1974), and Gregg (1975).

At the time that these local evolutionary models were proposed, a substantial amount of salvage work at Cahokia and a number of outlying sites such as Mitchell (Porter 1969, 1974), Kane Village (Munson and Anderson 1973), and Loyd (Hall and Vogel 1963) (Figs. 53, 54) had been completed, and the 1972 Cahokia Conference had produced a new chronological scheme for Cahokia (Fowler and Hall 1975). In addition, Vogel's (1975) ceramic analysis had been completed, as had the survey work by Munson (1971) and Harn (1971). O'Brien's research on the Powell Tract ceramics had been published (1972), and Chmurny's (1973) dissertation on environmental data from the reclaimed borrow pit below Mound 51 at Cahokia was available. In addition, Fowler had conducted extensive NSF funded research at Cahokia. A comprehensive literature review had been completed (Fowler 1969), a detailed site map had been developed (Fowler n.d.), and excavations had been carried out on the first terrace of Monks Mound (Benchley 1974), the east lobes of Monks Mound (Williams 1975), the stockade line just east of Monks Mound (Anderson 1969), and at Mound 72 (Fowler 1974). In addition, a controlled surface collection had been conducted on the Ramey Tract (Vander Leest 1980).

Other work at Cahokia included an annual field school conducted by the University of Illinois, Urbana-Champaign, under the direction of Charles J. Bareis. Bareis's investigations were conducted on the Powell Tract, Ramey Tract, Sub-51 borrow pit, and the first terrace of Monks Mound (Bareis 1975a, 1975b). Bareis was also involved in salvage excavations on the Powell Tract (including the Gem Store), Collinsville Airport (Bareis and Lathrap 1962), Master Seed and Mix (Bareis 1963), Dunham Tract (Bareis 1967), and Fingerhut (Bareis 1963). Outside of Cahokia, Bareis carried out salvage excavations at several interior upland sites in the Silver Creek drainage, including Knoebel (Bareis 1976), Faust (Bareis 1968), and Lienesch (Bareis 1972).

The initial Tract 15-A excavations resulted in definition of the Cahokia Woodhenge (Wittry 1969), which expanded into subsequent excavations centered on the definition of this large monument. Problem-oriented research was also conducted on the fourth terrace of Monks Mound by James Porter, Nelson Reed, and John Bennett of Washington University (Reed et al. 1968). This work was continued in the early 1970s by Reed and Browman of Washington University (Fischer n.d.). Finally, Beloit College under the direction of Robert Salzer was involved in the pursuit of the western stockade wall on the Merrell Tract (Salzer 1975; Kelly 1980).

A number of projects were also initiated by Fowler for

the area outside of Cahokia. Test excavations were carried out at the Horseshoe Lake site, a single mound center (Gregg 1975), and additional surveys of outlying areas of the American Bottom were undertaken (Brandt 1972).

While the studies cited above provide some indication of the research carried out from 1960 to the mid-1970s, is also true that only a small percentage of the data recovered has been analyzed and published.

Based on the information available at that time, Fowler (1974) proposed that by the Patrick and "unnamed" (now Loyd) phases (A.D. 600–900), populations at Cahokia were fully agricultural, and that they represented the "beginning of population expansion and in situ development that became part of the Mississippian cultural tradition at the Cahokia site" (1974: 19). While Fowler suggested the development of a number of Patrick phase villages at Cahokia, it was not until the Fairmount phase (A.D. 900–1050) that any degree of sociopolitical complexity was recognized. The Emergent Mississippian period and its developmental trajectory that linked the Patrick phase to the Early Mississippian portion of the Fairmount phase, was not, however, addressed by Fowler.

In a brief overview of Cahokia's development, Benchley (1974:40) stated:

> It seems more profitable at this stage of Cahokian and Mississippian research to view the rapid changes in ceramics and other aspects of culture in the Cahokia area during the Fairmount phase as part of an *in situ* evolutionary process. The Fairmount Phase represents a point at which increasingly dense populations become reorganized for the more efficient allocation of goods and services by means of a ranked sociopolitical order, differentiation in the form and function of settlements, and an increasing specialization of pursuits among the populace.

Although Benchley (1974:39–40) noted the presence of an exchange network, it was not discussed in detail, and she does not discuss population growth as a possible variable of cultural change.

Based on excavations at the Horseshoe Lake site, Gregg's thesis (1975) represented a test of one aspect of Fowler's (1974, 1975) four-level settlement system model of the Cahokia region. In Fowler's model Cahokia represented a single, very large, first-line settlement, with multiple mound and single mound centers forming the second and third levels of settlement, respectively. The remaining nonmound settlements comprised the last and lowest level of settlement. Gregg examined the possible specialized nature of third-line single mound centers, testing the hypothesis that Horseshoe Lake primarily functioned to supply Cahokia with an agricultural surplus of maize. Gregg also examined the initial development of Cahokia and its perceived four level settlement hierarchy (1975:-56–57). Following Fowler, population increase and agricultural dependence were identified as the basis for the initial development of the Cahokia settlement system of specialized third-line mound centers, with the beginning of this developmental trend recognized during the Patrick phase (A.D. 600–750). In the subsequent century (A.D. 750–900), intensification of bottomland agriculture and competition for agricultural land by an extensive system of farming communities presumably led to increasing territoriality and subsequent hereditary class stratification. By the beginning of the Fairmount phase (A.D. 900), platform mounds had emerged as a symbol of authority. Out of this sociopolitical context, Cahokia emerged as the dominant community within the system.

Hall (1966, 1973, 1975a) and Chmurny (1973) present two additional variations on a general internal evolutionary model of development for Cahokia, both of which include external influences of one kind or another. In his 1966 paper entitled *Cahokia Chronology,* Hall (1966:6) states:

> Mississippian culture may well have initially appeared at Cahokia with the baggage of some group that could be called original Mississippian, but if so these Mississippians need not have traveled from very far and it would be a mistake to think of Mississippian culture spreading only by the displacement of Woodland peoples.

Hall seems to indicate that Cahokia Mississippian culture was a local development. His perspective at that time was based largely on the data base resulting from the salvage work of the 1960s, especially the work conducted at Tract 15-A at Cahokia. Over the intervening years, Hall has written a number of articles that examine cultural process at Cahokia (1967, 1975b, 1980, 1985a), with a particular emphasis on the interaction

of Cahokia populations with those of the neighboring geographical areas to the north and northwest. Hall recognizes a number of elements as playing a central role in the development of Cahokia, and his position is best summarized in the following passage:

> Rooting the Cahokia Mississippian tradition exclusively within what we can see of the Patrick Phase at Cahokia is about as reasonable as generating Metropolitan Chicago from the Fort Dearborn community of 1812 without considering the contribution made by later arrivals (Hall 1975a:18).

Hall considers the Mississippian emergence to have probably begun locally with "organization changes within a society which was Woodland" (Hall 1975a: 23). Subsequent to this initial local beginning, Hall considers influence from the south initially, and increasingly from the north and northwest subsequent to A.D. 1000, to have played a critical role in the development of Cahokia cultural systems.

Hall also recognizes the role of climatic change in the initial development of Mississippian cultures in the Cahokia area, identifying the onset of the Neo-Atlantic climatic episode at A.D. 900 as bringing increased rainfall and temperature and a more favorable context for bottomland maize agriculture. Following Farnsworth (1973), Hall (1980) proposed that slash and burn agricultural techniques developed during the Late Woodland period, opening forested areas to cultivation.

While Chmurny's (1973) research did not focus specifically on Mississippian development in the American Bottom, his analysis of well-preserved floral and faunal assemblages from the Sub-mound 51 Lohmann phase borrow pit led him to formulate a model of cultural transformation for the American Bottom region in which "an agricultural system based on divided risks" led to the "formulation of a redistributive economy and a hierarchically ranked society."

A final model proposed to explain the development of Mississippian culture at Cahokia and within the American Bottom, which can be briefly outlined now under the general heading of "local evolution," is one that I presented ten years ago (Kelly 1980). This 1980 "Integration Model" was based primarily on insights gained from an analysis of excavated materials from the Merrell Tract at Cahokia, along with experience and ideas resulting from my involvement both in Porter's survey of the Mississippi Valley as far south as Cape Girardeau, Missouri, and the initial seasons of the FAI-270 project.

The explanation I proposed was labeled an "Integration Model" because it was "an attempt to integrate the evolutionary trends of increased complexity with patterns of increased interaction that were evident over a larger geographical area, i.e. the Mississippi River Valley" (Kelly 1980:170). The underlying basic premise of this Integration Model was that the emergence of Mississippian culture at Cahokia and the adjacent American Bottom could be

> . . .attributed to socio-economic developments occurring throughout the central and lower Mississippi River Valley. These developments were rooted in relatively large populations that formed permanent agricultural communities. While populations increased once the latter were attained, increased population density may have initially contributed to sedentism and agricultural intensification. Regardless, these factors were clearly interrelated to one another with no specific pattern of cause and effect evident at this time (Kelly 1980:171).

In marked contrast to the different models of local evolution briefly outlined above, a number of models of cultural development at Cahokia have been proposed that identify external variables as playing prime-mover roles in the initial development of Mississippian culture in the American Bottom region.

Migration-Contact Models

Migration-contact models of Mississippian development in the American Bottom consider "migrations and direct contacts with areas to the south as the prime factor whereby Late Woodland peoples were acculturated for purposes of the 'Cahokians'" (Porter 1974:7). Porter (1969, 1974), Vogel (1975), and Freimuth (1974) provide a number of different variations on this general, external influence, explanatory framework.

Freimuth (1974:83) perceived "the blending of local and Caddoan influences...as one part of the stimulus for the subsequent rise of the Mississippian culture in the American Bottom." The "Caddoan ceramics, mesquite, Alba points, calendrics, site planning, and possibly political organization" evident at Cahokia, Mitchell,

and Lunsford-Pulcher were the Caddoan influences that Freimuth suggested as contributing to the rise of Cahokia-Mississippian culture. Freimuth explicitly identified both the region (i.e., the Caddoan area) and the cultural elements constituting external causal factors in the initial development of Cahokia-Mississippian. As noted by Hall (1985a:40), Freimuth was undoubtedly influenced by Lathrap's unpublished theories concerning Mississippian developments in the Cahokia area. Lathrap suggested that the organizational principles for Cahokia-Mississippian were ultimately derived from Mexico, in the form of a "developed Mississippian culture through or from the Caddoan area" (Hall 1985a:40).

The developmental models proposed by Porter for the Cahokia area (1969, 1974) were similarly influenced by Lathrap. Although Porter's thesis did not directly focus on the origins of Cahokia and Mississippian culture in the American Bottom, he did review various interpretive models, and took the position that "the truth of Cahokia prehistory most likely lies somewhere in between, with a heavy preference toward the migration-contact view" (1974:7–8). Based on survey data from the American Bottom, Porter delineated a settlement system model composed of a series of Late Woodland/Mississippian "villages" with mounds, which were distributed along the Mississippi Valley to the south of the American Bottom as far south as the mouth of the Kaskaskia River. According to this "chain settlement" model, each of these mound centers was postulated to have emerged in response to certain economic factors that came into play when agriculture became important (Porter 1974:27–28). There was a subsequent shift from the chain pattern toward a central place theory hexagonal pattern that accompanied the appearance of a "merchant class." In an earlier publication, Porter (1969) presents a shorter description of this developmental process in which economic systems based on simple reciprocity evolved into redistribution systems and finally market-based systems.

Vogel provides an explanation for the initial development of Mississippian culture in the American Bottom that is based, in large part, on perceived changes in ceramic assemblages. His Cahokia ceramic sequence (1975) included both Late Woodland (Bluff) and subsequent Mississippian phases. The ceramic assemblage of the earliest phase he considered (Loyd) lacked any evidence of "Mississippian influence," while the succeeding Merrell phase not only contained evidence of Mississippian influence, but also exhibited considerable change in the Woodland (Bluff) component of the ceramic assemblage. From this, Vogel (1975:70)

> . . .postulated that Mississippian culture entered the American Bottom in a [sic] incipient form as part of an interaction situation no later than the A.D. 900s. The Mississippian phenomena at the Cahokia site were the product of the successful integration of many modes from a variety of sources, spread over as much as two centuries of Late Woodland Mississippian interaction, as well as the interaction to be expected between early Mississippian centers. The fathers of the 'Old Village' were many and included local antecedents.

Hall (1985a:32) suggests that Vogel was stimulated by Caldwell's (1964) essay on *Interaction Spheres*.

In each of the models outlined above, three general variables were identified by different researchers as central to the development of Mississippian sociopolitical systems in the American Bottom: population growth, agricultural intensification, and local and interregional changes in social interaction and organization. Because of the scattered, only partially reported, and largely poorly understood nature of the American Bottom archaeological data base prior to the inception of the FAI-270 project, these various models were based on "bits and pieces" of evidence, and were of necessity only broadly sketched. As a result of the FAI-270 project, and its deliberate focus on the delineation of prehistoric community plans in the American Bottom, however, a far more substantial and well-controlled data base is available from which a more detailed approximation of Mississippian emergence in the region can be proposed.

AN ALTERNATIVE MODEL

The description and explanation of Mississippian emergence in the American Bottom to be outlined below is firmly based in the past twenty-five years of research in the region, and pays particular attention to the research and interpretations derived from the FAI-270 project (Bareis and Porter 1984). It is also an explicit in situ developmental model in that it recognizes that Mississippian sociopolitical systems have deep developmental roots extending far back into indigenous Late Woodland cultural contexts. No longer is there any

need to perceive Mississippian culture in the American Bottom as having been introduced from somewhere else. This, however, does not mean that there were no external factors involved. Interaction with other regions was an integral aspect of the Mississippian emergence within the American Bottom. In proposing a trajectory of cultural development that spans the period of time from A.D. 600–1100 and outlines the relationships between different aspects of this complex process of change, population growth is as good an entry point as any.

It appears that there was a steady increase in population levels in the American Bottom throughout the Late Woodland period (A.D. 300–750). There are more and larger Patrick phase (A.D. 600–700) sites recorded in the region, especially on the floodplain, than are known for the Rosewood (A.D. 300–500) and Mund (A.D. 500–600) phases. It is not possible at the present time, however, to translate this increase in the size and number of sites during the Late Woodland period into accurate measures of rate of population growth or absolute measures of population density.

The increasing incorporation of starchy seeds into the diet can perhaps be identified as a factor allowing or encouraging this Late Woodland growth in population. The trend toward increasing reliance upon starchy seeds as a food source was apparently initiated prior to the Late Woodland period. Some changes in Late Woodland ceramic vessels may also be related to the improved processing of starchy seeds (Braun 1983). Buikstra et al. (1986) have recently proposed that improvements in the processing of starchy seeds resulted in "Gerber-like" gruels suitable for weaning infants; thereby decreasing the birth interval, and increasing fertility, thus resulting in population growth. In turn, the increased labor demands inherent in an increased reliance on cultivated plants may in turn have spurred population growth (cf. Braun 1977).

Despite population growth during the Late Woodland period, it does not appear that population had reached a density level sufficient to engender competition over certain limited resources. The basis for this supposition is the wide range of subsistence resources exploited by Patrick phase populations, especially in contrast to the subsequent Emergent Mississippian phases of A.D. 750–1000. During this two-century span, occupation space decreased along with the representation of certain subsistence items. At the Range site, for example, deer decrease in abundance from the Patrick phase into the Range phase, as do the number of small projectile points (Kelly et al. 1989b). Competition over resources may have begun to intensify during the Patrick phase, however, even though it is not clear in the archaeological record. There are some indications of individuals meeting a violent death at this time in the lower Illinois River valley (Perino 1973a, 1973b, 1973c), and increasing levels of tension and hostility both within and between settlements and larger communities may be reflected by the apparent frequent shifting of community size and organization at locations like the Range site. At the same time, however, similarities in ceramic assemblages over broad areas suggest broad-scale mechanisms of social interaction and communication. The discoidal, and the game within which it functioned, may have been one such mechanism of interaction. There are also some indications that some Patrick phase communities (e.g., P-4 at Range) had a ceremonial role, although it is not clear how positions of leadership were defined, attained, or maintained.

Although maize appears by the end of the Late Woodland period, one of the most important changes evident by the beginning of the Emergent Mississippian period at A.D. 750 was the increased importance of maize in the diet. At this point it is only possible to speculate why it was adopted. It clearly did not replace starchy seeds. Different species of starchy seeds would have been available for harvest at different periods of the year, with maygrass and little barley producing seed during the late spring, and knotweed and lambsquarter becoming available by mid-October. The indigenous starchy seed crops were labor intensive in terms of both harvesting and perhaps preparation, however (Braun 1977). Maize, in contrast, could have been picked in different forms throughout the summer and into the fall. Depending on the growing season, it might well have been double cropped or planted in staggered multiple crops. Over 42 types of maize dishes were known in the Southeast during the historic period (Swanton 1946:358). Maize could also have been stored in a variety of ways for later consumption—dried and stored on the cob or as shelled kernels, or as ground meal. Maize was clearly a more versatile crop than the indigenous starchy seed plants. Most importantly, it could produce large yields, with presumably less labor required to harvest and process it. Yet in spite of the ap-

parent advantages of maize, it was initially an addition to established field systems, rather than an outright replacement for local starchy seed crops.

Changes in other areas may also be related to the introduction and increasing importance of maize in the diet after A.D. 750. Changes in ceramic vessel morphology may relate to changes in the processing of maize. An increase in the number of large, deep pits with rectangular orifices, which parallels an overall decrease in the frequency of other features, and a marked decrease in earth ovens, may also be linked to the increasing dietary importance of maize.

The population increase evident in the American Bottom during the Late Woodland continues into the Emergent Mississippian period, based on an increase in the number of recorded Emergent Mississippian period sites relative to the preceding Late Woodland period (Kelly 1980). A number of indirect measures of population density also suggests continued population growth into the Emergent Mississippian period. Occupational areas decrease in size in a number of areas of the American Bottom, suggesting a premium is being placed on farmland adjacent to settlements. There may, in fact, be competition between settlements over available croplands. This economizing of space is particularly noticeable at the A.D. 750 transition point from Late Woodland to Emergent Mississippian. This economizing of habitation space may also reflect a need for additional cropland associated with the addition of maize to field systems. Again, it must be remembered that the rate and magnitude of demographic change is difficult to assess at this time.

Clearly the continuing growth in population during the Emergent Mississippian period influenced the manner in which cultural units were organized both internally and across the landscape. The emergence of *at least* two traditions out of an apparent single Late Woodland tradition is suggestive of the development of broad-scale social or ethnic boundaries. The distinctiveness of the ceramic assemblages in the area of these two traditions would seem to suggest that interaction and exchange of information between potters was limited, or that ceramic designs in the two areas were tightly tied to social identity. Whereas interaction during the Late Woodland was perhaps more widespread in terms of the number of individuals involved, interaction during the Mississippian period was perhaps restricted to a smaller segment of social units involved in the movement of certain commodities and raw materials across social boundaries. By the Range phase (A.D. 850–900), subsistence territories in the American Bottom appear to have shrunk considerably, based on the decrease in representation of upland species of animals such as deer, and a decrease in the representation of projectile points. It is also during the Range phase that Madison County shale jars reach a peak of representation in the Range site ceramic assemblage, indicating increased exchange with upland populations to the north.

The Dohack and Range phase community patterns at the Range site indicate, by A.D. 800–900, a very controlled and structured internal organization of space and people. As indicated earlier, certain features and symbols played a central role in this organization of space. The relatively small size and internal organization of each of these communities seems to indicate a social segment such as a lineage, with certain structures indicative of lineage authority. In turn, the distinctive central features may have reflected the village's ceremonial role within a larger group of similar villages. Such symbolism served to unify disparate communities.

A restructuring of communities appears to have begun during the George Reeves and Merrell phases (A.D. 900–1000). Settlements at the Range site reflect a larger population organized in a more constricted settlement area, while surveys in both upland and bottomland areas indicate a parallel dispersal of small social units across the landscape in hamlet and farmstead settlements. There is as yet no clear evidence of mound centers during this period. Sites such as Lunsford-Pulcher, which were well situated to control access to certain resources, would have been the most likely location for mound construction during this period, if it took place. The remaining multiple mound centers such as Washausen, Maeys, and Mathews were also positioned with respect to certain resources vis-à-vis the Mississippi River and streams exiting the Ozarks (Figs. 48, 53).

It would also have been at such settlements having control of access to certain limited resources where the critical transition to ranked social organization would have been most likely to have taken place. There is strong evidence in the organization of villages at the Range site and other similar settlements for strong lineage organization and authority structure centered on

hereditary lineage heads having been present in the American Bottom by A.D. 900–1000. Given this sociopolitical context, the next apparent change in organization would have involved the status separation and differential ranking of various lineages based on their relative wealth, power, and authority. An obvious basis for the emergence of differential ranking of lineages within the American Bottom would have involved differential access to, and control of, critical resources. The most likely resource to be "controlled" were the agricultural fields.

The initial basis, however, for such authority, as evinced at the Range site, was well rooted in the symbolism tied to the cross-in-circle. For certain southeastern groups the cross symbolized the position of the four logs of the sacred fire, which in turn was the earthy counterpart of the sun, the supreme sky being (Waring 1965; Hudson 1976). Thus, one's affiliation with this deity established the basis for religious and political authority. It was undoubtedly through such religious lines that control was established. Control not in a militaristic or hands-on manner, but one which was more a matter of perception on the part of the area's inhabitants.

Despite the availability of local cherts in the American Bottom area, there is a significant increase in Burlington cherts from the Crescent Hills quarry in lithic assemblages beginning in the George Reeves phase (A.D. 900–950). Access to the Burlington cherts of the Crescent Hills quarry could have been controlled by such emerging centers as Lunsford-Pulcher and Washausen. Numerous salt springs were also present in the area of the cherts (Kelly 1980). These settlements and others were well located with respect to the Mississippi River, an obvious corridor of movement downstream to a major Ozark river (the Meramec) that provides access to Ozark resources, as well as to streams exiting the Illinois bluffs such as Prairie du Pont and Fountain creeks.

The nucleated George Reeves/Lindeman phase village at the Range site was short-lived (50–75 years). Presumably it gave way to and was absorbed by a competing community at Lunsford-Pulcher. The layout of the Lunsford-Pulcher site may reflect the configuration of the large George Reeves village, reinforcing the possibility that this and other centers were being established at this time.

The smaller post A.D. 1000 Mississippian settlements

at Range may reflect continued nucleation and political centralization at centers such as Lunsford-Pulcher. The decrease in storage facilities at the smaller farmstead sites may in turn represent storage for immediate consumption. Surpluses may have been consolidated at the larger villages and centers. Whether these presumed surpluses entered tribute channels or were used in exchange for certain raw materials is, of course, difficult to ascertain. Certainly the variety of raw materials and commodities evident even at the small farmstead level points to some form of broad-scale exchange network.

While the developmental model outlined above follows the more general explanation proposed in 1980 (Kelly 1980), it also provides a more detailed consideration of the complex interaction between a number of causal variables. In summary, the emergence of Mississippian culture in the American Bottom was the result of a number of local processes that were initiated during the Late Woodland period. The developmental process was set in motion by certain demographic changes that involved an increase in population levels. This appears to be due to the preparation of certain gruels that permitted early weaning and thus a decrease in birth spacing and an increase in fertility. This in turn may have been tied to certain labor needs regarding the cultivation of starchy seeds. The addition of maize to field systems did not result in the abandonment of local seed crops, but the advantages of maize as a more reliable and versatile food plant eventually resulted in its increasing importance. Maize may have required less labor, both in harvesting and processing, while providing greater yields. As a result of increasing reliance upon cultivated crops, the need to manage available farmland resulted in territories and the development of authority along kinship lines. Such authority may have been through a mythical ancestor and sanctified through certain religious ceremonies performed at small villages. Continued population growth necessitated the economizing of habitation space in order to increase available farmland. Ultimately, there was a nucleation of populations into larger villages. These villages reflect centralization of political authority. The control of certain resources and exchange routes resulted in the emergence of status differentiation and unequally ranked social segments. The peak of settlement nucleation and political centralization is represented by the Early Mississippian (A.D. 1000–1200) center at Cahokia. The multiple mound complexes at

Cahokia may very well reflect various high-level lineages from elsewhere in the American Bottom and beyond coalescing at Cahokia.

FUTURE RESEARCH DIRECTIONS

Despite the very substantial nature of the data base, it should be evident from the preceding discussion that there are clear opportunities for future research on a number of important aspects of the developmental process leading to the emergence of Mississippian sociopolitical systems in the American Bottom area.

The magnitude and rate of population growth should be better quantified. Similarly, nutritional and demographic profiles of Late Woodland through Mississippian populations would provide much needed information on this process of demographic growth and change.

On a related topic, the nutritional impact of maize and its replacement of indigenous starchy seeds is an obvious area for future research. A better understanding is needed of the manner in which maize and the indigenous starchy seed crops were grown, processed, and consumed. Especially important in this context is the resultant implications for change in ceramic technology and the morphology and function of storage and processing features. Experimental work using these different data sets is certainly warranted.

In addition, further field research should be undertaken at the smaller mound centers to examine their initial development within the context of evidence for differential ranking among social segments such as lineages. More extensive investigations, especially of the mounds themselves, should provide evidence concerning the specific timing of such critical sociopolitical changes. These data could also be complemented by mortuary data from such mound centers or nearby burial sites.

Another obvious area for future research is the large and as yet unanalyzed collections from Cahokia and a number of other large sites within the American Bottom.

Finally, the northern half of the American Bottom continues to experience rapid development and modification of the land surface, resulting in a continued loss of archaeological sites and data sets relevant to the Mississippian emergence in the area. A realistic research and cultural resource management program that can stay ahead of the crest of destruction of the archaeological record needs to be developed and implemented.

ACKNOWLEDGMENTS

This chapter represents the work of numerous individuals who have been and some who are currently involved with the Mississippian emergence in the American Bottom. To those individuals acknowledged in the preceding chapter one must add the following. From the past, the work of Drs. James W. Porter, Robert L. Hall, Melvin B. Fowler, James B. Stoltman, and Robert Salzer have greatly influenced my thinking. My colleagues, Dale McElrath, Tom Emerson, Doug Jackson, Fred Finney, and Dr. George Milner, while at the UI, have shared in the fruits of this research. To my present colleagues, Bonnie Gums, Alan Brown, Drs. William I. Woods, George Holley, and Neal Lopinot among others at SIU-E, a great deal of gratitude is offered for their acceptance of me and my baggage. Mikels Skele of SIU-E drafted the original base maps for Figures 16 and 46. To Dr. Dan Morse and Phyllis, Drs. James B. Griffin, Stephen Williams, and Bruce Smith one must truly thank for their support from afar of the work in the American Bottom. Again, Dr. Bruce Smith is to be thanked for his patience and editorial prowess. I alone must bear the responsibility for the contents of this chapter.

REFERENCES CITED

Ahler, Steven R., and Peter J. DePuydt
  1987   *A Report on the 1931 Powell Mound Excavations, Madison County, Illinois.* Illinois State Museum Reports of Investigations 43. Springfield.

Anderson, James
  1969   A Cahokia Palisade Sequence. In *Explorations in Cahokia Archaeology,* edited by Melvin L. Fowler, pp. 89–99. Illinois Archaeological Survey Bulletin 7.

Bareis, Charles J.
  1963   University of Illinois Projects. In *Second Annual Report: American Bottom Archaeology, July 1, 1962–June 30, 1963,* edited by Melvin L. Fowler. Illinois Archaeological Survey. University of Illinois, Urbana.
  1967   *Interim Report on Preliminary Site Examination Undertaken in Archaeological Section A of FAI 255 South of Business 40 in the Interstate Portion of Area S-34-4 of the Cahokia Site, St. Clair County, Illinois.* University of Illinois Department of Anthropology Research Reports 1.
  1968   *Report on Salvage Work Undertaken at the Faust Site (S-69) on FAI-64, St. Clair County, Illinois (Phase 3 Excavations).* Urbana, Illinois.
  1971   *Report on Salvage Work Undertaken at the Diekemper Site (Ct-91) on FAI 64, Clinton County, Illinois (Phase 3 Excavations).* Urbana, Illinois.
  1972   *Reports on Preliminary Site Examinations Undertaken at the Holiday No. 2 site (S-68) and the Lienesch Site (S-67) on FAI 64, St. Clair County, Illinois (Phase 2 Testing).* Urbana, Illinois.
  1975a   Report of 1971 University of Illinois-Urbana Excavations at the Cahokia Site. In *Cahokia Archaeology: Field Reports,* edited by Melvin L. Fowler. pp. 9–11. Illinois State Museum Research Series Papers in Anthropology 3.
  1975b   Report of 1972 University of Illinois-Urbana Excavations at the Cahokia Site. In *Cahokia Archaeology: Field Reports,* edited by Melvin L. Fowler, pp. 11–15. Illinois State Museum Research Series Papers in Anthropology 3.
  1976   *The Knoebel Site, St. Clair County, Illinois.* Illinois Archaeological Survey Circular 1. Urbana, Illinois.

Bareis, Charles J., and Donald W. Lathrap
  1962   University of Illinois Projects. *First Annual Report: American Bottom Archaeology, July 1, 1961–June 30, 1962,* edited by Melvin L. Fowler. Illinois Archaeological Survey. Urbana, Illinois.

Bareis, Charles J., and Patrick J. Munson
  1973   The Linkeman Site (MS-108), Madison County, Illinois. In *Late Woodland Site Archaeology in Illinois I: Investigations in South-Central Illinois,* pp. 23–33. Illinois Archaeological Survey Bulletin 9.

Bareis, Charles J., and James W. Porter (editors)
  1984   *American Bottom Archaeology: A Summary of the FAI-270 Project Contributions to the Culture History of the Mississippi River Valley.* University of Illinois Press, Urbana and Chicago.

Batsell-Fuller, Neathery C.
  1985   *An Emergent Mississippian Farmstead at Thornhill 23SL220.* Unpublished M.A. thesis, Department of Anthropology, Washington University, St. Louis, Missouri.

Benchley, Elizabeth D.
  1974   *Mississippian Secondary Mound Loci: A Comparative Functional Analysis in a Time-Space Perspective.* Unpublished Ph.D. dissertation, Department of Anthropology, University of Wisconsin, Milwaukee.

Bentz, Charles, Dale L. McElrath, Fred A. Finney, and Richard B. Lacampagne
  1988   *Late Woodland Sites in the American Bottom Uplands.* American Bottom Archaeology, FAI-270 Site Reports 18. University of Illinois Press, Urbana.

Berres, Thomas Edward
  1984   *A Formal Analysis of Ceramic Vessels from the Schlemmer Site (11-S-382): A Late Woodland/Mississippian Occupation in St. Clair County, Illinois.* M.A. thesis, Department of Anthropology, Western Michigan University.

Blake, Leonard W.
  1949   The Missouri River Bluffs at Caulk's Creek in St. Louis County, Missouri. *The Missouri Archaeologist* 11(1):18–28.
  1955   The Lambert-St. Louis Airport Site. *The Missouri Archaeologist* 17(1):24–42.
  1964   An Indian House in Champ Industrial Village, St. Louis

County. *Missouri Archaeological Society Newsletter* 181:3–5.

Brandt, Keith A.
1972   American Bottom Settlements. Paper presented at the 37th Annual Meeting of the Society for American Archaeology, Bal Harbour, Florida.

Braun, David Phillip
1977   *Middle Woodland-(Early)Late Woodland Social Change in the Prehistoric Central Midwestern U.S.* Ph.D. dissertation, Department of Anthropology, University of Michigan. University Microfilms, Ann Arbor.
1983   Pots as Tools. In *Archaeological Hammers and Theories*, edited by James A. Moore and Arthur S. Keene, pp. 107–134. Academic Press, New York.

Brown, Alan J., James M. Collins, Bonnie L. Gums, George R. Holley, Mikels Skele, Christy L. Wells, and William I. Woods
1986   Recent Archaeological Investigations by Southern Illinois University at Edwardsville (May 1985–May 1986). *Illinois Archaeological Survey Newsletter* 1(1/2):2–6.

Buikstra, Jane E., Lyle W. Konegsberg, and Jill Burlington
1986   Fertility and the Development of Agriculture in the Prehistoric Midwest. *American Antiquity* 51(3):528–546.

Caldwell, Joseph R.
1964   Interaction Spheres in Prehistory. In *Hopewellian Studies*, edited by Joseph R. Caldwell and Robert L. Hall, pp. 133–143. Illinois State Museum, Scientific Papers 12(6). Springfield.

Chmurny, William Wayne
1973   *The Ecology of the Middle Mississippian Occupation of the American Bottom.* Unpublished Ph.D. dissertation, Department of Anthropology, University of Illinois, Urbana.

Denny, Sidney, Linda Carnes, and Annette Nekola
1978   *Archaeological Survey of the Gordon F. Moore Community Park, Alton, Illinois.* SIU-E Reports in Contract Archaeology Series 3.

Droessler, Judith
1981   *Craniometry and Biological Distance: Biological Continuity and Change at the Late Woodland-Mississippian Interface.* Center for American Archaeology, Northwestern University Research Series 1.

Emerson, Thomas E., and Douglas K. Jackson
1984   *The BBB Motor Site (11-Ms-595).* American Bottom Archaeology FAI-270 Site Reports 6. University of Illinois Press, Urbana.
1987   *Emergent Mississippian and Early Mississippian Homesteads at the Marcus Site (11-S-631).* American Bottom Archaeology FAI-270 Site Reports 17(2). University of Illinois Press, Urbana.

Emerson, Thomas E., and George R. Milner
1982   Community Organization and Settlement Patterns of Peripheral Mississippian Sites in the American Bottom, Illinois. Paper presented at the 47th Annual Meeting of the Society for American Archaeology, Minneapolis.

Esarey, Duane
1980   The Joan Carrie Site (11-Mo-663). In *Final Report on the Investigation of Three Archaeological Sites in Luhr Brother's Borrow Pit 4, Monroe County, Illinois*, by Duane

Esarey and Charles Moffat, pp. 52–102. Archaeological Research Laboratory, Western Illinois University, FAI-270 Archaeological Mitigation Project Report 35.

Esarey, Duane, with Timothy W. Good
1981   *Final Report on FAI-270 and Illinois Route 460 Related Excavation at the Lohmann Site (11-S-49), St. Clair County, Illinois.* Archaeological Research Laboratory, Western Illinois University, FAI-270 Archaeological Mitigation Project Report 39.

Farnsworth, Kenneth B.
1973   *An Archaeological Survey of the Macoupin Valley.* Illinois State Museum Reports of Investigations 26. Illinois Valley Archaeological Program Reseach Papers 7. Springfield.

Finney, Fred Austin
1985   The Carbon Dioxide Site (11-Mo-594). In *The Carbon Dioxide Site (11-Mo-594)*, by Fred A. Finney, and *The Robert Schneider Site (11-Ms-1177)*, by Andrew C. Fortier, pp. 1–167. American Bottom Archaeology FAI-270 Site Reports 11. University of Illinois Press, Urbana.

Fischer, Fred W.
n.d.   Recent Archaeological Investigations on the 4th Elevation of Monks Mound, Madison County, Illinois. Unpublished manuscript on file, Department of Anthropology, Washington University, St. Louis.

Fortier, Andrew C.
1985   The Robert Schneider Site (11-Ms-1177). In *The Carbon Dioxide Site (11-Mo-594)*, by Fred A. Finney, and *The Robert Schneider Site (11-Ms-1177)*, by Andrew C. Fortier, pp. 169–313. American Bottom Archaeology FAI-270 Site Reports 11. University of Illinois Press, Urbana.
1988   The Formation of Emergent Mississippian Cultures in the Cahokia Heartland: An Overview. Paper presented at the 50th Annual meeting of the Southeastern Archaeological Conference, New Orleans.

Fortier, Andrew C., Richard B. Lacampagne, and Fred A. Finney
1984   *The Fish Lake Site (11-Mo-608).* American Bottom Archaeology FAI-270 Site Reports 8. University of Illinois Press, Urbana.

Fortier, Andrew C., and Dale L. McElrath
1986   Archaeological Investigations at the University of Illinois (1985–1986). *Illinois Archaeological Survey Newsletter* 1(1/2):7–9.

Fowler, Melvin L.
1969   The Cahokia Site. In *Explorations into Cahokia Archaeology*, edited by Melvin L. Fowler, pp. 1–30. Illinois Archaeological Survey, Bulletin 7.
1974   *Cahokia: Ancient Capital of the Midwest.* Addison-Wesley Module in Anthropology 48.
1975   A Pre-Columbia Urban Center on the Mississippi. *Scientific American* 233(2):92–101.
n.d.   *A History of Investigations at the Cahokia Mounds Historic Site and Atlas of Mounds and other Aboriginal Features.* In press, Illinois Historic Preservation Agency.

Fowler, Melvin L., and James P. Anderson
1975   Report of 1971 Excavations at Mound 72, Cahokia Mounds State Park. In *Cahokia Archaeology: Field Reports*, edited by Melvin L. Fowler, pp. 25–27. Illinois State Museum Research Series, Papers in Anthropology 3. Springfield.

Fowler, Melvin L., and Robert L. Hall
1975   Archaeological Phases at Cahokia. In *Perspectives in Cahokia Archaeology*, pp. 1–14. Illinois Archaeological Survey Bulletin 10. University of Illinois, Urbana.

Freimuth, Glen A.
1970   Divers Site. *Illinois Association for the Advancement of Archaeology Newsletter* 2:38.
1974   The Lunsford-Pulcher Site: An Examination of Selected Traits and their Social Implications in American Bottom Prehistory. Unpublished predissertation paper, University of Illinois at Urbana-Champaign.

Gates, Richard I.
1966   *Historical Geography of Salt in the Old Northwest*. Unpublished M.A. thesis, Department of Geography, University of Wisconsin, Madison.

Gregg, Michael Lee
1975   *Settlement Morphology and Production Specialization: The Horseshoe Lake Site, A Case Study*. Unpublished Ph.D. dissertation, Department of Anthropology, University of Wisconsin, Milwaukee.

Griffin, James B.
1977   The University of Michigan Excavations at the Pulcher Site in 1950. *American Antiquity* 42:462–488.

Hajic, Edwin R.
1987   *Geomorphology of the Northern American Bottom as Context for Archaeological Site Survey: FAP-413, I-270 to Bluffline*. Report submitted to William I. Woods, Southern Illinois University, Edwardsville.

Hall, Robert L.
1966   Cahokia Chronology. Paper presented at the Annual Meeting of the Central States Anthropological Society, St. Louis.
1967   The Mississippian Heartland its Plains Relationship. *Plains Anthropologist* 12:175–183.
1973   An Interpretation of the Two-Climax Model of Illinois Prehistory. Paper presented at the IX International Congress of Anthropological and Ethnological Sciences, Chicago.
1975a   Chronology and Phases at Cahokia. In *Perspectives in Cahokia Archaeology*, pp. 15–31. Illinois Archaeological Survey Bulletin 10. University of Illinois, Urbana.
1975b   Some Problems of Identity and Process in Cahokia Archaeology. Revised version of paper prepared for advanced seminar on Mississippian cultural development at School of American Research, Santa Fe, New Mexico.
1980   An Interpretation of the Two-Climax Model of Illinois Prehistory. In *Early Native Americans: Prehistoric Demography, Economy, and Technology*, edited by David L. Brownman, pp. 401–462. Mouton, The Hague.
1985a   Cahokia Identity and Interaction Models of Cahokia Mississippian. Manuscript on file, Department of Anthropology, University of Illinois at Chicago Circle.
1985b   A Critique of the Time-Frame for the Mississippian Emergence in the Cahokia Area. Paper presented at the Sixth Mid-South Archaeological Conference, Starkville, Mississippi.

Hall, Robert L., and Joseph O. Vogel
1963   Illinois State Museum Projects. In *2nd Annual Report: American Bottoms Archaeology, July 1, 1962–June 30,*

1963, edited by Melvin L. Fowler, pp. 24–30. Illinois Archaeological Survey. University of Illinois, Urbana.

Hames, Raymond B.
1983   The Settlement Pattern of a Yanomamo Population Bloc: A Behavioral Ecological Interpretation. In *Adaptive Responses of Native Amazonians*, edited by Raymond B. Hames and William T. Vickers, pp. 393–427. Academic Press, New York.

Hanenberger, Ned
1986   *Late Archaic and Mississippian Occupations at the Olszewski Borrow Pit Site (11-S-465)*. Department of Anthropology, University of Illinois at Urbana-Champaign, FAI-270 Archaeological Mitigation Project, Report 73.

Harn, Alan D.
1971   An Archaeological Survey of the American Bottoms in Madison and St. Clair counties, Illinois. In *Archaeological Surveys of the American Bottoms and Adjacent Bluffs, Illinois*, pp. 19–39. Illinois State Museum, Reports of Investigations 21.

Hawks, Preston A.
1985   *Report of Supplemental Phase I Documentation and Survey and Phase II Archaeological Testing at Selected Sites for the Proposed FAP-413 Highway Project, Madison County, Illinois*. Report submitted to the Illinois Department of Transportation, Springfield. Illinois State University, Normal.

Hendrickson, Carl F.
1979   *The Ceramics of the Fenaia Site (M-1), Monroe County, Illinois*. Unpublished Master's thesis, Department of Anthropology, University of Wisconsin, Madison.

Holmes, William H.
1903   Traces of Aboriginal Operations in an Iron Mine near Leslie, Missouri. *American Anthropologist* 5:503–507.

Howard, James H.
1968   *The Southeastern Ceremonial Complex and its Interpretation*. Missouri Archaeological Society, Memoir 6, Columbia.

Hudson, Charles
1976   *The Southeastern Indians*. The University of Tennessee Press.

Hunt, William J., Jr.
1974   *Late Woodland-Mississippian Relationships at the River Bend East Site (23Sl79), St. Louis County, Missouri*. Unpublished M.A. thesis, Department of Anthropology, University of Nebraska, Lincoln.

Hus, Henri
1908   An Ecological Cross-Section of the Mississippi River in the Region of St. Louis. *Missouri Botanical Garden 19th Annual Report*, pp. 127–258. St. Louis, Missouri.

Ives, David J.
1975   *The Crescent Hills Prehistoric Quarrying Area*. Museum Brief 22, University of Missouri, Columbia.

Jackson, Douglas K.
1987   *Middle Woodland and Mississippian Short-Term Occupations at the Willoughby Site (11-Ms-610)*. Department of Anthropology, University of Illinois at Urbana-Champaign, FAI-270 Archaeological Mitigation Project, Report 76.
1988a   *Mississippian Occupations at the Esterlein Site (11-Ms-598)*. Department of Anthropology, University of Illinois at

Urbana-Champaign, FAI-270 Archaeological Mitigation Project, Report 77.

1988b Investigations at the Keller-Samson Borrow Pit: Early Emergent Mississippian Occupations in Madison County, Illinois. Paper presented at the Midwest Archaeological Conference, Urbana, Illinois.

Johannessen, Sissel
1987   Patrick Phase Plant Remains. In *The Range Site: Archaic through Late Woodland Occupations*, by John E. Kelly, Andrew C. Frontier, Steven J. Ozuk, and Joyce A. Williams. American Bottom Archaeology FAI-270 Site Reports, 16. University of Illinois Press, Urbana.

Kelly, John E.
1980   *Formative Developments at Cahokia and the Adjacent American Bottom: A Merrell Tract Perspective*. Unpublished Ph.D. dissertation, Department of Anthropology, University of Wisconsin, Madison.

1984   Late Bluff Chert Utilization on the Merrell Tract, Cahokia. In *Prehistoric Chert Exploitation: Studies from the Midcontinent*, edited by Brian M. Butler and Ernest E. May, pp. 23–44. Center for Archaeological Investigations, Southern Illinois University at Carbondale, Occasional Paper 2.

1985   Late Woodland. In *Illinois Archaeology*, edited by James W. Porter. Illinois Archaeological Survey Bulletin 1 (revised). University of Illinois, Urbana-Champaign.

1987   Emergent Mississippian and the Transition from Late Woodland to Mississippian: The American Bottom Case for a New Concept. In *The Emergent Mississippian*, edited by Richard A. Marshall. Proceedings of the sixth Mid-South Archaeological Conference, June 6–9, 1985. Cobb Institute of Archaeology, Mississippi State University, Occasional Papers 87–101.

1988   Coles Creek and the American Bottom: Patterned Interaction? Paper presented at the 50th Annual Meeting of the Southeastern Archaeological Conference, New Orleans, October 20, 1988.

1989   Cahokia and Its Role as a Gateway Center in Interregional Exchange. In *Cahokia and its Neighbors*, edited by Thomas E. Emerson and R. Barry Lewis. University of Illinois Press. In Press.

Kelly, John E., Fred A. Finney, Dale L. McElrath, and Steven J. Ozuk
1984a   Late Woodland Period. In *American Bottom Archaeology*, edited by Charles J. Bareis and James W. Porter, pp. 104–127. University of Illinois Press, Urbana.

Kelly, John E., Andrew C. Frontier, Steven J. Ozuk, and Joyce A. Williams
1987   *The Range Site (11-S-47): Archaic through Late Woodland Occupations*. American Bottom Archaeology FAI-270 Site Reports 16. University Press, Urbana.

Kelly, John E., Jean R. Linder, and Theresa J. Cartmell
1979   *The Archaeological Intensive Survey of the Proposed FAI-270 Alignment in the American Bottom Region of Southern Illinois*. Illinois Transportation Archaeology Scientific Reports 1. Illinois Department of Transportation, Springfield, and Illinois Archaeological Survey, Urbana.

Kelly, John E., James Mertz, and Larry Kinsella
1989a   Recent Salvage Investigations in the American Bottom. *Illinois Archaeological Survey Newsletter* 4(2).

Kelly, John E., Steven J. Ozuk, Douglas K. Jackson, Dale L. McElrath, Fred A. Finney, and Duane Esuary
1984b   Emergent Mississippi Period. In *American Bottom Archaeology. A Summary of the FAI-270 Project Contribution to the Culture of History of the Mississippi River Valley*, edited by Charles J. Bareis and James W. Porter, pp. 128–157. University of Illinois Press, Urbana.

Kelly, John E., Steven J. Ozuk, and Joyce A. Williams
1989b   *The Range Site 2 (11-S-47): The Emergent Mississippian Dohack and Range Phase Occupations*. Department of Anthropology University of Illinois at Urbana-Champaign, FAI-270 Archaeological Mitigation Project Report 81.

1989c   The Range Site 3(11-S-43): The Emergent Mississippian George Reeves and Lindeman Phase Occupations. Manuscript on file, Department of Anthropology, University of Illinois at Urbana-Champaign.

Kelly, Lucretia S.
1987   Patrick Phase Faunal Materials. In *The Range Site: Archaic through Late Woodland Occupations*, by John E. Kelly, Andrew C. Frontier, Steven J. Ozuk, and Joyce A. Williams, pp. 350–400. American Bottom Archaeology FAI-270 Site Reports 16. University of Illinois Press, Urbana.

Koldehoff, Brad
1987   The Cahokia Flake Tool Industry: Socioeconomic Implications for Late Prehistory in the Central Mississippi Valley, In *The Organization of Core Technology*, edited by J. Johnson and C. Morrow, pp. 151–188. Westview Press, Boulder.

1989   Cahokia's Immediate Hinterland: The Mississippian Occupation of Douglas Creek. Manuscript on file, American Resources Group, Carbondale.

Lopinot, Neal H., Joseph L. Harl, and Joseph M. Nixon
1987   *Archaeological Investigations at the Riverside Site (23SL481), Southern St. Louis County, Missouri*. Archaeological Survey, University of Missouri, St. Louis Research Report 52.

McElrath, Dale L., and Fred A. Finney
1987   *The George Reeves Site (11-S-650)*. American Bottom Archaeology FAI-270 Site Report 15. University of Illinois Press, Urbana.

McElrath, Dale L., Joyce A. Williams, Thomas O. Maher, and Michael C. Meinkoth
1987   *Emergent Mississippian and Mississippian Communities at the Radic Site (11-Ms-584)*. American Bottom Archaeology FAI-270 Site Reports 17(1). University of Illinois Press, Urbana.

McGimsey, Charles R., and Michael D. Conner (editors)
1985   *Deer Track: A Late Woodland Village in the Mississippi Valley*. Kampsville Archaeological Center, Center for American Archaeology, Technical Report 1. Kampsville, Illinois.

Mehrer, Mark W.
1982   *A Mississippian Community at the Range Site (11-S-47), St. Clair County, Illinois*. Department of Anthropology, University of Illinois at Urbana-Champaign, FAI-270 Archaeology Mitigation Project, Report 52.

Milner, George R.
1982   *The Palmer Creek Terrace Site (11-Mo-756)*. Department of Anthropology, University of Illinois at Urbana-Cham

paign, FAI-270 Archaeological Mitigation Project, Report 58.

1983 *The Turner (11-S-50) and DeMange (11-S-447) Sites.* American Bottom Archaeology FAI-270 Site Reports 4. University of Illinois Press, Urbana.

1984a *The Julien Site (11-S-63).* American Bottom Archaeology FAI-270 Site Reports 7. University of Illinois Press, Urbana.

1984b *The Robinson's Lake Site (11-Ms-582).* American Bottom Archaeology FAI-270 Site Reports 10. University of Illinois Press, Urbana.

Morgan, David T.
1985 Late Woodland Ceramics from the Fall Creek Locality, Adams County, Illinois. *The Wisconsin Archaeologist* 66: 265–281.

Munson, Patrick J.
1971 *An Archaeological Survey of the Wood River Terrace and Adjacent Bottoms and Bluffs in Madison County, Illinois.* Illinois State Museum Reports of Investigations 21(1). Springfield.

1974 Terraces, Meander Loops, and Archaeology in the American Bottoms, Illinois. *Transactions of the Illinois State Academy of Science* 67(4):384–392.

Munson, Patrick J., and James P. Anderson
1973 A Preliminary Report on Kane Village: A Late Woodland Site in Madison County, Illinois. In *Late Woodland Site Archaeology in Illinois I: Investigations in South-Central Illinois*, pp. 34–48. Illinois Archaeological Survey Bulletin 9.

Nixon, Joseph M., M. Colleen Hamilton, Laura E. Kling, Joseph L. Harl, and Neal Lopinot
1983 *Data Recovery Operations at Proposed VFW Bridge Relocation, Site 23JE514, Jefferson County, Missouri.* Archaeological Survey, University of Missouri, St. Louis Research Report 11.

O'Brien, Patricia Joan
1972 *A Formal Analysis of Cahokia Ceramics from the Powell Tract.* Illinois Archaeological Survey Monograph 3, Urbana.

Parker, Kathryn
1986 Family Gardens and Communal Fields: 600 years of Farming at the Range Site. Paper presented at the 51st Annual Meeting of the of the Society for American Archaeology, New Orleans, Louisiana.

Pauketat, Timothy R.
n.d. An Analysis of Pottery from the A.G. Church Site. Manuscript on file. University of Michigan Museum of Anthropology, Ann Arbor.

Perino, Gregory
1973a The Late Woodland Component at the Pete Klunk Site, Calhoun County, Illinois. In *Late Woodland Site Archaeology in Illinois I: Investigations in South-Central Illinois*, pp. 58–89. Illinois Archaeological Survey Bulletin 9. Urbana.

1973b The Late Woodland Component at the Schild Sites, Greene County, Illinois. In *Late Woodland Site Archaeology in Illinois I: Investigations in South-Central Illinois*, pp. 90–140. Illinois Archaeological Survey Bulletin 9.

1973c The Koster Mounds, Greene County, Illinois. In *Late*

Woodland Site Archaeology in Illinois I: Investigations in South-Central Illinois, pp. 141–210. Illinois Archaeological Survey Bulletin 9.

Porter, James W.
1963 *Bluff Pottery Analysis—Thin Section Experiment No. 2: Analysis of Bluff Pottery from the Mitchell Site, Madison County, Illinois.* Southern Illinois University Museum, Lithic Laboratory Research Report 4.

1969 The Mitchell Site and Prehistoric Exchange Systems at Cahokia: A.D. 1000 ± 300. In *Explorations into Cahokia Archaeology*, edited by Melvin L. Fowler, pp. 137–164. Illinois Archaeological Survey Bulletin 7. University of Illinois, Urbana.

1972 An Archaeological Survey of the Mississippi Valley in St. Clair, Monroe, and Randolph Counties. In *Preliminary Report of 1972 Historic Sites Survey Archaeological Reconnaissance of Selected Areas in the State of Illinois*, Part 1, Summary Section A, pp. 25–33.

1974 *Cahokia Archaeology as Viewed from the Mitchell Site: A Satellite Community at A.D. 1150–1200.* Ph.D dissertation, Department of Anthropology, University of Wisconsin, Madison, University Microfilms International.

1984 Thin Section Analysis of Ceramics. In *The Robinson's Lake Site (11-Ms-582)*, by George R. Milner, pp. 133–170. American Bottom Archaeology FAI-270 Site Reports 10. University of Illinois Press, Urbana.

Price, James E., and Cynthia R. Price
1984 *Phase II Testing of the Shell Lake Site, 23WE627, near Wappapello Dam, Wayne County, Missouri.* St. Louis District Cultural Resource Management Report 11. U.S. Army Corp of Engineers.

Reed, Nelson A., John W. Bennett, and James Warren Porter
1968 Solid Core Drilling of Monks Mound: Technique and Findings. *American Antiquity* 33(2).

Rose, Jerome, and James Wells
1972 Skeletal Analysis of Mound 72. Paper presented at the 37th Annual Meeting of the Society for American Archaeology, Bal Harbour, Florida.

Salzer, Robert J.
1975 Excavations at the Merrell Tract of the Cahokia Site: Summary Field Report, 1973. In *Cahokia Archaeology: Field Reports*, edited by Melvin L. Fowler, pp. 1–8. Illinois State Museum Research Series, Papers in Anthropology 3. Springfield.

Shippee, J. M.
1972b A Report of Salvage Investigations at St. Charles, Missouri. *The Missouri Archaeologist* 34(1–2):76–84.

Stahl, Ann Brower
1985 *The Dohack Site (11-S-642).* American Bottom Archaeology FAI-270 Site Reports 12. University of Illinois Press, Urbana.

Swanton, John R.
1946 *The Indians of the Southeastern United States.* Bureau of American Ethnology, Bulletin 137. Smithsonian Institution Press, Washington, D.C. Reprinted 1979.

Szuter, Christine R.
1979 *The Schlemmer Site: A Late Woodland-Mississippian Site in the American Bottom.* Unpublished Master's thesis, Department of Anthropology, Loyola University, Chicago.

Telford, Clarence J.
1927   *Third Report on a Forest Survey of Illinois.* Bulletin of the Illinois State Natural History Survey 16.

Vander Leest, Barbara J.
1980   *The Ramey Field, Cahokia Surface Collection: A Functional Analysis of Spatial Structure.* Unpublished Ph.D. dissertation, Department of Anthropology, University of Wisconsin, Milwaukee.

Vogel, Joseph O.
1975   Trends in Cahokia Ceramics: Preliminary Study of the Collections from Tracts 15-A and 15-B. In *Perspectives in Cahokia Archaeology,* pp. 32–125. Illinois Archaeological Survey Bulletin 10.

Walthall, John A.
1981   *Galena and Aboriginal Trade in Eastern North America.* Illinois State Museum, Scientific Papers 17. Springfield

Waring, Antonio J., Jr.
1965   The Southern Cult and Muskhogean Ceremonial. In *The Waring Papers: The Collected Works of Antonio J. Waring, Jr.,* edited by Stephen Williams. University of Georgia Press, Athens.

Welch, David
1975   *Wood Utilization at Cahokia: Identification of Wood Charcoal from the Merrell Tract.* Unpublished Master's thesis. University of Wisconsin, Madison.

Westover, Allan R., Mark E. Esarey, and Joseph S. Phillippe
1983   *Report of Testing at the Columbia Quarry Site, 11-S-629. In FAI-255 Borrow Pit # 2, Extension 3, St. Clair County, Illinois.* Midwestern Archaeological Research Center, Illinois State University, Research Report 5. Normal.

White, William P.
1983   *Geomorphic Research Conducted at the Fish Lake Site (11-Mo-608).* Department of Anthropology, University of Illinois at Urbana-Champaign, FAI-270 Archaeological Mitigation Project Geomorphical Report 10.

White, William P., Sissel Johannessen, Paula Cross, and Lucretia S. Kelly
1984   Environmental Setting. In *American Bottom Archaeology,* edited by Charles J. Bareis and James W. Porter, pp. 15–33. University of Illinois Press, Urbana.

Williams, Kenneth
1975   Preliminary Summation of Excavations at the East Lobes of Monks Mound. In *Cahokia Archaeology: Field Reports,* edited by Melvin L. Fowler, pp. 21–24. Illinois State Museum Research Series Papers in Anthropology 3.

Wittry, Warren L.
1969   The American Woodhenge. In *Explorations into Cahokia Archaeology,* edited by Melvin L. Fowler, pp. 43–48. Illinois Archaeological Survey Bulletin 7.

Wittry, Warren L., with John C. Arnold and Charles O. Witty
1982   The Holdener Site (11-S-685 in Borrow Pit25): An Early Late Woodland Mortuary. FAI-270 Archaeological Mitigation Project Report. Manuscript on file, Department of Anthropology, University of Illinois at Urbana-Champaign.

Wolforth, Thomas
1988   The Widman Site (11-Ms-866): A Small Havana Settlement in the Wood River Valley, Illinois. Paper presented at 1988 Midwest Archaeological Conference, Urbana.

Wright, Patti Jo
1986   *Analysis of Plant Remains from the Bridgeton Archaeological Site (23SL442): Late Woodland and Emergent Mississippian Assemblages.* Unpublished M.A. thesis, Department of Anthropology, Washington University, St. Louis.

Yerkes, Richard W.
1983   Microwear, Microdrills, and Mississippian Craft Specialization. *American Antiquity* 46:499–518.

Emergent Mississippian in the Central Mississippi Valley

INTRODUCTION

The central Mississippi Valley, as defined here, is that part of the alluvial valley between the Ohio and Arkansas Rivers (Fig. 65). The region is laterally bordered by and includes part of the Ozark Highlands on the west and the uplands immediately east of the Mississippi River, which include the Chickasaw Bluffs. Constituting approximately 40,000 sq km, the Central Valley is essentially oval in shape and oriented north-northeast to south-southwest. All major lowland streams are similarly oriented, and upland tributaries are perpendicular to the lowland drainage. The Central Valley is bifurcated into two lowlands, called "Eastern" and "Western," by an erosional remnant known as Crowley's Ridge. Sikeston Ridge segregates the Cairo Lowland from the rest of the Eastern Lowlands in the northeast. To be discussed later in this chapter, the Cairo Lowland portion of the Central Valley is considered by us to be of paramount importance in understanding the emergence and evolution of Mississippian culture in the central Mississippi Valley.

Extending across portions of five different states, the central Mississippi Valley is not a small homogeneous region, but rather supports a rich variety of different landforms and environmental settings (Morse and Morse 1983:1–15). Two basic kinds of soils and landforms can be identified within the Central Valley proper. Most of the region west of Crowley's Ridge, as well as substantial areas of the Eastern Lowland, have older braided stream terraces, formed during the

late Pleistocene and early Holocene, when the Mississippi River flowed as a braided stream west, then east, of Crowley's Ridge. These braided stream terraces, with their characteristic sand dune interfluve topography, are frequently interrupted by more recent meandering streams of various sizes. The eastern portion of the central Mississippi Valley, in contrast, is dominated by the more recent meander belt landscape of natural levees, oxbow lakes, and backswamps, reflecting the meandering nature of the Mississippi River after its course shifted east of Crowley's Ridge.

This central Mississippi Valley area, with its rich variety and abundance of plant and animal resources, and excellent agricultural soils, has long been proposed as a "heartland" of initial Mississippian development (Smith 1984). Yet it is only recently, with the excavation of the Zebree site (Morse and Morse 1980; Chapter 4, this volume) that an early period Mississippian presence in the Central Valley has been clearly and convincingly established.

The recognition and analysis of early Mississippian remains in the central Mississippi Valley constituted the primary goal of the classic *Archaeological Survey in the Lower Mississippi Alluvial Valley, 1940–1947*, by Phillips, Ford, and Griffin (1951:39–40). The earliest Mississippian remains found by them were plain shell-tempered ceramics, as exemplified by the lowest levels of a test pit at the Rose Mound site south of Parkin, Arkansas. This complex would today be classified within middle period Mississippian (A.D. 1000–1200)

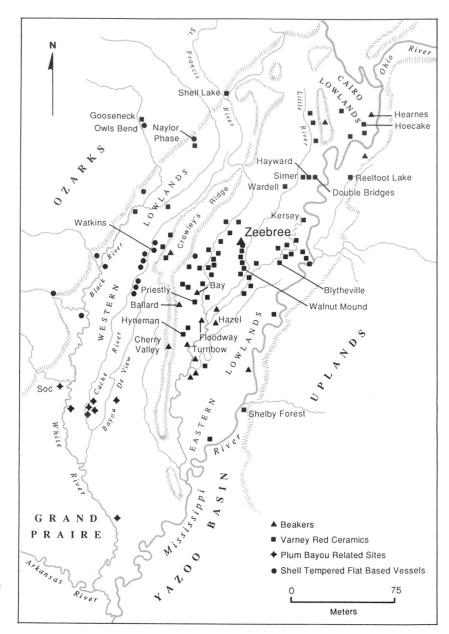

N

St. Francis River

OZARKS

CAIRO LOWLANDS

Ohio River

Little River

Shell Lake

Gooseneck
Owls Bend
Naylor Phase

Hearnes
Hoecake

Hayward
Simer
Wardell

Reelfoot Lake
Double Bridges

Watkins

Crowley's Ridge

LOWLANDS

Kersey

Zeebree

WESTERN

Black River

Priestly
Ballard
Hyneman
Cherry Valley

Bay

Hazel
Floodway
Turnbow

Blytheville

Walnut Mound

Cache River

Bayou De View

EASTERN

LOWLANDS

UPLANDS

Soc

Shelby Forest

White River

Mississippi River

GRAND
PRAIRE

▲ Beakers
■ Varney Red Ceramics
◆ Plum Bayou Related Sites
● Shell Tempered Flat Based Vessels

Arkansas River

YAZOO BASIN

0   75
Meters

Fig. 65. Map of the central Mississippi Valley showing the distribution of sites yielding Varney Red ceramics, Plum Bayou related materials, shell-tempered flat-based vessels, and beakers.

rather than early period Mississippian (A.D. 800–1000) (Fig. 66).

Even though Phillips, Ford, and Griffin did not recover artifactual evidence of an early Mississippian presence in the Central Valley, such evidence, in the form of Varney Red ceramics, was recovered and identified soon after the publication of their landmark study. Credit for the initial recognition of Varney Red ceramics (named after the Old Varney River site) and the interpretation that they dated early within the Mis-

sissippian period goes to Stephen Williams in his Ph.D. dissertation, *An Archeological Study of the Mississippian Culture in Southeast Missouri* (1954, table 1, 34, 210, 275).

Another decade would pass, however, before the first extensive report of excavations at an early period Mississippian site—the Kersey site located in the Missouri Bootheel (Fig. 65)—would appear (Marshall 1965a). Marshall placed "the early Mississippian component" at the Kersey site within his newly established Hayti

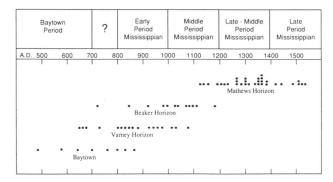

Baytown Period	?	Early Period Mississippian	Middle Period Mississippian	Late - Middle Period Mississippian	Late Period Mississippian

Fig. 66. Radiocarbon dates plotted by horizon. See Table 14 for specific dates. Data points represent corrected (via Damon et al. 1974) dates. Standard deviation values, which in some case are quite large (Table 14), are not illustrated.

phase (1965a:76). Marshall's account of an additional field season at the Kersey site remains unpublished (Marshall 1965b).

Marshall, Hopgood, and J. Raymond Williams subsequently did considerable work at the Hoecake site in the Cairo Lowland of Missouri (Fig. 65), where an early Mississippian component was recognized, although J. R. Williams (1974:86) classified the Hoecake phase as late Baytown.

Although an early period Mississippian ceramic marker had been identified and excavations at several early period Mississippian sites had been carried out, the first clear and convincing evidence for emergent Mississippian came with the excavation of the Zebree site in northeast Arkansas (Fig. 65) (see Chapter 4). The very large body of data resulting from almost a decade of research at Zebree forms, in large part, the basis for our understanding of the temporal, spatial, and cultural context of early period Mississippian in the central Mississippi Valley. The very basic question of temporal placement of emergent Mississippian complexes provides an excellent example of the importance of the Zebree data set in approaching the broader regional questions of Emergent Mississippian in the central Mississippi Valley.

CERAMIC COMPLEXES AND TEMPORAL CONTROL A.D. 700–1200

A large series of radiocarbon dates, along with a limited number of thermoluminescence and archaeomagnetic dates, span the Mississippian period in the central Mississippi Valley (Fig. 66, Table 14). However, only a very few dates pertain to the pre-Mississippian Baytown period (Table 14), and much tighter temporal control of Baytown assemblages is necessary for detailed examination of the period transition between Baytown (Woodland) and Mississippian.

A number of the Mississippian period radiocarbon dates are of questionable value for a number of reasons (Cottier 1977:310). At one time in archaeological investigation, radiocarbon dating was approached as a means of determining a date (and as a result, a cultural affiliation) instead of as a means to independently check a date hypothesized on the basis of seriation and stratigraphic data. In addition, samples of charcoal were often hurriedly gathered during a frustrating period of intensive salvage work rather than under the ideal conditions of a more relaxed and well-controlled recovery methodology.

As a result, a well-defined cultural sequence chart based on one- to two-century subperiods has not been established for most of the Central Valley. This is particularly true in the very critical eastern Missouri portion of the Central Valley despite a considerable amount of excavation (Lewis 1982:83). The best temporal control seems to be over the Eastern Lowlands of northeast Arkansas (Morse and Morse 1980) and the Western Lowlands of southeast Missouri (Price and Griffin 1979).

The chronological chart presented in Table 14 is primarily based on radiocarbon dates from western southeast Missouri and eastern northeast Arkansas. The dates in Figure 66 are represented by dots approximating the corrected (via Damon et al. 1974) date without reference to standard deviations, which in some cases are quite large. This chart is meant to be a list of dates demonstrating both clustering in support of the approximate subperiod borders and scatter beyond those borders as an indication of the built-in imperfections of dates on samples collected under a variety of circumstances. Dates that postdate A.D. 1000 from the Eastern Lowlands of Missouri, summarized in Cottier (1977), were omitted because there is some degree of difficulty deciding precisely what was actually dated.

The Baytown Period

Little investigation of the Baytown period has been ac-

Table 14. Radiocarbon Dates circa A.D. 700–1200 in the Central Mississippi Valley (see Fig. 66)

Lab/no.	Date (A.D.)	Site	Reference
Baytown			
GAK-1686	480 ± 140	Double Bridges	Cottier 1977:312
GAK-1685	572 ± 150	Double Bridges	Cottier 1977:312
M-2112	642 ± 138	Hyneman	Morse and Morse 1983:182
SMU-414	691 ± 74	Zebree	Morse and Morse 1980
M2113	761 ± 151	Hyneman	Morse and Morse 1983:182
Beta-?	800 ± 95	Brougham Lane	Klinger et al. 1983:637
SMU-415	829 ± 70	Zebree	Morse and Morse 1980
SMU-432	863 ± 84	Zebree	Morse and Morse 1980
Varney Horizon			
TX-3017	659 ± 200	23OR49	Lynott 1982
M-2212/2213	663 ± 184	Hoecake	S. Williams 1974:85
TX-3608	673 ± 87	23RI192	Lynott 1982
TX-3609	732 ± 121	23RI192	Lynott 1982
TX-4090	809 ± 95	Gooseneck	Lynott 1982
SMU-433	810 ± 80	Zebree	Morse and Morse 1980
SMU-445	836 ± 84	Zebree	Morse and Morse 1980
SMU-453	838 ± 86	Zebree	Morse and Morse 1980
RL-1418	840 ± 130	Robards	Dunnell 1982
SMU-411	876 ± 74	Zebree	Morse and Morse 1980
SMU-422	931 ± 57	Zebree	Morse and Morse 1980
SMU-450	941 ± 66	Zebree	Morse and Morse 1980
SMU-426	960 ± 63	Zebree	Morse and Morse 1980
TX-3074	978 ± 69	Mangrum	Morse and Morse 1983:238
SMU-460	1020 ± 74	Zebree	Morse and Morse 1980
TX-3073	1039 ± 61	Mangrum	Morse and Morse 1983:238
SMU-457	1076 ± 68	Zebree	Morse and Morse 1980
Beaker Horizon			
M-917	722 ± 137	Cherry Valley	Perino 1967:67
TX-700A	848 ± 92	Hazel	Morse and Morse 1983: 246
M-918	933 ± 160	Cherry Valley	Perino 1967:67
M-1954	990 ± 250	Obion	Garland 1966
M-1955	1000 ± 150	Obion	Garland 1966
M-1953	1044 ± 110	Obion	Garland 1966
M-1956	1044	Obion	Garland 1966
M-1162	1079 ± 87	Banks 3	Perino 1967:77
TX-845	1084 ± 111	Hazel	Morse and Morse 1983: 247
TX-844	1093 ± 74	Hazel	Morse and Morse 1983: 247
M-1486	1102 ± 120	Cherry Valley	Perino 1967:67
TX-704	1111 ± 92	Hazel	Morse and Morse 1983: 247
TX-878A	1186 ± 74	Hazel	Morse and Morse 1983 : 247
Matthews Horizon			
M-1158	1194 ± 160	Lawhorn	Moselage 1962
M-(N=8)	$\bar{x}$ = 1307	Turner	Price and Griffin 1979:186–187
M-1156	1308 + 160	Lawhorn	Moselage 1962
M-(N=5)	$\bar{x}$ = 1312	Powers Fort	Price and Griffin 1979:186–187
M-(N=15)	$\bar{x}$ = 1344	Snodgrass	Price and Griffin 1979:186–187
M-2434	1526	Flurry	Price and Griffin 1979:186–187
M-1157	1536 + 162	Lawhorn	Moselage 1962

complished within the Central Valley. The Zebree site contained a Dunklin phase component that was intensively investigated (Morse and Morse 1980). Excavation has also been carried out at the Baytown phase De Rossitt site (Spears 1978). In the Cairo Lowland where some investigators viewed Baytown as synonymous with Woodland (J. R. Williams 1974:1), it has been a little difficult to sort out what is meant by Baytown (Late Woodland). In southeast Missouri, several sites with Baytown components have been salvaged (J. R. Williams 1968, 1972; Marshall 1965a, 1965b) but little published substantive data have resulted. The eight Baytown period dates presented in Figure 66 are from the following sites: Double Bridges (2), Hyneman (2), Zebree (3) and Brougham Lake (1). Clearly, well-controlled and planned excavations at representative sites are needed before the upper boundary of the Baytown period can be tightly dated. This upper limit falls somewhere within the eighth century A.D.

The Varney Horizon

The Varney horizon is based on the presence, and in many cases the prevalence, of Varney Red ceramic styles. Type sites are Hoecake, Kersey, and of course, Zebree, from where most of the data known about this subperiod were derived (Morse and Morse 1980). There are nine radiocarbon dates from the Zebree site compared to ten radiocarbon and five thermoluminescence dates from all other sites.

Of the 19 radiocarbon dates and 5 thermoluminescence dates obtained from assumed Varney Red cultural contexts in the central Mississippi Valley, 15 fall within the "Zebree Cluster" of A.D. 809–1076 (Table 14, Fig. 66). In addition, the French site (22HO563) in northwest Mississippi has yielded a Varney Red associated date of A.D. 962 ± 59 (Beta-6874).

Two dates, both obtained from structure architectural elements at the recently excavated Shell Lake site adjacent to the Ozark escarpment in southeast Missouri (Fig. 65), fall into the fourteenth and sixteenth century (Table 14, Fig. 66) (Price and Price 1984:67). These dates have been judged to be in error by the Shell Lake excavators, however, and the site has been assigned to the ninth and tenth centuries A.D. (A.D. 800–1000) on the basis of similarity in the artifact assemblages of the Shell Lake site and other Varney Red components, including Zebree (Price and Price 1984:67).

Four radiocarbon dates fall prior to A.D. 800 and the Zebree cluster (Fig. 66). All but one of these early dates are from sites located in the eastern Ozarks. On the basis of these early dates Price and Price (1984:86) have proposed that ". . . Varney probably existed as early as ca. A.D. 650 . . . and that shell tempering probably developed even earlier than this, perhaps as early as A.D. 500." Three pre-A.D. 800 radiocarbon dates (from Gooseneck and Northfork, Table 14) resulted from charcoal samples recovered from the fill of one pit feature (two dates) and fill from a structural feature which also contained shell-tempered ceramics. The pre-A.D. 800 date from the Story Mound I excavations at the Hoecake site was obtained by combining charcoal samples from two separate log tombs. A total of four combined shell- and grog-tempered plain sherds were recovered from the Story Mound tomb fill, along with one Baytown period sherd (Baytown plain, Williams 1974:83; Marshall 1969). The standard deviation values of these four pre-A.D. 800 dates range from 121 to 200 years, and three of the four dates have single standard deviation ranges that extend into the ninth century A.D. (Table 14). Taken together, these pre-A.D. 800 dates do not provide much support for the Prices's suggested early initial development of Varney Red ceramics and shell tempering in general. Difficulties with

Ozark radiocarbon dates are exemplified by the middle period Mississippian dates from the Round Spring site (23SH19) (A.D. 1196, 1231, 1650, and modern, Lynott 1982). The A.D. 1650 and 1196 dates were obtained from the same sample. Considered to be contemporaneous with the Varney horizon, the "Owls Bend Tradition" has produced radiocarbon dates (Lynott et al. 1984) that also indicate that the Ozark early Varney dates are in error.

While the Varney horizon seems to date tightly within the A.D. 800–1000 time period, there is a possibility that a beginning date will fall late within the eighth century. Based on the available chronometric evidence, we tentatively place the early period Mississippian in the central Mississippi Valley at A.D. 800–1000. We suspect that eighth-century dates will not be characteristic of the Western Lowlands of Missouri once substantial data are at hand. As substantial work is carried out at Hoecake or a related site, we expect a pre-Varney ceramic complex to be identified that will fill the eighth-century gap (Fig. 66).

The Beaker Horizon

Middle period Mississippian is difficult to visualize for the whole Central Valley. It is during this period that Mississippian culture crystallized into what is often called "mature" Mississippian. The very nature of this development means that we should not expect to find broad-scale uniformity in change through time. In the Cairo Lowland, where we think the development of mature Mississippian was most rapid, the settlement centers are multiple component due to their existence throughout a time period of very significant changes. The archaeological picture is extraordinarily complex and is proving extremely difficult to unravel. Fortunately the middle portion of the Central Valley is the location of the Cherry Valley phase, characterized by mounds covering earth lodgelike structures and burials associated with specialized burial furniture. This furniture consists of plain simple jars with loop handles, simple true bottles, and beakers, the vessel form that is the most distinctive temporal marker of the early middle period Mississippian in the central Mississippi Valley. A Cherry Valley phase component was recognized at the Hazel site and similar ceramics are being recognized elsewhere, including the Obion site in Tennessee. Radiocarbon dates in Table 14 are on samples from the following sites: Cherry Valley (3), Banks (1), Obion (4) and Hazel (5). The Hazel dates are the least secure of these dates although they cluster nicely and are supported to a certain extent by archaeomagnetic dates processed from the lower (but not lowest) levels of the site by Dan Wolfman (1982). The three dates from the Cherry Valley site vary from A.D. 722 to 1102, and these two extremes are estimates on the structure beneath Mound 2. The latest date seems most reasonable to us. Dates from sites classified within this Beaker horizon subperiod help substantiate the Zebree C-14 results and allow us to make important observations concerning sociopolitical behavior into the twelfth century A.D.

The Matthews Horizon

Matthews Incised, *var. Matthews* and *Manly*, are marker ceramic types for the A.D. 1200–1400 late middle period Mississippian for most if not all of the Central Valley. At this time, tremendous change was taking place over much of the valley, culminating in abandonment of the braided stream surfaces with concurrent population nucleation onto the meander belt surfaces around A.D. 1400 (Morse and Morse 1983). All but three of the dates shown in Table 14 are from the Powers phase (Price and Griffin 1979). Most are from the Snodgrass site. No other site or phase has been as completely excavated or has been as intensively investigated in the Central Valley.

Dates in the Cairo Lowland suggest to Lewis (1982) that the Matthews ceramic tradition existed over a considerable period, from the eleventh through the sixteenth centuries. This degree of longevity for a single ceramic style is difficult for us to accept. However, it is possible that Matthews, as a ceramic tradition, began earlier and possibly lasted longer in the Cairo Lowland than elsewhere. But in the rest of the Central Valley, Matthews postdates A.D. 1200 and is replaced by Barton Incised and Parkin Punctated around A.D. 1400 or soon afterwards.

THE EMERGENCE OF MISSISSIPPIAN CULTURE A.D. 700–800

Based on evidence available at the present time, there were apparently three major Baytown period (A.D 400–700) complexes in the central Mississippi Valley. They are known as Dunklin or Barnes, Baytown, and Hoecake. Our view of the Baytown period undoubtedly is too simplistic, and conflicts in the interpretations of the emergence of Mississippian culture circa A.D 700–800 are related to attempts to resolve our unrealistic monothetic Baytown reconstruction. Phillips's Coles Creek period Beckwith, Black Bayou, Walnut Bend, and Peabody phases evidently have not held up, though; as he stated, "This is a very shaky proposition" (1970:912).

The Dunklin Phase

Centrally located in the region, the Dunklin phase dates immediately before and well into the eighth century based on radiocarbon dates from the Zebree site. The Dunklin phase is characterized by sand-tempered Barnes tradition ceramics, particularly Barnes Cord Marked, a minimal assemblage of lithics, including crude expanded-based points; and numerous but dispersed sites interpreted as single-family residence and small village locations thought to be indicative of seasonal rearrangements of populations within small watersheds (see the description of the Powell Canal site in Chapter 2). There is no good basis for supposing that the Dunklin phase could independently and rapidly evolve into Mississippian culture if the Zebree data base is truly representative of the Dunklin phase at or near the end of the eighth century.

However, according to Price and Price ". . . the Varney Tradition was an in situ development rising out of an indigenous sand tempered ceramic tradition that had existed almost 1,000 years" (1984:96). Price and Price interpret the presence of Varney Red at Hoecake as copies or as trade vessels derived from the Ozarks (1984:95). They also state that small projectile points assumed to reflect the initial appearance of the bow and arrow occur earlier in the Ozark foothills than elsewhere (1984:93), but these arrow points are invariably associated with shell-tempered ceramics. As mentioned above, the suggestion that by A.D. 650 the Varney tradition was widespread in the Western Lowlands and Ozark foothills of Missouri (but absent elsewhere) (1984:92), and that the use of shell as a tempering agent began as early as A.D. 500 (1984:69, 86) or A.D. 400 (Price 1981:493) in the Ozark foothills, is not supported by a very strong chronometric data set. As a result, while the association of arrow points and shell-tempered ceramics is clear, we believe that these complexes postdate A.D. 800.

Similarly, while we certainly agree that Early Mississippian (Naylor phase) sites exist in the Western Lowlands near Naylor, Missouri (Fig. 65), the idea that the sites predate the ninth century is based on a limited number of radiocarbon and thermoluminescence dates from the eastern Ozarks. As discussed above, a clear sequence represented by ample quantified data, checked against carefully selected and processed radiocarbon samples, is a necessary prerequisite to pushing any Varney Red complex and phase earlier than A.D. 800. Too much dependence is being placed on the selective application of a very few dates. The Naylor phase is characterized by Varney Red ceramics, although in low percentages (Lynott 1982:15). To date, little quantified documentation of the phase has been presented.

At the present time, we cannot see a local independent evolution nor can we yet accept pre-ninth-century dates for Varney Red ceramics near Naylor. Radiocarbon dates on the Dunklin phase overlap with those of early Mississippian culture at the Zebree site and there is absolutely no evidence of an evolution of one into the other.

The Baytown Phase, Plum Bayou Culture, and Flat-Based, Shell-Tempered Ceramics

In the southern portion of the Central Valley is a conglomeration of sites placed for convenience into the Baytown phase (Phillips 1970:903–904). These sites grade on the west and south into a complex formerly assigned to the Coles Creek tradition and now more specifically known as Plum Bayou culture (Rolingson 1982). Plum Bayou sites are, at least partially, contemporaneous with the Varney horizon. Plum Bayou is viewed as being contemporary with the earlier two-thirds of the Coles Creek period. The type site of Toltec is characterized by pyramidal mounds and is a major mound center (Chapter 3, this volume).

Plum Bayou culture dates around A.D. 700–900 (Rolingson 1982). Related sites are recorded along the lower White River (Moore 1910; Phillips 1970:916), the lower Cache River (House 1975:158–159), the

lower parts of Bayou de View (3CS118, AAS Collections) and the lower Little Red River (Figley 1968). These locations are to the south along major tributaries of the White/Arkansas rivers (Fig. 65). Pottery types tentatively identified include French Fork Incised, Mazique Incised, Coles Creek Incised, Evansville Punctated, *var. Rhinehart*, Baytown Plain, Coles Creek Plain, and unnamed punctated, overhang incised, and red filmed. "Of special interest [at the Soc site] were 2 shell-tempered sherds with Coles Creek-like decorations" (Figley 1968:48). Other artifacts include Poole-style stone pipes, boatstones, long narrow chisels, and copper (Moore 1910:341–348). The occurrence of red-filmed ceramics at the Toltec Mounds and at the Soc site, which postdates the demise of this trait further south (Belmont and S. Williams 1981, table 1), is of obvious interest. Red filming, of course, is very characteristic of the Varney ceramic complex.

At the Toltec site, shell-tempered pottery first appears in a late Plum Bayou context. Flat-based sherds from three vessels are in primary depositional association with Feature 1 in Mound D. This association dates to the late ninth and early tenth century (Rolingson, personal communication, June 12, 1985).

The early association at Toltec of flat-based, shell-tempered pottery is of particular importance. Other sites in Arkansas with flat-based jars occur in Izard (3IZ136), Independence (3IN39), Lawrence (3LWI00, 3LWI06, 3LW514), Jackson (3JA16), Greene (3GE47, 3GE346), and Craighead (3CG72, 3CG218, 3CG381, 3CG282, 3CG230, 3CG453) counties (Fig. 65). With one exception (3CG282), these sites are located west of Crowley's Ridge between Plum Bayou and Naylor (Fig. 65). Examples in Randolph and Clay counties and counties located to the west do not exist in our current collections, probably due both to their rarity as well as to the limited surveying that has been carried out in these counties. Price and Price (1984) have recognized components with flat-based vessels at the Scatters (3RA-19), Oneal Sullivan II (23Rl-37), and Owls Bend (23SH-10) sites (Fig. 65). House (1978:48) notes "It is clear that flat-based shell-tempered pottery is widespread and frequently occurring in the Ozarks, and . . . very complex in its variety and distribution." Dates, according to House (1978), appear to be very late, based on associations dating A.D. 1200–1300 and later.

One ovoid beaker found near Batesville (Morse and Morse 1983, fig. 11.7, 250–253) has strap handles, indicating a very late date. There are evidently two periods or one long period of manufacture of ovoid beakers, giving them questionable utility as a narrow-frame chronological marker.

Price and Price (1984) named the "Owls Bend Tradition" as a "Coles Creek" or "Emergent Mississippian" complex to accommodate the ovoid flat-based and shell-tempered jars, which are widely scattered in the Cache, White, and Black drainages. James Price had earlier established the Buckskull and Scatters "Late Woodland" phases for separate Ozark drainages (Price, Price, and Harris 1976:42, 45; Price 1981:484). We once had named this complex near Batesville the "Adams phase" (Morse 1969:22) but later quit using the name because we did not have good control over the data. Unfortunately, not much has been published about this "tradition." What is particularly needed is a detailed quantification of artifacts from good context. Only 25 sq m has been excavated at the Owls Bend site itself (Lynott et al. 1984). In Missouri simple stamped, check stamped, slipped, incised or textile impressed, and grit- or limestone-tempered ceramic attributes are characteristic of the "Owls Bend Tradition" (Price and Price 1984). Three sites in Arkansas (3LW106, 3GE346, and 3CG230) contain both Varney and "Owls Bend Tradition" sherds, and there is considerable overlap in space. These two ceramic complexes may be two partially contemporaneous (ninth and/or tenth to eleventh centuries) expressions of early Mississippian culture in different portions of the Central Lowlands. Four of five radiocarbon dates on samples from the Owls Bend site (Beta 7503–7507; Lynott et al. 1984) fall between about A.D. 800 and 1000 (the fifth date is about A.D. 600 but was run on a sample from Feature 3, which also produced an A.D. 1000 date). The specific dating of Owls Bend is unclear. However the dates do roughly correspond to an estimate of about A.D. 900 for the association of shell-tempered, flat-based vessels at Toltec. Varney in the Ozarks and Western Lowlands may predate Owls Bend where both occur, but that remains to be proved.

Although there is scant evidence regarding settlements of this time period, some information was recovered during the rapid destruction by land leveling of the Cleo Watkins site (3GE346) (Fig. 65) in the fall

Table 15. Selected Sites Reported with Major Varney Red Ceramics in the Central Mississippi Valley

Site	Major Reference
3CY72	Arkansas Archeological Survey Collections
3CY257	Arkansas Archeological Survey Collections
3CG29	Arkansas Archeological Survey Collections
3CG41	Arkansas Archeological Survey Collections
3CG64	Arkansas Archeological Survey Collections
3CG74	Arkansas Archeological Survey Collections
3CG105	Arkansas Archeological Survey Collections
3CG183	Arkansas Archeological Survey Collections
3CG213	Arkansas Archeological Survey Collections
3CG230	Arkansas Archeological Survey Collections
3CG300	Arkansas Archeological Survey Collections
3CG434	Arkansas Archeological Survey Collections
3CG438	Arkansas Archeological Survey Collections
3CG500	Arkansas Archeological Survey Collections
3CG504	Arkansas Archeological Survey Collections
3CG636	Klinger 1982
3CG903	Arkansas Archeological Survey Collections
3CT42	Arkansas Archeological Survey Collections
3GE34	Arkansas Archeological Survey Collections
3GE169	Arkansas Archeological Survey Collections
3GE316	Arkansas Archeological Survey Collections
3LW106	Arkansas Archeological Survey Collections
3LE3	House 1983
3MS2	Arkansas Archeological Survey Collections
3MS5	Arkansas Archeological Survey Collections
3MS16	Arkansas Archeological Survey Collections
3MS19	Morse and Morse 1980
3MS20	Morse and Morse 1980
3MS25	Morse and Morse 1980
3MS53	Arkansas Archeological Survey Collections
3MS59	Arkansas Archeological Survey Collections
3MS85	Arkansas Archeological Survey Collections
3MS93	Arkansas Archeological Survey Collections
3MS99	Arkansas Archeological Survey Collections
3MS114	Arkansas Archeological Survey Collections
3MS119	Morse and Morse 1980
3MS208	Morse and Morse 1980
3MS278	Arkansas Archeological Survey Collections
3MS304	Arkansas Archeological Survey Collections
3MS306	Arkansas Archeological Survey Collections
3MS312	Arkansas Archeological Survey Collections
3MS437	Arkansas Archeological Survey Collections
3MS469	Arkansas Archeological Survey Collections
3P074	Arkansas Archeological Survey Collections
3P0467	Morse 1986
3RA52	Arkansas Archeological Survey Collections
22H0565	Cottonlandia Collections
22TL501	Marshall 1983
23CT-54	Lynott 1982
23DU-5	S. Williams 1954:175–179
23DU-12	Marshall 1965c:21–38; Williams 1954:181–182 Arkansas Archeological Survey Collections
23DU-13	S. Williams 1954:182–184
Robards	Dunnell 1982
23MI-8	J. R. Williams 1974:55–88
23MI-55	Hopgood 1969b:141–147
23MI-68	Hopgood 1969b:163–168
23NM-52	Williams 1954:141–143
23NM-55	Hopgood 1969b:57–58
23NM-83	J. R. Williams 1974:86
23NM-96	Marshall 1965b
23NM-154	Hopgood 1969a:37–42
23NM-251	Marshall 1965b
23NM-501	Hopgood 1969a:47–48
23PM-2	Marshall 1965b
23PM-28	Arkansas Archeological Survey Collections
23PM-42	Marshall 1965b:43–137
23WE-627	Price and Price 1984
Wickliffe	Wesler 1985

of 1987. A later (circa A.D. 1250) village was superimposed almost exactly on an early component village (Morse 1988). Of interest here is that the early component, a compact village, covered about one hectare, and may have been fenced. The most common features observed during the rapid, and often dangerous, salvage operation at the Cleo Watkins site were deep 1–2 m diameter cylindrical storage pits. Of the 176 pit features recorded, only 15 percent were investigated. Structures were square or rectangular and of single-wall post construction. Burials were flexed. A large circular structure was reported by one of the dirt-buggy drivers but we were unable to verify its presence. Artifacts recovered included bone harpoons, small "Sequoyah"-style arrowheads, pottery gaming discs, bone awls, and shell-tempered handleless jars with flat (or occasionally round) bases. Red filming is prominent in the ceramic assemblage, primarily on interior surfaces, but sometimes on the exterior as well. Notching is the most common rim treatment. Of the 2,579 shell-tempered sherds recovered, 169 were rim sherds. Within the rim sherd sample, 25 had notched lips and 12 were red filmed. Red filming was observed on 177 body sherds.

The Baytown phase east of Crowley's Ridge is also past due for a reevaluation but that is not possible here. Radiocarbon dates from the Hyneman site in Poinsett County and Brougham Lake in Crittenden County indicate a basic seventh- and possibly eighth-century time period. Grog-tempered plain pottery, often in the form of flat-based bowls and jars, is characteristic. Crude stemmed points are also representative. Sites tend to be small and indicative of seasonal dispersal. It is becoming apparent that Varney Red and related ceramics do occur on sites located within the Baytown phase region (Table 15) although in some areas, their presence is obscured by proto-historic town sites. There is no evidence to date of transitional Mississippian sites, with the possible exception of Brougham Lake (Klinger et al. 1983).

The Baytown component at Brougham Lake (3CT98, located north of Parkin, Arkansas) has been radiocarbon dated at A.D. 780 ± 80 (F-83) but the same burned clay feature produced an archaeomagnetic date of circa A.D. 1200. Another radiocarbon date result was A.D. 1280 ± 100 (F-214). These results reflect the difficulty of interpreting context in shallow and disturbed multiple component sites. A total of 528 features (mostly post holes) were recorded within only 3,400 sq m. The poor C-14 results together with poor context also throw doubt on the assertion by Klinger and his associates that corn was associated with the Baytown component. The corrected date of the A.D. 780 estimate would be approximately A.D. 800, relatively late for Baytown but certainly within the Baytown range presented in Table 14.

Characteristic at Brougham Lake were semicircular and circular patterns of post holes, probably representing structures and/or wind-breaks ranging from 12.6–26.9 sq m in size. Pit features were basin shaped and relatively small (averaging 31.1 by 37.6 by 17 cm deep). Two burned, rectangular clay-lined pit features are unusual and of unknown function but are duplicated at other Baytown period sites. Besides Baytown Plain, the prevalent type, ceramic categories were identified by Klinger et al. as Mulberry Creek Cord Marked, Evansville Punctated, Larto Red, "Indian Bay Stamped" (probably Marksville period), Yates Net Impressed, "Alligator Incised," and "Kersey Incised." The various incised categories need to be carefully examined by someone familiar with identified types. Because only 42 rim sherds from features representative of the Baytown component were recovered (Klinger et al. 1983:15), the sherds are probably not numerous nor generally large.

Klinger and his associates identified a 10.6 sq m oval structure marked by 13 post holes and 4 nearby pit features, together with 11 other post holes, 9 pits, and 2 other features as possibly being early or transitional Mississippian. Ceramics included a small percentage of combined shell- and grog-tempered sherds. Most of the same features also contained Baytown Plain and about one-third of them also contained Mississippi Plain. A red-filmed sherd with combined temper and others with shell temper were recovered. All three paste groups involved rim sherds with notched lips and notched, folded, and applique rim strips. However, the same situation prevailed in other parts of the site as well, including wall trenches (1983:333), which are characteristic of middle period Mississippian. Primary questions concerning the Brougham Lake site include whether the Baytown and Mississippian component attributes of notching and rim strips are coincidental and respectively early and late, and how great a role was played by mechanical mixture. A radiocarbon date of A.D. 1285 ± 75 and a thermoluminescence date of A.D. 1500 ± 60 were derived from the possible Early Mississippian component.

The Hoecake Phase

Centered in the Cairo Lowland, the Hoecake phase is located in the northeast portion of the central Mississippi Valley. Radiocarbon dating at the Double Bridges site indicates a basic sixth-century time period and a date from the Hoecake site implies existence into the seventh century. The Hoecake phase is characterized by grog-tempered Baytown ceramics with an emphasis on cord marking, expanded-based points, and small sites as well as possible large multiple mound sites (Hoecake and Double Bridges). Evidence at the Hoecake site itself indicates that the Hoecake Baytown period phase developed into a "Hoecake" Mississippian period phase. Particularly impressive are the reported ceramics that include mixed pastes and surface treatments (J. R. Williams 1974:76–78). Also impressive are the significant shifts in ceramic categories from one part of the site to another. "In Area III, however [in contrast to Areas I, II, and IV], Mulberry Creek Cord-Marked composed only 5 to 17 percent of the total while Baytown Plain ranged from 52 to 67 percent. Larto Red Filmed constituted from 7 to 17 percent" (J. R. Williams 1974:74). Also: "In Area III, however [in contrast to Areas I, II and IV], shell tempered ceramics made up from 21 to 23 percent of the total" (J. R. Williams 1974:74, 79). Area III of the Hoecake site would appear to represent a transitional component between the earlier Hoecake phase and the later early period Mississippian occupation at the site. There seems to be little doubt that there is a change or transition, possibly occurring as early as the eighth century. We think that the "Hoecake phase" represents the earliest emergence of Mississippian culture in the Central Mississippi Valley.

We think the Cairo Lowland area is basic to the development of central Valley Mississippian culture during the eighth and early ninth centuries A.D. Major reasons for our taking this position concerning the Cairo Lowland include: (1) its proximity to the American Bottom (see Chapter 6) and to various important upland resources immediately north; (2) the immediate availability of a variety of important landforms (up-

lands, Braided Surface, prairie, and the Meander Belt); (3) its apparent role as a primary center for the subsequent development of Mississippian culture in the Central Valley; (4) the evidence for early transitional components; and (5) the evidence for highly developed early complexes. We do not necessarily believe that the Varney horizon and Early Mississippian began and solely existed in the Cairo Lowland for several centuries before appearing elsewhere. That is not an entirely logical expectation of cultural process. However, by the early to mid-ninth century A.D., a full Varney expression (Big Lake phase) existed at Zebree, located on a Braided Terrace and far removed from the Meander Belt and uplands. The same may be true of the Naylor phase, and the Shell Lake site area, where sites were close to or located within the uplands but at a considerable distance from the Meander Belt. The Naylor phase expression involves much less emphasis upon red filming, a characteristic thought to exist later in time east of Crowley's Ridge.

Both the Hoecake and Hayti phase concepts involve an unknown amount of mechanical mixture. In both cases it is extremely difficult to tell what is Baytown, transitional, or Mississippian. In both cases, similarity to the Big Lake phase is extremely close, with the exception of apparent transitional Baytown-Mississippian ceramics. The Big Lake phase is clearly not transitional in the sense of ceramics although obviously it is transitional in economic behavior (e.g., corn consumption). Similarities between the Missouri sites and Zebree include house type, storage pit shape, pottery shapes, discoidal shape, pottery objects, and arrow points. Differences include the presence at Zebree of the microlithic industry and harpoons, both of which are also characteristic of Early Mississippian complexes in the American Bottom (see Chapter 6). The evident ceramic transition at Hoecake roughly parallels that reconstructed for the American Bottom except in pottery paste.

Probably the most potentially important aspect of the Hoecake site is the presence of burial mounds with log tombs. An early radiocarbon date from these tombs indicates a date within or near the eighth century A.D. Hoecake thus reflects a state of development unparalleled in the Central Valley at this time with the possible exception of the Double Bridges site, a multiple mound Varney Red horizon site located between Hoecake and Zebree. In general, the Varney expression involves a population dispersed in "farmsteads" and small villages. Central burial centers are a later development except possibly for the Cairo Lowland and immediately south. From this time until the end of the fourteenth century, the Cairo Lowland seems to us to be central to development in Mississippian culture throughout the central Mississippi Valley.

EARLY MISSISSIPPIAN CULTURE:
A.D. 800–1000

The chronological placement of this period is based upon radiocarbon dates presented in Table 14, and particularly upon the "Zebree Cluster" dates for the Big Lake phase component at the Zebree site (Fig. 66). Varney Red-like ceramics in the American Bottom date to the ninth and tenth centuries (Kelly 1982:365–367). According to our Cahokia colleagues, "The Zebree site is viewed...as postdating the Merrell Tract assemblage primarily on the basis of the lack of grog tempered Baytown vessels" (Kelly 1982:366). This view restricts the Zebree assemblage to post A.D. 950. However, we view Zebree as an expression of Mississippian which, based on internal evidence, dates within the ninth and tenth centuries. The lack of grog-tempered pottery is not surprising because grog is not characteristic of this region at any time. Other significant traits at Zebree are characteristic of the American Bottom earlier than and/or contemporaneously with the radiocarbon-dated period of the Big Lake phase: arrowpoints, Mill Creek chert, maize, discoidals, small rectangular small post houses, pottery discs, and hooded bottles. The microlithic industry, however, at Cahokia evidently dates to a later period (tenth century) but this industry has not been emphasized in any investigation until very recently (Yerkes 1983). Probably the weakest part of our argument is the 200-year estimation for the occupation of Zebree by the Big Lake phase. The Varney Red horizon style itself may have lasted as much as 250–300 years (almost 400 according to Price) and evidently was a very long-lived ceramic style in comparison to later Mississippian ceramic horizon styles.

The Zebree site allowed us to examine a pristine phase, Big Lake, as representative of the Varney horizon. No other comparable assemblage has been reported in the Central Valley although it is now clear that probably hundreds of similar sites exist in southeast Missouri, northeast Arkansas, and northwest Mississippi. Table 15 lists sites with "major" Varney Red ceramics assemblages. Major can mean numerous large Varney Red potsherds, as at 3MS2 and 3GE316. It also means that on many sites, Varney Red constituted the major category of a small sherd sample. Several sites with one to four red-filmed sherds that might be Varney were not listed. This is not the place to review each individual site, but it is now evident that sites with Varney ceramics exist in a much broader area (Fig. 65) than indicated by Price and Price (1984) and by Morse and Morse (1983).

The invention and subsequent almost exclusive use of shell temper in a backswamp clay paste represents an important technological innovation (Morse and Morse 1983:208–210). When used with finely crushed grog, an even more superior ware was possible. There is no evidence from our experiments that salt was a necessary ingredient as suggested by Stimmell (1978). Shell and backswamp clay are typical lowland resources and it is logically expected that the marriage first took place in the valley lowland within the Mississippi Meander Belt. Shell-tempered paste is much lighter than sand-tempered paste (25–33 percent sand by weight compared with 10–15 percent shell by weight). The use of shell resulted in a more spherical and stronger jar, and eventually led to a revolution in shape and decoration.

It is probably no accident that grog and shell were used in the paste of many Hoecake vessels. The use of fine grog with shell continued throughout the Mississippian period, culminating in the superb protohistoric Bell Plain ware. Interestingly, the tradition of grog and shell began in the Cairo Lowland, continued there for many centuries (S. Williams 1954:98–99), and then increased in prevalence as the Cairo Lowland phase shifted downriver to become the dominant Nodena phase at about the beginning of the fifteenth century. We need microscopic examination of Hoecake sherds and experimentation with similar reconstructed pastes to say much more on this subject.

With the new ceramic technology, there was a period of uncertainty, a period of learning its potential. Rather than retreat into psychological speculations, we need to carefully examine why the new technology was so slow in fully developing. Large jars exhibit double rims or rimfolds. Presumably, this feature was for protection against cracking during drying and firing. It is also possible a folded rim aided in the attachment of a fabric cover. Red filming, a characteristic after which the Varney horizon is named, evidently was a process to add strength, or possibly to reduce porosity. Certainly the red-filmed sherds were stronger than plain sherds in the Zebree midden.

Corn was definitely present in the Zebree Big Lake deposit. Another attraction of shell (calcium carbonate) is that it aids in the digestion of corn. Particularly, the B vitamin niacin is freed when corn is soaked in a hot alkaline solution, preventing pellagra. This possible relationship must be further investigated.

Varney horizon ceramics are basically cooking jars, food and serving bowls, hooded bottles for storage, funnels and large pans for salt manufacture, and toys. They essentially copy basket and gourd (and wood?) containers. Changes in the sizes of cooking jars from the Baytown to the Mississippian period may have been due to either a shift from an extended family to a nuclear family size, or a shift to the cooking of corn. The evident need for salt, as reflected by the hypothesized salt manufacturing vessels, indicates a shift toward a more vegetarian diet, particularly corn. Osteological analyses, however, indicate that dependency upon corn was still not as significant as later. Human skeletal anomalies also suggest a transitional period toward, but not yet to, significant corn dependency.

Corn horticulture meant that Varney horizon sites were located on or adjacent to soils suitable for growing maize. The best soils, from the standpoint of fertility, drainage, and workability, are the sandy loams of river levees. A variety of soils can be exploited, and were. However, when faced with a choice, the levee soils would have been preferred, particularly because they are often located adjacent to oxbow lakes having extremely rich and varied protein sources. When Mississippian sites are found in non-natural levee settings, there often is another reason for the location. We do not believe it is wise to state that the meander belt adaptation of Mississippian populations is disproved because upland Mississippian sites exist, or that upland sites refute the postulated Mississippian adaptation to corn horticulture. Corn can be grown on many different soils; some are easier and more productive than others. Mississippian culture was able to adapt horticulture to a variety of environments by use of a dispersed settlement pattern. This pattern allowed, in addition, the easy acquisition of upland lithics, not available in the lowlands. Price and Price's (1984) reference to manufacturing debris at an early site adjacent to the Ozark Uplands emphasizes this important point.

Interestingly, white (Burlington?) chert is characteristic of sites as early as about A.D. 800. At Hoecake, there is considerable Burlington debitage present. At Zebree, quite a bit of Crescent Quarry chert was recovered. Burlington and Crescent Quarry cherts outcrop near St. Louis.

The three main early period Mississippian innovations involving lithics were the bow and arrow, the large hoe, and the discoidal. Additional innovations were in woodworking, particularly chert chisels, but also basalt celts and adzes. The bow and arrow not only meant the advent of a superior hunting and warfare implement but also was responsible for the bow drill, necessary for the production of large numbers of shell beads. The emphasis at Zebree and at Cahokia on the production of microliths used to drill shell beads underscores this importance. Shell beads probably functioned as trade items to help insure peaceful coexistence between different societies and as both an inter- as well as an intrachiefdom integration factor. The microlithic industry was also evidently important in the manufacture of another possible horizon marker, the bone and antler harpoon. Other than those excavated at the Zebree site, a single harpoon was recovered from the Watkins site (3GE346) (Fig. 65), and a large number of such artifacts have been reportedly found at the Reelfoot Lake site in Tennessee.

The large hoe, usually made of Mill Creek chert from Union County, Illinois, was particularly important to corn horticulture. In addition, the trade of finished hoes out of Illinois was important to interpersonal or intergroup relationships. Caches of these hoes have been found in Arkansas (*Central States Archaeological Journal*, January 1973, fig. 31). Conch shell for beads probably also was traded via Illinois. Cahokia is the location of tremendous amounts of conch shell debris, more than any other inland site in the eastern United States (Parmalee 1958).

The advent of discoidals has to have been important in terms of interchiefdom relationships. The game might have functioned as an integrating mechanism but the chunkey game certainly is not limited to chiefdoms (Culin 1907). The stone discoidal essentially is a Mississippian trait and the Zebree shape (Morse and Morse 1983:211) is both early and widespread in the region of Varney horizon sites and in the American Bottom. Zebree was reoccupied some two centuries later than the Big Lake phase component by a short-lived farmstead. Whatever importance the site might have had in the ninth and tenth centuries evidently was insufficient for continued use. Other sites located nearby continued in importance, particularly Walnut Mound (3MS2), Blytheville (3MS5), and Wardell (23PM28). Undoubtedly the continued investigation of many other later sites will reveal Varney Red horizon occupations.

How Zebree fits in a model of site hierarchy is really not known because we have little data beyond those obtained from the Zebree project. Zebree was a relatively small village. Other similar sites located nearby seem to be about as large or are smaller. There are, in addition, apparent single-structure sites ("farmsteads") and it is expected that these will be recorded in much larger numbers than multiple-structure sites ("villages") of up to 1 ha in size.

We do not know if Zebree functioned as a primary center. Certainly any village of comparable size would function as a central place to neighboring farmsteads—socially, politically, and economically. The presence of a major microlithic industry is obviously unusual and an important indication of village craft specialization. Immediately adjacent to the Zebree site was a Varney Red ceramic location and a microlithic location, an indication that Zebree was one component of a broader community with spatially separate units. Perhaps mounds once existed within this broader community; certainly the region has undergone extensive land modification during the twentieth century. Local tales of mounds reference any natural knoll as a "mound" and cannot be accepted as an indication of burial mounds.

The Kersey site (Marshall 1965a, 1965b) was evidently similar to Zebree. Its total size and the existence of possible sister communities is not known. There was apparently a central post pit similar to the one found at Zebree. Artifact and feature traits, with the exception of the evident lack of the microlithic industry, are very similar to Zebree. The ceramics are shell tempered. There are some grog-tempered sherds present that may constitute part of the Hayti phase but most grog-tempered pottery seems to belong to an earlier Baytown period occupation. Some minor amounts of Barnes pottery were also recovered. A structure associated with bundle burials may be post-Hayti phase, but the loop-handled jar and true bottle recovered were

intrusive into the deposit and one bundle of bones was lined with Varney Red sherds. Like the group burial at Zebree, no burial furniture was in primary association. A second bundle burial group was also found at Kersey by Marshall.

Three sites along Portage Open Bay in Missouri have produced significant concentrations of Varney Red ceramics (Hopgood 1969a). Hayward is a "small village" while Simer is recorded as 3 1/4 ha in size with a 7.5 m high mound. Double Bridges contained between 7 (Adams and Walker 1942:11) and 23 (Moore 1916: 502) mounds and covered 11 ha (J. R. Williams 1968, fig. 26). "Perforators" are also characteristic of Double Bridges (Hopgood 1969a:29). The recent discovery of Varney Red pottery at Wardell by us and Richard Marshall has resulted in the recognition of a linear pattern of sites leading south toward Zebree. Double Bridges is characterized by the presence of grog-tempered ceramics, but only a minor percentage at this time can be tentatively associated with the post-Baytown component characterized by Varney Red.

The most impressive Varney Red horizon site is Hoecake, located in the Cairo Lowland. It is about 80 ha in extent and originally contained between 31 and 54 mounds (Marshall 1965b; J. R. Williams 1974; Hopgood 1969b; Houck 1908:64; Morse and Morse 1983). Artifact and feature similarities to Zebree and Kersey are remarkable. The microlithic industry has not been recognized or reported, if indeed it exists at Hoecake. Two extended burials with associated pottery jars have been recovered from Village Area III. One vessel with Burial 1 is similar to Varney Red types in shape but the two found with Burial 2 have angular shoulders. The mounds at Hoecake cover log-lined tombs. Pottery at Hoecake is primarily grog tempered. Shell-tempered pottery does occur in significant concentrations as does a combined shell and grog paste. Red filming is mostly on a grog paste; Varney Red is relatively rare. Hoecake is significantly different from Zebree and Kersey in most of its ceramics but not in other Mississippian traits.

We interpret this to mean that much of Hoecake is slightly earlier in time than other Varney sites, but it could be that contemporary indigenous populations are undergoing slightly different responses to the same stimuli.

The makeup of the Hoecake site is of residential units separated from each other. The site actually appears to be a large complex community of sites. Whether components of the site are contemporaneous or not is not known (for a similar situation, see the Range site description, Chapter 5). The areas tested can be organized sequentially in time but there is a real need for additional intensive investigation at Hoecake. We interpret the large size of the site to be due to multiple occupation or community shifts through time. Most of the site seems to have been destroyed but substantial areas yet remain.

THE EVOLUTION OF MISSISSIPPIAN CULTURE: A.D. 1000–1200

By at least A.D. 1000 Mississippian sites were distributed throughout the central Mississippi Valley. In contrast to the earlier Varney and later Matthews horizons, the ceramics of the period are very difficult to recognize. This has resulted in statements in the past such as: "[the Powers phase] . . . is not indigenous to the Little Black River area but came there fully developed" (Price and Griffin 1979:3).

Red filming, particularly the thick polished interior Varney variety, probably disappeared during the first half of the eleventh century. Plain undecorated pottery seems to have been the basic kitchenware and there are sites (e.g., in Clay County, Arkansas, and near Naylor, Missouri) with plain Varney-shape jar fragments. Settlements evidently are mainly dispersed neighborhood communities of farmsteads. Pre-late twelfth-century centers are not readily identified because they are rare and/or because they continued to be used in subsequent centuries.

In Craighead and Poinsett counties, Arkansas, red-filmed and sandy paste shell-tempered ceramics occur at 3PO490, 3PO192, 3PO54, 3PO52, and 3CG67. These are not strictly Varney, based on the Zebree sample, but are relatively early and possibly indicative of a regional adaptation. We infer that the components at those sites date somewhat later in time than classic Varney sites, about A.D. 1000, but we have no solid evidence for this hypothesis. The sandy paste sherds with notched lips found at the group of leveled sites (3PO52, 3PO54, 3PO192) in Poinsett County may represent a variation on the Varney theme. When found they were employed to establish the "Hyneman phase" (Morse 1969:21), but there are only three closely situated sites representative of this "phase." We quit using the term because we felt we had jumped too far ahead of our

data. The salvage of 3CG67, which had a similar but not identical ceramic complex, convinced us that we simply lacked good control over the development of "emergent" Mississippian. However, the recent partial salvage excavation of the Priestly site (3PO490) by David Benn of Southwest Missouri State University has reinforced the concept of a Hyneman phase with relationships to the Early Mississippian component at Brougham Lake. At Priestly, a very large circular structure was partially excavated that may have been a charnel structure characteristic of a slightly later period.

At the Bay Mounds site (3CG29), which seems to date A.D. 1050–1200, there are Varney Red sherds indicating either (1) a Varney horizon component at this site, or (2) Varney Red vessels continued to be manufactured for a very short period after A.D. 1000. The same seems to be true of 3CG636 (Klinger 1982), where most of the Varney Red sherds were recovered from a single feature, indicating the probability of a multiple component occupation. Our rule-of-thumb standard that red filming disappeared overnight at A.D. 1000 or even A.D. 1000–1050 is, after all, simply an archaeological construct to help isolate Varney horizon sites. With a mass of new site data now becoming known, this rule-of-thumb has to be refined and recognized for what it is, a tool to seriate site assemblages. All this would be easier if people simply would have abandoned forever all former site locations every one to two generations.

The Cairo Lowland region is more complex than the remainder of the Central Valley in terms of the identification of a progressional sequence of events after A.D. 1000. Most sites are multicomponent and have received only minimal excavation or analyses. In the center of the Central Valley—northeast Arkansas—is a basic clue, we believe, to the general situation characteristic of the eleventh and twelfth centuries A.D. This clue is the Cherry Valley phase, based on the type site location near Cherry Valley, Arkansas, on the west flank of Crowley's Ridge (Fig. 65).

Three of the original five mounds at the Cherry Valley location were salvaged by Gregory Perino (1967) after a period of vandalism destroyed much of the site. No residential debris was identified at the location. The mounds constituted a central burial place for a population evidently living nearby in farmsteads and small villages. The mounds were 4–4.5 m high and 18–20.5 m in diameter. A typical Cherry Valley mound was built over a structure. The structure was used, perhaps only partially, as a charnel house, and the primary mound is usually associated with bundle burials. As the mound was enlarged, both bundle and primary burials were included. The mounds presumably were sequential at any one location and evidently most burials found in one mound were actually associated with ceremonies initiated in an unmounded structure located nearby. The upper levels of mounds often contained later burials that we think were interred into a traditionally sacred burial place.

The major aspects of Cherry Valley phase burial locations are (1) the structure beneath the mound, (2) bundle burials as the predominant mode of burial, and (3) the type of burial furniture. The best preserved structure was found at the base of Mound 2 at Cherry Valley. It is simply extraordinary. There once existed, before Mound 2 was constructed, a 10 m diameter circular building with a 6 m long entryway. This structure probably functioned as a men's council house. Similar structures were characteristic of the eighteenth-century Southeastern Indians who were organized as simple chiefdoms as opposed to the complex chiefdoms described by the De Soto expedition (DePratter 1983: 204–211). There evidently was a full development of chiefdomship before the time of the De Soto expedition, with subsequent decline due to intrusive historic events. In the central Mississippi Valley, the seventeenth-eighteenth century Quapaw are interpreted by us as representing remnant populations of one or more earlier powerful chiefdoms now subsumed within a single decentralized chiefdom or tribal confederacy.

The Cherry Valley Mound 2 structure is similar to the Macon, Georgia, earth lodge (Fairbanks 1946) in many respects and both are reminiscent of Le Moyne's painting *A Council of State*. An early circular structure was found at the contemporaneous Banks Mound 3 (Perino 1967), located north of Memphis and a considerable distance from Cherry Valley, indicating that this circular structure feature probably was widespread within the Central Valley.

The consistent association of bundle burials with Cherry Valley phase mounds seems to us to be a very important trait. To be "bundled" the corpse first has to be defleshed. The loss of soft tissue may be due simply to temporary storage in an environment conducive to skeletonization.

. . .in climates similar to Florida, on the surface defleshing may occur in a minimum of two weeks to a maximum of about eight months. . . . Buried bodies decompose much slower. . . . Cooler weather in the Winter and Fall will materially slow down decomposition (Morse 1983:125).

Unfortunately, studies of bundle burials have not to our knowledge included an investigation of the temporary storage environment or an estimation of time needed for decomposition or even an appraisal of the nature of the skeletonization process. Cleaning and other current curation techniques have destroyed much or all of the data needed for such an investigation utilizing extant remains.

The conscious act of skeletonization implies a need for the proper ceremonial disposal of remains at appropriate and predicted dates. Evidently for the Cherry Valley and other contemporary phases in the Central Valley, a central burial mound served as the end point of the mortuary program of dispersed residential units. We do not know any population statistics for the Cherry Valley phase skeleton assemblages. There also, unfortunately, are no population statistics for the Hearnes site skeletal assemblage in the Cairo Lowland (Klippel 1969:64–76), mainly due to poor preservation. Hearnes may date slightly later in time than the Cherry Valley phase but does suggest that a mortuary practice involving bundle burial was widespread at this general time period.

Cherry Valley phase ceramic burial furniture is very instructive, both from the standpoint of technology and of functional categories. The Le Moyne painting referenced earlier shows the consumption of a tea as an integral part of the ceremony. "Black drink, a ritual beverage, was a necessary part of all important council meetings" (Hudson 1976:226). Cherry Valley ceramics primarily consist of beakers, bottles, and small jars. Plates and nonbeaker bowls are present but in small numbers. At the Floodway site (3P046), we recovered a bottle with a beaker placed upside down over the bottle neck. The beaker evidently functioned as a cup and was filled with a beverage stored in the bottles. The jars could have functioned to brew the drink and hearths associated with structures might have been used to cook the brew in these jars. In the Cherry Valley phase, ceremonial libation was apparently associated

Table 16. Beakers Reported from the Central Mississippi Valley

Sites	References
Bay Mounds Craighead Co., AR (3CG29)	Smithsonian Collections
Middle Craighead Co., AR (3CG102)	Arkansas Archeological Survey Collections
Banks Mound 3 Crittenden Co., AR (3CT16)	Perino 1967:82
Cherry Valley Cross Co., AR (3CS40)	Perino 1967:48–60
Parkin Cross Co., AR (3CS29)	Perino 1967:60
Rose Mound Cross Co., AR (3CS27)	Phillips, Ford, and Griffin 1951: fig. 100-J
Turnbow Cross Co., AR (3CS61)	Arkansas Archeological Survey Collections
Vernon Paul Cross Co., AR (3CS25)	Perino 1967:60; Hathcock 1976: fig. 116
Floodway Poinsett Co., AR (3PO46)	Arkansas Archeological Survey Collections
Ballard Poinsett Co., AR (3PO115)	Arkansas State University Collections
Hazel Poinsett Co., AR (3PO6)	Morse and Smith 1973: figs. 15a, 28e, 30; Perino 1967:60
McClellan Poinsett Co., AR (3PO32)	Arkansas Archeological Survey Collections
Arkansas (unknown site)	Riggs Collection, Buffalo Museum of Science
Campbell Fulton Co., KY	Hathcock 1976: fig. 115
Hanna New Madrid Co., MO (23NM68)	Hathcock 1976: fig. 113
Crosno Mississippi Co., MO (23MI1)	S. Williams 1954: fig. 63a
Obion Henry Co., TN (40 HY14)	Baldwin 1966

with the final disposition of human remains and perhaps also the temporary storage of human remains in charnel structures. As Hudson (1976:320–336) points out, there was widespread concern in the eighteenth century over the burial of a kinsman, and it is not unreasonable to visualize the council house, the curated human remains, and the practice of drinking a special ceremonial broth as part of a single mortuary program. It is also possible that changes in kinship status due to death were extremely important and complex.

The technology of Cherry Valley phase ceramics is also informative and at least provides clues for the recognition of a similar technology elsewhere in the Central Valley despite the rarity of beakers. Jars have "loop" handles. These were riveted into the vessel wall in contrast to later "strap" handles, which were applied to the vessel wall. Riveting reflects a general lack of confidence in one's ability to successfully manufacture and fire an appliqued ceramic component. More importantly, riveting is easily recognized and can provide an important dating criterion if future investigation does indeed demonstrate that it is a horizon style within the Central Valley. Simple bowl, true bottle, and jar outlines are characteristic. Simple rim effigies are present but very little variation in ceramic shape is evident. Mound Place Incised and variations of O'Byam Incised (on plates) are rare decorations, and most pottery is plain.

We have coined the term "Beaker horizon" to describe the period of time occupied by the Cherry Valley phase. Beakers are rare in the Central Valley (Table 16) and presumably date to this period. Until the excavation of the Cherry Valley site by Perino the beaker form was "a type hitherto unreported for Arkansas" (1967: 9, 60). The main recorded burial sites of this time period are located in northeast Arkansas: Cherry Valley (3CS40), Floodway (3PO46), Ballard (3PO115), Bay (3CG29), and probably Turnbow (3CS61). Bay Mounds and Turnbow are unusual because villages are present. We are not really certain of the exact location or circumstances of the Smithsonian discoveries at the Bay (Webb) Mounds. But the collection is available for analysis although it had to be "rediscovered" after Perino's 1967 report; obviously collections of this nature are very valuable.

There were two mounds dug completely away at the Ballard site by the Arkansas State University Museum. A number of typical Cherry Valley phase ceramic artifacts exist from one mound but no field notes are extant. It is possible that there was only one actual mound that contained several burials, mostly bundle. At Floodway, at least six mounds were leveled. One was salvaged by D. Morse and the others were subsequently bulldozed—unmonitored—after assurances were received they would be preserved. From the salvaged mound were recovered a good representative Cherry Valley phase ceramic assemblage, bundle burials, and evidence of a circular structure. Inferences about Turnbow are based on the presence of disturbed mounds at that site and a collection of beaker handles in the Arkansas Archeological Survey collections.

Beakers have been reported from other sites, from the Cairo Lowland south almost to Forrest City, Arkansas (Fig. 65). The clear indication is that beakers occupy a large geographical area of the Central Valley and probably more examples could be recorded simply by an examination of local collections. It is amazing to us that they were not recognized until so late in our archaeological investigation of the Central Valley. Beakers similar to those found in the Central Valley postdate A.D. 1000 in the American Bottom.

Indications are that during the twelfth century A.D., fortification became characteristic of Mississippian sites. This is particularly noticeable in the Cairo Lowland where very large centers developed and continued to develop well into the fourteenth century (Morse and Morse 1983:262–266). The extreme complexity of major sites such as Lilbourn, Sandy Woods, Matthews, Towosahgy, and Sikeston, together with a strong range of C-14 dates from the twelfth through the fourteenth centuries, forms the primary evidence for this development. Sites in the southern portion of the Central Valley are not nearly so impressive as those in the northern portion for this time period. Interestingly, the exact reverse occurred after the fourteenth century, to the extent that braided stream surfaces and the Cairo Lowland are essentially abandoned in terms of permanent habitation. This population nucleation process evidently began in the twelfth century and climaxed at the end of the fourteenth century with an abrupt shift in settlement pattern. Fortification, centralization of authority, and population nucleation began as related events in the twelfth century. This also appears to be the period of a very significant increase in the dependence upon corn agriculture. It is also, perhaps not coincidentally, a period of decreased summer precipitation (Bryson et al. 1970:64–70). However, we do not know what precise effects the rest of the ecosystem sustained at this time. Corn does not need continuous or high precipitation. It needs precipitation at specific times of its development. In any event, the nature of Mississippian society after A.D. 1200 seems quite different than before A.D. 1100. We postulate that there was a development during this century from a local or simple chiefdom to a regional or complex chiefdom (Smith 1978; Steponaitis 1978), or from a "minimal" to a

"typical" chiefdom (Carneiro 1981). This shift does not seem to have taken place everywhere in the Central Valley at the same time. The Powers phase seems to have achieved the status of a typical chiefdom possibly near the beginning of the fourteenth century (Price and Griffin 1979; Morse and Morse 1983:256–262) or approximately one century after the Cairo Lowland societies.

THEORIES OF ORIGIN AND DEVELOPMENT

The essence of anthropological archaeology is to understand behavioral changes as reflected by cultural sequence reconstructions. This is a very elusive goal because we really do not yet fully understand the archaeological sequence or its environmental and cultural context. We are forced to work with imperfectly preserved material culture garbage, recovered as inadequate samples by human beings with a limited knowledge of archaeological midden formation and modification. We tend to grope at simple explanations of very complex social-political and economic matters. We cannot help but get better at interpretation but it seems to be taking a very long time.

The simplest explanation for cultural change is a catastrophic one. Either the environment suddenly changed or the migration of a superior society took place. Such explanations do have the merit of being testable. But often, the tests are negative. A Mexican origin for Mississippian culture in the Central Valley region has been advocated by many, mostly by county society historians but also by respected archaeologists (Porter 1969). Very few, if any, trained Eastern United States archaeologists today seriously consider a migration from Mexico as the reason for the origin of Mississippian culture (see Smith 1984 for a good discussion of migration theories). Similarly, interregional migration as a cause of the beginning of Mississippian culture is no longer as popular as it once was.

Recent investigations in the American Bottom and within the Central Valley have resulted in the recognition of concurrent but distinctive developmental sequences. Rather than try any more to cope with the overall origin of Mississippian culture in the eastern woodlands, we now have focused on trying to explain the initiation and subsequent development of Mississippian culture within a specific region such as the central Mississippi Valley.

Human beings are formed into societies that are components of ecosystems. Any change within a ecosystem can result in change in the social behavior of human beings. The Hypsithermal surely must have been witness to some relatively significant behavioral changes, although this hypothesis has not yet been proved. Postulating an environmental shift as the reason for the origin of Mississippian culture is too simple and almost certainly invalid. We really do not know specifically what environmental changes took place within the valley during the past millennium and a half. It is doubtful that anything really significant occurred during the century we postulate behavioral change took place—the eighth century A.D. Yet it is possible that something environmentally occurred because a major Mississippi River crevasse channel may have originated in northeast Arkansas at this time. It is difficult to see any significant result beyond the local scene, and crevasse channels do not require significant shifts in the regional environment to be created. Clearly, we cannot now invoke an environmental change to explain the emergence of Mississippian culture.

Ecological change, however, did take place after A.D. 400. Corn cultivation and the advent of the bow and arrow probably began to cause some changes in species selection in the eastern United States. The only published study to our knowledge concerning species stress in the Central Valley was by Smith (1975) and he concluded that wolves, not humans, constituted critical population control of white-tailed deer in the Central Valley. Recent studies (e.g., Cross 1985) do not detect any significant changes in faunal composition from the sixth century into the eleventh century. However, during the eighth and ninth centuries A.D., an increase in species selection may have taken place due to the introduction of the Mill Creek hoe and its wide acceptance as an efficient farming tool, together with almost universal use of the bow and arrow. In addition, there was an acceleration in the exploitation of wood resources, as reflected in new house construction technology and the appearance of more sophisticated and greater numbers of woodworking tools. It is certainly a puzzle why faunal and floral assemblages do not reflect what must have been significant changes.

Population probably increased during the Early Mississippian period although there are no hard data on which to base population estimates. Varney Red sites are inferred to be permanent year-round settlements, at least in terms of slash-and-burn agriculture, while Baytown sites are interpreted as being of a seasonal nature. Large Varney Red sites appear to have contained more people than large Baytown sites, based on the Zebree site investigation. However, small Baytown sites may have contained more people than comparable Varney Red sites. If population did increase significantly, species selection may also have increased, with an ever-increasing prevalence of forest-edge environment. Species selection also would have extended directly to shellfish procurement for pottery paste. Farming communities are more prone to population increase (extra farmhands and shorter nursing periods) than hunting-gathering communities. Population increase, together with a growing importance of land stewardship, may have contributed to the development of chiefdom social organization, but it probably cannot account solely for it, based on ethnographically known groups.

In the lowlands of the Central Valley, upland lithics constituted a critical resource. Successful farming, woodworking, and hunting were completely dependent upon the successful procurement of this class of raw material. Increased population must have significantly increased this need. Land stewardship, increasing awareness of concept of territory, and a potentially hostile frontier together with land and resource competition may have significantly contributed to the development of chiefdomship. Procurement and consumption of scarce resources evidently was directed by chiefs in an atmosphere of increasing authoritarianism.

Once ecological changes were set in motion, there was a kind of inertia in place toward authoritarianism and population nucleation. The catalyst seems to have been the acceptance of a single cereal (maize) after A.D. 400 in the eastern United States. Some environments proved extremely conducive to its adaptation, and once adopted, corn could be grown virtually everywhere. Adaptation involved social-political changes, particularly where critical upland resources were absent. Increasing population within a newly created and ever-changing ecotone contributed to increasing centralized authority.

Phillips (1970:912) lamented that there was nothing really comparable in the Central Valley to the southern Coles Creek period. That problem has been solved in that there is now abundant evidence of ninth- and tenth-century cultural developments comparable to the Coles Creek over much of the central Mississippi Valley.

The eighth century is still largely unknown, but the only evident independent emergence recognized to date appears to have taken place in the Cairo Lowland. The American Bottom was almost certainly a major region of influence for the central Mississippi Valley as a neighboring, very complex, social-political entity. This region was, by about the end of the time of the Varney horizon, the location of the largest site and the largest mound ever constructed in the United States. By the time the Big Lake phase occupation took place at Zebree, the American Bottom already had witnessed most of the innovations of Mississippian culture with the exception of pottery paste. But the important lesson from this review is that whatever the stimuli, the occupants of the central Mississippi Valley responded as an indigenous population participating fully in the emergence of Mississippian culture in the eastern United States.

There is an emerging picture in the central Mississippi Valley of at least two early complexes: Plum Bayou and Varney, with the possibility of a third, "Owls Bend." Plum Bayou and Varney ceramics are associated with multiple-mound sites, and an evident site hierarchy thought to be characteristic of, but not proof of, chiefdoms. Varney first emerged in the Cairo Lowland region, probably in the eighth century, and was evidently the primary base for post-A.D 1000 Mississippian culture throughout the Central Valley. Mississippian culture continued to evolve during the eleventh and twelfth centuries, when fortification, population nucleation, high dependence upon corn, and chiefly exotic artifacts known as the Southeastern Ceremonial Complex became characteristic.

ACKNOWLEDGMENTS

We wish to particularly thank the following individuals, who helped to make this paper possible: Elizabeth Garland, Eric van Hartesveldt, John House, Richard Marshall, Robert Mainfort, James Price, Martha Rolingson, Bruce Smith, Marvin Smith, Kit Wesler, and most of all, Marvin Jeter.

REFERENCES CITED

Adams, Robert M., and Winslow M. Walker
1942   Archaeological Surface Survey of New Madrid County, Missouri. *The Missouri Archaeologist* 8(2).

Baldwin, Elizabeth E.
1966   *The Obion Site: An Early Mississippian Center in Western Tennessee.* Ph.D. dissertation, Department of Anthropology, Harvard University, Cambridge.

Belmont, John S., and Stephen Williams
1981   Painted Pottery Horizons in the Southern Mississippi Valley. Traces of Prehistory, edited by F. West and R. Neuman. *Geoscience and Man* 22:19–42. Baton Rouge.

Bryson, Reid A., David A. Baerreis, and Wayne M. Wendland
1970   The Character of Late-Glacial and Post-Glacial Climatic Changes. In *Pleistocene and Recent Environments of the Central Great Plains*, edited by Wakefield Dort, Jr. and J. Knox Jones, Jr., pp. 53–74. University Press of Kansas.

Carneiro, Robert L.
1981   The Chiefdom: Precursor of the State. In *The Transition to Statehood in the New World*, edited by Grant D. Jones and Robert R. Kautz, pp. 37–75. Cambridge University Press, Cambridge.

Cottier, John W.
1977   Radiocarbon Dates from the Lilbourn Site and a Check List of Dates from the Eastern Lowlands of Southeast Missouri. *The Missouri Archaeologist* 38:308–314. Columbia.

Cross, Paula
1985   On Mississippian Hunting Practices. Paper presented at the sixth Mid-South Archaeological Conference, June 8–9, 1985, Starkville, Mississippi.

Culin, Stewart
1907   *Games of the North American Indians.* Bureau of American Ethnology Annual Report 24. Washington, D.C.

Damon, P. E., C. W. Ferguson, A. Long, and E. I. Wallick
1974   Dendrochronologic Calibration of the Radiocarbon Time Scale. *American Antiquity* 39:350–366.

DePratter, Chester Burton
1983   *Late Prehistoric and Early Historic Chiefdoms in the Southeastern United States.* Unpublished Ph.D. dissertation, Department of Anthropology, University of Georgia, Athens.

Dunnell, Robert
1982   Missouri. In Current Research. *American Antiquity* 47: 225–226.

Fairbanks, Charles
1946   The Macon Earthlodge. *American Antiquity* 12(2): 94–108.

Figley, Charles Jr.
1968   The Soc Site, 3Wh34. *Arkansas Archeologist* 9:41–57.

Hathcock, Roy
1976   *Ancient Indian Pottery of the Mississippi River Valley.* Hurley Press. Camden, Arkansas.

Hopgood, James F.
1969a   *An Archaeological Reconnaissance of Portage Open Bay in*

Southeast Missouri. Missouri Archaeological Society Memoir, No. 7.

1969b *Continuity and Change in the Baytown Pottery Tradition of the Cairo Lowland, Southeast Missouri.* M.A. thesis, Department of Anthropology, University of Missouri. Columbia.

Houck, L. B.
1908 *A History of Missouri.* (3 vols.) Chicago.

House, John H.
1975 Summary of Archeological Knowledge Updated with Newly Gathered Survey Data. In *The Cache River Archeological Project,* chap. 15, assembled by M. B. Schiffer and J. H. House. Arkansas Archeological Survey Research Series, No. 8.

1978 Flat-based Shell-tempered Pottery in the Ozarks: A Preliminary Discussion. *The Arkansas Archeologist, Bulletin of the Arkansas Archeological Society* 19:45–49.

1983 Emergency Salvage at Barrett Mound A, Lee County, Arkansas. *Field Notes, Newsletter of the Arkansas Archeological Society* 192:3–10.

Hudson, Charles
1976 *The Southeastern Indians.* The University of Tennessee Press, Knoxville.

Kelly, John Edward
1982 *Formative Developments at Cahokia and the Adjacent American Bottom: A Merrell Tract Perspective.* Archaeological Research Laboratory, Western Illinois University, Macomb.

Klippel, Walter E.
1969 The Hearnes Site: A Multicomponent Occupation Site and Cemetery in the Cairo Lowland Region of Southeast Missouri. *The Missouri Archaeologist* 31.

Klinger, Timothy C.
1982 *The Mangrum Site: Mitigation through Excavation and Preservation.* Arkansas Archaeological Survey Research Series. No. 20.

Klinger, Timothy C., Steven M. Imhoff, and Roy J. Cochran, Jr.
1983 *Brougham Lake.* Historic Preservation Associates Reports 83-7. Submitted to the Department of the Army, Memphis District, Corps of Engineers, Contract No. DACW66-80-C-0082.

Lewis, R. Barry
1982 *Two Mississippian Hamlets: Cairo Lowland, Missouri.* Illinois Archaeological Survey, Special Publication, No. 2, Urbana.

Lynott, Mark J.
1982 Mississippian Archaeology of the Upper Current River, Southeast Missouri. *Southeastern Archaeology* 1(1):8–21.

Lynott, Mark J., Susan M. Mond, and James E. Price
1984 The Owls Bend Site, 23SH10: An Emergent Mississippian Occupation in the Eastern Ozarks, Southeast Missouri. *Missouri Archaeological Society Quarterly* 1(1):12–15.

Marshall, Richard A.
1965a *An Archaeological Investigation of Interstate Route 55 Through New Madrid and Pemiscot Counties, Missouri, 1964.* Highway Archaeology Report, No. 1, University of Missouri. Columbia.

1965b Highway Salvage Archaeology at Two Village Sites in Pemiscot and New Madrid Counties, Missouri, 1965.

Manuscript on file, American Archaeology Division, University of Missouri. Columbia.

1965c Test Excavations at the J.R. Marret Site, 23Du12, Southeastern Missouri. *Arkansas Archeologist* 6(2–3):21–28.

1969 The Story Mound Excavation at the Hoecake Site. Manuscript on file.

1983 A Brief Comparison of Two Early Mississippi Substage Settlement Patterns in Southeast Missouri and Northwest Mississippi. Paper presented at the Society for American Archaeology Annual Meeting, Pittsburgh.

Moore, Clarence B.
1910 Antiquities of the St. Francis, White and Black Rivers, Arkansas. *Journal of the Academy of Natural Sciences of Philadelphia* 14:255–364.

1916 Some Aboriginal Sites on Green River, Kentucky, Certain Aboriginal Sites on Lower Ohio River, Additional Investigation on Mississippi River. *Journal of the Academy of Natural Sciences of Philadelphia* 16:429–511.

Morse, Dan F.
1969 Introducing Northeast Arkansas Prehistory. *Arkansas Archeologist* 10:12–28.

1986 McCarty (3PO467): A Tchula Period Site Near Marked Tree, Arkansas. In *The Tchula Period in the Mid-South,* edited by David Dye and Ronald Brister, pp. 70–92. Mississippi Department of Archives and History Archaeological Report 17. Jackson.

1988 Salvage of the Cleo Watkins Site (3GE346). *Field Notes, Newsletter of the Arkansas Archeological Society* 220:7–9.

Morse, G. Daniel
1983 The Time of Death. In *Handbook of Forensic Archaeology and Anthropology,* edited by D. Morse, J. Duncan, and J. Stoutamire, pp. 124–144. Rose Printing Company, Tallahassee.

Morse, Dan F., and Phyllis A. Morse (editors)
1980 *Zebree Archeological Project.* Submitted to the U.S. Army Corps of Engineers, Memphis, by the Arkansas Archeological Survey.

1983 *Archaeology of the Central Mississippi Valley.* Academic Press, New York.

Morse, Dan F., and Samuel D. Smith
1973 The Hazel Site: Archaeological Salvage during the Construction of Route 308. *The Arkansas Archaeologist* 14:36–77.

Moselage, John
1962 The Lawhorn Site. *The Missouri Archaeologist* 24:1–104.

Parmalee, Paul
1958 Marine Shells of Illinois Indian Sites. *Nautilus* 71:129–139.

Perino, Gregory
1967 *The Cherry Valley Mounds and Banks Mound 3.* Central States Archaeological Societies, Memoir No. 1.

Phillips, Philip
1970 *Archaeological Survey in the Lower Yazoo Basin, Mississippi, 1949–1955.* Papers of the Peabody Museum 60. Harvard University, Cambridge.

Phillips, Philip, James A. Ford, and James B. Griffin
1951 *Archaeological Survey in the Lower Mississippi Alluvial Valley, 1940–1947.* Papers of the Peabody Museum 25. Harvard University, Cambridge.

Porter, James
1969 The Mitchell Site and Prehistoric Exchange Systems at Cahokia: A.D. 1000 ± 300. In *Explorations into Cahokia Archaeology,* edited by Melvin L. Fowler, pp. 137–164. Illinois Archaeological Survey Bulletin 7.

Price, James E.
1981 Analysis of the Prehistoric Cultural Materials. In *Changing Settlement Systems in the Fourche Creek Watershed in the Ozark Border Region of Southeast Missouri and Northeast Arkansas, Project CAR-251,* chap. 11, edited by James E. Price and Cynthia R. Price. Submitted to USDA-Soil Conservation Service, Interagency Archaeological Services-Denver, Contract No. C35001.(79), by Center for Archaeological Research, Springfield.

Price, James E., and Cynthia R. Price
1984 *Phase II Testing of the Shell Lake Site, 23WE-627 near Wappapello Dam, Wayne County, Missouri, 1984.* St. Louis District Cultural Resource Management Report No. 11. U.S. Army Corps of Engineers, St. Louis District. Contract No. DACW43-82-D-0083.

Price, James E., and James B. Griffin
1979 *The Snodgrass Site of the Powers Phase of Southeast Missouri.* Museum of Anthropology, University of Michigan Anthropological Papers No. 66.

Price, James E., Cynthia R. Price, and Suzanne E. Harris
1976 *An Assessment of the Cultural Resources of the Fourche Creek Watershed.* Soil Conservation Service, Columbia.

Rolingson, Martha Ann (editor)
1982 *Emerging Patterns of Plum Bayou Culture.* Arkansas Archeological Survey Research Series 18, Fayetteville.

Smith, Bruce D.
1975 *Middle Mississippi Exploitation of Animal Populations.* Museum of Anthropology, University of Michigan Anthropological Papers No. 57. Ann Arbor.
1978 Variation in Mississippian Settlement Patterns. In *Mississippian Settlement Patterns,* edited by B. D. Smith. Academic Press, New York.
1984 Mississippian Expansion: Tracing the Historical Development of an Explanatory Model. *Southeastern Archaeology* 3(1):13–32.

Spears, Carol S.
1978 *The Derossitt Site (3SF49): Applications of Behavioral Archeology to a Museum Collection.* Master's thesis, Department of Anthropology, University of Arkansas, Fayetteville.

Steponaitis, Vincas
1978 Location Theory and Complex Chiefdoms: A Mississippi Example. In *Mississippian Settlement Patterns,* edited by Bruce D. Smith. Academic Press, New York.

Stimmell, Carole
1978 A Preliminary Report on the Use of Salt in Shell Tempered Pottery of the Upper Mississippi Valley. *The Wisconsin Archeologist* 59(2):266–274.

Wesler, Kit W.
1985 Early Mississippian at Wickliffe Mounds, 15BA4. In *The Emergent Mississippian,* edited by Richard Marshall, pp. 149–159. Occasional Papers 87-01. Cobb Institute of Archaeology, Mississippi State University, Starkville.

Williams, J. Raymond
1968 *Southeast Missouri Land Leveling Salvage Archaeology: 1967.* National Park Service. Department of Anthropology, University of Missouri, Columbia.
1972 *Land Leveling Salvage Archaeology in Missouri: 1968.* National Park Service, Department of Anthropology. University of Missouri, Columbia.
1974 The Baytown Phases in the Cairo Lowland of Southeast Missouri. *The Missouri Archaeologist* 36:1–109.

Williams, Stephen
1954 *An Archaeological Study of the Mississippian Culture in Southeast Missouri.* Ph.D. dissertation, Yale University, New Haven.

Wolfman, Daniel
1982 Archeomagnetic Dating in Arkansas and the Border Areas of Adjacent States. In *Arkansas Archeology in Review,* edited by N. L. Trubowitz and M. D. Jeter, pp. 277–300. Arkansas Archeological Survey Research Series No. 15. Fayetteville.

Yerkes, Richard
1983 Microwear, Microdrills and Mississippian Craft Specialization. *American Antiquity* 48:499–518.

Gerald F. Schroedl, C. Clifford Boyd, Jr., and R. P. Stephen Davis, Jr. Chapter **8**

Explaining Mississippian Origins in East Tennessee

INTRODUCTION

T. M. N. Lewis and Madeline Kneberg (1946) made the first formal attempt to describe and explain the origins and development of Mississippian cultures in east Tennessee. Population migration was the basis for their explanation. Lewis and Kneberg's work was consistent with Webb's (1938) general approach to archaeological interpretation and his analyses of archaeological data from the Norris Basin, which included associating archaeological remains with specific ethnic groups. Earlier researchers, such as Cyrus Thomas (1894), C. B. Moore (1915), and M. R. Harrington (1922), had shared this interest, but Lewis and Kneberg concluded, as had Webb, that Muskogean rather than Cherokee people were responsible for the Mississippian cultures of east Tennessee (see Smith 1984). The Midwestern Taxonomic System was used to organize the east Tennessee archaeological record into a chronological sequence of cultural foci and aspects characteristic of the Woodland and Middle Mississippi patterns in the area (Kneberg 1952; Lewis and Kneberg 1946). In constructing this sequence, Lewis and Kneberg included comparative data from Webb's work in the Norris Basin and from the investigations of Cyrus Thomas, M. R. Harrington, and others. Archaeological excavations conducted in the Chickamauga Basin, most importantly at Hiwassee Island (40MG31), but also at the Hixon (40HA3), Dallas (40HA1), Sale Creek (40HA10), and Davis (40HA2) sites as well as other sites (see Fig. 67) provided the essential elements for

the Lewis and Kneberg culture-historical scheme (Lewis and Kneberg n.d., 1941, 1946; also see Kneberg 1952; Rowe 1952; Whiteford 1952).

Through the 1950s and 1960s, the culture history of east Tennessee was embellished with greater descriptive detail, but neither its structure nor its explanatory framework was challenged by researchers. In the late 1960s the first signs of dissatisfaction and need for fundamental revision began to appear (Faulkner 1972; Salo 1969). Contributing to this situation was evidence that Middle Woodland period cultures in east Tennessee shared previously unrecognized affinities with contemporary cultures in western North Carolina (Chapman 1973; Gleeson 1970). Furthermore, it became increasingly difficult to fit the growing radiocarbon chronology with the existing culture-historical sequence for the Late Woodland and Early Mississippian periods. Too many radiocarbon dates from Late Woodland period burial mounds indicated Early Mississippian period burial mound use (Schroedl 1973, 1978a). Artifacts found with mound interments, furthermore, were comparable to Early Mississippian styles. At the same time, excavations of sealed stratigraphic contexts at the Martin Farm site (40MR20) produced sherd assemblages that were difficult to accommodate within the existing culture chronology and accepted explanation for change in the archaeological record (Faulkner 1972; Salo 1969). Accompanying the difficulties in accounting for geographical, temporal, and material content variability were fundamental changes in archaeo-

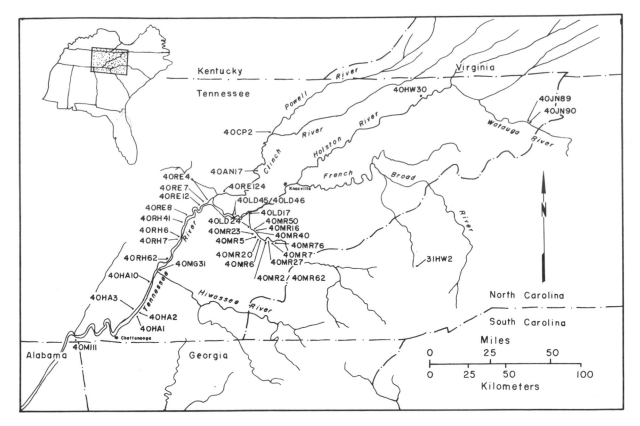

Fig. 67. Archaeological sites in east Tennessee discussed in the text.

logical methods and attempts to develop alternative theoretical approaches for archaeological explanation (e.g., Binford and Binford 1968; Clarke 1968; Flannery 1968). Concepts of ethnic and culture material uniformity with migration responsible for culture change in the archaeological record were replaced by concepts of culture adaptation and evolutionary change.

While the Chickamauga Basin project of the 1930s was the source of archaeological data for the interpretations of Lewis and Kneberg, the Tellico Archaeological Project, conducted in the lower Little Tennessee River valley between 1967 and 1982, has provided most of the data used to reevaluate and revise the definitions of Woodland and Mississippian period culture-historic units in east Tennessee (Kimball 1985; Kimball and Baden 1985; Schroedl et al. 1985). The development of alternative models for interpreting the transition between these cultures has been inspired by excavations and detailed analyses of the Martin Farm site (Schroedl et al. 1985). A revised perspective on the chronology of burial mound use has come from the series of radio-

carbon dates obtained at the McDonald site (40RH7) on the Tennessee River and at 40RE124 on the lower Clinch River (Schroedl 1973, 1978a).

The orientation presented here is decidedly biased toward analyses and interpretations generated by the Tellico Archaeological Project. Geographically, comparative data is largely restricted to the Tennessee River valley between Knoxville and Chattanooga and the lower reaches of three of its major tributaries, the Little Tennessee, Hiwassee, and Clinch rivers. Thus included are sites in the Chickamauga, Watts Bar, and Tellico Reservoirs. The upper valley of the Clinch River within the Norris Basin is also considered here. The Tennessee Valley north of Knoxville is generally excluded for lack of available comprehensive excavations and data analyses. Such studies, however, have been recently initiated, and although far from complete, they suggest strong cultural affinities with western North Carolina during the Mississippian period (Boyd 1985). Woodland period relationships may have had greater continuity with the rest of east Tennessee. Besides

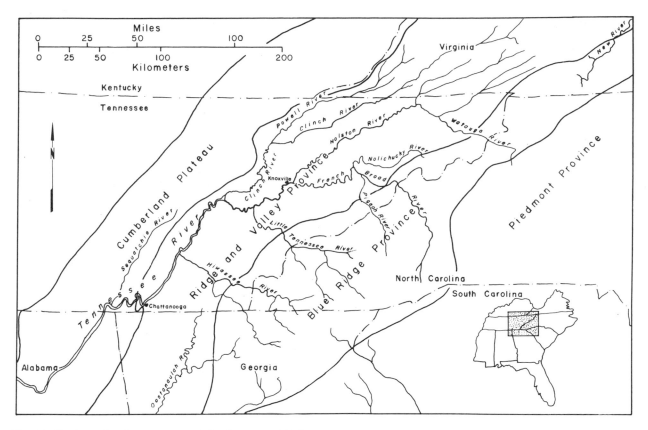

Fig. 68. Physiography of east Tennessee (after Fenneman 1938).

apparent differences in archaeological records, there are also physiographic and environmental contrasts for which Knoxville serves as an approximate southern boundary.

ENVIRONMENT

East Tennessee makes up most of the southern section of the Ridge and Valley physiographic province (Fenneman 1938:265–278). This section, consisting of folded and dissected Paleozoic sediments, is 50 to 120 km wide and extends from the Tennessee-New River divide in southwest Virginia to the coastal plain and piedmont areas in northern Georgia and Alabama (Fig. 68). From northeast to southwest, the number of ridges, their elevations, and the degree of relief they form with adjoining valleys gradually diminishes. North of Knoxville, long, parallel ridges and valleys are closely spaced with valley floors 250 to 275 m in elevation and ridges 100 to 125 m higher. In contrast, the ridges south of Knoxville seldom exceed 300 m in elevation and there are

far greater areas of smooth rolling lowlands with elevations around 250 m. Here major river valleys, particularly the Tennessee and Hiwassee, are as much as 8 to 10 km wide. Having elevations from 1,250 to 1,850 m, the Unaka and Smoky Mountains of the Blue Ridge Province bound the Ridge and Valley Province to the east. To the west are the Cumberland Mountains and Cumberland Plateau. These features ascend to elevations of 450 to 650 m, with Powell Mountain, Wallen Ridge, Walden Ridge, and Lookout Mountain forming particularly prominent escarpments.

East Tennessee has a temperate continental climate with a mean annual temperature of 58 degrees F and overall average annual precipitation of 55 inches (140 cm) (USDA 1941). January and July mean temperatures are respectively 38 degrees F and 76 degrees F and an average of 190 frost-free days occur between mid-April and mid-October. Winter and summer months are wettest, while fall and spring months are comparatively dry. Because of topographic differences the amount and pattern of precipitation may markedly

Table 17. East Tennessee Culture Chronology for the Woodland and Mississippian Periods

Period	Culture	Dates
Cherokee	Overhill	A.D. 1700–A.D. 1838
Late Mississippian	Dallas, Mouse Creek	A.D. 1200–A.D. 1600
Early Mississippian	Hiwassee Island	A.D. 1000–A.D. 1200
Late Woodland	Hamilton, Roane-Rhea	A.D. 600–A.D. 900
Middle Woodland	Candy Creek	A.D. 200–A.D. 600
Early Woodland	Watts Bar, Long Branch	900 B.C.–A.D. 200

(based on Lewis and Kneberg 1946)

vary over the area, particularly during the summer when locally heavy thunderstorms occur. Because of greater elevation, the Cumberland Plateau and Blue Ridge areas, in general, receive about 10 inches (25 cm) more precipitation and average 5 degrees to 10 degrees F cooler than the Ridge and Valley of east Tennessee.

Although chestnut is now virtually extinct due to blight, oak-chestnut forests characterized east Tennessee (Braun 1950:192–258). Oak, particularly white oak *(Quercus alba)*, tends to prevail on valley floors and has become more abundant on ridges as chestnut has declined. Oak-chestnut forests also covered the adjacent Unaka and Smoky Mountains. Sheltered ravines and coves in the mountains and ridges contained mixed mesophytic or hemlock forest communities. Mixed mesophytic forests, consisting of a complex mosaic of forest communities, characterize the Cumberland Plateau and Cumberland Mountain escarpments. South of Knoxville the oak-chestnut forests made a gradual transition to oak-pine forests, which predominate in northwestern Georgia and northeastern Alabama.

Essentially modern climate and forest conditions were established in east Tennessee by 4,000 years ago. Recent pollen and botanical studies, however, show that the impact of aboriginal populations on the biotic environment was greater than previously imagined (Chapman et al. 1982; Cridlebaugh 1984). Cultigens such as squash, gourd, and sunflower are known from Late Archaic period (2500–1300 B.C.) contexts and evidence of corn occurs in Middle Woodland period (A.D. 200–550) sites (Chapman and Shea 1981; Cridlebaugh 1981, 1984). Pollen data suggest possible cultivation of corn on older alluvial terraces at this time. These data also show probable widespread forest clearance in the lower Little Tennessee River valley about A.D. 900, marked by increased abundance of successional

species and distinct *Ambrosia* pulses characteristic of disturbed habitats (Cridlebaugh 1984). Although vegetational change was accelerated by Euro-American settlement in the eighteenth century, it is significant that this process coincides with the transition to the Mississippian period. While detailed documentation of this impact is limited to the lower Little Tennessee River, the abundance of Mississippian period sites elsewhere in east Tennessee suggests considerable aboriginal modification of the biotic environment throughout the region.

CULTURE CHRONOLOGY

The Woodland and Mississippian period chronology developed by Lewis and Kneberg is given in Table 17. Of particular interest is that the cultural sequence includes Middle and Late Woodland, Candy Creek, and Hamilton foci, respectively, succeeded by the Early Mississippian, Hiwassee Island focus. Although Lewis (1959) and Kneberg (1961) suggested changes in other portions of the culture history, only Kneberg's (1961) addition of the Roane-Rhea ceramic complex as a Late Woodland culture unit distinct from the Hamilton focus has relevance to the problem of Woodland-Mississippian transition.

The chronology was modified further when major archaeological excavations were begun in the Tellico Reservoir in the late 1960s. This involved partitioning previously defined archaeological cultures, expanding the geographic distribution of cultures to include other portions of east Tennessee, and defining new cultures never before recognized in the area. Early and late divisions of the Candy Creek culture were hypothesized (Chapman 1973), but Connestee culture, well known from work in western North Carolina (Keel 1972, 1976), quickly came into use in lieu of more formal consideration of a late Candy Creek designation (McCollough and Faulkner 1973). In 1969, Salo (1969) proposed a new culture unit to describe archaeological materials from the Martin Farm site. Initially the materials were called Emergent Mississippian, but were subsequently referred to as the Martin Farm phase (Faulkner 1972). Thereafter the term "emergent" was retained as a modifier instead of a formal cultural division.

Culture units were designated by Midwestern Taxonomic System labels until the 1960s, although the As-

Table 18. Alternative East Tennessee Culture Chronology for the Woodland and Mississippian Periods

Period	Culture	Dates
Mississippian IV	Overhill Cherokee	A.D. 1600–A.D. 1838
Mississippian III	Dallas, Mouse Creek	A.D. 1300–A.D. 1600
Mississippian II	Hiwassee Island	A.D. 1000–A.D. 1300
Mississippian I	Martin Farm	A.D. 900–A.D. 1000
Woodland III	Icehouse Bottom, Westmoreland-Barber	A.D. 350–A.D. 900
Woodland II	Patrick I, II	200 B.C.–A.D. 350
Woodland I	Bacon Bend	900 B.C.–200 B.C.

(after Kimball 1985)

pects (e.g., Upper Valley aspect) that had been defined were never widely used (see Kneberg 1952). Thus the culture-historical sequence was a geographic and temporal arrangement of foci, representing the east Tennessee expression of Archaic, Woodland, and Mississippian periods. Radiocarbon dates were used to establish and then monitor the duration of each focus. Beginning in the 1960s, Willey and Phillips's (1958) terminology was substituted for the Midwestern Taxonomic System designations, and foci became phases. In a variety of contexts, horizon and tradition were employed, but were seldom formally defined or widely incorporated into the east Tennessee culture-historical sequence.

The Woodland and Mississippian cultures of east Tennessee are defined by the occurrence of specific historic ceramic types and their comparative frequencies in stratigraphic deposits or archaeological facilities with cultural integrity. The most abundant ceramic types are considered diagnostic for a specific phase. Lithic artifacts, except for one or two projectile point types such as Hamilton and Madison triangular types, are seldom considered crucial to phase definitions. Structures, burials, and other site facilities are included in phase descriptions, but they also usually make little difference in the definition of these units. The important exceptions are burial mounds, which are Late Woodland period, Hamilton phase occurrences only in the Lewis and Kneberg chronology.

The first serious proposal to revise or replace the Lewis and Kneberg culture history was made in 1980 (Kimball 1985). As shown in Table 18, most culture designations in this scheme use familiar terminology, which makes the sequence superficially resemble its predecessor. In contrast to the intuitive assessment of ceramic type frequencies, the culture units constitute sherd assemblage profiles defined using statistical

methods (Kimball and Baden 1985). This included using (1) varimax rotated principal component analysis to identify covariation among the ceramic categories and to assign new numerical values to specific assemblages; (2) Ward's H-GROUP single-linkage hierarchical clustering procedure to establish significant assemblage clusters; and (3) discriminant analysis to evaluate the distinctiveness of each assemblage cluster to all other clusters similarly defined.

Thirty-eight sherd assemblages (having 135 to 39,132 sherds) from eight sites, five of which are located on the lower Little Tennessee River, were used to define the Woodland period temporal units. The Mississippian period temporal units were derived from the study of 73 sherd assemblages (having 235 to 22,991 sherds) from 11 sites in the Tellico Reservoir and 9 sites in the Chickamauga Basin. Diagnostic projectile points were identified for each temporal unit, while the temporal duration of the units was established by critical evaluation of all available radiocarbon dates.

There are two very important things to realize about the culture sequence presented in Table 18. First, it was specifically created to date surface collections recovered in the lower Little Tennessee River valley (Davis et al. 1982; Kimball 1985). The culture units are explicitly defined from ceramic assemblage studies and radiocarbon dates. No other archaeological data categories are defining criteria. Such data, however, must necessarily be included when considering the emergence of Mississippian period cultures in east Tennessee.

This culture-historic sequence is used here, as a result, more in the sense of archaeological phases than ceramic assemblage complexes as originally defined. By doing so, a conflict between the available archaeological data and the ceramic assemblage temporal units becomes evident. In Kimball's culture sequence there is no unit comparable to Lewis and Kneberg's Late Woodland, Hamilton phase. Instead, the period A.D. 600 to A.D. 900 is included in the Woodland III period, Icehouse Bottom and Westmoreland Barber-Moccasin Bend temporal units. The archaeological record dating between A.D. 600 and A.D. 900 is especially critical to understanding the development of Mississippian culture in east Tennessee, since there is now ample evidence for the comparatively rapid development of this culture between A.D. 900 and A.D. 1000. Because of the implications for defining Late Woodland period cul-

Table 19. Middle and Late Woodland Period Radiocarbon Dates

		Carbon Years Uncorrected			Damon et al. 1974 Corrected			
Site	Lab No.	BP	s	Age	BP	s	Age	Reference
40MR40	GX-5243	1365	145	A.D. 585	1342	147	A.D. 608	Schroedl 1978b
40MR40	GX-5246	1430	155	A.D. 520	1408	157	A.D. 542	Schroedl 1978b
40MR23	GX-2487	1345	90	A.D. 605	1323	93	A.D. 627	Gleeson 1970
40MR23	GX-2154	1365	90	A.D. 585	1342	93	A.D. 608	Chapman 1973
40MR23	GX-5046	1480	135	A.D. 470	1459	137	A.D. 491	Chapman and Keel 1979
40MR23	UGa-1881	1515	110	A.D. 435	1496	112	A.D. 454	Chapman and Keel 1979
40MR23	GX-5047	1545	160	A.D. 405	1526	162	A.D. 424	Chapman and Keel 1979
40MI11	GX-573	1325	105	A.D. 625	1302	107	A.D. 648	Faulkner and Graham 1966
40JN89	GX-10245	1290	155	A.D. 660	1267	163	A.D. 683	Riggs 1985
40JN90	GX-10246	1320	150	A.D. 630	1297	154	A.D. 653	Riggs 1985
40HW30	DIC-982	1370	65	A.D. 580	1347	69	A.D. 603	Lafferty 1981
40MR5	GX-7733	1260	135	A.D. 690	1238	144	A.D. 712	Baden 1983
40MR76	GX-7728	1550	135	A.D. 400	1531	137	A.D. 419	this paper
40MR76	GX-7730	1250	130	A.D. 700	1228	140	A.D. 722	Schroedl et al. 1985
40MR76	GX-7729	720	120	A.D. 1230	728	124	A.D. 1222[a]	this paper
31HW2	GX-593	1145	85	A.D. 805	1126	99	A.D. 824	Keel 1976

[a] Date is considered too recent for associated ceramic assemblage.

tures and characterizing the period A.D. 600 to A.D. 900, a brief review of the Middle Woodland period in east Tennessee is necessary.

WOODLAND PERIOD

The Candy Creek phase was defined by Lewis and Kneberg (n.d., 1941, 1946) as the Middle Woodland culture of east Tennessee. They recognized this culture from the occurrence of limestone-tempered plain, fabric-marked, and fine-cordmarked sherds as well as limestone-tempered checked, complicated and simple stamped pottery. Sand-tempered plain, fabric-marked, and complicated, simple, and checked-stamped sherds were important constituent types.

Excavations at Icehouse Bottom (40MR23) (Chapman 1973; Cridlebaugh 1981), the Patrick site (40MR40) (Schroedl 1978b), the Higgs site (40LD45) (McCollough and Faulkner 1973), and comparative data from Connestee phase sites in western Carolina, particularly Garden Creek Mound No. 2 (Keel 1972, 1976), prompted investigation of the temporal and cultural relationships of limestone- and sand-tempered ceramics. The Higgs and Patrick site studies suggested that sand-tempered ceramics were temporally later than limestone-tempered types and thus the Candy Creek phase and the succeeding Connestee phase represented distinct Middle Woodland cultures in east Tennessee. Radiocarbon dates at Icehouse Bottom and Garden Creek Mound No. 2 range from A.D.

424 to A.D. 824, with most circa A.D. 400 to A.D. 500 (Table 19). Keel's (1976:239) proposed age range for Middle Woodland cultures in east Tennessee is, as a result, A.D. 200 to A.D. 600.

Although Keel suggests a distinct Late Woodland culture dating A.D. 600 to A.D. 900, he identifies no such specific culture in east Tennessee. Kimball's (1985) analyses of the same data indicate contemporaneity of Candy Creek and Connestee phase ceramics, and because no additional ceramic assemblages were distinct enough to warrant separate culture period designations, Kimball favored a Middle Woodland-Late Woodland continuum dating A.D. 350 to A.D. 900.

Is there a distinct Late Woodland period culture as first proposed by Lewis and Kneberg and endorsed by Keel, or is there a ceramic continuum, and by implication, no distinct Late Woodland culture in east Tennessee? Answering this question is difficult because of the problems researchers have had identifying Late Woodland period occupation sites, the reevaluation of burial mounds as defining criteria of the Late Woodland period, and the occurrence of diagnostic Middle Woodland ceramic types in apparent Late Woodland contexts. Despite these difficulties, data gathered in the last five years may warrant creating a distinct Woodland IV period temporal unit dating A.D. 600 to A.D. 900. There are insufficient quantitative analyses of the kind performed by Kimball and Baden (1985), however, to specify to what degree this unit might resemble their Westmoreland Barber-Moccasin Bend designation or previously defined Hamilton or Roane-Rhea ceramic complexes (Kneberg 1961). Associated radiocarbon dates and qualitative contextual data support a Late Woodland or Woodland IV period culture unit for which a name is not proposed, but for which the name Hamilton is inappropriate.

Kneberg (1961) documented Hamilton culture ceramic variability with data from Hiwassee Island (40MG31, Units 38, 46, and 112), Sale Creek (40HA10, Unit 62), and the Dallas site (40HA1, Unit 7, 8, and 63). According to Lewis and Kneberg (1946) and others (e.g., Rowe 1952:200–201) limestone-tempered plain and cordmarked ceramic types were diagnostic of the Candy Creek and Hamilton phases. They and other researchers (Chapman 1973; Cridlebaugh 1981; Keel 1976; McCollough and Faulkner 1973) argue that limestone-tempered cordmarked followed by limestone-tempered plain and brushed types dominate Late Woodland period Hamilton occupations. There is agreement too that limestone-tempered stamped types and sand-tempered types, so common in Candy Creek/Connestee contexts, are rare Late Woodland occurrences. Lewis and Kneberg also indicate that wider and shallower impressions distinguish Hamilton from Candy Creek cordmarked types, and even suggest that Hamilton cordmarked is an intermediate or transitional type between the earlier Candy Creek cordmarked and later Hamilton Plain types (also see McCollough and Faulkner 1973:120). The difficulties distinguishing these types, and thus telling Middle Woodland from Late Woodland period occupations, is further complicated by the use of undesignated cordmarked and plain type names for sherds that cannot be satisfactorily assigned to either Candy Creek or Hamilton types (Salo 1969:123–125). Recent research shows differences in the type of cord (S-twist or Z-twist) and degree of smoothing on limestone-tempered cordmarked sherds. Identifying a particular limestone-tempered cordmarked type on a single sherd basis, however, is virtually impossible (Schroedl et al. 1985:165). Individual limestone-tempered plain types are just as difficult to separate.

Besides the Hamilton phase and ceramic complex, Kneberg (1961) also described a terminal Late Woodland period cultural manifestation that she called the Roane-Rhea ceramic complex after its frequent occurrence at sites in these two counties. Data from four sites, the Wilson site (40RE7, Unit 17), the Alford site (40RE4, Unit 4), the Montgomery site (40RE8, Unit 73), and Upper Hampton Place (40RH41, Units VT2 and 85), were the basis for the complex. Abundant limestone-tempered plain ceramics and correspondingly fewer limestone-tempered cordmarked sherds characterized these occurrences. Stamped pottery is absent in the complex. More importantly, Kneberg noted similarities between Roane-Rhea complex and Early Mississippian vessel morphology (Kneberg 1961:8). She pointed out, for example, that vessels tended to have globular rather than conoidal or tetrapodal bases and that jars with constricted necks and shallow bowls occurred in the Roane-Rhea complex.

In the Chickamauga and Watts Bar basins, Lewis and Kneberg (n.d., 1941, 1946) identified numerous shell heaps, measuring as large as 10 by 25 m, as "individual household" middens of the Hamilton culture. No contemporary structures were ever identified in or around these deposits, leading Lewis and Kneberg (1946:36) to conclude that the buildings were of such light construction that they left no detectable archaeological evidence. The middens were thought to represent year-round occupations. From the abundance of shell and near absence of vertebrate remains, Lewis and Kneberg were convinced that "the fresh water mussel was the staple protein source" (1946:44). Native plants were considered part of the Hamilton culture diet; the possibility of agriculture was viewed as an unlikely or peripheral subsistence activity. The overall settlement pattern consisted of households "strung out along the river banks" (Lewis and Kneberg 1946:36) with individual or clustered burial mounds located in the vicinity away from the river. Burial mounds were assumed to represent "centralization points for Hamilton communities which otherwise were rather loosely organized as to their plan of settlement" (Lewis and Kneberg 1946:36).

Since the 1930s only two additional Hamilton shell middens have been investigated in east Tennessee, and both the Doughty site (40LD46) and 40RH62 investigations were used to evaluate Lewis and Kneberg's ideas about Hamilton settlement-subsistence patterns (McCollough and Faulkner 1973; Prescott 1977). While neither excavation produced evidence of an associated structure, faunal and botanical studies provide alternative perspectives on this topic.

McCollough and Faulkner (1973:124–129) propose that small shell middens, like the Doughty site, found on higher river terraces are winter and early spring base camps occupied by small family groups represented primarily by women and children. They further suggest that caves and rockshelters in upland areas, particularly the Cumberland Plateau, were used as hunting camps by male members of the society to supply the riverine base camps. "Summer and fall settlements of band size were located in the floodplain zone, often on the T-1 [first river terrace], where some type of incipient horticulture was practiced and the wild plant and animal foods of the riverine environment could be exploited" (McCollough and Faulkner 1973:127). This model is considered a working hypothesis by the authors because no specific comparative data for summer-fall riverine and winter-spring upland settlements are presented.

Faunal and botanical data from 40RH62 do not completely support the settlement models of Lewis and Kneberg or McCollough and Faulkner. Prescott (1977: 43) indicates that reptile and fish remains at the site are evidence for spring-summer occupation oriented toward riverine resources. Arboreal nuts from the midden suggest a probable fall occupation (Prescott 1977: 43–49). The near absence of larger mammal and bird remains such as deer and turkey at 40RH62, however, is consistent with the Doughty site and other Hamilton occupation sites. Prescott uses this and functional indices for lithic artifacts to argue for distinct female and child related activities at 40RH62. Prescott (1977: 43–44), in summary, does not believe that 40RH62 was a permanent habitation area as predicted by the Lewis and Kneberg model, but neither is the site a winter-spring occupation in accordance with the McCollough and Faulkner view.

A comprehensive Late Woodland period settlement-subsistence model is still far from completely developed. Hamilton shell middens are confined primarily to the Chickamauga and Watts Bar areas on the main Tennessee River. None are reported from major tributaries such as the Little Tennessee River, and the character of Late Woodland period sites in these areas is virtually unknown. Ceramic collections from cave and rockshelters in the Cumberland Plateau suggest frequent intense use of the area during the Late Woodland period. However, almost none of these materials have been recovered or studied by professional archaeologists.

Late Woodland shell middens often occur amidst deposits containing earlier or later cultural remains, raising questions about the stratigraphic and cultural integrity of Hamilton phase occupation areas. Available studies, however, document distinct Middle Woodland and Early Mississippian period shell deposits (Chapman 1977; Parmalee et al. 1982). Parmalee et al. (1982) show, furthermore, that there is little perceptible difference in species diversity and abundance among the mollusks from such sites regardless of culture period. This means that systematic exploitation of river mussel resources remained virtually identical during Late Woodland and Early Mississippian times. The few studies of faunal and botanical remains are inconclusive, although reptiles, fish, small mammals, and arboreal nut shells occur at either the Doughty site or at 40RH62. Larger animal species are infrequent in the available samples. Corn is well represented in Late Woodland context at the Westmoreland-Barber site (40MI11) (Faulkner and Graham 1966, 1967). Chenopod, knotweed, maygrass, and the remains of arboreal nuts also occur in recently analyzed samples from Westmoreland-Barber (Gremillion and Yarnell 1985). Corn and other cultigens will surely be identified when additional Late Woodland period sites are investigated.

Radiocarbon dates for Late Woodland occupations are scarce, and none, unfortunately, is available from a shell midden. Faulkner and Graham (1966:114) obtained an A.D. 648 date (Table 19) from Feature 50 at the Westmoreland-Barber site. Although they considered the pottery representative of the Hamilton ceramic complex, Kimball (1985) indicates that the relative frequencies of limestone-tempered plain and cordmarked sherds more closely resemble Kneberg's (1961) Roane-Rhea complex. Walthall (1980:135), however, believes the Feature 50 ceramics represent the Late Woodland period Flint River culture, which is predominantly found in northern Alabama. At Jones Ferry (40MR76) in the lower Little Tennessee River valley, Feature 80, containing nearly equal proportions of limestone-tempered cordmarked and plain ceramics (respectively 47 percent and 45 percent of the total sherds), was radiocarbon dated at A.D. 722 (also see Chapman 1980: 43–58). Comparable dates come from sites 40HW30 (Lafferty1981:491), 40JN89, and 40JN90 (Riggs 1985) in upper east Tennessee (Table 19). Nearly all the sherds (81 of 86 specimens) from Feature 8 at 40HW30 are limestone-tempered plain; limestone-tempered sherds are predominant in the radiocarbon dated contexts at 40JN89 and 40JN90, but associated cord-roughened and coarse sand-tempered sherds indicate cultural patterns not found elsewhere in east Tennessee (Boyd 1985).

In contrast to occupation areas, the most distinctive and best-documented features of the Late Woodland period are burial mounds. To the virtual exclusion of other archaeological data, burial mounds and their associated grave goods have become the diagnostic trait of the Hamilton phase. Although abundant in most areas of east Tennessee, few burial mounds are recorded in the Norris Basin and their numbers in general diminish north of Knoxville. In contrast, nearly 200 burial mounds are recorded for the Watts Bar Reservoir area (Cole 1975, table 2) and 50 or more are found in Tellico Reservoir (Thomas 1894; Kimball 1985). Such mounds occur alone or in clusters and are usually situated on higher river terraces. Occasionally, a burial mound is found on a bluff or ridge overlooking a river valley. Because burial mounds have been the object of both clandestine as well as professional investigations for well over 100 years, it is difficult to obtain accurate estimates of mound size and burial populations. Mound height and diameter vary considerably with most examples about 2 m high and 20 m in diameter. The number of associated interments also ranges widely from as few as a single individual to over 100 burials (see Lewis and Kneberg n.d., 1946; Schroedl 1978a). Most examples perhaps contain 10 to 20 interments.

In most cases mound construction was initiated by burning the surface vegetation or scraping away the upper few centimeters of soil. On the prepared surface a pit was excavated or a log tomb was built, in which the initial burial, usually an adult male, was placed and covered with a low earthen mound. Additional burials or mound construction stages were sometimes covered or marked by limestone slabs or deposits of river mussel shells. Use of river mussel shells is more common at sites to the south while limestone slabs are found more often with mounds in northerly areas of the distribution (Cole 1975:70). Small log covers mark burial locations in a few mounds; individual logs also are sometimes laid horizontally at the base of the mound slope. Drilled conch columellae (*Busycon* sp.) and Hamilton triangular projectile points are common grave associations. Small celts, steatite pipes, stemmed projectile points, and bone artifacts also are associated with mound burials. Despite the variety of known burial associations, most burials contain no grave goods (Cole 1975; Lewis and Kneberg 1946; Schroedl 1978a). Cole's (1975:72) study also suggests a tendency for the number of burials with grave goods to decrease over time.

From the detailed analysis of site 40RE124 and a selected sample of 14 additional mounds, Cole (1975) attempted, through a variety of multivariate statistical tests, to infer properties of Late Woodland social organization from mortuary patterning. Her study identified three geographical mound clusters whose properties suggest subregional Late Woodland groups perhaps organized at a tribal level. Age, sex, and grave association data indicate egalitarian societies with achieved status. Individual mounds or mound groups may have been built and maintained by particular lineage groups and may have served as territorial markers. Exotic artifacts, especially conch columellae (*Busycon* sp.), indicate cultural contact and exchange well beyond the east Tennessee region. Their association with comparatively few interments suggested to Cole (1975:81) that such artifacts marked higher status individuals who might have controlled or influenced the trade or manufacture of shell ornaments. No significant correlation, however, occurs between conch shell columellae and age and sex groups (Cole 1975:85).

That burial mounds were exclusive Late Woodland occurrences was not questioned until a radiocarbon chronology for their use was constructed beginning in the 1970s (Schroedl 1973). The dates now available (Table 20) are ample evidence for burial mound use in east Tennessee from A.D. 700 to A.D. 1200, clearly showing their use during the subsequent Early Mississippian period. Hamilton mounds, for this reason, are no longer considered a defining criterion or exclusive association of the Late Woodland period. The Hamilton burial mound complex is a more appropriate designation for this phenomenon.

As noted above, occupation sites dating between A.D. 600 and A.D. 900 are not nearly as well understood as burial mounds. The settlement models proposed by Lewis and Kneberg (1946) and by McCollough and Faulkner (1973) with the exception of Prescott's work (1977) remain largely untested. Extensive exploitation of river mussels and the accumulation of shell middens is evident along the Tennessee River below Knoxville. Such exploitation, however, is dated before A.D. 600 and continued after A.D. 900 in the same area. Else-

Table 20. Hamilton Burial Mound Complex Radiocarbon Dates

Site	Lab No.	Carbon Years Uncorrected			Damon et al. 1974 Corrected			Reference
		BP	s	Age	BP	s	Age	
40RH7	GX-2596	1135	100	A.D. 815	1116	112	A.D. 834	Schroedl 1978a
40RH7	GX-2597	850	100	A.D. 1100	848	105	A.D. 1102	Schroedl 1978a
40RH7	GX-2598	730	95	A.D. 1220	737	100	A.D. 1213	Schroedl 1978a
40RH7	GX-2599	595	100	A.D. 1355	615	104	A.D. 1335	Schroedl 1978a
40RH7	GX-2600	805	95	A.D. 1145	806	100	A.D. 1144	Schroedl 1978a
40RH7	GX-2601	795	100	A.D. 1155	797	104	A.D. 1153	Schroedl 1978a
40RH7	GX-2602	1030	95	A.D. 920	1017	100	A.D. 933	Schroedl 1978a
40RH7	GX-2603	1150	130	A.D. 800	1131	140	A.D. 819	Schroedl 1978a
40RH7	GX-2604	1275	105	A.D. 675	1253	117	A.D. 697	Schroedl 1978a
49RH7	GX-2605	1145	120	A.D. 805	1126	130	A.D. 824	Schroedl 1978a
40RH7	GX-2606	855	95	A.D. 1095	853	100	A.D. 1097	Schroedl 1978a
40RE4	M-730	930	150	A.D. 1020	922	153	A.D. 1028	Faulkner 1967
40RE124	GX-3463	1265	170	A.D. 685	1243	177	A.D. 707	Schroedl 1978a
40RE124	UGa-738	1030	60	A.D. 920	1017	68	A.D. 933	Schroedl 1978a
40RE124	GX-3462	1020	120	A.D. 930	1008	124	A.D. 943	Schroedl 1978a
40RE124	GX-3460	970	160	A.D. 980	960	163	A.D. 990	Schroedl 1978a
40RE124	GX-3461	725	160	A.D. 1225	733	163	A.D. 1217	Schroedl 1978a
40RE124	GX-3459	1070	180	A.D. 880	1054	185	A.D. 896	Schroedl 1978a
40MR16	GX-8609	840	115	A.D. 1110	839	119	A.D. 1111	Davis et al. 1982

where along major tributaries, and in general north of Knoxville, comparable shell middens are absent, although in the lower Little Tennessee River valley increased exploitation of river mussels is evident by A.D. 900 (see Bogan 1982; Bogan and Bogan 1985). The possibility of Late Woodland occupation sites without accompanying shell middens along the main Tennessee River, however, has never been suggested or included in any proposed settlement model.

Kneberg's (1961) analysis remains the model of ceramic assemblage composition for Late Woodland occupations in east Tennessee. The distinctness of particular ceramic types as chronological markers, however, has been shown less secure than Kneberg proposed, and the consistent separation of site collections into Hamilton, Candy Creek, and Roane-Rhea ceramic complexes using Kneberg's methods have proven difficult. Quantitative methods assessing the affinities of sherd assemblages as used by Kimball and Baden (1985) have produced more acceptable results.

Kimball's Woodland III period and its temporal units dating A.D. 350 to A.D. 900, however, probably include too much ceramic variability for a single culture period. It perhaps makes more sense to consider Kimball's Westmoreland Barber-Moccasin Bend temporal unit as a distinct Woodland IV phenomenon. Although a quantitative ceramic study has not been made, the Jones Ferry Feature 80 and perhaps 40RH62 data are proposed as examples of this unit. The 40JN89 and 40JN90 as well as the 40HW30 ceramics may constitute a contemporary but geographically distinct temporal unit.

A proposed Woodland IV context at Jones Ferry contains small quantities of shell-tempered ceramics. Feature 20 contained a ceramic assemblage identical to Feature 80 except that about 3 percent of the sherds were shell tempered. Both limestone- and shell-tempered loop handles also were found in Feature 20 (Schroedl et al. 1985:243). A radiocarbon date of A.D. 1222 is considered much too recent for such an assemblage. At the Doughty site, although McCollough and Faulkner (1973) considered it a Late Woodland Hamilton occupation, small numbers of nonintrusive shell-tempered sherds occurred in the deposits (McCollough and Faulkner 1973:121–122). Both shell-tempered and limestone-tempered sherds occurred with a mortuary area of processing and secondary disposal pits at Tomotley (40MR5) (Baden 1983; Glassman 1983, fig. III.2). It was suspected at first that this represented an emergent Mississippian Martin Farm phase occurrence (Schroedl 1978a:197). A radiocarbon date now places the burial area at A.D. 712 (Baden 1983, table 4.6) raising the possibility of a mortuary pattern alternative to burial mound use rather than subsequent to it as originally proposed. No comparable mortuary area has been excavated in east Tennessee.

Because of the radiocarbon dates and associated ceramics, deciding whether to label contexts such as

Table 21. Early Mississippian Period Radiocarbon Dates

		Carbon Years Uncorrected			Damon et al. 1974 Corrected			
Site	Lab No.	BP	s	Age	BP	s	Age	Reference
Martin Farm Components								
40MR20	GX-4213	960	120	A.D. 990	950	124	A.D. 1000	Schroedl 1978a
40MR20	GX-4208	935	130	A.D. 1015	927	134	A.D. 1023	Schroedl 1978a
Hiwassee Island Components								
40MR20	GX-4209	930	140	A.D. 1020	922	143	A.D. 1028	Schroedl 1978a
40MR20	GX-4210	930	140	A.D. 1020	922	143	A.D. 1028	Schroedl 1978a
40MR20	GX-4211	755	140	A.D. 1195	761	143	A.D. 1189	Schroedl 1978a
40MR20	GX-4212	790	130	A.D. 1160	792	133	A.D. 1158	Schroedl 1978a
40MR5	GX-7732	985	125	A.D. 965	974	129	A.D. 976	Baden 1983
40MR50	UGa-1245	1090	65	A.D. 860	1074	83	A.D. 876	Schroedl 1978a
40RH6	GX-2594	850	100	A.D. 1100	848	105	A.D. 1102	Schroedl 1978a
40MR27	GX-1572	700	95	A.D. 1250	710	100	A.D. 1240	Salo 1969
40CP2	M-729	760	150	A.D. 1190	765	153	A.D. 1185	Schroedl 1978a
40RE12	M-731	670	150	A.D. 1280	683	153	A.D. 1267	Schroedl 1978a
40MR6	GX-6077	735	130	A.D. 1215	742	133	A.D. 1208	Polhemus 1987

Jones Ferry and Tomotley as Woodland IV or Mississippian I (in the Kimball chronology) is difficult. Here it is proposed to label them Woodland IV with dates of A.D. 600 to A.D. 900. It is conceivable that future researchers may wish to consider them Mississippian I, but revise the dates for this period to A.D. 800 to A.D. 1000. This is also more appropriate to the precision of radiocarbon dating.

EMERGENT AND EARLY MISSISSIPPIAN PERIODS

The work at Martin Farm and additional comparative studies in the lower Little Tennessee River valley now make it possible to describe the emergence of Mississippian culture in east Tennessee (see Schroedl et al. 1985). Additional detailed studies when made elsewhere in the region are not likely to change the general patterns observed in the lower Little Tennessee River valley. Intraregional variability is expected, but to a degree no greater than known for other cultural periods. Martin Farm or Mississippian I cultural components date A.D. 900 to A.D. 1000. Subsequent Mississippian II or Hiwassee Island manifestations date A.D. 1000 to A.D. 1300 (Table 21). Both cultural components have received exhaustive study at the Martin Farm site.

Analysis to identify Mississippian I (Martin Farm) and Mississippian II (Hiwassee Island) ceramic assemblages at Martin Farm used 23,598 sherds from 31 proveniences, each containing 100 or more specimens. The relative frequencies of the ceramic types were reduced to a smaller number of variables using principal component analysis and were, in turn, used to generate new component scores for each provenience. Mississippian I and II ceramic assemblage groups were defined from the clustered component scores using Ward's H-Group cluster analysis. This produced two Mississippian I and three Mississippian II ceramic assemblage groups whose sherd frequencies are illustrated in Figure 69.

The constituent types of each assemblage group are virtually identical, yet the percentage composition of the Martin Farm (Mississippian I) and Hiwassee Island (Mississippian II) groups are distinctly different. The Martin Farm ceramics are predominantly limestone-tempered plain (30–35 percent), limestone-tempered cordmarked (20–25 percent), and shell-tempered plain (35–40 percent), with minor amounts of other ceramic types. Limestone-tempered loop handles also are found in Mississippian I contexts. The Hiwassee Island ceramic assemblage groups are comprised of shell-tempered plain (65–85 percent), cordmarked (1–15 percent), fabric-marked (3–5 percent), and red-filmed (1–3 percent) sherds, and limestone-tempered plain (5–11 percent) and cordmarked (3–6 percent) pottery, with no limestone-tempered loop handles. In comparison, the Mississippian II assemblages have greater ceramic type diversity. Shell-tempered types are dominant, but limestone-tempered ceramics are well-represented in the assemblages. The differences are thus in assemblage composition rather than in historic type occurrence.

Quantitative studies of the lithic artifacts show virtually no differences between the Mississippian I and

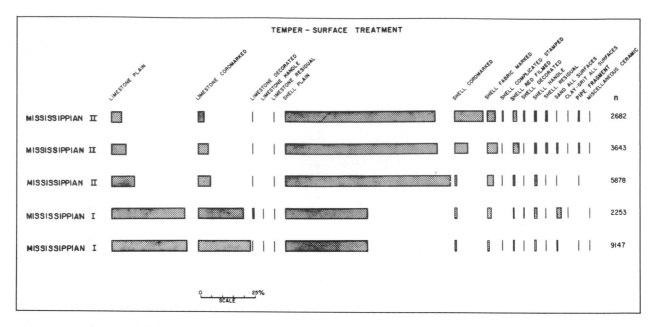

Fig. 69. Composition of Mississippian I and II ceramic assemblage groups at Martin Farm (40MR20) (from Schroedl et al. 1985, fig. 109).

Mississippian II assemblages (Schroedl et al. 1985: 248–368). The artifacts are made from locally available cherts using mostly bifacial or bipolar reduction technologies. Debitage analysis shows nearly identical technological as well as morphological characteristics. Blades and ground stone implements are rare in both assemblages. Cluster analysis of projectile points from the Mississippian I and II components shows that specimens from the temporally different assemblages cluster together. Small triangular Hamilton, Madison, and incurvate blade types are the characteristic projectile points in both components. All analyses demonstrate near-identical technological, functional, stylistic, and raw material characteristics for the Mississippian I and II lithic artifacts at Martin Farm.

Comparative analyses of botanical and faunal remains also indicate few differences between the Mississippian I and II occupations at Martin Farm (Bogan and Bogan 1985:369–410). Extensive use of local aquatic habitats, as evidenced by the number and variety of mollusk, turtle, and fish remains, and the acquisition of a diversity of terrestrial species such as deer, raccoon, and squirrel occurred during both occupations. The species composition of the Jones Ferry faunal samples, although small, is essentially no different from Martin Farm as are the faunal remains from

later Mississippian period occupations at Chota-Tanasee(40MR2–40MR62), Citico (40MR7), and Toqua (40MR6) in the lower Little Tennessee River valley. One important distinction is that the Early Mississippian faunal assemblages contain no remains of bear. While the analyzed Early Mississippian faunal assemblages are few and comparatively small, the absence of bear bones seems significant, albeit unexplained.

Analyzed Mississippian I and II botanical remains at Martin Farm are no different in proportions of hickory nutshell, acorn shell, walnut shell, and maize (Schroedl et al. 1985:411–456). Both 8 and 10-rowed maize varieties are found in the botanical assemblages as are other cultigens or potential cultigens including squash, gourd, sunflower, smartweed, chenopod, and sumpweed. The Martin Farm Mississippian I and II botanical assemblages are similar to those from Jones Ferry, and Early Mississippian contexts at Tomotley and Icehouse Bottom. None of these contexts contains domesticated beans. Wood charcoal analysis indicates general exploitation of all woodland habitats in the immediate site vicinity as well as higher river terraces and upland areas.

The area of Mississippian I occupation at Martin Farm is comparatively small, probably covering no more than 0.5 ha. Nevertheless, important site facilities

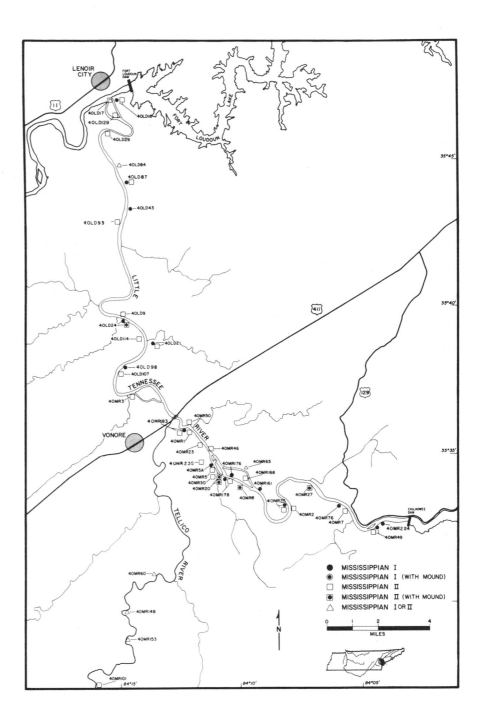

Fig. 70. Location of Mississippian I and II site components in the lower Little Tennessee River valley (from Schroedl et al. 1985, fig. 154).

include four structures, with both wall-trench and single-post wall construction types represented, and a platform mound, measuring about 14 m in diameter and 1.8 m high. A refuse-filled trench, 1.75 m wide and .50 m deep, which was traced over a distance of 16 m, is also a prominent Mississippian I component association. The placement of this feature near the plat-

form mound and the overall relation of these features to structures and other facilities, including probable storage pits, suggest a degree of site complexity not heretofore recognized for occupations dating circa A.D. 900 in east Tennessee.

The size and probable complexity of the Martin Farm site increased during the Mississippian II occupation.

The occupation area grew to about 4.5 ha, and a second mound, about 15 m in diameter but only 10 cm high and with at least four superimposed wall-trench structures, was built at the site. Elsewhere at the site, superimposed single-post wall construction buildings and probable storage pits suggest domestic activities not evident in the mound vicinity.

The Mississippian I and II occupations at Martin Farm are similar in terms of their construction of single-post and wall-trench structures, use of substructure mounds, production of similar lithic artifact classes, and use of faunal and botanical resources. Except for the bones of an infant found in the Mississippian I midden, neither occupation contains human interments. The major differences between the two occupations are the composition of the ceramic assemblages and the increased site size and organizational complexity of the Mississippian II occupation.

The Martin Farm site is one of 42 sites with Mississippian I or II components presently identified in the lower Little Tennessee River valley (Fig. 70). Based on ceramic assemblage composition, Mississippian I components occur at 17 sites including Martin Farm. Thirteen of these sites are situated on the first alluvial river terrace and the other four sites are found on higher and older terrace surfaces. Data from most sites are from surface collections, and site size and intrasite pattern are difficult to estimate. Most occupations, however, likely represent residence sites of limited areal extent. Evidence for the construction of substructure mounds is restricted to Martin Farm, although Mississippian I occupations at Bat Creek (40LD24) and Bussell Island (40LD17) may be associated with initial mound construction stages at these sites.

Mississippian II period occupations are identified at 30 sites in the lower Little Tennessee River valley, and where excavations have been made, site facilities considered characteristic of the Hiwassee Island phase are present. Besides Martin Farm, platform mounds are recorded at Mayfield II (40MR27), Toqua (40MR6), and Bat Creek (40LD24). The earliest mound construction stages at Citico (40MR7) and Bussell Island (40LD17) also may be Mississippian II in age, but this relationship is uncertain.

In contrast to Mississippian I occupations, only a little more than half of the Mississippian II sites are found on the first river terrace, with the remainder situated on second or higher river terraces. This same pattern in general contrasts Woodland period with Mississippian period occupations in the lower Little Tennessee River. Significantly, the transition between Mississippian I and II is marked by a shift in residence location away from the Little Tennessee River to higher ground.

Increased site size, complexity, and permanence is evidenced for the Mississippian II period by well-defined architectural features and associated site facilities. No Woodland sites with comparable characteristics are known in the area, despite the moderately large excavations at Patrick (40MR40) and Icehouse Bottom (40MR23) and surface collection data from nearly 200 additional sites (see Davis et al. 1982; Kimball 1985). Second and higher river terraces are protected from periodic, seasonal flooding, and for this reason are more appropriate locations for permanent habitation and the construction of buildings.

By Mississippian II times, partial abandonment of first terraces for residential use also may reflect increased need for rich and easily tilled soils suitable for intensive maize agriculture. First terrace soils, consisting largely of loams and sandy loams, are the most agriculturally productive soils in the area (Elder 1959, 1961; Hall et al. 1981). Population increase, evident from the Early Mississippian through Historic periods, implies a progressively greater use of rich agricultural land for food production.

The Mississippian I occupation at Martin Farm was once regarded as a unique or anomalous cultural manifestation in east Tennessee (e.g., Salo 1969; Schroedl 1978a). This is no longer so. Besides the sites now recognized in the lower Little Tennessee River valley, Martin Farm components are identified at Hiwassee Island and surely occur at the Hixon, Sale Creek, Dallas, and Davis sites in the Chickamauga Basin (Kimball and Baden 1985). In the Norris Basin, ceramics indicate such an occupation at Lea Farm (40AN17) (Griffin 1938). The Martin Farm culture unit includes shell- and limestone-tempered ceramics, Mississippian style structures, and the earliest evidence of platform mounds in the region. The only essential material development in the subsequent Hiwassee Island culture, which is abundantly well documented from numerous sites (see Lewis and Kneberg n.d.; Whiteford 1952), is the elaboration of a shell-tempered ceramic technology. Differences in settlement location, size, and complexity, however, show that major social and economic changes accompanied the change to the Hiwassee Island culture. Radiocarbon dates indicate that the change was rapid, perhaps occurring in less than 100 years (see Table 21).

THE WOODLAND-MISSISSIPPIAN TRANSITION

The change from the Woodland to Mississippian archaeological records reflects major social, economic, and cultural developments. Material culture differences and their total and abrupt replacement once thought so distinct are now known to be less dramatic. Although the material culture assemblages, particularly for the Late Woodland period, are not yet fully described, it is still possible to assess the nature of the Woodland-Mississippian transition from available archaeological studies and to place these data in the context of contemporary archaeological theory. Models describing agricultural origins and intensification, accompanied by increased populations and social complexity, are appropriate in this regard.

At least three models have been proposed to describe the Woodland-Mississippian transition in east Tennessee. Lewis and Kneberg (1946) used an ethnic replacement model based on culture group migration, territorial invasion, sometimes violent confrontation, and indigenous culture extinction or absorption. Faulkner (1972, 1975) and Schroedl et al. (1985) have entertained a more subtle, and perhaps as a result more vague, process of culture diffusion or Mississippianization that tends to include elements of both the migration model and the in situ culture development model, the third perspective. Faulkner (1972, 1975) and Schroedl et al. (1985) also consider in situ cultural development with minimal external influence. This view has enjoyed the greatest recent support (Boyd et al. 1983; Helmkamp 1985; Schroedl 1978a; Schroedl and Boyd 1985; Schroedl et al. 1985). All these approaches tend to describe or explain culture change in an historical rather than evolutionary sense. Historical models are event oriented, while evolutionary models are process oriented.

Lewis and Kneberg (1946:9–10) proposed that a migration of Middle Mississippian Muskogean-speaking peoples invaded east Tennessee and replaced the indigenous Late Woodland Hamilton culture. Shell-tempered pottery, maize agriculture, and platform mounds were among the culture traits introduced by the new group. Each group thus employed distinct and mutually exclusive material culture. The archaeological result was that limestone- and shell-tempered ceramics respectively became the diagnostic traits of the Woodland and Mississippian periods, and by definition, neither Hamilton nor Hiwassee Island cultures could contain both ceramic wares. Contexts that contained both wares were considered deposits of poor integrity and culturally mixed. When such contexts could not be ignored, as occurred when Kneberg (1961) described Mississippian ceramic traits with the Late Woodland Roane-Rhea complex, they were explained as the acquisition of new traits by remnant Late Woodland groups.

Other archaeological characteristics presented similar difficulties. No diagnostic artifacts or contexts, for example, made it possible to identify Hiwassee Island culture burials. Hamilton burial mounds were considered temporally earlier and ethnically distinct, and it was inconceivable that burial mounds also were in use in Hiwassee Island times. Lewis and Kneberg (1946) could conclude only that Hiwassee Island burials were absent for lack of adequate archaeological exploration rather than adequate explanatory models.

The migration model is appealing for the simple and direct connection it makes between archaeological materials and ethnic groups in terms of historic events. Lewis and Kneberg formulated their description of Mississippian origins in east Tennessee within a more general model for the Southeast in which the expansion of Mississippian cultures was identified with Muskogean migrations. Smith's (1984:13–32) critical review adequately discusses the development and demise of this model. While now largely rejected, Smith concludes that no equally broad explanation has replaced the migration model (1984:30).

In east Tennessee an alternative view is the diffusion or Mississippianization model. It differs from the culture replacement model in only one major respect: the diffusion of new ideas rather than the migration of new people is responsible for differences observed in the archaeological record. Substituting ideas for people makes it easy to interpret mixed contexts as the result of Mississippian influence.

The Mississippianization model is prominent in Faulkner's (1972, 1975) discussions of the Woodland-Mississippian transition in east Tennessee. For Faulkner, however, Mississippianization includes elements of both the migration and in situ development models, and it is not entirely clear whether this process is predominantly due to internal change or external influence. Faulkner states:

> The most reasonable conclusion is that the appearance of the Mississippian tradition in the eastern Tennessee Valley can be explained largely by internal change. . . . [The] early and rapid appearance of the Mississippian tradition throughout the Tennessee Valley suggests the Mississippianization of Late Woodland groups rather than migration to explain all this culture change. Nevertheless, it is difficult to adequately explain the marked changes in subsistence patterns, settlement patterns, and burial practices as resulting solely from internal culture development. This would suggest some intrusions of expanding Mississippian or more likely Mississippianized Woodland populations particularly into marginal areas along smaller tributaries (1975:27–28).

The original interpretations of the Martin Farm site followed the same general logic.

> The Emergent Mississippian [at Martin Farm may] represent an intrusive group in the throes of a Mississippian transition which [was] located in the Little Tennessee valley (Salo 1969:138).

Alternatively, Salo (1969:138) suggested

> . . . the Emergent Mississippian represents an indigenous Late Woodland group under influence from a very early Mississippian group based outside the valley.

In any case, external influence is crucial to both the Mississippianization and cultural replacement models. Each has had limited utility as an historical explanation because the source, kind, and motive for influence or migration is seldom identified or discussed. The expectation of these models, as Smith has summarized (1984:13–32), is that they necessitate the identification of a source from which cultural influence radiates. It is widely accepted and well documented that Mississippian cultures developed essentially simultaneously circa A.D. 800 or 900 throughout the Southeast, "making local development a more reasonable interpretive framework than site unit intrusion [i.e., migration]" (Smith 1984:30) or cultural diffusion as Mississippianization.

The formal recognition of in situ culture development is comparatively recent in east Tennessee (Faulkner 1975; Schroedl 1973, 1978a). No attempts, however, have been made to associate the archaeological record of the Woodland-Mississippian transition with a specific model of internal culture change. Instead, chronology and artifact assemblage pattern studies have been made as convincing evidence that such a model is both plausible and appropriate (see Kimball 1985; Davis et al. 1982; Schroedl et al. 1985).

The model of in situ Mississippian culture evolution is supported by continuity in numerous archaeological traits and patterns from the Woodland to Mississippian periods. Among these are the use of small triangular projectile points that first appear in Middle Woodland contexts, and in fact continue to be used through the Historic period. This is surely related to the widespread use of the bow and arrow. Although few detailed comparative studies have been made, substantive changes in lithic artifact technology or function are not likely to have occurred from the Middle Woodland period until after Euro-American contact.

Changes in the kinds and frequencies of ceramic temper and surface treatment attributes are the most sensitive indicators of temporal variability from the Middle Woodland through Early Mississippian periods. Nevertheless, continuity is exhibited in the persistence of limestone-tempered plain and cordmarked ceramics into the Hiwassee Island phase. Shell-tempered plain and cordmarked ceramics, furthermore, exhibit gradual rather than abrupt increased frequencies from Martin Farm to Hiwassee Island occupations. Different vessel forms and their increased variety are well expressed in Early Mississippian period assemblages.

The Hamilton burial mound complex, which first dates near the beginning of the Late Woodland period, continues through the Martin Farm and into the Hiwassee Island phases. At Martin Farm a substructure mound is dated well before the widespread use of such earthworks in Hiwassee Island contexts. Rectangular single-post wall and wall-trench construction houses occur in both Martin Farm and Hiwassee Island culture contexts. Late Woodland period houses are undocumented in east Tennessee. Thus, there is abundant evidence for developmental continuity in material culture from the Late Woodland to Early Mississippian periods. This suggests that models of in situ cultural development are appropriate for the description of Mississippian origins in east Tennessee.

The problem of east Tennessee Mississippian origins is regarded here as a regional-scale question of the origins of complex agricultural societies. Numerous regional-scale models have been proposed to explain the origins of agriculture or the development of complex societies (see Hassan 1981:209–230 for a review). Among more recent proposals are Binford's (1968: 313–341, 1983:210–213) packing model and Rindos's (1984) evolutionary constructs. Extending these approaches to the east Tennessee archaeological record is an opportunity to expand the cases covered by these explanations and thereby make them more general in their application. The possibility also exists for showing which models require modification if their uses are not to remain restricted in some fashion. An explanation of Mississippian origins in east Tennessee, whatever its form, must necessarily have wider regional application because Mississippian cultures were simultaneously established throughout the Southeast by A.D. 800 or A.D. 900 (see Smith 1984:30). Satisfactory resolution of the problem cannot be constrained by local variability in the southeastern archaeological record and cannot avoid addressing the mechanisms of culture change by appealing to external conditions such as migration or diffusion. Such conditions are unavoidably considered normal or acceptable variability rather than exceptional causal agents.

There are numerous potential forms that a model of Mississippian origins in east Tennessee and the Southeast might take. The current emphasis is on approaches that focus on demographic and economic variables, particularly population growth, sedentism, food storage, and agricultural intensification. These variables are most often expressed in cultural systems or culture-ecological frameworks (e.g., Flannery 1968, 1972; Sanders and Price 1968). Other perspectives emphasizing demographic variables such as warfare (Carneiro 1970:733–738) or sociopolitical and socioreligious complexity also are available, as are models focusing on economic considerations of regional interaction and trade (see Redman 1978). All such approaches have received considerable criticism respecting their limitations and explanatory power (e.g., Dunnell 1980; Wenke 1981). More recently, as a result, alternative evolutionary models have been developed that may be useful in explaining Mississippian agricultural development, socioreligious elaboration, and sociopolitical complexity (e.g., Rindos 1984).

Whatever explanatory framework is proposed for east Tennessee and the Southeast, it is surely necessary to consider specific demographic and economic variables ignored or believed unimportant in most models of agricultural development and increased social complexity now available. Plant domestication, for example, is not always adequately distinguished from horticulture and agriculture. Plant domestication, beginning in the Archaic period and eventually involving a variety of local as well as exotic species, is well documented for the Southeast, and east Tennessee is part of this overall pattern (Chapman and Shea 1981). During the Woodland period, garden horticulture was probably common throughout the area. Corn was among a variety of plants grown as early as the Middle Woodland period and was a familiar plant by the time its intense and widespread cultivation was established during the Early Mississippian period. In east Tennessee this process was underway by A.D. 900 and was firmly in place by A.D. 1100 or 1200, as indicated by the abundance of corn in botanical samples from Mississippian I and II contexts. It is significant that agricultural intensification is coincident with the replacement of tropical flint varieties by eastern flint varieties of corn whose yields are potentially much greater than their predecessors (Ford 1981:16; Gary Crites, personal communication 1985). Palynological data indicate accompanying human impact on the local biotic environment from forest clearing (Cridlebaugh 1984).

The degree of sedentism, population density, and the form and nature of sociopolitical complexity also are elements important to describing Mississippian origins. Defined territories with at least semisedentary populations likely existed in east Tennessee by the Middle Woodland period. Their response to Hopewellian decline and the eventual form and organization of Late Woodland populations is virtually unknown. Hamilton burial mounds suggest moderately dense populations with well-established, but perhaps comparatively small, territories. Social and religious status were well defined, and it is conceivable that status positions were semihereditary. Associations with lineage groups were surely well marked and well understood. Sedentism and population densities may have exceeded levels usually considered in describing agricultural development and increased cultural complexity.

Attempting to explain Mississippian origins in east Tennessee, as complex as it is, includes agricultural intensification and increased settlement size with accompanying greater social differentiation. In this respect, Late Woodland groups were organized at a level appropriate to a hunting/gathering/horticultural economy. Population levels perhaps fluctuated about an optimal mean. The potential for further population growth could not be realized without increased economic efficiency, with economic success in turn difficult to maintain without organizational changes in sociopolitical as well as socioreligious institutions. The introduction of eastern flint corn varieties around A.D. 800 potentially was an important element to overall culture development (Ford 1977, 1981:16). Increased yields could be produced by this plant within the existing horticultural system. By focusing on the selective advantages of this plant, the food supply was improved with no great additional cost in labor. If this became correlated with population peaks over several generations, it is conceivable that a population threshold might have been reached beyond the previous optimal mean. The available Late Woodland sociopolitical and socioreligious organizations were not suitable or capable of managing this situation. Only greater social differentiation with power and access to resources restricted to fewer individuals and groups and more explicitly defined social roles would work. Once in place this system was self-reinforcing until it, too, reached optimal efficiency. This was achieved by the Late Mississippian period.

Helmkamp (1984, 1985) has independently arrived at a similar view of Mississippian origins in east Tennessee. He suggests first that the tropical cultigens grown by Late Woodland groups were far more susceptible to microclimatic variations than native adapted species. Agriculture production, furthermore, became increasingly concentrated and hence restricted to the most fertile river bottom lands. Competition for land and the risk of uncertain production thus are important in Helmkamp's perspective.

Late Woodland groups, according to Helmkamp (1985:158), were "small-scaled localized non-hierarchical systems with highly impermeable boundaries and cooperative decision-making" that "may not have had the information and material processing capacities and, probably more importantly, means of implementation necessary to cope with the increasing volume and complexity of a maturing agricultural economy." This encouraged the evolution of "centralized systems and ranking access to roles of power" (Helmkamp 1985:158) characteristic of Mississippian societies. Despite the differences in initial premises, Helmkamp's model, like the perspective developed here, describes Mississippian origins in terms of processes generated from within the culture systems of east Tennessee.

No formal model for Mississippian origins has been presented here. Instead, an evolutionary and culture systems perspective has been used to connect economic and demographic variables in a logical process that describes the Woodland-Mississippian transition. No contradiction in available data are evident and no external influences are employed as extraordinary causative agents. The description can also be expanded beyond east Tennessee.

CONCLUSIONS

The investigation of Mississippian origins in east Tennessee has prompted revisions in how the archaeological record is conceptualized, in how archaeological cultures are defined and labeled, and in how chronological differences are related to models of culture change. Characteristics once considered diagnostic of mutually exclusive archaeological cultures are now known to have significant occurrences in two or more cultures. The most serious result is that the Late Woodland period Hamilton culture, as defined by Lewis and Kneberg, is greatly altered because virtually every one of its diagnostic traits, including Hamilton project points, limestone-tempered plain and cordmarked ceramics, and burial mounds, are now well documented for earlier or later contexts. Not even shell middens are restricted to the Late Woodland period. More recent proposals from ceramic assemblage data for a Middle-Late Woodland continuum or Woodland III period, may prove unworkable. As a culture phase designation, a Woodland IV period dating A.D. 600 to A.D. 900 is probably justified, but it should be clear that this is not a substitution for Lewis and Kneberg's Hamilton culture.

Because of work at the Martin Farm site and because of the ceramic assemblage analyses now available, the period A.D. 900 to A.D. 1300 is well described. The Martin Farm culture unit (A.D. 900 to A.D. 1000) is the initial Mississippian cultural expression in east Tennessee. It includes both shell- and limestone-tempered ceramics, Mississippian-style structures, and the first evidence of platform mounds. The only essential material development in the subsequent Hiwassee Island culture (A.D. 1000 to A.D. 1300) was the elaboration of a shell-tempered ceramic technology. Residential settlement size and complexity increased. This and changes in settlement location suggest agricultural intensification with accompanying sociopolitical development. The cultures of east Tennessee changed from independent local segments to regionally integrated complexes (see also Helmkamp 1984, 1985).

What happened about A.D. 900 has been described; how and why this happened is more difficult to specify. Migration and culture replacement, at least as envisioned by Lewis and Kneberg, is difficult to support with available data and contemporary theory. The Mississippianization or culture-diffusion model also is difficult to accept in its present form. Alternative models for agricultural origins and development of complex sociopolitical structures may prove useful for describing the origins of Mississippian culture in east Tennessee. These may require modification appropriate to probable Late Woodland economic and social institutions. Any model that proposes to explain Mississippian origins in east Tennessee necessarily has relevance elsewhere in the Southeast. One possible approach described here attempts to link higher yield corn agriculture with a degree of sedentism and population size, which Late Woodland organizational structures were incapable of managing.

ACKNOWLEDGMENTS

We wish to thank Bruce Smith for asking us to contribute to this volume. Vincas Steponaitis, Christopher Peebles, and Charles Faulkner reviewed our chapter and we appreciate their comments and suggestions for improving it. Kim Johnson worked her usual magic with the IBM word processor.

REFERENCES CITED

Baden, William W.
1983   *Tomotley: An Eighteenth Century Cherokee Village.* Report of Investigations No. 36. Department of Anthropology, The University of Tennessee, Knoxville.

Binford, Lewis R.
1968   Post-Pleistocene Adaptations. In *New Perspectives in Archaeology,* edited by Sally R. Binford and Lewis R. Binford, pp. 313–341. Aldine Publishing Company, Chicago.

1983   *In Pursuit of the Past: Decoding the Archaeological Record.* Thames and Hudson, New York.

Binford, Sally R., and Lewis R. Binford (editors)
1968   *New Perspectives in Archaeology.* Aldine Publishing Company, Chicago.

Bogan, Arthur E.
1982   Archaeological Evidence for Subsistence Patterns in the Little Tennessee River Valley. *Tennessee Anthropologist* 7:38–50.

Bogan, Arthur E., and Cynthia M. Bogan
1985   Faunal Remains. In *Archaeological Contexts and Assemblages at Martin Farm,* by Gerald F. Schroedl, R. P. Stephen Davis, Jr., and C. Clifford Boyd, Jr., pp. 369–410. Report of Investigations No. 39. Department of Anthropology, University of Tennessee, Knoxville.

Boyd, C. Clifford, Jr.
1985   *Archaeological Investigations in the Watauga Reservoir; Carter and Johnson Counties, Tennessee.* Report of Investigations No. 44. Department of Anthropology, The University of Tennessee, Knoxville.

Boyd, C. Clifford, Jr., Gerald F. Schroedl, and R. P. Stephen Davis, Jr.
1983   Early Mississippian Culture Development at Martin Farm in the Little Tennessee River Valley. Paper presented at the 40th Annual Meeting of the Southeastern Archaeological Conference, Columbia, South Carolina.

Braun, E. Lucy
1950   *Deciduous Forests of Eastern North America.* The Free Press, New York.

Carneiro, R. L.
1970   A Theory of the Origin of the State. *Science* 169:733–738.

Chapman, Jefferson
1973   *The Icehouse Bottom Site, 40MR23.* Report of Investigations No. 13. Department of Anthropology, University of Tennessee, Knoxville.

1980   The Jones Ferry Site (40MR76). In *The 1979 Archaeological and Geological Investigations in the Tellico Reservoir,* edited by Jefferson Chapman, pp. 43–58. Report of Investigations No. 29. Department of Anthropology, University of Tennessee, Knoxville.

Chapman, Jefferson, Paul A. Delcourt, Patricia A. Cridlebaugh, Andrea B. Shea, and Hazel R. Delcourt
1982   Man-Land Interaction: 10,000 Years of American Indian Impact on Native Ecosystems in the Lower Little Tennessee River Valley, Eastern Tennessee. *Southeastern Archaeology* 1:115–121.

Chapman, Jefferson, and Bennie C. Keel
1979   Candy Creek-Connestee Components in Eastern Tennessee and Western North Carolina and Their Relationship with Adena-Hopewell. In *Hopewell Archaeology: The Chillicothe Conference,* edited by David S. Brose and N'omi Greber, pp. 157–161. The Kent State University Press, Kent, Ohio.

Chapman, Jefferson, and Andrea Brewer Shea
1981   The Archaeobotanical Record: Early Archaic Period to Contact in the Lower Little Tennessee River Valley. *Tennessee Anthropologist* 6:61–84.

Chapman, Lloyd N.
1977   Report on Archaeological Survey and Testing Blair Bend Industrial Park Loudon, Tennessee. Manuscript on file, Frank H. McClung Museum, University of Tennessee, Knoxville.

Clarke, David L.
1968   *Analytical Archaeology.* Methuen and Company, Ltd., London.

Cole, Patricia E.
1975   *A Synthesis and Interpretation of the Hamilton Mortuary Pattern in East Tennessee.* Unpublished M.A. thesis, Department of Anthropology, University of Tennessee, Knoxville.

Cridlebaugh, Patricia A.
1981   *The Icehouse Bottom Site (40MR23): 1977 Excavations.* Report of Investigations No. 35. Department of Anthropology, University of Tennessee, Knoxville.
1984   *American Indian and Euro-American Impact Upon Holocene Vegetation in the Lower Little Tennessee River Valley, East Tennessee.* Unpublished Ph.D. dissertation, Department of Anthropology, University of Tennessee, Knoxville.

Damon, P. E., C. W. Ferguson, A. Long, and E. I. Wallick
1974   Dendrochronologic Calibration of the Radiocarbon Time Scale. *American Antiquity* 39:350–366.

Davis, R. P. Stephen, Jr., Larry R. Kimball, and William W. Baden (editors)
1982   *An Archaeological Survey and Assessment of Aboriginal Settlement Within the Lower Little Tennessee River Valley.* Report submitted to the Tennessee Valley Authority, Norris, Tennessee.

Dunnell, Robert C.
1980   Evolutionary Theory and Archaeology. In *Advances in Archaeological Method and Theory,* vol. 3, edited by Michael B. Schiffer, pp. 38–99. Academic Press, New York.

Elder, Joe A.
1959   *Soil Survey of Blount County.* Soil Conservation Service, United States Department of Agriculture, Washington, D.C.
1961   *Soil Survey of Loudon County, Tennessee.* Soil Conservation Service, United States Department of Agriculture, Washington, D.C.

Faulkner, Charles H.
1967   Tennessee Radiocarbon Dates. *Tennessee Anthropologist* 23:12–30.
1972   The Mississippian-Woodland Transition in the Middle South. *Proceedings: Southeastern Archaeological Conference, Bulletin* 15:38–45.
1975   The Mississippian-Woodland Transition in the Eastern Tennessee Valley. *Proceedings: Southeastern Archaeological Conference, Bulletin* 18:19–30.

Faulkner, Charles H., and J. B. Graham
1966   *Westmoreland-Barber site (40MI11), Nickajack Reservoir: Season II.* Report of Investigations No. 3. Department of Anthropology, University of Tennessee, Knoxville.
1967   Plant Food Remains on Tennessee Sites: A Preliminary Report. *Proceedings of the 22nd Annual Southeastern Archaeological Conference, Bulletin* No. 5. Morgantown.

Fenneman, Nevin M.
1938   *Physiography of Eastern United States.* McGraw-Hill Book Company, Inc., New York.

Flannery, Kent V.
1968   Archaeological Systems Theory and Early Mesoamerica. In *Anthropological Archaeology in the Americas,* edited by Betty J. Meggers, pp. 67–87. The Anthropological Society of Washington, Washington, D.C.
1972   The Cultural Evaluation of Civilizations. *Annual Review of Ecology and Systematics* 3:399–426.

Ford, Richard I.
1977   Evolutionary Ecology and the Evolution of Human Ecosystems: A Case Study from the Midwestern U.S.A. In *Explanation of Prehistoric Change,* edited by James N. Hill, pp. 153–184. University of New Mexico Press, Albuquerque.
1981   Gardening and Farming Before A.D. 1000: Patterns of Prehistoric Cultivation North of Mexico. *Journal of Ethnobiology* 1:6–27.

Glassman, David M.
1983   Appendix III: Burial Analysis. In *Tomotley: An Eighteenth Century Cherokee Village,* by William W. Baden, pp. 210–236. Report of Investigations No. 36. Department of Anthropology, University of Tennessee, Knoxville.

Gleeson, Paul F. (editor)
1970   *Archaeological Investigations in the Tellico Reservoir: Interim Report 1969.* Report of Investigations No. 8. Department of Anthropology, University of Tennessee, Knoxville.

Gremillion, Kristen J., and Richard A. Yarnell
1985   Plant Remains from the Westmoreland-Barber and Pittman-Alder sites, Marion County, Tennessee. Paper presented at the 42nd Annual Meeting of the Southeastern Archaeological Conference, Birmingham, Alabama.

Griffin, James B.
1938   The Ceramic Remains from Norris Basin, Tennessee. In *An Archaeological Survey of the Norris Basin in Eastern Tennessee,* by W. S. Webb, pp. 253–358. Bureau of American Ethnology, Bulletin 118.

Hall, William G., Bedford W. Jackson, and Theodore R. Love
1981   *Soil Survey of Monroe County, Tennessee.* Soil Conservation Service and Forest Service, United States Department of Agriculture, Washington, D.C.

Harrington, M. R.
1922   *Cherokee and Earlier Remains on Upper Tennessee River.* Indian Notes and Monographs No. 24. Museum of the American Indian, Heye Foundation.

Hassan, Fekri A.
1981   *Demographic Archaeology.* Academic Press, New York.

Helmkamp, Richard C.
1984   Intraregional Social Boundaries in Late Woodland and Mississippian Eastern Tennessee. Paper presented at the Central States Anthropological Society Meeting, Lincoln, Nebraska.
1985   *Biosocial Organization and Change in East Tennessee Late Woodland and Mississippian.* Unpublished Ph.D. dissertation, Department of Anthropology, Purdue University, Lafayette, Indiana.

Keel, Bennie C.
1972 *Woodland Phases of the Appalachian Summit.* Ph.D. dissertation, Department of Anthropology, Washington State University, Pullman.
1976 *Cherokee Archaeology: A Study of the Appalachian Summit.* The University of Tennessee Press, Knoxville.

Kimball, Larry R. (editor)
1985 *The 1977 Archaeological Survey: An Overall Assessment of the Archaeological Resources of Tellico Reservoir.* Report of Investigations No. 40. Tellico Archaeological Survey, Report No. 1. Department of Anthropology, University of Tennessee, Knoxville.

Kimball, Larry R., and William W. Baden
1985 Quantitative Model of Woodland and Mississippian Ceramic Assemblages for the Identification of Surface Collections. In *The 1977 Archaeological Survey: An Overall Assessment of the Archaeological Resources of Tellico Reservoir,* edited by Larry R.Kimball, pp. 121–274. Report of Investigations No. 40. Tellico Archaeological Survey, Report No. 1. University of Tennessee, Knoxville.

Kneberg, Madeline
1952 The Tennessee Area. In *Archaeology of Eastern United States,* edited by James B. Griffin, pp. 190–198. The University of Chicago Press, Chicago.
1961 Four Southeastern Limestone Tempered Pottery Complexes. *Newsletter of the Southeastern Archaeological Conference* 7(2):3–14.

Lafferty, Robert H., III
1981 *The Phipps Bend Archaeological Project.* Research Series No. 4. Office of Archaeological Research, University of Alabama, University, Alabama.

Lewis, T. M. N.
1959 Additional Camp Creek Artifacts. *Tennessee Archaeologist* 15:68–69.

Lewis, T. M. N., and Madeline Kneberg
1941 *The Prehistory of the Chickamauga Basin in Tennessee.* Tennessee Anthropology Papers No. 1.
1946 *Hiwassee Island.* University of Tennessee Press, Knoxville.
n.d. The Prehistory of the Chickamauga Basin. Manuscript on file, Frank H. McClung Museum, University of Tennessee, Knoxville.

McCollough, Major C. R., and Charles H. Faulkner
1973 *Excavation of the Higgs and Doughty Sites: I-75 Salvage Archaeology.* Tennessee Archaeological Society Miscellaneous Paper No. 12.

Moore, Clarence B.
1915 Aboriginal Sites on Tennessee River. *Journal of the Academy of Natural Sciences of Philadelphia* 16(3):169–428.

Parmalee, Paul W., Walter E. Klippel, and Arthur E. Bogan
1982 Aboriginal and Modern Freshwater Mussel Assemblages (Pelecypoda: Unionidae) from the Chickamauga Reservoir, Tennessee. *Brimleyana* 8:75–90.

Polhemus, Richard R.
1987 *The Toqua Site (40MR6): A Late Mississippian Dallas Phase Town.* Report of Investigations No. 41. Department of Anthropology, The University of Tennessee, Knoxville.

Prescott, Douglas
1977 *Phase II Intensive Survey and Testing of the Proposed Tenna-*

Tech, Inc. Industrial Site in Rhea County, Tennessee. Report submitted to Tenna-Tech, Inc.

Redman, Charles L.
1978 *The Rise of Civilization: From Early Farmers to Urban Society in the Ancient Near East.* W. H. Freeman and Company, San Francisco.

Riggs, Brett H.
1985 Dated Contexts from Watauga Reservoir: Cultural Chronology Building for Northeast Tennessee. In *Exploring Tennessee Prehistory: A Dedication to Alfred K. Guthe,* edited by Thomas R. Whyte, C. Clifford Boyd, Jr., and Brett H. Riggs, pp. 214–234. Report of Investigations No. 42. Department of Anthropology, University of Tennessee, Knoxville.

Rindos, David
1984 *The Origins of Agriculture: An Evolutionary Perspective.* Academic Press, New York.

Rowe, Chandler W.
1952 Woodland Cultures of Eastern Tennessee. In *Archaeology of Eastern United States,* edited by James B. Griffin, pp. 199–206. The University of Chicago Press, Chicago.

Sanders, William T., and Barbara J. Price
1968 *Mesoamerica: The Evolution of a Civilization.* Random House, New York.

Salo, Lawr V. (editor)
1969 *Archaeological Investigations in the Tellico Reservoir, Tennessee, 1967–968: An Interim Report.* Report of Investigations No. 7. Department of Anthropology, University of Tennessee, Knoxville.

Schroedl, Gerald F.
1973 Radiocarbon Dates from Three Burial Mounds at the McDonald Site in East Tennessee. *Tennessee Archaeologist* 29:3–11.
1978a *Excavations of the Leuty and McDonald Site Mounds.* Report of Investigations No. 22. Department of Anthropology, University of Tennessee, Knoxville.
1978b *The Patrick Site (40MR40), Tellico Reservoir, Tennessee.* Report of Investigations 25. Department of Anthropology, University of Tennessee, Knoxville.

Schroedl, Gerald F., and C. Clifford Boyd, Jr.
1985 Mississippian Origins in East Tennessee. Paper presented at the 6th Mid-South Archaeological Conference, Starkville, Mississippi.

Schroedl, Gerald F., R. P. Stephen Davis, Jr., and C. Clifford Boyd, Jr.
1985 *Archaeological Contexts and Assemblages at Martin Farm.* Report of Investigations No. 39. Department of Anthropology, University of Tennessee, Knoxville.

Smith, Bruce D.
1984 Mississippian Expansion: Tracing the Historical Development of an Explanatory Model. *Southeastern Archaeology* 3:13–32.

Thomas, Cyrus
1894 Report on the Mound Explorations of the Bureau of American Ethnology. *Twelfth Annual Report of the Bureau of American Ethnology 1890–91.*

United States Department of Agriculture
1941 *Climate and Man: Yearbook of Agriculture.* United States Department of Agriculture, Washington, D.C.

Walthall, John A.
    1980   *Prehistoric Indians of the Southeast*. University of Alabama
            Press, University, Alabama.
Webb, William S.
    1938   *An Archaeological Survey of the Norris Basin in Eastern
            Tennessee*. Bureau of American Ethnology, Bulletin 118.
Wenke, Robert J.
    1981   Explaining the Evolution of Cultural Complexity: A Re-
            view. In *Advances in Archaeological Method and Theory*,
            vol. 4, edited by Michael B. Schiffer, pp. 79–127. Aca-
            demic Press, New York.

Whiteford, Andrew H.
    1952   A Frame of Reference for the Archaeology of Eastern
            Tennessee. In *Archaeology of Eastern United States*, edited
            by James B. Griffin, pp. 207–225. University of Chicago
            Press, Chicago.
Willey, Gordon R., and Philip Phillips
    1958   *Method and Theory in American Archaeology*. University
            of Chicago Press, Chicago.

Paul D. Welch Chapter 9

Mississippian Emergence in West-Central Alabama

INTRODUCTION

In west-central Alabama between A.D. 950 and 1100[1] a number of societal units changed from Late Woodland to Mississippian forms of organization. One of these units built the great Mississippian center at Moundville, with its 40 ha plaza and 20 large platform mounds. Moundville, however, was not the only Mississippian community in the area, and while much has been published about the nature of Moundville society, little information about its neighbors or predecessors has been widely available. This paper describes the Late Woodland-Mississippian transition in the Moundville district and in two other nearby districts, one centered around the Bessemer site and the other extending along the central portion of the Tombigbee River (Fig. 71).

Aside from its culture-historical aspect, the emergence of Mississippian societies is of anthropological interest primarily as an example of the transformation of acephalous tribal organization to hierarchical social organization. Most, and by some definitions all, Mississippian societies were chiefdoms (e.g., Peebles and Kus 1977; Smith 1978; Griffin 1985). Because the theoretical literature on chiefdoms has tended to focus on the characteristics of well-developed, relatively complex chiefdoms (e.g., Peebles and Kus 1977; Carneiro 1981; Wright 1984), the characteristics of simple chiefdoms are reviewed here.

My usage of the term 'simple chiefdom' follows Steponaitis (1978:420) and Wright (1984), and is similar

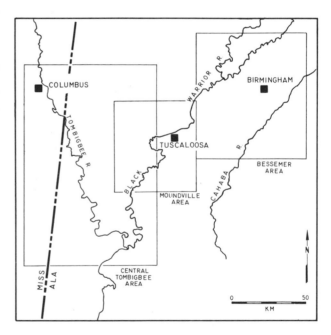

Fig. 71. Map of west-central Alabama, showing the three study areas.

to Smith's (1978:494–498) notion of chiefdoms at a "local center level of organization." Ethnographically, simple chiefdoms have only one level of superordinate political offices, for which recruitment is restricted to an ascribed subgroup of the particular sociopolitical entity (for examples see Firth 1957, 1965; Sahlins 1962; Mitchell 1956; Southall 1956). Just as in more complex chiefdoms, chiefs in simple chiefdoms act as foci for the religious and ceremonial life of their communities by virtue of their closer connection to the supernatural or more potent supernatural lore. Chiefs also receive tribute and use it to sponsor production of sumptuary goods, establish and maintain external political and economic ties, and support military action. Unlike complex chiefdoms, in simple chiefdoms the chiefly households are expected to be self-sufficient. The archaeological correlates of simple chiefdoms are a subset of the list presented by Peebles and Kus (1977). There must be no more than two levels of settlement hierarchy. Chiefly households or compounds will be distinguished from those of commoners by size, capacity of storage facilities, and quality of facilities for the assemblage of groups. There will also be a distinction between subordinate and superordinate classes of mortuary program. The three Mississippian societies described in this chapter possessed these characteristics, insofar as relevant data are available and our analytic concepts adequate.

Despite their proximity and similarity of material culture, these three Mississippian societies differed considerably. This fact alone warrants that the development of each society be considered separately. In addition, the Mississippian societies developed from different Late Woodland precursors, in different environments. After a sketch of these environments, I describe the Late Woodland-Mississippian transition in each area, starting with the area from which the most complete data are available. In a concluding section, the different trajectories of the three cases are compared and suggestions are made for future research on chiefdom origins in west-central Alabama.

ENVIRONMENT

Harper (1943:63) noted that "[i]n Alabama . . . the geological formations influence the soil and topography so directly that a map of forest regions does not differ much in its broader features from a geological map." The Moundville and central Tombigbee districts are geologically and biotically similar, but they contrast with the Bessemer district. The following outline is based on Harper (1943), and examinations of General Land Office witness tree records from the first half of the nineteenth century (Caddell 1981; Scarry 1986: 70–113).

The Bessemer district straddles the western edge of the folded Appalachian Ridge and Valley province. It thus includes linear sandstone-capped ridges and limestone-floored valleys, and in its western part deeply dissected unfolded sandstones and shales. Alluvial soils occur only infrequently, with most soils being fine sandy loams on the ridges, loam and clay loam in the linear valleys, and various loams in the dissected western part of the district. The residual soils of the limestone-floored valleys, along with the patches of alluvial soils, are moderately to highly fertile. Forests of the Bessemer district were dominated by oaks, with pine predominant on xeric ridgetops and chestnut prominent elsewhere (Scarry 1986:89–99).

Both the Moundville and central Tombigbee districts are relatively broad (about 5 km) stretches of floodplain and river terrace. Both rivers, the Tombigbee and the Black Warrior, are below their fall line in these districts, and have meandering courses with the attendant oxbow lakes, sloughs, and swamps. Excepting stands of bald cypress in permanently inundated soils, the forests are almost entirely hardwoods. These range from sweet gum and tupelo in permanently wet soils, through large tracts of oaks in seasonally wet soils, to mixed hardwoods on natural levees and terrace edges. On both sides of the Black Warrior floodplain and on the east side of the Tombigbee floodplain are low, dissected uplands of marine gravels, sands, and clays. General Land Office witness tree records show these uplands to have been clad in oak-hickory and oak-pine forests in the early 1800s (Caddell 1981:15; Scarry 1986:89–99). To the west of the relevant portion of the Tombigbee floodplain and terraces lies the Black Belt, a region of heavy residual soils overlying chalk and marl. These soils supported a prairie vegetation with patches of blackjack and post oaks. Though the reasons for these prairies are a matter of debate (see Jones and Patton 1966), their presence was noted as early as 1775 (Bartram 1955:318–320).

Despite differences in the biota of the three districts, they share substantial similarities. All have frost-free seasons in excess of 200 days and average annual precipitation of roughly 120 cm. All have substantial amounts of fertile soils. Though differentially abundant, the same plant species occur in each district. This is particularly true of plant species of direct economic importance prehistorically, such as hickories, oaks, grapes, mulberries, cane, and so on. The Black Belt afforded the Tombigbee inhabitants a different set of plants, yet as Cole noted (1983:47), few of those plants provide food for humans. It seems, then, that the significant floristic differences between the districts were quantitative rather than qualitative, and this is also true of the fauna.

Each area supported largely the same set of terrestrial fauna. Deer, bear, raccoon, and turkey would have been available in each area, and to some extent differential population densities of such economic species could have been evened out by manipulation of the forests with fire. The abundance of aquatic and avian fauna, however, differed sharply between the Bessemer district and the two floodplain districts. The streams of the Bessemer district are smaller and generally swifter than the floodplain streams, and the Bessemer area lacks oxbow lakes. Human inhabitants of the area would have had limited access to backwater species of fish and turtles. Waterfowl would also have been conspicuously less abundant in the Bessemer district than in the floodplain districts, even though west central Alabama does not lie along a major migratory waterfowl flyway. In terms of easily acquired animal protein, the two floodplain districts are far more attractive than the Bessemer district. Further, as the central Tombigbee floodplain is larger and more complex than the Black Warrior floodplain in the Moundville district, the Tombigbee district can be ranked somewhat more attractive than the Moundville district. As will be shown below, this ranking is mirrored by Late Woodland population densities.

MISSISSIPPIAN EMERGENCE ALONG THE CENTRAL TOMBIGBEE RIVER

History of Research

Until federally mandated cultural resource management projects in the 1970s, the central Tombigbee area (Fig. 72) was largely ignored by archaeologists. Clarence B. Moore steamed through the area in 1901 and excavated at a dozen sites (Moore 1901). There were sporadic archaeological forays into northeast Mississippi in the middle of the century (e.g., Ford 1936; Jennings 1944; Cotter and Corbett 1951; Bohannon 1972). The next research actually in the river valley, however, did not come until 1970, when Walthall and

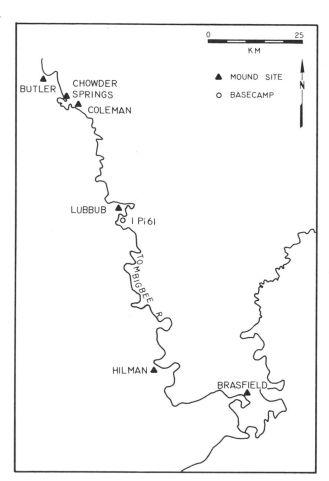

Fig. 72. Locations of central Tombigbee sites mentioned in text.

Jenkins began a preliminary site survey in the proposed Tennessee-Tombigbee Waterway. The ensuing decade of research by University of Alabama archaeologists in the Gainesville Reservoir area is presented in a five-volume final report (Jenkins and Ensor 1981; Jenkins 1981, 1982; Ensor 1981; Caddell et al. 1981). Additional extensive excavation of the Mississippian components in the Lubbub Creek Archaeological Locality (Lubbub for short) is reported in Peebles (1983a, 1983b, 1983c). Information from upriver comes from a series of reports, mostly by Mississippi State University archaeologists (e.g., Rucker 1974; Blakeman 1975a, 1975b; Blakeman et al. 1976; Atkinson 1978; Atkinson et al. 1980; O'Hear et al. 1981; Bense 1982). Sheldon et al. (1982) present data from the area downriver of the Gainesville Reservoir. There are dozens of other contract reports on research in this area, many of them preliminary and nearly all of them of extremely limited

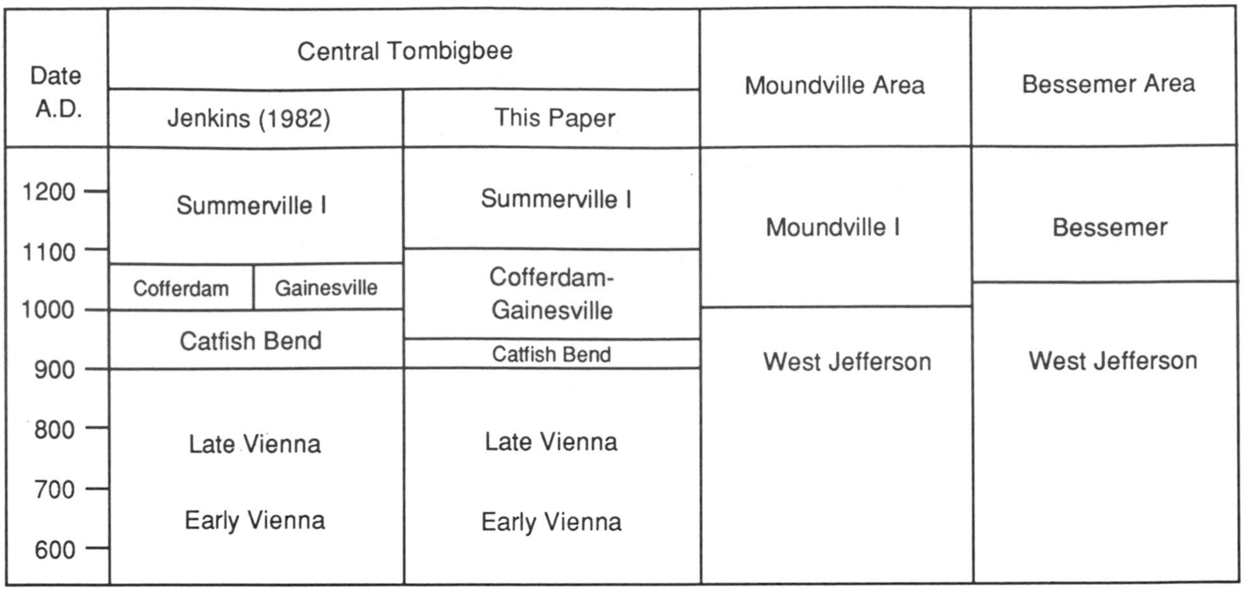

Date A.D.	Central Tombigbee		Moundville Area	Bessemer Area
	Jenkins (1982)	This Paper		
1200 — 1100 —	Summerville I	Summerville I	Moundville I	Bessemer
1000 —	Cofferdam | Gainesville	Cofferdam-Gainesville		
900 —	Catfish Bend	Catfish Bend	West Jefferson	West Jefferson
800 — 700 —	Late Vienna	Late Vienna		
600 —	Early Vienna	Early Vienna		

Fig. 73. Chronologies of the central Tombigbee, Moundville, and Bessemer areas.

distribution. Fortunately many of them are superceded by the Gainesville Reservoir final reports, so the bibliographic tangle can be kept to a minimum.

The archaeological site survey coverage along the central Tombigbee was dictated by the location of areas to be impacted by the Waterway construction. Consequently, the survey coverage is biased toward the alluvial portion of the valley, underrepresenting the valley margins. Within the alluvial valley all principal topographic settings were sampled. Despite the biases inherent in a survey of this sort, the resulting picture of settlement distribution is probably fairly accurate.

Complementing the survey data were test excavations at many sites (Nielsen and Moorehead 1972; Nielsen and Jenkins 1973; Jenkins 1975) and large-scale excavation at five sites (Jenkins and Ensor 1981; Peebles 1983a). These large-scale excavations were accomplished by mechanical removal of the plow zone, and in some cases undifferentiated midden, followed by hand excavation of intact features. The scope of these excavations ranged from merely extensive (1Gr50: 575 sq m) to monumental (Lubbub: 22,000 sq m), and the overall total exceeded 3.2 ha. By the completion of archaeological mitigation in the Gainesville Reservoir around 1980, the long archaeological neglect of this area had been amply redressed.

Chronology

It is generally agreed that shell-tempered ceramics had completely replaced grog-tempered ceramics in the Gainesville Reservoir by A.D. 1100. This simple statement glosses over some perplexing archaeological data. The construction of the Late Woodland to Mississippian chronology for this area has been managed almost single-handedly by Ned Jenkins. To accomplish the task, he grouped excavated features into archaeological phases on the basis of distinctive patterns in relative ceramic frequencies within each feature. He then ordered the phases in accordance with the associated radiocarbon dates. For the Late Woodland Miller III period, A.D. 600–1000, Jenkins distinguished four phases (actually he called them subphases of the Miller III phase): Vienna, Catfish Bend, Cofferdam, and Gainesville. Radiocarbon dates suggested considerable overlap of the last three phases.

In Jenkins's (1982) formulation (see Fig. 73), the Vienna phase was subdivided into early and late subphases, and was followed by the Catfish Bend phase. The Cofferdam phase branched off the Catfish Bend phase. At this time or perhaps slightly later, the Catfish Bend phase developed into the Gainesville phase. The Cofferdam and Gainesville phases were thus contemporary. The radiocarbon determinations on which this

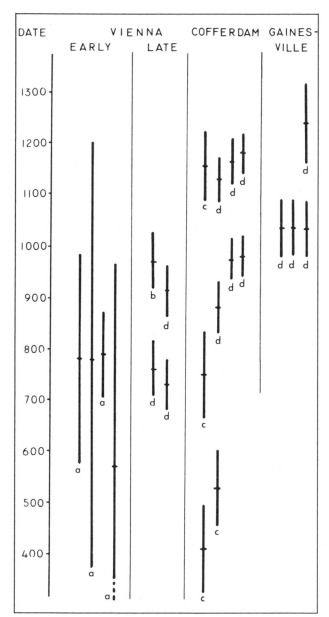

Fig. 74. Radiocarbon dates for Late Woodland phases in the central Tombigbee area. Sources for dates: (a) Atkinson et al. 1980; (b) O'Hear et al. 1981; (c) Blakeman et al. 1976; (d) Jenkins 1981.

Table 22. Ceramic Frequencies of the Cofferdam and Gainesville Phases

	Cofferdam	*Gainesville*
Tempering agent		
Grog (%)	94–95	93–94
Sand (%)	5–6	6–7
Shell (%)	much rarer than 1	1
Grog and Shell (%)	—	.5
Surface Treatment		
Plain (%)	15–30	35–45
Cordmarked (%)	55–75	35–45
Other (%)	10–20	10–20
Grog-tempered loop handles	absent	Infrequently found on plain grog-tempered vessels

(Source: Jenkins 1982:101–103)

quently" found on plain grog-tempered vessels but were absent in the Cofferdam phase. Third, a very few Gainesville phase vessels had shell tempering (or mixed grog and shell), while shell tempering was "much rarer" in the Cofferdam phase. Jenkins saw these differences as an indication that the Gainesville phase was more 'Mississippianized' than the Cofferdam phase:

> Two Late Woodland complexes developed by the end of the Catfish Bend subphase at A.D. 1000. One of these, the Gainesville subphase ceramic complex, may have developed out of the Catfish Bend subphase complex either as a result of contact with Mississippian groups, or development toward Mississippian norms. The other, the Cofferdam subphase complex, may represent a direct development out of the Catfish Bend subphase without Mississippian influence. This complex contains very few Mississippian attributes (Jenkins 1982:101–102).

After assigning components to the Cofferdam or Gainesville phase on the basis of their ceramic frequencies, Jenkins found that base camps of the two phases consistently differed in other respects (see Table 23). These differences did not represent geographical patterning, as components of the two phases were interspersed. Unlike the Cofferdam phase, Gainesville phase base camps had houses similar to Mississippian structures. This is consistent with Jenkins's interpretation as quoted above. Other differences, however, had no clear relationship to 'Mississippianization.' Compared to Gainesville phase components, Cofferdam phase components had less deer bone, less bird bone, and more turtle and fish bone. Cofferdam components had

sequence was based are presented in Figure 74.

In distinguishing between Cofferdam and Gainesville phase ceramic assemblages (see Table 22), Jenkins (1982:101–103) emphasized three points. First, compared with the Cofferdam phase, Gainesville phase ceramics were more frequently plain surfaced. Second, in the Gainesville phase loop handles were "infre-

Table 23. Differences Between Cofferdam and Gainesvile Base Camps

	Cofferdam	*Gainesville*
Structures	no substantial architecture	rectangular single-post houses with shallow floors and central hearths
Burials	semiflexed (1/2) orientation unspecified	semiflexed (22/33) heads east (25/33)

Faunal (% of identified bone)

	Cofferdam		*Gainesville*	
deer	71	deer	77[a]
other mammal	4.7	other mammal	5.3
bird	4.2	bird	9.0
turtle	16	turtle	7.2
fish	4.1	fish	2.1

Bone and shell abundance (g/m^3)

	Cofferdam		*Gainesville*	
bone	0.18–0.44	bone	0.95–1.46
shell	1.18–1.99	shell	18.9–60.9

Bone:shell ratio	.09–.38		.02–.08

[a] Faunal data for the Gainesville phase may include some Catfish Bend phase material (Jenkins 1982:107)

(*Source:* Jenkins 1982:105–108)

far lower overall bone and mussel shell abundances, and less shell relative to bone. In other respects, Jenkins contended, Cofferdam and Gainesville base camps were similar. In particular, he took the presence of summer- and fall-harvested plant food remains in base camps of both phases to indicate identical seasons of occupation.

Jenkins's interpretation is not the only one consistent with these data. Rather than being normative differences between interspersed communities lasting up to 200 years, I suggest these differences were due to differing seasons of occupation. The botanical data, after all, only indicate when the plant foods were harvested, not when they were consumed. In my interpretation, the Catfish Bend phase was followed by a single phase that had transitory camps, base camps occupied during late fall and winter, and other base camps occupied during warmer months. As with any aspect of foragers' mobility patterns, the timing and length of stay in winter or summer quarters would be affected by year-to-year climatic variation. I do not suggest cold season and warm season base camps were mutually exclusive loci. Rather, I suggest "Gainesville" components were those sites with the longest, most frequent cold season occupations, and "Cofferdam" components were those that

tended to have been occupied during the warm months.

Components of the "Gainesville phase" had the characteristics expectable for cold season occupations. They had substantial houses with central hearths. Deer, which are more easily procurable at this time of year, were relatively abundant. Both of the two deer mandibles from "Gainesville" contexts for which age at death could be assessed were killed during December–February, based on a 1 August birth date (Woodrick 1981:124; cf. Davis 1979). Fish and turtles, which are much less easy to procure in the cold season, were relatively scarce. On the other hand, if Jenkins (1982:111) is correct that mussels were more likely to have been procured in the warm season, the higher relative and absolute abundance of mussel shell in "Gainesville" contexts appears inconsistent with my interpretation (Jenkins, personal communication).

In contrast, "Cofferdam" components had characteristics of warm season occupations. Fish and turtles were relatively abundant. Scott's analysis of "Cofferdam" faunal remains at the Lubbub site concluded that "fauna from [Cofferdam] samples in the Lubbub Creek Archaeological Locality strongly suggest an occupational hiatus extending from mid-fall to early or mid-winter" (Scott 1983:322). Faunal remains in general were relatively scarce at "Cofferdam" components, which is not surprising if these sites were occupied during the season when fresh plant foods were available. Substantial dwellings do not appear to have been built. Nuts and nutshells, which would most likely be used as fuel during or shortly after the fall nut harvest, were not as abundant in "Cofferdam" as in "Gainesville" components. By weight, 10–13 percent of charcoal in features at "Cofferdam" components was nut or nutshell, compared with 16–48 percent from the analyzed "Gainesville" components (Caddell 1981, tables 9, 14, 20, 27).

This interpretation also accounts for the other differences between these putative phases. With demonstrably different sorts of food being prepared at the seasonally differentiated sites, we might expect vessels of different shapes and sizes to have been used in different frequencies. Jenkins (1982:103) noted that there is a strong correlation in Miller III between surface finish and vessel forms. The predominance of cordmarked sherds over plain sherds in "Cofferdam" assemblages equates to a predominance of large, shallow hemi-

Table 24. Radiocarbon Dates for Summerville I Phase Components

Possible Summerville I Contexts		
Pit associated with Summerville I house, Lubbub (Peebles and Mann 1983:78–79)	Beta-1096	A.D. 900 ± 105
Smudge pit associated with pre-mound house, Lubbub (Blitz 1983a:238)	Beta-1103	A.D. 980 ± 90
Secure Summerville I Contexts		
Summerville I house, Lubbub (Blitz 1983b:261)	Beta-1095	A.D. 1190 ± 80
Summerville I house, Lubbub (Blitz 1983b:269)	Beta-1097	A.D. 1070 ± 125
Pit with diagnostic sherds, 22Lo527 (Blakeman 1975a:95–98)	UGa-910	A.D. 1175 ± 70
Pit with diagnostic sherds, 22Lo564 (Blakeman 1975a:95–98)	UGa-911	A.D. 1185 ± 60
Pit with charred maize cobs, 22Lo527 (Atkinson et al. 1980:237)	UGa-2764	A.D. 1185 ± 90
Hearth on platform mound, 22Lo507 (Rucker 1974:34, 56)	UGa-680	A.D. 1265 ± 105

spherical bowls and deep hemispherical or semiconoidal containers, as compared with plain-surfaced, flat-based beakers. The relative scarcity of loop handles at "Cofferdam" components is also to be expected, because loop handles were found only "infrequently" on the plain-surfaced vessels that were in turn infrequent at these sites. As for the difference between "less than 1 percent" and "much rarer" frequencies of shell-tempered sherds in the different "phases," all of these sites had subsequent Mississippian occupations. It would be surprising if some later items had *not* been intruded into earlier contexts, either by natural or cultural agencies. The remaining difference between the two "phases" proposed by Jenkins is in the mortuary data. If, as Saxe (1970) suggests, cemeteries function to establish claims on territory or property, it would be more likely for such cemeteries to be associated with the permanent structures of the cold season camps rather than the presumably ephemeral facilities at the warm season camps.

The result of my rearrangement of the Late Woodland chronology is a Miller III culture with three phases. The Vienna phase, A.D. 600–900, is not changed from Jenkins's (1982) description. It is followed by the Catfish Bend phase. Because there are no radiocarbon dates for this phase, its duration is not known. The following phase, which can be called Cofferdam-Gainesville, lasts from around A.D. 950 to

1100 (Fig. 73). This termination date for Cofferdam-Gainesville excludes several later radiocarbon dates. This exclusion minimizes or eliminates the chronological overlap of the Cofferdam-Gainesville and Summerville I phases. Unlike Jenkins (1982) I see no compelling evidence of any protracted overlap. However, perhaps the only certain aspect of the Late Woodland chronology is that without the painstaking work of Jenkins and his colleagues there would be nothing to argue about.

The Mississippian chronology for the central Tombigbee valley has not been very controversial. Four phases are recognized in the Gainesville Reservoir: Summerville I through IV (Peebles and Mann 1983; Jenkins 1982). Summerville I is usually dated A.D. 950 or 1000 to 1200. Summerville II and III differ so little from each other ceramically that they are usually treated as a single unit, dating A.D. 1200 to 1450 or 1500. The Summerville IV phase is largely protohistoric, as it lasts from A.D. 1450 or 1500 to A.D. 1650 or 1700. I suggest one revision to this scheme. Despite the popularity of A.D. 950–1000 for the inception of Summerville I, the available radiocarbon dates for demonstrably Summerville I contexts are all after A.D. 1050 (see Table 24). On this basis I argue that Summerville I follows Cofferdam-Gainesville at A.D. 1050–1100. The result of my reinterpretation of the Late Woodland-Mississippian chronology for the central Tombigbee is shown in Figure 73.

Miller III Culture

We have unusually complete data for a reconstruction of Miller III culture. The only significant gap in the data is the lack of even a partial layout of a single community. Midden deposits and features extend across considerable areas (›1 ha) at the base camps, but we have no idea of the size or layout of an occupation at any one time.

Throughout Miller III there were two fundamental site types: large base camps and small transitory camps. The small transitory camps range in size from a few hundred to a few thousand square meters. Because ceramics are usually sparse at these sites and few have been excavated to any extent, little can be said about their seasonality or their specific chronology. Transitory camps were located in the alluvial valley and in the lands east and west of the valley (Jenkins 1982: 110–111; DeJarnette et al. 1975a, 1975b; J. Blitz, personal communication). In addition to varying in terms of physiographic and ecological setting, transitory camps also varied in relative artifact frequencies. Some had extremely abundant lithic debris, while others had more even lithic to ceramic ratios. It remains to be seen just how these camps fitted into the resource procurement and settlement location strategy.

Subsistence remains from Miller III base camps have been analyzed in considerable detail. Plant food remains seem to have varied little through Miller III. Charred nutshells were the most abundant byproduct of plant food processing. Hickory nutshell comprised 75–95 percent of all nutshell by weight, with most of the remainder being acorn shell (all data from Caddell 1981, 1983). Maize was recovered from one feature of early or late Vienna phase date, the earliest context for maize in the Tombigbee valley. Maize increased in abundance slightly through time: 1 out of 12 (8 percent) of Vienna phase samples contained maize; 10 out of 35 (29 percent) samples of Catfish Bend or Cofferdam-Gainesville date contained maize; and 17 out of 57 (30 percent) of Cofferdam-Gainesville samples contained maize. Excluding two Cofferdam-Gainesville smudge pits, maize constituted less than 2 percent of all botanical remains by weight in each of these 104 samples. In tandem with the increase in maize abundance, there was an apparent increase in the number of species of wild plant seeds, from 6 taxa in Vienna samples to 15 or more in Cofferdam-Gainesville contexts. These numbers may be misleading, however, because a much larger number of Cofferdam-Gainesville samples has been analyzed. Species present included grape, persimmon, maypop, blackberry or dewberry, and sumac, as well as potential food species such as pigweed, goosefoot, sumpweed, panic grass, and maygrass. There was also one possible common bean in a Cofferdam-Gainesville feature, though Caddell reported the identification as uncertain and noted that the specimen could be intruded from a subsequent Mississippian occupation. Caddell summarized the Late Woodland vegetable diet as dominated by wild species with maize as a minor, supplementary carbohydrate source.

Faunal remains from Miller III contexts have been studied in similar detail (Woodrick 1981, 1983; Scott 1983). From early to late there was a decrease in the relative abundance of deer, from 88 percent of all bone by weight in the Vienna phase to 74 percent in combined Catfish Bend and Cofferdam-Gainesville samples (Woodrick 1981, table 37, in which Catfish Bend and "Gainesville" data were grouped and "Cofferdam" data were reported separately). Other mammals, turtles, fish, and birds all increased in abundance over this period, with little change in proportions among themselves. Whether this progressively increasing utilization of smaller species was paralleled by a shift in prey size within individual taxa is not known, but Scott (1983, Appendix C) showed that the fish caught by Cofferdam-Gainesville occupants at Lubbub were surprisingly small. The average weight over 61 individuals was .52 kg with a median of .25 kg, and this only included material recovered from one-quarter inch mesh screens.

The botanical and faunal data present clear evidence of a downward shift in the size of food items in Miller III times. Typically we would expect such a shift towards energetically costlier "second-line" resources to accompany human population increase. Gainesville Reservoir data confirm a higher population density for Miller III than for the preceding Miller II period (A.D. 300–600). Only 5 Miller II base camps were recorded compared to 25 Miller III base camps. Furthermore, the Miller III base camp middens were larger and denser than their Miller II counterparts. Unfortunately we have phase attributions for only five of the Miller III sites, so little is known about the rate or timing of population increase within the 450-year-long Miller III period.

The increasing use of smaller but more abundant resources in Miller III was not an adequate response to the higher population density. The mortuary remains from the Vienna phase (n = 2) are too scant to permit generalization, but we have larger samples of Catfish Bend (n = 45) and Cofferdam-Gainesville (n = 33) burials. Cole et al. (1982) examined the human skeletal remains for porotic hyperostosis and cribra orbitalia—indicators of nutritional stress. Evidence of systemic infection and degenerative pathology—osteoarthritis, vertebral osteophytosis, and osteoporosis—was also recorded. By all these measures there was a marked decline in health status from the Catfish Bend phase[2] to the Cofferdam-Gainesville phase (see Table 25). This decline was also evident in the death rate: only 38 percent of Catfish Bend individuals died before age 20, while in the Cofferdam-Gainesville population 52 percent died young. Life,

Table 25. Health Status of Catfish Bend, Cofferdam-Gainesville, and Summerville I Mortuary Populations

Phase	Sample Size	Percent of population with:			
		Nutritional Stress[a]	Degenerative Pathologies	Systemic Infection	Evidence of Violence[b]
Catfish Bend	45	27	27	36	13 (9)
Cofferdam-Gainesville	33	42	30	67	6 (0)
Summerville I	19	11	21	26	5 (5)

[a] Based on presence of porotic hyperostosis, cribra orbitalia, or cribra parietalis. Note that this differs from the definition of nutritional stress used in Cole et al. 1982, table 14.

[b] Based on evidence of 'parry' fractures or projectile point wounds. Numbers in parentheses are percentages of population with evidence of projectile point wounds.

(*Source:* Cole et al. 1982)

it seems, became shorter and more painful during Miller III.

Paralleling the declining health status, evidence of violent conflict diminished from Catfish Bend phase to Cofferdam-Gainesville phase (see Table 25). This is true whether we consider only the incidence of projectile point wounds, or we include evidence of 'parry' fractures. The unexpectedness of declining incidence of violent conflict during a period when there must have been increasing competition for vital resources indicates this is a topic deserving further research.

The mortuary remains also provide information on social structure. The most common mortuary items were shell beads and shell pendants. The only other common artifacts were triangular projectile points, most if not all of which were the cause of death rather than mortuary items, per se. Most burials lacked grave goods altogether: 71 percent in Catfish Bend and 63 percent in Cofferdam-Gainesville. Such summary statements, however, belie the patterning in the data.

The Catfish Bend burials were found in three loose clusters at 1Pi61. All the burials in one cluster (n = 11) lacked grave goods. As their attribution to this phase was not certain (Cole et al. 1982:206) I omit them from the following discussion. The other two clusters (n = 16 and n = 18) were remarkably similar to each other. Most of the burials were unaccompanied (86 percent and 58 percent respectively). The age and sex distribu-

tion of unaccompanied burials was nearly the same as for accompanied burials. Shell beads and shell pendants were the only accompaniments, aside possibly from one projectile point found with an adult female. All the shell pendants (n = 4) were found with women, in two burials of one cluster and one in the other. Most of the shell beads in each cluster were made of freshwater species, though one cluster had 0.4 percent (6/1,402) marine shell beads and the other 10.6 percent (181/1,692) marine shell beads. Except for two unusual burials, subadults had more beads than adult females (114–294 per subadult versus 6–54 per adult female), and adult females had more beads than adult males (6–54 per adult female versus 2–26 per adult male). Over 80 percent of the 3,094 beads were found with the two unusual burials (n = 1,399 and n = 1,142), one burial in each cluster. Each of these two burials was a young woman, ages 16 and 21, buried in a seated position. These were the only seated burials, and one of them apparently had been placed against a framework of three posts set upright in the bottom of the grave. No other graves had internal structures. Except for the two unusual burials there was no indication of status differentiation other than by age and gender. Nevertheless, because not all young women had grave goods or were buried in unusual positions, the two exceptional burials indicate that age and gender were not the only components of status differentiation. Exactly what status the two young women had, or how they came to have it, is not at all clear. It could plausibly have been the result of their manner or time of death, or their descent, to name only a few possibilities.

The Cofferdam-Gainesville burials at 1Pi61 present a different picture. Again there were two clusters of burials, one with 19 individuals and the other with 14. Again most burials were unaccompanied, 63 percent and 64 percent respectively. Shell beads were the most common accompaniments, but beads were less abundant and were distributed differently than before. Subadults again had relatively plentiful beads (from 5 to 395 in the accompanied burials) but not more than adult males (19–493). Adult females had few beads, one individual with a single bead and another with two beads. These were the only items accompanying women. Not only did some men have more accompanying items than before, relatively more men had accompaniments: 25 percent (2/8) in Catfish Bend compared to 36 percent (4/11) in Cofferdam-Gainesville.

There was also a broader range of accompanying arti-facts. One male was buried with 2 turtle shells, and another had 2 drilled bear canines, 1 greenstone celt, and 1 shell pendant in addition to 493 shell beads. A greenstone celt was also buried with a 10–11-year-old child, along with 395 shell beads.

It can, of course, be objected that the differences be-tween Catfish Bend burials and Cofferdam-Gainesville burials were due only to changes in mortuary symbol-ism without any modification of the society's system of roles and statuses. I think this unlikely, however, on the basis of a pattern of redundancy in the data. Not only did women in general receive less preferential treatment in the later phase burials, but also the un-usual status of the Catfish Bend seated young female burials disappeared. Not only did men receive larger quantities and a greater variety of goods than before, but also these increases primarily involved goods from nonlocal sources. Marine shell beads increased from 6 percent of all Catfish Bend beads to 58 percent of Cofferdam-Gainesville beads. Greenstone celts are also of nonlocal origin, the closest stone source thought to be 200 km to the east. In short, I argue that the unusual status position previously open to some young women had changed or disappeared and that adult males were involved in intercommunity exchange relationships to a greater extent than before. The Cofferdam-Gainesville burials do not indicate any marked status hierarchy, nor is there any suggestion of status ascription on any basis besides age and gender.

Altogether, the Late Woodland survey and excava-tion data from the Gainesville Reservoir consistently indicate increasing economic stress preceding the ap-pearance of Mississippian culture. From A.D. 600 to 1100 there was increasing consumption of small fauna, possibly an increased consumption of nondomesticated small seeds, and a growing though still minor use of at least one cultivated crop. This dietary shift was ac-companied by deteriorating health status and a change in settlement pattern. The base camp-transitory camp dichotomy of the Vienna phase gave way to a pattern of warm season and cold season base camps, probably with continuing use of transitory camps. As yet we do not know whether this settlement pattern change im-plies population nucleation for longer portions of the year. The size and/or number of nucleated communities increased through time. Intercommunity exchanges in-creased in frequency or volume, and the addition of

a new item of exchange may indicate an expansion in the geographical scope of exchanges. Adult males seem to have been the agents in these exchange rela-tionships, and as their activity increased there was a shift in the expression of achieved status at death from females to males. In addition, one unusual status previ-ously open to some women either ceased to exist or was no longer expressed at death. Throughout the per-iod there is no indication of strong status hierarchies, nor is there any evidence of mound construction, vil-lage fortification, or other corporate labor projects.

Summerville Culture

Like much of the Southeast, Mississippian culture ap-pears to be dramatically different from the preceding Late Woodland culture in the central Tombigbee valley. The differences include a variety of functionally interre-lated aspects of material culture as well as changes in social structure. While the temporal ordering of these changes remains an open issue, there are indications that in the Gainesville Reservoir area the social trans-formation began before the wholesale adoption of agri-culture and its attendant effects on material culture.

Our knowledge of early Mississippian culture in the central Tombigbee valley is somewhat uneven, as it is based on excavations at a single large site. Small Missis-sippian sites with low artifact density are present all along the central Tombigbee River, both upstream and downstream of the Gainesville Reservoir (Sheldon et al. 1982; Jenkins et al. 1975; Atkinson 1978). Though little firm data exist to indicate site functions, these sites are thought to be farmsteads or small hamlets (e.g., Kellogg Village, Atkinson et al. 1980), field houses, and transitory camps. A limited number of larger sites ex-isted, each with a platform mound. Between Colum-bus, Mississippi, and Demopolis, Alabama, there were six sites with at least one platform mound (see Fig. 72). The two southernmost mounds are of unknown age, despite repeated visits by archaeologists (Moore 1901:505–507; Nielsen et al. 1973:36–37; Sheldon et al. 1982:4). Of the three northernmost mound sites, only the Coleman mound has had test excavations since Moore's visit. The mound had been constructed in at least two episodes, and a hearth below the last mound fill layer yielded a radiocarbon date of A.D. 1265 ± 105 (Rucker 1974:53–56). On this basis the mound is considered to have existed in Summerville

I times. Based on the morphology of a vessel recovered by Moore (1901:503) from Mound B at Chowder Springs, this site also has a Summerville I component. Age of the Butler mound is unknown, though like the Hilman and Brasfield mounds it is probably Mississippian. The mound at Lubbub is the only excavated one along the central Tombigbee, though by virtue of a landowner's effort to level it, we have data only from below the second of at least six fill layers. The mound construction was initiated during Summerville I. The occupation associated with this mound is also the only extensive Mississippian occupation along the central Tombigbee River to have had any significant excavation.

Two major excavations were conducted at Lubbub. The first, directed by Ned Jenkins, exposed a Summerville I cemetery and located the (levelled) mound (Jenkins and Ensor 1981:68–93). Christopher Peebles (1983a, 1983b, 1983c) directed the second project, which excavated over 2 ha in a stratified systematic unaligned sample of the site. Unless stated otherwise, Summerville I data in the following discussion are taken solely from the final reports of these two projects.

The difference between Cofferdam-Gainesville subsistence strategy and that of Summerville I is distinct and abrupt. Members of Summerville I society were fully dependent on cleared-field maize agriculture. This is attested by several independent lines of evidence. First, the absolute and relative abundance of carbonized maize fragments increased. Of the charred botanical material in refuse-filled pits of the Cofferdam-Gainesville phase, 10–40 percent was nutshell and ≤ 0.1 percent was maize, by weight. For the same context in Summerville I the figure for nutshell is 6 percent while maize has risen to 51 percent (Caddell 1981, 1983). Smudge pits, in which maize is overrepresented, are excluded from these figures. The difference was more extreme if counts are used rather than weights, or if only food plants are included in the totals (Caddell 1983:231–244). Second, along with the increase of maize relative to nutshell, there was a change in the proportions of nut species collected. In the Cofferdam-Gainesville pits acorn and hickory nutshell were equally abundant: 52 percent and 48 percent by count, respectively (being denser and less fragmented, hickory overwhelmingly dominated by weight, but for this comparison Caddell suggested counts are more informative). In Summerville I pits, the proportions were

8 percent acorn and 92 percent hickory, again by count (Caddell 1983, table 27). In discussing this contrast, Caddell (1983:240–244) noted that on a per gram basis, acorn is high in carbohydrates and low in protein, oils, and calories when compared with hickory nuts. Thus, for the Cofferdam-Gainesville population, acorns were the major source of carbohydrates, but had been replaced by maize in Summerville I times.

The faunal remains provide supporting evidence of a major shift to cultivated foods. First, the progressive shift to smaller prey species during Miller III was reversed in Summerville I. From 25 percent of all bone by weight in Cofferdam-Gainesville samples, deer bone increased to 41 percent in Summerville I samples.[3] Fish and turtle remains declined in abundance, though bird remains increased slightly. The increase in prey size is also found within a single prey class. Average captured fish weight rose from 0.52 kg in Cofferdam-Gainesville to 1.58 kg in Summerville I; the median also rose from 0.25 to 0.7 kg (Scott 1983, appendix C). Scott interprets these data as showing a shift towards higher-return-per-energy-investment prey species concomitant with an overall reduction in dependence on hunting. In other words, hunters could now afford to concentrate on larger prey. Other evidence of the substantial difference between Cofferdam-Gainesville and Summerville I subsistence comes from squirrels, rabbits, and rats (Scott 1983:361–363). The ratios of climax forest species to field or successional species is higher in Cofferdam-Gainesville refuse than in Summerville refuse (Summerville I–IV data combined due to low sample sizes and problems of phase attribution). This is true for each of the following species pairs: gray squirrel/fox squirrel; swamp rabbit/cottontail; wood rat/hispid cotton rat; wood rat/marsh rice rat. In comparison to the Cofferdam-Gainesville fauna, the Summerville I fauna "indicate relatively large scale land clearance" (Scott 1983:361).

The large-scale cultivation of maize improved the population's health substantially. Cole et al. (1982) presented data on 19 Summerville I burials as well as the Miller III burials described above. From Cofferdam-Gainesville to Summerville I there was a decline in the incidence of nutritional stress, degenerative pathologies, and systemic infection (see Table 25). The incidence of death before age 20 years also fell, from 52 percent to 32 percent. In one respect, however, the Summerville I population was less healthy than their predecessors. Cole et al. (1982) do not present data on caries rates, but 18 percent of Cofferdam-Gainesville burials had severe dental abscesses, compared with 32 percent of Summerville I individuals. The relatively greater incidence of dental pathology in Summerville I burials is indicative of the greater importance of carbohydrates in their diet.

A number of changes in material culture were more or less directly related to the shift in subsistence strategy. In concert with change in the nature and probably the amount of stored plant food, the use of subsurface pits was discontinued in favor of some form(s) of above-ground facility. Free-standing granaries may have been used (cf. Blitz 1983b:261–263) or perhaps maize was stored inside habitations. This latter possibility may in part account for the increase in house size from Cofferdam-Gainesville to Summerville I. Four Cofferdam-Gainesville structures at 1Pi61 averaged 10 sq m (Jenkins and Ensor 1981:131–139), while the three Summerville I houses excavated at Lubbub averaged 35 sq m (Peebles 1983:399). Summerville I structures were rectangular, and both wall-trench and single-post constructions were present. The most visible difference between the Cofferdam-Gainesville phase and Summerville I is in the ceramic assemblage. Crushed shell tempering was used nearly exclusively in Summerville I vessels, and vessel surfaces were no longer cordmarked. Beakers and deep conoidal jars were no longer made, while subglobular jars and bottles were added to the vessel assemblage. Incision and burnishing were new decorative treatments. Commenting on these changes, Peebles (1983:396) stated: "The reasons for these developments were straightforward: changes in foods, food preparation and storage, and the use of ceramics in a wider variety of tasks. In brief, the context of ceramic production, distribution, and use changed radically."

The changed social context of the Summerville I phase is revealed by mortuary data and community layout. Mention has already been made of the relatively good health status of the population represented by the burials. Many of the excavated Summerville I burials were in a formal cemetery consisting of three or four rows of parallel (heads oriented east) extended inhumations. The cemetery contained 21 individuals in 19 graves.[4] Subadults and older males predominated, though three adult females were also present. The distribution of grave goods suggests that the cemetery represents a limited segment of the community.

As a group, the cemetery burials differ from the 14 Summerville I burials found in the village area (Powell 1983:455, appendix A). Among these village burials 43 percent were unaccompanied, and the only accompaniments were pottery vessels (maximum of three per burial) and one bone pin. In contrast, only 16 percent of the cemetery burials were unaccompanied. Accompaniments included pots, bone awls, projectile points, and a few other items also probably of local origin. Eleven of the cemetery burials (58 percent) contained items of nonlocal origin, including objects of copper, galena, greenstone, and marine shell. The distribution of items conforms with age and gender. Subadults either had no accompaniments or had items of shell and pottery. Adult females were buried with pots or shell beads. Adult males were buried with a range of utilitarian and nonutilitarian items. Thus, the cemetery burials contrast with the village burials in two respects: unlike the village burials they constituted a formal cemetery, and only burials in the cemetery contained exotic, nonutilitarian goods. The cemetery apparently contained adult males of high status, along with females and subadults somehow associated with these males. Possibly the cemetery contains the members of a chiefly lineage, though an equally plausible alternative is that the cemetery contains the close relatives of a set of unrelated adult members of achieved high status. In short, Summerville I society was ranked, though not strongly nor necessarily ascriptively.

In tandem with the ranked social organization indicated by the mortuary remains, Lubbub had a characteristically Mississippian mound-plaza layout. As reconstructed by Peebles and his coworkers (Peebles 1983:399; Blitz 1983a, 1983b; Cole and Albright 1983), the Summerville I community spread over 8.5 ha within a 19 ha area bounded by the Tombigbee River and a bastioned palisade. Residences formed an arc around the mound, leaving a plaza to the east of the mound. On the south side of the mound was an inner palisade separating the residential zone from the plaza and the mound ramps. As the mound was largely bulldozed away twenty years ago nothing is known about the structures that once surmounted it. Moore's excavations (1901:504–505) on the mound plateau exposed hearths "here and there." Recent excavation of the mound remnant (Blitz 1983a) showed the mound to have had at least six fill layers, though there may not have been structures atop each of the sequent layers. The intact, lowest layer, at any rate, had no trace of a structure. Structure patterns were found underneath the lowest fill layer, however, and they provide us with an intriguing glimpse at the development of mound ceremonialism at the site.

There were six pre-mound structures, apparently constructed in three sequent pairs. The earliest pair, Nos. 3 and 4, were square to rectangular with no internal features, and appear to be common domestic dwellings. Overlying these were two structures, Nos. 2 and 5A. Structure 2 was square with a carefully constructed central hearth. Structure 5A had two rooms with a hearth in the center of the "inside" room and the "outside" room open on the side of the plaza. Just as Structures 3 and 4 had been carefully razed before construction of Nos. 2 and 5A, the latter two were razed before construction of Nos. 1 and 5B. Structure 1 was square with a carefully prepared central hearth. Structure 5B almost precisely repeated the design of 5A, though this time the posts were singly set and the "outside" room was closed on all sides. The "outside" room had a central, raised, circular, fired clay platform and another raised but unfired clay platform carefully shaped but of irregular outline. The "inside" room also had a central, raised, burnt clay platform. The function of these burnt clay platforms is not clear; aside from their brick-like consistency, no trace of fire remained. The walls of Structures 1 and 5B, though not the clay platforms, were razed like the previous structures, and a rectangular yellow clay cap was spread over the area. This was the first of the mound fill layers.

All six structures, the yellow clay cap, all subsequent mound fill layers, and the inner palisade line demarcating the plaza had identical orientations (sides E 26 degrees S, fronting southeast). The series of construction episodes appears to represent the gradual transformation of a particular domestic compound to a communally constructed public edifice. The latest stages of this transformation—the upper mound stages—were of Summerville II-III date, but the initial yellow clay cap and the later two pairs of premound structures were of Summerville I date as judged by associated ceramics. The date of the earliest pair of structures unfortunately is not well established. A smudge pit beside one of these buildings was radiocarbon dated A.D. 980 ± 90, which is in the Cofferdam-Gainesville phase according to the chronology presented above. There were no ce-

ramics unambiguously associated with this earliest pair of structures, but there is nothing about their construction inconsistent with a Cofferdam-Gainesville origin. If they were contemporaneous with the smudge pit and the radiocarbon date is accurate, the social or religious functions that later were centered around the mound and plaza already were developing in the Cofferdam-Gainesville phase.

In summary, the Mississippian emergence along the central Tombigbee was a successful response to the increasing subsistence stress of the Late Woodland period. The response had technological and social dimensions as well as the strictly economic one. The basic economic response was a sudden shift from a foraging-gardening strategy to dependence on large-scale field agriculture. The new economic strategy required new technologies in cooking utensils, storage facilities, and housing. The social dimension of the response included the development of social ranking. The difficulty of achieving fine chronological resolution in the archaeological record leaves the issue in doubt, but the modification of the earliest premound structures suggests that the reorganization of society began before the economic shift. In any case, the development of ranking did not lag far behind the economic shift, indicating that the new organization probably was not a response to the uncertainties of crop dependence. Rather, in this instance, the development of rank organization was part of the adaptive response to the stresses of life in the Late Woodland period.

MISSISSIPPIAN EMERGENCE ALONG THE BLACK WARRIOR FLOODPLAIN

History of Research

The Moundville site has been excavated sporadically for over 140 years. The history of this research has been presented elsewhere (Peebles 1979, 1981; Steponaitis 1983a, 1983b). Thus, I will only describe the nature of the available data. The bulk of our information about Moundville comes from the efforts of C. B. Moore (1905, 1907) and D. L. DeJarnette (see Wimberly 1956; Peebles 1979). Moore attacked all of the visible mounds and large parts of the site's high status precincts. His reports and field notes almost exclusively provide information on mortuary associations. In con-

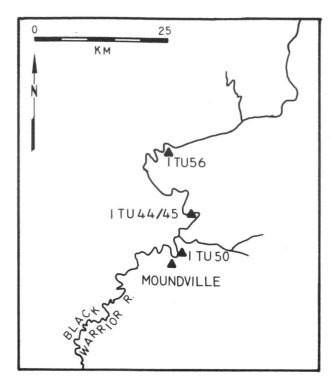

Fig. 75. Locations of Moundville I mound sites.

trast, DeJarnette's excavations focused on the non-mound area and provide information on nonmortuary aspects of the site. Excavations by DeJarnette and his successors at the University of Alabama have continued to the present, with the labor crews of the Relief era being replaced in more recent times by field school students. These extensive excavations (roughly 5 ha) in general lacked tight stratigraphic control and, as sediments were rarely screened, artifact recovery was strongly biased toward complete, large, and unusual items. Recently these 'extensive' data have been complemented by 'intensive' data from microstratigraphic excavations employing fine-mesh waterscreening and flotation. These excavations were directed by M. Scarry (1981b, 1986) as part of C. S. Peebles's program for expanding our knowledge of the Moundville culture.

The allure of the large, impressive Moundville site has not forestalled investigation of its environs (Fig. 75). Moore (1905) tested half a dozen platform mounds on the Black Warrior floodplain between Tuscaloosa and Eutaw, Alabama, and found nothing to interest him. In the 1930s the Alabama Museum of Natural History began compiling an archaeological site file.

In addition to visiting all the Warrior floodplain sites, the Alabama Museum also excavated cemetery areas at two single-mound sites near Moundville (DeJarnette and Peebles 1970; Jones and DeJarnette n.d.; DeJarnette, field notes on file at Mound State Monument). Aside from a few, very minor salvage expeditions and the excavation of some Protohistoric cemeteries not of concern here, the outlying sites received no further attention until the 1970s. At that time many of the floodplain sites were revisited and small surface collections were taken (Nielsen et al. 1973). Subsequently, John Walthall directed the intensive survey of a 6 sq km section of floodplain and valley margin as well as the excavation of a small portion of a Late Woodland occupation site (Walthall, field notes on file at Mound State Monument; Bozeman 1982:157–159). This was followed by controlled surface collections and mound stratigraphy testing as part of Peebles's Moundville project (Bozeman 1982). Another section of the floodplain (4.45 sq km) was intensively surveyed by Lawrence Alexander (1982). Further, informal site surveys by both professional and avocational archaeologists have covered much of the remaining floodplain. In short, we have good survey coverage of the floodplain near Moundville, but extremely scarce excavation data.

Chronology

Chronological control for the Late Woodland period in the Moundville area is based on cross-dating to radiocarbon-dated sequences nearby. Research in the Gainesville Reservoir of the Tombigbee River has provided the majority of relevant data, but additional information comes from the upper reaches of the Black Warrior River. To date, all the Late Woodland sites in the Moundville area have been ascribed to the West Jefferson phase (Jenkins 1978; Welch 1981b; Bozeman 1982; Knight 1982). The description of this phase (Jenkins and Nielsen 1974; O'Hear 1975; Jenkins 1978) was based on material from sites in the upper Warrior drainage. The fundamental diagnostic characteristic of this phase is a ceramic assemblage consisting almost entirely of plain-surfaced, grog-tempered vessels. Radiocarbon dates from the upper Black Warrior sites establish an A.D. 850 or 900 to A.D. 1000 range for the phase (Jenkins and Nielsen 1974; Ensor 1979). No earlier Late Woodland phases have been defined anywhere in the Black Warrior drainage.[5] On this basis it appears that in the Moundville area there was no permanent occupation in the Late Woodland period prior to the West Jefferson phase ca. A.D. 850. This will not be certain, however, until there has been far more excavation at Late Woodland sites.

The West Jefferson phase is followed by the Moundville I phase in the Moundville area. On the basis of ceramic cross-dating and a limited number of radiocarbon dates from Moundville, Steponaitis (1978, 1983a) defined Moundville I as beginning about A.D. 1050. Subsequently, available radiocarbon dates from Moundville suggest Moundville I commenced 'slightly earlier' (Scarry 1981b:90, see her table 1 and figure 3), around A.D. 1000. The end of the phase is set at A.D. 1250 (Steponaitis 1983a:104–106), resulting in a 250-year-long phase. Fortunately morphological and stylistic change in ceramics permits discrimination of the earlier end of the phase from the later end. As closely as we can determine, Moundville I is fully Mississippian throughout its time span, not only in terms of its shell-tempered ceramics, but also in terms of maize-dependency, architectural style, platform mound construction, and ranked social organization.

West Jefferson Culture in the Moundville Area

The available data for the Late Woodland in the Moundville area are far less complete than for this period in the central Tombigbee area. Survey and test excavation data provide the outlines of subsistence strategy and settlement pattern, but the lack of extensive excavation severely limits our understanding of community organization. An additional constraint is the nearly total lack of mortuary remains.

Settlement pattern is the best-known aspect of the West Jefferson phase in the Moundville area. Site sizes range from light sherd scatters 10 m in diameter to multihectare middens (Bozeman 1982:159; Alexander 1982:117). This broad range, however, is misleading. Controlled surface collection of several of the larger sites shows them to be composed of contiguous smaller clusters of debris, each well under 1 ha in area (e.g., Bozeman 1982, figs. 15, 18). Most likely large sites, such as 1Tu426 (9.6 ha) and 1Tu427 (8.8 ha, Alexander 1982), were actually multiple, partially overlapping reoccupations of a particularly favorable landform—in this case a terrace close to the Black Warrior River,

above the mean annual flood level, and immediately downstream of the Fall Line shoals at Tuscaloosa. Generalizing from Bozeman's data (1982), the smaller clusters, which overlap to form the multihectare sites, are each .2 to .5 ha. I take this to be the modal size of the floodplain communities. There are also at least a few villages on the hilltops overlooking the floodplain, but this landform has received such scant inspection that little is known about the number or size of these sites. Test excavations at several of the .2 to .5 ha floodplain components permit the admittedly speculative reconstruction of seasonal resource scheduling and settlement movement.

Subsistence remains have been analyzed from one refuse-filled, bell-shaped storage pit at each of two sites. Obviously additional data would be desirable, but none are yet available. In both features the faunal subsistence remains were quite diverse, including shellfish, deer, various birds, fishes, small and medium size mammals, and turtles. Based on the presence of a 4–6 month old fawn in one of the pits (1Ha39, Feature 1), Scott (personal communication) assigned a late fall/winter date to the pit's refuse fill. Vegetal subsistence remains from this pit were dominated by nutshell. Hickory shell (91 percent of food remains by weight) was much more abundant than acorn (8 percent), with minor amounts of maize cob (1 percent) and a variety of grass and fruit seeds present (Scarry 1981a). The same site also yielded the only excavated West Jefferson phase house from the Moundville area. The structure was a roughly rectangular,[6] single-post dwelling, 3–4 m on a side, with a central hearth. No intact floor level was found. Altogether, the material from this site closely resembles the subsistence and seasonality pattern of the 'cold season' aspect of the Cofferdam-Gainesville phase along the Tombigbee River.

In an earlier synthesis of West Jefferson phase data (Welch 1981b) I suggested the floodplain villages were occupied during the warm season and at least partially abandoned during the winter. Current data are insufficient to evaluate this suggestion. One line of evidence, however, indicates the villages were not year-round, permanent occupations; most of the large floodplain sites are at elevations below the Black Warrior five-year flood level and only marginally, if at all, above the two-year flood level (Peirce 1962:48–50). Floods are most likely to occur from January through April (Peirce 1962:44). Summarizing the available data in the

Moundville area, the West Jefferson phase settlement pattern included villages of .2 to .5 ha that may have been abandoned or partially abandoned for some part of the year, most likely in the late winter-early spring. During the village abandonment, the population may have dispersed to scattered, small campsites on the higher river terraces or in the surrounding hills. Throughout the year, subsistence was based on a wide variety of collected and hunted resources. Maize was cultivated, but only on a small scale.

Discussion of West Jefferson phase social organization is even more speculative than reconstruction of the settlement system. By transforming the multihectare sites to an equivalent number of .2 to .5 ha villages, a very crude estimate of the number of such villages is 50–100. Assuming each community relocated their village every 20 years, there would have been 7–15 villages at any one time during the 150-year-long phase. Further, assuming five people per house and one house per 200 sq m, each village would have comprised roughly 50–125 people. These figures yield a population of 350–1,900, with a density on the floodplain (about 400 sq km) of .9–4.75 persons per square kilometer. These figures should not be taken too seriously, as several of the parameters may be wrong by a factor of two or three. The figures do show, however, that the population was not particularly large. By hunting/gathering standards the floodplain population density was high, although this is misleading because the population probably seasonally exploited not only the floodplain but also thousands of square kilometers of surrounding hills. Certainly the West Jefferson phase population was neither so large nor so dense as to presuppose a complex, hierarchical social organization.

More direct evidence of the nature of social organization is not available. Artifact inventories from surface collections do vary between sites—including, for instance, abundance of nonlocal chert and greenstone—but it is not certain which component(s) at these usually multicomponent sites was responsible for such variation. Only two burials of this phase have been excavated, and they contained few or no grave goods (Walthall, personal communication). In short, our information on social organization is negative evidence: there is no reason to believe there was marked social ranking.

Without further excavation, little more can be said about the West Jefferson phase in the Moundville area. There is a strong tendency to view the West Jefferson phase as being very similar to the Catfish Bend or Cofferdam-Gainesville phases in the central Tombigbee area. Because the post-Woodland developments in the Moundville area were significantly different from those along the Tombigbee, such an analogy may be misleading. Though many details of Late Woodland culture in the Moundville area are not known, a number of very visible changes took place about A.D. 1000.

Moundville I Culture

Like the Gainesville Reservoir area, the transition from forager/gardeners producing grog-tempered pottery to field agriculturalists using shell-tempered ceramics occurred rapidly in the Moundville area. Settlement pattern changes also occurred during or very close to this brief period. The scarcity of excavation data outside Moundville, and the unanalyzed state of most of the Moundville excavation data, leave us with blank areas in our picture of Moundville I culture. The outlines of the picture, however, are clear.

Subsistence in the Moundville I phase was based on maize agriculture. Of 9 features and 20 midden and floor deposits from Moundville analyzed by M. Scarry (1981a), all contained maize fragments. By weight, maize averaged 47 percent of vegetal subsistence remains in features and 58 percent in the midden and floor deposits. This is roughly comparable to the contemporary data from Lubbub (Caddell 1983, tables 6–8). Other cultigens present in the Moundville I samples were common beans, squash seeds, and sunflower seeds. Nutshell was also abundant in the samples, but instead of hickory predominating over acorn, as was the case in West Jefferson contexts, the Moundville I samples have a roughly even hickory to acorn ratio. This is precisely the reverse of nutshell ratios in the central Tombigbee area from Late Woodland to Mississippian. We have no satisfactory explanation for the difference between the two areas. Faunal remains from Moundville I contexts at Moundville were dominated by deer in terms of meat weight contribution, with fish, small mammals, and turkey providing significant though far lower contributions (Michals 1981). Like Summerville I contexts, the cottontail/swamp rabbit ratio suggests extensive field clearance, though the grey squirrel/fox squirrel ratio suggests the opposite. Assessment of the Moundville subsistence remains, however, is beset by two difficulties.

The analyzed subsistence remains from Moundville come from what may be a high status precinct of the site (Scarry 1986). This raises the possibility that the subsistence remains are systematically skewed away from the commoner's diet by sumptuary rules. A further difficulty is that the Moundville site lies at the edge of the floodplain rather than being well away from the surrounding hills. Its 1 km radius catchment is significantly different from the catchments of the Black Warrior and central Tombigbee sites with which we compare it. Until other Moundville I contexts are examined, these potential biasing factors remain imponderable.

The diet of the Moundville I population was adequately nutritious. Powell's (1984) conclusion after a thorough examination of Moundville burials is that the population was notably healthy. Though the sample of definitely Moundville I burials was small, they seemed no different from the remainder of the burials.

The switch from grog- to shell-tempered pottery occurred very close to the same time as the change in subsistence strategy. Though it is unwise to put much reliance on a single sample, the shift to field agriculture may have preceded the ceramic change. A refuse-filled, bell-shaped pit, such as are common at Late Woodland sites in the area, was excavated at 1Tu44/45. Included ceramics were grog tempered (Bozeman, unpublished data; Welch, field notes), and the feature originated in a West Jefferson phase midden level. The botanical subsistence remains were 34 percent maize, 41 percent acorn, and 25 percent hickory by weight (Scarry 1981a, table 1). These proportions are much more similar to Moundville I samples than to other West Jefferson phase samples. The A.D. 1150 ± 70 (Beta-1109) radiocarbon date from the feature is two standard deviations later than the proposed termination of the West Jefferson phase, yet I remain convinced the pit was a West Jefferson phase feature. To the extent that this sample accurately reveals local developments, late West Jefferson phase villages adopted field agriculture before altering their pottery production.

Temporal precedence of the subsistence shift over the ceramic change would help account for the fact that there are no known Moundville I villages. Four sites are known to have early Moundville I components. The extent of early Moundville I occupation at two (1Tu50 and Moundville; see Fig. 74 for site locations) is not known precisely, but is quite small (<.1 ha) at the other two (1Tu56 and 1Tu44/45; Bozeman 1982). These four sites are thought to be political and religious centers for dispersed 'neighborhoods' of farmsteads and hamlets:

> The evidence is that the majority of the population was distributed across the landscape in dispersed farmsteads and hamlets usually on or adjacent to the best floodplain agricultural soils. The habitat of these Mississippian farmers, like the Late Woodland population before them, was the environmentally rich meander-belt zone of the Warrior River. Here the Mississippian population had access to a variety of wild plants, animals, and backwater species of fish in addition to easily tilled alluvial soils (Bozeman 1982:304).

Each of the four Moundville I centers had a platform mound. Moundville may have had more than one, but at least during early Moundville I only one mound was definitely present (Steponaitis 1983a:152–156).[7] Though test excavations at the other three sites were inconclusive (Moore 1905:127, 243–244; Bozeman 1982:142–149, 173–174), at 1Tu56 the mound was built in multiple stages, with at least one structure atop each stage (Bozeman 1982:59–68). Unfortunately, the test excavation revealed nothing about these structures except that one had an internal, prepared clay hearth. Testing at two sites further revealed that shell-tempered ceramics were present in the submound soil. We do not know whether special purpose 'public' buildings preceded mound construction like we do at Lubbub. Nevertheless, it is clear that the shift to agriculture, village dispersal, and the change to shell-tempered ceramics all preceded the beginning of mound construction.

Mortuary data indicative of the degree of ranking are available only from Moundville. Because the majority of all Moundville burials were unaccompanied, their assignment to phases can be difficult. Based on grave goods where present, and otherwise on the location at the site, Peebles (1986:27) estimated that "approximately one percent of the population, all of whom are adults, were interred in places and with items that marked them as having superordinate status." The items indicative of superordinate status include a few imported vessels and a very few items of imported shell, greenstone, and copper.[8]

The Moundville I phase seems to be a set of simple chiefdoms. Each polity consisted of a dispersed set of farmsteads and hamlets. Sometime, apparently shortly after this settlement pattern was established, each polity began construction and use of a platform mound that served as the focus of the political and ceremonial life of the community. At this point, none of the four mound centers appears in any way distinct from the others, though Moundville may well have been "first among equals." Hierarchical social ranking was present, and was marked by access to nonlocal sociotechnic items. Ranking was not strongly developed, however, and because no subadults received superordinate mortuary distinction, high rank may not have been strongly ascriptive.

Though not strictly germane to the topic of Mississippian emergence, the subsequent trajectory of the Moundville culture is of considerable interest. By the end of the Moundville I phase Moundville was qualitatively different from the other mound sites. The large central plaza may already have been laid out (see Steponaitis 1983a, fig. 32), whether or not additional mounds had been constructed. Greenstone, mica, copper, and imported vessels were present in quantities far exceeding those of the other sites, and residences were spread over several hectares. Based on the absolute dates from M. Scarry's excavations (Scarry 1981b), Moundville had passed from "first among equals" to primate status by A.D. 1150 or 1200. For the next 300 years the Moundville site was the center of a complex chiefdom. Population at the center grew to around 3,000 (Peebles and Kus 1977:436), with the elite expanding to 5 percent of the Moundville population (Peebles 1986:28). An additional several thousand people resided in farmsteads dispersed around single-mound sites on the Black Warrior floodplain within 20 km of Moundville. Though mostly distributed north of Moundville in the Moundville I phase, southward expansion of the population progressively rationalized the settlement pattern, producing by early Moundville III the optimal distribution hypothesized by Steponaitis (1978; Bozeman 1982:291–300). At about the same time, a fortification wall was built around the Moundville site (Peebles 1986:29). In mid-Moundville III, however, the complex chiefdom began to disintegrate. The abundance of nonlocal items and raw materials

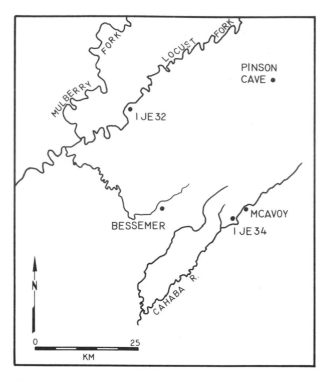

Fig. 76. Locations of Bessemer area sites mentioned in text.

declined, Moundville declined in importance relative to the single-mound sites, and by A.D. 1540 the large, central, multimound site was virtually abandoned (Steponaitis 1983a:160; Peebles 1986; Welch 1983, 1986).

MISSISSIPPIAN EMERGENCE IN THE BESSEMER AREA

History of Research

Much less is known about the Mississippian emergence in this area than in the central Tombigbee or Moundville areas. It is included here because of the prominence of the Bessemer site in previous discussions of the Late Woodland-Mississippian interface in Alabama (e.g., DeJarnette 1952:280; Jenkins 1978; Peebles 1978; Walthall 1980:196–211; Schnell et al. 1981:242; Steponaitis 1983a:165–167). A history of investigations at Bessemer through 1941 is provided in DeJarnette and Wimberly's site report (1941). Other research in the area (Fig. 76) includes excavation at West Jefferson phase sites (Jenkins and Nielsen 1974), along with a reanalysis of that material (O'Hear 1975). Survey and test excavations along the upper reaches of the Cahaba River provide additional information (Ensor 1979; Shaffield 1975, 1977), as do excavations at Pinson Cave (Oakley 1971; Bunn 1972) and 1Je37 (Brooms 1980). Recent reanalysis of the Bessemer collection (Walthall and Wimberly 1978; Welch 1981a) provides further chronological information.

Chronology

The Late Woodland period in the Bessemer area is represented by the West Jefferson phase. Just as in the Moundville area, there is scant evidence of earlier Late Woodland occupation. Ten radiocarbon dates (Jenkins and Nielsen 1974:155–158; Ensor 1979:8) fix the West Jefferson phase in this area from A.D. 875 to 1050. Ceramics were predominantly grog-tempered plain, but a significant proportion of feature fills also contained a very few sherds with shell tempering. O'Hear (1975:24–30) calculated weighted averages of the radiocarbon dates from features with shell-tempered sherds and those without such sherds, and showed the average date for the grog-only features was significantly earlier than for the features with mixed ceramics ($t = 1.64$, $p = .05$; inclusion of the radiocarbon date from Ensor [1979:8] lowers the t value just below the 5 percent significance level [procedures from Long and Rippeteau 1974]). O'Hear (1975:30) concluded that "the shell tempered wares are late elements in West Jefferson phase assemblages otherwise dominated by clay tempered ceramics."

The West Jefferson phase was succeeded by a Mississippian occupation referred to as the Bessemer phase (Jenkins 1978; Walthall 1980:196–211) or as Moundville I at Bessemer (Steponaitis 1983a:165–167). As used by Walthall and Jenkins, all the material excavated at Bessemer is, ipso facto, Bessemer phase material. Hence, for them the Bessemer phase had roughly equal proportions of grog-tempered and shell-tempered ceramics (see sherd counts in DeJarnette and Wimberly 1941:80). They do postulate a gradual replacement of grog tempering by shell tempering, in line with O'Hear's analysis. In contrast, I have argued (Welch 1981a) that the bulk of the grog-tempered sherds at Bessemer come from a West Jefferson phase component that preceded such Mississippian traits as wall-trench architecture, mound construction, superor-

dinate burial status, and wholesale adoption of shell-tempered ceramics. As used in this paper, the Bessemer phase has these latter characteristics. A radiocarbon date of A.D. 1070 ± 55 (Walthall and Wimberly 1978: 118–120) from a relatively secure Bessemer phase context suggests a beginning date for the phase around A.D. 1050. The Bessemer site and, as far as we know, the entire area, was abandoned by A.D. 1250 because no artifacts diagnostic to post-Moundville I times have been found.

West Jefferson Culture in the Bessemer Area

Contract archaeology has provided most of the data on the West Jefferson phase in this area. At six sites, large tracts of plow zone/topsoil have been stripped off to reveal feature patterns. Of these six, 1Je37 (Brooms 1980) produced no features, while at Bessemer none of the excavated features was diagnostic of the West Jefferson phase. The remaining four sites, therefore, provide most of the available data on subsistence, settlement pattern, and social organization.

Each of the four sites with excavated features was a locus for seasonal encampment of a small social group. Two of the sites were well under .2 ha in area, with few features and sparse artifacts. The other two sites were relatively large (approximately .4 ha), but artifacts and features were sparse. O'Hear's outstanding reanalysis (1975) of one of these large sites showed it to contain two seasonally and spatially discrete components, and the larger of the two components contained two chronologically distinct occupations. None of these three (at least) separate occupations covered more than .1 ha. Post molds were relatively abundant but only one possible structure pattern was discerned. This was a vaguely circular alignment roughly 3 m in diameter (O'Hear 1975:118–119), with no clear feature associations. This is similar to the only other known West Jefferson phase structure in this area, a 4.5 by 5 m oval, single-post structure at 1Je34 (Ensor 1979). Though the scarcity of archaeological survey and the extent of modern urbanization make the issue difficult to resolve, Late Woodland population density in the Bessemer area seems to have been considerably lower than in the central Tombigbee or Moundville areas.

Information on subsistence strategy and site seasonality comes almost solely from botanical remains, as preservation of faunal remains was extremely poor at the excavated sites. Botanical remains from refuse-filled pits were dominated by hickory nutshell, 69–93 percent by weight, with 4–18 percent acorn shell, and usually 2–6 percent maize fragments (Scarry 1981a, table 1). Though maize appears to be a minor component of the diet, it is noteworthy that maize remains are more abundant in these features than in contemporary Late Woodland contexts in the Moundville or central Tombigbee areas. This may indicate that cultigens played a greater role in this hilly area than in the food-rich floodplains (Scarry 1986). Small numbers of a wide variety of nondomesticated seeds were also present. Except for one pit fill in which 26 percent of subsistence remains were maize fragments, these data indicate wild foods predominated in the vegetal diet, with maize commonly present but usually in small amounts. Though both early and late maturing species were represented, no seasonal patterning has been noted among the plant remains. O'Hear (1975), however, noted that mussel shell and nutshell never co-occurred in the fills of cylindrical pits at 1Je32. He plausibly suggested this distribution stemmed from seasonal dietary differences. These scant data are consistent with a strategy of seasonal mobility and resource scheduling such as sketched above for the Late Woodland phases in the Gainesville Reservoir and Moundville areas. Nevertheless, the accuracy of this model for the West Jefferson phase in the Bessemer area remains conjectural.

Reconstruction of the character of this society's social organization is similarly tenuous. Aside from the apparently small community size and seasonal mobility of residence, two lines of evidence warrant attention. First, one West Jefferson phase cemetery[9] has been partially excavated. Its unusual nature in comparison with other Late Woodland mortuary programs in the Southeast provokes interpretive caution. Pinson Cave (Oakley 1971), a limestone dissolution chamber, was the repository for an estimated 90 individuals. Fully or partially articulated cadavers were dropped down a vertical shaft into the cave. Excavation of roughly half the cave deposit yielded remains of a minimum of 46 individuals. Both sexes and all age groups were represented. Post-burial disarticulation and downslope movement of the remains prevented identification of individual burials and their associations, but there were few artifacts in the deposit. Utilitarian items included 50 projectile points and a few other chipped stone

tools, 10 pecked or ground stone tools, and a variety of bone pins, awls, and antler flakers all present in very low numbers. Eighty-five shell beads and pendants were the only nonutilitarian items present, aside from one canine tooth pendant and a small greenstone object of unknown function. All but one of the shell items were made of marine shell. This assemblage of artifacts is similar in nature to the artifacts in Cofferdam-Gainesville burials in the Gainesville Reservoir, though the overall quantity of items is lower here. The number of projectile point wounds (n = 7) is also roughly comparable to the incidence in the Cofferdam-Gainesville burials. To the extent that comparison with the Cofferdam-Gainesville phase mortuary program is meaningful, and assuming the Pinson Cave remains represent normal West Jefferson phase mortuary practice, the West Jefferson phase in the Bessemer area was similar to the Cofferdam-Gainesville phase in terms of the nature and abundance of exotic goods, absence of a superordinate mortuary dimension, and incidence of violent conflict.

The second line of evidence concerning West Jefferson social organization is the abundance of stone discoidals, frequently called 'chunkey stones,' at occupation sites. Compared with the Cofferdam-Gainesville phase sites or with West Jefferson phase sites in the Moundville area, West Jefferson sites in the Bessemer area had an unusually large number of these small (usually < 10 cm diameter), ground stone discoidals. Flat, plano-concave, and biconcave forms were present. Arguing for the contemporaneity of ethnically distinct Late Woodland and Mississippian populations, Jenkins (1978:22; Seckinger and Jenkins 1982) has suggested West Jefferson inhabitants of the Bessemer area manufactured discoidals for exchange with Mississippian groups, specifically the Bessemer site community. Jenkins suggested such exchange as a plausible medium through which the Late Woodland population acculturated to Mississippian norms. Most of the discoidals in the area were certainly locally made —they were mostly made of local raw materials and the unfinished examples formed 75 percent of the total recovered sample (n = 72 [Jenkins and Nielsen 1974:30, 77, 131; Ensor 1979:12]). Jenkins's proposition does not seem consistent, however, with the low number (n = 3) of discoidals found at the Bessemer site (DeJarnette and Wimberly 1941:76). Whatever discoidals were used for, it seems they were used locally by the West Jefferson phase population.

Based on the available information, in the Bessemer area the West Jefferson phase had a foraging/gardening economy with small, seasonally shifting social groups. There is no evidence for marked differences in social rank. Exchange relationships beyond the local area introduced a small number and variety of items made from exotic materials, neither more than nor different in nature from those available to contemporary populations elsewhere in west-central Alabama. Like those neighbors, a small but significant percentage of the population was exposed to, and died of, violent conflict. The scant available data do not reveal any trends through the phase, other than the first appearance of shell-tempered pottery late in the phase.

Bessemer Phase Culture

Beginning near A.D. 1050 the Bessemer area rapidly acquired a population culturally Mississippian in such respects as mound-plaza community layout, rectangular wall-trench architecture, shell-tempered pottery, and some degree of social rank differential. Unfortunately, aside from the absence of Late Woodland-like storage pits, we have no information at all on the subsistence base for this phase. Because nearly all the available data for the phase come from late 1930s excavations at one site, and that excavation focused on what was probably the high status precinct of the site, there are a number of such gaps in our understanding of this phase.

So little archaeological survey and excavation has been done in the Bessemer area, and so much of the area is now urbanized, that we know only one sizeable Bessemer phase site. This is the Bessemer site itself, which had three mounds and a village area probably of several hectares. From the surveys of Shaffield (1975, 1977) we know that some of the population resided outside the Bessemer site. For example, at the McAvoy I site a burial containing perhaps four individuals included a large fragment of a diagnostically Bessemer phase vessel (Shaffield 1977). Though no architectural remains were found, the site had a light scatter of Bessemer phase domestic debris. Combined with the sparse Bessemer phase debris at other sites, this suggests the presence of scattered farmsteads.

Stratigraphic information from the Bessemer site re-

veals that its final layout emerged gradually. There was a West Jefferson phase occupation of unknown extent at the north end of the site. After the adoption of shell-tempered ceramics and rectangular, wall-trench architecture, the village assumed an arcuate shape around a plaza. At this time there may have been ceremonial structures in the plaza—a rock platform and a structure with an adjacent fenced courtyard—but the inner edge of the arc had at least two buildings of 'public' character. One measured 16.5 by 10.7 m, the other 11.9 by 9.2 m. Neither had any preserved internal features except a few random post molds. Unlike the 'public' buildings at Lubbub, these two large structures do not appear to be modifications of previous domestic dwellings; rather, they were communal structures from the outset. Several smaller, possibly domestic structures were built after destruction of these public buildings, and they align with another public building (18.6 by 11.9 m). Immediately beside, and apparently after demolition of this latter building, a rectangular platform mound was constructed on the same alignment. At least one large building (10.1 by 8.5 m) topped this mound. The mound underwent five subsequent fill episodes, each of which was topped by one or more large structures. Significantly, there was evidence of considerable erosion between a few of the fill episodes.

The chronological relationship between this construction series and the construction of the other two mounds is not definite. The so-called ceremonial mound, of wholly unknown function (see details in DeJarnette and Wimberly 1941), may slightly postdate the beginning of the platform mound. The burial mound and its enclosing screen more probably postdate the initial platform mound. In any case, the plaza and the 'public' buildings fronting it predate any of the mounds. The mound construction preserved the plaza outline, with 'public' buildings, now located atop the mound(s), continuing to front on the plaza.

Given the size of the site and its structures, the 22 individuals in the burial mound cannot have represented the entire community. With the exception of one burial in the ceremonial mound, no other burials definitely of Bessemer phase date were encountered. Thus we have no local comparisons for the mound burials. The mound burials themselves were mostly extended inhumations. Fifteen burials contained the 22 individuals, mostly poorly preserved. The site report (DeJarnette and Wimberly 1941:63–70) does not specify how or by whom age and sex determinations were made. To the extent the reported assessments were accurate, the adult sex ratio was even, and four children were present. Three of the children, however, were interred with a single adult female. Fifty percent of the individuals were described as either 'young adult' or 'adolescent.' This high percentage of youthful individuals suggests burial in the mound was not restricted to individuals of achieved high status. Indeed, two of the three individuals buried with articles of (probably) nonlocal origin were young adults. One of these two had a small, embossed copper plate over the mouth. The other, an isolated skull, had two pots, possibly of nonlocal manufacture. The only other nonlocal goods were 38 shell beads included with an adult female, along with one pot, a limestone discoidal, and two bundled adult males. The only other grave goods in the cemetery were locally produced ceramic vessels, from one to four per burial. Nine of the fifteen graves had no accompaniments. Altogether, the mound burials do not evince strong rank differentials, either in terms of restricted access to exotic goods or complexity of mortuary treatment. Nevertheless, their placement in a communally constructed, restricted access cemetery located at the margin of the plaza marks these burials as a class symbolically distinct from, and likely superordinate to, the rest of the community.

In all, the Bessemer phase appears to have been a society with moderate rank differential. The overall settlement pattern is not known, but the Bessemer site clearly served as the ceremonial and/or political center throughout the phase's 200-year duration. Evidence of erosion between mound construction episodes indicates the site or the platform mound may have been disused at times. This in turn suggests that however the site served as a focus for social integration, the strength of this function(s) varied through time. The data are consistent with a model in which ascriptive hierarchical status distinctions are superimposed by relatively strong idiosyncratic differences in the ability to manipulate and exercise these distinctions.

CONCLUSION

The most detailed interpretation of Mississippian emergence in west-central Alabama is that formulated by Ned Jenkins. In essence, he argues that Mississippian communities, most likely derived from northeast Alabama, moved into the region and settled at Bessemer, Moundville, Lubbub, and perhaps elsewhere. These communities coexisted with surrounding Late Woodland communities for an extended period, 200 years or more. Some of the Late Woodland groups interacted with the Mississippian communities in such a way that they gradually acquired the intrusive material culture, subsistence practices, and other cultural norms. In unpublished discussions Jenkins has further stated that the intrusive Mississippian culture need not have been brought by entire communities, but could have been carried by a relatively small number of elite individuals brought into 'progressive' Late Woodland communities (see Southall 1956 for an ethnographic parallel). The size of the intrusive groups is not important. Rather, the lengthy acculturation of the indigenous population to a new, foreign culture is the chief feature of his interpretation.

The interpretation advanced in this paper is that the transition from Late Woodland to Mississippian culture was rapid and more or less uniform within each of the three areas, though not synchronous between areas (A.D. 1000 in the Moundville area, A.D. 1050 in the Bessemer area, and A.D. 1050–1100 along the central Tombigbee). Obviously this interpretation hinges on the accuracy of the chronological frameworks presented above. An accurate chronology, however, is not an explanation of culture change.

The emergence of Mississippian culture in west-central Alabama actually involved change in two distinct cultural subsystems, i.e., subsistence and social integration. The abrupt switch from foraging/gardening to field agriculture entailed changes in the seasonal mobility of the population, the character of storage facilities and residential architecture, and even the size and shape of cooking vessels (though not their decoration). The other aspect of Mississippian emergence was the development of hierarchical social organization. Such hierarchy is manifest in, and reproduced by, dimensional differences in mortuary treatment, control of extralocal exchange, and control of communal labor. Not only are the changes in subsistence and social organization separable at the theoretical level, they were neither synchronous nor did they occur in the same order in the three areas considered here.

A review of the data presented above reveals the differing relationship of subsistence and social organizational changes. In the Moundville area the shift to a dispersed, presumably agricultural settlement pattern and Mississippian material culture preceded the initiation of mound building at ca. A.D. 1000. Though mounds per se do not indicate hierarchical social organization, in the Moundville area the mounds are the earliest indicators of a form of social integration distinct from the Late Woodland form. In the Bessemer area the changing organization of the Bessemer site shows that hierarchical social organization developed after the settlement pattern, architecture, and storage technology indicate an agricultural subsistence base at ca. A.D. 1050. In the central Tombigbee, however, the subsistence and social organizational changes occurred a little later, A.D. 1050–1100, but unlike the other two areas the adoption of agriculture seems to have come after a form of social ranking had emerged. My explanation of the emergence of Mississippian culture in the three areas accounts for these chronological relationships by distinguishing between several causes and mechanisms of change.

The subsistence change, I argue, was a rational response to subsistence stress. In the central Tombigbee area the subsistence remains and health status of the Cofferdam-Gainesville population unequivocally indicate the foraging/gardening strategy had reached its productive limits. Even without further population increase the mortality rate would have made desirable an alternative subsistence strategy that produced higher yields. In the Moundville area the Late Woodland population density was comparable to that along the central Tombigbee, and was faced with a smaller, less productive floodplain. In this situation it is expectable that the subsistence transition occurred earlier in the Moundville area than along the Tombigbee. Mortuary remains of the West Jefferson phase in the Moundville area, when found, should show the same pattern of health status as the Cofferdam-Gainesville phase. The Bessemer area is the least productive of the three for a foraging strategy, but the Late Woodland population apparently was not as dense as in the floodplain areas. Subsistence change in this area could have been caused by subsistence stress, in which case the Pinson Cave mortuary remains should also indicate poor health status. Alternatively, warfare could have mandated population nucleation and an increased demand for stored food. This proposition could be tested, for instance, by further excavation at Bessemer. Ongoing research by Margaret Scarry on botanical remains from Late Wood-

land and Early Mississippian contexts in the Moundville and Bessemer areas will also help evaluate these propositions.

The causes of the emergence of ranked societies in west-central Alabama are less certain. Though this article is primarily descriptive rather than explanatory, certain relationships sketched here provide a framework for research on the causes of chiefdom formation. Following Flannery (1972), I distinguish between the process of chiefdom development and the mechanisms by which this development may occur. The central figures in simple chiefdoms have both a special relationship to the supernatural, which confers on them a sanctified authority, as well as a set of political and economic roles in which their decisions and actions are bolstered by this authority. There are abundant ethnographic examples of societies with either one or the other aspect of chiefly office. On one hand, numerous tribal cultures have religious roles with considerable authority, though this authority does not extend to political and economic decision-making. On the other hand, the political and economic activities of classic "big men" differ little from those of chiefs, though the scope of action of "big men" is constrained by their lack of real authority. From an analytical viewpoint, then, we can conceive of simple chiefdoms developing by two contrasting mechanisms. The chiefly office may arise by an extant sanctified role acquiring political and economic functions. Alternatively, a central political and economic role may acquire sanctified authority. Other mechanisms of chiefdom formation may exist, but at present I consider only these two and their contrasting archaeological correlates.

In west-central Alabama there seems to have been an example of each mechanism. At Bessemer, large, centrally located public buildings preceded indications of superordinate rank. The sodality organization indicated by these buildings apparently persisted, presumably with some modification, through the emergence of hierarchical political and economic control. This is consistent with the promotion of a sanctified role or an office in the sodality system to a politically and economically dominant position. In contrast, at Lubbub a common domestic compound was converted by stages to a public structure, subsequently erected on a mound, but strong indications of superordinate rank did not appear. This is consistent with a political and economic role acquiring a modest degree of sanctification. In the Moundville area, unfortunately, data are yet too incomplete to indicate which mechanism operated.

It can also be postulated that the contrasting mechanisms would operate in response to contrasting stimuli. Rappaport (1979) showed that there is a relationship between the level of a cosmological statement and the rate at which the statement may change: the higher or more central the cosmological import, the lower the variation through time. Taking a chief's central religious and ritual role to be encoded at a higher cosmological level than are the economic and political roles (see Rappaport 1979:14–23, 223–246), the sanctification mechanism should operate slowly. Sanctification of a political and economic role should occur only after protracted stress during which that role was vital to the society's reproduction. The long duration of subsistence stress in the Late Woodland along the Tombigbee, the progressive increase in the volume and geographical scope of extralocal exchange, and the gradual conversion of a domestic dwelling to a public building, are consistent with the sanctification mechanism. In contrast, the addition of political and economic dimensions to a sanctified office should occur when exogenous political stresses exceed the coping capacity of the sodality system. Such a situation is likely to have existed in the Bessemer area ca. A.D. 1050, when the society rather suddenly found itself interacting with chiefdom societies to its south (Moundville I phase) and north (Langston phase, cf. Walthall 1980:200–205). Extant political institutions may have been incapable of adjusting to interaction with hierarchically organized societies, as has been argued for a similar situation in central Europe (Frankenstein and Rowlands 1978). In the Moundville area the causes and mechanisms of the development of hierarchical social organization remain unclear, and should be among the principal foci of future research.

A final note of caution is appropriate. Much of the cultural description in this paper is predicated on uncertain chronological relationships. We employ ceramics as the principal measure of chronology, and the absolute chronology of the ceramics is provided by radiocarbon dates whose relation to the ceramics often is not clear. Much of the current debate over Late Woodland-Mississippian chronology in this region might well be obviated if the ceramics themselves were to be dated by thermoluminescence techniques. Meanwhile, the debate has served the very useful purpose of exposing the extent to which all of us have imposed our preconceptions on the archaeological record. As a result, the rigor with which interpretations have been tied to data has improved greatly, as study of the sources cited herein amply proves.

ACKNOWLEDGMENTS

This paper has been improved by the thoughtful comments of J. Blitz, N. Jenkins, C. B. Mann, C. S. Peebles, T. R. Rocek, M. Scarry, C. M. Sinopoli, V. Steponaitis, and H. T. Wright. Unpublished data have been provided most generously by T. Bozeman and M. Scarry. My most heartfelt thanks go to Christopher Peebles and Ned Jenkins, who have responded graciously and constructively to my mauling of their data and ideas. The faults of the paper are, of course, uniquely mine.

NOTES

1. All dates in this paper are in uncorrected radiocarbon years.
2. The Catfish Bend phase data in Table 25 include the Catfish Bend South burial cluster (Cole et al. 1982:206, table 6). All 11 burials in this cluster lacked grave goods, so their phase attribution was not certain. Their exclusion from Table 25 would not alter the direction of the observed trends in health status. Without the South burial cluster, Catfish Bend health status data are: nutritional stress, 26 percent; degenerative pathologies, 24 percent; systemic infection, 35 percent; evidence of violence, 15 percent; proportion dying before age 20, 38 percent.
3. These data are percentages of all bone and thus are not comparable with the percentages of identified bone as listed in Table 23. Recalculating Scott's (1983, appendixes 1, 2) data in an approximation of the procedures used by Woodrick (1981:103), the contribution of deer to identified bone at Lubbub was 48 percent in Cofferdam-Gainesville contexts and 79 percent in Summerville I contexts. Though the value for Cofferdam-Gainesville phase is low compared to Woodrick's data, these adjusted data do show an increased consumption of deer in the Summerville I phase.
4. In different portions of this chapter, different sets of Summerville I burials are used. The health status figures for the Summerville I population used in this paper were those presented by Cole et al. (1982), based in turn on the burial phase attributions of Jenkins and Ensor (1981, table 9). Powell (1983) presented data about additional Summerville I burials from outside the formal cemetery, but I have not included these data because they were neither coded nor presented in the same categories as used by Cole et al. (1982). Their inclusion would not change the conclusions drawn about the Summerville I health status, since Cole et al. state that these

village burials were healthier than the cemetery burials. For my discussion of the Summerville I mortuary program I rely on the cemetery burials, but not exactly the same list of burials as used by Cole et al. Most of the burials with diagnostic Summerville I grave goods occurred in a cemetery with three or four rows of parallel, usually extended inhumations. Not all the Summerville I burials used by Cole et al. were in this cemetery, nor were all the burials in the cemetery considered by them to be of Summerville I date. None of the burials in the formal cemetery had grave goods diagnostic of any other period, though two were in a typically Cofferdam-Gainesville burial position. Except for these two possible Late Woodland burials, I have departed from Jenkins and Ensor (1981) and Cole et al. (1982) and include all the cemetery burials but none of the burials outside the pattern of serried rows. The burials included are: 4, 5, 11, 15–19, 20a–d, 24–27, 28a–b, 29–31, 34, 36.

5. Surface collections from Late Woodland sites between Moundville and the Black Warrior-Tombigbee confluence progressively depart from West Jefferson ceramic type frequencies in the direction of Miller III type frequencies (Sheldon et al. 1980; Bozeman 1982; Welch, unpublished field notes). Without excavation data, however, it is not possible to determine whether this pattern resulted from synchronic variation in ceramic production or a progressive spread of occupation up the Black Warrior River combined with diachronic change in ceramic production.

6. Numerous post molds from recent fences and farm sheds confound this excavation. The rectangular shape of the structure may be due to modern post alignments rather than prehistoric ones. Indeed, there are so many post molds it is as easy to fit a circle over some as a square over others. Nevertheless, the cluster of post molds has a roughly rectangular outline overall.

7. The fact that Moore (1905, 1907) normally excavated little deeper than 1 m (4 ft) from the top of the mounds may bias Steponaitis's (1983:152–161) account of the development of the Moundville site. Had Moore excavated deeper, it is possible that the plaza outline could be shown to develop during Moundville I rather than during Moundville II (Steponaitis, personal communication). In any case, by late Moundville I, Moundville was already qualitatively different from the other Moundville I mound sites.

8. Specific quantities of these items are not given here because in most cases the burial's precise chronological position is somewhat ambiguous. One greenstone spud and two nonlocal vessels were included among burials listed by Steponaitis (1983a, table 35) as no later than Moundville I. A few copper and shell items were included with burials that date to Moundville I or early Moundville II. Based on their location at the site, Peebles (1984, personal communication) feels a few of these burials are most likely of Moundville I date.

9. The assignment of this cemetery to the West Jefferson phase is tenuous. Three potsherds, most likely of Late Woodland date (Oakley 1971:54, 88), plus an A.D. 1040 ± 80 radiocarbon date on bone (Oakley, personal communication) are the basis for this assignment. All other artifacts with the burials are types found in both Late Woodland and Mississippian contexts. The only evidence against a Late Woodland assignment is the remarkably high caries rate: 57 percent of all teeth

(n = 999) had caries (Bunn 1972:57). Not only is this a high rate for Late Woodland populations in the region, it is even high for the generally more caries-prone Mississippian populations (Powell 1983, tables 5, 6).

REFERENCES CITED

Alexander, Lawrence S.
1982   *Phase I Archaeological Reconnaissance of the Oliver Lock and Dam Project Area, Tuscaloosa, Alabama.* University of Alabama Office of Archaeological Research Report of Investigations No. 33.

Atkinson, James R.
1978   A Cultural Resources Survey of Selected Construction Areas in the Tennessee-Tombigbee Waterway: Alabama and Mississippi, vol. 1. Report submitted to U.S. Army Corps of Engineers, Mobile District.

Atkinson, James R., John C. Phillips, and Richard Walling
1980   *The Kellogg Village Site Investigations, Clay County, Mississippi.* Report submitted to U.S. Army Corps of Engineers, Mobile District.

Bartram, William
1955   *Travels of William Bartram.* Dover, New York.

Bense, Judith A.
1982   *Archaeological Testing Excavations at 58 Sites in the River and Canal Sections of the Tennessee-Tombigbee Waterway.* University of Alabama Office of Archaeological Research Report of Investigations No. 18.

Blakeman, Crawford H., Jr.
1975a   *Archaeological Investigations in the Upper Central Tombigbee Valley: 1974 Season.* Report submitted to U.S. Department of Interior, National Park Service.
1975b   *A Cultural Resources Survey of the Aberdeen Lock and Dam and Canal Section Areas of the Tennessee-Tombigbee Waterway: 1975.* Report submitted to U.S. Department of Interior, National Park Service.

Blakeman, Crawford H., Jr., James R. Atkinson, and G. Gerald Berry
1976   *Archaeological Excavations at the Cofferdam Site, 20Lo599, Lowndes County, Mississippi.* Report submitted to U.S. Army Corps of Engineers, Mobile District.

Blitz, John H.
1983a   The Summerville Mound. In *Excavations in the Lubbub Creek Archaeological Locality,* edited by C. S. Peebles, pp. 128–139, vol. 1, Prehistoric Agricultural Communities in West Central Alabama. Report submitted to the U.S. Army Corps of Engineers, Mobile District.
1983b   The Summerville I Community. In *Excavations in the Lubbub Creek Archaeological Locality,* edited by C. S. Peebles, pp. 253–277, vol. 1, Prehistoric Agricultural Communities in West Central Alabama. Report submitted to the U.S. Army Corps of Engineers, Mobile District.

Bohannon, Charles F.
1972   *Excavations at the Pharr Mounds, Prentiss and Itawamba Counties, Mississippi, and Excavations at the Bear Creek Site, Tishomingo County, Mississippi.* Report submitted to the U.S. Department of Interior, National Park Service.

Bozeman, Tandy K.
1982 *Moundville Phase Communities in the Black Warrior River Valley, Alabama.* Unpublished Ph.D. dissertation, Department of Anthropology, University of California, Santa Barbara.

Brooms, B. MacDonald
1980 Investigations at 1Je37: A West Jefferson Phase Site in Jefferson County, Alabama. *Journal of Alabama Archaeology* 26:87–98.

Bunn, Ralph H., Jr.
1972 *An Analysis of the Dental Material from Pinson Cave(1Je20).* Unpublished M.A. thesis, Department of Anthropology, University of Alabama.

Caddell, Gloria M.
1981 Plant Resources, Archaeological Plant Remains, and Prehistoric Plant-Use Patterns in the Central Tombigbee River Valley. In *Archaeological Investigations in the Gainesville Lake Area of the Tennessee-Tombigbee Waterway,* vol. 4, pp. 1–90. University of Alabama, Office of Archaeological Research Report of Investigations No. 14.
1983 Floral Remains from the Lubbub Creek Archaeological Locality. In *Studies of Material Remains from the Lubbub Creek Archaeological Locality,* edited by C. S. Peebles, pp. 194–271, vol. 2, Prehistoric Agricultural Communities in West Central Alabama. Report submitted to the U.S. Army Corps of Engineers, Mobile District.

Caddell, Gloria M., Anne Woodrick, and Mary C. Hill
1981 Biocultural Studies in the Gainesville Lake Area, vol.4, In *Archaeological Investigations in the Gainesville Lake Area of the Tennessee-Tombigbee Waterway.* University of Alabama Office of Archaeological Research Report of Investigations No. 14.

Carneiro, Robert L.
1981 The Chiefdom: Precursor of the State. In *The Transition to Statehood in the New World,* edited by G. D. Jones and R. R. Kautz, pp. 37–79. Cambridge University Press, New York.

Cole, Gloria
1983 Environmental Background. In *Excavations in the Lubbub Creek Archaeological Locality,* edited by C. S. Peebles, pp. 10–63, vol. 1, Prehistoric Agricultural Communities in West Central Alabama. Report submitted to the U.S. Army Corps of Engineers, Mobile District.

Cole, Gloria, and Caroline H. Albright
1983 Summerville I–II Fortifications. In *Excavations in the Lubbub Creek Archaeological Locality,* edited by C. S. Peebles, pp. 140–196, vol. 1, Prehistoric Agricultural Communities in West Central Alabama. Report submitted to the U.S. Army Corps of Engineers, Mobile District.

Cole, Gloria, Mary C. Hill, and H. Blaine Ensor
1982 Bioarchaeological Comparisons of the late Miller III and Summerville I Phases in the Gainesville Lake Area. In *Archaeological Investigations in the Gainesville Lake Area of the Tennessee-Tombigbee Waterway,* vol. 5. University of Alabama Office of Archaeological Research Report of Investigations No. 23.

Cotter, John L., and John M. Corbett
1951 *Archaeology of the Bynum Mounds, Mississippi.* National Park Service, Archaeological Research Series 1. Washington, D.C.

Davis, J. R.
1979 *The White-tailed Deer in Alabama.* Alabama Department of Conservation and Natural Resources, Special Report No. 8.

DeJarnette, David L.
1952 Alabama Archaeology: A Summary. In *Archaeology of Eastern United States,* edited by J. B. Griffin, pp. 272–284. University of Chicago Press.

DeJarnette, David L., and Christopher S. Peebles
1970 The Development of Alabama Archaeology: The Snow's Bend Site. *Journal of Alabama Archaeology* 16:77–119.

DeJarnette, David L., John A. Walthall, and Steve B. Wimberly
1975a Archaeological Investigations in the Buttahatchee River Valley, Lamar County, Alabama. *Journal of Alabama Archaeology* 21:1–37.
1975b Archaeological Investigations in the Buttahatchee River Valley, II: Excavations at Stucks Bluff Rockshelter. *Journal of Alabama Archaeology* 21:99–119.

DeJarnette, David L., and Steve B. Wimberly
1941 *The Bessemer Site: Excavation of Three Mounds and Surrounding Village Areas near Bessemer, Alabama.* Geological Survey of Alabama, Alabama Museum Paper 17.

Ensor, H. Blaine
1979 Archaeological Investigations in the Upper Cahaba River Drainage, North Central Alabama. *Journal of Alabama Archaeology* 25:1–60.
1981 Classification and Synthesis of the Gainesville Lake Area Lithic Materials: Chronology, Technology, and Use. In *Archaeological Investigations in the Gainesville Lake Area of the Tennessee-Tombigbee Waterway,* vol. 3. University of Alabama Office of Archaeological Research Report of Investigations No. 13.

Firth, Raymond
1957 *We, the Tikopia: Kinship in Primitive Polynesia.* Second edition. Beacon Press, Boston.
1965 *Primitive Polynesian Economy.* Norton, New York.

Flannery, Kent V.
1972 The Cultural Evolution of Civilizations. *Annual Review of Ecology and Systematics* 3:399–426.

Ford, James A.
1936 *Analysis of Indian Village Site Collections from Louisiana and Mississippi.* Louisiana Department of Conservation, Anthropological Studies No. 2.

Frankenstein, Susan, and Michael J. Rowlands
1978 The Internal Structure and Regional Context of Early Iron Age Society in Southwestern Germany, 73–112. *University of London Institute of Archaeology Bulletin 15.*

Griffin, James B.
1985 Changing Concepts of the Prehistoric Mississippian Cultures of the Eastern United States. In *Alabama and the Borderlands,* edited by Reid Badger and Lawrence A. Clayton, pp. 40–64. University of Alabama Press, Tuscaloosa.

Harper, Roland M.
1943 *Forests of Alabama.* Geological Survey of Alabama, Monograph 10.

Jenkins, Ned J.
1975 *Archaeological Investigations in the Gainesville Lock and*

Dam Reservoir: 1974. Report submitted to the U.S. Department of Interior, National Park Service.

1978 Terminal Woodland-Mississippian Interaction in Northern Alabama: The West Jefferson Phase. *Southeastern Archaeological Conference Special Publication* 5:21–27.

1981 Gainesville Lake Area Ceramic Description and Chronology. In *Archaeological Investigations in the Gainesville Lake Area of the Tennessee-Tombigbee Waterway,* vol. 2. University of Alabama Office of Archaeological Research Report of Investigations No. 12.

1982 Archaeology of the Gainesville Lake Area: Synthesis. In *Archaeological Investigations in the Gainesville Lake Area of the Tennessee-Tombigbee Waterway,* vol. 5. University of Alabama Office of Archaeological Research Report of Investigations No. 23.

Jenkins, Ned J., Cailup B. Curren, and Mark DeLeon
1975 *Archaeological Site Survey of the Demopolis and Gainesville Lake Navigation Channels and Additional Construction Areas.* Report submitted to the U.S. Army Corps of Engineers, Mobile District.

Jenkins, Ned J., and H. Blaine Ensor
1981 The Gainesville Lake Area Excavations. In *Archaeological Investigations in the Gainesville Lake Area of the Tennessee-Tombigbee Waterway,* vol. 1. University of Alabama Office of Archaeological Research Report of Investigations No. 11.

Jenkins, Ned J., and Jerry J. Nielsen
1974 *Archaeological Salvage Investigations at the West Jefferson Steam Plant Site.* Report submitted to the Alabama Power Co., copy on file at Mound State Monument, Moundville, Alabama.

Jennings, Jesse D.
1944 The Archaeological Survey of the Natchez Trace. *American Antiquity* 4:408–414.

Jones, Alice S., and E. Gibbes Patton
1966 Forest, 'Prairie,' and Soils in the Black Belt of Sumter County, Alabama, in 1832. *Ecology* 47:75–80.

Jones, Walter B., and David L. DeJarnette
n.d. *Moundville Culture and Burial Museum.* Geological Survey of Alabama, Museum Paper 13.

Knight, Vernon L., Jr.
1982 Document and Literature Review. In *Phase I Archaeological Reconnaissance of the Oliver Lock and Dam Project Area, Tuscaloosa, Alabama,* by Lawrence S. Alexander, pp. 27–102. University of Alabama Office of Archaeological Research Report of Investigations No. 33.

Long, Austin, and Bruce Rippeteau
1974 Testing Contemporaneity and Averaging Radiocarbon Dates. *American Antiquity* 39:205–215.

Michals, Lauren
1981 The Exploitation of Fauna During the Moundville I Phase at Moundville. *Southeastern Archaeological Conference Bulletin* 24:91–93.

Mitchell, J. Clyde
1956 *The Yao Village: A Study in the Social Structure of a Nyasaland Tribe.* Manchester University Press.

Moore, Clarence B.
1901 Certain Aboriginal Remains of the Tombigbee River.

Journal of the Academy of Natural Sciences of Philadelphia 11:504–505.

1905 Certain Aboriginal Remains of the Black Warrior River. *Journal of the Academy of Natural Sciences of Philadelphia* 13:124–244.

1907 Moundville Revisited. *Journal of the Academy of Natural Sciences of Philadelphia* 13:334–405.

Nielsen, Jerry J., and Ned J. Jenkins
1973 *Archaeological Investigations in the Gainesville Lock and Dam Reservoir: 1972.* Report submitted to the U.S. Department of Interior, National Park Service.

Nielsen, Jerry J., and Charles Wesley Moorehead
1972 *Archaeological Salvage Investigations Within the Proposed Gainesville Lock and Dam Reservoir, Tennessee-Tombigbee Waterway.* Report submitted to the U.S. Department of Interior, National Park Service.

Nielsen, Jerry J., John W. O'Hear, and Charles W. Moorehead
1973 *An Archaeological Survey of Hale and Greene Counties, Alabama.* Report submitted to the Alabama Historical Commission.

Oakley, Carey B., Jr.
1971 *An Archaeological Investigation of Pinson Cave (1Je20).* Unpublished M.A. thesis, Department of Anthropology, University of Alabama.

O'Hear, John W.
1975 *Site 1Je32: Community Organization in the West Jefferson Phase.* Unpublished M.A. thesis, Department of Anthropology, University of Alabama.

O'Hear, John W., Clark Larsen, Margaret Scarry, John Phillips, and Erica Simons
1981 *Archaeological Salvage Excavations at the Tibbee Creek Site (22Lo600), Lowndes County, Mississippi.* Report submitted to the U.S. Army Corps of Engineers, Mobile District.

Peebles, Christopher S.
1978 Determinants of Settlement Size and Location in the Moundville Phase. In *Mississippian Settlement Patterns,* edited by Bruce Smith, pp. 369–416. Academic Press, New York.

1979 *Excavations at Moundville, 1905–1951.* University Microfilms International, Ann Arbor.

1981 Archaeological Research at Moundville: 1840–1980. *Southeastern Archaeological Conference Bulletin* 24:77–81.

1983 Summary and Conclusions: Continuity and Change in a Small Mississippian Community. In *Excavations in the Lubbub Creek Archaeological Locality,* edited by C. S. Peebles, pp. 393–407, vol. 1, Prehistoric Agricultural Communities in West Central Alabama. Report submitted to the U.S. Army Corps of Engineers, Mobile District.

1986 Paradise Lost, Strayed, and Stolen: Prehistoric Social Devolution in the Southeast. In *The Burden of Being Civilized: An Anthropological Perspective on the Discontents of Civilization,* edited by Miles Richardson and Malcolm Webb, pp. 24–40. Southern Anthropological Society Proceedings No. 20.

Peebles, Christopher S. (editor)
1983a *Excavations in the Lubbub Creek Archaeological Locality,* vol. 1, Prehistoric Agricultural Communities in West Central Alabama. Report submitted to the U.S. Army Corps of Engineers, Mobile District.

1983b *Studies of Material Remains from the Lubbub Creek Archae-*

ological Locality, vol. 2, Prehistoric Agricultural Communities in West Central Alabama. Report submitted to the U.S. Army Corps of Engineers, Mobile District.

1983c *Basic Data and Data Processing in the Lubbub Creek Archaeological Locality*, vol. 3, Prehistoric Agricultural Communities in West Central Alabama. Report submitted to the U.S. Army Corps of Engineers, Mobile District.

Peebles, Christopher S., and Susan M. Kus
1977 Some Archaeological Correlates of Ranked Societies. *American Antiquity* 42:421–448.

Peebles, Christopher S., and Cyril B. Mann, Jr.
1983 Culture and Chronology in the Lubbub Creek Archaeological Locality. In *Excavations in the Lubbub Creek Archaeological Locality*, edited by C. S. Peebles, pp. 64–78, vol. 1, Prehistoric Agricultural Communities in West Central Alabama. Report submitted to the U.S. Army Corps of Engineers, Mobile District.

Peirce, L. B.
1962 *Surface Water in Tuscaloosa County, Alabama*. Geological Survey of Alabama County Report 9.

Powell, Mary Lucas
1983 Biocultural Analysis of Human Skeletal Remains from the Lubbub Creek Archaeological Locality. In *Studies of Material Remains from the Lubbub Creek Archaeological Locality*, edited by C. S. Peebles, pp. 430–477, vol. 2, Prehistoric Agricultural Communities in West Central Alabama. Report submitted to the U.S. Army Corps of Engineers, Mobile District.

1984 Patterned Associations Between Social Rank and Skeletal Pathology at Moundville. Paper presented at the 41st Annual Meeting of the Southeastern Archaeological Conference, Pensacola.

Rappaport, Roy
1979 *Ecology, Meaning, and Ritual*. North Atlantic Books, Richmond, California.

Rucker, Marc D.
1974 *Archaeological Survey and Test Excavations in the Upper-Central Tombigbee River Valley: Aliceville-Columbus Lock and Dam Impoundment Areas, Alabama and Mississippi*. Report submitted to the U.S. Department of Interior, National Park Service.

Sahlins, Marshall D.
1962 *Moala: Culture and Nature on a Fijian Island*. University of Michigan Press, Ann Arbor.

Saxe, Arthur A.
1970 *Social Dimensions of Mortuary Practices*. University Microfilms International, Ann Arbor.

Scarry, Margaret M.
1981a Plant Procurement Strategies in the West Jefferson and Moundville I Phases. *Southeastern Archaeological Conference Bulletin* 24:94–96.

1981b The University of Michigan Moundville Excavations: 1978–1979. *Southeastern Archaeological Conference Bulletin* 24:87–90.

1986 *Change in Plant Procurement and Production During the Emergence of the Moundville Chiefdom*. Ph.D. dissertation, Department of Anthropology, University of Michigan. University Microfilms, Ann Arbor.

Schnell, Frank T., Vernon J. Knight Jr., and Gail S. Schnell
1981 *Cemochechobee: Archaeology of a Mississippian Ceremonial Center on the Chattahoochee River*. University of Florida Press, Gainesville.

Scott, Susan L.
1983 Analysis, Synthesis, and Interpretation of Faunal Remains from the Lubbub Creek Archaeological Locality. In *Studies of Material Remains from the Lubbub Creek Archaeological Locality*, edited by C. S. Peebles, pp. 272–379, vol. 2, Prehistoric Agricultural Communities in West Central Alabama. Report submitted to the U.S. Army Corps of Engineers, Mobile District.

Seckinger, Ernest W., Jr., and Ned J. Jenkins
1982 A Plural Society in Prehistoric Alabama. Revised version of a paper presented at the 37th Annual Meeting of the Southeastern Archaeological Conference, New Orleans.

Shaffield, L. M., Jr.
1975 The Cahaba River Valley: A Survey of Sites Found in Jefferson County, 1973 to 1974. Unpublished manuscript in possession of the author.

1977 1Je49, The McAvoy Site: A Summary of Test Excavations, 1974–1976. Unpublished manuscript in possession of the author.

Sheldon, Craig T., Jr., D. W. Chase, G. Waselkov, T. L. Paglione, and E. S. Sheldon
1982 *Cultural Resources Survey of Demopolis Lake, Alabama: Fee Owned Lands*. Auburn University Archaeological Monograph 6.

Smith, Bruce D.
1978 Variation in Mississippian Settlement Patterns. In *Mississippian Settlement Patterns*, edited by Bruce Smith, pp. 479–503. Academic Press, New York.

Southall, Aidan
1956 *Alur Society: A Study in Process and Types of Domination*. W. Heffer and Sons, Cambridge, England.

Steponaitis, Vincas P.
1978 Location Theory and Complex Chiefdoms: A Mississippian Example. In *Mississippian Settlement Patterns*, edited by Bruce Smith, pp. 417–453. Academic Press, New York.

1983a *Ceramics, Chronology, and Community Patterns: An Archaeological Study at Moundville*. Academic Press, New York.

1983b The Smithsonian Institution's Investigations at Moundville in 1869 and 1882. *Midcontinental Journal of Archaeology* 8:127–160.

Walthall, John A.
1980 *Prehistoric Indians of the Southeast: Archaeology of Alabama and the Middle South*. University of Alabama Press.

Walthall, John A., and Steve B. Wimberly
1978 Mississippian Chronology in the Black Warrior Valley: Radiocarbon Dates from Bessemer and Moundville. *Journal of Alabama Archaeology* 24:118–124.

Welch, Paul D.
1981a Restudy of the Grog and Shell Tempered Ceramics from the Bessemer Site, Central Alabama. Paper presented at the 38th Annual Meeting of the Southeastern Archaeological Conference, Asheville, North Carolina.

1981b The West Jefferson Phase: Terminal Woodland Tribal Society in West Central Alabama. *Southeastern Archaeological Conference Bulletin* 24:81–83.

1983   Research at a Moundville Phase Subsidiary Site. Paper presented at the 40th Annual Meeting of the Southeastern Archaeological Conference, Columbia, South Carolina.

1986   *Models of Chiefdom Economy: Prehistoric Moundville as a Case Study.* Ph.D. dissertation, Department of Anthropology, University of Michigan. University Microfilms, Ann Arbor.

Wimberly, Steve B.

1956   A Review of Moundville Pottery. *Southeastern Archaeological Conference Newsletter* 5(1):17–20.

Woodrick, Anne

1981   An Analysis of the Faunal Remains from the Gainesville Lake Area. In *Archaeological Investigations in the Gainesville Lake Area of the Tennessee-Tombigbee Waterway*, vol. 4, pp. 91–168. Univ. of Alabama Office of Archaeological Research Report of Investigations No. 14.

1983   Molluscan Remains and Shell Artifacts. In *Studies of Material Remains from the Lubbub Creek Archaeological Locality*, edited by C. S. Peebles, pp. 391–429, vol. 2, Prehistoric Agricultural Communities in West Central Alabama. Report submitted to the U.S. Army Corps of Engineers, Mobile District.

Wright, Henry T.

1984   Prestate Political Formations. In *On the Evolution of Complex Societies: Essays in Honor of Harry Hoijer, 1982*, edited by Timothy Earle, pp. 41–78. Undena Publications, Malibu, California.

John F. Scarry Chapter **10**

Mississippian Emergence in the Fort Walton Area

The Evolution of the Cayson and Lake Jackson Phases

INTRODUCTION

Explaining the emergence of social hierarchies and politically complex societies is one of the most intriguing of archaeological problems. The development of chiefdoms, hierarchical societies with one generalized type of political control, is one aspect of this problem. In chiefly societies political control (decision-making) is vested in a specialized subsystem of the society that is itself not internally specialized (Wright 1984:42). Chiefdoms are thus less complex than state societies, although they can be large and complex.

The southeastern United States is a good arena for the study of chiefly societies. The Mississippian chiefdoms of that area evolved without stimulus from state societies. They also survived to historic times, so we have ethnohistorical descriptions of them and their archaeological remains have not been obscured by later states that evolved from them. The Mississippian chiefdoms varied in size, internal complexity, and history, but they shared basic organizational and subsistence procurement strategies (J. B. Griffin 1967, 1985; Peebles and Kus 1977; B. D. Smith 1978). The variation seen in the Mississippian polities was a function of the diversity of the environments they occupied, the cultural bases from which they developed, and the evolutionary paths they followed in their development.

Several independent Mississippian chiefdoms, which shared the general Fort Walton material culture, formed the Fort Walton regional system (Scarry 1981a, 1984a:332–360). Like other Mississippian societies, they varied in size, complexity, and history. And, like other Mississippian societies, they can tell us something about the development and evolution of hierarchical societies.

In this chapter, I discuss the development of two Fort Walton systems, the Cayson phase of the Apalachicola Valley and the Lake Jackson phase of the Tallahassee Hills. The Cayson phase was one of the earliest Fort Walton polities. It marked the initial appearance (in the Fort Walton area) of the basic features of the Mississippian adaptation, cleared-field agriculture and hierarchical decision-making organizations. The Lake Jackson phase emerged somewhat later than (and may have developed from) the Cayson phase. The Lake Jackson phase was one of the largest and most complex of the Fort Walton polities. It marked the development of complex chiefdoms in the Fort Walton area.

In my discussion I try to identify those historical factors that might have triggered or selected for the changes in subsistence and organization we can see in these two developments. I also suggest general processes involved in the developments and try to show why those processes took place, using general models proposed by Gregory Johnson (1978, 1982), Timothy Earle (1980), and Henry Wright (1984). I hasten to add that my models are speculative. They are in accord with the available data, and I am confident of the general developmental sequences outlined, but the data on the origins of the Cayson and Lake Jackson

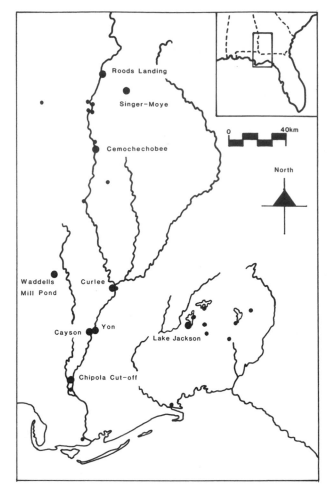

Fig. 77. The Fort Walton area, showing major sites and subareas (large circles, major sites mentioned in text; small circles, other Fort Walton centers) (after Scarry and Payne 1986).

phases are limited, and my conclusions must be viewed with caution.

FORT WALTON MISSISSIPPIAN

The Fort Walton regional system was a group of independent polities whose interactions caused them to share a distinct material culture, as well as the Mississippian organizational and subsistence procurement strategies. The territory occupied by the Fort Walton systems was bounded by the Fall Line, the Aucilla River, and the Chipola River Valley (Fig. 77). North of the Fall Line on the Chattahoochee River, sites with Fort Walton (Rood or Bull Creek phase) assemblages

are rare. The few that do exist are small, and there are no major Rood or Bull Creek phase centers north of the Fall Line (McMichael and Kellar 1960). The Aucilla River was the boundary of the historic Apalachee (descendants of the Lake Jackson phase) and this boundary appears to have had considerable time depth. East of the Aucilla, Fort Walton ceramics are rare and there are no Fort Walton centers. The western boundary is less well marked, but the late prehistoric occupations of the lower Choctawhatchee River valley (the drainage immediately to the west of the Chipola River valley) were Pensacola (Knight 1984), not Fort Walton. Within the Fort Walton area, Mississippian societies occupied the alluvial valleys of the Apalachicola and Chattahoochee rivers (and perhaps the Flint) and the Marianna Lowlands and Tallahassee Hills, two nearby areas with fertile agricultural soils.

The Fort Walton societies shared a ceramic technology that differed from those of Mississippian societies to the north and west; in fact, this is their most distinguishing characteristic. Fort Walton vessels are, by and large, not shell tempered. Fort Walton vessels are morphologically distinct; the collared jars and collared and carinated bowls found in Fort Walton assemblages are not found in neighboring Mississippian assemblages (Knight 1980; Scarry 1984a:127–146; Sears 1967). Fort Walton ceramics are also typologically distinct from those of neighboring Mississippian systems (Scarry 1985), although some Fort Walton types are found in Pensacola contexts (see Fuller and Stowe 1982; Lazarus and Hawkins 1976).

The Fort Walton societies did not form a single united polity. This is clear from the ethnohistoric records (see, inter alia, Smith 1968; Swanton 1922, 1985; Hann 1988); the Apalachee, the Apalachicolas, and the Chatot were politically distinct, although they were all Fort Walton polities. Simulations of Fort Walton political boundaries (Scarry and Payne 1986) suggest there were five to ten independent polities in the Fort Walton area. Differences among assemblages from various portions of the Fort Walton area may also reflect political divisions within the Fort Walton area (Scarry 1985).

The Fort Walton area can be divided into several subareas: the lower Chattahoochee Valley, the Marianna Lowlands, the Apalachicola Bay Coast, the upper Apalachicola Valley, and the Tallahassee Hills (Fig. 77). These areas are marked by differences in the frequencies of specific ceramic design motifs and temper types. They are also marked by the distribution of Fort Walton sites (e.g., there is a definite gap between the Tallahassee Hills and the Apalachicola Valley that does not appear to contain any Fort Walton sites).

The lower Chattahoochee Valley extends from the Fall Line to roughly the Florida-Alabama border. The Fort Walton manifestations of this area belong to the Rood and Bull Creek phases (McMichael and Kellar 1960:213–216; F. Schnell 1981). Early Rood phase assemblages lack the check-stamped ceramics found in the roughly contemporaneous Cayson phase assemblages to the south and contain higher frequencies of Cool Branch Incised, *var. Cemochechobee,* and Lake Jackson Incised, *var. Walter George.* Simulations (Scarry and Payne 1986) suggest that the Rood phase consisted of two or more independent polities, including a complex chiefdom centered on the Rood's Landing and Singer-Moye sites. We cannot, however, discern these units on material culture criteria.

The Marianna Lowlands area includes the upper Chipola River valley and portions of the surrounding Marianna Lowlands. It was occupied by the Waddells Mill Pond phase (Gardner 1966, 1969, 1971; Scarry 1984a:375–379). Assemblages of this phase are marked by high percentages of Lake Jackson Plain, *var. Waddells Mill Pond* (Scarry 1985). In the seventeenth century, the Marianna Lowlands area was occupied by the Chatot, a politically and linguistically independent group (Gardner 1969; Hann 1988). Radiocarbon dates for the distinct Waddells Mill Pond phase ceramic assemblage suggest that this separation from other Fort Walton groups may have had considerable time depth (B. C. Jones, personal communication).

The Apalachicola Bay Coast includes the barrier islands and coastal areas of Apalachicola Bay and portions of the lower Apalachicola River valley. The Fort Walton manifestations of this area are poorly known. Sites occur on the barrier islands, the mainland coast, the levees of the lower Apalachicola, and the interior swamps of the Coastal Lowlands (Braley 1982; Forney 1985; Miller et al. 1981). Several mound centers are located in the area, e.g., the Pierce and Cool Spring sites at the mouth of the Apalachicola (Moore 1902: 216–229; Sears 1962:23–26) and the Jones-Daniel site several kilometers up the Apalachicola River (B. C.

Jones, personal communication). The intriguing Chipola Cut-off site (Moore 1903:445–466; Willey 1949: 254–256; Brose and Percy 1978:100), with its historic burials accompanied by Fort Walton pottery, lies at the northern edge of this area.

The upper Apalachicola Valley extends from the Florida-Alabama border to slightly south of the Cody Scarp. It corresponds to the territories occupied by the Cayson, Sneads, and Yon phases (Scarry 1984a: 408–416). Early Fort Walton assemblages in this area contain Wakulla Check Stamped and Alachua Cob Marked ceramics more frequently found in Late Woodland contexts (see Scarry 1985). They also contain high frequencies of Marsh Island Incised, Lake Jackson Incised (particularly *var. Lake Lafayette*), and Fort Walton Incised, *vars. Cayson* and *Sneads.* The upper Apalachicola Valley area is separated from the lower Chattahoochee Valley area by a gap (from the Curlee site at river mile 102 to the Omussee Creek site at river mile 148) that contains no Fort Walton mound centers, and from the Tallahassee Hills by an area in central Gadsden County, Florida, that contains no Fort Walton sites (although it does contain large tracts of fertile soils) (Payne 1981).

The Tallahassee Hills area includes the land between the Aucilla and Ochlockonee rivers. It corresponds to the area occupied by the Lake Jackson, Velda, and San Luis phases (Scarry 1984a:381–398). It is also the territory of the Apalachee chiefdom visited by Narvaez and de Soto (Hann 1988; Smith 1968; Swanton 1985). Simulations (Scarry and Payne 1986) suggest that the area was occupied by one or two complex chiefdoms centered on the Lake Jackson and Letchworth sites.

PRIOR ARCHAEOLOGICAL RESEARCH

Moore and Brannon: The Early Investigators

During the latter portion of the nineteenth century and the first forty years of the twentieth century, several archaeologists worked in the Fort Walton area. These included such notable figures as John Rogan, Matthew Stirling, and S. T. Walker. Only two of the early investigators, Clarence B. Moore (1902, 1903, 1907, 1918) and Peter A. Brannon (1909), had major impacts on later work, however.

Moore's work in particular had a profound effect on later syntheses of the archaeology of the Fort Walton culture. His demonstration of the association of Fort Walton ceramics and European materials at Marsh Island (1902:274–281) and Chipola Cut-off (1903: 445–466) colored early efforts to construct chronological frameworks for the Fort Walton area. Indeed, I think that the preoccupation of later investigators with these and similar finds from the Pensacola area contributed to the tenacity of the model of Fort Walton as a chronologically late, Mississippian development (Sears 1977).

Willey: Synthesis and Foundation

Gordon Willey's stature as the most significant figure in the development of Fort Walton archaeology has not been challenged since the publication of his *Archeology of the Florida Gulf Coast* (1949). This monumental work is still the reference on the archaeology of the Pensacola, Fort Walton, and Safety Harbor areas.

Willey compiled and synthesized the available data and constructed frameworks that, although modified, have endured to this day. He defined ceramic types, series, and complexes. He arranged those units into a chronological framework. He defined cultural units (e.g., Fort Walton) that corresponded to his ceramic complexes but incorporated many additional traits (see Willey 1949:512–513 for the Fort Walton trait list). Finally, he proposed cultural-historical models to explain the changes he observed in the archaeological record.

Willey argued the Fort Walton societies were Mississippian and assumed they possessed well-developed agricultural economies. He reasoned that the reduction in the ratio of mound centers to habitation sites from the Weeden Island period to the Fort Walton period reflected a trend toward politico-religious cohesion and the emergence of a few autonomous political units. He inferred from the appearance of pyramidal substructure mounds and the virtual disappearance of conical burial mounds that there was a ". . . decline in the importance of the death cult and a concomitant rise in the significance of tribal leaders . . ." (1949:445). These phenomena, the increase in the size of independent polities and the increased significance of leaders, suggested that the powers and functions of the leaders had increased over earlier periods. Given the data base available to Willey and the analytical and theoretical development of the

discipline at that time, these were perceptive and innovative conclusions.

The Post-Willey Era

With the publication of *Archeology of the Florida Gulf Coast,* archaeologists working in the Fort Walton area had an established framework they could use to interpret their data. Most of the researchers following Willey used that framework, and their work was more narrowly focused than his broad synthesis.

Surveys in the Chattahoochee and Apalachicola Valleys (Belovich et al. 1983; Bullen 1950; Hurt 1975; Huscher 1959a, 1959b, 1959c; Kelly 1950; Kohler et al. 1980; White et al. 1981), the Interstate 10 corridor across northern Florida (Fryman 1971), and Leon County, Florida (Bryne 1986; Tesar 1980, 1981) have added to our knowledge of the distribution of Fort Walton and earlier sites and the demographics of Fort Walton polities (e.g., Payne 1981, 1982). Excavations at Fort Walton mound centers have provided data on chronological change in ceramic assemblages (Caldwell 1955; Fairbanks 1955; Griffin 1950; Knight 1979; Kurjack 1975; White 1981, 1982), spatial organization (Brose et al. 1976; Huscher 1964, 1971; Schnell et al. 1981), site development (Schnell et al. 1981), subsistence (Brose et al. 1976; Neuman 1961; Schnell et al. 1981), and the role of Fort Walton polities in the Southern Cult network (Jones 1982; Schnell et al. 1981). Excavations at Fort Walton farmsteads (Alexander 1984; Bierce-Gedris 1981; Brose 1980; Broyles 1962, 1971; Bullen 1958; Jones and Penman 1973; Scarry 1984b, 1984c; Tesar 1980:726–749, 777–794) have provided data on how the majority of the Fort Walton populations lived. Finally, studies of ethnohistoric accounts of the Apalachee and their neighbors have contributed invaluable insights into the operation of Late Fort Walton societies and their eventual demise (e.g., Boyd 1951; Bushnell 1978, 1979; Deagan 1976; Hann 1986a, 1986b, 1988; Jones 1972).

While there have been no recent works comparable in scale to Willey's *Archeology of the Florida Gulf Coast,* there have been important studies. Sears (1967) and more recently Schnell et al. (1981) and Scarry (1985) have presented major revisions of Willey's Fort Walton ceramic typology. Sears (1964, 1977), Brose and Percy (Brose 1984a, 1984b, 1985; Brose and Percy 1974; Percy and Brose 1974), Scarry (1981b, 1984a), and

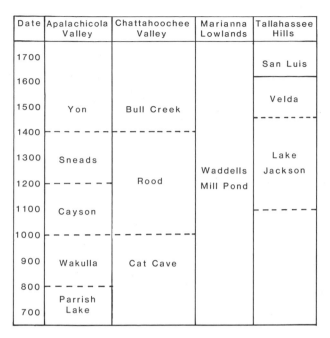

Date	Apalachicola Valley	Chattahoochee Valley	Marianna Lowlands	Tallahassee Hills
1700				San Luis
1600				
1500	Yon	Bull Creek		Velda
1400				
1300	Sneads			Lake Jackson
1200		Rood	Waddells Mill Pond	
1100	Cayson			
1000				
900	Wakulla	Cat Cave		
800				
700	Parrish Lake			

Fig. 78. General chronology for the Fort Walton area (after Scarry 1984a and Brose 1984b).

White (1982, 1985) have presented models of Woodland and Mississippian period culture change in the southern portion of the Fort Walton area. Brose and Percy (1978), Fairbanks (1971), and Payne (1981, 1982) have presented syntheses of Fort Walton settlement patterns. Finally, Jones (1982) has shown the significant role the Lake Jackson system played in the Southern Cult network.

CULTURE HISTORY IN THE SOUTHERN PORTION OF THE FORT WALTON AREA

The General Fort Walton Chronology

The chronological framework within which I have structured my discussion of Fort Walton evolution comprises 12 phases, which form the four regional chronologies shown in Figure 78 (Brose 1984b; Knight and Mistovich 1984; Scarry 1984a:361–416; F. Schnell 1981). There are three phases in the lower Chattahoochee Valley sequence, the Late Woodland Cat Cave complex, and the Mississippian Rood and Bull Creek phases. Only one phase, the Mississippian Waddells Mill Pond phase is defined for the Marianna Lowland

area. The upper Apalachicola Valley sequence consists of five phases: the late Middle Woodland Parrish Lake phase, the Late Woodland Wakulla phase, and the Mississippian Cayson, Sneads, and Yon phases. The Tallahassee Hills sequence consists of three phases: the Mississippian Lake Jackson and Velda phases, and the historic San Luis phase. At this time, no phases have been defined for the Apalachicola Bay coast area. The chronological positions of these phases are based on radiocarbon assays and cross-dated ceramic types. The development and evolution of the Fort Walton societies and the Fort Walton regional system took place during the life of these phases. They can be placed into categories—Woodland, Early Fort Walton, Middle Fort Walton, and Late Fort Walton—that represent four broad stages in the evolution of the Fort Walton societies and the Fort Walton regional system. These stages are not chronological periods, of course, and transitions from one stage to another are not contemporaneous across the Fort Walton area.

Woodland

The Woodland stage represents the base from which the later Fort Walton societies developed. During this stage, those processes that eventually produced the Fort Walton culture were set in motion. It is here that we must look for causes.

The Woodland societies of the Fort Walton area were egalitarian systems. There is archaeological evidence of status differentiation, but not of ascriptive political statuses. The differences observed in the archaeological record are not inconsistent with those expected of bigman societies. There is also evidence that they grew maize and squash, but these crops do not appear to have been dietary mainstays.

In the southern portion of the Fort Walton area (the area I address here) there is a single late Middle Woodland phase, Brose's Parrish Lake phase (1984b). The geographic extent of the Parrish Lake phase outside the Apalachicola Valley is not known. If it does not extend outside the valley, similar manifestations do. There are no radiocarbon dates for the Parrish Lake phase, but based on the available dates from the preceding Woodland manifestations and the subsequent Wakulla phase it should date to circa A.D. 500 to 750.

Two Late Woodland manifestations have been recognized in the Fort Walton area: the Cat Cave complex

(Knight and Mistovich 1984:221–222) and the Wakulla phase (Scarry 1984a:400–404). The Cat Cave complex occupied the lower Chattahoochee Valley in the southern portion of the Walter F. George Reservoir (i.e., that portion of the valley passing through the Fall Line Hills) (F. Schnell 1981). We have no absolute dates for the Cat Cave complex, but ceramic cross dating suggests that it lasted from circa A.D. 800 to perhaps as late as A.D. 1000 (the marker type Wakulla Check Stamped appears on Cat Cave complex sites). The Wakulla phase occupied the upper Apalachicola Valley. Available radiocarbon dates indicate that it lasted from circa A.D. 750 until A.D. 1000 (see Milanich 1974).

There are Late Woodland occupations in the Marianna Lowlands, the Apalachicola Bay area, and the Tallahassee Hills, but these have not been defined. Their material cultures appear to be similar to the Wakulla phase.

Early Fort Walton

The Early Fort Walton stage marks the emergence of Mississippian societies in the Fort Walton area. These societies possessed social organizations, subsistence procurement strategies, and material cultures unlike those of the earlier societies of the area (although the Early Fort Walton Cayson phase is marked by Woodland elements in its ceramic assemblage). They were simple chiefdoms, with clear social distinctions between high status and low status individuals—distinctions revealed in residential segregation and the extraction and allocation of community surplus labor. The people relied on cleared-field agriculture for a significant portion of their diet. Their material cultures (i.e., their ceramic assemblages) suggest that they formed separate, bounded systems, although there were clearly significant interactions among the Early Fort Walton societies. Their material cultures also indicate that these emergent chiefdoms exchanged information and perhaps material goods with Mississippian societies outside the Fort Walton area.

There are two manifestations, the Cayson phase of the Apalachicola Valley and the early Rood phase of the lower Chattahoochee Valley, that can be definitely assigned to the Early Fort Walton stage. Two other phases, the early Waddells Mill Pond phase of the Marianna Lowlands and the early Lake Jackson phase of the Tallahassee Hills, may be Early Fort Walton stage

manifestations. The Rood phase (McMichael and Kellar 1960:213–214; Scarry 1984a:365–371; F. Schnell 1981; Schnell et al. 1981:235–251; G. Schnell 1981) began perhaps as early as A.D. 950 and lasted until A.D. 1350. In its earliest stages, the Rood phase probably consisted of several independent simple chiefdoms. Later a Middle Fort Walton period stage complex chiefdom (sensu Steponaitis 1978; Wright 1984) centered on the Rood's Landing and Singer-Moye sites emerged, subsuming many if not all the earlier polities (Scarry and Payne 1986). The Cayson phase (Scarry 1984a: 408–412) began about A.D. 1000 and lasted until circa A.D. 1200. It consisted of one or perhaps two simple chiefdoms.

Middle Fort Walton

During the Middle Fort Walton stage, the Fort Walton systems grew in size and complexity and the Fort Walton culture spread throughout the region. Complex chiefdoms appeared in the Tallahassee Hills (Lake Jackson) and the lower Chattahoochee Valley (Rood's Landing and Singer-Moye). Most Woodland elements disappeared from ceramic assemblages. Interregional trade in prestige items, many of which can be tied to the Southeastern Ceremonial Complex, played a prominent role in the growth and maintenance of the complex chiefdoms. At the end of the Middle Fort Walton stage we see drastic changes in Fort Walton material culture and the abandonment of many mound centers, including the Lake Jackson site. Middle Fort Walton stage systems appear circa A.D. 1100–1200.

Middle Fort Walton systems are known from all portions of the Fort Walton area: the late Rood phase from the lower Chattahoochee Valley; the Sneads phase from the upper Apalachicola Valley; the Waddells Mill Pond phase from the Marianna Lowlands; and the Lake Jackson phase from the Tallahassee Hills. In addition, undefined Middle Fort Walton manifestations occur along the Apalachicola Bay coast.

Late Fort Walton

In the Late Fort Walton stage, striking changes took place in the Fort Walton material culture. I believe these changes reflect the disruption of interregional trade networks (particularly those involving prestige goods used by the elite to reinforce their authority), the collapse (or restructuring) of individual Fort Walton polities, and the establishment of new systems of alliance and exchange with other Mississippian systems. At the end of this stage, the entrance of Europeans into the Fort Walton area marked the end of the Fort Walton societies and the Fort Walton culture. Late Fort Walton stage systems first appear circa A.D. 1400.

Late Fort Walton manifestations are known from all portions of the area. The Marianna Lowlands and Apalachicola Bay Coast systems have not been formally defined but they clearly exist. In the lower Chattahoochee Valley the Late Fort Walton manifestation is the Bull Creek phase. In the upper Apalachicola Valley it is the Yon phase. And in the Tallahassee Hills it is the Velda phase.

WOODLAND-MISSISSIPPIAN CULTURE HISTORY IN THE UPPER APALACHICOLA VALLEY AND THE TALLAHASSEE HILLS

The Parrish Lake Phase: Early Weeden Island in the Upper Apalachicola Valley

The Parrish Lake phase (Brose 1984b) represents the Early Weeden Island occupation of the upper Apalachicola Valley. There are no radiocarbon dates for the phase, but Brose estimates that it lasted from ca. A.D. 500 to ca. A.D. 800 (a reasonable estimate given the available dates for the prior and succeeding phases in the valley). The Parrish Lake phase replaced the Middle Woodland Bird Hammock phase (Brose 1984b), from which it appears to have developed. It was followed by the Late Woodland Wakulla phase (Scarry 1984a: 400–405), which developed from it.

The Parrish Lake phase was a Woodland system (sensu Griffin 1967; Ford 1974, 1977), an egalitarian society that relied on wild plants and animals for the bulk of its subsistence. The subsistence procurement strategy did incorporate domesticated plants (i.e., maize and squash, see Penton 1970:48; Percy 1976, table 1; Percy and Brose 1974:11), but they were supplemental resources not staples. The Parrish Lake phase practiced gardening (Ford 1979), not cleared-field agriculture. According to Percy and Brose (1974:16), Parrish Lake phase sites are largely restricted to three major habitats: the levees (both current and former) of the Apalachicola River, the slightly higher ground

at the western edge of the valley, and the edge of the Marianna Lowlands overlooking the valley. They also used the sandy uplands east of the valley (see Jones 1974; Percy and Jones 1976).

Available evidence indicates that the Parrish Lake phase was an egalitarian system. The mortuary programs seen in the Sampson's Landing and Aspalaga mounds (Moore 1903:481–491)—i.e., multiple, unaccompanied secondary burials—do not suggest the presence of a superordinate dimension of ascriptive status cross-cutting age and sex distinctions. Some Parrish Lake phase mounds, for example Davis Field (Moore 1903:468–473), possess central features containing a single adult interment besides the typical scattered secondary burials. While the individuals in the central features were accorded special status at the time of burial, there is no indication that they held ascriptive status.

There was a functional dichotomy between burial mounds and habitation sites but no settlement hierarchy. The variation in settlement size (typically from one to five household units) was minor (Percy and Brose 1974). The one site that could possibly be seen as a higher order center is the Aspalaga site (Moore 1903: 481–488; Sears 1962:31–33; Milanich 1974). Aspalaga resembles the McKeithen site (a roughly contemporaneous Weeden Island site in north-central Florida) in size, structure, and complexity (see Kohler 1978, 1980; Milanich 1980; Milanich et al. 1984). Both Kohler (1978, 1980) and Sigler-Lavelle (1980) have argued convincingly that the McKeithen system was not a chiefdom but more closely resembled a big-man system.

There is no evidence from the Parrish Lake phase that suggests the existence of organized productive activities that transcended the capabilities of the household group. Parrish Lake phase mounds were small (approximately 1–3 m high and 10–25 m in diameter with a volume of about 150 cu m). These are clearly within the organizational and manpower capabilities of lineage segments (see Scarry 1984a:217). There was surplus labor, but its extraction and allocation do not appear to have been controlled by an elite segment of the society, nor do the products of that labor seem to have been allocated to a group of high status individuals.

Brose and Percy (1974) characterize the Parrish Lake phase as a tribal system. Settlements would have consisted of related families (i.e., lineage segments) and

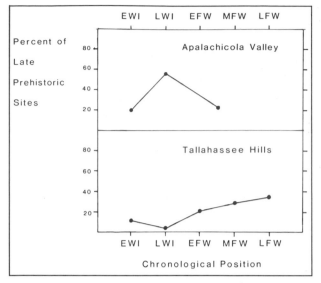

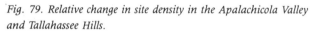

Fig. 79. Relative change in site density in the Apalachicola Valley and Tallahassee Hills.

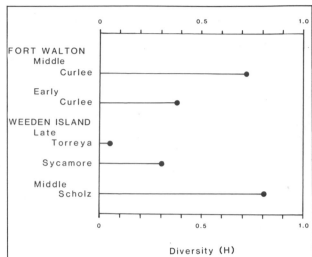

Fig. 80. Change in diversity of decorated ceramic assemblages in the Apalachicola Valley (data drawn from Milanich 1974; Percy 1976; White 1982).

several such segments would have shared a single burial mound (see Brose and Percy 1974:4; Percy and Brose 1974:12; Sigler-Lavelle 1980:28). Societal integration would have been based in large part on kin groupings (both real and putative). Individual status would have been conditioned by age, gender, and personal ability. Data from contemporaneous sites outside the Apalachicola Valley (e.g., Kolomoki and McKeithen) suggest that status distinctions did arise and were reflected in mortuary programs (Sears 1956; Milanich et al. 1984) but these distinctions can easily be accommodated within a big-man model (see Braun 1979).

The Wakulla Phase and Late Woodland in the Tallahassee Hills

The Wakulla phase and similar systems known from the Tallahassee Hills and Marianna Lowlands were the last Woodland societies in the southern Fort Walton area. They emerged about A.D. 750 and lasted until perhaps as late as A.D. 1000. They were preceded by Middle Woodland Weeden Island systems throughout the region (e.g., the Parrish Lake phase) and they were succeeded by systems that were clearly Mississippian in character (e.g., the Cayson and Lake Jackson phases).

The Wakulla phase population appears to have been

larger than that of the Parrish Lake phase. Certainly there were more sites in the bottomlands (see Fig. 79). Brose and Percy (1978:16) suggest that the increase may have been as great as fivefold. Given the available survey data (which are limited, cf. White 1985) it is difficult to determine if the increase represents an absolute increase for the valley or merely an increase in population density in the alluvial bottomlands and the uplands to the east of the river (cf. Kohler 1984). But survey data from the Torreya Ravines area east of the valley (Jones 1974; Percy and Jones 1976) and from the Apalachicola National Forest to the southeast (Forney 1985) show similar trends. There is no indication of this apparent population growth in the Tallahassee Hills, however (see Fig. 79).

The Wakulla phase material culture differs, qualitatively and quantitatively, from those of earlier Weeden Island and later Fort Walton systems. The type Wakulla Check Stamped dominates Wakulla phase assemblages; at the Sycamore site (Milanich 1974, table 4), it formed 47.6 percent of the total assemblage and 81.5 percent of the decorated assemblage and at the Torreya site (Percy 1976, table 9), the frequencies were even higher —66.3 percent and 97.7 percent respectively. This domination by a single type makes Wakulla phase assemblages individually less diverse and as a group more homogeneous than earlier assemblages (see Fig. 80). Coupled with this trend toward assemblage simplicity is an accompanying trend toward greater regional similarities. Many Late Woodland assemblages on the Gulf Coastal Plain contain high frequencies of check-stamped ceramics. These ceramics are virtually identical from Florida to Louisiana, e.g., the Mississippi Delta type Ponchartrain Check Stamped cannot be distinguished from Wakulla Check Stamped on the basis of photographs or rim profiles (compare the sherds illustrated in Brown 1982, figs. 15, 16, and 17, and Bullen 1958).

The Wakulla phase peoples appear to have followed subsistence procurement strategies much like those followed by their Early Weeden Island ancestors (see Percy 1974, 1976; Percy and Brose 1974). The hunting and gathering of wild food resources provided the bulk of the subsistence base, although domesticated plant foods were available. At the Wakulla phase Sycamore site (Milanich 1974, table 7), maize constituted 0.2 percent (by weight) of the ethnobotanical food remains, while acorn fragments (96.6 percent of the sample by weight) and hickory nut shell (2.9 percent) dominated the food remains. There is no evidence Wakulla phase peoples cleared extensive bottomland areas for corn fields; palynological data from the Yon site suggest the levee was not cleared during the Wakulla phase occupation of the site (Brose et al. 1976). Like earlier Weeden Island peoples, they gardened and did not rely on maize to the extent later Fort Walton peoples did.

The Wakulla phase was an egalitarian system. There is no evidence of settlement hierarchies. Settlements vary slightly in size but not in kind; there are no sites that appear to represent administrative centers. Even the larger sites (e.g., Torreya see Percy 1971, 1972) show no signs of internal differentiation like that seen in earlier Weeden Island sites or later Fort Walton centers.

The limited mortuary data also support a picture of the Wakulla phase as an egalitarian system. There is no evidence of ascriptive ranking of individuals. In fact, there is little evidence of any kind to suggest that status differentiation comparable to that seen in earlier Weeden Island systems (e.g., Kolomoki, Sears 1951, 1952, 1954, 1956; or McKeithen, Kohler 1978; 1980; Milanich 1980; Milanich et al. 1984) existed in the Wakulla phase. Wakulla phase mortuary assemblages contain fewer nonlocal goods and fewer specialized mortuary ceramics than earlier Weeden Island assemblages (Kolomoki is an extreme example of elaboration in Early Weeden Island mortuary assemblages, but compare the description of the Early Weeden Island Davis Field Mound in Calhoun County, Florida [Moore 1903: 468–473], with the description of the Late Weeden Island Mound below Bristol in Liberty County, Florida, across the Apalachicola [Moore 1903:473–474]). Those grave goods that do appear are frequently domestic ceramics.

Wakulla phase corporate labor projects were less prominent than those of earlier Weeden Island systems of the Apalachicola Valley. In fact, they appear to have been limited to the construction of small burial mounds. No sites with multiple mounds and plazas like McKeithen or Aspalaga have been found. Even Wakulla phase burial mounds are less elaborate and generally smaller than earlier mounds. There are no specialized central features like those found at Kolomoki or the Davis Field Mound. Clearly, the allocation of surplus labor provided by the Wakulla phase peoples was different from that seen in earlier Weeden Island systems.

The Cayson Phase

The Cayson phase was the earliest Fort Walton system in the upper Apalachicola Valley. Available radiocarbon dates (Table 26) indicate that it emerged about A.D. 1000 and lasted until about A.D. 1200. It was preceded by the Wakulla phase system and followed by the Sneads phase, a Middle Fort Walton manifestation distinguished from the Cayson phase largely on the basis of changes in ceramic design motifs.

The Cayson phase population may not have been appreciably larger than that of the Wakulla phase (see Fig. 79). There are roughly comparable numbers of Cayson phase and Wakulla phase sites in the Jim Woodruff Reservoir area, although some of the Cayson phase sites (e.g., Curlee, see White 1982) may have been larger than the Wakulla phase sites.

The Cayson phase material culture contained both Woodland and Mississippian elements. Weeden Island ceramic types and Woodland vessel forms are commonly found in Cayson phase contexts along with Fort Walton types and Mississippian vessel forms. At the

Table 26. Radiocarbon Dates for Fort Walton Components

Site	Lab Number	Age	Error	Damon et al. 1974	Ralph et al. 1973	Klein et al. 1982 Range	Midpoint

(Tree-ring Corrected Dates header spans Damon et al. 1974, Ralph et al. 1973, and Klein et al. 1982. Klein et al. 1982 spans Range and Midpoint.)

Apalachicola Valley

YON PHASE
Yon	DIC-655	640	70	1295	1320	1255–1405	1330

SNEADS PHASE
J-5	M-392	534	100	1389	1390	1270–1500	1387

CAYSON PHASE
Curlee	DIC-1048	760	50	1185	1230	1205–1325	1265
Cayson	DIC-46	770	60	1175	1220	1200–1320	1260
Cayson	DIC-45	840	65	1111	1180	1050–1265	1157
Yon	DIC-95	900	120	1056	1090	910–1270	1090
Cayson	DIC-94	900	100	1056	1090	910–1270	1090
Cayson	DIC-44	940	145	1018	1050	865–1295	1080
Yon	DIC-114	980	105	981	1020	880–1240	1060
Cayson	DIC-93	1000	70	962	1010	895–1195	1045
Yon	DIC-656	1030	105	933	980	800–1220	1010
Yon	DIC-658	1110	70	857	910	785–1035	910

Tallahassee Hills

VELDA PHASE
Velda	I-13,613	430	80	1485	1430	1340–1645	1492
Velda	I-6583	445	90	1472	1430	1330–1640	1485
High Ridge	I-13,611	550	80	1376	1390	1265–1490	1377
High Ridge	I-13,612	630	80	1302	1330	1235–1420	1327

LAKE JACKSON PHASE
Lake Jackson	I-9919	365	80	1543	1460–1500	1395–1660	1527
Lake Jackson	I-9920	715	80	1227	1225	1180–1400	1290
Lake Jackson	I-9918	1025	80	842	980-1000	800–1225	1012
Lake Jackson	I-9922	1035	80	834	975	790–1215	1005

Marianna Lowlands

WADDELLS MILL POND PHASE
Waddells	I-13,614	410	80	1503	1440	1345–1650	1497
Waddells	I-13,626	460	80	1457	1420	1330–1630	1480
Waddells	I-13,624	490	80	1431	1410	1315–1520	1417
Waddells	I-13,625	790	80	1158	1200–1220	1040–1335	1187
Waddells	I-13,615	910	80	1046	1080	905–1265	1087

Lower Chattahoochee Valley

BULL CREEK PHASE
Gary's Pond	SI-263	530	120	1393	1390	1275–1500	1387
Singer-Moye	UGa-357	550	60	1376	1390	1320–1425	1372

ROOD PHASE
Cemochechobee	UGa-1847	395	60	1518	1450	1405–1630	1517
Cemochechobee	UGa-1848	525	55	1398	1395	1325–1430	1377
Cemochechobee	UGa-1946	630	125	1302	1330	1235–1420	1327
Cool Branch	SI-261	660	280	1277	1310	885–1665	1275
						1770–1790	1780
Singer-Moye	UGa-356	680	80	1257	1260–1290	1215–1385	1300
Cemochechobee	UGa-1849	720	70	1222	1250	1225–1340	1282
Cemochechobee	UGa-1942	750	60	1193	1230	1210–1330	1270
Cemochechobee	UGa-1941	765	55	1180	1225	1200–1325	1262
Cemochechobee	UGa-1939	790	55	1158	1200–1220	1175–1310	1242
Cemochechobee	UGa-2001	870	90	1083	1110–1140	920–980	950
						1010–1290	1200
Cemochechobee	UGa-1945	895	55	1060	1095	1025–1250	1157
Cemochechobee	UGa-1707	940	55	1018	1050	920–1230	1075
Cemochechobee	UGa-1995	955	55	1005	1035	910–1225	1062
Cemochechobee	UGa-1998	960	80	1000	1030	885–1245	1065
Cemochechobee	UGa-2041	970	55	990	1030	905–1215	1060
Cemochechobee	UGa-1944	1005	70	957	1005	890–1195	1042
Cemochechobee	UGa-1943	1020	60	942	980–1000	890–1170	1030
Cemochechobee	UGa-2000	1055	65	910	955	875–1055	965
Cemochechobee	UGa-1996	1100	60	867	920	790–1035	912
Cemochechobee	UGa-1997	1240	95	732	700–790	600–915	757

Curlee site, White (1982, table 5) found that over 20 percent of the earliest Cayson phase assemblage consisted of types generally assigned to the Weeden Island period (e.g., Wakulla Check Stamped and Alachua Cob Marked). Cayson phase assemblages clearly indicate both continuity with earlier Woodland systems *and* the influence of Mississippian groups (see Knight 1980 for a differing opinion of the early Rood phase assemblage).

Cayson phase subsistence procurement strategies differed from those of the preceding Wakulla phase, with the main point of difference appearing to be a greater reliance on maize. Maize is commonly found in Cayson phase contexts (e.g., Bullen 1950, 1958; Brose et al. 1976; White 1982). At the Cayson site, limited palynological evidence suggests that the general site area was cleared in the eleventh century, with maize accounting for as much as 14 percent of the pollen in the samples (Brose et al. 1976). This contrasts with the Yon site where pollen evidence suggests that the site was wooded during the tenth-century Wakulla phase occupation (Brose et al. 1976).

The Cayson phase was hierarchically structured, probably as a simple chiefdom. There was a clear settlement hierarchy, but no indication of more than one level of control hierarchy above the local community. There may have been some residential segregation. There were corporate labor projects (i.e., mound construction), and the control and allocation of surplus labor differed from that seen in earlier Woodland societies. Two site types can be distinguished. These differ in size, degree of internal organization, and evidence of corporate labor projects. At one end are the Cayson phase mound centers—Cayson, Curlee, and Yon—at the other are small farmsteads (e.g., the Scholz Steam Plant Parking Lot site, see Brose and Wilkie 1980). The mound centers were much larger than the farmsteads; the occupation area at the Cayson site covered at least 10 ha while the Parking Lot site covered less than 1 ha. The mound centers were internally differentiated. At Cayson, a curved wall separated a central precinct from the general habitation area. Within the central precinct were several large rectangular structures, a pyramidal mound, a low conical mound(?) that supported a circular structure, and a cleared plaza. The earthworks at the Cayson phase centers are not large but they reflect a pattern of extraction and allocation of surplus labor not found in either the earlier Wakulla

phase sites or in contemporaneous Cayson phase farmsteads.

The Lake Jackson Phase

The Middle Fort Walton Lake Jackson phase was the earliest Mississippian manifestation in the Tallahassee Hills (I place the Lake Jackson phase in my Middle Fort Walton unit because of the lack of significant percentages of Woodland ceramic types in assemblages assigned to this phase). I believe the phase began ca. A.D. 1100—slightly later than the Cayson phase—and lasted until ca. A.D. 1400, but since there are only two good radiocarbon dates for the phase (see Table 26), my dating is far from secure. It followed a Late Woodland manifestation presently indistinguishable from the Wakulla phase of the upper Apalachicola Valley. It was followed by the Late Fort Walton Velda phase.

The population of the Tallahassee Hills appears to have been much larger during the Lake Jackson phase than during the Late Woodland (see Fig. 79), unlike the pattern seen in the upper Apalachicola Valley. Tesar (1981:27) reports 35 early Lake Jackson phase sites but only five Late Woodland sites from five survey areas in northern Leon County, Florida. Similar trends can be seen if all recorded sites in Leon County are considered (see Tesar 1980:602–625).

The Lake Jackson phase ceramic assemblage is, in general, similar to those of the contemporaneous Cayson, Sneads, and Rood phases, although certain features serve to distinguish it from those assemblages. The dominant decorated types and varieties are Lake Jackson Incised, *var. Lake Lafayette*, Marsh Island Incised, *vars. Marsh Island* and *Columbia*, Fort Walton Incised, *vars. Cayson, Sneads,* and *Crowder*, and Cool Branch Incised, *var. Cool Branch* (see Scarry 1985). It lacks the Woodland features (i.e., vessel forms and the ceramic types Wakulla Check Stamped and Alachua Cob Marked) that mark Cayson phase assemblages. Also, the Lake Jackson assemblage is largely grog tempered, the commonest variety of Lake Jackson Plain is *var. Tallahassee*.

Our knowledge of other facets of the Lake Jackson phase material culture is limited, and largely derives from investigations of elite burials and specialized contexts at the Lake Jackson site itself. Calvin Jones excavated elite burials from Mound 3 at Lake Jackson, finding repoussé copper plates and headdress elements, shell beads and gorgets, and greenstone and copper celts (Jones 1982). Louis Hill's excavations of Mound 6 at Lake Jackson revealed numerous specialized ceramics from a submound structure, including Andrews Decorated beakers and elbow pipes. The beakers from Mound 6 are virtually indistinguishable from beakers found at the Yon site in the Apalachicola Valley and the Cemochechobee site, a minor Rood phase center in the lower Chattahoochee Valley (Schnell et al. 1981).

We assume that the Lake Jackson phase peoples relied on maize agriculture for the bulk of their subsistence. Substantial deposits of maize were found in Mound 3 at Lake Jackson (Alexander 1984). Maize has also been recovered from the Winewood and Bear Grass sites (Jones and Penman 1973:80; Tesar 1980: 789).

The Lake Jackson phase was hierarchically organized, and for much of its existence, it was a complex chiefdom. This organization is reflected in the products of surplus labor, in the mortuary treatment afforded certain individuals, and the variation in settlement size and complexity (see Wright 1984:43–44).

The most obvious products of surplus labor in the Lake Jackson phase are the pyramidal earthen mounds found at the largest Lake Jackson phase sites. These mounds are unlike the earlier Woodland mounds. They are much larger, they served different functions, and they resulted from radically different patterns of surplus labor extraction and allocation. Some of these mounds served as substructures for rectangular wall-trench structures, perhaps temples or the residences of high status individuals, that are unlike the round residential structures found on smaller Lake Jackson phase sites (Payne 1982; Scarry 1984c).

Lake Jackson phase burials have been excavated at the Lake Jackson (Jones 1982), Winewood (Jones and Penman 1973), and Borrow Pit (B. C. Jones, personal communication) sites. These data indicate that individuals were accorded different treatments after death. I assume these treatments reflect differences in the status the individuals possessed when alive (cf. Saxe 1971, Peebles 1971). At Winewood, Jones and Penman found a series of shallow pits filled with domestic refuse and primary human interments. Some burials were unaccompanied; others were accompanied by whole and broken utilitarian ceramics. At Borrow Pit, a larger site with five structures, Jones found nine burials inside a large circular structure that he interpreted as a special-ized civic building (B. C. Jones, personal communication). None of these burials had accompaniments. At Lake Jackson, approximately 20 individuals were buried in Mound 3. Each was buried in a deep (about 2 m) grave excavated through the floor of the structure atop Mound 3. Following the burial, the structure was burned, a fresh cap of earth was added to the mound and a new structure was built. The burials were also accompanied by exotic grave goods: repoussé copper plates and headdress ornaments, engraved shell gorgets, copper and greenstone celts, and shell beads. Several of the repoussé copper items and the shell gorgets bore examples of Southeastern Ceremonial Complex iconography (Jones 1982).

Lake Jackson phase settlement patterning was hierarchical. Four classes of sites can be identified: the small farmsteads with one or two houses (e.g., Winewood); larger hamlets with five to ten houses and a larger (specialized?) structure (e.g., Borrow Pit); minor centers with a single pyramidal mound (e.g., Velda); and the major multiple mound center (Lake Jackson). The Lake Jackson phase settlement pattern seems to indicate that there was considerable residential segregation, with the elite residing at the mound centers and the bulk of the populace residing at farmsteads and hamlets (Payne 1982).

MODELS OF FORT WALTON EMERGENCE

General Considerations

The emergence of the Fort Walton societies involved changes in subsistence procurement, social organization, and group interactions. Maize replaced wild nuts and meats as the primary food source, as cleared-field agriculture superceded gardening. Decision-making and social control systems increased in complexity. Formal, permanent political offices appeared, and authority was concentrated in those offices. An ascribed elite emerged and monopolized access to political office. Holders of political office assumed control of the extraction and allocation of surplus labor, and probably received many of the products of that labor. Alliances and exchange systems among the various elite did much to structure interactions among polities.

We can see indications of these changes in subsistence remains, site sizes, settlement patterning, site organization, mortuary patterning, and material culture.

Palynological data suggest that land was cleared, presumably for maize fields, and macrobotanical remains suggest that maize played a more important role in the diet. Settlement pattern data indicate an increased association of settlements with fertile agricultural soils and the appearance of large, internally complex administrative centers. Settlement hierarchies may indicate the emergence of social hierarchies. The earthen mounds found at the larger centers mark changes in the patterns of extraction and allocation of surplus labor. Material culture data reflect patterns of interaction.

To explain these changes—and, thus, explain the emergence of individual Fort Walton societies and the Fort Walton regional system—we must seek to determine why they occurred, how they occurred, and why they endured so successfully. We must identify the external factors that pressed for change and the internal sources of variability on which those pressures acted. We must show how the changes occurred by identifying the processes, mechanisms, and historical events that produced the observed changes. Finally, we must identify the selective advantages of the final product.

The Emergence of the Cayson Phase: Subsistence Costs and Information

The evolution of the Cayson phase began perhaps as early as A.D. 700 and was completed by A.D. 1050–1100. During that period, a simple chiefdom with a subsistence economy based on cleared-field agriculture developed from a tribal society with a hunting-gathering-gardening subsistence economy. This chiefdom was the result not of large-scale population movements into the Apalachicola Valley but of the evolution of resident populations (see Scarry 1984a).

The institutions and technology needed to produce the Cayson phase were present in (or readily available to) the Parrish Lake and Wakulla phases. The staple agricultural crop, maize, was already being grown, although in much smaller quantities. Decision-making positions that could be modified into the chiefly offices of the Cayson phase were present in the Woodland societies, although their authority, scope, and accessibility were much different. Lineage leaders, religious practitioners, and situational leaders existed and had the potential to become the permanent political leaders of the Cayson phase.

Increases in the costs of subsistence procurement, in-

formation processing, and social integration exerted pressures on the Woodland systems of the Apalachicola Valley and can be seen as leading to the changes that produced the Cayson phase system. Population densities in the upper Apalachicola Valley grew during the Woodland period, particularly during the later portions of the period (i.e., the Parrish Lake and Wakulla phases). This growth altered the costs of procuring adequate food supplies and the system's ability to effectively and efficiently process information, make and implement decisions, and maintain social integration.

The evolutionary trajectory that led from the Wakulla phase to the Cayson phase comprised a series of adaptive responses to changes in the efficiency and efficacy of the society's subsistence procurement and organizational strategies. The increase in population density that occurred in the upper Apalachicola Valley during the Woodland period had predictable effects on subsistence procurement and organizational systems. It increased the overall costs of subsistence procurement and changed relationships among the costs of alternative strategies. It may have increased the risks of localized production shortfalls. It increased the amount of essential information that had to be processed to maintain system integration.

The Wakulla phase organizational and subsistence procurement strategies were responses to these factors. Settlements appear in habitats not previously exploited or exploited at much lower levels. The mix of specific subsistence procurement strategies did not change dramatically, but they expanded into new or less intensively exploited habitats. Tribal integrative mechanisms were strengthened, possibly at the expense of individual community or group leaders. Vertical status differentiation was reduced (or at least made less obvious to us).

The Cayson phase organizational and subsistence procurement strategies were responses to the same factors. Settlements were concentrated in the alluvial bottomlands of the Apalachicola and Chattahoochee rivers. The mix of specific subsistence procurement strategies was dramatically altered. The labor devoted to agriculture was increased, and cleared-field maize agriculture became the dominant subsistence procurement strategy. Vertically specialized decision-making and information-processing institutions appeared, and political authority was concentrated in those institutions. Vertical status differentiation increased, and an ascriptive elite arose.

The available survey data for the upper Apalachicola Valley show a marked increase in site density from Early Weeden Island to Late Weeden Island (see Fig. 79). If we assume the number of sites correlates with population, this suggests there was a significant growth in population density during the Late Woodland period. Such growth would have increased the overall cost of subsistence procurement, increased the marginal costs (i.e., the costs required to raise the yield of a procurement strategy by one unit of output, Earle 1980) of specific procurement strategies, and increased the amount of information that had to be processed to maintain system integration. If they were of sufficient magnitude and duration, these increases could have prompted the changes that led to the Cayson phase.

An increase in population density within the upper Apalachicola Valley would have caused overall subsistence procurement costs and the marginal costs of specific procurement strategies to rise because it would have required more intensive exploitation of *limited resources*. Search and transportation costs would have risen as food sources became harder to find near habitation sites. Average yields would have declined as hunters settled for smaller prey and gatherers exploited smaller or less productive stands. Also, because cost is not a linear function of exploitation and maximum yields vary for different procurement strategies, marginal costs would not have risen at the same rate for all strategies (see Earle 1980:10–12). Any significant increase in exploitation levels would, therefore, have led to marked differences in marginal costs of specific procurement strategies.

Timothy Earle (1980) has constructed a model of subsistence change that relates such changes in marginal costs to changes in the mix of alternative procurement strategies. He argues that in stable systems the mix of specific procurement strategies is such that alternative strategies have equal marginal costs (a situation arising, according to Earle, from a rational pattern of labor allocation). Strategy mixes change as systems try to maintain equal marginal costs. For example, if the marginal cost of one strategy becomes greater than that of another strategy (for whatever reason), labor would be shifted from the higher cost strategy to the lower cost. Because marginal costs vary with intensity of exploitation, this shift would cause the marginal costs of the higher cost strategy to decrease and the lower cost strategy to increase. Eventually a stable point would

be reached where all marginal costs were once again equal. The important thing is that the resulting mix might not be the same as the starting point.

Earle's model is simple, and it undoubtedly ignores many factors that work to shape subsistence procurement systems. Not all resources are exploited for the same reason. I doubt we can assume that resources supplying calories were evaluated on the same basis (or exploited at the same marginal cost) as resources supplying protein. I also doubt that the allocation of labor to alternative strategies was perfectly rational. Ideational values placed on resources probably played important roles in allocation decisions. Nevertheless, I feel Earle's model is an important tool for examining and explaining subsistence change. It does not require subsistence stress to initiate change, any factors that modify marginal costs will do (e.g., changes in procurement technology, changes in types of resources, changes in the environment, or changes in the demand for some or all subsistence goods). Of course, the changes had to be of sufficient magnitude to overcome social inertia and conservatism.

Given this model, we might expect two responses to the increasing demand for subsistence goods during the Late Woodland. The first would be expansion of the existing strategy mix into new areas; the second, reallocation of labor and modification of the strategy mix. The more conservative of these is expansion, and if the new areas are similar to the original environment in distribution and abundance of resources there would be little change in marginal costs. If, on the other hand, the new environment differed from the old, or if expansion did not reduce population densities in the old areas to earlier levels, then marginal costs would change and there would be pressure to modify the strategy mix.

The archaeological data from the Apalachicola Valley indicate the resident Weeden Island society initially expanded into previously underutilized habitats. During the Wakulla phase, sites were situated in several habitats not previously occupied—the sandy uplands east of the Apalachicola River and the Tate's Hell Swamp of the Coastal Lowlands east of the river (Forney 1985; Jones 1974; Percy and Jones 1976). This response might have allowed easy return to the earlier homeostasis if population densities had returned to earlier values, but they did not (see Fig. 79).

A population density increase would also have required that the system process more information to maintain system integration, and as a result it would have raised the overall costs of maintaining system integration and stability. The additional people and settlements to be integrated would have been a major cause of this increased information load. The expansion of the subsistence economy into new areas would have produced information. It is possible that risks of localized production shortfalls would have produced critical information. Finally, there were many other Woodland societies in the Southeast that were also evolving toward the Mississippian pattern. The peoples of the Apalachicola Valley were probably in contact with some of them. These evolving societies could have been significant sources of information for the Apalachicola Valley society.

Gregory Johnson (1978, 1982) has constructed a model that relates changes in essential information that a society has to process to changes in its social organization. He argues that a major driving force for organizational change is relative efficiency of information processing. On theoretical grounds, Johnson argues that increases in the variety of decisions required to integrate a set of units or activities select for increases in the complexity of decision-making organizations (1978:88). Drawing from the literature on organization theory, he identifies two basic processes by which decision-making organizations increase in complexity (1978:87). The first is horizontal specialization, which increases the number of decision-making units at a given level of the decision-making organization. The second is vertical specialization, which increases the number of hierarchical levels of the organization. Making an assumption of cost-benefit optimization, and assigning arbitrary values to the costs of information transfer (channel monitoring) and information processing (source integration), Johnson produced a model that suggests that evolution would proceed in a step-wise fashion, and that suppression of either vertical or horizontal specialization would produce marked increases in work loads and costs of system integration.

Johnson's model is, like Earle's, simplified. It ignores many factors that work to shape organizational structures. But, it does allow us to examine organizational change and to propose testable explanations of such changes.

Given Johnson's model, we might expect that the initial response to the changes in population density seen in the Apalachicola Valley would be horizontal specialization of information-processing and decision-making institutions. If such horizontal specialization were effected by the creation of sequential (Johnson 1982) hierarchies (i.e., individuals to family units to lineages to clans) instead of simultaneous hierarchies (i.e., commoner to chief) it would produce a strengthening of tribal integrative mechanisms. I would argue that this is exactly what we see in the archaeological record. The material culture changes that mark the Wakulla phase and related manifestations across the Gulf Coastal Plain (e.g., increased stylistic homogeneity at the regional level and reduced stylistic diversity at the assemblage level) reflect the strengthening of tribal social networks (cf. Braun and Plog 1982).

The Wakulla phase adaptation was ultimately unsuccessful. It failed to return the system to its earlier homeostasis and it did not establish a new homeostasis. It did not reduce the costs of subsistence procurement, and it did not maintain balance among the marginal costs of alternative strategies. As disparities in marginal costs increased, labor was reallocated and the subsistence strategy mix was radically altered.

Subsistence procurement costs continued to rise because (1) the intensity of exploitation within the Apalachicola Valley remained higher than earlier levels (population levels within the Apalachicola Valley did not decline) and (2) the new areas exploited by the Wakulla phase (i.e., the sandy uplands east of the Apalachicola River and the Coastal Lowland swamps) were less productive than the Apalachicola Valley. The marginal costs of those strategies dependent on wild resources eventually reached levels comparable to those of cleared-field agriculture. At that point, labor was shifted from those strategies to agriculture. This reallocation did not simply lead to the expansion of household gardens, however. As labor was shifted to agriculture, the environmental changes that cleared-field agriculture produces (i.e., environmental simplification and elimination of alternative resources, Ford 1974, 1977) acted to accelerate the process, increasing the costs of alternate strategies and lowering the cost of agricultural products. This process could have been accomplished quickly because it did not require a new technology.

The Wakulla phase organization was also unsuccessful. I think the lack of success was due, not to its inabil-

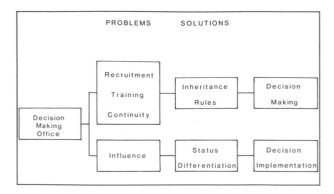

Fig. 81. Relationship of inheritance rules and status differentiation to decision-making (after Johnson 1978).

ity to maintain system integration, but to its inability to efficiently and effectively process essential environmental information. The sequential hierarchies (e.g., clans) that served to integrate the Wakulla phase society endured and formed the framework for the later Fort Walton chiefdoms. These tribal institutions were not so capable at information processing and decision making, particularly when the sources of information were external to the society and the decisions to be made went beyond the integration of individuals and groups into the society.

During the Wakulla phase, the costs of information management and decision making rose to the point that higher-order decision makers and information managers would have lowered costs. Two organizational configurations found in the prehistoric Southeast possessed such higher-order institutions: big-man societies and chiefdoms (Sahlins 1963). Big-man societies appear throughout the Woodland period (e.g., Kolomoki in the Fort Walton area), and the Wakulla phase may have been a poorly centralized big-man system. In any event, I believe that the status positions that could at least temporarily assume the functions of higher-order control units existed in the Wakulla phase (e.g., religious functionaries, lineage and community headmen).

The evolution of the Wakulla phase organization to that of the Cayson phase involved the promotion (sensu Flannery 1972) of one or more of these positions. Paul Welch (this volume) has proposed two distinct mechanisms (once again sensu Flannery) for the promotion of tribal status positions to chief. The first of these involves the assumption of secular authority

by a religious functionary; the second involves the religious sanctification of a secular position. Unfortunately, the data from the Apalachicola Valley do not allow us to distinguish between these two alternatives.

Antonio Gilman (1981) has suggested that a crucial question in the development of ranked societies like the Cayson phase has to do with why people would acquiesce to the centralization of authority in the chiefly office. He proposes that one possible reason lies in the capital investment represented by agricultural fields. This investment can be threatened by the emerging elite and it acts to lessen the ability of people to move away from a power-hungry chief. Gilman's model is also appealing because it suggests an explanation for why chiefly organizations emerged from Late Woodland societies like the Wakulla phase, but not from earlier big-man systems (e.g., Kolomoki).

Gregory Johnson (1978:101) has argued that we should expect a high degree of association among the development of higher-order control units, ascriptive status differences, and effective influence. He presents a cybernetic model relating these factors that makes intuitive sense. This model is shown in Figure 81. If Johnson's and Gilman's models are correct, we would expect that the organizational transition from the Wakulla phase to the Cayson phase would have occurred rapidly, perhaps in as few as two or three generations.

The Cayson phase adaptation that was the end product of this trajectory was selectively advantageous compared to the Woodland adaptation it replaced. It provided greater amounts of food from a given area. It could provide surplus foods to support specialized leaders. It could process larger amounts of information more efficiently. It could make and implement decisions more efficiently. These advantages were counterbalanced by the greater costs of the Cayson phase subsistence procurement strategy and social organization.

The Emergence of the Lake Jackson Phase: Demographic Expansion and Elite Alliances

The evolution of the Lake Jackson phase began ca. A.D. 1100, after the emergence of simple chiefdoms in the Apalachicola and Chattahoochee valleys. By A.D. 1250, the Lake Jackson phase was a complex chiefdom and it had assumed a dominant role in the southern portion of the Fort Walton area. It maintained that position until it was submerged beneath the tide of European colonization in the seventeenth century. The initial step in the evolution involved the movement of peoples into the Tallahassee Hills. The subsequent development of the Lake Jackson phase, however, was an in situ process—the product of local demographic and organizational factors, shaped by the interactions of the Lake Jackson elite with the elite of other chiefdoms in the lower Southeast.

The factors that initiated the evolution of the Lake Jackson phase occurred outside the Tallahassee Hills. The adoption of agricultural subsistence economies and hierarchical organizations by the emergent Fort Walton chiefdoms of the Apalachicola and Chattahoochee valleys gave those societies considerable advantages over their Woodland neighbors (see Ford 1974, 1977 and Peebles and Kus 1977 for discussions of the competitive advantages held by Mississippian societies). They also reduced selective pressures against population growth. Systems contracted, drawing their populations into the fertile bottomlands; neighboring Woodland groups (e.g., the Late Woodland inhabitants of the Tallahassee Hills) may have been absorbed; and reproductive rates increased. As a result, population densities increased beyond those of the Woodland period.

The growth in population size and density increased the amount of information the early Fort Walton chiefs had to process to effectively integrate their societies. This increase eventually taxed the abilities of the emergent Fort Walton chiefdoms (with their simple hierarchies) to effectively make and implement decisions and maintain social integration. One way to ameliorate this stress was to increase the number of decision makers (i.e., chiefs).

Three processes could have produced an increase in the number of chiefs: segmentation, horizontal specialization, and vertical specialization. Each of these processes could have arisen from structural mechanisms inherent in chiefly societies.

Segmentation could result from the rebellion of lesser elite who exerted claim on the chiefly office. Because the number of elite with some tie to the chiefly office would grow, disputes over the office would be common. Rebellions resulting from such disputes would occur with greater frequency and have greater chances of success in times of administrative stress. They would also have greater chances of success if there were territories available for the rebellious segment of the society to occupy.

Horizontal specialization could result from the division of the authority of the chief. The promotion of a lesser noble to chiefly office and his assumption of some of the authority of the paramount would have accomplished this. Horizontal specialization would produce several chiefs with more or less equal standing but whose decision-making and administrative authority did not overlap. This is perhaps what we see in the historic linking of "White Towns" and "Red Towns" among the Muskogean groups of the Southeast, or the separation of the Great Sun and the Tattooed Serpent among the Natchez (Swanton 1911:100–107).

Vertical specialization could result from the promotion of several lesser elite to positions of chiefly authority over portions of the polity but without diminution of the authority of the paramount. The granting of fiefs by the paramount could have accomplished this. In vertically specialized systems, only the paramount retains societywide authority and he has authority over subchiefs and extracts tribute and processed information from them.

The emergent Fort Walton chiefdom in the Apalachicola Valley appears to have segmented, and one segment then entered the Tallahassee Hills as the early Lake Jackson phase. The ceramic assemblages of the early Lake Jackson phase and the Cayson and Sneads phases are very similar. Nevertheless, I do not believe that they were parts of a single polity. The geography of the Apalachicola Valley would have promoted fissioning (see below), and the presence of an apparently uninhabited buffer zone between the Cayson phase and the Lake Jackson phase suggests that they were not part of a single vertically specialized system.

The early Lake Jackson phase polity was a simple chiefdom, but it possessed the institutions and technology required for the development of the late Jackson phase complex chiefdom. It had a subsistence procurement system based on cleared-field maize agriculture. It had an ascriptive elite. It had a hierarchical organization with political authority concentrated in a permanent political office. The evolution of the Lake Jackson phase required elaboration of this existing political structure and vertical specialization of the elite, it did not require revolutionary changes in organization or subsistence.

The Lake Jackson phase polity experienced substantial population growth after its entry into the Tallahassee Hills (Fig. 79). Tesar (1980:609) reports an increase from 29 pure and 6 mixed component sites for his early Apalachee Fort Walton phase to 47 pure and 6 mixed component sites for his late Apalachee Fort Walton phase (Tesar's early and late Apalachee Fort Walton phases are subsumed by and are equivalent to my Lake Jackson phase). These data were obtained from surveys in the western portion of the Lake Jackson phase territory, where earlier sites appear to be more common, and I think they may actually underestimate the true growth.

This population growth eventually stressed the information processing and managerial capabilities of the early Lake Jackson phase simple chiefdom—just as it had done earlier for the Cayson phase in the Apalachicola Valley. The evolutionary changes that resulted in the Lake Jackson phase were different from those that took place in the Cayson phase, however. I believe that the reasons for this derive, at least in part, from differences between the Tallahassee Hills and Apalachicola Valley environments.

These two areas have several important similarities. They have fertile soils capable of supporting high population densities if cleared-field maize agriculture is used (consider, for example, the role of Apalachee Province in the provisioning of seventeenth-century St. Augustine and Havana, Hann 1988). They contain rich and productive aquatic habitats. They support abundant nut-producing trees. But the spatial organizations of the two areas are different, and these differences helped shape the evolution of the societies that occupied the two areas.

The Apalachicola Valley is a linear environment, effectively one dimensional. The valley is, particularly in its upper portion, narrow and the Apalachicola does not have a wide meander belt zone. The linear organization of the valley restricts the amount of agricultural soils within the catchment of an individual settlement, although it may increase the environmental diversity within catchments. For the Fort Walton societies, this limited the size of many settlements. Cayson phase settlements, like those of many other Mississippian groups (cf. Ward 1965) were largely confined to fertile agricultural soils (Brose and Percy 1978:97–98). The distribution of these soils in the Apalachicola Valley imposed a linear pattern on the Cayson phase settlements.

The Tallahassee Hills environment is two dimensional and contains large tracts of fertile agricultural soils. It could support a larger total population than the Apalachicola Valley (as it did in the protohistoric and early historic periods, Hann 1988; Swanton 1979), although population densities per acre of agricultural soil were no higher. It could support larger individual settlements because it had larger tracts of agricultural land. It could support a more compact polity than linear river valley environments (compare the dimensions of the sixteenth-century Coosa [Hudson et al. 1985] and Apalachee chiefdoms).

The early Lake Jackson phase polity responded to the administrative stress induced by population growth by increasing the number of administrators. It did so not by fissioning but by forming a two-tiered administrative hierarchy (i.e., by vertical specialization of its political structure). I believe this response was prompted by two factors. First, the Lake Jackson phase did not have a nearby area like the Tallahassee Hills into which a seceding group could withdraw. Second, the compact organization of the Lake Jackson phase polity would have made it much easier for a chief to monitor and control the lesser elite.

Vertical specialization of the Lake Jackson phase political organization involved two promotions. Lesser elite assumed positions of authority over portions of the polity's territory. One chief assumed a paramount position vis-à-vis the others, with authority over the entire polity. This paramount chief may have been the original chief, and both processes may have occurred as the result of the elevation of lesser elite to new positions under that individual (through a process analogous to the granting of fiefs). Alternatively, the processes could have occurred sequentially, with lesser elite assuming positions of administrative authority over geographically restricted areas as the polity expanded, daughter communities formed, and the polity segmented. Competition among such local leaders could then have led to the promotion of one such local office to a paramount position (see Wright 1984:49–50 for a discussion of this process). Of these two trajectories, I believe that the latter was more likely because it would not involve the unlikely (it seems to me) ceding of authority by an individual already in a paramount position.

The Lake Jackson phase shared a common "culture" with other Fort Walton polities. This is not surprising if, as I believe, the Lake Jackson phase originated as a result of the fissioning of an early Fort Walton chiefdom. Part of this "culture" involved the ritual sanctification of the authority of the elite. Indications of this "culture" can be seen in the use of specialized ceramics (particularly beaker and bottle forms of the types Andrews Decorated, Fort Walton Incised, and Point Washington Incised [Scarry 1985]) and copper status markers. Andrews Decorated beakers have been found in a presumably ceremonial context beneath Mound 6 at the Lake Jackson site and associated with a mound construction episode and used as mortuary furniture at the early Fort Walton Cemochechobee site on the Chattahoochee River (Schnell et al. 1981:206–207). The Andrews Decorated beakers from these two sites (as well as from the Yon site on the Apalachicola River) are virtually indistinguishable. Another indication of this common Fort Walton "culture" is the similar copper headdress ornaments found associated with elite (paramount?) burials at Lake Jackson (Jones 1982, table 2) and Cemochechobee (Schnell et al. 1981:218–226).

Alliances and exchanges of marriage partners among the elite of the several Fort Walton polities may have been another part of this common "culture" (e.g., in the late seventeenth century, an Ustagan chief was the nephew of the Apalachee chief of Ivitachuco, Hann 1988). If this were the case during the prehistoric period, the Fort Walton elite probably had social networks different from those of commoners. Henry Wright (1984:48–50) has suggested that competition among elite for status positions within a given polity will involve emphasis on ". . . geographically distant prestigious links or temporally distant divine links . . ." (these being differing interpretations of equivalent phenomena). These links could be demonstrated through genealogies or through the possession of exotic status markers.

Differences in links to foreign elite and consequent differences in access to exotic prestige goods would help promote status differences among local elite. Once one chiefly lineage assumed a superior position vis-à-vis the other elite, i.e., once one chief was clearly promoted to a paramount position, the new paramount would be able to further bolster his prestige (both local and regional) by commanding tribute from the lesser elite, controlling locally manufactured prestige items, and thus using resources beyond his own to obtain exotic prestige goods for his own use and to distribute to the lesser elite. Wright (1984:50) has suggested that "the centripetal flow of tribute must aggrandize the

center, simultaneously giving the paramount the possibility of becoming more than a first among equals and making the other office holders permanent political and ritual subsidiaries."

This whole process could have been accomplished over a few generations. Several consecutive strong leaders within a single elite lineage might have been enough to produce the Lake Jackson complex chiefdom, while the absence of such leaders might have contributed to the fissioning of the Cayson phase.

CONCLUSIONS

I have proposed explanations for the emergence of Mississippian chiefdoms in the Apalachicola Valley and the Tallahassee Hills. The societies that occupied these areas were independent and possessed political organizations differing in scale and complexity. I have argued that the evolutionary trajectories and mechanisms that produced these polities were different. The general processes involved were similar, and the evolution of the Lake Jackson and Cayson phases can be explained in terms of general evolutionary models (Earle 1980; Johnson 1978; Wright 1984), but they were discrete events and require separate specific explanations.

My models are speculative. I have only limited data relating to the emergence of the Lake Jackson and Cayson phase chiefdoms, and those data are of uneven quality. All in all, however, I feel that the models are accurate, at least in broad outline. I also believe that my explanations for the changes we can see in the archaeological record are better than alternative models. They do not conflict with the data that are available, and they account for several facets of the archaeological record not addressed by other models. My explanations suggest specific mechanisms to account for observed changes, and are testable, although not with the data we have now.

I am not the first archaeologist to speculate about the origins of the Fort Walton societies. Gordon Willey proposed an invasion model in *Archeology of the Florida Gulf Coast* (1949). John Griffin suggested that the Fort Walton ceramic complex evolved from the Weeden Island as Mississippian decorative styles diffused into the Fort Walton area (1950). Joseph Caldwell argued for Willey's invasion model based on his analysis of the early ceramic component at the Rood's Landing site (1955). Ripley Bullen argued against total replacement of peoples, citing apparent transitional Weeden Island-Fort Walton assemblages in the Apalachicola Valley (1958). William Sears forcefully advocated a population movement explanation, and argued that the Fort Walton societies were chronologically late and not of local origin (1962, 1964, 1967, 1977). David Brose argued against external causes and for in situ evolution (Brose 1984a, 1984b, 1985; Brose and Percy 1978; Percy and Brose 1974).

The quality and quantity of our data have limited all attempts to explain "Fort Walton origins." In particular, the early studies were constrained by the available data. Radiocarbon dates, detailed stratigraphic sequences, settlement pattern models, and fine-grained studies of ceramic variability were not available when the earlier models were formulated. The currently available data do allow us to reject several of the previous models. We now know the first Fort Walton societies were not chronologically late. It is also evident the Fort Walton societies were not marginal Mississippian systems. It seems clear there was not a large-scale movement of peoples into the Fort Walton area nor was there a replacement of the indigenous Woodland groups. It is apparent the emergence of the Fort Walton societies was not a single, simple event, explicable by a single, simple model.

Not all previous models can be refuted so easily. Brose's proposals (particularly 1984a) are a valid alternative to my models. We now have models that are detailed enough, and specific enough to be tested. What we must do next is collect data that will permit us to evaluate these models. I think the testing of these models will be an exciting process and will help us to say with some surety why and how chiefly societies appeared in the southeastern United States.

REFERENCES CITED

Alexander, Michelle
  1984 *Paleoethnobotany of the Fort Walton Indians: High Ridge, Velda, and Lake Jackson Sites.* Unpublished M.S. thesis, Department of Anthropology, Florida State University, Tallahassee.

Belovich, Stephanie, David S. Brose, and Russell Weisman, with Nancy M. White
  1983 *Archaeological Survey at George W. Andrews Lake, Alabama and Georgia.* Archaeological Research Report 37. Cleveland Museum of Natural History, Cleveland.

Bierce-Gedris, Katharine
  1981 *Apalachee Hill: The Archaeological Investigation of an Indian Site of the Spanish Mission Period.* Unpublished M.A. thesis, Department of Anthropology, Florida State University, Tallahassee.

Boyd, Mark F.
  1951 Fort San Luis: Documents Describing the Tragic End of the Mission Era. In *Here They Once Stood: The Tragic End of the Apalachee Missions,* by M. F. Boyd, H. G. Smith, and J. W. Griffin, pp. 1–104. University of Florida Press, Gainesville.

Braley, Chad O.
  1982 *Archaeological Testing and Evaluation of the Paradise Point Site (8Fr71), St. Vincent NWR, Franklin County, Florida.* Southeastern Wildlife Services, Athens, Georgia.

Brannon, Peter A.
  1909 Aboriginal Remains in the Middle Chattahoochee Valley of Alabama and Georgia. *American Anthropologist* 11: 186–198.

Braun, David P.
  1979 Illinois Hopewell Burial Practices and Social Organization: A Reexamination of the Klunk-Gibson Mound Group. In *Hopewell Archaeology: The Chillicothe Conference,* edited by D. S. Brose and N. Greber, pp. 66–79. Kent State University Press, Kent, Ohio.

Braun, David P., and Stephen Plog
  1982 Evolution of "Tribal" Social Networks: Theory and Prehistoric North American Evidence. *American Antiquity* 47:504–525.

Brose, David S.
  1980 Coe's Landing (8Ja137) Jackson County, Florida: A Fort Walton Campsite on the Apalachicola River. *Bureau of Historic Sites and Properties Bulletin* 6:1–31.
  1984a Mississippian Period Cultures in Northwestern Florida. In *Perspectives on Gulf Coast Prehistory,* edited by D. Davis, pp. 165–197. Ripley P. Bullen Monographs in Anthropology and History 6. University Presses of Florida, Gainesville.
  1984b "Willey-Nilly" or the Archaeology of Northwest Florida and Adjacent Borderlands Revisited. Paper presented at the 41st Annual Southeastern Archaeological Conference, Pensacola.
  1985 "Willey-Nilly" or the Archaeology of Northwest Florida and Adjacent Borderlands Revisited. In *Archaeology of Northwest Florida and Adjacent Borderlands: Current Research Problems and Approaches,* pp. 156–162. Florida Anthropological Society Publication 11. The Florida Anthropologist 38.

Brose, David S., and George W. Percy
  1974 An Outline of Weeden Island Ceremonial Activity in Northwest Florida. Paper presented at the 39th Annual Meeting of the Society for American Archaeology, Washington.
  1978 Fort Walton Settlement Patterns. In *Mississippian Settlement Patterns,* edited by B. D. Smith, pp. 81–114. Academic Press, New York.

Brose, David S., and Duncan C. Wilkie
  1980 A Fort Walton Campsite (8Ja201) at the Scholz Steam Plant Parking Lot, Jackson County, Florida. *The Florida Anthropologist* 33:172–206.

Brose, David S., Patricia S. Essenpreis, John F. Scarry, Helga Bluestone, and Anne Forsythe

1976   Contributions to the Archaeology of Northwestern Florida: Investigations of Early Fort Walton Sites in the Middle Apalachicola River Valley. Manuscript on file, Florida Bureau of Archaeological Research, Tallahassee.

Brown, Ian W.
1982   *The Southeastern Check Stamped Pottery Tradition: A View from Louisiana.* MCJA Special Paper 4. Kent State University Press, Kent, Ohio.

Broyles, Bettye J.
1962   A Lamar Period Site in Southwest Georgia, 9Cla51. In *Survey of Archaeological Sites in Clay and Quitman Counties, Georgia,* by A. R. Kelly, R. Nonas, B. Broyles, C. de Baillou, D. W. Chase, and F. T. Schnell, Jr., pp. 29–35. Series Reports 5. University of Georgia Laboratory of Archaeology, Athens.
1971   A Lamar Site in Southwest Georgia. *Southeastern Archaeological Conference Newsletter* 10(2):55–56.

Bryne, Stephen Cowles
1986   *Apalachee Settlement Patterns.* Unpublished M.S. thesis, Department of Anthropology, Florida State University, Tallahassee.

Bullen, Ripley P.
1950   An Archaeological Survey of the Chattahoochee River Valley in Florida. *Journal of the Washington Academy of Science* 40:101–125.
1958   Six Sites near the Chattahoochee River in the Jim Woodruff Reservoir Area, Florida. *Bureau of American Ethnology Bulletin* 169:315–376.

Bushnell, Amy T.
1978   "That Demonic Game": The Campaign to Stop Indian Pelota Playing in Spanish Florida, 1675–1684. *The Americas* 35:1–19.
1979   Patricio de Hinachuba: Defender of the Word of God, the Crown of the King, and the Little Children of Ivitachuco. *American Indian Culture and Research Journal* 3(3): 1–21.

Caldwell, Joseph R.
1955   Investigations at Rood's Landing, Stewart County, Georgia. *Early Georgia* 2:22–49.

Damon, P. E., C. W. Ferguson, A. Long, and E. I. Wallick
1974   Dendrochronological Calibration of the Radiocarbon Time Scale. *American Antiquity* 39:350–366.

Deagan, Kathleen A.
1976   The Apalachee. In *Handbook of North American Indians,* vol. 13, *The Southeast,* edited by R. D. Fogelson. Smithsonian Institution, Washington, D.C. (In Press)

Earle, Timothy K.
1980   A Model of Subsistence Change. In *Modeling Change in Prehistoric Subsistence Economies,* edited by T. K. Earle and A. Christenson, pp. 1–29. Academic Press, New York.

Fairbanks, Charles H.
1955   The Abercrombie Mound, Russell County, Alabama. *Early Georgia* 2:13–19.
1971   The Apalachicola River Area of Florida. *Southeastern Archaeological Conference Newsletter* 10(2):38–40.

Ford, Richard I.
1974   Northeastern Archeology: Past and Future Directions. *Annual Review of Anthropology* 4:385–414.
1977   Evolutionary Ecology and the Evolution of Human Ecosystems: A Case Study from the Midwestern U.S.A. In *Explanation of Prehistoric Change,* edited by J. N. Hill, pp. 153–184. University of New Mexico Press, Albuquerque.
1979   Gathering and Gardening: Trends and Consequences of Hopewell Subsistence Strategies. In *Hopewell Archaeology: The Chillicothe Conference,* edited by D. S. Brose and N. Greber, pp. 234–238. Kent State University Press, Kent, Ohio.

Forney, Sandra Jo
1985   Prehistoric Settlement and Subsistence System of the Apalachicola National Forest, Florida. In *Archaeology of Northwest Florida and Adjacent Borderlands: Current Research Problems and Approaches,* pp. 98–103. Florida Anthropological Society Publication 11. The Florida Anthropologist 38.

Fryman, Frank B.
1971   Highway Salvage Archaeology in Florida. *Archives and History News* 2(1):1–4.

Fuller, Richard, and Noel R. Stowe
1982   A Proposed Typology for Late Shell Tempered Ceramics in the Mobile Bay/Mobile-Tensaw Delta Region. In *Archaeology in Southwestern Alabama: A Collection of Papers,* edited by C. Curren, pp. 45–93. Alabama Tombigbee Regional Commission, Camden, Alabama.

Gardner, William M.
1966   The Waddells Mill Pond Site. *The Florida Anthropologist* 19:43–64.
1969   An Example of the Association of Archaeological Complexes with Tribal and Linguistic Grouping: The Fort Walton Complex of Northwest Florida. *The Florida Anthropologist* 22:1–11.
1971   Ft. Walton in Inland Florida. *Southeastern Archaeological Conference Newsletter* 10(2):48–50.

Gilman, Antonio
1981   The Development of Social Stratification in Bronze Age Europe. *Current Anthropology* 22:1–23.

Griffin, James B.
1967   Eastern North American Archaeology: A Summary. *Science* 156:175–191.
1985   Changing Concepts of the Prehistoric Mississippian Cultures of the Eastern United States. In *Alabama and the Borderlands: From Prehistory to Statehood,* edited by R. Badger and L. Clayton, pp. 40–63. University of Alabama Press, University.

Griffin, John W.
1950   Test Excavations at the Lake Jackson Site. *American Antiquity* 16:99–112.

Hann, John H.
1986a   Translation of Governor Rebolledo's 1657 Visitation of Three Florida Provinces and Related Documents. *Florida Archaeology* 2:81–145.
1986b   Translation of Alonso de Leturiodo's Memorial to the King of Spain. *Florida Archaeology* 2:165–225.
1988   *Apalachee: The Land Between the Rivers.* Ripley P. Bullen Monographs in Anthropology and History 7. University Presses of Florida, Gainesville.

Hurt, Wesley R.
1975   The Preliminary Archaeological Survey of the Chatta-

hoochee Valley Area in Alabama. In *Archaeological Salvage in the Walter F. George Basin of the Chattahoochee River in Alabama*, edited by D. L. DeJarnette, pp. 6–85. University of Alabama Press, Tuscaloosa.

Hudson, Charles, Marvin Smith, David Hally, Richard Polhemus, and Chester DePratter
1985   Coosa: A Chiefdom in the Sixteenth-Century Southeastern United States. *American Antiquity* 50:723–737.

Huscher, Harold
1959a   Appraisal of the Archeological Resources of the Columbia Dam and Lock Area, Chattahoochee River, Alabama and Georgia. Manuscript on file, National Park Service Southeast Archeological Center, Tallahassee.
1959b   Appraisal of the Archeological Resources of the Oliver Basin, Chattahoochee River, Alabama and Georgia. Manuscript on file, National Park Service Southeast Archeological Center, Tallahassee.
1959c   Appraisal of the Archeological Resources of the Walter F. George Reservoir Area, Chattahoochee River, Alabama and Georgia. Manuscript on file, National Park Service Southeast Archeological Center, Tallahassee.
1964   The Cool Branch Site, 9Qu5, Quitman County, Georgia: A Fortified Mississippian Town with Tower Bastions. *Eastern States Archeological Federation Bulletin* 23:11.
1971   Two Mississippian Mound Sites in Quitman County, Georgia. *Southeastern Archaeological Conference Newsletter* 10(2):35–38.

Johnson, Gregory A.
1978   Information Sources and the Development of Decision-Making Organizations. In *Social Archeology: Beyond Subsistence and Dating*, edited by C. Redman, M. Berman, E. Curtin, W. Langhorne, N. Versaggi, and J. Wanser, pp. 87–112. Academic Press, New York.
1982   Organizational Structure and Scalar Stress. In *Theory and Explanation in Archaeology: The Southampton Conference*, edited by C. Renfrew, M. J. Rowlands, and B. A. Segraves, pp. 389–421. Academic Press, New York.

Jones, B. Calvin
1972   Colonel James Moore and the Destruction of the Apalachee Missions in 1704. *Bureau of Historic Sites and Properties Bulletin* 2:25–33.
1982   Southern Cult Manifestations at the Lake Jackson Site, Leon County, Florida: Salvage Excavation of Mound 3. *Midcontinental Journal of Archaeology* 7:3–44.

Jones, B. Calvin, and John T. Penman
1973   Winewood: An Inland Fort Walton Site in Tallahassee, Florida. *Bureau of Historic Sites and Properties Bulletin* 3:65–90.

Jones, M. Katherine
1974   *Archaeological Survey and Excavation in the Upper Sweetwater Creek Drainage of Liberty County, Florida.* Unpublished M.A. thesis, Department of Anthropology, Florida State University, Tallahassee.

Kelly, Arthur R.
1950   Survey of the Lower Flint and Chattahoochee Rivers. *Early Georgia* 1:26–33.

Klein, Jeffrey, J. C. Lerman, P. E. Damon, and E. K. Ralph
1982   Calibration of Radiocarbon Dates: Tables Based on the Consensus Data of the Workshop on Calibrating the Radiocarbon Time Scale. *Radiocarbon* 24:103–150.

Knight, Vernon J., Jr.
1979   Ceramic Stratigraphy at the Singer-Moye Site, 9Sw2. *Journal of Alabama Archaeology* 25:138–151.
1980   Interregional Relationships and the Study of Fort Walton Mississippian Ceramic Style. Paper presented at the 37th Annual Southeastern Archaeological Conference, New Orleans.
1984   Late Prehistoric Adaptation in the Mobile Bay Region. In *Perspectives on Gulf Coast Prehistory*, edited by D. Davis, pp. 198–215. Ripley P. Bullen Monographs in Anthropology and History 6. University Presses of Florida, Gainesville.

Knight, Vernon J., Jr., and Tim S. Mistovich
1984   *Walter F. George Lake: Archaeological Survey of Fee Owned Lands, Alabama and Georgia.* Report of Investigations 42. University of Alabama Office of Archaeological Research, Moundville.

Kohler, Timothy A.
1978   *The Social and Chronological Dimensions of Village Occupation at a North Florida Weeden Island Period Site.* Unpublished Ph.D. dissertation, Department of Anthropology, University of Florida, Gainesville.
1980   The Social Dimensions of Village Occupation of the McKeithen Site, North Florida. *Southeastern Archaeological Conference Bulletin* 22:5–11.
1984   Behavioral Correlates of Population Growth: A Speculative Example from the Middle Chattahoochee. *Southeastern Archaeology* 3:153–163.

Kohler, Timothy A., Thomas P. DesJeans, C. Feiss, and D. E. Thompson
1980   Survey of Selected Portions of the Fort Benning Military Reservation, Alabama and Georgia. Manuscript on file, National Park Service, Southeastern Archeological Center, Tallahassee.

Kurjack, Edward B.
1975   Archaeological Investigations in the Walter F. George Basin. In *Archaeological Salvage in the Walter F. George Basin of the Chattahoochee River in Alabama*, edited by D. L. DeJarnette, pp. 87–198. University of Alabama, Tuscaloosa.

Lazarus, Yulee W., and Carolyn B. Hawkins
1976   *Pottery of the Fort Walton Period.* Temple Mound Museum, Fort Walton Beach, Florida.

McMichael, Edward V., and James H. Kellar
1960   *Archeological Salvage in the Oliver Basin.* Series Report 2. University of Georgia Laboratory of Archaeology, Athens.

Milanich, Jerald T.
1974   Life in a 9th Century Indian Household: A Weeden Island Fall-Winter Site on the Upper Apalachicola River, Florida. *Bureau of Historic Sites and Properties Bulletin* 4:1–44.
1980   Conclusions from the McKeithen Site, an Early Weeden Island Mound-Village Complex in Northern Florida. Paper presented at the 45th Annual Meeting of the Society for American Archaeology, Philadelphia.

Milanich, Jerald T., Ann S. Cordell, Vernon J. Knight, Jr., Timothy A. Kohler, and Brenda Sigler-Lavelle
1984   *McKeithen Weeden Island: The Culture of Northern Florida, A.D. 200–900.* Academic Press, New York.

Miller, James J., John W. Griffin, Mildred L. Fryman, and Frank W. Stapor
 1981 *Archeological and Historical Survey of St. Vincent National Wildlife Refuge, Florida.* Cultural Resource Management, Tallahassee, Florida.

Moore, Clarence B.
 1902 Certain Aboriginal Remains of the Northwest Florida Coast, Part II. *Journal of the Academy of Natural Sciences of Philadelphia* 12:127–358.
 1903 Certain Aboriginal Mounds of the Apalachicola River. *Journal of the Academy of Natural Sciences of Philadelphia* 12:439–492.
 1907 Mounds of the Lower Chattahoochee and Lower Flint Rivers. *Journal of the Academy of Natural Sciences of Philadelphia* 13:426–456.
 1918 The Northwestern Florida Coast Revisited. *Journal of the Academy of Natural Sciences of Philadelphia* 16:513–581.

Neuman, Robert
 1961 Domesticated Corn from a Fort Walton Mound Site in Houston County, Alabama. *The Florida Anthropologist* 14:75–80.

Payne, Claudine
 1981 A Preliminary Investigation of Fort Walton Settlement Patterns in the Tallahassee Red Hills. *Southeastern Archaeological Conference Bulletin* 24:29–31.
 1982 Farmsteads and Districts: A Model of Fort Walton Settlement Patterns in the Tallahassee Hills. Paper presented at the 39th Annual Southeastern Archaeological Conference, Memphis.

Peebles, Christopher S.
 1971 Moundville and Surrounding Sites: Some Structural Considerations of Mortuary Practices II. In *Approaches to the Social Dimensions of Mortuary Practices,* edited by J. Brown, pp. 68–91. Memoirs of the Society for American Archaeology 25.

Peebles, Christopher S., and Susan M. Kus
 1977 Some Archaeological Correlates of Ranked Societies. *American Antiquity* 42:421–448.

Penton, Daniel T.
 1970 *Excavations at the Early Swift Creek Component at Bird Hammock (8Wa30).* Unpublished M.A. thesis, Department of Anthropology, Florida State University, Tallahassee.

Percy, George W.
 1971 Preliminary Report to the Division of Recreation and Parks, Department of Natural Resources, State of Florida, on Archaeological Work at Torreya State Park during the Year 1971 by the Department of Anthropology at Florida State University. Manuscript on file, Florida Division of Historical Resources, Tallahassee.
 1972 A Preliminary Report on Recent Archaeological Investigations in Torreya State Park, Liberty County, Florida. Paper presented at the 24th Annual Meeting of the Florida Anthropological Society, Winter Park.
 1974 A Review of Evidence for Prehistoric Indian Use of Animals in Northwest Florida. *Bureau of Historic Sites and Properties Bulletin* 4:65–93.
 1976 *Salvage Investigations at the Scholz Steam Plant Site, a Middle Weeden Island Habitation Site in Jackson County, Florida.* Miscellaneous Project Report Series 35. Florida Bureau of Historic Sites and Properties, Tallahassee.

Percy, George W., and David S. Brose
 1974 Weeden Island Ecology, Subsistence, and Village Life in Northwest Florida. Paper presented at the 39th Annual Meeting of the Society for American Archaeology, Washington.

Percy, George W., and M. Katherine Jones
 1976 An Archaeological Survey of Upland Locales in Gadsden and Liberty Counties, Florida. *The Florida Anthropologist* 29:105–125.

Ralph, E. K., H. N. Michael, and M. C. Han
 1973 Radiocarbon Dates and Reality. *MASCA Newsletter* 9:1–20.

Sahlins, Marshall D.
 1963 Poor Man, Rich Man, Big-Man, Chief: Political Types in Melanesia and Polynesia. *Comparative Studies in Society and History* 3:285–303.

Saxe, Arthur A.
 1971 Social Dimensions of Mortuary Practices in a Mesolithic Population from Wadi Halfa, Sudan. In *Approaches to the Social Dimensions of Mortuary Practices,* edited by J. Brown, pp. 39–57. Memoirs of the Society for American Archaeology 25. Society for American Archaeology, Manasha.

Scarry, John F.
 1981a Fort Walton Culture: A Redefinition. *Southeastern Archaeological Conference Bulletin* 24:18–21.
 1981b Subsistence Costs and Information: A Model of Fort Walton Development. *Southeastern Archaeological Conference Bulletin* 24:31–32.
 1984a *Fort Walton Development: Mississippian Chiefdoms in the Lower Southeast.* Ph.D. dissertation, Department of Anthropology, Case Western Reserve University, Cleveland. University Microfilms, Ann Arbor.
 1984b The Spatial Organization of a Late Fort Walton Farmstead at the Velda Site, Leon County, Florida. Paper presented at the 36th Annual Meeting of the Florida Anthropological Society, Palm Beach.
 1984c Spatial Organization and Refuse Disposal Patterns at a Late Prehistoric Velda Phase Farmstead in the Tallahassee Hills. Paper presented at the 41st Annual Southeastern Archaeological Conference, Pensacola.
 1985 A Proposed Revision of the Fort Walton Ceramic Typology: A Type-variety Approach. *The Florida Anthropologist* 38:199–233.

Scarry, John F., and Claudine Payne
 1986 Mississippian Polities in the Fort Walton Area: Application and Evaluation of the Renfrew-Level XTENT Model. *Southeastern Archaeology* 5:79–90.

Schnell, Frank T., Jr.
 1981 Late Prehistoric Ceramic Chronologies in the Lower Chattahoochee Valley. *Southeastern Archaeological Conference Bulletin* 24:21–23.

Schnell, Frank T., Jr., Vernon J. Knight, Jr., and Gail S. Schnell
 1981 *Cemochechobee: Archaeology of a Mississippian Ceremonial Center on the Chattahoochee River.* Ripley P. Bullen Monographs in Anthropology and History. University Presses of Florida, Gainesville.

Schnell, Gail S.
1981   A Preliminary Political Model for the Rood Phase. *Southeastern Archaeological Conference Bulletin* 24:23–24.

Sears, William H.
1951   *Excavations at Kolomoki: Season I—1948.* Series in Anthropology 2. University of Georgia, Athens.
1952   An Archaeological Manifestation of a Natchez-type Burial Ceremony. *The Florida Anthropologist* 5:1–7.
1954   The Sociopolitical Organization of Precolumbian Cultures on the Gulf Coastal Plain. *American Anthropologist* 56:339–346.
1956   *Excavations at Kolomoki, Final Report.* Series in Anthropology 5. University of Georgia, Athens.
1962   An Investigation of Prehistoric Processes on the Gulf Coastal Plain. Manuscript on file, National Science Foundation, Washington.
1964   The Southeastern United States. In *Prehistoric Man in the New World,* edited by J. D. Jennings and E. Norbeck, pp. 259–287. University of Chicago Press, Chicago.
1967   The Tierra Verde Burial Mound. *The Florida Anthropologist* 20:25–74.
1977   Prehistoric Culture Areas and Culture Change on the Gulf Coastal Plain. In *For the Director: Research Essays in Honor of James B. Griffin,* edited by C. E. Cleland, pp. 152–185. Anthropological Papers 61. University of Michigan Museum of Anthropology, Ann Arbor.

Sigler-Lavelle, Brenda J.
1980   On the Non-Random Distribution of Weeden Island Period Sites in North Florida. *Southeastern Archaeological Conference Bulletin* 22:22–29.

Smith, Bruce D.
1978   Variations In Mississippian Settlement Patterns. In *Mississippian Settlement Patterns,* edited by B. D. Smith, pp. 479–503. Academic Press, New York.

Smith, Buckingham
1968   *Narratives of De Soto in the Conquest of Florida as Told by a Gentleman of Elvas and in a Relation by Luys Hernandez de Biedma.* Palmetto Books, Gainesville, Florida.

Steponaitis, Vincas P.
1978   Location Theory and Complex Chiefdoms: A Mississippian Example. In *Mississippian Settlement Patterns,* edited by B. D. Smith, pp. 417–453. Academic Press, New York.

Swanton, John R.
1911   *Indian Tribes of the Lower Mississippi Valley and Adjacent Coast of the Gulf of Mexico.* Bureau of American Ethnology Bulletin 43. Smithsonian Institution, Washington.
1922   *Early History of the Creek Indians and their Neighbors.* Bureau of American Ethnology Bulletin 73. Smithsonian Institution, Washington.

1979   *The Indians of the Southeastern United States.* Bureau of American Ethnology Bulletin 137. Classics of Smithsonian Anthropology, Smithsonian Institution, Washington. (A reprint of the 1946 edition.)
1985   *Final Report of the United States De Soto Expedition Commission.* Classics of Smithsonian Anthropology. Smithsonian Institution, Washington. (A reprint of the 1939 edition.)

Tesar, Louis D.
1980   *The Leon County Bicentennial Survey Report: An Archaeological Survey of Selected Portions of Leon County, Florida.* Miscellaneous Project Report Series 49. Florida Bureau of Historic Sites and Properties, Tallahassee.
1981   Fort Walton and Leon-Jefferson Cultural Development in the Tallahassee Red Hills Area of Florida: A Brief Summary. *Southeastern Archaeological Conference Bulletin* 24: 27–29.

Ward, Trawick
1965   Correlation of Mississippian Sites and Soil Types. *Southeastern Archaeological Conference Bulletin* 3:42–48.

White, Nancy M.
1981   The Curlee Site (8Ja7) and Fort Walton Development in the Upper Apalachicola—Lower Chattahoochee Valley in Florida, Georgia, and Alabama. *Southeastern Archaeological Conference Bulletin* 24:24–27.
1982   *The Curlee Site and Fort Walton Development in the Upper Apalachicola—Lower Chattahoochee Valley.* Ph.D. dissertation, Department of Anthropology, Case Western Reserve University, Cleveland. University Microfilms, Ann Arbor.
1985   Nomenclature and Interpretation in Borderland Chronology: A Critical Overview of Northwest Florida Prehistory. In *Archaeology of Northwest Florida and Adjacent Borderlands: Current Research Problems and Approaches* pp. 163–174. Florida Anthropological Society Publication 11. The Florida Anthropologist 38.

White, Nancy M., Stephanie J. Belovich, and David S. Brose
1981   *Archaeological Survey at Lake Seminole: Jackson and Gadsden Counties, Florida, Seminole and Decatur Counties, Georgia.* Archaeological Research Reports 29. Cleveland Museum of Natural History, Cleveland.

Willey, Gordon R.
1949   *Archeology of the Florida Gulf Coast.* Smithsonian Miscellaneous Collections 113. Smithsonian Institution, Washington.

Wright, Henry T.
1984   Prestate Political Formations. In *On the Evolution of Complex Societies: Essays in Honor of Harry Hoijer, 1982,* edited by T. K. Earle, pp. 41–78. Undena Publications, Malibu, California.

James A. Brown, Richard A. Kerber, and Howard D. Winters Chapter 11

Trade and the Evolution of Exchange Relations at the Beginning of the Mississippian Period

INTRODUCTION

The subject of intergroup trade holds a minor place in Mississippian period archaeology. In only a handful of studies has this subject been related in any significant way to larger topics of economy, society, and ecology. As a consequence, it has been relegated to a subsidiary place in portrayals of the period (Griffin 1967, 1985). A measure of its unimportance is the short notice given in two recent overviews (Smith 1986; Steponaitis 1986a). The status of trade, however, needs to be upgraded, if for no other reason than to provide information on the relationship between the growth of political centralization and the development of trade networks, which are central topics in most discussions of hierarchical societies in other parts of the world.

There are three aspects of trade that require systematic research before the subject can begin to yield useful information. First, the raw materials of traded objects need to be accurately sourced to develop a pattern of exchange relations (Plog 1977). Second, the relative value of objects has to be identified, and third, the objects have to be distinguished by context of manufacture, use, and consumption. On all fronts, some advances have been made in recent years that hold hope for the development of more sophisticated approaches to a subject that has long been dominated by a trait list approach (Holmes 1919).

In this chapter various strands of admittedly incomplete and problematical data are brought together in an effort to demonstrate how certain approaches to the exchange relations underlying trade can contribute to a sharper understanding of the social and political changes heralded by the beginning of the Mississippian period. Trade is not necessarily conceived of as providing the crucial answers to questions posed by these changes. Merely, that the subject of trade is probably as important to their solution as the traditionally central subjects of subsistence and settlement changes.

The subject of this chapter is intergroup exchange, which archaeologically is accessible mainly through evidence of trade. For purposes here it will be equated with the movement of durable goods and other objects rather than as a specific type of such transfer, such as truck or barter (Renfrew 1975:4). Trade is only an aspect of external relations. It clearly has to share a place with warfare and intermarriage. As Dalton stated, "Warfare, trade, and marriage meant external relationships of hostility and alliance, relations of antagonism and dependence, the opposite of isolation and self-sufficiency" (Dalton 1977:200). Thus, food, marriage mates, and valuables become simply alternative spheres of the larger political economy (Dalton 1977). Because exchange is the major vehicle by which small-scale societies conduct external relations, the trade part of exchange provides us with an instrument to investigate the changing relations of societies with each other and the changes within components of individual societies (Friedman 1975; Service 1975).

This chapter will offer a perspective on trade in the early phases of the Mississippian period by relying on a handful of artifact distributions to address some selected questions about the prehistory of this period. The area of study is confined to part of the eastern Woodlands that includes the Southeast (according to the definition in *The Handbook of North American Indians*) and the Mississippi River valley to the west and north. Excluded are the Great Lakes and the drainage of the Atlantic seaboard. The principal example—Mill Creek chert hoes—rests on data collected by Howard Winters.

THE PLACE OF TRADE IN MISSISSIPPIAN PERIOD STUDIES

Discussion of the changes around the A.D. 1000 timeline is best begun by reviewing the perspectives for trade in the Mississippian period. Two distinct areas of scholarship have been established that have only occasionally been brought together (Brown 1983; Winters 1981). First, there has been an interest in sourcing objects imported into sites, particularly those of distant origin (Bell 1947; Jones 1939; Peebles 1971). Second, there has been a fascination with the objects of the Southeastern Ceremonial Complex as a cultural phenomena, complete with the necessity that it has a distinct areal distribution and a proper time slot (Waring 1968; Waring and Holder 1945). By making the Complex possess all these essential properties of a culture (cult in shorthand), its artifacts and subject matter are almost entirely excluded from the economic sphere. As a consequence, the separation from exchange is made all the more complete, and consideration of ordinary imports is left to dominate the study of trade. However, as it will become clear, the study of flint sources and foreign pottery derivation cannot be divorced from the sources, uses, and consumption of elaborately crafted marine shell and copper artifacts that have come to represent the heart of the Southeastern Ceremonial Complex. Both are traded in the same exchange networks. Without each other, a portrayal of Mississippian period trade would be incomplete.

Although a great deal of miscellaneous information has accumulated about quarries, saltworks, and highly refined crafts, this information has had remarkably little impact on models of the Mississippian period as a whole, to say nothing of its beginnings (cf. Muller 1987). Rather, it is the subject of external relations that has dominated the literature on the Mississippian period. Warfare and intersocietal competition are aspects of local-level external relations that have assumed prime importance in models of these past systems (Gibson 1974; Larson 1972; Peebles and Kus 1977). The archaeological literature on trade as a vehicle for change in this period is small (e.g., Muller 1987; Peebles 1987; Porter 1969, 1974).

Before considering specific lines of inquiry on intergroup trade, a discussion of models applicable to the Mississippian period is in order. Trade has held a widely regarded role in understanding the social processes in the development of social and political complexity (Flannery 1968, 1972; Renfrew 1975:4). Historically, trade has played specific roles in thinking about key features of this complexity, ranging from the accumulation of surplus and the stratification of society, to the centralization of state powers. In a recent review, Brumfield and Earle (1987) have organized this thought into three major perspectives. First is the commercial development model, which views trade as a means for capital accumulation. This model assumes that land and labor are commodities. Because there is no basis for this line of thought in aboriginal eastern woodland economies, it need not concern us further.

The second perspective is more central to Mississippian studies. Brumfield and Earle (1987) label this the adaptationist model, which is really a set of models with a common perspective. The third basic perspective Brumfield and Earle (1987) consider can be appropriately described as political. Both of these will be addressed for their potential to use trade information in elucidating the social and cultural changes that took place in the centuries preceding and following A.D. 1000.

TRADE AND SOCIETY

Archaeological evidence for trade is often so infrequent that it leads to the false impression that trade among small-scale agricultural communities is rare and that cultural isolation predominates. This impression is undoubtedly a consequence of the relative invisibility of trade in the archaeological record due to arbitrary samples and adverse preservation (cf. Muller 1987; Wright 1967, 1968). When comparable social settings are examined by cultural anthropologists, external relations, often extending considerable distances, turn out to be integral to provisioning activities of these societies. Indeed, access to foreign items, through either trade or direct acquisition, often is discovered to be a critical vehicle for local-level transactions of all kinds (Wright 1968).

In eastern woodlands archaeology, the site, and the cultural tradition it represents, can no longer be regarded as the remains of an isolated, self-sustaining community. Although it has been commonplace to ascribe the provisioning of peoples who left these sites solely in terms of their immediate resources, a wider sphere exists from which useful and economically significant items are derived. Only a very parochial view of the economy treats this wider sphere as somehow outside the subject of prehistoric economies.

The place of items acquired externally to the local economy is no mystery. Settled populations regularly resort to the use of foreign materials or finished items as a means of validating social transactions. Exotic items can be expected to be so employed. Even simple hunter-gatherers employ exotic materials to express social differences and mark individual distinction. The principles involved are worth stating here in Hirth's (1984b:1) words:

> Because economic activities embody and reinforce social categories and statuses, reconstructing economic relationships has become one of the principle ways of examining social relationships. Mauss, for example, pointed out that in many instances the exchange of commodities is a physical manifestation of the social relationships found in society. . . . By moving commodities within the society, individuals reinforce those relationships of mutual dependency that are necessary for survival.

The transfer of items outside of the community is the basis of that quintessential political activity, alliance formation. Dalton (1977) has trenchantly argued that in aboriginal economies of stateless (or acephalous) societies, trade held a particular role in alliance relations among primary descent groups. These alliance relations were simultaneously political, economic, and social. The exchanges in these alliance relations were undertaken with primitive valuables—the Kula bracelets of the Trobriand economy. Dalton states some of the ways in which these valuables were important:

> The kula valuables were more than sentimental symbols or tokens, like crown jewels or sports trophies. They were spent, transacted, paid out, but in noncom-

mercial ways, that is in political and social ways, such as death compensation, bridewealth, and war alliance formation. Primitive valuables, such as kula bracelets in the Trobriands and pearl shells in the Highlands, are of most interest to us because they were intimately connected to statelessness, to ceremonial exchanges, and to alliance formation; in short, they were the most important sort of money-like thing in aboriginal economies in stateless societies employing ceremonial exchange. It was primitive valuables that were used by big-men and lineage leaders for important political and social transactions: death compensation, payments to allies, bridewealth, and, occasionally, for emergency conversion . . ., as when the precolonial Tobrianders traded off kula valuables for seed yams in time of famine (Dalton 1977:198).

A number of salient points have been made that require reiteration. Trade can be assumed to have been pervasive whether or not exotics have been recovered archaeologically. Groups that conduct marriage alliances outside of their subsistence catchment are automatically involved in trade. Where alliances and exchange partnerships exist, warfare can be expected to follow as an alternative state of external relations. Finally, trade objects themselves possess value as tokens in solely internal social transactions, thereby laying the basis for a purely local demand.

TRADE AND REDISTRIBUTION

Through the influence of Sahlins (1958) and Service (1962) the second of Brumfield and Earle's perspectives has received widespread attention among American scholars. Sahlins employed the exchange typology of Polanyi (1957)—reciprocal, redistributive, and market relations—as the economic mainsprings of certain social evolutionary types identified as bands, tribes, chiefdoms, and states. Implicit in the Sahlins application of Polanyi was the equation between a redistributive economy and a chiefdom (Carneiro 1981).

Service (1962) took the model of a redistributive system one step further and proposed a thesis, which has since become popular in thinking, about the evolution of chiefly political organizations. In this model, the key to the economy of the chiefdom was the managerial service provided by the central leader to even out through redistribution the unequal productivity of individual farming units. This meant that irrespective of the relative success achieved each year, every community would be assured an adequate food supply through the gifts provided by the chief in redistributive rites as long as they submitted to his demands for contributions to the common pool. The redistributive activity of the central manager became a key process by which the food supply system was rationalized in the absence of a supply-and-demand market. As a result of this emphasis on the major managerial function of central leadership, economics became the theoretical route by which political centralization was achieved. Through his regulatory role, the chief assumed power by contributing to the benefit of participating communities. An adaptationist argument clearly underlies this model, which rests on the unstated proposition that the adaptive fitness of the participants was enhanced by economic centralization, thereby contributing to individual reproductive success and the consequent spread of the chiefly institution as an evolutionary sociopolitical type. This model, whether or not all of its features have been subscribed to, has been employed in a number of theoretical versions to explain the adaptation of Mississippian period social systems to their natural and social environment (e.g., Peebles 1971).

An influential version of this line of thinking by Peebles and Kus (1977) shifted the characterization of chiefdoms from the solely economic process per se to a generalized central function. In keeping with the adaptive perspective, they defined a chiefdom as a political organization in which the basic residential social units delegate certain decision-making functions to a central leader. Minimally, these functions include those that deal with risk and uncertainty in the social and natural environment. This centralization would have conferred greater adaptive fitness than would otherwise be possible on the level of independent subsistence communities.

> If, for example, the variables affecting food production (rainfall, first and last frost, floods, etc.) were least predictable, then there should be evidence either of a mixed strategy of exploitation or of storage and distribution of foodstuffs to even out the fluctuations in production. If warfare is a major unpredictable environmental variable, then there should be evidence of defensive organization. If intersocietal trade in essential items is a critical variable, then there should be some evidence for the "management" of this trade. In sum, there should be a correlation between the complexity of organization of the chiefly establishment (Sahlins's degree of stratification) and the complexity of information inputs with which this regulator had to deal (Peebles and Kus 1977:433).

From the perspective of intergroup trade as a means by which group success is managed by chiefs, certain positions follow. If trade has an important role in intersocietal trade, then part-time craft production should have sprung up in response to chiefly demands, and such production should exhibit signs of coordination. Thus, specialization to some degree can be expected as a correlate of the administrative functions assumed by central leaders (Peebles and Kus 1977:432).

In the context of the Moundville site example, Peebles and Kus (1977:442–3) argue that some degree of specialization was present as evidenced by concentrations of (1) finished shell beads, unworked shell, and beadworking tools at the northeast corner of the site, (2) large bone awls and sharpening stones for hide processing in the northeast quadrant, and (3) large fired hearths, caches of shell, clay and fullers earth for pottery production at the western edge of the site. Low variability in shape and volume of ceramic vessels was further evidence for nonhousehold directed craft production. Some of the items important in intersocietal trade were thought to have been produced by resident craftsmen.

Intersocietal trade was evidenced by the foreign ritual objects interred with the elite in and around Mound C at Moundville. Following Flannery (1968), exchange of these ritual items, identified with objects of the Southeastern Ceremonial Complex, was the vehicle by which elites created obligations among peers in other polities. From the adaptationist perspective, these obligations ultimately served to buffer and balance any differential productivity of subsistence goods between these societies. For Moundville the exchange of ritual objects was a principal means of successful higher-level coordination of foreign relations by centralized leadership (Peebles and Kus 1977:443–444). These objects eventually became removed from trade circulation through burial, thereby dampening the inflationary tendencies of overproduction (Brown 1975).

Following the centralized control feature of the Sahlins and Service models, central chiefly control was visualized as a widespread characteristic of Mississippian period polities (Smith 1978). Trade, likewise, was a critical resource to be controlled. Indirect evidence has been cited in the spatial positioning of towns within the Moundville phase polity (Steponaitis 1978). Lesser towns were observed to have clustered either around central Moundville or near the frontier in such a pattern as to suggest that tribute demands had a centripetal effect on town and village location nearby and a centrifugal effect outside of the sphere of immediate domination.

However, the inference that external trade was commonly centralized has been challenged by Muller (1987). He argues that in the Black Bottom area of the Ohio River a small but persistent presence of painted pottery (a specialized product) in central towns and small hamlets alike was a pattern that did not conform to centralized control of privileged objects. Further, he observes that access to saltworks in southern Illinois were likewise without evidence of control by nearby centers. Not only does use of these works appear to be part-time, but access could easily have been direct, without interference from nearby fortified settlements. Muller raises the question of whether craft production was subject to central control to any degree. His arguments reveal that support of this thesis by archaeological evidence is conspicuously weak. Thus, the extent and degree to which central control is manifest in the Southeast is problematical. As a consequence of this critique, one is led naturally to question whether management-type models of political organization have any force in explaining developments in the prehistoric Southeast. Muller's criticisms are not isolated, but coincide with the arguments of others that redistribution and centralized control have rarely been associated with chiefly political formations (Brumfield and Earle 1987; Carneiro 1981; Earle 1977, 1987; Feinman and Neitzel 1984).

PRESTIGE GOODS ECONOMY

Criticism of the place of redistribution in chiefdom models encourages us to examine Brumfield and Earle's (1987) third basic perspective. Under the "political economy" rubric lies many distinct models that are united by the place that the allocation and flow of wealth has in social control and political manipulation (e.g., Brumfield and Earle 1987; Renfrew and Shennan 1982; Renfrew and Cherry 1986). Unlike the adaptationist perspective, trade is essentially an instrument of political activity that does not satisfy specific needs, whether they are the accumulation of wealth or the buffering of shortfalls in the local food supply.

Of the different approaches available we prefer to focus on a political economic model that is far removed from the Service model. In what has become known as the Prestige Goods Economy, stress has been placed on the function of imported valuables in an economy in which families have to compete for a limited supply of the necessary wealth essential to discharging ordinary social obligations (Ekholm 1977; Friedman and Rowlands 1977:132–143). For an economy in which agricultural productive capacity defines the ranking of households, Friedman (1975) argued that such wealth will preferentially gravitate to the higher ranking households possessing the greatest capacity to mobilize goods and produce food.

Not all such systems that are covered by Friedman's model make use of long-distance exchange to anchor the top of the wealth pyramid in exotic artifacts. But those that do, depend upon the monopoly that a dominating elite have on extrasocietal exchange relations with distant peers (Friedman and Rowlands 1977). Monopoly is enhanced by the conduct of all forms of ceremonial gift exchange and warfare-waging functions by chiefs. But crucial to the success of their monopoly is the services they perform in other social arenas.

> Command over valuables can only participate in the evolution of political hierarchies where it can be used to support claims to preeminent honour of another kind, the right to perform special functions for a wider community. 'Wealth' and prestige as such can only indicate the fitness of such a claim in the eyes of society. Furthermore, where control over imports remains de facto rather than de jure, it may be fragile . . . (Gledhill 1978:260).

Such a monopoly stimulates expansion of long-distance trade in exclusive status-markers as exchange mates join the network as peers. With this expansion comes the opportunity for paramount chiefs to acquire items that are increasingly beyond the reach of less advantageously positioned minor elite. Both are factors contributing to the expansion of the inter-peer exchange network. Because competition between neighbors fosters a proliferation of participants in the network, and because local-level status promotion by the elite places a premium upon exotics from remote or preeminently prestigious sources, such networks, consequently, will tend to expand to the geographical limit to which polities can participate.

Out of this network comes the capacity of elite patronage to stimulate the florescence of arts and crafts. Similarly, the consumption of utilitarian and nonutilitarian (but commonly used objects) stimulates the production of local crafts. In developed economies this same control over foreign relations gives rise to a form of centralized finance (Brumfield and Earle 1987). An important feature of the Prestige Goods Economy is the role that elite demands on local-level production has in accelerating the consumption of ordinary items through inflating the requirements of local social transactions of all kinds, such as bride wealth, funerary offerings, and blood compensation (Gledhill 1978:261). Thus, production and consumption at all social levels is expanded through elite financial manipulations and control (Brumfield and Earle 1987).

Indirectly Muller (1987) has provided a case in support of the political perspective. He argues that craft specialization in the Mississippian period was structurally undeveloped and that there was little evidence to support a level of coordination above that of purely local-level control of production and distribution (Muller 1987:20). As a major point, he raises the possibility that salt procurement, evidenced by salt-making equipment at salt springs, was available through direct access to the source and may not have been under any local monopoly. In his point-by-point argument, Muller undermines the managerial theory of chiefly social formations by pointing to the threadbare justification for either subsistence production or prestige goods distribution to be under central coordination. Although he held out for the importance of the coordination of information in chiefdoms, his critique amounts to a brief for the political perspective. On a theoretical level, centralized control is not a feature of the model reviewed here. Substantively, it is difficult to find examples whereby chiefs actually instituted centralization or coordination of production at the local level (Feinman and Neitzel 1984). Certainly, the finance of their products in most ethnohistoric situations does not rest on such management. Torrence (1986) has marshalled cases where resource procurement remained direct in access, even where the material was useful to emerging state formations. It would appear that centralization is not a necessary feature of developing economies anywhere. It is probably a secondary development and one that emerges unevenly at that (Carneiro 1981). The political perspective outlined here does not entail centralization of any kind of function. It is a political economy in which privilege, power, and hierarchy evolve as an outcome to the consequences in how important resources are allocated to alternative ends.

MODELS OF TRADE AND SOCIAL CHANGE

In the context of the critical centuries in which social formations typical of Mississippian period evolved, the two models presented above have some significant statements to make.

Both models specify an important relationship between the external economy and food production. For the Service model, external trade and other foreign relations are administrative functions requiring centralization in order to ensure success. Maize agriculture increases the necessity for coordination of foreign affairs because of the increased risk of conflict brought on by expansion of population. This increase is a consequence of more effective administration of food disparities among producers. In the Prestige Goods Economy external trade introduces exotic objects that become a means of implementing and validating status changes among lineages. Preeminent status, which carries with it the means of establishing extrasocietal exchange, attracts gifts through the honor and sacred association attached to such status. With the growth of power that such honor instills comes the recourse to exactions of outright tribute. Both gifts and tribute constitute funds out of which projects of a less sacred character can be financed. The kind and quality of these gifts can differ, with ordinary quality items returned into the local economy and high-quality items consumed as status items or traded to elites in other polities. But the organization of production ultimately rests with local-level decision makers. This activity is concentrated on the manufacture of wealth as well as goods useful for gifts. In this system elite patronage of arts and crafts can easily become the basis for creating new types of objects or items of extraordinary design out of reach of ordinary craft knowledge.

In both models any change in the internal subsistence economy can be anticipated to have a related impact on the external relations. More specifically, the two models have very different expectations of the early conditions under which wealth is created and goods become circulated, whether at the level of local or inter-elite exchange. Under the centralized control model, density-dependent factors are the trigger to change (Dumond 1972). Centralization is seen as arising in response to the necessity for relieving internal stresses brought about principally by the unequal distribution of food. However, the problems raised by external conflict offer almost as much a scope for centralization of authority for the prosecution of war and the building of alliances. The same principle of control constitutes the basis for wealth, mainly through restricted access to critical resources. Once created, wealth production is capable of central stimulation. Thus, the production of all manner of high-demand items, such as salt, shell valuables, or coppers, can be expected to be jealously protected and access rigorously controlled in this model. Furthermore, as the chiefly polities become larger, the more numerous would be the sources controlled in order to keep pace with the outflow of prestige goods and the internal redistribution of useful necessities.

In the Prestige Goods Economy, population-dependent factors are not critical. The process of expansion in production of goods of all kinds ensues from inter-household competition for marriage mates in order to increase the size of the workforce. Competition has the effect of distributing relative honor and social importance among lineages. In this system, the more productive lineage becomes the more attractive to the most able bodied workers and prestigious individuals, thereby ensuring success politically and economically. Where wealth is used as an instrument for conducting bride price and other forms of debt payment, households compete in amassing wealth through production and debt claims. Here again, productive might is self-reinforcing. In this competition there comes a point when prestigious lineages will reach out to more distant peers and seek to consolidate their elevated honor through acquiring rare, prestige-enhancing artifacts. A rather uninhibited competition for honor can be expected in the early, formative phases of social hierarchies. Upon consolidation around an entrenched chiefly line, interlineage competition can be expected to level off and perhaps even decline.

So, in the matter of trade, the two models take very different positions toward social and political implications. In one, trade waxes and wanes along with population compaction and political strength. In the other, it grows in response to competition among weakly unified local lineages and changes its character after hierarchies consolidate. Both models articulate with the long-held position that Mississippian period trade was a consequence of the production of a storable food supply in stable maize-based economies (Griffin 1967, 1985). For one model this connection affects trade through the intervening variable of social stability and centralization of administration and craft patronage. For the other, trade is a direct reflection of the deployment of wealth as an instrument of social advancement of autonomous lineages. Production is uncoordinated and capacity is governed by household size and clientele. Elaborate prestige goods are not the design of centralized functionaries but an emergent creation of households bent on elevating themselves at the expense of their neighbors. Food production is the basis for supporting larger households and attracting client households in what is essentially a prestige-driven model.

THE CONTEXT OF TRADE BETWEEN A.D. 800 AND 1200

What are the conditions in which trade might play a role in the cultural, economic, and demographic changes that took place between 800 and 1200? The changes in cultural form and the appearance of new and enhanced technologies, different settlement patterns, and a specific ceremonial architecture signals far-reaching changes in other domains. Of long-held significance is the transformation of maize agriculture from a minor crop at the beginning of this 400-year transitional period to a dominant source of food at the end. This economic shift, of course, is very significant because the supplanting of noncereals by a cereal grain implies an increase in calories per unit effort (Reidhead 1980, 1981). More problematical is the timing of this shift in labor efficiency. Contrary to hallowed belief, demographics, settlement patterns, and architectural patterns change before maize agriculture is well entrenched (Lynott et al. 1986; Smith 1986; Steponaitis 1986a), thus undermining the presumed priority of subsistence change in its causal relationship to cultural change. Other important changes take place at the same time, further complicating the picture. In the

American Bottom area where a well-controlled series of completely mapped sites exists, settlements undergo a sequence of change in layout. At the Range site the number of structures per unit area rises during the first few centuries. Throughout the 400 years the average habitation structure increases in size and village layouts shift from irregular or circular to well-defined alignments of structures (Bareis and Porter 1984). The actual number of such structures per century rises in the first half of the period, briefly stabilizes and declines at the end, thus leading to the conclusion that the resident population was growing to about A.D. 1100 before a progressive decline set in (Milner 1986). In this single area the factors of subsistence, demography, and the social discipline of settlement organization change in a complicated manner very different from a simple cause-effect relationship.

Certainly the prestige good trade networks had been undergoing a renaissance during the Emergent Mississippian period. Burial data for the lower Illinois Valley (then a cultural extension of the American Bottom) show an unmistakable rise in both the number and proportion of burials with shell beads after A.D. 800 (Kerber 1986). These are mostly *Anculosa,* but a substantial number of marine shell beads are present. This increase is spread over all age/sex categories (juveniles are especially prominent as recipients) and all sites. Other categories of grave wealth are too infrequent, and too varied, to show any trends. It is unfortunate that the sources of *Anculosa* beads have not been pinpointed. *Anculosa* beads go back a long way as occasional finds, however, and their sudden increase in popularity suggests that new social and/or economic arrangements had substantially altered their value or availability.

The changes in prestige good networks were paralleled during the Emergent Mississippian period by an increased self-assertiveness on the part of local polities, as evidenced in the divergent styles of cemetery building that take root after A.D. 800. Political competition among local communities is apparent at least as far back as Early Bluff times, where there is ample evidence of warfare. It is probably not coincidence that long-distance trade reappears with the establishment of strong local polities, and the ebbing of local warfare. As new political structures grew, increased power could both cause and benefit in turn from reduced warfare. The development of new, and the revival of old, trade

networks could encourage political growth. At perhaps the most fundamental level, the adoption (in many places) during the Emergent Mississippian period of maize cultivation offered further support in the form of increased labor demands, increased sedentism, increased local production risks, and increased possibility of surplus production. Observations similar to Cahokia have been marshalled for Moundville by Peebles (1987). Trade in exotics rises to a peak at A.D. 1200, only to drop later in relation to locally crafted items.

Trade-based models have something to contribute to these and other observations for the period. Under the centralized control model, valuables can be expected to be hoarded and used for conducting foreign exchange. Special craft areas can be expected to be located close to and under the control of chiefly leadership. Major changes in craft production should be visible when settlement patterns change or when other changes signal the establishment of centralized control. Under the Prestige Goods Economy, dramatic rises in the amount of valuables manufactured locally and disposed of in graves and other locations should appear early. Prestige goods will make their appearance in small spheres of regionally produced items first and gradually increase in distribution and exoticness as competitively advantaged lineages gain hegemony over a district and begin to forge alliances with distant peers.

Aside from these differences in timing, the two models are distinguished by their approach to trade goods. In the central control model, external trade is not well-differentiated by value and function, being mainly determined by a single social function. In the Prestige Goods Economy model, fast turnover valuables (shell bead wealth), items obtained for use (hoe blades), and slow turnover sumptuary goods (headdress plates) will have distinct patterns of distribution and abundance. In sum, trade goods have the distinct potential to enlighten us about the social bases of the transformations between A.D. 800 and 1200.

RAW MATERIAL SOURCES AND THEIR IDENTIFICATION

The subject of trade has not occupied a prominent position in Mississippian period studies, despite the fact, long recognized in the literature, that certain raw materials and finished goods moved thousands of kilometers. In the Woodland (Seeman 1979; Spence 1982;

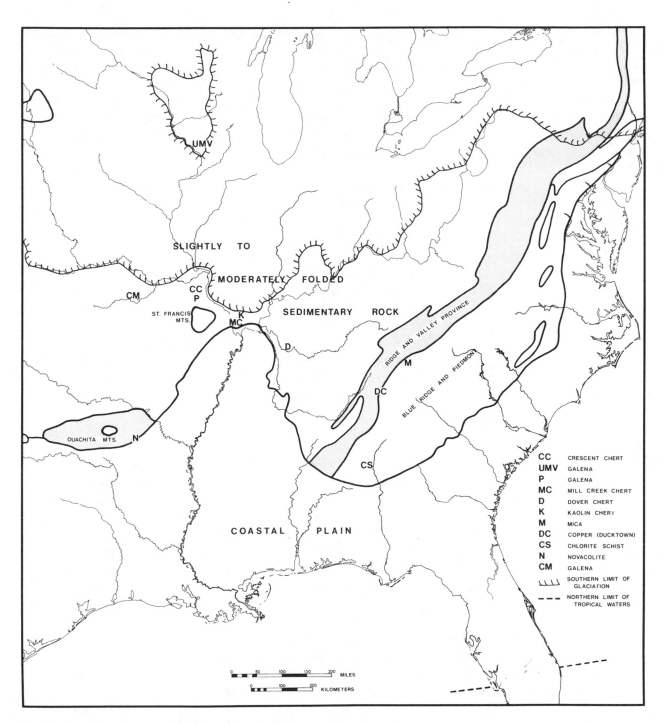

Fig. 82. Geography of common minerals and important resource zones.

Wright 1974) and even the Archaic periods (Winters 1968) this subject has been of more central concern. Valuable observations have been marshalled for the Historic period as well (Wright 1967, 1968). Irrespective of the status of trade research, certain observations

appear warranted although much of what will be said here is tentative pending more systematic fingerprinting of objects from dated contexts.

This chapter will neither attempt to summarize previous research on the subject of Mississippian trade nor will it itemize instances of exotics that have been recorded in the literature. In the first place, the itemization of detail would threaten to blur the patterns we have chosen. In the second place, many of the exotic identifications will not bear up under expert scrutiny. They do not rest on the necessary groundwork that takes into consideration the range and variability of particular rocks and minerals. To complicate matters, many raw materials have multiple sources potentially, and only a few can be unquestionably identified to a single source, particularly from the inspection of hand specimens.

The source of raw materials continues to constitute a major hurdle to pinpointing trade networks. In the Mississippian period, copper, marine shell, pearls, mica, red pipestones (bauxite), greenstones, glauconite, fluorite, galena, and various flints have been sought for crafting prestigious as well as utilitarian objects. The sources of the animal and mineral resources exploited for trade in the Early Mississippian period are indicated in Figure 82 together with the major resource zones they are found in. Arguably the three highest valued materials, native copper, large marine shells, and freshwater pearls, are among the most difficult to source, each erecting very different problems of identification.

Copper sourcing is very intractable (Goad 1980; Goad and Noakes 1978; Rapp et al. 1980, 1984; Woolverton 1974). The crystalline state of native copper is so pure that careful sampling of diagnostic trace elements have to be undertaken to discriminate between possible sources. Only recently has sophisticated equipment been developed that can adequately cope with the problem. The Ducktown area has been pinpointed as a southeastern source of native copper (Goad 1980; Hurst and Larson 1958), otherwise glacial drift is likely to be the major source of placer nuggets. Rapp and associates (1984) have identified the gravels of the Snake River in Minnesota as one source, but undoubtedly the gravel trains of the Mississippi and Illinois rivers are likely to be others. Given the proximity of nugget-bearing river gravels to major Mississippian period earthworks along the upper Mississippi River, this source cannot be dismissed. At this stage in our knowledge the most that can be said about copper sources is the relative potential of certain districts to yield usable nuggets.

Marine shells used in the fabrication of artifacts are found over a wide stretch of coastline from Cape Hatteras to Mexico. *Busycon contrarium*, the most extensively used large gastropod, is most common on the west coast of Florida (Hale 1976). Other species can only be found in tropical waters. For this reason and because the size of the more catholic and cold-tolerant taxa reach exceptional size in warmer tropical waters, the large size of many archaeologically recovered shells indicates a predominance of a peninsular Florida provenience. Today tropical waters wash only as far north as Tampa Bay (Fig. 82). The sources of freshwater pearls are even more dispersed, being from the various locations that produce abundant mussels. Subtle differences in pearl sheen are recognized by jewelers today as providing indication of the river beds in which the shell hosts lived, but unfortunately, burial of pearls destroys this distinctive coloration (Vertrees 1913).

Lesser valued rocks and minerals offer different problems in source identification, but they are ones that long-term research can make more reliable (Speilbauer 1976). Unfortunately, most of the materials found in Mississippian sites have not been adequately provenienced. Although the mineral may be properly identified, the identification of the source or sources is quite another matter. Research findings on galena sources are very instructive (Walthall 1981; Walthall, Stow, and Karson 1980). Walthall and his collaborators showed that one must thoroughly investigate all possible sources because out-of-hand attribution of rocks and minerals to the closest available deposit can lead to ignoring the possibility of long-distance trade from a much more distant source. The opposite may also be true. Just because material resembles a well-known mineral, such as catlinite, does not mean it is this material, nor does it point to the same source used historically (Gundersen and Tiffany 1986). Not only can the distance to the source be grossly underestimated (or in the rare instance, overestimated), one can be lulled into thinking that a single source is involved. Detailed work on sourcing invariably leads to the discovery that multiple sources are possible, if not highly likely.

All told, there is a general structure to the distribution of raw materials used in long-distance trade. Copper sources are present most abundantly in the Great Lakes area or in the northern drift-derived deposits of the Till Plains mantling the Midwest (Fig. 82). Marine

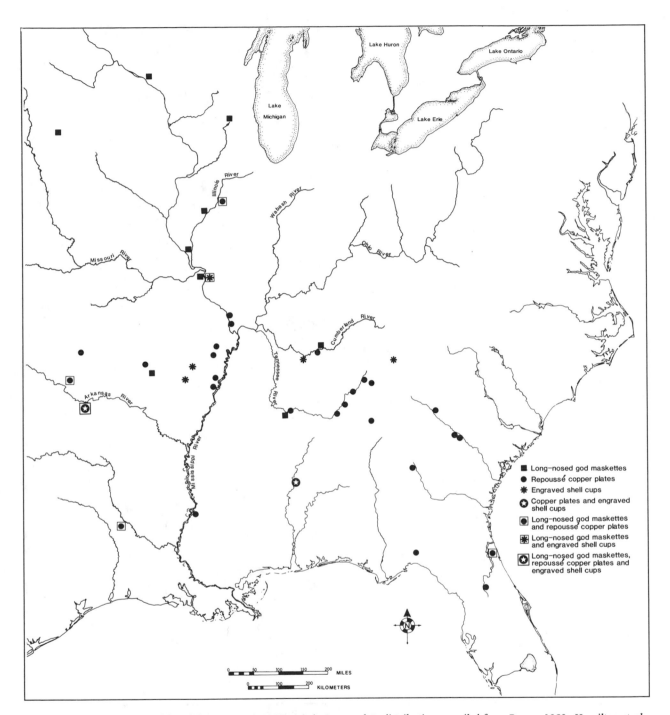

Fig. 83. Distribution of valuables of the A.D. 1000–1200 period. Copper plate distribution compiled from Brown 1983; Hamilton et al. 1974; Jones 1982. Engraved shell cups from Phillips and Brown 1978. Long-nosed god maskettes from Hall (n.d) and Kelly (1980).

shells are found in the shallow waters and beaches of the Gulf and south Atlantic. In between are to be found pigments, mainly on the edge of the Gulf Coastal Plain. Igneous rocks are found concentrated in the glacial drift and the beds of the folded Appalachians, and to a lesser extent, the Ozarks and Ouachitas. But otherwise it is evident that many of the rocks and minerals made use of can be found in a multitude of locations. What is

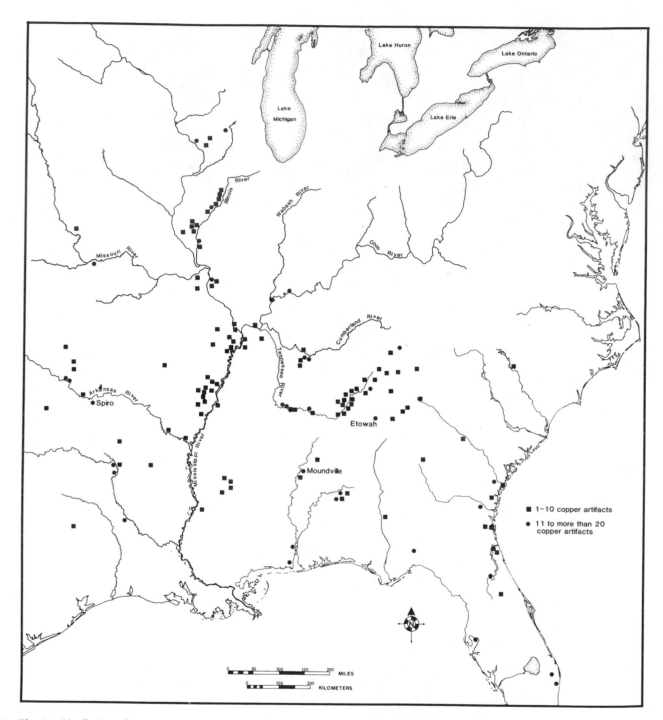

Fig. 84. Distribution of copper artifacts among Mississippian period sites (after Goodman 1984).

noteworthy, following the discoveries of galena finger-printing, is that only a selection of the total number of possible sources were utilized. Further, these tend to be located near major concentrations of farming communities.

ARTIFACT-ORIENTED RESEARCH

At this stage in the study of Mississippian trade, mapping of distinctive artifact distributions remains one of the most common vehicles for exploring trade connections (e.g., Brown 1983; Goodman 1984), although

Trade and the Evolution of Exchange Relations 263

distribution maps have been placed more often in the service of typology (e.g., Moorehead 1917; Webb and DeJarnette 1942:286–300) and chronological integration (e.g., Griffin 1952; Williams and Goggin 1956) than anything else. Distributional plots of long-nosed god maskettes have led the way (Hall n.d.; Kelly 1980:212–213; Williams and Goggin 1956), but similar potential in other items, such as engraved shell cups and gorgets and repoussé copper plates remains unrealized (Fig. 83). Some of this potential is indicated by the far-flung distribution of look-alike copper plates (Griffin 1952). The density of Mississippian period copper artifacts is indicated by Figure 84.

Site-oriented studies of raw material sources, chiefly chippable stone, have gained in favor (e.g., Bell 1943; Brown 1983; Kelly 1984; Perttula 1984; Southard 1973). Sourcing of particular raw materials remains very unusual for any period (Goad 1978; Otteson 1978; Walthall 1981). Museum-oriented distributional studies are not much more common (Goodman 1984; Winters 1981). Lists of marine shells from different inland sites convey some information about trade, but the subject has yet to be dealt with systematically (Brown 1983; Hale 1976; Parmalee 1958; Van der Schalie and Parmalee 1960).

A more common topic is the provenience of trade vessels (Bareis and Porter 1965; Brown 1983; O'Brien 1972; Steponaitis 1983; Williams 1979). This effort has been undertaken with different degrees of precision. It is a subject that requires detailed microscopic effort, particularly where plain wares are concerned (Ferring and Perttula 1987). Elaborately decorated pottery is less open to erroneous assignment, although here too identification is not error-free (Bareis and Porter 1965).

TRADE IN THE SOUTHEAST

The circulation of prestige goods among distinct regional entities has not been widely accepted. Waring and Holder (1945) in their classic formulation of the Southeastern Ceremonial Complex were willing to accept trade in raw materials, such as marine shell and native copper, but were averse to accepting the same in prestige goods, arguing that the degree of stylistic and motif localism on decorated items from Etowah, Moundville, and Spiro was much too great to support an argument for exchange among them.

Bell (1947) was one of the few who stressed the significance of the trade in his preliminary review of exotic materials from Spiro. He found that almost all of the items assignable to the Southeastern Ceremonial Complex were of exotic material and that these items were accompanied by other equally foreign objects. Thus, in contrast to the view advanced by Waring (Waring and Holder 1945; Waring 1968), Bell raised the point that the presence of objects of this complex was part of a larger trade pattern that included many more objects of exotic raw material than was encompassed in the Southeastern Ceremonial Complex lists. Some of this same residue of exotic artifacts (e.g., elongate spatulate celts, pulley-shaped earspools) became the platform on which Baerreis (1957) proposed another ceremonial complex identified principally with the Spiro site. They were widely distributed prestige goods in the Caddoan, upper Mississippian drainage, and Southeastern areas proper. However, this proposal has not met with acceptance because the objects are insufficiently separated in time from the more traditional core of the Southeastern Ceremonial Complex. But the point is well taken that long-distance trade of well-crafted objects in many exotic materials is a characteristic of the Mississippian period throughout its duration. Some of these objects, which are more time-sensitive than others, such as the pulley-shaped earspools and other ornaments, have the potential of being good markers of phases of prestige goods within the Mississippian period. The implications of this perspective toward prestige goods has been, however, slow to influence our thinking of the period (Brown 1975, 1983; Peebles 1971, 1987).

For the early parts of the Mississippian period, discussion of exchange relations centers almost solely on the relationships between Cahokia, the American Bottom, and the northern hinterland (Anderson 1987; Fowler and Hall 1978; Gibbon 1974; Hall n.d.). Trade to the north has been seen as the means whereby Cahokia implanted its influence on the up-river hinterland. Domination of the Midwest was accomplished through trade, slaving, ceremonial feasting, and gift-exchange relations. Although migration is held to have a role in a few Cahokian connections, war and ceremonial domination apply to the majority. Material expression of these relations was evident in the marine shell artifacts, ceramics, and prestige goods deriving from or funnelled through Cahokia. Some of the importance of Cahokia as a regional town center is thought to derive from its trade position (Fowler and Hall 1978; Gibbon 1974). However, the northern trade only focuses on a limited part of the exchange network. The subcontinental scope of this network is left undeveloped, although marine shell stockpiled at Cahokia and elsewhere obviously derived from coastal waters far to the south. Thus the trading activities of Cahokia to its upstream neighbors has a less well known counterpart to the southeast.

Although our knowledge of Mississippian period trading networks is scant, it consists primarily of prestige goods that are usually classified as objects of the Southeastern Ceremonial Complex, particularly those current in the period between A.D. 1200 and 1400. On the basis of trade linkages in this period it is possible to state that the main corridor of intergroup trade described a lazy-J shape with the stem lying just above the 35th Parallel, from the Great Plains to the Appalachians, and the hook descending through Georgia into Florida (Brown 1983). The Arkansas Valley, Memphis region, Nashville Basin, and southern Appalachian Valley lie along this corridor containing most of the famous mound centers yielding prestige goods of repoussé copper and engraved shell. The notable exception is Moundville, which has yielded abundant prestige goods and at least 14 percent of its grave ceramics from foreign locations (Steponaitis 1983, 1986a). The sourceable pottery indicates that Moundville controlled a rival corridor from the Memphis region to the Gulf Coast (Brown 1983).

PRESTIGE GOODS

The economics of scarcity among societies in which valuables affirm a status derived from noneconomic pursuits dictates that these valuables will be employed primarily as emblems of the rank derived from personal exploits and inherited honor. In the Mississippian period principal among them are the columnella pendants, sheet copper hair ornaments and headdresses, robes, pearls, nonfunctional weapon-derived artifacts (including the mace, axes, and long-sword bifaces), ear ornaments, and discoidals (Brown 1976a, 1984; Larson 1971; Peebles 1971; Peebles and Kus 1977). Copper ax heads and pearl beads are among the more precious in the later centuries of the Mississippian period.

Out of the many items of highly valued raw materials of marine shell and copper that were traded in the early part of the Mississippian period, there are several that deserve particular attention here. These are the long-nosed god maskette ornaments suspended in the earlobes, the exaggerated ax heads of spatulate form and exotic material that point to nonutilitarian use, and the repoussé copper plates employed mainly as hair ornaments and headdress pieces. Other items are undoubtedly certain engraved shell cups of the Braden style (Phillips and Brown 1978), ordinary and exaggerated (hypertrophic) arrowheads, found usually in quiver-load batches (Brown 1976b; Fowler 1969), stone discoidals, and mica cutouts (Fowler 1969).

Long-Nose God Maskettes

Ear ornaments in the shape of a small long-nosed human face are well known, amounting to a type fossil for the pre-1200 period (Anderson 1975; Bareis and Gardner 1968; Harn 1975; Kelly 1980; Williams and Goggin 1956). The most up-to-date distribution map follows Kelly (1980). These maskettes tend to be copper in the south and marine shell in north, thus representing the principal exotic material in the place of deposition. They are not uniform in size, detail, or mode of construction, which leads one to conclude that a number of production localities are represented. Maskettes are found far north of Cahokia, somewhat further than the Mill Creek hoes, but about the same distance as Powell Plain and Ramey Incised pottery. They are found in much smaller numbers than the pottery in a manner consistent with the sumptuary contexts of these prestige objects.

Spatulate Celts

Several distinct styles of nonfunctional stone ax heads are dated to this time (Brown 1976b; Pauketat 1983). These include the classic spatulate form (class A of Moorehead 1917)—commonly misnamed spuds, after a potato-digging tool. This is the most broadly distributed of this category of ax head and is commonly made from a greenstone (mostly chlorite schist) of southern Appalachian derivation. A prominent source is the Hillabee formation (Brown 1983). Examples have been found from such widely dispersed localities as Harlan (Bell 1972, 1984), Spiro (Brown 1976b), Gahagan (Webb and Dodd 1939), Cahokia (Titterington 1938), Rudder (Webb and Wilder 1951:235), Ocmulgee (Fairbanks 1956), and Mount Royal (Moore 1894:22, fig. 9). A shorter and palmate-bitted Jersey type (class B of Moorehead 1917) is made of igneous rock typical of the midwestern locations where this form is found (C. Brown 1902, 1926). Another distinctive early ax head form is the bell-shaped type, chipped and polished from Kaolin and occasionally Mill Creek cherts (Moorehead 1917). The latter type was widely traded (Brown 1976b; Titterington 1938) within the sphere of Mill Creek hoe blades.

Repoussé Copper Plates

Embossed sheet copper in the form of headdress plates is widely distributed through the Southeast prior to A.D. 1400 (Fig. 83). Trade is clearly involved in this distribution. Griffin (1952) has cited the near identity of two large plates from Spiro in Oklahoma and Mount Royal in Florida. Much of the other copper was not made at the sites in which they were deposited, including the famous Rogan plates from Etowah (Thomas 1894). One of us has argued that the mixture of styles from individual sites has to be the product of trade and the source of these pieces is indicated by the style connections to readily traceable pottery via engraved shells and other stylistic intermediates (Brown 1989). Although much of this decorated sheet copper is recorded in contexts post-dating the time under consideration here, it is likely that some of it was produced much earlier than the time it was deposited (Brown 1989). In this regard it is instructive that many of the more fragile copper hair ornaments are repaired with riveted patches after heavy wear and tear (Hamilton et al. 1974). Furthermore, it is not unknown for plates to be encrusted with patches embossed in different subjects and even different styles that speak of extended recycling long after initial plate making.

In the pre-A.D. 1200 period, a different pattern of subcontinental trade emerges from the distribution of well-dated prestige goods. Location of long-nosed god maskettes describe a north-south band that points to the existence of a trade corridor along the Mississippi River valley (Fig. 83). The distribution of other prestige goods expands on this picture by bringing in the Southeast and peninsular Florida. The areas involved include those that conform to the patterns of the post-A.D. 1200 period. However, the east-west linkages do not appear to be as strong. Thus, it is problematical whether the later pattern is representative of pre-A.D. 1200 conditions.

UTILITARIAN GOODS—THE MILL CREEK HOE CASE

At the more utilitarian end of the scale are hoes that do not appear to have any prestige attached to them. Because these tools are recovered in large numbers, their distribution provides us with more information than prestige goods on the sphere within which these goods were acquired.

Mill Creek chert deposits, lying in easily accessible beds of residual clay, began to be exploited largely for the production of chert hoe and spade blades as early as 900, when bifaces begin to show up in Merrell phase contexts at Cahokia some 120 km to the northwest (Bareis and Porter 1984:151). Production rose markedly by 1000 to become the single most common material for the making of hoe blades in the Mississippi Valley. This high level of production was sustained for two centuries before it either began to decline or was supplanted, perhaps by production from the Dover quarries to the south.

Mill Creek hoes were produced over a long period. The ovate and side-notched and truncated ovate forms make their appearance as early as A.D. 900 (Fig. 85). The trapezoidal or flared form is much later, only appearing about A.D. 1200 (Bareis and Porter 1984; Lewis 1982:39). A stemmed type is unplaced (Winters 1981).

Mill Creek hoes were distributed over a considerable range (Fig. 86). A hoe chip was discovered on the surface of the Lake George site, Yazoo County, Mississippi (Williams and Brain 1983:252–253). Presumably, this piece belongs to the Crippin Point phase at that site when Ramey Incised and Powell Plain pottery from Cahokia make their appearance. Griffin (1986) places this exchange contact during the Stirling phase (A.D. 1050–1150). At approximately the same time, during Moundville I time, Mill Creek hoes reached a site (1TU50) near Moundville where a hoe chip of this material was found (Steponaitis 1986b).

Although Mill Creek chert was a heavily used resource for the manufacture of hoes, other materials were important (Fig. 86). Probably the next most common is the Ft. Payne chert from the Dover quarry, Stewart County, Tennessee. Kaolin chert from the Iron Mountain deposit of Union County, Illinois, is next

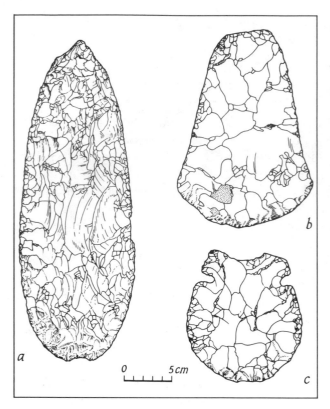

Fig. 85. Mill Creek chipped stone hoe blade forms (from Bareis and Porter 1984, fig. 59); (a) simple ovate form, (b) simple trapezoidal or flared form, (c) side-notched, truncated ovate type.

(Billings 1984). Local use of Crescent (Jefferson County, Missouri [Ives 1984]) and Burlington cherts are known in the Missouri and Illinois areas. Outside the Mill Creek and Dover distributions other materials were used, including orthoquartzite (silicified siltstone), sandstone, limestone, and volcanic rocks.

The production of hoe blades from chert of the Salem formation in the upper drainage of Mill Creek, astraddle the Alexander-Union county line, constituted the single most important source of these implements. This hard, granular flint is well suited to heavy use in tilling and general earth moving of heavy, clay-rich soils in the major inland river valleys. It occurs as nodules and flagstone-shaped pieces that are easily chipped into large bifaces (Winters 1981). Innumerable workshops are scattered over an area approximately 6.5 km by 3.0 km in an unconcentrated pattern without clear indications of coordinated use. Enormous deposits of broken blanks are present throughout the quarry zone (May 1984). This dispersed pattern points to heavy but uncoordinated exploitation over a long time span and perhaps even relatively open access to the quarry beds. It is all the more distinctive because it is so different from the exploitative pattern reported of other contemporary chert quarries nearby (e.g., Kaolin, May 1984).

Phillips's (1900) investigations revealed the chert to have been obtained through open-pit mining. On the surface are depressions 4 to 13 m in diameter and 1.3 m deep. The depth of the pits they mark was discovered in a 21 m long excavation through three depressions. Five pits discovered ranged, in their slumped condition, from 3 to 4.3 m wide and 3.3 to 6.1 m deep. One of the five was part of a freshly filled pit disclosed in a straight-cut, inslanting walled pit extending 3.4 m. Quarry tools and chipped blank pieces were found in the fill. Phillips observed that the knapping done in the vicinity of the pits was really just preliminary shaping. The more refined stages of flintwork were executed at workshops removed from the quarry pits (1899). These workshops are numerous and highly variable in size. Snyder (1910) reported that they ranged from .5 to 2 ha in extent. One workshop stood out as exceptional.

> There are several groups of quarry pits west and north of the town of Mill Creek, where the Hale site is located. This site appears to have been a distributive center for Mill Creek tools, and may even be tied into an exchange network that includes the Linn-Heilig and Ware mound groups. The latter sites are located in the Mississippi floodplain several kilometers to the west (May 1984:76).

The Hale site, a 6 ha center with one small platform mound and a low, rounded burial mound, has been regarded as a village concentrating on the finished production of Mill Creek tools. Located on the foreslope and floodplain of Mill Creek, the midden of debitage, food refuse, and pottery was described as 1 to 2 m deep (Thomas 1894:148). Numerous stone box burials were found there, some containing large bifacial tools, chert preforms, and antler flakers as grave goods (Thomas 1894:149, 150). May states that

> Phillips and Holmes proposed that the Hale Site was a workshop where later stages of tool production were executed, while the primary steps were completed in the hills adjacent to the quarry pits. They made this proposal on the basis of: (1) differences in the kinds

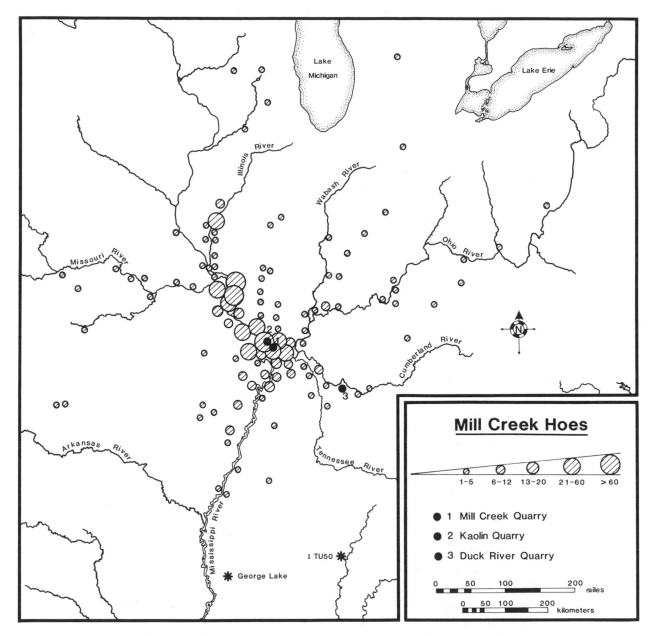

Fig. 86. Distribution of Mill Creek hoe blades. Circles are sized proportionately to number of blades reported for each county; stars indicate the presence of excavated hoe chips of the same chert.

and sizes of debitage found on the Hale Site and quarry sites; (2) the blades found at the Hale Site showed evidence of edge grinding in preparation for secondary chipping; (3) the array of knapping implements found on the Hale Site—including one concentration of antler flakers near the banks of Mill Creek—in contrast to the uniformity of knapping tools encountered at quarry sites; and (4) the fact that grinding stones, assumed to be used in the preparation

of edges for secondary chipping and final retouch, were present on the Hale site but were lacking on upland quarry sites. . . (May 1984:77–8).

From these observations we can conclude that the inhabitants of the Hale site were heavily involved in the manufacture of Mill Creek bifaces of all types. However, it would be premature to conclude that they mo-

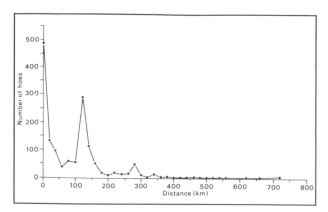

Fig. 87. Fall-off curve of the total number of Mill Creek hoe blades in counties within 20 km intervals from the quarry source.

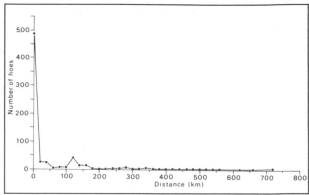

Fig. 88. Fall-off curve of the average number of Mill Creek hoe blades in county centers within 20 km intervals from the quarry source.

nopolized exploitation of the chert beds. Given the lack of more comprehensive information on the archaeology of the area, one can only conclude from the dispersed character of the quarry pits that access to the quarry was shared by a larger group of exploiters than resident at the Hale site.

FALL-OFF CURVE STUDY

Additional light can be shed on the exploitation of the famous Mill Creek quarries by studying the locations that have yielded hoe blades of this material. The source of these records are museums that have amassed large collections of hoe blades of all types (Winters 1981). The Mill Creek hoe blades are of particular interest here because the distribution is relatively complete in all compass directions and because this chert stands the best chance of unambiguous identification.

By simply taking the number of Mill Creek hoes recorded by county, which happens to be the minimal reliable provenience location for 95 percent of all records, a general picture of distribution can be developed. As an index of the total trade effort involved in amassing a particular county's hoe total from the source, we have calculated the hoe distance for each county. Hoe distance is simply the number of hoes multiplied by kilometers.

The incidence of hoes from Union County would be a smooth fall-off curve but for the influence of Cahokia, which produces a strong secondary peak (Fig. 87). A third peak occurs at the 280 km interval, which consists

almost entirely of Cass County's contribution. A tiny peak at 340 km is basically Fulton County, Illinois. Some sites along the Ohio River drainage contribute importantly to the 120–160 km totals, especially Posey County, Indiana. Although the influence of these hot spots is dampened by averaging the county numbers within sets of common distance intervals from Union County, nonetheless the first two are sufficiently strong to remain expressed (Fig. 88). The averaged incidence of Mill Creek hoe blades by distance probably provides a less biased picture of hoe blade fall-off.

Although Cahokia so dominates the distributional pattern to suggest that it may have been a major center from which hoes were distributed, a separate fall-off curve eliminating the Union County records shows that this site does not explain the hoe numbers to the south. A fall-off curve drawn in terms of distance from Cahokia indicates that such a hypothesis cannot account for the generally high level of hoes in the counties surrounding Union County. In fact, it takes 190 km from Union County for hoe levels to reach the same value attained only 50 km from Cahokia. This argues for the Mill Creek region exercising a stronger influence on the hoe total in southern Illinois than Cahokia. Thus a substantial amount of the trade in Mill Creek hoes was carried out by one or more Union County centers.

Another way to view the trade is by river system (see Fig. 86). Excluding Union County, a pattern is revealed by a comparison of the upper Mississippi drainage (embracing all tributaries above Union County) with the Ohio drainage (consisting of the Wabash, Tennessee, and Cumberland) and the lower Mississippi system (made up of the remaining tributaries below Union County). Both the Ohio and upper Mississippi drainages have produced far more hoes than the lower Mississippi drainage, even if the contribution of Madison and St. Clair counties is removed to compensate for the effect of Cahokia. Although hoes traveled slightly farther up the Mississippi, differences with other drainages are probably not significant.

One can examine the fall-off by river system. Here we have attempted to discover whether the individual peaks in the overall fall-off curves were replicated for each of the river systems—as might be the case if trading centers were distributed in some regular fashion up and down river valleys. These results are inconclusive, though they dramatize once again Cahokia's importance to the hoe trade. Hoe distance is probably the best way to pinpoint hot spots, and the list discussed above highlights most counties at the mouth of a major tributary (e.g., St. Clair, Cass, St. Louis, Fulton, Posey counties).

In terms of Renfrew's (1975) models of fall-off curves, Mill Creek hoes fit the directional trade model very well indeed. Clearly, the American Bottom region exerted a very strong directional influence on trade in Mill Creek hoes. This result raises the question of whether the size and proximity or gravitational pull of Cahokia are by themselves enough to account for Cahokia's influence on the hoe trade, or whether other factors such as the location with respect to major rivers or high demand for trade goods may have played an equal role. In order for a gravitational model to account for Cahokia's dominance of the hoe trade, Cahokia would have to represent more than 20 percent of the population of the study area. Moreover, if hoe totals were moving in a strictly gravitational fashion (according to Berry's model cited in Hodder [1978:167]), Cass County would have to have possessed a population equal to Cahokia's.

Since $I_{ij} = a\dfrac{P_j + P_i}{D_{ij}^b}$, then $P_{j + Pi} = \dfrac{I_{ij}D_{ij}^b}{a}$,

where I_{ij} is the interaction between sites i and j; D_{ij} is the distance between the sites; P_i and P_j are the populations of sites i and j, and a and b are constants (a is a scaling factor, and b is usually taken to be 2 [for discussion of approaches to this parameter, see Hodder

1978:167]). If we take P_i to be the population of Union County, and I_{ij} to be the number of hoes exchanged from Union County to some other county j, and we let a = 1.6093, then

$$P_j = \text{Hoes} * \text{Km}^2 - P_i$$

For our purposes, P_i is a constant, so

$$P_j = \text{Hoes} * \text{Km}^2$$

Note that the units of population are not meaningful in themselves under this formulation, but the P_js calculated may be compared to one another. Thus,
St. Clair County: 256 hoes * 121.45^2 km = 3.77×10^6; and Cass County: 45 hoes * 289.32^2 km = 3.77×10^6.

To bring the numbers down to earth, the standardized scores are: St. Clair, 5.89 and Cass, 5.87. Of course, the standardized gravity scores are just another formulation of hoe distance, in this case with distance weighted more heavily.

It seems unlikely that the standardized gravity scores reflect actual population levels although it would be nice to be able to provide some kind of test. Thus, hoes are not moving through the system solely on the basis of the proximity of population centers to Union County. Certain sites exert an influence on hoe movement disproportionate to their size. These centers of trade appear to be located primarily at or near the mouths of major tributaries of the river system on which they are located. Obviously, the data we have are not ideal for pinpointing site locations, but they seem to point to geographical nodes in the exchange network.

The dispersion sphere of Mill Creek hoe blades is about 700 km. Although the size of this exchange sphere may appear to argue for some degree of centralization of exchange relations, the data by itself does not. Larger exchange spheres of stone ax heads are even better documented in southeastern Australia among groups that are not even sedentary (McBryde 1987). This sphere of exchange was maintained without the benefit of water transport, which has undoubtedly extended the fall-off curves (Little 1987).

In parallel fashion hoe blades from rival quarries of Kaolin chert and Dover chert appear to move in an orderly fashion away from their respective centers of production toward trade centers favorably located with respect to river systems and population concentrations (Fig. 86). Very often the trade centers and the population centers are one and the same. Cahokia, the largest and most favorably placed trade center, dominates the hoe trade by volume, but does not maintain an exclusive control over it. This leads to the question of the mode in which hoes were distributed. No answer is possible with the data in hand. Further investigations with standardize values will be required even to approach the question of whether down-the-line, center-to-center, or a mixture of the two fit the distributional data (Hodder 1980; Hodder and Lane 1982).

SHELL BEAD VALUABLES

Shell bead wealth holds an important place in the Prestige Goods Economy. A stock of readily accepted, locally manufactured, exchange valuables are essential to make payments for all manner of social debts. The specific form that these valuables might take is not important, nor does it have to be naturally scarce. The objects should be within the capacity of unskilled manufacturers to produce with simple, but time-consuming, methods. The volume of items produced should be commensurate with the size of the household. The items themselves should be widely found, and occasionally in considerable concentrations.

Beads made from the walls and columnella of large marine gastropods and from pierced small gastropods conform to these specifications. In the early centuries of the Mississippian period, *Marginella* and *Anculosa* beads are particularly common examples of small marine and freshwater shells converted into beads. A number of different shapes occur archaeologically, but the disc bead from the wall of *Busycon* and other large shells is the most common and ubiquitous. Great numbers of beads are reported from particular burials throughout the Southeast (Fowler 1969; Lewis and Kneberg 1946; Prentice 1987).

In keeping with the ordinariness of shell bead production, work areas are known in both large and small sites. At Cahokia large areas of shell bead production are known although inadequately investigated (Mason and Perino 1961). In one area, many shell beads, shell scrap, and burned whelk columnella are found together with small chipped stone drills of the Cahokia microblade industry. The Ramey Tract east of Monks Mound has been a rich source of these materials. A structure filled with shell debris was partially uncovered in the stockade excavations that is early in the Cahokia sequence and antecedent to the stockade (Vander Leest

1980:122). These special spicule-shaped tools were evidently employed in great numbers to drill the holes to make marine shell beads. Experiments reported by the Morses (1980) and associates have demonstrated these tools to be effective shell bead drills. This does not rule out other uses because the surface of some tool-rich areas of Cahokia lack shell debris connected with bead manufacture (Mason and Perino 1961). Activity areas of microdrills and shell detritus are known not only for areas of Cahokia but also in small hamlets belonging to the hinterland of Cahokia (Pauketat 1987; Prentice 1983, 1985, 1987; Yerkes 1983, 1986). The same activities were reported for the Zebree (Morse and Morse 1980) and Chemochechobee sites (Schnell et al. 1981). Complementary to this evidence of shell bead production is the accumulation of marine shell cups and other artifacts, and in shell raw material in graves and associated mortuary features in the Cahokian locale (Fowler 1974; Milner 1984; Pauketat 1987; Winters 1974, n.d.).

CONTEXTS OF PRODUCTION

The Organization of Production

Following the outline of Hirth (1984a), production and consumption will be discussed under the headings of organization of production, the spheres of utility and value, and the factors of distribution. Muller (1987) has argued at length that acquisition of raw materials was organized mainly on the household level. Many rocks and minerals, including native copper, are the sort of resource that is likely to be picked up opportunistically while undertaking other tasks. Certainly, the extent to which resources scattered in placer gravels were the objects of accumulation is likely to be matched by decentralization of the task of primary acquisition. On the other hand, the more that effort is sunk into quarrying, particularly at great depths, the more likely resource acquisition will be undertaken as a coordinated effort. Concentrated effort on a few shafts has not been widely documented. Even at sources as extensively quarried as the Mill Creek locale, there are few pits that qualify as deep shafts, although some are sizable. Although deep mines represent an investment more typical of the organized efforts of patron chiefs, less organized work is not thereby excluded as ethnographic cases testify (Torrence 1986). Decentralization of acquisition appears to be pronounced in the Mississippian period.

Pearls are a particularly good case. This resource remained a highly valuable item from the Middle Woodland to the early Historic period. Yet it is a resource that obviously cannot be predicted and its exploitation depends on the attention of many mussel eaters. To mount a deliberate search would entail an extraordinary labor effort. Without the efforts of many mussel foragers looking for food, it would take more than a single lifetime to amass the number of pearls present in archaeological caches. Because mussels were widely consumed throughout the eastern woodlands, the simplest way to accumulate a large number of these rare gems is to rely on the labor of foragers operating in dispersed localities for supply. Although the collecting of pearls imposes many critical restrictions on accumulation, differences in value do not simply amount to labor value. Pearls are subtly colored according to the valley or river segment source (Vertrees 1913). This is potentially a source of distinction, which if valid, would have further narrowed prime collecting opportunities to areas producing valuable colorations.

Craft production areas appear to have been widely distributed among local self-sufficient farmers. Hamlet localities that contain craftworking debris and tools are known in the American Bottom and Black Bottom. What is interesting is that such craft production is evident in some sites but not in others. Larger centers contain examples of craft debris and tool areas. Workshops have been tentatively identified on a few sites although none has been investigated thoroughly.

Craft production exists for different spheres of trade. Shell bead production fits a requirement of the Prestige Goods Economy—there exists a commonly available medium for wealth accumulation and the discharge of debts (Ceci 1982). Marine shell is a naturally scarce material in the deep interior of North America that limits the amount of material reaching the use areas. In small pieces it makes a good medium of exchange; in large pieces, preserving as much as possible of the larger marine univalves intact (as in cups), it serves well as a major prestige good.

Cahokia was probably a prominent center for production of all manner of trade goods. Large amounts of copper, mica, galena, and quartz on the surface of portions of Cahokia point to either production of arti-

facts from these materials or simple on-site consumption of the same (Vander Leest 1980:122). Of the large centers Cahokia is not alone. The Toltec site in east-central Arkansas has yielded large amounts of debris of rocks and minerals from the Gulf Coastal Plain and the Ouachitas to the south (Rolingson 1982).

At the lower end of the exchange scale is the evidence of trade in utilitarian objects and commodities. In the Emergent Mississippian period, locally manufactured pottery within the American Bottom area was traded internally (Porter 1974). This is a noteworthy example of an intermediate sphere of exchange within communities that gains ground at A.D. 850 and proceeds to include production areas well outside the American Bottom by A.D. 1000 before it ceases (Bareis and Porter 1984; Porter 1969, 1974).

Quarry-working, however, yields one of the more provocative examples of intermediate level of trade. Many quarries are known to have been utilized in the period under consideration, the most famous being the Mill Creek quarry. Other sources exploited before A.D. 1200 are the Crescent, the Kaolin, Arkansas Novaculite (Baker 1982), and probably the Dover quarries. The mica mines of western North Carolina were presumably in use at this time because this material finds its way into the American Bottom (Fowler 1969; Winters n.d.).

Production for food use arises during this period. Saltworks are located adjacent to major salt springs, commonly in the Mississippi River valley (I. Brown 1980). Occupation definitely extends back to the early phases of the Mississippi period (Keslin 1964). One of the few systematically investigated of these saltworks is the Great Salt Spring of southern Illinois (Muller 1984). Many of the saltworks of the interior Mississippian River valley were likewise in production (Keslin 1964).

The procurement strategies of quarrying, mining, and salt spring exploitation are something we know little about. It has sometimes been thought that major regional centers controlled quarry production. Cahokia has been held to have controlled the distribution of Mill Creek chert (Morse and Morse 1983). However, the distribution of chert hoes shows that the site can be demonstrated to have controlled only a small surrounding zone. Acquisition was probably mainly through trade of various types since it is doubtful that a large amount of Mill Creek chert was acquired directly through long-distance treks to the sources. Within these limits, however, there remains a great deal of latitude for the existence of mixed modes of acquisition. Some local-level control over production and distribution could have existed side-by-side with direct access by nearby groups. Examples are reviewed by Torrence (1986).

It is on the matter of craft specialization that the sharpest debate on production has centered (Muller 1984, 1986, 1987; Prentice 1983, 1985; Yerkes 1983, 1986). Although this controversy has concentrated on the degree of specialization, the assumptions held in common disclose how fundamental the political centralization model is to current thinking about the political and economic organization of societies in the Mississippian period.

In the American Bottom (as well as other localities) the production of marine shell artifacts appears in contexts that suggest the engagement of new economic forces (Prentice 1983, 1985; Yerkes 1983, 1986). Not only are specific limited activity areas of major sites given over to extensive craftwork, but certain small farmsteads have yielded similar evidence of bead production (Prentice 1983; Yerkes 1983) and marine-shell caching (Pauketat 1987). It is significant that the production of items from this obviously exotic material takes place in dispersed farmsteads, although it is overstating the place of this production to label it as a "cottage industry" or "craft specialization." While production in these locales is evidently small in scale, the potential importance of such units of production cannot be undervalued. If such a pattern of dispersion should be strengthened through additional fieldwork, it would undermine the thesis that craft production was controlled through a central office.

On the basis of available information, Muller (1984, 1987) effectively argued the same point although he viewed the issue as one in which the degree of craft specialization was indicative of the level of political centralization, and hence the importance of chiefly social organization. In his expectations, Muller was joined by Prentice and Yerkes. For both sides in the debate the amount of work effort allocated to craft production instead of subsistence is an important issue. Archaeological data were enlisted to draw different lines of inference about the degree of centralized control exercised. But as the Prestige Goods Economy would

have it, centralized control is not a function that is responsible for the rise of chiefly institutions (Earle 1977, 1978, 1987). Hence, the quest for evidence that craft production is organized under the control, direction, or coordination of a central political agent does not contribute to the understanding of how these institutions have arisen. For these reasons, the question of the degree to which craftwork is specialized represents an obsolete problem for small-scale polities (Clark 1979).

The pattern of production debris is interesting because of the potential light it may shed on the development of local economies (Pauketat 1987; Yerkes 1983). Not all households are involved and furthermore the byproducts of production indicate a small-scale effort at any one location (the Ramey Tract of the Cahokia site may prove to be an exception). At the same time, marine shell raw material is encountered in cached deposits, at least one of which is associated with a very rich grave at Mitchell Mound A (Winters 1974, n.d.). Such stockpiles of raw material and finished goods are not uncommon in the American Bottom. Although we have little information to rely upon to infer the organization of production, caches of raw materials in sacred precincts contrast with the widespread distribution of small-scale craftsmen. This suggests a hierarchy of access to exotic resources and a use of shell beads as gifts of all kinds in every level of society—but with the lowest on the social hierarchy least capable of competing with the highest echelons for this scarce resource that everyone needs (Brumfield and Earle 1987:8; Ceci 1982).

Spheres of Utility and Value

The best information on relative value lies in patterns of disposition of grave goods. In the Early Mississippian period, burial mounds at the George C. Davis site (Shafer 1978; Story 1972), Spiro (Brown 1975), Gahagan (Webb and Dodd 1939), Mitchell (Winters 1974, n.d.), Kane mound (Melbye 1963; Milner 1982), and Hamilton sites (Lewis and Kneberg 1946) provide abundant information on the relative value of objects used as mortuary gifts. Copper and marine shell artifacts, together with pearl beads, occupy the apogee of value (Goad 1976). The principal burials at Etowah, Moundville, and Spiro monopolize the goods of these types

(Brown 1975; Larson 1971; Peebles and Kus 1977). In the later part of the Mississippian period, to which these sites apply most strongly, the heavier copper items, such as ax heads, are more valuable than sheet copper emblems, and the marine shell cups are concentrated with the larger and richer central burials at the expense of the less prestigious. Shell beads and even shell gorgets are intermediate in value (Hatch 1976) along with chipped and ground stone emblems. An indication of the relative value of shell beads and gorgets is the way they were sometimes made at Spiro from recycled engraved cups and other ruined shell art (Brown 1976b; Phillips and Brown 1978). All of this points toward a value proportional to the material's scarcity or artifact's labor input, which is, strictly speaking, not part of the socially determined standard of value of the Prestige Goods Economy. Nevertheless, by A.D. 1300 the relative value of prestige goods is well ordered.

In the first centuries of the Mississippian period similar organization of wealth seems to emerge from a consideration of grave goods disposal. One of the best known is the burial furnishings of Cahokia Mound 72 (Fowler 1974). During the Lohmann phase this mound was founded and added to in a location that was of ritual significance in the mound alignments at the site. After the fifth episode, some major elite burials were interred with considerable shell wealth and other prestige goods. An extended skeleton rested on a bed of shell disc beads that had the appearance of a mass sewn onto a large cape. Nearby were some bone bundles and partially disarticulated individuals next to a rolled sheet of copper, uncut mica, chunkey stones, and arrowhead caches of exotic styles. Somewhat later in Mitchell Mound A, a central burial was outfitted with a bison skull headdress and a cape of copper ornaments. Other burials were accompanied by a cache of Kaolin chert ax heads, numerous copper ornaments, and a variety of freshwater and marine shell beads. According to Winters (1974, n.d.), two categories of grave associations are apparent. One consists of ritual paraphernalia, costumery, and weapons. The second was quantities of marine shell in various stages of alteration for manufacture of goods.

Caches offer another indication of hoarding. While these contexts are more difficult to interpret, nonetheless they are highly indicative of the scale of consumption. At the bottom of this scale are the single offerings (e.g., discoidals, Ramey bifaces) commonly placed in the wall trenches of structures built in the American Bottom. At the high end are caches of the sort described by Rau (1869:402–403). In the 1860s three cache pits were found together by construction workers in East St. Louis. Each of the pits was stocked with quantities of a specific raw material or finished goods that were commonly employed in long-distance trade. One contained 70 or more neatly stacked hoe blades. Some at least were of Mill Creek chert, and 20 were said to have been sharp edged and unused. The second contained about a bushel of partly pierced small freshwater and marine gastropods destined to become beads. The third contained chunks of flint, greenstone, and diorite. Although it is difficult to determine whether these items were stockpiled for future use or were deliberately consumed by interment, the unfinished state of the raw materials and the unused state of the craft items point to a value, either ritual or economic, to the accumulation of these goods.

Factors of Distribution

Historically, the coast and the interior have played complementary roles in trade (Larson 1980). Beginning from about 4000 B.C. marine shells, primarily from Florida west coast waters, have been part of an archaeologically visible chain of long-distance exchange with native copper artifacts from the Great Lakes area (Brose 1979; Winters 1968).

Two different levels of intergroup trade are known for the period. Long-distance trade of scarce objects from sources greater that 300 km (Brown 1983) contrasts with intravalley trade spheres of utilitarian items. The former is visibly marked by exotics, the latter is more subtle. Perhaps the clearest case is in the American Bottom where some degree of microregional specialization in the production of limestone-tempered ceramic vessels at the southern end of the immediate Cahokia economic catchment and grit- and grog-tempered jars of distinct pastes in the northern end. This specialization is known from widely distributed examples of each within common refuse areas of many sites dating from the Range and Loyd phases, circa A.D. 850 (Bareis and Porter 1984). This local-level trade appears in the record before far-distant exotic vessels from southern Illinois make their appearance.

At the most exclusive level a network of interconnections is revealed by a pattern of exotics. Cahokia appears to have dominated trade as indicated by the extent of its imports. Ceramic data from the site and its satellites disclose imports from central Iowa and eastern and southwestern Arkansas (Bareis and Porter 1984; Fowler and Hall 1975; O'Brien 1972). A strong connection with the eastern Ozarks is disclosed by the point styles in the quiver-loads of exotics in the Mound 72 central burials. The appearance of exotics is reciprocal. Cahokian pottery is found at Mill Creek sites, at Azatlan, and other northern Midwestern sites, in the Yazoo River basin (Williams and Brain 1983) and at Spiro (Brown 1983). At the latter site, Cahokia notched points, and Kaolin and Mill Creek chipped stone ax heads appear in Harlan phase contexts (Brown 1976b). Although Cahokia clearly dominated this pattern, it is doubtful if it controlled it. Caddoan pottery from Texas is found in Mill Creek contexts (Anderson and Tiffany 1987), and Smokey Hill jasper bifaces made their way from Nebraska to Spiro (Brown 1983). The exchange network was clearly extended into the South although specifics are more difficult to come by. In the east, Mount Royal has yielded repoussé copper identical to that found at Spiro. In the west, central burials at George C. Davis yielded exotic bifaces, ax heads, and carved pipes that derive from the Arkansas region.

SUMMARY AND CONCLUSIONS

In the last few years the tempo of trade-related research in Mississippian period studies has quickened. With it has come a lively debate on the degree of craft specialization in the early centuries of the period. Out of this debate has come a better appreciation of the contribution that trade can make to our understanding of the social and political developments of the period through an analysis of production, consumption, and exchange. The debate, likewise, has disclosed the hold that the centralized polity model has on thinking about the economy. In an effort to liberate us from the confines of an obviously restrictive model, considerable attention is devoted here to delineating the Prestige Goods Economy and the ways in which it anticipates very different relationships between social formations and the rise of maize agriculture. In the particularly nonadaptationist form developed by Friedman (1975), the Prestige Goods Economy contributes much to the understanding of the complex interactions of this subsistence change and contemporary changes in population and settlement organization. As a consequence, difficult-to-resolve issues on the matter of craft specialization become obsolete when centralization of decision making is removed as the basis of chiefdom formation.

A review of some of the information available on raw material sources and prestige goods points to some revealing ways in which fall-off curves can be of aid in examining the rise of exchange networks. Particularly useful would be the separate delineation of the distribution of high-ranking valuables, circulating shell wealth, and utilitarian objects. In one example of Mill Creek hoe blade dispersion from quarries, an extensive, largely river-borne traffic was described that linked a 700 km region to the production center. Based on preliminary data it is evident that Cahokia exercised great importance in the hoe blade trade to the north, but contrary to the inflated role made of this center, it did not exercise a dominant role in traffic south into the lower Mississippi Valley.

Our knowledge of the whole network at any one time in the Mississippian period is woefully inadequate to move beyond the instructive insights that one relatively well-controlled case affords. It is of particular importance to the models of trade introduced in this paper that other trade spheres be documented in similar detail, both at the level of high-value prestige goods and at the level of utilitarian items—both those in heavy demand (Mill Creek hoe model) and those of relatively limited demand. Our notions of Mississippian period economy depends on a full investigation of all types of trade, not simply resting on the extraordinary cases. Essential to this will be the establishment of strategically useful programs on sourcing key raw materials.

ACKNOWLEDGMENTS

The authors wish to thank Charles Cobb for his contribution to the description of the Hale site.

REFERENCES CITED

Anderson, Duane C.
1975   A Long-Nosed God Mask from Northwest Iowa. *American Antiquity* 40:326–329.
1987   Toward a Processual Understanding of the Initial Vari-

ant of the Middle Missouri Tradition: The Case of the Mill Creek Culture of Iowa. *American Antiquity* 52:522–537.

Anderson, Duane C., and Joseph A. Tiffany
1987 A Caddoan Trade Vessel from Northwestern Iowa. *Plains Anthropologist* 32:93–96.

Baerreis, David A.
1957 The Southern Cult and the Spiro Ceremonial Complex. *Bulletin of the Oklahoma Anthropological Society* 5:23–38.

Baker, Charles M.
1982 A Brief Study of the Arkansas Novaculite Quarries. In *Fancy Hill, Archeological Studies in the Southern Ouachita Mountains*, edited by Ann M. Early and W. Frederick Limp, pp. 306–334. Arkansas Archeological Survey Research Series 16.

Bareis, Charles J., and William M. Gardner
1968 Three Long-Nosed God Masks from Western Illinois. *American Antiquity* 33:495–498.

Bareis, Charles J., and James W. Porter
1965 Megascopic and Petrographic Analyses of a Foreign Pottery Vessel from the Cahokia Site. *American Antiquity* 31:95–101.

Bareis, Charles J., and James W. Porter (editors)
1984 *American Bottom Archaeology.* University of Illinois Press, Urbana.

Bell, Robert E.
1943 *Lithic Analysis as a Method in Archaeology.* M.A. thesis, Department of Anthropology, University of Chicago.
1947 Trade Materials at Spiro Mound as Indicated by Artifacts. *American Antiquity* 12:181–184.
1972 *The Harlan Site, Ck-6, A Prehistoric Mound Center in Cherokee County, Eastern Oklahoma.* Oklahoma Anthropological Society, Memoir 2.
1984 Arkansas Valley Caddoan: The Harlan Phase. In *Prehistory of Oklahoma*, edited by Robert E. Bell, pp. 221–240. Academic Press, New York.

Billings, Deborah A.
1984 *An Analysis of Lithic Workshop Debris from Iron Mountain, Union County, Illinois.* Center for Archaeological Investigations Research Paper 47. Southern Illinois University at Carbondale.

Brose, David S.
1979 A Speculative Model of the Role of Exchange in the Prehistory of the Eastern Woodlands. In *Hopewell Archaeology: The Chillicothe Conference*, edited by David S. Brose and N'omi Greber, pp. 3–8. Kent State University Press, Kent.

Brown, Charles E.
1902 The Stone Spud. *Wisconsin Archaeologist* n.s. 2(1):15–28.
1926 Additional Stone Spuds. *Wisconsin Archaeologist* 5(3):79–82.

Brown, Ian W.
1980 *Salt and the Eastern North American Indian, an Archaeological Study.* Lower Mississippi Survey, Bulletin 6.

Brown, James A.
1975 Spiro Art and its Mortuary Contexts. In *Death and the Afterlife in Pre-Columbian America*, edited by Elizabeth P. Benson, pp. 1–32. Dumbarton Oaks Research Library and Collections, Washington, D.C.

1976a The Southern Cult Reconsidered. *Midcontinental Journal of Archaeology* 2:115–135.
1976b *Spiro Studies*, vol. 4. The Artifacts. Second Part of the Third Annual Report of Caddoan Archaeology—Spiro Focus Research. University of Oklahoma Research Institute, Norman.
1983 Spiro Exchange Connections Revealed by Sources of Imported Raw Materials. In *Southeastern Natives and Their Pasts: A Collection of Papers Honoring Dr. Robert E. Bell*, edited by Don G. Wyckoff and Jack L. Hofman, pp. 129–162. Oklahoma Archeological Survey, Studies in Oklahoma's Past, No. 11.
1984 Arkansas Valley Caddoan: The Spiro Phase. In *Prehistory of Oklahoma*, edited by Robert E. Bell, p. 241–263. Academic Press, New York.
1989 On Style Divisions of the Southeastern Ceremonial Complex—A Revisionist Perspective. In *Southern Ceremonial Complex, Artifacts and Analysis: The Cottonlandia Conference*, edited by Patricia Galloway, pp. 183–204. University of Nebraska Press, Lincoln.

Brumfield, Elizabeth M., and Timothy K. Earle
1987 Specialization, Exchange, and Complex Societies. In *Specialization, Exchange, and Social Complexity*, edited by Elizabeth Brumfield and Timothy Earle, pp. 1–9. Cambridge University Press, Cambridge.

Carneiro, Robert L.
1981 The Chiefdom: Precursor of the State. In *The Transition to Statehood in the New World*, edited by Grant D. Jones and Robert R. Kautz, pp. 37–79. Cambridge University Press.

Ceci, Lynn
1982 The Value of Wampum Among the New York Iroquois: A Case Study in Artifact Analysis. *Journal of Anthropological Research* 38:97–107.

Clark, J. R.
1979 Modelling Trade in Non-Literate Archaeological Contexts. *Journal of Anthropological Research* 35:170–190.

Dalton, George
1977 Aboriginal Economies in Stateless Societies. In *Exchange Systems in Prehistory*, edited by Timothy K. Earle and Jonathon E. Ericson, pp. 191–212. Academic Press, New York.

Dumond, Don E.
1972 Population Growth and Political Centralization. In *Population Growth: Anthropological Implications*, edited by Brian Spooner, pp. 286–310. MIT Press, Cambridge.

Earle, Timothy K.
1977 A Reappraisal of Redistribution: Complex Hawaiian Chiefdoms. In *Exchange Systems in Prehistory*, edited by Timothy K. Earle and Jonathan E. Ericson, pp. 213–229. Academic Press, New York.
1978 *Economic and Social Organization of a Complex Chiefdom: the Halelea District, Kaua'i, Hawaii.* University of Michigan, Department of Anthropology, Anthropological Papers 63.
1987 Chiefdoms in Archaeological and Ethnohistorical Perspective. *Annual Review of Anthropology* 16:279–308.

Ekholm, Karen
1977 External Exchange and the Transformation of Central

African Systems. In *The Evolution of Social Systems*, edited by Jonathan Friedman and M. J. Rowlands, pp. 115–136. Duckworth, London.

Fairbanks, Charles H.
1956   *Archaeology of the Funeral Mound, Ocmulgee National Monument, Georgia.* National Park Service, Washington, D.C.

Feinman, Gary, and Jill Neitzel
1984   Too Many Types: An Overview of Sedentary Prestate Societies in the Americas. In *Advances in Archaeological Method and Theory*, vol. 7, edited by M. B. Schiffer, pp. 39–102. Academic Press, New York.

Ferring, C. R., and T. K. Perttula
1987   Defining the Provenance of Red Slipped Pottery from Texas and Oklahoma by Petrographic Methods. *Journal of Archaeological Sciences* 14:437–456.

Flannery, Kent V.
1968   The Olmec and the Valley of Oaxaca: A Model for Interregional Interaction in Formative Times. In *Dumbarton Oaks Conference on the Olmec*, edited by Elizabeth P. Benson, pp. 79–110. Washington, D.C.
1972   The Cultural Evolution of Civilizations. *Annual Review of Ecology and Systematics* 3:399–426.

Fowler, Melvin L.
1969   The Cahokia Site. In *Explorations into Cahokia Archaeology*, edited by Melvin L. Fowler, pp. 1–30. Illinois Archaeological Survey Bulletin 7.
1974   *Cahokia: Ancient Capital of the Midwest.* Addison-Wesley Module in Anthropology 48.

Fowler, Melvin L., and Robert L. Hall
1975   Archeological Phases at Cahokia. In *Perspectives in Cahokia Archaeology*, pp. 1–14. Illinois Archaeological Survey, Bulletin 10.
1978   Late Prehistory of the Illinois Area. In *The Handbook of North American Indians*, vol. 15, Northeast, edited by Bruce G. Trigger, pp. 560–568. Smithsonian Institution, Washington, D.C.

Friedman, Jonathan
1975   Tribes, States, and Transformations. In *Marxist Analyses and Social Anthropology*, edited by Maurice Bloch, pp. 161–202. Tavistock Publications, New York.

Friedman, Jonathan, and M. J. Rowlands
1977   Notes Towards an Epigenetic Model of Civilization. In *The Evolution of Social Systems*, edited by Jonathan Friedman and M. J. Rowlands, pp. 201–276. Duckworth, London.

Gibbon, Guy
1974   A Model of Mississippian Development and its Implications for the Red Wing Area. In *Aspects of Upper Great Lakes Archaeology*, edited by Eldon Johnson, pp. 129–137. Minnesota Historical Society.

Gibson, Jon L.
1974   Aboriginal Warfare in the Proto-historic Southeast: An Alternative Perspective. *American Antiquity* 39:30–133.

Gledhill, John
1978   Formative Development in the North American Southwest. In *Social Organisation and Settlement: Contributions from Anthropology, Archaeology and Geography*, edited by David Green, Colin Haselgrove, and Matthew Spriggs,

pp. 241–290. BAR International Series (Supplementary) 47. Oxford.

Goad, Sharon I.
1976   Copper and the Southeastern Indians. *Early Georgia* 4:49–67.
1978   *Exchange Networks in the Prehistoric Southeastern United States.* Unpublished Ph.D. dissertation, Department of Anthropology, University of Georgia, Athens.
1980   Chemical Analysis of Native Copper Artifacts from the Southeastern United States. *Current Anthropology* 21:270–271.

Goad, Sharon I., and John Noakes
1978   Prehistoric Copper Artifacts in the Eastern United States. In *Archaeological Chemistry II*, edited by G. F. Carter, pp. 335–346. Advances in Chemistry 171, American Chemistry Society, Washington, D.C.

Goodman, Claire Garber
1984   *Copper Artifacts in Late Eastern Woodlands Prehistory*, edited by Anne-Marie Cantwell. Center for American Archeology, Evanston, Illinois.

Griffin, James B.
1952   An Interpretation of the Place of Spiro in Southeastern Archaeology. In The Spiro Mound, by H. W. Hamilton. *The Missouri Archaeologist* 14:89–106.
1967   Eastern North American Prehistory: A Summary. *Science* 156:175–191.
1985   Changing Concepts of the Prehistoric Mississippian Culture of the Eastern United States. In *Alabama and the Borderlands from Prehistory to Statehood*, edited by R. Reid Badger and Lawrence A. Clayton, pp. 40–63. University of Alabama Press.
1986   Review of Excavations at the Lake George Site, Yazoo County, Mississippi, by Stephen Williams and Jeffrey P. Brain. Papers of the Peabody Museum of Archaeology and Ethnology 74, Harvard University, 1983. *Southeastern Archaeology* 5:71–73.

Gundersen, James N., and Joseph A. Tiffany
1986   Nature and Provenance of Red Pipestone from the Wittrock Site (13OB4), Northwest Iowa. *North American Archaeologist* 7:45–67.

Hale, Howard Stephen
1976   *Marine Shells in Midwestern Archaeological Sites and the Determination of Their Most Probable Source.* Unpublished Master's thesis, College of Social Science, Florida Atlantic University, Boca Raton.

Hall, Robert L.
n.d.   Cahokia Identity and Interaction Models of Cahokia Mississippian. In *Cahokia and Its Neighbors: Mississippian Cultural Variation in the American Midwest*, edited by Thomas E. Emerson and R. Barry Lewis. University of Illinois Press, Urbana (in press).

Hamilton, Henry W., Jean Tyree Hamilton, and Eleanor F. Chapman
1974   *Spiro Mound Copper.* Missouri Archaeological Society, Memoir 11.

Harn, Alan D.
1975   Another Long-Nosed God Mask from Fulton County, Illinois. *The Wisconsin Archeologist* 56:2–8.

Hatch, James W.
1976   *Status in Death: Principles of Ranking in Dallas Culture*

Mortuary Remains. Ph.D. dissertation, Department of Anthropology, Pennsylvania State University.

Hirth, Kenneth G.
1984a The Analysis of Prehistoric Economic Systems: A Look to the Future. In *Trade and Exchange in Early Mesoamerica,* edited by Kenneth G. Hirth, pp. 281–302. University of New Mexico Press, Albuquerque.
1984b Early Exchange in Mesoamerica: An Introduction. In *Trade and Exchange in Early Mesoamerica,* edited by Kenneth G. Hirth, pp. 1–15. University of New Mexico Press, Albuquerque.

Hodder, Ian
1978 Some Effects of Distance on Patterns of Human Interaction. In *The Spatial Organisation of Culture,* edited by Ian Hodder, pp. 155–178. Duckworth, London.
1980 Trade and Exchange: Definitions, Identification and Function. In *Models and Methods in Regional Exchange,* edited by Robert E. Fry, pp. 151–156. Society for American Archaeology Papers No. 1.

Hodder, Ian, and Paul Lane
1982 A Contextual Examination of Neolithic Axe Distribution in Britain. In *Contexts for Prehistoric Exchange,* edited by Jonathan E. Ericson and Timothy K. Earle, pp. 213–235. Academic Press, New York.

Holmes, William H.
1919 Introduction, The Lithic Industries. In *Handbook of Aboriginal American Antiquities.* Bureau of American Ethnology Bulletin 60(1).

Hurst, Vernon J., and Lewis H. Larson, Jr.
1958 On the Source of Copper at the Etowah Site, Georgia. *American Antiquity* 24:177–181.

Ives, David J.
1984 The Crescent Hills Prehistoric Quarrying Area: More Than Just Rocks. In *Prehistoric Chert Exploitation: Studies from the Midcontinent,* edited by Brian M. Butler and Ernest E. May, pp. 187–195. Center for Archaeological Investigations, Occasional Paper No. 2, Southern Illinois University at Carbondale.

Jones, B. Calvin
1982 Southern Cult Manifestations at the Lake Jackson Site, Leon County, Florida: Salvage Excavation of Mound 3. *Midcontinental Journal of Archaeology* 7:3–44.

Jones, Walter B.
1939 Geology of the Tennessee Valley Region of Alabama, with Notes on the Topographic Features of the Area and the Effect of Geology and Topography upon Aboriginal Occupation. In *An Archaeological Survey of Wheeler Basin on the Tennessee River in Northern Alabama,* by William S. Webb, pp. 9–20. Bureau of American Ethnology Bulletin 122.

Kelly, John E.
1980 *Formative Developments at Cahokia and the Adjacent American Bottom: The Merrell Tract Perspective.* Unpublished Ph.D. dissertation, University of Wisconsin, Madison.
1984 Late Bluff Chert Utilization on the Merrell Tract, Cahokia. In *Prehistoric Chert Exploitation: Studies from the Midcontinent,* edited by Brian M. Butler and Ernest E. May, pp. 23–44. Center for Archaeological Investigations, Occasional Paper No. 2, Southern Illinois University at Carbondale.

Kerber, Richard A.
1986 *Political Evolution in the Lower Illinois Valley:* A.D. *400–1000.* Unpublished Ph.D. dissertation, Northwestern University, Illinois.

Keslin, Richard O.
1964 Archaeological Implications on the Role of Salt as an Element of Cultural Diffusion. *The Missouri Archaeologist* 26:1–181.

Larson, Lewis H.
1971 Archaeological Implications of Social Stratification at the Etowah Site, Georgia. In *Approaches to the Social Dimensions of Mortuary Practices,* edited by James A. Brown, pp. 58–67. Society for American Archaeology, Memoir 25.
1972 Functional Consideration of Warfare in the Southeast during the Mississippian Period. *American Antiquity* 37:383–392.
1980 *Aboriginal Subsistence Technology on the Southeastern Coastal Plain During the Late Prehistoric Period.* University Presses of Florida, Gainesville.

Lewis, R. Barry
1982 *Two Mississippian Hamlets: Cairo Lowland, Missouri.* Illinois Archaeological Survey, Special Publication 2.

Lewis, Thomas M. N., and Madeline Kneberg
1946 *Hiwassee Island.* University of Tennessee Press, Knoxville.

Little, Elizabeth A.
1987 Inland Waterways in the Northeast. *Midcontinental Journal of Archaeology* 12:55–76.

Lynott, Mark J., Thomas W. Boulton, James E. Price, and Dwight E. Nelson
1986 Stable Carbon Isotopic Evidence for Maize Agriculture in Southeast Missouri and Northwest Arkansas. *American Antiquity* 51:51–65.

McBryde, Isabel
1987 Wil-im-ee Moor-ring: Or, Where do Axes Come From? *Mankind* 11:354–382.

Mason, Ronald J., and Gregory Perino
1961 Microblades at Cahokia, Illinois. *American Antiquity* 26:553–557.

May, Ernest E.
1984 Prehistoric Chert Exploitation in the Shawnee Hills. In *Cultural Frontiers in the Upper Cache Valley, Illinois,* edited by Veletta Canouts, Ernest E. May, Neal H. Lopinot, and Jon D. Muller, pp. 68–90. Center for Archaeological Investigations, Research Paper No. 16, Southern Illinois University at Carbondale.

Melbye, F. Jerome
1963 *The Kane Burial Mounds.* Southern Illinois University Museum, Archaeological Salvage Report 15.

Milner, George R.
1982 *Measuring Prehistoric Levels of Health: A Study of Mississippian Period Skeletal Remains from the American Bottom, Illinois.* Unpublished Ph.D. dissertation, Department of Anthropology, Northwestern University, Illinois.
1984 Social and Temporal Implications of Variation Among American Bottom Mississippian Cemeteries. *American Antiquity* 49:468–488.
1986 Mississippian Period Population Density in a Segment

of the Central Mississippi River Valley. *American Antiquity* 51:227–238.

Moore, Clarence B.
1894   Certain Sand Mounds of the St. John's River, Florida, Part I. *Journal of the Academy of Natural Sciences of Philadelphia* 10(1).

Moorehead, Warren K.
1917   *Stone Ornaments of the American Indian*. Andover Press, Andover, Massachusetts.

Morse, Dan F., and Phyllis A. Morse
1983   *Archaeology of the Central Mississippi Valley*. Academic Press, New York.

Morse, Dan F., and Phyllis A. Morse (editors)
1980   *Zebree Archaeological Project*. Report submitted to Memphis District, U.S. Army Corps of Engineers, by the Arkansas Archeological Survey.

Muller, Jon
1984   Mississippi Specialization and Salt. *American Antiquity* 49:489–507.
1986   Pans and a Grain of Salt: Mississippian Specialization Revisited. *American Antiquity* 51:405–409.
1987   Salt, Chert, and Shell: Mississippian Exchange and Economy. In *Specialization, Exchange, and Social Complexity*, edited by E. Brumfield and Timothy Earle, pp. 10–21. Cambridge University Press, Cambridge.

O'Brien, Patricia J.
1972   *A Formal Analysis of Cahokia Ceramics from the Powell Tract*. Illinois Archaeological Survey, Monograph 3.

Otteson, Ann I.
1978   *A Preliminary Study of Acquisition of Exotic Raw Materials by the Late Woodland and Mississippian Groups*. Unpublished Ph.D. dissertation, New York University.

Parmalee, Paul W.
1958   Marine Shells of Illinois Indian Sites. *Nautilus* 71:132–139.

Pauketat, Timothy R.
1983   A Long-Stemmed Spud from the American Bottom. *Midcontinental Journal of Archaeology* 8:1–16.
1987   Mississippian Domestic Economy and Formation Processes: A Response to Prentice. *Midcontinental Journal of Archaeology* 12:77–88.

Peebles, Christopher S.
1971   Moundville and Surrounding Sites: Some Structural Considerations of Mortuary Practices, II. In *Approaches to the Social Dimensions of Mortuary Practices*, edited by James A. Brown, pp. 68–91. Society for American Archaeology, Memoirs 25.
1987   Moundville from 1000 to 1500 A.D. as Seen from 1540 to 1985 A.D. In *Chiefdoms in the Americas*, edited by Robert D. Drennan and Carlos A. Uribe, pp. 21–42. University Press of America, Lanham, Maryland.

Peebles, Christopher S., and Susan M. Kus
1977   Some Archaeological Correlates of Ranked Societies. *American Antiquity* 42:421–448.

Perttula, Timothy K.
1984   Patterns of Prehistoric Lithic Raw Material Utilization in the Caddoan Area: The Western Gulf Coastal Plain. In *Prehistoric Chert Exploitation: Studies from the Midconti-*

nent, edited by Brian M. Butler and Ernest E. May, pp. 129–148. Center for Archaeological Investigations, Occasional Paper No. 2, Southern Illinois University at Carbondale.

Phillips, Philip, and James A. Brown
1978   *Pre-Columbian Shell Engravings from the Craig Mound at Spiro, Oklahoma (Part 1)*. Peabody Museum of Archaeology and Ethnology, Harvard University, Cambridge.

Phillips, W. A.
1899   The Aboriginal Quarries and Shops at Mill Creek, Union County, Illinois. *Proceedings of the American Association for the Advancement of Science* 48:361–363.
1900   Aboriginal Quarries and Shops at Mill Creek, Illinois. *American Anthropologist* n.s. 2:37–52.

Plog, Fred
1977   Modeling Economic Exchanges. In *Exchange Systems in Prehistory*, edited by Timothy K. Earle and Jonathon E. Ericson, pp. 127–140. Academic Press, New York.

Polanyi, Karl
1957   The Economy as Instituted Process. In *Trade and Market in the Early Empires*, edited by Karl Polanyi, M. Arensberg, and H. Pearson, pp. 243–270. Free Press, Glencoe.

Porter, James Warren
1969   The Mitchell Site and Prehistoric Exchange Systems at Cahokia: A.D. 1000 ± 1300. In *Explorations into Cahokia Archaeology*, edited by Melvin L. Fowler, pp. 137–164. Illinois Archaeological Survey Bulletin 7.
1974   *Cahokia Archaeology as Viewed from the Mitchell Site: A Satellite Community at A.D. 1150–1200*. Unpublished Ph.D. dissertation, University of Wisconsin, Madison.

Prentice, Guy
1983   Cottage Industries: Concepts and Implications. *Midcontinental Journal of Archaeology* 8:17–48.
1985   Economic Differentiation Among Mississippian Farmsteads. *Midcontinental Journal of Archaeology* 10:77–122.
1987   Marine Shells as Wealth Items in Mississippian Societies. *Midcontinental Journal of Archaeology* 12:193–223.

Rapp, George, Jr., James Allert, and Eiler Henrickson
1984   Trace Element Discrimination of Discrete Sources of Native Copper. In *Archaeological Chemistry III*, edited by Joseph B. Lambert, pp. 273–293. Advances in Chemistry 205, American Chemistry Society, Washington, D.C.

Rapp, George, Jr., E. Henrickson, M. Miller, and S. Aschenbrenner
1980   Trace-Element Fingerprinting as a Guide to the Geographic Sources of Native Copper. *Journal of Metals* 32:35–44.

Rau, Charles
1869   A Deposit of Agricultural Flint Implements in Southern Illinois. *Smithsonian Institution Annual Report for 1868*, pp. 401–407. Washington, D.C.

Reidhead, Van A.
1980   The Economics of Subsistence Change: Test of an Optimization Model. In *Modeling Change in Prehistoric Subsistence Economies*, edited by T. K. Earle and A. L. Christenson, pp. 141–186. Academic Press, New York.
1981   *A Linear Programing Model of Prehistoric Subsistence Optimization: A Southeastern Indiana Example*. Prehistoric

Research Series, Indiana Historical Society 6(1), Indianapolis.

Renfrew, Colin
1975 Trade as Action at a Distance: Questions of Integration and Communication. In *Ancient Civilization and Trade,* edited by Jeremy A. Sabloff and C. C. Lamberg-Karlovsky, pp. 3–59. University of New Mexico Press, Albuquerque.

Renfrew, Colin, and John F. Cherry (editors)
1986 *Peer Polity Interaction and Socio-political Change.* Cambridge University Press, Cambridge.

Renfrew, Colin, and Stephen Shennan (editors)
1982 *Ranking, Resources and Exchange: Aspects of the Archaeology of Early European Society.* Cambridge University Press, Cambridge.

Rolingson, Martha A.
1982 The Concept of Plum Bayou Culture. In *Emerging Patterns of Plum Bayou Culture,* edited by Martha Ann Rolingson, pp. 87–93. Arkansas Archeological Survey Research Series 18.

Sahlins, Marshall
1958 *Social Stratification in Polynesia.* University of Washington Press, Seattle.

Schnell, Frank T., Vernon J. Knight, and Gail S. Schnell
1981 *Chemochechobee: Archaeology of a Mississippian Ceremonial Center on the Chattahoochee River.* University Presses of Florida, Gainesville.

Seeman, Mark F.
1979 *The Hopewell Interaction Sphere: The Evidence for Interregional Trade and Structural Complexity.* Indiana Historical Society, Prehistoric Research Series 5(2).

Service, Elman R.
1962 *Primitive Social Organization.* Random House, New York.
1975 *Origins of the State and Civilization: The Process of Cultural Evolution.* W. W. Norton, New York.

Shafer, Harry J.
1978 *Lithic Technology at the George C. Davis Site, Cherokee County, Texas.* Ph.D. dissertation, Department of Anthropology, University of Texas, Austin.

Smith, Bruce D.
1978 Variation in Mississippian Settlement Patterns. In *Mississippian Settlement Patterns,* edited by Bruce D. Smith, pp. 479–503. Academic Press, New York.
1985 Mississippian Patterns of Subsistence and Settlement. In *Alabama and the Borderlands from Prehistory to Statehood,* edited by R. Reid Badger and Lawrence A. Clayton, pp. 64–79. University of Alabama Press.
1986 The Archaeology of the Southeastern United States: From Dalton to de Soto, 10,500–500 B.P. In *Advances in World Archaeology* 5:1–92.

Snyder, John F.
1910 Prehistoric Illinois: The Primitive Flint Industry. *Journal of the Illinois State Historical Society* 3(2):11–25.

Southard, Michael D.
1973 Sources of Chert Present at Towosahgy State Archaeological Site. *Missouri Archaeological Society, Newsletter* 273:2–7.

Spence, Michael W.
1982 The Social Context of Production and Exchange. In *Contexts for Prehistoric Exchange,* edited by Jonathan E. Ericson and Timothy K. Earle, pp. 173–197. Academic Press, New York.

Spielbauer, Ronald H.
1976 *Chert Resources and Aboriginal Chert Utilization in Western Union County, Illinois.* Ph.D. dissertation, Department of Anthropology, Southern Illinois University at Carbondale.

Steponaitis, Vincas P.
1978 Location Theory and Complex Chiefdoms: A Mississippi Example. In *Mississippian Settlement Patterns,* edited by Bruce D. Smith, pp. 417–453. Academic Press, New York.
1983 *Ceramics, Chronology, and Community Patterns: An Archaeological Study at Moundville.* Academic Press, New York.
1986a Prehistoric Archaeology in the Southeastern United States, 1970–1985. *Annual Review of Anthropology* 15:363–404.
1986b The University of Alabama Excavations at 1TU50, a Moundville I Phase Center in the Black Warrior Valley. Paper presented at the 43rd Southeastern Archaeological Conference, Nashville, Tennessee.

Story, Dee Ann
1972 *A Preliminary Report of the 1968, 1969, and 1970 Excavations at the George C. Davis Site, Cherokee County, Texas.* Report of Field Research Conducted under National Science Foundation and Interagency Contracts, University of Texas at Austin.

Titterington, Paul F.
1938 *The Cahokia Mound Group and its Village Site Materials.* Privately printed, St. Louis, Missouri.

Torrence, Robin
1986 *Production and Exchange of Stone Tools.* Cambridge University Press, Cambridge.

Vander Leest, Barbara J.
1980 *The Ramey Field, Cahokia Surface Collection: A Functional Analysis of Spatial Structure.* Unpublished Ph.D. dissertation, University of Wisconsin, Milwaukee.

Van der Schalie, Henry, and Paul W. Parmalee
1960 Animal Remains from the Etowah Site, Mound C, Bartow County, Georgia. *The Florida Anthropologist* 13:37–57.

Vertrees, Herbert H.
1913 *Pearls and Pearling.* Fur News Publishing Company, New York.

Walthall, John A.
1981 *Galena and Aboriginal Trade in Eastern North America.* Illinois State Museum, Scientific Papers 17.

Walthall, John A., Stephen H. Stow, and Marvin J. Karson
1980 Copena Galena: Source Identification and Analysis. *American Antiquity* 45:2–42.

Waring, Antonio J., Jr.
1968 The Southern Cult and Muskhogean Ceremonial. In *The Waring Papers, the Collected Works of Antonio J. War-*

ing, Jr., edited by Stephen Williams, pp. 30–69. Papers of the Peabody Museum of Archaeology and Ethnology 58. Harvard University.

Waring, Antonio J., Jr., and Preston Holder
1945   A Prehistoric Ceremonial Complex in the Southeastern United States. *American Anthropologist* 47:1–34.

Webb, Clarence H., and Monroe Dodd, Jr.
1939   Further Excavations of the Gahagan Mound: Connections with a Florida Culture. *Texas Archeological and Paleontological Society, Bulletin* 11:90–128.

Webb, William S., and David L. DeJarnette
1942   *An Archeological Survey of Pickwick Basin in the Adjacent Portions of the States of Alabama, Mississippi and Tennessee.* Bureau of American Ethnology Bulletin 129. Washington, D.C.

Webb, William S., and Charles G. Wilder
1951   *An Archaeological Survey of Guntersville Basin on the Tennessee River in Northern Alabama.* University of Kentucky Press, Lexington.

Williams, Stephen
1979   Some Negative Painted Pottery: A Possible Horizon Marker in the Southeast. Paper presented at the 36th Southeastern Archaeological Conference, Atlanta, Georgia.

Williams, Stephen, and Jeffrey P. Brain
1983   *Excavations at the Lake George Site, Yazoo County, Mississippi, 1958–1960.* Papers of the Peabody Museum of Archaeology and Ethnology 74. Harvard University.

Williams, Stephen, and John M. Goggin
1956   The Long Nosed God Mask in Eastern United States. *The Missouri Archaeologist* 18(3).

Winters, Howard D.
1968   Value Systems and Trade Cycles of the Late Archaic in the Midwest. In *New Perspectives in Archeology*, edited by S. R. Binford and L. R. Binford, pp. 175–221. Aldine, Chicago.

1974   Some Unusual Grave Goods from a Mississippian Burial Mound. *Indian Notes* 10(2):34–36. Museum of the American Indian, Heye Foundation, New York.

1981   Excavating in Museums: Notes on Mississippian Hoes and Middle Woodland Copper Gouges and Celts. In *The Research Potential of Anthropological Collections in Museums*, edited by Anne-Marie Cantwell, James B. Griffin, and Nan A. Rothschild, pp. 17–34. Annals of the New York Academy of Sciences 376.

n.d.   A Commentary on the Contents of a Mississippian Burial Mound at the Mitchell Site, Madison County, Illinois. Manuscript in author's possession.

Woolverton, Donald G.
1974   Electron Microprobe Analysis of Native Copper Artifacts. In *Spiro Mound Copper*, by Henry W. Hamilton, Jean Tyree Hamilton, and Eleanor F. Chapman, pp. 207–212. Missouri Archaeological Society Memoir 11.

Wright, Gary A.
1967   Some Aspects of Early and Mid-seventeenth Century Exchange Networks in the Western Great Lakes. *Michigan Archaeologist* 13:181–197.

1968   A Further Note on Trade Friendship and Gift Giving: The Western Great Lakes. *Michigan Archaeologist* 14:165–166.

1974   *Archaeology and Trade.* Addison-Wesley Module in Anthropology 49.

Yerkes, Richard W.
1983   Microwear, Microdrills, and Mississippian Craft Specialization. *American Antiquity* 48:499–518.

1986   Licks, Pans, and Chiefs: A Comment on "Mississippian Specialization and Salt." *American Antiquity* 51:402–404.